# Microsoft® SQL Server®
# 2008 Administrator's
# Pocket Consultant

*William R. Stanek*

PUBLISHED BY

Microsoft Press

A Division of Microsoft Corporation

One Microsoft Way

Redmond, Washington 98052-6399

Library of Congress Control Number: 2008929782

Printed and bound in the United States of America.

1 2 3 4 5 6 7 8 9   QWE   3 2 1 0 9 8

Distributed in Canada by H.B. Fenn and Company Ltd.

A CIP catalogue record for this book is available from the British Library.

Microsoft Press books are available through booksellers and distributors worldwide. For further information about international editions, contact your local Microsoft Corporation office or contact Microsoft Press International directly at fax (425) 936-7329. Visit our Web site at www.microsoft.com/mspress. Send comments to mspinput@microsoft.com.

Microsoft, Microsoft Press, Access, Active Directory, ActiveX, BitLocker, Excel, Expression, Internet Explorer, MS, Outlook, SharePoint, SQL Server, Visual Basic, Visual Studio, Win32, Windows, Windows PowerShell, Windows Server and Windows Vista are either registered trademarks or trademarks of the Microsoft group of companies. Other product and company names mentioned herein may be the trademarks of their respective owners.

The example companies, organizations, products, domain names, e-mail addresses, logos, people, places, and events depicted herein are fictitious. No association with any real company, organization, product, domain name, e-mail address, logo, person, place, or event is intended or should be inferred.

This book expresses the author's views and opinions. The information contained in this book is provided without any express, statutory, or implied warranties. Neither the authors, Microsoft Corporation, nor its resellers, or distributors will be held liable for any damages caused or alleged to be caused either directly or indirectly by this book.

**Acquisitions Editor:** Martin DelRe
**Developmental Editor:** Karen Szall
**Project Editor:** Melissa von Tschudi-Sutton
**Project Management:** Publishing.com
**Compositor:** Curtis Philips
**Technical Reviewer:** Randall Galloway; Technical Review services provided by Content Master, a member of CM Group, Ltd.
**Cover:** Tom Draper Design

Body Part No. X15-04055

# Table of Contents

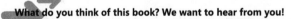

**What do you think of this book? We want to hear from you!**

Microsoft is interested in hearing your feedback so we can continually improve our books and learning resources for you. To participate in a brief survey, please visit:

**www.microsoft.com/learning/booksurvey**

## Part III   Microsoft SQL Server 2008 Data Administration

## Part IV   Microsoft SQL Server 2008 Optimization and Maintenance

**What do you think of this book? We want to hear from you!**

Microsoft is interested in hearing your feedback so we can continually improve our books and learning resources for you. To participate in a brief survey, please visit:

**www.microsoft.com/learning/booksurvey**

# Acknowledgments

You know you've been at this thing called writing for a long time when people ask how many books you've written and you just have no idea. For many years, my bio stated that I was the author of over 25 books. Several times my publishers have asked me to update the bio with a more precise number, so at around number 61 I started counting to keep everyone happy. That was about five years ago; I'm now somewhere over 70, 75, or 90 depending on how you count. ;-).

For me, it's always been about the craft of writing. I love writing, and I love challenging projects most of all. Some of the most challenging books I ever wrote were the *SQL Server 7.0 Administrator's Pocket Consultant*, published in 1999, the *SQL Server 2000 Administrator's Pocket Consultant*, published in 2000, and the *SQL Server 2005 Administrator's Pocket Consultant*, published in 2005. Writing *SQL Server 2008 Administrator's Pocket Consultant* was no less challenging.

The challenge in writing a day-to-day administrator's guide to SQL Server is that there's so much I'd like to cover but pocket consultants aren't meant to be all-in-one references. Pocket consultants are meant to be portable and readable—the kind of book you use to solve problems and get the job done wherever you might be. With that in mind, I have to continually make sure I focus on the core of SQL Server 2008 administration. The result is the book you hold in your hand, which I hope you'll agree is one of the best practical, portable guides to SQL Server 2008.

As I've stated in the three dozen or so pocket consultants I've written, the team at Microsoft Press is top-notch. Melissa von Tschudi-Sutton was instrumental throughout the writing process. She was my primary contact at Microsoft. Martin DelRe was the acquisitions editor for the project. He believed in the book from the beginning and was really great to work with. Completing and publishing the book wouldn't have been possible without their help! Thank you so much!

Unfortunately for the writer (but fortunately for readers), writing is only one part of the publishing process. Next came editing and author review. I must say, Microsoft Press has the most thorough editorial and technical review process I've seen anywhere—and I've written a lot of books for many different publishers. Randall Gallaway was the technical editor for the book. He helped with testing to ensure that things worked as expected. Roger LeBlanc managed the copyediting and ensured consistency of style. He did an excellent job and went above and beyond. Curt Philips managed the editorial process and helped out many times to ensure this was a great book. As proofreader, Andrea Fox also did a top-notch job and was very attentive to screens and overall continuity. Together, they were a terrific team to work with.

Colin Lyth, a technologist with Microsoft Learning, helped to ensure that I had the resources I needed. Indy Crowley, SQL Server 2008 Release Team & Data Programmability Native Components Release Manager, was also very helpful when it came to crunch time. Thank you Colin and Indy!

I would like to thank Chris Nelson for his help during this project! Chris is terrific to work with and always willing to help any way he can. Thanks also to everyone else at Microsoft who has helped at many points of my writing career and been there when I needed them the most.

Thanks also to Studio B, The Salkind Agency, and my agent Neil Salkind!

Hopefully, I haven't forgotten anyone but if I have, it was an oversight. *Honest.* ;-)

# Introduction

*Microsoft SQL Server 2008 Administrator's Pocket Consultant* is designed to be a concise and compulsively usable resource for SQL Server 2008 administrators. It covers everything you need to perform the core administrative tasks for SQL Server and is the readable resource guide that you'll want on your desk at all times. Because the focus is on giving you maximum value in a pocket-sized guide, you don't have to wade through hundreds of pages of extraneous information to find what you're looking for. Instead, you'll find exactly what you need to get the job done.

This book is designed to be the one resource you turn to whenever you have questions about SQL Server administration. To this end, the book zeroes in on daily administration procedures, frequently used tasks, documented examples, and options that are representative while not necessarily inclusive. One of the key goals is to keep content concise enough so that the book is compact and easy to navigate while also ensuring that the book contains as much information as possible. Instead of a 1000-page tome or a 100-page quick reference, you get a valuable resource guide that can help you quickly and easily perform common tasks, solve problems, and implement advanced SQL Server technologies such as replication, distributed queries, and multiserver administration.

## Who Is This Book For?

*Microsoft SQL Server 2008 Administrator's Pocket Consultant* covers the Standard, Enterprise, Developer, Web, and Workgroup Editions of SQL Server. The book is designed for

- Current SQL Server 2008 database administrators
- Accomplished users who have some administrator responsibilities
- Administrators migrating to SQL Server 2008 from previous versions
- Administrators transitioning from other database architectures

To include as much information as possible, I had to assume that you have basic networking skills and a basic understanding of SQL Server. With this in mind, I don't devote entire chapters to understanding SQL Server architecture or running simple SQL queries. But I do cover SQL Server installation, configuration, enterprise-wide server management, performance tuning, optimization, maintenance, and much more.

I also assume that you're fairly familiar with SQL commands and stored procedures as well as the standard Microsoft Windows user interface. If you need help learning SQL basics, you should read other resources (many of which are available from Microsoft Press).

# How Is This Book Organized?

*Microsoft SQL Server 2008 Administrator's Pocket Consultant* is designed to be used in the daily administration of SQL Server and, as such, the book is organized according to job-related tasks rather than SQL Server features. Before you use this book, you should be aware of the difference between the Administrator's Pocket Consultant titles and the Administrator's Companion titles. Although both types of books are designed to be a part of an overall administrator's library, books in the Administrator's Pocket Consultant series are the down-and-dirty, in-the-trenches books and Administrator's Companion titles are the comprehensive tutorials and references that cover every aspect of deploying a product or technology in the enterprise.

Speed and ease of reference are essential parts of this hands-on guide. The book has an expanded table of contents and an extensive index for finding answers to problems quickly. Many other quick reference features have been added to the book as well. These features include quick step-by-step procedures, lists, tables with fast facts, and cross-references. The book is broken down into both parts and chapters. The parts contain a part-opener paragraph or two about the chapters grouped in that part.

Part I, "Microsoft SQL Server 2008 Administration Fundamentals," covers the fundamental tasks you need for SQL Server administration. Chapter 1 provides an overview of SQL Server administration tools, techniques, and concepts. Chapter 2 discusses deploying SQL Server. Chapter 3 shows you how to configure SQL Server's services, components, and networking capabilities. Chapter 4 examines the structures available for configuring and tuning SQL Server. The chapter looks at SQL Server 2008's system catalog and then continues with a discussion of catalog queries and stored procedures.

In Part II, "Microsoft SQL Server 2008 Administration," you'll find the essential tasks for administering SQL Server. Chapter 5 details management techniques for server groups and servers. Chapter 6 explores configuring and tuning SQL Server using SQL Server Management Studio. You'll learn about optimizing memory usage, parallel processing, authentication, auditing, and more. The core administration tasks for creating and managing databases are covered in Chapter 7. Chapter 8 discusses the essential techniques for managing full-text catalogs, full-text indexes, stopwords, stoplists, thesaurus files, and other components of full-text search. Chapter 9 focuses on SQL Server security. To manage server security, you'll create user logins, configure login permissions, and assign roles. The permissions and roles you assign determine the actions users can perform as well as what types of data they can access.

SQL Server data administration is the subject of Part III. Chapter 10 covers techniques for creating, managing, and optimizing schemas, tables, indexes, and views. In Chapter 11, you'll find tasks for importing and exporting data, as well as the old standby bulk copy program (BCP). Chapter 12 focuses on integrating SQL Server databases with other SQL Server databases and with other data sources. You'll find detailed discussions on distributed queries, distributed transactions, Microsoft Distributed

Transaction Coordinator (MS DTC), and linked servers. Chapter 13 explores data replication. You'll learn all about the latest replication techniques, including merge replication and immediate-updating subscribers.

Part IV, "Microsoft SQL Server 2008 Optimization and Maintenance," covers administration tasks you'll use to enhance and maintain SQL Server. Chapter 14 provides the essentials for working with server logs, monitoring SQL Server performance, and solving performance problems. Chapter 15 starts by explaining how to create a backup and recovery plan. Afterward, the chapter dives into common tasks for creating and restoring backups. Chapter 16 explores database automation and maintenance, showing how to create alerts, schedule jobs, handle operator notifications, and more. You'll also learn how to create maintenance plans and resolve database consistency problems. Chapter 17 begins with a discussion about log shipping and database mirroring. Log shipping and database mirroring are disaster recovery solutions designed to help improve availability and quickly recover SQL Server 2008. In Chapter 18, you'll learn about essential tasks for implementing Policy-Based Management. Policy-Based Management defines policies that not only configure SQL Server settings but also control whether and how settings can be changed. Before you deploy SQL Server 2008, you should familiarize yourself with the available options and determine whether your servers will be put into specific management groups.

## Conventions Used in This Book

I've used a variety of elements to help keep the text clear and easy to follow. You'll find code terms and listings in monospace type, except when I tell you to actually type a command. In that case, the command appears in **bold** type. When I introduce and define a new term, I put it in *italics*.

Other conventions include the following:

- **Note**   To provide additional details on a particular point that needs emphasis.
- **Tip**   To offer helpful hints or additional information.
- **Caution**   To warn you when there are potential problems you should look out for.
- **Real World**   To provide real-world advice when discussing advanced topics.
- **Best Practice**   To explain the best technique to use when working with advanced configuration and administration concepts.

I truly hope you find that *Microsoft SQL Server 2008 Administrator's Pocket Consultant* provides everything you need to perform essential administrative tasks on SQL Server as quickly and efficiently as possible. Your thoughts are welcome at *williamstanek@aol.com* or visit *http://www.williamstanek.com/*. Thank you.

# Support

Every effort has been made to ensure the accuracy of this book. Microsoft Press provides corrections for books through the World Wide Web at the following address:

*http://mspress.microsoft.com/support/.*

If you have comments, questions, or ideas regarding this book, please send them to Microsoft Press using either of the following methods:

Postal mail:

Microsoft Press
Attn: *Microsoft SQL Server 2008 Administrator's Pocket Consultant* Editor
One Microsoft Way
Redmond, WA 98052-6399

E-mail:

*mspinput@microsoft.com*

Please note that product support is not offered through the above mail addresses. For support information, visit Microsoft's Web site at *http://support.microsoft.com/default.aspx.*

## Find Additional Content Online

For more great information from Microsoft Press, visit the new Microsoft Press Online sites—your one-stop online resource for access to updates, sample chapters, articles, scripts, and e-books related to our industry-leading Microsoft Press titles. Check out the following sites: *http://www.microsoft.com/learning/books/online/developer* and *http://www.microsoft.com/learning/books/online/serverclient.*

# Part I
# Microsoft SQL Server 2008 Administration Fundamentals

Part I of this book examines the fundamental tasks you need for Microsoft SQL Server 2008 administration. Chapter 1 provides an overview of SQL Server administration concepts, tools, and techniques. Chapter 2 provides planning, installation, and deployment details to help you roll out SQL Server 2008. Chapter 3 shows you how to manage surface security, access, and networking. Chapter 4 examines the structures available for configuring and tuning SQL Server. This chapter provides the essential background for understanding how to configure and tune SQL Server 2008.

# Chapter 1
# Microsoft SQL Server 2008 Administration Overview

Microsoft SQL Server 2008 builds on the base provided by Microsoft SQL Server 2005 and finally makes the vision of SQL Server as an end-to-end data platform a reality. By functioning as a mission-critical data platform, allowing dynamic development, providing pervasive business intelligence, and going beyond relational data, SQL Server 2008 proides the bedrock foundation on which small, medium, and large organizations can build their next generation IT infrastructure. At the core of SQL Server 2008, you will find the following:

- **Database Engine Services** Includes the core database, notification, replication, and full-text search components. The core database, the Database Engine, is the heart of SQL Server. Replication increases data availability by distributing data across multiple databases, allowing you to scale out the read workload across designated database servers. Full-text search allows plain-language queries on data stored in SQL Server tables.

- **Analysis Services** Delivers Online Analytical Processing (OLAP) and data-mining functionality for business intelligence applications. Analysis Services allows your organization to aggregate data from multiple data sources, such as relational databases, and work with this data in a wide variety of ways.

- **Integration Services** Provides an enterprise data transformation and integration solution for extracting and transforming data from multiple data sources and moving it to one or more destination sources. This functionality allows you to merge data from heterogeneous data sources, load data into data warehouses and data marts, and more.

2

- **Reporting Services**   Includes Report Manager and Report Server to provide a complete, server-based platform for creating, managing, and distributing reports. The Report Server is built on standard Internet Information Services (IIS) and .NET framework technology, allowing you to combine the benefits of SQL Server and IIS to host and process reports.

- **Service Broker**   Provides reliable queuing and messaging as a core part of the database. Queues can be used to stack work, such as queries and other requests, and perform them as resources allow. Messaging allows database applications to communicate with each other. The Database Engine uses Service Broker to deliver notification messages. This notification functionality doesn't require or use Notification Services, which has been removed from SQL Server 2008.

- **Sync Framework**   Enables data synchronization for collaboration and offline use. Developers can use Sync Framework to synchronize databases and other types of data stores as well as files, folders, and metadata.

As you get started with Microsoft SQL Server 2008, you should concentrate on these areas:

- How SQL Server 2008 works with your hardware

- What versions and editions of SQL Server 2008 are available and how they meet your needs

- How SQL Server 2008 works with Microsoft Windows–based operating systems

- What administration tools are available

# SQL Server 2008 and Your Hardware

Successful database server administration depends on three things:

- Good database administrators

- Strong database architecture

- Appropriate hardware

The first two ingredients are covered: you're the administrator, you're smart enough to buy this book to help you through the rough spots, and you've enlisted SQL Server 2008 to provide your high-performance database needs. This brings us to the issue of hardware. SQL Server 2008 should run on a system with adequate memory, processing speed, and disk space. You also need an appropriate data and system protection plan at the hardware level.

**Note**   Having well-written database applications and proper database design makes a database administrator's job much easier. Poor performance is more often caused by poor application and data structure design than by anything a database administrator can remedy. So in a way, this makes the overall design a fourth ingredient for success—but it's an ingredient that's largely beyond your control as a database administrator.

Key guidelines for choosing hardware for SQL Server are as follows:

- **Memory**   All non-Express editions of SQL Server 2008 require a minimum of 512 MB of RAM and have a recommended RAM of 2048 MB. In most cases, you will want to have at least twice the recommended minimum amount of memory. The primary reason for this extra memory is performance. SQL Server 2008 and standard Windows services together use about 512 MB of memory as a baseline on Windows Server 2003 and 1 GB of memory as a baseline on Windows Server 2008.

  Additional database features—such as Analysis Services, Reporting Services, and Integration Services—increase the baseline memory requirements (by about 30 MB of RAM each). Running either management studio on the SQL Server uses 50 MB to 60 MB of RAM as a baseline. Also, consider the number of user connections. User connections consume about 24 KB each. Data requests and other SQL Server processes use memory as well, and this memory usage is in addition to all other processes and applications running on the server.

- **CPU**   The 32-bit versions of SQL Server 2008 run on Intel *x*86 or compatible hardware. The 64-bit versions run on Intel Itanium (IA-64) and the X64 family of processors from AMD and Intel, including AMD64 and Intel Extended Memory 64 Technology (Intel EM64T). SQL Server provides solid benchmark performance with dual-core and quad-core processors using AMD Opteron, Intel Xeon processor 5000 sequence, and Intel Xeon processor 7000 sequence. Any of these CPUs provide good starting points for the average SQL Server system. You can achieve significant performance improvements with a high-level on-processor cache. Look closely at the L1, L2, and L3 cache options available—a higher cache can yield much better performance overall.

  The primary advantages of 64-bit processors over 32-bit processors have to do with memory limitations and data access. Because 64-bit processors can exceed the 4-GB memory limit of 32-bit processors, they can store greater amounts of data in main memory, providing direct access to and faster processing of data. In addition, 64-bit processors can process data and execute instruction sets that are twice as large as 32-bit processors. Accessing 64 bits of data (versus 32 bits) offers a significant advantage when processing complex calculations that require a high level of precision. However, not all applications are optimized for 64-bit processors, which can present an implementation and maintenance challenge.

- **SMP**   SQL Server 2008 supports symmetric multiprocessors and can process complex parallel queries. Parallel queries are valuable only when relatively few users are on a system and you're processing large queries. On a dedicated system that runs only SQL Server and supports fewer than 100 simultaneous users who aren't doing complex queries, a single CPU should suffice. If the server supports more than 100 users or doesn't run on a dedicated system, you might want to consider adding processors (or using a system that can support additional processors as your needs grow). Keep in mind that the size of the queries and data sets being processed affects how well SQL Server scales. As the size of jobs being processed increases, you will have increasing memory and CPU needs.

- **Disk drives**  The amount of data storage capacity you need depends entirely on the number and size of the databases that the server supports. You need enough disk space to store all your data plus work space, indices, system files, virtual memory, and transaction logs. For log shipping and mirroring, you need space for the backup share, and, in the case of a cluster, the quorum disk. I/O throughput is just as important as drive capacity. For the best I/O performance, FC (Fiber Channel) is the recommended choice for high-end storage solutions. Instead of using a single large drive, you should use several smaller drives, which allows you to configure fault tolerance with RAID (redundant array of independent disks). I recommend separating data and logs and placing them on separate spindles. This includes the backup share for log shipping and the quorum disk for clustering.

- **Data protection**  You should add protection against unexpected drive failure by using RAID. For data, use RAID 0 + 1 or RAID 5. For logs, use RAID 1. RAID 0 (disk striping without parity) offers good read/write performance, but any failed drive results in SQL Server not being able to continue operation on an affected database until the drive is replaced and data is restored from backup. RAID 1 (disk mirroring) creates duplicate copies of data on separate drives, and you can rebuild the RAID unit to restore full operations. RAID 5 (disk striping with parity) offers good protection against single drive failure but has poor write performance. For best performance and fault tolerance, RAID 0 + 1 is recommended, which consists of disk mirroring and disk striping without parity.

- **Uninterruptible Power Supply (UPS)**  SQL Server is designed to maintain database integrity at all times and can recover information using transaction logs. This does not protect the server hardware, however, from sudden power loss or power spikes. Both of these events can seriously damage hardware. To prevent this, get an uninterruptible power supply that conditions the power. A UPS system gives you time to shut down the system properly in the event of a power outage, and it is also important in maintaining database integrity when the server uses write-back caching controllers.

If you follow these hardware guidelines, you will be well on your way to success with SQL Server 2008.

# Microsoft SQL Server 2008 Editions

SQL Server 2008 is distributed in four main editions: Workgroup, Standard, Enterprise, and Developer. In all of these editions, you will find instance features and shared features for installation. The instance features include the full version of SQL Server and support services. The shared features include the client tools, development tools, and documentation required for working with SQL Server from a workstation, as well as Microsoft Sync Framework and Integration Services.

Workgroup Edition is designed as an entry-level database solution. This edition is ideal for small departments in large enterprises and for small businesses that need a robust database solution but do not need the extended business intelligence features of the Standard Edition and Enterprise Edition. The Workgroup Edition

■ Runs on multiple versions of the Microsoft Windows operating system, including Windows XP Professional, Windows Vista, Windows Server 2003, and Windows Server 2008.

> **Note**   For all editions of SQL Server 2008 running on Microsoft Windows Server 2003 and Windows XP Professional, Service Pack 2 (SP2) or later must be installed. For additional requirements pertaining to the operation of SQL Server 2008 on Windows Server 2003 and Windows XP Professional, refer to the SQL Server 2008 Books Online.

■ Supports an unlimited database size, up to the operating system maximum for RAM, two CPUs for symmetric multiprocessing, limited replication publishing, and full-text search.

■ Enables log shipping, which allows SQL Server to send transaction logs from one server to another. Use this feature to create a standby server.

The most widely deployed edition is the Standard Edition, which is designed for the average-sized organization. The Standard Edition

■ Runs on multiple versions of the Microsoft Windows operating system, including Windows XP Professional, Windows Vista, Windows Server 2003, and Windows Server 2008.

■ Supports an unlimited database size, an unlimited amount of RAM, four CPUs for symmetric multiprocessing, full replication publishing, and full-text search.

■ Provides basic features for Analysis Services, Reporting Services, and Integration Services.

■ Includes database mirroring (single-threaded), log stream compression, and two-node failover clustering.

■ Supports limited data encryption and auditing features.

Although the Standard Edition is a strong database server solution, large organizations will want to consider the Enterprise Edition. The Enterprise Edition adds

■ Unlimited scaling and partitioning, which provides for exceptional performance and the ability to scale SQL Server to support very large database installations. By horizontally partitioning tables across multiple servers, you can configure a group of servers to work together to support a large Web site or enterprise data processing.

- Advanced database mirroring for complete online parallel operations and advanced analysis tools for data mining and full-featured OLAP.

- Failover clustering for up to 16 nodes, multi-instance support, database snapshots, indexed views, online page and file restore, backup compression, and hot-add memory and CPU support.

- Extended data encryption and auditing features, including Transparent Data Encryption (TDE) and C2-compliant tracing.

- Multiserver administration, unlimited virtualization, automatic server group management, and mirrored backup media.

As you might expect, the SQL Server 2008 Enterprise Edition runs on multiple versions of the Microsoft Windows operating system, including Windows XP Professional, Windows Vista, Windows Server 2003, and Windows Server 2008. The Developer Edition supports all the features of the Enterprise Edition but is licensed for development/test use only.

Other editions of SQL Server 2008 are available. These editions include the Web Edition, the Compact Edition (which replaces the Mobile Edition in SQL Server 2005), the Express Edition (which includes the redistributable Database Engine), and the Express Edition with Advanced Services. The Compact Edition allows you to use SQL Server as the data store for mobile devices, desktops, and Web clients. The Express Edition is the version you run when you want an easy-to-use, low-end database solution for desktop and small server applications. The Express Edition is free and can be distributed with third-party applications. Both editions support up to a 4-GB database size, up to 1 GB of RAM, and a single CPU.

> **Note**  With the exception of the Express and Compact Editions, most of the differences between various editions of SQL Server are below the surface and don't affect the interface. Therefore, this text refers to specific editions and differentiates between their installation only when necessary. As you would expect, the Express and Compact Editions have simple management interfaces.

Like SQL Server 2005, all editions of SQL Server 2008 automatically and dynamically configure user connections. This behavior is different from SQL Server 7.0 and earlier versions, in which specific limitations were placed on the number of simultaneous user connections. Therefore, you don't have to worry about managing user connections as much as in early versions. Just keep in mind that as the number of user connections increases, so does the amount of resource usage on the server. The server has to balance the workload among the many user connections, which can result in decreased throughput for user connections and the server as a whole.

Like SQL Server 2005, SQL Server 2008 uses the Windows Installer and has a fully integrated installation process. This means you can configure SQL Server 2008 components much like you can any other application you install on the operating system. You can perform the installation remotely from a command shell as well as locally.

SQL Server 2008 uses the same modular component architecture found in Windows Vista and Windows Server 2008. Because of this modular architecture, all non-Express editions of SQL Server 2008 can be part of a single build with the installed edition determined by the key. Further, while you could not upgrade earlier releases of SQL Server from one edition to another, you now can upgrade from one edition to another edition. For example, you can upgrade from Developer Edition to Enterprise Edition.

Chapter 2, "Deploying Microsoft SQL Server 2008," provides detailed instructions for installing SQL Server 2008. For an initial installation, the installer will first check the system configuration to determine the status of required services and components, which includes checking the configuration and availability of the operating system, operating system service packs, installation permissions for the default install path, memory, and hardware.

After checking the system configuration, the installer offers a choice of components to install. Whether you use the Developer, Workgroup, Standard, or Enterprise Edition, you have similar options. You can install instance features, shared features, or both. With instance features—such as Database Engine Services, Analysis Services, and Reporting Services, you can install one or more instances of each on Enterprise and Developer Editions. Each instance of SQL Server consists of a distinct set of services that have specific settings for collation and other options. Directory structures in the file system and in the registry reflect instance names, as do the names associated with SQL Server support services. Shared features, on the other hand, are shared across all instances of SQL Server and include the client tools, development tools, Microsoft Sync Framework, and Integration Services.

SQL Server Replication and Full-Text Search are part of Database Engine Services. Unlike SQL Server 2005 and earlier releases of SQL Server, Full-Text Search is fully integrated into the Database Engine. Additionally, if you choose to install Reporting Services, SQL Server Setup will configure the server as a report server. Unlike SQL Server 2005 and earlier releases of SQL Server, Reporting Services does not require or use IIS.

By installing Client Tools, you can work with remote computers running SQL Server from your workstation. When you install the Client Tools, you might also want to install the SQL Server Books Online and Business Intelligence Development Studio. Books Online provides extended help documentation. Business Intelligence Development Studio allows you to develop business solutions for SQL Server.

> **Tip**   The SQL Native Client header and library files are installed with Database Engine instances of SQL Server. You'll find them under %*ProgramFiles*%\Microsoft SQL Server\100\SDK. When you are developing business solutions for SQL Server, you'll need to ensure you copy and install all of the required files.

# SQL Server and Windows

When you install SQL Server on server operating systems, SQL Server makes several modifications to the environment. These modifications include new system services, integrated authentication, new domain/workgroup accounts, and registry updates.

## Services for SQL Server

When you install SQL Server on Windows, several services are installed on the server. These services include the following:

- **Distributed Transaction Coordinator**   The Distributed Transaction Coordinator service coordinates distributed transactions between two or more database servers.

- **SQL Active Directory Helper**   MSSQLServerADHelper100 adds and removes objects used to register SQL Server and Analysis Server instances. It also Updates object permissions related to SQL Server service accounts.

- **SQL Full-Text Filter Daemon Launcher**   Starts the full-text filter daemon process. This process performs document filtering and word breaking for SQL Server full-text search.

- **SQL Server**   The SQL Server service is the primary database service. For the default database instance, this service is named SQL Server (MSSQLServer). When multiple instances of SQL Server are installed, you will also see MSSQL$*instancename*, where *instancename* is the name of the SQL Server instance.

- **SQL Server Agent**   The SQL Server Agent is used with scheduling and alerting. For the default database instance, this service is named SQLServerAgent. When multiple instances of SQL Server are installed, you will also see SQLAgent$*instancename*, where *instancename* is the name of the SQL Server instance.

- **SQL Server Analysis Services**   The Microsoft SQL Server Analysis Services are used for OLAP and data mining. For the default database instance, this service is named MSSQLServerOLAPService. When multiple instances of SQL Server are installed, you will also see MSOLAP$*instancename*, where *instancename* is the name of the SQL Server instance.

- **SQL Server Browser**   The SQL browser (SQLBrowser) provides connection details and information to clients.

- **SQL Server Integration Services 10.0**   MsDtsServer100 provides an enterprise data transformation and integration solution for extracting and transforming data.

- **SQL Server Reporting Services**   Microsoft Reporting Services creates, manages, and delivers reports. For the default database instance, this service is named ReportServer. When multiple instances of SQL Server are installed, you will also see ReportServer$*instancename*, where *instancename* is the name of the SQL Server instance.

- **SQL Server VSS Writer**   SQLWriter provides the necessary interfaces for backing up and restoring SQL Server using the Volume Shadow Copy Service (VSS).

**Note**   You will learn more about managing services and configuring service-related options in Chapter 5, "Managing the Enterprise."

## SQL Server Logins and Authentication

SQL Server authentication allows authentication using simple connection strings containing user IDs and passwords—a technique that is compatible with non-Windows clients and applications. Integrated Windows Authentication provides a more robust solution for authentication using Windows domain accounts and local computer accounts. Completely integrating SQL Server security with Windows domain security allows for authentication based on user and group memberships as well. Together, these authentication techniques make it much easier to manage access and security. You can do the following:

- Combine Windows and SQL Server authentication so that users in Windows domains can access the server using a single account and other users can be logged on using a SQL Server login ID.

- Use authentication based on Windows domain accounts only so that only users with a domain account can access the server.

For SQL Server 2008, SQL Server authentication supports encryption by default using certificates generated by SQL Server to encrypt the channel when transmitting log-in packets. Because of this, you do not have to acquire and install a valid Secure Sockets Layer (SSL) certificate to ensure that SQL credentials are secure and encrypted regardless of whether SQL logins or Windows logins are used.

When running on Windows Server 2003 or Windows Server 2008, the Database Engine also uses Group Policy for password policy enforcement rules on SQL Server logins. SQL Server validates passwords automatically during authentication and whenever you set or reset passwords, unless you suspend enforcement for a specific login. For more information, see Chapter 9, "Managing SQL Server 2008 Security."

## Service Accounts for SQL Server

When using Windows Server 2003 and Windows Server 2008, SQL Server services can be configured either to log on as Local System, Local Service, or Network Service or to use Windows logon accounts. There are advantages and disadvantages to each of these techniques, as follows:

- **Local system accounts**   This option provides administrative privileges to SQL Server on the local system but no privileges on the network. If the server requires resources on the local server only, use the local system account. Use local system accounts when you want to isolate SQL Server and restrict it from interacting with other servers.

- **Local service accounts**   This option provides the same level of access to resources and objects as members of the Users group. Services that run under this account access network resources as a null session without credentials. Use this account when a SQL Server service doesn't need access to other servers.

- **Network service accounts**   This option provides the same level of access to resources and objects as members of the Users group and also allows Services that run under this account to access the network and thereby communicate with other servers. Specifically, processes running under this account can interact throughout a network using the credentials of the computer account.

- **Domain accounts**   This option sets the service to use a standard domain account with privileges you configure. Use domain accounts when the server requires resources across the network, when you need to forward events to the application logs of other systems, and when you want to configure e-mail or pager notification.

You should configure SQL Server services with the lowest possible privileges, making sure only those privileges required are assigned. Table 1-1 provides a summary of the account types under which specific SQL Server services can run as well as the standard default account. Although SQL Server and SQL Server Agent can run under the Network Service account, Microsoft doesn't recommend this when other services that use the account are installed on the computer.

**Table 1-1   Account Types for SQL Server Services**

| Service Name | Domain User | Local System | Network Service | Local Service | Default Account |
|---|---|---|---|---|---|
| SQL Server | Yes | Yes | Yes | No | Domain User |
| SQL Server Agent | Yes | Yes | Yes | No | Domain User |
| Analysis Services | Yes | No | Yes | Yes | Domain User |
| Reporting Services | Yes | Yes | Yes | Yes | Domain User |
| Integration Services | Yes | Yes | Yes | Yes | Network Service |
| SQL Server Browser | Yes | Yes | Yes | Yes | Domain User |
| SQL Server Active Directory Helper | No | Yes | Yes | No | Domain User |
| SQL Writer | No | Yes | No | No | Local System |

**Note**   Security in SQL Server is managed through logins, server roles, database access permissions, and object permissions. Windows domain accounts can be used for user authentication and logging in to SQL Server. You can, for example, specify a Windows account to use for authentication and log in to SQL Server. You will learn more about SQL Server logins, server roles, and security in Chapter 8, "Full-Text Search Administration."

# Using the Graphical Administration Tools

SQL Server 2008 provides several types of tools for administration. The graphical administration tools are the ones you will use most often. You can access these tools by selecting Start, choosing All Programs, and then using the Microsoft SQL Server 2008 menu. With a full instance and shared feature installation, the Microsoft SQL Server 2008 menu has the following options and suboptions:

- Import And Export Data
- SQL Server Business Intelligence Studio
- SQL Server Management Studio
- Analysis Services
    - ❏ Deployment Wizard
- Configuration Tools
    - ❏ Reporting Services Configuration Manager
    - ❏ SQL Server Configuration Manager
    - ❏ SQL Server Error And Usage Reporting
    - ❏ SQL Server Installation Center
- Documentation And Tutorials
    - ❏ Microsoft SQL Server Samples Overview
    - ❏ SQL Server Books Online
    - ❏ SQL Server Tutorials
- Integration Services
    - ❏ Data Profile Viewer
    - ❏ Execute Package Utility
- Performance Tools
    - ❏ Database Engine Tuning Advisor
    - ❏ SQL Server Profiler

SQL Server Management Studio is the tool you'll use to perform most of your core SQL Server administration tasks. SQL Server Management Studio provides several different views. When you first start working with this tool, you will see the Object Explorer view as shown in Figure 1-1. If it is not displayed, this and other views can be accessed from the View menu, and the following descriptions explain how to use each view:

- **Object Explorer**   Allows you to view and connect to SQL Server, Analysis Services, Integration Services, Reporting Services, and SQL Server Compact Edition. Once connected to a particular server, you view its components as an object tree and can expand nodes to work your way to lower levels of the tree.

- **Registered Servers**   Shows the currently registered servers. The top bar of the view allows you to quickly switch between servers of a particular type (SQL Server, Analysis Server, Integration Server, Report Server, SQL Compact Edition).

- **Template Explorer**   Provides quick access to the default Query Editor templates and any custom templates you have created. You can create templates in any script language supported by SQL Server Management Studio. SQL Server, Analysis Server, and SQL Server Compact Edition support templates.

- **Solutions Explorer**   Provides quick access to existing SQL Server, Analysis Server, and SQL Compact Edition projects. Projects detail connections, queries, and other functions to perform when the project is executed.

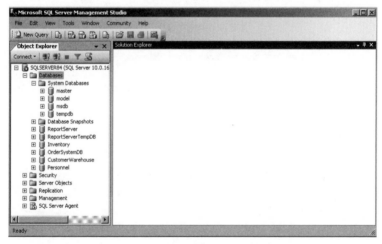

**Figure 1-1**   Use SQL Server Management Studio to perform core administration tasks.

If you have worked with early versions of SQL Server, you will find that SQL Server Management Studio is very different from the tools it replaces. Most of the friendly wizards are gone, and they have been replaced with nonmodal dialog boxes that provide quick access to configuration elements. As shown in Figure 1-2, Script and Help options are provided on the top bar of these dialog boxes to make it easy for you to generate a script based on your configuration choices and get help when you need it.

**Figure 1-2**   Use the top bar options to quickly perform key tasks.

Another important tool is SQL Server Configuration Manager, shown in Figure 1-3. SQL Server Configuration Manager replaces Server Network Utility, Client Network Utility, and Services Manager. This means you can use SQL Server Configuration Manager to perform many essential service setup and network configuration tasks. When you select a service under the Services node, you can manage the service in the details pane by right-clicking it and then choosing an appropriate option, such as Start, Stop, or Restart. You can also choose Properties to configure the related settings, such as startup mode, login account, and login account password.

**Figure 1-3**   Use SQL Server Configuration Manager to manage services and network configurations.

SQL Server 2008 is designed for local and remote management. You can use most of the tools to manage local resources as well as remote resources. For example, in SQL Server Management Studio, you can register a new server and then connect to it. Afterward, you can remotely manage the server and all its databases from your system. Table 1-2 provides a summary of the graphical administration tools discussed, as well as other useful graphical tools.

**Table 1-2   Quick Reference for Key SQL Server 2008 Administration Tools**

| Administration Tool | Purpose |
|---|---|
| Analysis Services Deployment Wizard | Allows you to deploy the output from an Analysis Services project to a target server using specified deployment configuration settings and options. |
| Business Intelligence Development Studio | Allows you to develop and manage Business Intelligence objects. This feature includes SSIS Designer, which you can use to create and maintain SQL Server Integration Services (SSIS) packages. |
| Database Engine Tuning Adviser | Helps you tune the performance of SQL Server databases. |
| Import And Export Data Wizard | Allows you to define SSIS Services packages for importing and exporting data. |
| SQL Server Configuration Manager | Allows you to configure the client and server network libraries and manage SQL Server services. Replaces Server Network Utility, Client Network Utility, and Services Manager. This feature is covered in Chapter 2. |
| SQL Server Installation Center | Provides a central interface for upgrading to SQL Server 2008 from SQL Server 2000 or SQL Server 2005, installing instance and shared features and configuring SQL Server clusters. |
| SQL Server Management Studio | The main administration tool for SQL Server 2008. This feature manages SQL servers, databases, security, and more. Key aspects are discussed in Chapter 4, "Configuring and Tuning Microsoft SQL Server 2008." It replaces SQL Server Enterprise Manager, Query Analyzer, and Analysis Manager. |
| SQL Server Profiler | Allows you to analyze user activity and generate audit trails. SQL Profiler is a graphical interface to SQL Trace. This feature is covered in Chapter 14, "Profiling and Monitoring Microsoft SQL Server 2008." |

# Using the Command-Line Tools

The graphical administration tools provide just about everything you need to work with SQL Server. Still, there are times when you might want to work from the command line, especially if you want to automate installation, administration, or maintenance with scripts. The primary command-line tool is SQLCMD.EXE, which replaces OSQL.EXE and ISQL.EXE. Another command-line tool you'll use is BCP.EXE.

## BCP

BCP is the bulk copy program. You can use BCP to import and export data or copy data between instances of SQL Server 2008. The major advantage of BCP is its speed. It is much faster than standard database import/export procedures. Unfortunately, its command-line syntax makes it much harder to use.

The syntax for BCP is shown in Sample 1-1.

**Sample 1-1**   BCP Syntax

```
bcp {dbtable | view | query} {in | out | queryout | format} datafile
  [-m maxerrors] [-f formatfile] [-e errfile]
  [-F firstrow] [-L lastrow] [-b batchsize]
  [-n native type] [-c character type] [-w Unicode characters]
  [-N keep non-text native] [-V file format version] [-q quoted id]
  [-C code page specifier] [-t field terminator] [-r row terminator]
  [-i inputfile] [-o outfile] [-a packetsize]
  [-S server name\instance name] [-U username] [-P password]
  [-T trusted connection] [-v version] [-R regional enable]
  [-k keep null values] [-E keep identity values]
  [-h "load hints"] [-x generate xml format file]
```

## SQLCMD

SQLCMD is an SQL query tool that you can run from the command line. Unlike OSQL and ISQL, which SQLCMD replaces, SQLCMD communicates with SQL Server only through the OLE DB application programming interface (API). Like OSQL and ISQL, SQLCMD has very little overhead, making it a good choice when system resources are a concern. Sample 1-2 shows the syntax for SQLCMD.

**Sample 1-2**   SQLCMD Syntax

```
sqlcmd [-U login id] [-P password]
  [-S servername[\instancename]] [-H hostname] [-E trusted connection]
  [-d use database name] [-l login timeout] [-t query timeout]
  [-h headers] [-s colseparator] [-w screen width]
  [-a packetsize] [-e echo input] [-I Enable Quoted Identifier]
  [-c cmdend] [-L[c] list servers[clean output]]
  [-q "cmdline query"] [-Q "cmdline query" and exit]
  [-m errorlevel] [-V severitylevel] [-W remove trailing spaces]
```

```
[-u unicode output] [-r[0|1] msgs to stderr]
[-i inputfile] [-o outputfile] [-z new password]
[-f <codepage> | i:<codepage>[,o:<codepage>]] [-Z new password and
    exit]
[-k[1|2] remove[replace] control characters]
[-y variable length type display width]
[-Y fixed length type display width]
[-p[1] print statistics[colon format]]
[-R use client regional setting]
[-b On error batch abort]
[-v var = "value"...] [-A dedicated admin connection]
[-X[1] disable commands[and exit with warning]]
[-x disable variable substitution]
```

**Note**   Unlike ISQL, SQLCMD does support connecting to named instances of SQL Server 2008. By default, SQLCMD connects to the default instance of SQL Server. If you specify the instance name as well as the server name, SQLCMD will connect to the specified instance name on the designated server.

When you start SQLCMD, you can issue Transact-SQL statements to run queries, execute stored procedures, and perform additional tasks. Because you are working at the command line, these commands aren't executed automatically, and you need to use additional commands to tell SQLCMD when to execute statements, when to ignore statements, and so on. These additional statements must be entered on separate lines and are summarized in Table 1-3.

**Note**   With some commands the colon [:] is optional to maintain compatibility with OSQL scripts. This is indicated by the [:] notation in the table.

**Table 1-3   SQLCMD Commands**

| Command | Description | Supported by Invoke-SQLCmd |
| --- | --- | --- |
| Ctrl+C | Ends a query without exiting from SQLCMD. | Yes |
| Go [count] | Executes all statements entered up to the previous GO or RESET. If count is used, the cached statements are executed the number of times specified in count as a single batch. | Yes |
| :!! *command* | Executes the specified system command or script. | No |
| :connect | Connects to an instance of SQL Server, or closes the current connection. The syntax is: connect [timeout] [*ServerName\InstanceName*] [*Username*] [*Password*] | No |

Table 1-3    SQLCMD Commands

| Command | Description | Supported by Invoke-SQLCmd |
|---|---|---|
| :ed | Calls the text editor, which is defined by the SQLCMDEDITOR environment variable, such as **SET SQLCMDEDITOR=notepad**. | No |
| :error *filename* | Redirects all error output to the specified file. | No |
| :exit *statement* | Sets the exit statement. The batch or query is executed, and then SQLCMD quits. | Yes |
| :help | Displays a list of available commands. | Yes |
| :list | Prints the contents of the statement cache. | No |
| :listvar | Lists currently set variables. | No |
| :out *filename* | Redirects all query results to the specified file. | No |
| :perftrace *filename* | Redirects all performance trace information to the specified file. | No |
| :quit | Exits SQLCMD. | Yes |
| :r *filename* | Sets the name of a file containing Transact-SQL statements to execute, which can include the GO command. | Yes |
| :reset | Clears statements you've entered so that they aren't executed. | No |
| :serverlist | Lists the locally configured servers and any network servers. | No |
| :setvar | Sets variables. | Yes |

In early editions of SQL Server, you used ODBCPING to verify an ODBC connection between a client and server. In SQL Server 2008, OLE DB is the preferred technique for establishing database connections. You can establish a connection to a server for the purposes of testing and troubleshooting using SQLCMD –A.

## Other Command-Line Tools

Table 1-4 provides a summary of key command prompt utilities included in SQL Server 2008. As the table shows, most command-line executables are stored in the %ProgramFiles%\Microsoft SQL Server\100\Tools\Binn directory or in the directory for the SQL Server component to which they relate. On a 64-bit computer, you'll find a separate Program Files folder for 32-bit tools. For example, on X64 computers, you'll find a Program Files folder with 64-bit tools and a Program Files (x86) folder with 32-bit tools.

Table 1-4    Key Command-Line Tools for SQL Server 2008

| Name | Description | Location |
|---|---|---|
| Bulk Copy Utility (bcp.exe) | Used to import and export data or to copy data between instances of SQL Server. | %*ProgramFiles*%\Microsoft SQL Server\100\Tools\Binn |
| Database Maintenance Plan Utility (sqlmaint.exe) | Used to execute database maintenance plans created in previous versions of SQL Server. | %*ProgramFiles*%\Microsoft SQL Server\MSSQL10.*InstanceName*\ MSSQL\Binn |
| Replication Monitor (sqlmonitor.exe) | Used to start Replication Monitor from a command line. | %*ProgramFiles*%\Microsoft SQL Server\100\Tools\Binn |
| Reporting Services Configuration Manager (rsconfigtool.exe) | Used to start Reporting Services Configuration Manager from a command prompt. | %*ProgramFiles*%\Microsoft SQL Server\100\Tools\Binn |
| Reporting Services Configuration Utility (rsconfig.exe) | Used to configure a report server connection. | %*ProgramFiles*%\Microsoft SQL Server\100\Tools\Binn |
| Reporting Services Key Management Utility (rskeymgmt.exe) | Used to manage encryption keys on a report server. | %*ProgramFiles*%\Microsoft SQL Server\100\Tools\Binn |
| Reporting Services Utility (rs.exe) | Used to run Reporting Services scripts. | %*ProgramFiles*%\Microsoft SQL Server\100\Tools\Binn |
| SQL Diagnostics Utility (sqldiag.exe) | Used to perform comprehensive diagnostics testing for troubleshooting. | %*ProgramFiles*%\Microsoft SQL Server\100\Tools\Binn |
| SQL Query Command-Line Utility (sqlcmd.exe) | Used to perform administration and enter T-SQL statements at the command prompt. | %*ProgramFiles*%\Microsoft SQL Server\100\Tools\Binn |
| SQL Server Agent (sqlagent.exe) | Used to start SQL Server Agent from a command prompt. | %*ProgramFiles*%\Microsoft SQL Server\MSSQL10.*InstanceName*\ MSSQL\Binn |
| SQL Server Database Engine (sqlservr.exe) | Used to start and stop an instance of the SQL Server Database Engine. | %*ProgramFiles*%\Microsoft SQL Server\MSSQL10.*InstanceName*\ MSSQL\Binn |
| SQL Server Database Engine Tuning Advisor (dta.exe) | Used to analyze workloads and recommend optimization changes for that workload. | %*ProgramFiles*%\Microsoft SQL Server\100\Tools\Binn |

Table 1-4    Key Command-Line Tools for SQL Server 2008

| Name | Description | Location |
|------|-------------|----------|
| SQL Server Execution Package Utility (dtexec.exe) | Used to configure and execute a SQL Server Integration Services (SSIS) package. The corresponding GUI tool is DTExecUI. | *%ProgramFiles%*\Microsoft SQL Server\100\DTS\Binn |
| SQL Server Log Shipping Agent (sqllogship.exe) | Used to configure and manage log shipping. | *%ProgramFiles%*\Microsoft SQL Server\100\Tools\Binn |
| SQL Server PowerShell (sqlps.exe) | Used to start the SQL Server PowerShell and load the SQL Server provider. | *%ProgramFiles%*\Microsoft SQL Server\100\Tools\Binn |
| SQL Server Profiler (profiler.exe) | Used to start SQL Server Profiler from a command prompt. | *%ProgramFiles%*\Microsoft SQL Server\100\Tools\Binn |
| SQL Server Replication Diff Tool (tablediff.exe) | Used to compare the data in two tables and display differences. | *%ProgramFiles%*\Microsoft SQL Server\100\COM |
| SQL Server Service Broker Diagnostics Utility (ssbdiagnose.exe) | Used to diagnose communication and configuration issues related to SQL Server Service Broker. | *%ProgramFiles%*\Microsoft SQL Server\100\Tools\Binn |
| SQL Server SSIS Package Utilities (dtutil.exe) | Used to manage SQL Server Integration Services (SSIS) packages. | *%ProgramFiles%*\Microsoft SQL Server\100\DTS\Binn |

# Using the SQL Server PowerShell

Windows PowerShell is increasingly being used in enterprises, and SQL Server 2008 includes extensions to help you take advantage of this powerful shell environment. By default, when you install the Database Engine, SQL Server Setup installs Windows PowerShell and then configures extensions for SQL Server 2008. However, if you've already installed the appropriate version of Windows PowerShell, SQL Server Setup installs only the necessary extensions for SQL Server 2008.

## Running and Using Cmdlets

Windows PowerShell introduces the concept of a cmdlet (pronounced *commandlet*). A cmdlet is the smallest unit of functionality in the Windows PowerShell. You can think of a cmdlet as a built-in command. Rather than being highly complex, most cmdlets are quite simple and have a small set of associated properties.

You use cmdlets the same way you use any other commands and utilities. Cmdlet names are not case-sensitive. This means you can use a combination of both uppercase and lowercase characters. After starting Windows PowerShell, you can enter the name of the cmdlet at the prompt and it will run in much the same way as a command-line command.

For ease of reference, cmdlets are named using verb-noun pairs. The noun tells you specifically what the cmdlet works with. For example, the get-variable cmdlet gets a named Windows PowerShell environment variable and returns its value. If you don't specify which variable to get as a parameter, get-variable returns a list of all Windows PowerShell environment variables and their values.

You can work with cmdlets by executing commands directly at the shell prompt or by running commands from within scripts. You can enter any command or cmdlet you can run at the Windows PowerShell command prompt into a script by copying the related command text to a file and saving the file with the .ps1 extension. You can then run the script in the same way you would any other command or cmdlet. However, when you are working with Windows PowerShell, the current directory might not be part of the environment path. For this reason, you might need to use "./" when you run a script in the current directory, such as

```
./runtasks
```

From the Windows command-line environment or a batch script, you can execute Windows PowerShell cmdlets with the –command parameter. Generally, you will also want to suppress the Windows PowerShell logo with the –nologo parameter and stop execution of profiles with the –noprofile parameter. For example, at a command prompt or in a .BAT script, you could get a list of running processes using the following command:

```
msh -nologo -noprofile -command get-process
```

> **Note**   Windows PowerShell also includes a rich scripting language and allows the use of standard language constructs for looping, conditional execution, flow control, and variable assignment. Discussion of these features is beyond the scope of this book. A good resource is *Windows PowerShell Administrator's Pocket Consultant* (Microsoft Press, 2008).

## Running and Using the SQL Server PowerShell

SQL Server PowerShell (sqlps.exe) is a version of the Windows PowerShell with extensions for SQL Server 2008. You use SQL Server PowerShell to work with instances of the SQL Server Database Engine and the objects in those instances.

To invoke the SQL Server PowerShell, you must first open a command prompt window and then start the SQL Server PowerShell by typing **sqlps** at the command line. To exit the SQL Server PowerShell and return to the command prompt, type **exit**.

Usually, when the shell starts, you will see a message similar to the following:

```
Microsoft SQL Server PowerShell
Version 10
Microsoft Corp. All rights reserved.
```

You can disable this message by starting the shell with the –nologo parameter, such as

```
sqlps -nologo
```

Regardless of how you start the shell, you know you are using the SQL Server Power-Shell because the command prompt title bar changes to Command Prompt – sqlps and the current path is preceded by PS.

The current execution policy for SQL Server PowerShell controls whether and how you can run scripts. Although the default configuration depends on which operating system and edition you've installed, you can quickly determine the execution policy by entering **get-executionpolicy** at the PowerShell prompt.

To set the execution policy to require that all scripts have a trusted signature to execute, enter the following command:

```
set-executionpolicy allsigned
```

To set the execution policy so that scripts downloaded from the Web execute only if they are signed by a trusted source, enter:

```
set-executionpolicy remotesigned
```

To set the execution policy to run scripts regardless of whether they have a digital signature and work in an unrestricted environment, you can enter the following command:

```
set-executionpolicy unrestricted
```

## Working with SQL Server Cmdlets

When you are working with the SQL Server PowerShell, the available cmdlets are different than when you are working with the standard Windows PowerShell. The reason for this is that the set of registered snap-ins is different. Additional SQL Server–specific cmdlets are available, and some standard PowerShell cmdlets might not be available.

In the original implementation of SQL Server PowerShell, the following additional cmdlets are included:

- **Convert-UrnToPath** Converts a SQL Server Management Object Uniform Resource Name (URN) to a SQL Server provider path. The URN indicates a management object's location within the SQL Server object hierarchy. If the URN path has characters not supported by PowerShell, the characters are encoded automatically.

- **Decode-SQLName**    Returns an unencoded SQL Server identifier when given an identifier that has been encoded.

- **Encode-SQLName**    Encodes special characters in SQL Server identifiers and name paths to formats that are usable in PowerShell paths. The characters encoded by this cmdlet include \:/%<>*?[]|. If you don't encode these characters, you must escape them using the single quote (') character.

- **Invoke-PolicyEvaluation**    Evaluates management policies applied to SQL Server instances. By default, this command reports compliance but does not enforce compliance. To enforce compliance, set –AdHocPolicyEvaluationMode to Configure.

- **Invoke-SQLCmd**    Runs a Transact-SQL or XQuery script containing commands supported by the sqlcmd utility. By default, this cmdlet doesn't set any sqlcmd variables by default or return message output. As shown in Table 1-3, many sqlcmd commands aren't supported.

Because the set of available cmdlets and cmdlet options will change as new versions of SQL Server PowerShell are released by Microsoft, you can use the following techniques to discover new cmdlets and determine how they are used:

- To view a list of all cmdlets, type **get-command** at the shell prompt.

- To get detailed information about a cmdlet, type **get-help** *CmdletName* **–detailed** where *CmdletName* is the name of the cmdlet you want to examine.

- To get detailed information about the SQL Server provider, which provides the SQL Server functionality for PowerShell, type **get-help sqlserver | more**.

# Chapter 2

# Deploying Microsoft SQL Server 2008

With SQL Server Setup, you can create new instances of SQL Server, add components, rebuild the SQL Server registry, uninstall SQL Server, and perform other common setup tasks. Prior to setup and configuration, you need to decide how SQL Server 2008 will be used in your environment. When you have decided on the role SQL Server 2008 will have, you can plan for your deployment and then roll out SQL Server.

## SQL Server Integration Roles

SQL Server 2008 is designed as a comprehensive Business Intelligence platform that can be used for

- Extraction, Transformation, and Loading (ETL)
- Relational data warehouses
- Multidimensional databases and data mining
- SQL Server Analysis Services
- Managed reporting

### Using SQL Server Integration Services

SQL Server Integration Services (SSIS) provides a complete enterprise ETL platform that is fully programmable and extensible. Although basic SSIS packages can be created using SQL Server Management Studio, true ETL packages can be created only with the Business Intelligence Development Studio. With the redesigned SSIS, you no longer have to write self-modifying packages. Instead, you should use package variables and the package configuration framework to customize the way the package runs in different circumstances.

This book will use the terms *DTS 2000* and *SSIS* to differentiate between SSIS packages designed for SQL Server 2000 and SSIS packages designed for SQL Server 2008. You can use the DTS 2000 Package Migration Wizard to migrate DTS packages designed for SQL Server 2000 to SSIS packages for SQL Server 2008. A DTS 2000 runtime is also provided so that you can run DTS 2000 packages without upgrading them.

SQL Server 2008 improves ETL performance through the following features:

- **Lookup cache enhancements**   A lookup builds a cache of retrieved rows taken from the dataset you are working with. SQL Server 2005 has several lookup limitations. It can populate the cache only by using an SQL query. It can get data only from specific OLE DB connections. It reloads the cache every time it is used. With SQL Server 2008, you can populate the cache using a separate pipeline in the same package or a different package and use any available source data. To reuse the cache easily, you can save the cache to virtual memory or file storage. Lookup performance has been enhanced in many other ways as well, including a miss-cache feature that loads key values that have no matching entries in the reference dataset into the cache to save time.

- **Pipeline parallelism**   Normally, SQL Server 2005 SSIS processes execution trees serially even if you split the data flow. This occurs because all output paths of a multicast belong to the same execution tree and SQL Server 2005 SSIS doesn't use more than one processor thread per execution tree even if there are more processor threads available. With pipeline parallelism, SQL Server 2008 can take full advantage of multiple processors or multiple processor cores using shared thread pools that allow multiple outputs of a multicast to be executed simultaneously. Further, because each output has an active buffer and not just one buffer and one active thread, this can result in parallel execution that ensures all processors and processor cores are fully utilized.

**Note**   You will find complete details for working with SSIS in Chapter 11, "Importing, Exporting, and Transforming Data."

## Using SQL Server 2008 for Relational Data Warehousing

SQL Server 2008 continues to provide a best-of-class relational data warehouse platform in the tradition of SQL Server 2000 and SQL Server 2005. Integration with the .NET Framework enables you to build database applications that use managed code rather than Transact-SQL.

Your managed code can be organized into classes and namespaces for ease of management and maintenance. In many cases, you will find that managed code is better than Transact-SQL at processing numbers, managing complicated execution logic, and manipulating data strings with regular expressions. Transact-SQL remains a good choice to perform data access with little or no procedural logic.

As with Transact-SQL, managed code runs on the computer running SQL Server. This approach keeps the server functionality and the data close together without requiring an additional layer in your infrastructure. It also allows you to take advantage of the server's processing power while reducing network traffic between the database servers and the middle tier.

SQL Server 2008 Enterprise Edition has made significant enhancements to the relational database management system (DBMS) that was used in earlier releases. These enhancements allow SQL Server 2008 to perform better when you create, manage, and query large data warehouses and include

- **Partitioned table parallelism**   SQL Server 2005 includes logic that allows allocation of all available processor threads to a single-partition query. However, queries that work with more than one partition use one thread (and one processor core) per partition even if there are more processor threads available. With partitioned table parallelism, SQL Server 2008 can take full advantage of multiple processors or multiple processor cores when processing queries across multiple partitions and more predictably use available processor resources to improve query performance. Now, when a query works with more than one partition, SQL Server 2008 can assign all available threads to the partitions, and it does so in round-robin fashion to boost performance. This functionality can result in parallel execution plans that ensure all processors and processor cores are fully utilized.

- **Partition-aligned indexed views**   Normally, when you have a fact table that is partitioned by date or by another element, you use indexed views to help speed up queries. With SQL Server 2005, you must drop any indexed views defined on a partitioned table before using the ALTER TABLE SWITCH statement to switch a partition in or out. With partitioned-aligned indexed views in SQL Server 2008, you bring along the indexed views for the partition when you switch in a partition. This means you don't have to rebuild indexed views on an entire partitioned table, and that helps to automatically maintain indexed views and automatically rewrite queries to use indexed views to resolve queries that refer only to the base tables.

- **GROUPING SET statements**   Normally, when you want to examine multiple summary aggregates (indexed views), you have to run multiple queries and then use the UNION ALL statement to combine the queries into one result set. With the GROUP BY GROUPING SETS statement, you can write one query against multiple aggregates and return a single result set. You can then order the result set using the ORDER BY statement.

- **Merge operations**   Normally, when you want to perform multiple insert, update, and delete operations on the same data, you must perform each operation in turn using separate INSERT, UPDATE, and DELETE statements, which can tie up computer resources. With the MERGE statement, SQL Server 2008 joins the target table or view with a data source and then performs the insert, update, and delete operations on the results of the join. Because the merge operation requires only a single pass over the data, MERGE statements offer much better performance than running separate insert, update, and delete operations.

- **Change data capture**   Normally, when you need to track changes made to a database, you must use triggers, timestamp columns, or resource-intensive queries to determine what changed. Change data capture eliminates the need for these techniques by tracking changes made to user tables for you. The auxiliary data SQL Server 2008 gathers when using change data capture, in turn, makes it easy to determine what was changed and when.

- **Minimally logged inserts**   Normally, when you write data to a database, SQL Server must write it twice: once to the log and once to the database. This is because you might need to be able to undo or redo transactions. To bypass this write-twice approach, you can use minimal logging with existing tables to log only the information that is required to roll back the transaction while writing all the related data directly to the database. Although this approach makes it impossible to do point-in-time recovery, it does speed up the write process considerably. SQL Server 2005 allows you to minimally log bulk import operations, index creation operations, index rebuild operations, and SELECT INTO statements. SQL Server 2008 extends minimal logging to include INSERT INTO...SELECT FROM statements, provided that you are inserting into an empty table that has a clustered index and no nonclustered indexes or that you are inserting into a nonempty heap that has no indexes.

SQL Server 2008 supports resource controls, data compression, and backup compression. Resource controls implemented in the Resource Governor allow you to control the amount of CPU and memory resources allocated to various parts of the database workload. It also allows you to reserve resources by prioritizing the workload. Data compression at the page and row level reduces the size of tables while requiring additional processing power to compress and uncompress data. Backup compression reduces the amount of data SQL Server 2008 has to write and the size of your SQL backups.

## Using SQL Server 2008 for Multidimensional Databases and Data Mining

In SQL Server 2008, Analysis Services has been enhanced to provide better support for multidimensional databases and data mining. Analysis Services has two key components: an Online Analytical Processing (OLAP) engine and a data-mining engine. You can build an analytic database from any data source, including a relational database. You then define the analytic structure, the data-mining models, and the views into this structure.

SQL Server 2008 Analysis Services uses the Unified Dimension Model (UDM). UDM combines the best features of the relational and OLAP data models, serving to blur the lines between traditional relational databases and multidimensional OLAP databases. A set of cubes and dimensions defined in SQL Server 2008 is referred to as a *Unified Dimension Model*. This model improves query performance and flexibility.

The data definition language for SQL Server 2008 Analysis Services is XML. Because of this, the metadata repository is removed and replaced by XML files that are stored and managed on the SQL Server 2008 Analysis Services server. Additionally, unlike SQL Server 2000 Analysis Services, SQL Server 2008 Analysis Services performs all calculations on the server rather than on the client. This eliminates the need for client-side caching and can improve query performance for complex calculations. To reduce latency and improve performance, proactive caching is used. The way proactive caching works can be customized so that you can configure how often the cache is rebuilt, how queries are answered while the cache is being rebuilt, and whether the cache is automatically refreshed when transactions occur, and you can control other characteristics of the cache as well.

With dimensionally modeled data warehouses, queries that join the fact table with one or more dimension tables are known as *star join queries*. Most star join queries express filter conditions on nonkey columns of the dimension tables and perform an aggregation on a column of the fact table. SQL Server 2008 uses a series of hash joins to optimize the star join, building a hash table for each dimension table. SQL Server 2008 also uses the hash tables to reduce the join information, using a bitmap filter that eliminates nonqualifying fact table rows. Together these enhancements can reduce CPU processing time considerably.

During MDX queries, SQL Server 2008 Analysis Services improves block computation performance in two ways:

- By evaluating only non-null values in the cube space
- By recognizing where the same work needs to be redone

Normally, regardless of whether the data is sparse or dense, cells in a cube always are evaluated on a cell-by-cell basis. This means if the data is sparse, cells in a cube are calculated regardless of whether they will return a null value, and if data is dense, the same work is redone over and over. To speed up multidimensional query processing, SQL Server 2008 calculates only cells that will return non-null values and moves the evaluation process up the execution tree rather than performing it at the cell level. This behavior allows SQL Server 2008 to work down the execution tree to determine what cells need to be filled and then to obtain the necessary storage engine data for base measures that are required to fill spaces as SQL Server 2008 works up the tree. Combined, these behaviors allow for fast and efficient processing.

Another area of Analysis Services that has been improved is cell writeback. When users update cell values at leaf or aggregate levels, they are using the cell writeback feature.

With cell writeback, each measure group has a special writeback partition that stores the difference between an updated cell value and a cell's original value. When a multidimensional query requests cell data from a measure group, Analysis Services accesses all partitions, including the writeback partition, and aggregates the results to produce the correct cell value. In SQL Server 2005, Analysis Services requires writeback partitions to use relational OLAP storage. In SQL Server 2008, Analysis Services can use writeback partitions with multidimensional OLAP storage, and this improves performance.

SQL Server 2008 Analysis Services has a new backup storage subsystem that introduces an enhanced backup format. While you previously had to use raw file system utilities to back up large databases, you can now use the backup subsystem that is integrated into Analysis Services.

The scalable shared database (SSD) feature allows you to mark a database as read only and share it across multiple server instances from a storage area network (SAN). Previously, you needed to use a load-balancing solution, such as network load balancing (NLB), and replicate the data between the servers to scale out in this way. With SSD, you scale out processing, queries, data, and cache management to new servers while eliminating the need to replicate data by using a central read-only database on a shared SAN drive. This saves time and disk space.

A typical SSD deployment for Analysis Services involves

- A network load-balancing solution between the clients and the servers
- SQL Server Analysis Services servers connected to a SAN
- A read-only database on a shared SAN drive

As with SQL Server 2005, you can apply a similar SSD solution to your relational database needs.

## Using SQL Server 2008 for Managed Reporting

SQL Server 2008 Reporting Services is designed to help you create a complete solution for creating, distributing, and managing reports. Reporting Services includes a set of tools for working with and viewing reports, an engine for hosting and processing reports, and an extensible architecture for integration with existing IT infrastructure. For example, Reporting Services can be integrated easily with Microsoft Office SharePoint Server so that a SQL Server 2008 report server can deliver automatically generated reports to a SharePoint portal.

As an administrator, you can use the report server Web application to do the following:

- Define role-based security for reports
- Schedule report generation and delivery
- Track reporting history

Reports can be delivered in a variety of ways and formats. You can configure Reporting Services to deliver reports to a portal on a server running SharePoint, send reports by e-mail to users, or allow users to access reports on the Web-based report server. Reports can be created in HTML, PDF, TIFF, Microsoft Office Excel, XML, and CSV, as well as other formats. HTML reports are ideal for viewing on the Web. Adobe PDF and TIFF are good formats to use for reports that will be printed. Excel, XML, or CSV reports work well if the data in a report needs to be stored in a database or if the user needs to manipulate the report data.

For SQL Server 2008, Microsoft has done a major rewrite of the reporting engine. The rewrite allows the reporting engine to create much larger and much more complex reports. Because Reporting Services no longer runs within Internet Information Services (IIS) and manages its own memory, you have many more configuration options. These changes to Reporting Services allow you to configure it to run more efficiently with other database services.

# Planning for Your SQL Server 2008 Deployment

As a SQL Server 2008 administrator or developer, you'll fill several different roles, including database designer and database architect. The organization where you work might have dedicated database designers and database architects, but so much has changed in SQL Server that it is critical that you understand the new configuration and setup options before deploying servers that run SQL Server.

## Building the Server System for Performance

You have many basic options for deploying SQL Server 2008. You need to choose an edition of SQL Server and the version of Microsoft Windows on which SQL Server will run. After you make this decision, you should spend some time thinking about the system configuration. In Chapter 1, "Microsoft SQL Server 2008 Administration Overview," you learned some key guidelines, but do not overlook the importance of the I/O subsystem.

The I/O subsystem is one of the most fundamental components of the server system, and you should give considerable thought to its configuration. Start by choosing drives or storage systems that provide the appropriate level of performance. There really is a substantial difference in speed and performance between various drive specifications. When given a choice for the internal drives of a computer running SQL Server, look closely at both SATA II or higher and Ultra SCSI (preferably Ultra320 SCSI or higher).

Consider not only the capacity of the drive, but also its rotational speed and average seek time. The rotational speed is a measurement of how fast the disk spins. The average seek time is a measurement of how long it takes to seek between disk tracks during sequential I/O operations. Generally speaking, when comparing drives that conform to the same specification, such as SATA II or Ultra320 SCSI, the higher the rotational speed (measured in thousands of rotations per minute) and the lower the average seek time (measured in milliseconds, or msec) the better. As an example, a drive with a rotational speed of 15,000 RPM will give you 45 percent to 50 percent more I/O per second than the average 10,000-RPM drive, all other things being equal. A drive with a seek time of 3.5 msec will give you a 25 percent to 30 percent response time improvement over a drive with a seek time of 4.7 msec.

Other factors to consider include the maximum sustained data transfer rate and the mean time to failure (MTTF). Most drives of comparable quality will have similar transfer rates and MTTF. For example, if you compare Ultra320 SCSI drives with a 15,000-RPM rotational speed, you will probably find similar transfer rates and MTTF. As an example, the Maxtor Atlas 15K II has a maximum sustained data transfer rate of up to 98 MBps. The Seagate Cheetah 15K.4 has a maximum sustained data transfer rate of up to 96 MBps. Both have an MTTF of 1.4 million hours.

Transfer rates can also be expressed in gigabits per second. A transfer rate of 1.5 gigabits per second is equivalent to a data rate of 187 MBps. A transfer rate of 3.0 gigabits per second is equivalent to 374 MBps. Sometimes you'll see a maximum external transfer rate (per the specification to which the drive complies) and an average sustained transfer rate. The average sustained transfer rate is the most important factor. The Seagate Barracuda 7200 SATA II drive has a rotational speed of 7200 RPM and an average sustained transfer rate of 58 MBps. With an average seek time of 8.5 msec and an MTTF of 1 million hours, the drive performs comparably to other 7200-RPM SATA II drives. However, most Ultra320 SCSI drives perform better.

**Note**   Temperature is another important factor to consider when you are selecting a drive—but it is a factor few administrators take into account. Typically, the faster a drive rotates, the hotter it will run. This is not always the case, but it is certainly something you should consider when making your choice. For example, 15K drives tend to run hot, and you must be sure to carefully regulate temperature. Both the Maxtor Atlas 15K II and the Seagate Cheetah 15K.4 can become nonoperational at temperatures of 70 degrees Celsius or higher (as would most other drives were they to reach these temperatures).

## Configuring the I/O Subsystem

When configuring your server system, you will typically have to make a choice between hardware RAID (redundant array of independent disks) and software RAID for the server's internal disk drives. You must make this choice, in most cases, even if your server will use external storage. Cost and performance are the two key issues to consider for internal RAID.

Hardware RAID is more expensive than software RAID because it requires RAID controller cards. The expense of hardware RAID, however, is offset by the performance boost it offers. With software RAID, the server's operating system manages the RAID implementation, which requires system resources: CPU processing power, memory, and so on. With hardware RAID, the server's RAID controllers manage the RAID implementation.

Hardware RAID might also give you additional fault-tolerance options. For example, Microsoft Windows Server 2003 and Windows Server 2008 support software RAID levels 0 (disk striping), 1 (disk mirroring), and 5 (disk striping with parity). With hardware RAID, you might have additional options, such as RAID 0 + 1 (which is also referred to as RAID 10, and combines disk striping and mirroring).

The operating system drive of a SQL Server system is often configured with RAID 1, as are drives used for SQL Server's transaction logs. RAID 1 provides a full duplicate (or mirror) of a drive that can be used in case of failure of a primary drive. Because all data writes must go to two drives, disk mirroring doesn't have the best write performance. Read performance is improved over that of a single disk because seeks typically can be split over both disks in the set, which means you could essentially get twice as many reads as with a single disk.

> **Note**   RAID can be configured in many ways. Sometimes it is more efficient to use both hardware and software RAID. For example, you could use hardware RAID controllers to do parity calculations and software RAID to stripe across the disks. Sometimes, you'll want to use two drive controllers with mirroring (a technique referred to as *disk duplexing*). Disk duplexing has the same write performance as a single disk.

With RAID 1, failure recovery is easier and quicker than with other RAID options because you have a full duplicate disk. This is also why RAID 1 is recommended for the operating system drive. RAID 1 is recommended for drives containing transaction logs because transaction logs are sequentially written and read only in the case of a rollback operation. Thus, when you put a transaction log on its own mirrored drive, you can achieve good performance and have fault tolerance.

Drives containing SQL Server's data files are often configured with RAID 5 or RAID 0 + 1. RAID 5 provides fault tolerance by striping data across multiple disks and storing parity information as data is written. Sections of data and parity information are written to each disk in the set in turn. In the case of disk failure, the parity information can be used to re-create the data on any lost disk. It is important to point out that this parity information can be used to recover only from the loss of a single drive in the array. If multiple drives fail simultaneously, the entire array will fail.

RAID 5 has advantages and disadvantages. With RAID 1, you can mirror a 150-GB drive onto another 150-GB drive. When you do this, there is a 50-percent overhead requirement, meaning that you use double the number of disks and gain no additional storage space. With a three-disk RAID 5 array, the amount of overhead required is about one-third (33 percent) of the total disk space. As you add volumes to a RAID 5 array, the overhead requirement decreases. Because reads are performed across multiple drives, RAID 5 offers better read performance than RAID 1. Essentially, you can perform as many reads as with a single disk multiplied by the number of disks in the array, meaning an array with five disks would have a read capacity of five times that of a single disk.

RAID 5 has poorer write performance than RAID 1 because whenever data is written to a RAID 5 array, four I/O operations are required: two reads and two writes. The target disk stripe and the parity stripe must be read first. The parity is then calculated. Then the target stripe and the parity stripe are written to disk.

RAID 0 + 1 is a combination of disk striping and mirroring. With RAID 0 + 1, you mirror a disk stripe, ensuring that there is a duplicate for each striped disk while gaining the performance of pure disk striping. As with RAID 1, each RAID 0 + 1 write operation requires two I/O operations: a write to each disk in the mirror (as with RAID 1). Read operations typically are spread across multiple disks, offering high performance (as with RAID 0 or RAID 5).

RAID 0 + 1 offers very high fault tolerance. Unlike RAID 1 and 5, the array can continue to operate in many cases even if more than one disk fails. In fact, all the disks on one side of the mirror could fail and the array would continue to operate. Failure of both sides of the mirror would result in a complete failure of the set, however.

> **Note**   A disadvantage of RAID 0 + 1 is the number of disks required. You need twice as many disks as you would need with a striped set. To mirror a 450-GB stripe set, you need another 450-GB stripe set, but the total capacity of the mirror does not change. It remains 450 GB.

When choosing between RAID 5 and RAID 0 + 1, and without considering the comparative cost, the key factor should be the way the disks will be used. RAID 5 works well when there is a high percentage of reads and few writes. RAID 0 + 1 offers better performance compared to RAID 5 as the amount of write operations increases. Specifically, with 90-percent reads and 10-percent writes, RAID 5 is the better choice. As the ratio of writes to reads increases, you will see improved performance if you select RAID 0 + 1.

> **Tip**   When using RAID 1, 5, and 0 + 1, be sure that the disks have a battery-backed write cache. A battery-backed write cache can help protect data because it still can be written to disk even in the event of power interruption or failure. This back-up power source is important to have when the same data must be written to multiple disks, as with RAID 1 and 0 + 1, and when parity information must be written accurately to ensure fault tolerance.

## Ensuring Availability and Scalability

Not long ago, your options for ensuring the availability and scalability of SQL Server were limited. This is no longer the case. You have many options—and most of these options do not require expensive storage subsystems or SANs. To ensure availability of

SQL Server, you can use log shipping to establish a standby server that you have to manually bring online if the primary server fails. SQL Server 2008 includes log stream compression, which can significantly reduce the amount of data transmitted during log shipping. You can use the Cluster service to create a failover server—one that could automatically come online if the primary server fails. For scalability, you can use distributed partition views to horizontally distribute tables across multiple servers. To improve read-ahead performance, you can use indexed views.

The key drawback to server clustering is that it is expensive, both in terms of required equipment and in resources required for setup. SQL Server 2008 uses an extended form of log shipping called *database mirroring*, which works on standard server hardware and requires no special storage or controllers. Database mirroring allows you to continuously stream a transaction log from a source server to a destination server. If the source server fails, applications can reconnect to the database on the secondary server within a matter of seconds. Unlike server clustering, transaction logs used with database mirroring can be fully synchronized between the servers. This approach allows changes to be synchronized in both directions.

Database mirroring requires three servers running SQL Server 2008:

- A source server, also referred to as the principal. The *principal server* is the one to which applications connect and where transactions are processed.

- A destination server, also referred to as the mirror. The *mirroring server* is the target of the shipped transaction logs, and it operates in a standby state that does not allow read operations.

- A tracking server, also referred to as the witness. The *witness server* tracks which server currently is acting as the principal and which is acting as the mirror. It is used when automatic failover is needed. Whenever there is contention between which server has which role, the witness makes a decision.

As transaction log records are generated on the principal, they can be compressed and are replayed either synchronously (at the same time) or asynchronously (at different times, such as after a short delay) on the mirror. This behavior ensures that the mirror server is exactly in sync or very close to being in sync with the principal server. For example, there might be no write lag between the two servers, or there might be one or more transaction write lags between the two.

From the client's point of view, failover from the principal to the mirror is automatic and nearly instantaneous. If the principal goes offline, the application fails over to the mirror. The mirror then becomes the principal. When the failed server comes back online, it becomes the mirror and receives transaction log records.

**Note**   SQL Server replication can also be used to create copies of a database. You can use replication to distribute data across multiple databases. SQL Server supports several types of replication, including snapshot replication, transactional replication, and merge replication. For more information on replication, see Chapter 13, "Implementing Snapshot, Merge, and Transactional Replication."

## Ensuring Connectivity and Data Access

SQL Server 2008 has two features that can help ensure consistent connectivity and data access:

- **Dedicated administrator connection**   Designed to ensure that administrators can get consistent access to SQL Server

- **Multiple active result sets**   Designed to ensure that users accessing the database have consistent access to SQL Server

Unlike early editions of SQL Server, in which administrators could be locked out if SQL Server became unresponsive, SQL Server 2008 uses dedicated administrator connections to provide a way for administrators to access a server that is not responding or is otherwise unavailable. With this feature, administrators are able to establish a connection that can be used to troubleshoot and resolve problems.

Any administrator who is a member of the sysadmin fixed server role can establish a dedicated server connection using the SQLCMD command prompt utility with the –A parameter. Consider the following example:

```
sqlcmd –U wrstanek –P moreFunPlease –S corpdbsvr05 –A
```

Here, the user wrstanek, who is a member of the sysadmin fixed server role, is connecting to the default instance on CorpDBSvr05. You could also connect to a named instance, such as

```
sqlcmd –U wrstanek –P moreFunPlease –S corpdbsvr05\webapp05 –A
```

where webapp05 is the name of the SQL Server instance.

Multiple Active Result Sets (MARS) have improved SQL Server connectivity markedly for users as well. With SQL Server 2000, you could have at most one pending request in a given situation. Although server-side cursors and other techniques can be used to work around this limitation, you still do not have a direct way to handle multiple result sets in a single session. MARS corrects this problem by providing the programming interfaces necessary to represent a connection and a request executed under that connection separately. As an example, with Open Database Connectivity (ODBC) you represent connections and executed requests within connections using handles:

- The SQL_HANDLE_DBC type represents connection handles.

- The SQL_HANDLE_STMT type represents executed statements within connections.

The SQLODBC and SQLOLEDB drivers included in the SQL Native Client Installation for SQL Server 2008 are MARS-enabled, as is the SqlClient .NET Data Provider included in the Microsoft .NET Framework, version 2.0 or later. By default, these drivers establish connections and handle requests using MARS. Technically, execution requests can be a single T-SQL statement, a batch of T-SQL statements, or the name of a stored procedure or function to run, along with any appropriate parameter values. Regardless, SQL Server sequentially executes the statements as it iterates through them, and the statements might or might not produce results. Thus, you can have more than one pending request under a given connection and more than one default result set.

> **Tip**   Native drivers for SQL Server 2000 or earlier do not support MARS. MARS works by interleaving execution of multiple requests and not by parallel execution. MARS allows a statement, batch, or procedure to run and within the execution allows other requests to run. Interleaving works with SELECT, FETCH, READTEXT, RECEIVE, and BULK INSERT. It also works with asynchronous cursor population.

In contrast to SQL Server 2000, in which implicit spawning of connections under OLE DB and additional requests under ODBC are not allowed, SQL Server 2008 allows both to occur. This means that if a session has an active transaction, all new requests run under the transaction. When there is no active transaction, batches run in auto-commit mode, in which each statement is executed under its own transaction.

The SqlClient .NET Data Provider has separate SqlConnection, SqlCommand, and Sql-Transaction objects. SqlConnection objects represent connections established to a server. SqlCommand objects represent commands (requests) executed under the connection. SqlTransaction objects represent active transactions. When you begin a transaction within the context of a specific connection, a SqlTransaction object is returned to represent this transaction.

## Managing SQL Server Configuration and Security

SQL Server configuration and security administration tasks have changed considerably over earlier releases. As I'll discuss in detail in Chapter 3, "Managing the Surface Security, Access, and Network Configuration," SQL Server 2008 introduces a new configuration architecture called Policy-Based Management. Like Group Policy, Policy-Based Management defines management policies that not only configure SQL Server settings but also control whether and how settings can be changed. Before you deploy SQL Server 2008, you might want to familiarize yourself with the available options and determine whether your servers will be put into specific management groups.

SQL Server 2008 has many security enhancements. For data encryption solutions, you have many options. You can use any of the following:

- Cell-level encryption, as in SQL Server 2005
- File-level encryption using Encrypting File System (EFS)
- Volume-level encryption using BitLocker Drive Encryption
- Full database-level encrypting using Transparent Data Encryption (TDE)
- Upgrading your edition of SQL Server 2008

When you are using Windows Server 2003 or Windows Server 2008, SQL Server 2008 also enforces the password policy requirements you've configured in Group Policy. Even if you aren't using Windows Server 2003 or Windows Server 2008, SQL Server still enforces some password strength rules to help enhance security. This means you won't be able to use null or empty passwords, passwords that have the same name as the computer or login name, any password of "password," "admin," "administrator," "sysadmin," or "sa." The only way to override this feature is to use the CHECK_POLICY = OFF setting when creating or altering a login. For more information, see Chapter 9, "Managing SQL Server 2008 Security."

> **Tip**   SQL Server 2008 Enterprise Edition supports hot-add memory and hot-add CPU functionality when running on Enterprise or Datacenter editions of Windows Server 2003 or Windows Server 2008. There are several caveats. Your server hardware also must support this functionality. Only 64-bit editions of SQL Server Enterprise Edition support both hot-add memory and hot-add CPU. With 32-bit editions of SQL Server 2008 Enterprise Edition, you can hot-add memory provided that Address Windowing Extensions (AWE) is enabled and that SQL Server was started using the –h option.

# Running and Modifying SQL Server Setup

SQL Server Installation Center, shown in Figure 2-1, is the utility you use to perform key installation tasks for SQL Server. You use SQL Server Installation Center to launch SQL Server Setup so that you can create new instances of SQL Server. Other tasks you can perform with SQL Server Installation Center include the following:

- Upgrading from SQL Server 2000 or SQL Server 2005

- Determining hardware and software requirements for your edition of SQL Server 2008

- Creating a single-node failover cluster

- Adding or removing cluster nodes

- Upgrading your edition of SQL Server 2008

When you first start working with SQL Server 2008, the Setup process will launch SQL Server Installation Center for you. After you install SQL Server 2008, you'll find a related option on the Start menu under All Programs\Microsoft SQL Server 2008\ Configuration Tools. SQL Server Installation Center has the following wizard pages:

- **Planning**   Provides links to planning documentation and helpful planning tools.

- **Installation**   Includes options for installing SQL Server instances, upgrading from earlier versions, and adding features.

- **Maintenance**   Includes options for upgrading your SQL Server edition, repairing your installation, and removing cluster nodes.

■ **Tools**   Includes options for checking the system configuration prior to installation, reporting the current configuration of SQL Server products, and upgrading Integration Services packages.

■ **Resources**   Provides links to additional documentation that might be helpful.

■ **Advanced**   Includes an option for installing SQL Server using a configuration file as well as advanced clustering options.

■ **Options**   Allows you to specify the root directory for SQL Server media, such as would be required if you want to install from a shared folder.

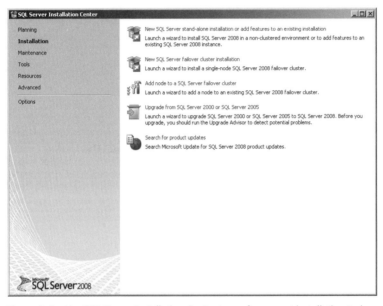

**Figure 2-1**   Use SQL Server Installation Center to perform most installation tasks.

## Creating New Instances of SQL Server

You can install multiple instances of the SQL Server 2008 Database Engine on a single computer. Each Database Engine instance has its own integrated replication and full-text search functionality. Running multiple instances of the Database Engine is ideal in the following circumstances:

■ You need to support multiple test and development environments on a single large server.

■ You need to run multiple applications on a desktop, and each application installs its own instance of the SQL Server 2008 Database Engine.

■ You need to securely isolate the databases that are available on a single server.

In most other situations, however, you should not run multiple instances of the SQL Server 2008 Database Engine. Each instance of the SQL Server 2008 Database Engine has its own set of system and user databases. Each instance has separate SQL Server and SQL Server Agent services, and as applicable, separate Analysis Services and Reporting Services as well. All other components and services are shared, and this adds to the overhead on the server due to management of the shared resources.

When running SQL Server 2008 on Windows Server 2008, an additional option you have is virtualization. Virtualizing your SQL Server 2008 deployments helps to isolate one deployment from another. The virtual machine must run an operating system supported for the specific SQL Server 2008 edition.

### Understanding SQL Server Instances

When you install SQL Server 2008, you have the option of installing a default instance of the SQL Server 2008 Database Engine or a named instance of the SQL Server 2008 Database Engine. In most cases, you will want to install the default instance first and then install additional named instances of the SQL Server Database Engine as necessary. There is no limit to the number of named instances that you can run on a single computer.

A default instance is identified by the name of the computer on which the SQL Server 2008 Database Engine is running; it does not have a separate instance name. Applications connect to the default instance by using the computer name in their requests. Only one default instance can run on any computer, and this default instance can be any version of SQL Server.

All instances of SQL Server other than the default instance are identified by the instance name that you set during installation. Applications connect to a named instance by specifying the computer name and the instance name in the format *computer_name\instance_name*. Only the SQL Server 2000, SQL Server 2005, and SQL Server 2008 Database Engines can run as named instances. Earlier versions of SQL Server do not support named instances.

> **Note**   When you run SQL Server 2008 Enterprise Edition, you can create multi-node server clusters. Applications connect to the default instance on a SQL Server cluster by specifying the virtual server name. Applications connect to a named instance on a SQL Server cluster by specifying the virtual server name and the named instance in the format *virtual_server_name\instance_name*.

### Installing a SQL Server Instance

The SQL Server 2008 installation process has changed considerably since SQL Server 2000. The installation process now requires the .NET Framework version 3.5 SP1 or later, SQL Server Native Client, SQL Server Setup support files, Windows Installer 4.5 or later, and Microsoft Data Access Components (MDAC) 2.8 SP1 or later. If these components aren't installed, the installation process will install them and any other prerequisites.

Not only does using Windows Installer help streamline and stabilize the installation process, it also makes modification of installed components easier. You can

- Perform upgrades directly using the Installation Wizard.

- Install additional components or instances by rerunning the Installation Wizard.

- Maintain installed components. With Windows Server 2003, use Add Or Remove Programs in Control Panel. With Windows Server 2008, use the Programs And Features page under Control Panel\Programs.

- Resume a failed installation or modification. With Windows Server 2003, use Add Or Remove Programs in Control Panel. With Windows Server 2008, use the Programs And Features page under Control Panel\Programs.

For administration purposes, you can install the SQL Server client tools, development tools, and Books Online on a workstation computer running Windows XP Service Pack 2 or later. This workstation must also have Windows PowerShell installed.

To install an instance of the SQL Server 2008 Database Engine, complete the following steps:

1. Log on to the server using an account with administrator privileges. Then insert the SQL Server 2008 DVD into the DVD drive.

   **Tip**  Be sure to keep a detailed record of the actions you perform. These actions should explicitly state the server, server instance, and installation options you are using. You might need this information later.

2. If Autorun is enabled, the SQL Server 2008 Setup program should start automatically. Otherwise, double-click the appropriate executable in the base folder of the DVD.

3. Setup determines the status of required components. If Setup can install the required components, it will begin doing so and prompt you to confirm by clicking OK. Because required components might be downloaded from the Internet, you might need to connect the computer to the Internet. Follow the prompts to install the required additional components. In some cases, you might need to restart the computer to complete the installation of required components. If so, you'll need to restart Setup.

4. Review the items on the Planning page as necessary. Click New SQL Server Stand-Alone Installation... on the Installation page to continue.

5. Setup attempts to verify that the computer meets all other requirements for successful installation. When it finishes, you'll see a status of Operation Completed, as shown in Figure 2-2. If any tests failed, you received warnings, or tests were skipped, click Show Details to see detailed information and any errors. Note any errors, and take the necessary corrective actions before continuing. If there are no required corrective actions, click OK to proceed with the installation.

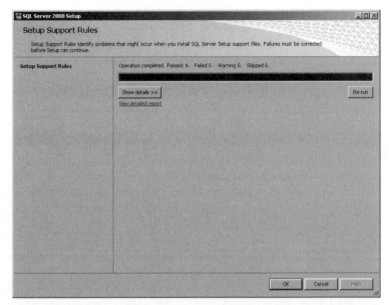

**Figure 2-2**   SQL Server 2008 Setup scans the computer where SQL Server 2008 will be installed.

6. If you are prompted to enter a product key, enter the product key for the SQL Server edition you want to install. Remember, all non-Express editions of SQL Server 2008 can be part of a single build with the installed edition determined by the key you enter.

7. If you agree to the license terms, click I Accept The License Terms and then click Next to continue.

8. If Setup needs to install any additional support files, you'll see the Setup Support Files page. Click Install. When Setup finishes, you'll see a status of Operation Completed. If there are any issues, click Show Details to see detailed information. Note any errors or issues, and take the necessary corrective actions before continuing. If there are no required corrective actions, click Next to proceed with the installation. If you installed additional support files, Setup checks for problems again before continuing. Click Next.

9. On the Feature Selection page, shown in Figure 2-3, select the components to install, including

   ❑ **Database Engine Services**   Allows you to install a SQL Server instance. You can also install SQL Server 2008 instances on cluster nodes. To install replication or full-text search components as well, select the related check boxes.

   ❑ **Analysis Services**   Allows you to install an Analysis Services instance. You can also install Analysis Services instances on cluster nodes.

❑ **Business Intelligence Development Studio**   Allows you to install SQL Server developer tools, including the related command-line tools.

❑ **Integration Services**   Allows you to install SSIS for the purposes of ETL.

❑ **Management Tools**   Allows you to install SQL Server management and configuration tools, including the command-line and PowerShell tools.

❑ **Microsoft Sync Framework**   Allows you to install the Sync Framework to synchronize databases and other types of data stores, as well as files, folders, and metadata.

❑ **Reporting Services**   Allows you to configure the server as a report server. Report servers no longer require IIS. You will, however, need to install a Simple Mail Transfer Protocol (SMTP) server for sending reports or know the name of your organization's Microsoft Exchange gateway.

❑ **SQL Server Books Online**   Allows you to install SQL Server Books Online.

**Figure 2-3**   Select the features to install, and set the shared component path.

10. The Shared Feature Directory path shows where shared features will be installed. Click the Options button to the right of the path to browse for a new path, or type the desired path in the text box provided. Click Next to continue.

> **Note**   On 64-bit systems, you'll have two path boxes: Shared Feature Directory, for specifying where 64-bit components should be stored, and Shared Feature Directory (X86), for specifying where 32-bit components should be stored.

11. As shown in Figure 2-4, you must now determine the instance type to install. To install a default instance of SQL Server, select Default Instance and then click Next. Otherwise, select Named Instance, type the instance name in the field provided, and then specify the instance root directory. Click Next to continue.

> **Note**   You can install only one default instance on a computer. If a default instance already exists, you cannot select the Default Instance check box. The instance name can be up to 16 characters in length and must follow the naming rules for nondelimited identifiers. If you type an invalid instance name, you will see an error message and you will have to change the instance name before you can continue.

**Figure 2-4**   Use the options to select the instance type as either default or named.

12. On the Disk Space Requirements page, review the required and available disk space. If you determine that you need to change the installation paths, you can use the Back button to return to earlier pages.

13. On the Server Configuration page, determine how the SQL Server services will run, as shown in Figure 2-5, and then click Next. You have the following options:

❑ **Customize the service accounts**   You can configure each service account individually. Type a user name and password for each service before continuing. For domain accounts, be sure to enter names in *Domain\ UserName* format, such as Cpandl\WilliamS. For local computer accounts, simply enter the account name.

❑ **No customization of service accounts**    You assign a built-in system account or a specific domain user account for all SQL Server services. If the server requires resources on the local server only, use the Local System account. Otherwise, use a Domain User account. See Table 1-1 on page 11.

❑ **Configure service startup**    Use the drop-down lists to configure service startup. In most deployments, the SQL Server Agent service is set to manual startup and most other services are set to automatic startup by default.

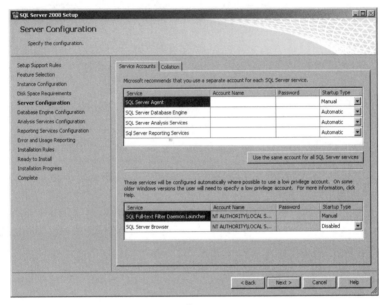

**Figure 2-5**    Server Configuration page with login options for SQL Server services.

**Note**    Use a local system account when you are configuring a SQL Server database instance that will be isolated from other servers—that is, one that will operate independently and not connect to other servers over the network. The permissible actions, of course, depend on the permissions granted to the Local System account. If interaction with other servers is required, rather than granting additional permissions to the Local System account, you should use Domain User accounts and grant the appropriate level of permissions to these accounts.

**Note**    Although the SQL Server service does not require administrator account privileges, the SQL Server Agent service does require them in some cases. Specifically, if you create CmdExec and ActiveScript jobs that belong to someone other than a SQL Server administrator or if you use the AutoRestart feature, the SQL Server Agent service does require administrator privileges. Additionally, if you are configuring Reporting Services and the report server database is on a remote server, you should use a Domain User account.

14. If you want to customize the collation settings, click the Collation tab. The Collation tab provides settings that enable you to define the sorting behavior for the server. (See Figure 2-6.) By clicking Customize and making the appropriate selections, you can specify separate collation settings for the Database Engine and Analysis Services instances before continuing.

> **Note**   The default Collation Designator is the Microsoft Windows locale setting for the server, such as Latin1_General. Typically, you want to use the default locale setting. Binary and Case-Sensitive are the fastest sorting orders. If the sort order is set to Binary, the other options are not available. SQL collations are used for compatibility with earlier versions of SQL Server and are not used for Analysis Services.

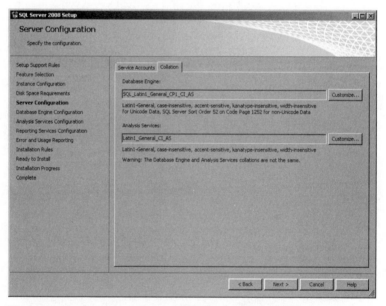

**Figure 2-6**   Configure the collation settings on the Collation tab.

> **Caution**   Although you can change the collation settings on individual databases, you cannot change the collation settings on an existing SQL Server installation without rebuilding the master database. Rebuilding the master database detaches all other databases on the server, making them unusable. For more information about this process, see "Changing Collation and Rebuilding the *master* Database" on page 174.

15. If you are installing a Database Engine instance, on the Database Engine Configuration page, you have the following options tabs, as shown in Figure 2-7:

   ❑ **Account Provisioning**   Use the Security Mode settings to configure the authentication settings. The SQL Server instance can run under Windows authentication or Mixed Mode authentication. With Windows authentication, you use only Domain User accounts to authenticate connections to the SQL Server instance. With Mixed Mode authentication, users can access the SQL Server instance using Domain User accounts or SQL Server IDs. If you've selected Mixed Mode authentication, enter a strong password for the sa account. Strong passwords use a mix of numbers, letters, and special characters to make them difficult to crack.

Specify users that have administrative permissions for the Database Engine instance. You can add the currently logged-on user as an administrator by clicking Add Current Users. To add other users as administrators, click the Add button.

❑ **Data Directories**   Use the options provided to specify the directories for system databases, user databases, temporary databases, and backup. By default, all subdirectories build off of the Data Root Directory. Because of this, you should set the root directory first and then customize the other directories as needed.

❑ **FILESTREAM**   Use the options provided to specify file-streaming options. File streaming allows SQL Server to work with binary large objects (BLOBs) that are stored outside the database. When you enable file streaming, SQL Server stores pointers to BLOBs in the database. By default, BLOBs can be stored only on local disk volumes. Also, you cannot use tables that contain file streams in database snapshots or database mirroring sessions.

Figure 2-7   Configure a Database Engine instance.

16. If you are installing an Analysis Services instance, on the Analysis Services Configuration page, you have the following options tabs, as shown in Figure 2-8:

   ❑ **Account Provisioning**   Specify users that have administrative permissions for Analysis Services. You can add the currently logged-on user as an administrator by clicking Add Current User. To add other users as administrators, click the Add button.

   ❑ **Data Directories**   Use the options provided to specify the directories for data, logs, temporary files, and backup. By default, all subdirectories build off of a common Data Root Directory.

**Figure 2-8**   Configure an Analysis Services instance.

17. If you are installing a Reporting Services instance, on the Reporting Services Configuration page, select an installation mode. As shown in Figure 2-9, you can specify Native mode or SharePoint mode with a default configuration or you can install but not configure the server. The virtual directories to use for the report server and Report Manager can be accessed in a Web browser as follows:

   ❑ For the default SQL Server instance, use *http://ServerName/Directory-Name*, where *ServerName* is the host name or Domain Name System (DNS) name of the server computer and *DirectoryName* is the name of the virtual directory for either the report server or Report Manager, such as *http://corprs17/reports*.

❑   For the default SQL Server instance, use *http://ServerName/Directory-Name$InstanceName*, where *ServerName* is the host name or DNS name of the server computer, *DirectoryName* is the name of the virtual directory for either the report server or Report Manager, and *InstanceName* is the SQL Server instance to which you are connecting, such as *http://corprs17/reports$webapp05*.

**Note**   With the default configuration, the report server is installed on the SQL Server instance you are configuring and the names of various components reflect that instance name. So if you are installing a named SQL Server instance called CustData on EngDbSrv12, the default report server name would be ReportServer$CustData and the default virtual directories would be *http://engdbsvr12/ReportServer$CustData* and *http://engdbsvr12/Reports$CustData*, respectively. If you don't want to use the default configuration, you can install but not configure the report server at this time and then later use the Reporting Services Configuration Manager to configure the report server.

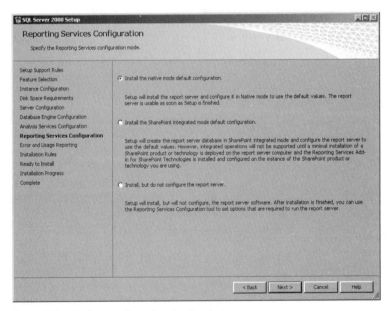

**Figure 2-9**   Configure a Reporting Services instance.

18. On the Error And Usage Report Settings page, choose whether to automatically report fatal error messages and feature usage data, and then click Next. Error information is sent over Secure HTTP (HTTPS) to Microsoft by default or to a designated corporate error reporting server if you have configured one in Active Directory Group Policy. When Feature Usage Reporting is configured, reports about component usage are generated and reported to Microsoft. The intent of these reports is to help Microsoft better understand how components and

features are being used. This feature is also referred to as Customer Feedback Reporting.

19. Setup attempts to identify problems that might occur when you install SQL Server with the current selections. When it finishes, you'll see a status of Operation Completed. If any components failed to install, you received warnings, or components were skipped, click Show Details to see detailed information on the installation process and any errors. Note any errors, and take the necessary corrective actions before continuing. If there are no required corrective actions, click OK to proceed with the installation.

20. On the Ready To Install page, review the configuration options you've chosen. Click Install to begin the installation process. The Installation Progress page tracks the components that are being installed and the progress of the installation. When Setup finishes, note the status of each installed component and click the link provided to check the setup log file if there are any problems. For future reference, you might want to save the install log to a save folder. Click Next, and then click Close to complete the installation process.

## Adding Components and Instances

SQL Server keeps track of components you have installed and those you have not installed. If you ever want to add components and instances, you can do so by completing the following steps:

1. Start SQL Server Installation Center by clicking the related option under Start, All Programs, Microsoft SQL Server 2008, Configuration Tools.

2. Click New SQL Server Stand-Alone Installation on the Installation page.

3. As necessary, insert the SQL Server 2008 media. If you are prompted to browse for the installation media, use the Browse For Folder dialog box to select the root folder for the installation media and then click OK.

4. As when you are installing SQL Server for the first time, Setup attempts to verify the computer configuration and also checks to ensure required components are installed. You'll need to proceed through each phase of the checks as appropriate.

5. On the Installation Type page, specify whether you want to perform a new installation or add features to an existing instance. If you want to add features to an existing instance, use the drop-down list to select the instance of SQL Server to update. You cannot add features to a failover cluster instance and must instead perform a new installation to install a separate instance.

**Tip**   Although you can install multiple instances of Instance features, you need to install Shared features only once. If you already installed the SQL Server Database Services and have an existing instance of SQL Server, the Installation Type and Instance Configuration pages will list installed instances of SQL Server, Analysis Services, and Reporting Services.

## Repairing a SQL Server 2008 Installation

You can repair SQL Server 2008 installations by completing the following steps:

1. Start SQL Server Installation Center by clicking the related option under Start, All Programs, Microsoft SQL Server 2008, Configuration Tools.

2. Click Repair on the Maintenance page.

3. As necessary, insert the SQL Server 2008 media. If you are prompted to browse for the installation media, use the Browse For Folder dialog box to select the root folder for the installation media and then click OK.

4. As when you are installing SQL Server for the first time, Setup attempts to verify the computer configuration and also checks to ensure required components are installed. You'll need to proceed through each phase of the checks as appropriate.

5. On the Select Instance page, select the repair option. If you want to repair an instance of SQL Server 2008 and all related components, select that instance. If you want to repair only the management tools and shared features, select Repair Shared Features Only.

6. Setup attempts to verify that the repair process will work. Review any issues and make corrections as necessary before clicking Next to continue.

7. Click Repair to begin the repair process. The Repair Progress page tracks the components that are being repaired and the progress of the repair. When Setup finishes, note the status of each repaired component. Click Next. Click the link provided to review the summary log and then click Close to complete the repair process.

## Upgrading Your Edition of SQL Server 2008

All non-Express editions of SQL Server 2008 are part of a single build with the installed edition determined by the key. You can upgrade from one edition to another edition using SQL Server Installation Center. Select the Maintenance page, click Edition Upgrade, and then follow the prompts.

## Uninstalling SQL Server

The way you uninstall SQL Server depends on whether you are working with Windows Server 2003 or Windows Server 2008.

With Windows Server 2003, use Add Or Remove Programs in Control Panel to uninstall SQL Server or any of its components. You must uninstall each instance of the SQL

Server Database Engine separately. To uninstall an instance of SQL Server, complete these steps:

1. Select the SQL Server instance in Add Or Remove Programs, and then click Change/Uninstall. In the SQL Server 2008 dialog box, click Remove.

2. Setup attempts to verify that the uninstall process will work. Note any issues and then click OK when you are ready to continue.

3. On the Select Instance page, select an uninstall option. If you want to uninstall an instance of SQL Server 2008 and related components, select that instance. If you want to uninstall only the management tools and shared features, select Remove Shared Features Only.

4. On the Select Features page, select the components to remove and then click Next

5. Setup attempts to verify that the uninstall process will work. Note any issues and then click Next when you are ready to continue.

6. Click Remove. Setup will remove the selected instances, components, or both.

With Windows Server 2008, you use the Programs And Features page in Control Panel. Again, you must uninstall each instance of the SQL Server Database Engine separately. To uninstall an instance of SQL Server, complete these steps:

1. In Control Panel, click the Uninstall A Program link under Programs. In Programs And Features, select the SQL Server 2008 entry to display the Change/Uninstall button. In the SQL Server 2008 dialog box, click Remove.

2. Follow steps 2 through 6 of the previous procedure.

Chapter 3

# Managing the Surface Security, Access, and Network Configuration

To control access to your server, few things are more important than the configuration of Microsoft SQL Server's services, components, and networking capabilities. Every SQL Server installation has a specific configuration for the services, components, and network, and the configuration determines security levels that control access in the surface area of the server such as

- Who can access the server and by what means

- What SQL Server services run automatically at startup or manually as needed

- Where and by what means SQL Server components can connect to (or be connected from) remote resources

By limiting these who, what, and where aspects of the server's configuration, you reduce the server surface area, which improves the server security and can also enhance overall performance because you are running only necessary services and components.

Client access to SQL Server is managed through SQL Native Client Configuration parameters. SQL Server access to local and remote resources is managed through the SQL Server 2008 services and the SQL Server 2008 network configuration. You can manage client access, SQL Server services, and the network configuration using SQL Server Configuration Manager.

# Managing SQL Server Component Feature Access

To reduce the server surface area and improve server security, you should enable only the features needed by your clients and applications. This will limit the ways the server can be exploited by malicious users and close avenues of potential attack. Table 3-1 details the surface area features you can manage for the SQL Server Database Engine, Analysis Services, and Reporting Services. In SQL Server 2008, you manage these surface area features using Policy-Based Management policies, as discussed in Chapter 18, "Implementing Policy-Based Management." By default, these features are all disabled.

**Table 3-1   Component Features for Managing Surface Area Access**

| Component/Facet | Description/Usage |
| --- | --- |
| **Database Engine** | |
| AdHocRemoteQueries-Enabled | The OPENROWSET and OPENDATASOURCE functions can use ad hoc connections to work with remote data sources without an administrator specifically configuring linked or remote servers. If your applications or scripts use these functions, you should enable OPENROWSET and OPEN-DATASOURCE support. Otherwise, this functionality should be disabled. |
| ClrIntegrationEnabled | With Common Language Runtime (CLR) Integration, you can write stored procedures, triggers, user-defined types, and user-defined functions using Microsoft Visual Basic .NET, C#, and any other .NET Framework language. If your applications or scripts use .NET Framework languages, enable this feature. Otherwise, this feature should be disabled. |
| DatabaseMailEnabled | Database Mail replaces SQL Mail as the preferred technique for sending e-mail messages from SQL Server using Simple Mail Transfer Protocol (SMTP). Enable this feature if you have created a mail host database (by running the %*ProgramFiles*%\Microsoft SQL Server\MSSQL.1\MSSQL\Install\Install_DBMail_Upgrade.sql script on the server) and the necessary database mail profiles, and you want applications and scripts to be able to use the sp_send_dbmail stored procedure to send e-mail messages from SQL Server. Otherwise, this feature should be disabled. |
| RemoteDacEnabled | Using the SQLCMD command-line utility with the –A parameter, administrators can maintain SQL Server installations using a dedicated connection from the command line, either locally or remotely. By default, only local dedicated connections are permitted. If you want to authorize remote dedicated connections, enable this feature. Otherwise, this feature should be disabled. |

**Table 3-1**   Component Features for Managing Surface Area Access

| Component/Facet | Description/Usage |
|---|---|
| SoapEndpointsEnabled | With Native Web Services, you can access SQL Server over HTTP using Simple Object Access Protocol (SOAP) messaging. SOAP messages contain text-based commands that are formatted with XML. If you plan to use SOAP for data exchange and have configured the necessary HTTP endpoints, you can configure the state of each endpoint as Started, Stopped, or Disabled. Note that the SQL Server Reporting Services, SQL Server Service Broker, and Database Mirroring components make use of Native Web Services, but they have separate configurations. |
| OleAutomationEnabled | OLE Automation provides the ability to use Transact-SQL batches, stored procedures, and triggers to reference SQL DMO and custom OLE Automation objects. Enable this feature if you want to be able to use OLE Automation, including the extended stored procedures sp_OACreate, sp_OADestroy, sp_OAGetErrorInfo, sp_OAGetProperty, sp_OAMethod, sp_OASetProperty, and sp_OAStop. Otherwise, this feature should be disabled. |
| ServiceBrokerEndpoint-Active | Service Broker provides queuing and messaging for the Database Engine. Applications can use Service Broker to communicate across instances of SQL Server. If your applications use Service Broker and you have configured the necessary HTTP endpoints, you can configure the state of each endpoint as Started, Stopped, or Disabled. |
| SqlMailEnabled | SQL Mail can be used with legacy applications for sending e-mail messages from SQL Server using SMTP. Enable this feature if you want legacy applications and scripts to be able to use the xp_sendmail stored procedure to send e-mail messages from SQL Server. Otherwise, this feature should be disabled. |
| XPCmdShellEnabled | The xp_cmdshell executes command strings using the operating system command shell and returns the results as rows of text. If you want applications and scripts to run operating system commands, you must enable this feature. By default, only members of the sysadmin fixed server role can execute xp_cmdshell. You can grant execution permission to other users. For sysadmin users, xp_cmdshell is executed under the security context in which the SQL Server service is running. For other users, xp_cmdshell will impersonate the command shell proxy account (as specified using xp_cmdshell_proxy_account). If the proxy account is not available, xp_cmdshell will fail. |

Table 3-1   Component Features for Managing Surface Area Access

| Component/Facet | Description/Usage |
| --- | --- |
| WebAssistantEnabled | In previous versions of SQL Server, Web Assistant stored procedures that could be used to generate HTML files from SQL Server data. In SQL Server 2005 and SQL Server 2008, Reporting Services takes the place of these stored procedures because this feature is more robust and has more configuration options. If you have legacy applications or scripts that use Web Assistant, enable this feature. Otherwise, this feature should be disabled. |
| **Analysis Services** | |
| AdHocDataMiningQueries-Enabled | The Data Mining Extensions OPENROWSET function establishes a connection to a data source object by using a provider name and connection string. This permits ad hoc connections to remote data sources without an administrator specifically configuring linked or remote servers. Enable this feature if your applications or scripts use OPENROWSET with Data Mining. Otherwise, this feature should be disabled to prevent applications and scripts from passing a provider name and connection string when using the OPENROWSET function. |
| AnonymousConnections-Enabled | With anonymous connections, unauthenticated users can establish connections with Analysis Services. Enable this feature if your applications and scripts require unauthenticated user access. Otherwise, disable this feature. |
| LinkedObjectsLinksFrom-OtherInstancesEnabled | With Analysis Services, you can use linked objects to link dimensions and measure groups between servers. If you want this instance to be linked from other servers, enable this feature. Otherwise, disable this feature. |
| LinkedObjectsLinksTo-OtherInstancesEnabled | With Analysis Services, you can use linked objects to link dimensions and measure groups between servers. If you want Analysis Server to link to other servers, select Enable Links To Other Instances. Otherwise, disable this feature. |
| ListenOnlyOnLocal-Connections | Analysis Services can work with remote resources as well as local resources. When you allow Analysis Services to work with remote resources, Analysis Services listens for TCP/IP connections from both local and remote server instances, which allows connections from remote computers. When you restrict Analysis Services from working with remote resources, Analysis Services opens a TCP/IP port on the server but listens only for connections from local server instances. If you want Analysis Services to only work with local resources, enable this feature. Otherwise, disable this feature. |

**Table 3-1    Component Features for Managing Surface Area Access**

| Component/Facet | Description/Usage |
|---|---|
| UserDefinedFunctions-Enabled | Analysis Services is integrated with the .NET Framework and can load assemblies containing user-defined functions. These functions can be written using the CLR or component object model (COM) objects. CLR objects and functions have an integrated security model. COM objects do not use this model, and they are therefore less secure inherently. Enable this feature if your applications and scripts require user-defined COM functions. Otherwise, disable this feature to permit only CLR functions. |
| **Reporting Services** | |
| ScheduledEventsAnd-ReportDeliveryEnabled | With Reporting Services, you can use ad hoc, on-demand reports and scheduled reports. Typically, when you have installed Reporting Services, both types of reports are enabled. If you do not use scheduled reports, you can disable this aspect of report generation and delivery by disabling this feature. |
| WebServiceRequests-AndHTTPAccessEnabled | Reporting Services components use SOAP messaging over HTTP for communications and HTTP for URL access requests. These features are handled by the Report Server Web Service and permit you to work with Reporting Services through Report Manager, Report Designer, and SQL Server Management Studio. Typically, if Reporting Services are installed, the server will handle HTTP and Web Service requests. Enable this feature if your client applications use the Report Server Web Service or if you use Report Manager, Report Designer, or SQL Server Management Studio with this Reporting Services installation. Otherwise, disable this feature. |
| ReportManagerEnabled | Report Manager is a Web-based application for viewing reports, managing report server content, and controlling access to report servers running in Native Mode. Enable this feature if you use Report Manager with this Reporting Services installation. Otherwise, disable this feature. |

# Configuring SQL Server Services

SQL Server Configuration Manager is implemented in a custom Microsoft Management Console and also available as a snap-in that you can add to your own custom consoles. You can start SQL Server Configuration Manager using one of the following techniques:

- Log on to the database server through a local or remote login, and then start SQL Server Configuration Manager by clicking the Start button; pointing to All Programs, Microsoft SQL Server 2008, Configuration Tools; and then selecting SQL Server Configuration Manager. You can also start this tool by clicking Start, typing **sqlservermanager10.msc** in the Search box, and then pressing Enter.

■ In SQL Server Management Studio, open the Registered Servers view by pressing Ctrl+Alt+G. Use the Registered Servers toolbar to select the top-level group, and then expand the group nodes by double-clicking them. Right-click the server entry and then select SQL Server Configuration Manager.

When you start SQL Server Configuration Manager, you will see the main window shown in Figure 3-1. You can use SQL Server Configuration Manager to perform several main tasks:

■ Manage the services configuration of related SQL Server instances

■ Manage the connections configuration of related SQL Server instances

■ Manage the configuration of SQL Native Client on the computer running SQL Server

**Note**   On 64-bit computers, you'll find multiple nodes for managing network and client configuration settings. You use the nodes with the suffix (32bit) to manage 32-bit settings and the other nodes to manage 64-bit settings.

**Figure 3-1**   SQL Server Configuration Manager main window.

## Managing the Services Configuration

You can use SQL Server Configuration Manager to view and manage the startup state of SQL Server services. After you start SQL Server Configuration Manager, click the SQL Server Services node to view the critical SQL Server services configured for all running instances of SQL Server 2008 on the computer to which you are currently connected. The services available depend on the components you have installed. Keep the following in mind:

■ **Active Directory Helper**   Runs as the SQL Server Active Directory Helper service. The executable file for this service is Sqladhlp.exe, specified with the service startup command line, such as:

```
"C:\Program Files\Microsoft SQL Server\100\Shared\sqladhlp.exe"
```

You cannot configure this service in SQL Server Configuration Manager. Use the Services utility instead.

- **Analysis Services** Runs as the SQL Server Analysis Services (*InstanceName*) service. The executable file for this service is Msmdsrv.exe, and the service runs a specific initialization file specified in the startup command line, such as:

```
"C:\Program Files\Microsoft SQL Server\MSAS10.CUSTDATAW\OLAP\bin\
    msmdsrv.exe" -s "C:\Program Files\Microsoft SQL Server\
    MSAS10.CUSTDATAW\OLAP\Config"
```

The initialization file (Msmdsrv.ini) is defined using XML and should not be edited directly.

- **Database Engine** Runs as the SQL Server (*InstanceName*) service. The executable file for this service is Sqlservr.exe, and the service runs under an instance specified in the startup command line, such as (for the default instance, MSSQLSERVER):

```
"C:\Program Files\Microsoft SQL Server\MSSQL10.MSSQLSERVER\MSSQL\
    Binn\sqlservr.exe" -s MSSQLSERVER
```

> **Note** Although some components, such as the Database Engine, can be started directly from the command line, services typically are started with the appropriate tool or with NET START. If you manually start up the Database Engine, you can set specific startup parameters as discussed in Chapter 4, "Configuring and Tuning Microsoft SQL Server 2008."
>
> You can also set startup parameters using SQL Server Configuration Manager. Double-click the SQL Server service for the instance with which you want to work. In the Properties dialog box, on the Log On tab, click Stop to stop the service. Then on the Advanced tab, enter the startup parameters in the Startup Parameters field. Finally, on the Log On tab, click Start to start the service.

- **Integration Services** Runs as the SQL Server Integration Services service. The executable file for this service is Msdtssrvr.exe, specified with the service startup command line, such as:

```
"C:\Program Files\Microsoft SQL Server\100\DTS\Binn\MsDtsSrvr.exe"
```

- **Reporting Services** Runs as the Report Server (*InstanceName*) service. The executable file for this service is ReportingServicesService.exe, specified with the service startup command line, such as:

```
"C:\Program Files\Microsoft SQL Server\MSRS10.CUSTDATAW\
    Reporting Services\ReportServer\bin\ReportingServicesService.exe"
```

- **SQL Server Agent** Runs as the SQL Server Agent (*InstanceName*) service. The executable file for this service is Sqlagent.exe, and the service runs under an instance specified in the startup command line, such as:

```
"C:\Program Files\Microsoft SQL Server\MSSQL10.MSSQLSERVER\MSSQL\
    Binn\SQLAGENT.EXE" -i MSSQLSERVER
```

- **SQL Server Browser**    Runs as the SQL Browser service. The executable file for this service is Sqlbrowser.exe, specified with the service startup command line, such as:

  ```
  "C:\Program Files\Microsoft SQL Server\100\Shared\sqlbrowser.exe"
  ```

- **SQL Writer**    Runs as the SQL Server VSS Writer service. The executable file for this service is Sqlwriter.exe, specified with the service startup command line, such as:

  ```
  "C:\Program Files\Microsoft SQL Server\100\Shared\sqlwriter.exe"
  ```

  You cannot configure this service in SQL Server Configuration Manager. Use the Services utility instead.

After you select the SQL Server Services node, you will see a detailed entry for each service that includes the following information:

- **Name**    The common name for the service shown in the user interface.

- **State**    The status of the service as of the last refresh, such as Running or Stopped.

- **Start Mode**    The startup state of the service—Automatic, Manual, or Disabled.

- **Log On As**    The user account under which the service runs. For services running under system accounts, you will see the name of the system account used, such as NT AUTHORITY\LOCAL SERVICE for a service running under the LOCAL SERVICE account, NT AUTHORITY\NETWORK SERVICE for a service running under the NETWORK SERVICE account, or LocalSystem for a service running under the Local System account.

- **Process ID**    The identification number of the system process under which the service is running.

- **Service Type**    The type of SQL Server component to which the service relates, such as Report Server.

Any SQL Server services not being used or not required for your installation should be set to manual startup and stopped if they are running. If you want to prevent a service from running, you should set the Start Mode to Disabled. Keep in mind that the SQL Server Browser service provides connection information to client computers. If clients connect to SQL Server remotely, this service is required (in most instances).

> **Note**    You can also use the Services utility to manage SQL Server services. The advantage that SQL Server Configuration Manager has over the Services utility is that it streamlines the information and provides access only to SQL Server services rather than all system services.

When you install SQL Server, SQL Server Setup creates user groups for the SQL Server services and adds the service accounts to these groups as appropriate. These groups are meant to simplify the process of granting permissions required to run SQL Server services and related executables. Table 3-2 lists the user groups created by SQL Server Setup, the related SQL Server services, and the default permissions. These groups also are assigned access permissions for numerous files and folders used by SQL Server.

**Table 3-2    Related Groups and Assigned Permissions for Services**

| Service | Related Group or Groups | Assigned Permissions |
|---|---|---|
| SQL Server | Default instance: SQLServerMSSQLUser-$*ComputerName*$MSSQLSERVER<br>Named instance: SQLServerMSSQLUser-$*ComputerName*$*InstanceName* | Log on as a service<br>Log on as a batch job<br>Replace a process-level token<br>Bypass traverse checking<br>Adjust memory quotas for a process<br>Permission to start SQL Server Active Directory Helper<br>Permission to start SQL Writer |
| SQL Server Active Directory Helper | Default or named instance: SQLServerMSSQLServerADHelperUser-$*ComputerName* | N/A |
| SQL Server Agent | Default instance: SQLServerSQLAgent-User$*ComputerName*$MSSQLSERVER<br>Named instance: SQLServerSQLAgent-User$*ComputerName*$*InstanceName* | Log on as a service<br>Act as part of the operating system (only on Microsoft Windows 2000)<br>Log on as a batch job<br>Replace a process-level token<br>Bypass traverse checking<br>Adjust memory quotas for a process |
| SQL Server Analysis Services | Default instance: SQLServerMSASUser$*ComputerName*-$MSSQLSERVER<br>Named instance: SQLServerMSASUser$*ComputerName*-$*InstanceName* | Log on as a service |
| SQL Server Browser | Default or named instance: SQLServer-SQLBrowserUser$*ComputerName* | Log on as a service |

**Table 3-2   Related Groups and Assigned Permissions for Services**

| Service | Related Group or Groups | Assigned Permissions |
|---|---|---|
| SQL Server Integration Services | Default or named instance: SQLServer-DTSUser$*ComputerName* | Log on as a service<br>Permission to write to application event log<br>Bypass traverse checking<br>Impersonate a client after authentication |
| SQL Server Reporting Services | Default instance:<br>SQLServerReportServerUser$*Computer-Name*$MSSQLSERVER and SQLServer-ReportingServicesWebServiceUser-$*ComputerName*$MSSQLSERVER<br><br>Named instance:<br>SQLServerReportServerUser$*Computer-Name*$*InstanceName* and SQLServer-ReportingServicesWebServiceUser-$*ComputerName*$*InstanceName* | Log on as a service |
| SQL Writer | N/A | N/A |

## Managing Service State and Start Mode

You can use the Services utility or SQL Server Configuration Manager to manage SQL Server services. With the Services utility, you manage SQL Server services as you would any other service. With SQL Server Configuration Manager, you can manage the service login account, the start mode, and status. If applicable, you can also manage advanced features such as dump directory, error reporting, and startup parameters. The advantage that SQL Server Configuration Manager has over the Services utility is that it streamlines the information available so that you see only SQL Server services rather than all system services. Additionally, some advanced options, such as the dump directory, can be configured only by using SQL Server Configuration Manager.

Using SQL Server Configuration Manager, you can stop, start, pause, or restart a server service by completing the following steps:

1. Start SQL Server Configuration Manager, and then select the SQL Server Services node.

2. In the right pane, you will see a list of services used by SQL Server and its configured components, as shown previously in Figure 3-1. You can work with services in several ways:

   ❑ Click the name of the service to select it. Use the Start, Pause, Stop, and Restart buttons on the menu bar to manage the service run state, or click the Properties button to view the service properties.

❑   Right-click the service, and then use the shortcut menu to manage the service run state, or click Properties to view the service properties.

❑   Double-click the service to view the service properties.

You can set a service's start mode by following these steps:

1. Start SQL Server Configuration Manager, and then select the SQL Server Services node.

2. In the right pane, right-click a service, and then select Properties from the shortcut menu.

3. On the Service tab of the Properties dialog box, use the Start Mode drop-down menu to select the desired start mode as shown in Figure 3-2. Options include Automatic, Disabled, and Manual.

4. Click OK.

**Figure 3-2**   Service tab options for start mode.

## Setting the Startup Service Account

SQL Server and its components have specific rights and permissions from the startup service account. These permissions are used whenever the Database Engine or another SQL Server component performs tasks on the local system or across the network. As you learned in "Service Accounts for SQL Server" on page 10, you can configure services to use three different types of built-in accounts: Local Service, Local System, and Network Service. You also can configure services to use domain accounts.

You can specify a built-in account for a SQL Server service by completing the following steps:

1. Start SQL Server Configuration Manager, and then select the SQL Server Services node.

2. In the right pane, right-click a service to select it, and then select Properties.

3. On the Log On tab of the Properties dialog box, select Built-In Account and then use the drop-down list to choose the service to use.

4. If the service is running, you must restart the service by clicking Restart. This stops the service and starts it again using the new credentials.

5. Click OK.

You can specify a domain account for a SQL Server service by completing the following steps:

1. Start SQL Server Configuration Manager, and then select the SQL Server Services node.

2. In the right pane, right-click a service to select it, and then select Properties.

3. On the Log On tab of the Properties dialog box, choose the This Account option, as shown in Figure 3-3. Then type the designated account name and password. For domain accounts, specify the domain as part of the account name, such as **CPANDL\sqlprimary**, where *CPANDL* is the domain name and *sqlprimary* is the account name. For local computer accounts, enter .\ followed by the name of the account, such as **.\sqlaccount**. Click Browse if you want to use the Select User Or Group dialog box to select an account.

4. If the service is running, you must restart the service by clicking Restart. This stops the service and starts it again using the new credentials.

5. After you click OK to close the Properties dialog box, ensure you've granted the specified domain account the appropriate permissions and privileges. Refer to Table 3-2 to determine the groups to which you should add the domain account to ensure the account has the appropriate access permissions for files and folders used by SQL Server.

**Figure 3-3**  Setting the startup account for a selected service.

## Configuring File Streaming

File streaming allows the SQL Server Database Engine to work with binary large objects (BLOBs) that are stored outside the database. To distinguish between standard BLOBs stored in database tables, BLOBs stored outside the database are called FILESTREAM BLOBs. Like standard BLOBs, FILESTREAM BLOBs are specified in the database as varbinary(max) data types and can include any type of unstructured data from Microsoft Office documents to videos to digital images. Unlike standard BLOBs, FILESTREAM BLOBs do not have a 2-gigabyte (GB) file size limit. You distinguish a FILESTREAM BLOB from a standard BLOB by setting the FILESTREAM attribute on a varbinary(max) column. This tells the Database Engine to store the data for that column on the file system rather than in the database. SQL Server is able to locate the BLOB data because it stores pointers to BLOBs in the database.

Transact-SQL statements can insert, update, query, search, and delete file-stream data. The SQL Server Database Engine uses the features of the NTFS file system for caching file data while streaming files rather than the SQL Server buffer pool. This helps ensure memory is available for processing queries and also helps maintain Database Engine performance.

Although you can use an insert operation to prepopulate a FILESTREAM field with a null value, empty value, or a limited amount of inline data, a large amount of data is more efficiently streamed into a file that uses Win32 interfaces. Here, the Win32 interfaces work within the context of a SQL Server transaction and you use the Path-name intrinsic function to obtain the logical Universal Naming Convention (UNC) path of the BLOB file on the file system. You then use the OpenSqlFilestream application programming interface (API) to obtain a file handle and operate on the BLOB via the file system using the following Win32 file streaming interfaces: ReadFile, Write-File, TransmitFile, SetFilePointer, SetEndOfFile, and FlushFileBuffers. Close the handle by using CloseHandle. Because file operations are transactional, you cannot delete or rename FILESTREAM files through the file system.

When you update a FILESTREAM field, you modify the underlying BLOB data in the file system. When a FILESTREAM field is set to NULL, the BLOB data associated with the field is deleted. To perform partial updates to the data, you cannot use a Transact-SQL chunked update, implemented as UPDATE.Write(). Instead, use a device FS control (FSCTL_SQL_FILESTREAM_FETCH_OLD_CONTENT) to fetch the old content into the file that the opened handle references, which will trigger a content copy. When you delete a row or delete or truncate a table that contains FILESTREAM data, you delete the underlying BLOB data in the file system.

FILESTREAM data must be stored in FILESTREAM filegroups. A FILESTREAM file-group is a special filegroup that contains file system directories instead of the files themselves. These file system directories are called data containers and act as the interface between Database Engine storage and file system storage.

When working with FILESTREAM data, you should also keep in mind the following:

- You can create database snapshots only of standard (non-FILESTREAM) file-groups. The FILESTREAM filegroups are marked as offline for those snapshot databases. Further, a SELECT statement that is executed on a FILESTREAM table in a snapshot database must not include a FILESTREAM column.

- Log shipping supports file streaming as long as the primary and secondary servers are running SQL Server 2008, or a later version, and have file streaming enabled.

- Database Mirroring does not support file streaming. You cannot create a FILESTREAM filegroup on the principal server and cannot configure Database Mirroring for a database that contains FILESTREAM filegroups.

- Full-text indexing works with a FILESTREAM column in the same way that it does with a varbinary(max) column as long as the FILESTREAM table has a column that contains the file name extension for each FILESTREAM BLOB. The full-text engine indexes the contents of the FILESTREAM BLOBs, and whenever a FILESTREAM BLOB is updated, it is reindexed.

- A varbinary(max) column that has the FILESTREAM attribute enabled at the Publisher can be replicated to a Subscriber with or without the FILESTREAM attribute. You can specify the way in which the column is replicated using the

Article Properties - <Article> dialog box or the @schema_option parameter of sp_addarticle or sp_addmergearticle.

■ For failover clustering, FILESTREAM filegroups must be put on a shared disk. You also must enable file streaming on each node in the cluster that will host the FILESTREAM instance.

You can enable and configure file streaming by completing the following steps:

1. Start SQL Server Configuration Manager, and then select the SQL Server Services node.

2. In the right pane, right-click the instance of the Database Engine service that you want to configure, and then select Properties.

3. On the FILESTREAM tab of the Properties dialog box, shown in Figure 3-4, you can now use the Enable FILESTREAM For Transact-SQL Access check box to enable or disable file streaming for Transact-SQL. Select this check box to allow file streaming to be used; clear this check box to prevent file streaming from being used. If you disabled file streaming, click OK and skip the remaining steps.

4. If you want to enable file I/O streaming access by local clients, select Enable FILESTREAM For File I/O Streaming Access and then specify the name of the Windows Share from which files will be streamed. The default share name is MSSQLSERVER, which sets the global root for file streaming as \\?\GLOBAL-ROOT\Device\RsFx0101\<localmachine>\MSSQLSERVER.

**Figure 3-4** Configuring FILESTREAM for a Database Engine instance.

5. If you enabled local file streaming and want to enable file I/O streaming access by remote clients, select Allow Remote Clients To Have Streaming Access To FILESTREAM Data. Remote file system access to FILESTREAM data is enabled over the Server Message Block (SMB) protocol. If the client is remote, no write operations are cached by the client side, which means write operations will always be sent to the server where they can be cached if necessary.

6. If you have made changes and the service is running, you must restart the service by clicking Restart on the Log On tab. This will stop the service and then restart it using the new settings.

7. Click OK.

## Configuring Service Dump Directories, Error Reporting, and Customer Feedback Reporting

You can use advanced service configuration options to configure reporting and error-logging features. When you install SQL Server, you are asked whether you want to enable two types of reports:

- Error reports
- Feature reports (also called Customer Feedback Reporting)

When error reporting is enabled, error reports are generated and sent to Microsoft or a designated corporate error-reporting server whenever fatal errors cause a service to terminate. Error reports help determine the cause of the fatal error so that it can be corrected, and they contain details to identify what caused the error, including the version of SQL Server being used, the operating system and hardware configuration, and data from the memory or files of the process that caused the error.

Error information is also logged in a designated dump directory. The dump directory used depends on the component and its related instance. For example, the dump directory for the default SQL Server instance might be located under *%ProgramFiles%*\ Microsoft SQL Server\MSSQL10.MSSQLSERVER\MSSQL\LOG, and the Reporting Services dump directory might be located under *%ProgramFiles%*\Microsoft SQL Server\MSRS10.CUSTDATAWAREHOUS\Reporting Services\LogFiles.

Customer Feedback Reporting generates reports about component usage that are sent to Microsoft when this feature is configured. These reports help Microsoft understand how components and features are being used.

You can manage reporting and error dumps for each service individually. To do so, complete the following steps:

1. Start SQL Server Configuration Manager, and then select the SQL Server Services node.

2. In the right pane, right-click a service to select it, and then select Properties.

3. Select the Advanced tab in the Properties dialog box. Using the properties boxes shown in Figure 3-5, you can now do the following:

   ❏ Use the Dump Directory box to view the current dump directory. To change the dump directory, simply enter the new directory to use. Be sure that the logon account for the selected service has appropriate read and write access to this directory.

   ❏ Use the Error Reporting and Customer Feedback Reporting drop-down menus to enable or disable reporting as appropriate. Select Yes to enable reporting. Select No to disable reporting.

4. If you have made changes and the service is running, you must restart the service by clicking Restart on the Log On tab. This stops the service and starts it again using the new settings.

5. Click OK.

**Figure 3-5**   Setting advanced options for a selected service.

# Managing the Network and SQL Native Client Configuration

SQL Server installations can be configured to allow local and remote connections. SQL Server can use several protocols, including Shared Memory, Named Pipes, TCP/IP, and Virtual Interface Architecture (VIA). These protocols all have separate server and client configurations.

As shown in Figure 3-6, network configuration is set separately for each server instance through SQL Server Network Configuration. The client configuration is set on a per-client basis through SQL Native Client Configuration.

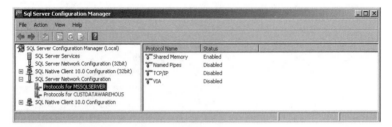

**Figure 3-6**   Viewing network configuration settings for a SQL Server instance.

When multiple client protocols are available and configured for use, clients use the protocols in a specified priority order. As Figure 3-7 shows, the default order is

1. Shared Memory

2. TCP/IP

3. Named Pipes

4. VIA

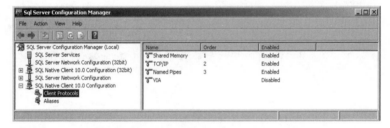

**Figure 3-7**   Clients attempt to use network protocols in a specific order.

> **Note**    Any system on which you have installed SQL Native Client is a SQL Server client. This can include systems running Windows XP Professional, Windows Vista, Windows Server 2003, and Windows Server 2008.

## Managing the Connections Configuration

SQL Server installations can be configured to provide local, remote, and dedicated connections. Local connections are used by applications running on the computer that is also running SQL Server. Remote connections are used by clients connecting to the server, by applications running on other servers, and by other SQL servers. Dedicated connections are a special feature used by administrators to maintain SQL Server installations (and managed as a configurable feature rather than as a permissible connection type).

> **Note**   The default configuration for connections depends on how you have con-
> figured service accounts, what components are installed, and other installation
> options, such as whether you performed an upgrade or new installation. Typically, a
> new installation will be configured for local connections only. However, if you have
> installed additional components, such as Reporting Services, the configuration will
> usually permit local and remote connections.

Although a configuration for only local connections provides obvious security advantages, you cannot always run SQL Server in this configuration. Often, and more typically, you will need to allow incoming connections from remote clients and servers, and in this case, the permitted connection protocols can affect the amount of resources used and the relative security of the server. For remote connections, SQL Server 2008 can use TCP/IP, Named Pipes, or both.

TCP/IP is a widely used protocol suite consisting of Transmission Control Protocol (TCP) and Internet Protocol (IP). SQL Server listens on and communicates over dynamic, static, or both port types, depending on its configuration. SQL Server 2008 supports both IP version 4 (IPv4) and IP version 6 (IPv6). The IP addresses SQL Server uses for network communications depend on its configuration as well. TCP/IP includes standards for routing traffic that help to ensure data packets reach their destination and standards for communications security that help protect sensitive information. This makes TCP/IP ideal for use on both local area networks (LANs) and wide area network (WANs).

Named Pipes is a protocol designed for LANs. With Named Pipes, a part of memory is used by one process to pass information to another process so that the output of one process becomes the input of another process. The second process can be local, meaning it is on the same computer as the first process, or it can be remote, meaning it is on a different computer than the first process. Although local named pipes run in kernel mode and are very fast, remote named pipes don't work well on slow networks. The reason for this is that named pipes typically generate a lot of message traffic over the network.

Because TCP/IP and Named Pipes require specific and different ports to be open across a firewall, you can limit the server to one protocol or the other to reduce the potential attack surface. Before you change the permissible connection types, however, you should make sure that all clients and applications are configured to use the appropriate network library.

With TCP/IP, SQL Server can communicate using standard IP and the TCP/IP Sockets Net-Library. The default listen port for the default instance is TCP port 1433. The default listen port for named instances is set dynamically, unless otherwise assigned. TCP port 1434 is used for client connections. When you use named pipes, SQL Server 2008 uses the Named Pipes Net-Library to communicate over a standard network address: \\.\pipe\sql\query for the default instance and \\.\pipe\MSSQL$*instance-name*\sql\query for a named instance. Named pipes require a range of ports to be open for communication across a firewall. With named pipes, the server will listen on TCP port 445.

SQL Server 2008 also supports the Shared Memory protocol for local connections and VIA for both local and remote connections. NWLink IPX/SPX and AppleTalk are no longer supported

## Specifying the Shared Memory Network Configuration

The Shared Memory protocol is used for local connections only. If the protocol is enabled, any local client can connect to the server using this protocol. If you don't want local clients to use the Shared Memory protocol, you can disable it.

You can enable or disable the Shared Memory protocol by completing the following steps:

1. Start SQL Server Configuration Manager. Expand the SQL Server Network Configuration node, and then select the Protocols For entry for the SQL Server instance you want to work with.

2. Right-click Shared Memory and do one of the following:

   ❑ Select Enable to enable the protocol to be used.

   ❑ Select Disable to prevent the protocol from being used.

## Specifying the Named Pipes Network Configuration

The Named Pipes protocol is used primarily for local or remote connections by applications written for early versions of the Windows operating system. When you enable Named Pipes, SQL Server 2008 uses the Named Pipes Net-Library to communicate over a standard network address: \\.\pipe\sql\query for the default instance and \\.\pipe\MSSQL$*instancename*\sql\query for a named instance. In addition to enabling or disabling the use of Named Pipes, you can configure properties of this protocol to change the named pipe to use.

You can manage the Named Pipes network configuration by completing the following steps:

1. Start SQL Server Configuration Manager. Expand the SQL Server Network Configuration node, and then select the Protocols For entry for a SQL Server instance.

2. Right-click Named Pipes and select Properties.

3. You can now do the following:

   ❑ Use the Enabled drop-down menu to enable or disable the protocol. Select Yes to allow the protocol to be used; select No to prevent the protocol from being used.

❑ Change the name of the default pipe by typing a new value in the Pipe Name field. (Don't forget to update the client configuration.)

4. Click OK.

## Specifying the TCP/IP Network Configuration

The TCP/IP protocol is the preferred protocol for local or remote connections to SQL Server. When you use TCP/IP, SQL Server listens on a specific TCP port and IP address for requests. By default, SQL Server listens on TCP port 1433 on all IP addresses that are configured for its network cards. For security reasons, you might want SQL Server to use a different TCP/IP configuration, and you have several options. You can

■ Configure SQL Server to listen on all configured IP addresses and to use the same TCP port configuration across however many IP addresses this includes.

■ Configure SQL Server to listen to only specifically enabled IP addresses and then configure each TCP listen port separately for each IP address.

With either configuration approach, you can configure the TCP listen ports manually or dynamically. When you manually assign a TCP listen port, the TCP port is static and changes only if you assign a new value. When you dynamically assign a TCP listen port, the related SQL Server instance dynamically assigns the TCP listen port whenever you start the related service. Because the TCP listen port is dynamically assigned at startup, client applications need a helper server to determine the incoming listen port, and this is where the SQL Server Browser service comes into the picture. When SQL Server instances are using dynamically assigned TCP ports, the SQL Server Browser service checks for incoming connections and directs them to the current port for the related SQL Server instance.

**Note**   You shouldn't use dynamically assigned ports when clients are connecting through a firewall. If you do, clients might experience connection problems whenever the dynamically assigned port changes.

### Disabling, Enabling, and Configuring TCP/IP

You can disable or enable and configure TCP/IP by completing the following steps:

1. Start SQL Server Configuration Manager. Expand the SQL Server Network Configuration node, and then select the Protocols For entry for a SQL Server instance.

2. Right-click TCP/IP and select Properties. This displays the TCP/IP Properties dialog box.

3. On the Protocol tab, you can now use the Enabled drop-down menu to enable or disable the protocol. Select Yes to allow the protocol to be used; select No to prevent the protocol from being used. If you disabled TCP/IP, click OK and skip the remaining steps.

4.  On the Protocol tab, you can configure parameters that control whether and how the SQL Server instance tries to maintain idle TCP/IP connections. Two parameters are used:

    ❑ **Listen All**   Controls whether SQL Server listens on all IP addresses that are configured for its network cards. If you set this value to Yes, the settings of the IPAll properties box on the IP Addresses tab apply to all active IP addresses. If you set this value to No, you must configure each IP address separately using the related properties boxes on the IP Addresses tab.

    ❑ **Keep Alive**   Controls how often SQL Server tries to verify that the computer at the end of a remote connection is still available. By default, SQL Server checks a remote connection after it has been idle for 30,000 milliseconds (30 seconds). In most cases, a value between 30 and 60 seconds will suffice. Depending on how busy the server is and the importance of client activity, you might want to verify and maintain idle connections more quickly, which can ensure that idle connections are not terminated. For example, you could use a smaller value, such as 15,000 or 20,000 milliseconds, to ensure that idle connections are validated faster.

5.  Click OK.

### Using Static TCP/IP Network Configurations

You can configure a SQL Server instance to use a static TCP/IP network configuration by completing the following steps:

1.  Start SQL Server Configuration Manager. Expand the SQL Server Network Configuration node, and then select the Protocols For entry for a SQL Server instance.

2.  Right-click TCP/IP and select Properties. On the IP Addresses tab of the TCP/IP Properties dialog box, you should see entries representing the IPv4 and IPv6 addresses configured on the server. Individual IP address entries, in numerical order—such as IP1, IP2, IP3, and so on—are for when SQL Server is listening for specific IP addresses. The IPAll entry is used when SQL Server is listening on all IP addresses on the server.

    **Note**   The IP addresses 127.0.0.1 and ::1 are the local loopback addresses for IPv4 and IPv6, respectively. These addresses are used to listen for connections from local clients.

3.  If you want SQL Server to listen on all configured IP addresses on the server, you should do the following:

    a.  On the Protocol tab, set Listen All to Yes.

    b.  On the IP Addresses tab, scroll down and set a specific TCP listen port for IPAll. The default is 1433. To change the TCP listen port, type the desired TCP listen port in the field provided.

4. If you want to enable listening on specific IP addresses and TCP ports, you should do the following:

    a. On the Protocol tab, set Listen All to No.

    b. On the IP Addresses tab, specify the IP addresses that SQL Server should actively listen on by setting their IP address entries to Active Yes and Enabled Yes. Then type the desired TCP listen port for each IP address in the fields provided.

    c. On the IP Addresses tab, specify the IP addresses that SQL Server shouldn't actively listen on by setting their IP address entries to Active No and Enabled No.

5. Click OK.

**Tip**   SQL Server can listen to multiple TCP ports on the same IP address. Simply list the desired ports separated by commas, such as 1433,1533,1534. Ensure that you don't insert a space between the comma and the values. The TCP Port field is limited to a total of 2047 characters.

### Using Dynamic TCP/IP Network Configurations

You can configure a SQL Server instance to use a dynamic TCP/IP network configuration by completing the following steps:

1. Start SQL Server Configuration Manager. Expand the SQL Server Network Configuration node, and then select the Protocols For entry for a SQL Server instance.

2. Right-click TCP/IP and select Properties. On the IP Addresses tab of the TCP/IP Properties dialog box, you should see entries representing the IPv4 and IPv6 addresses configured on the server. Individual IP address entries, in numerical order—such as IP1, IP2, IP3, and so on—are for when SQL Server is listening for specific IP addresses. The IPAll entry is used when SQL Server is listening on all IP addresses on the server.

    **Note**   The IP addresses 127.0.0.1 and ::1 are the local loopback addresses for IPv4 and IPv6, respectively. These addresses are used to listen for connections from local clients.

3. If you want SQL Server to listen to the same dynamic port on all configured IP addresses on the server, you should do the following:

    a. On the Protocol tab, set Listen All to Yes.

    b. On the IP Addresses tab, scroll down and then type **0** (zero) in the TCP Dynamic Ports box.

4. If you want to enable listening on specific IP addresses, you should do the following:

   a. On the Protocol tab, set Listen All to No.

   b. On the IP Addresses tab, specify the IP addresses that SQL Server should actively listen on by setting their IP address entries to Active Yes and Enabled Yes. Then type 0 (zero) in the related TCP Dynamic Ports field.

   c. On the IP Addresses tab, specify the IP addresses that SQL Server shouldn't actively listen on by setting their IP address entries to Active No and Enabled No.

5. Click OK.

## Configuring Security for Native Client Configurations

By default, clients do not use Secure Sockets Layer (SSL) or attempt to validate server certificates. You can force protocol encryption, server certificate validation, or both by completing the following steps:

1. Start SQL Server Configuration Manager. Expand SQL Server Network Configuration, SQL Native Client Configuration.

2. Right-click SQL Native Client Configuration and then select Properties.

3. For Force Protocol Encryption, select Yes to force clients to use SSL; select No to use unencrypted connections.

4. For Trust Server Certificate, select Yes to force clients to validate server certificates; select No to skip validation of server certificates.

## Configuring the Native Client Protocol Order

Shared Memory is always the preferred local connection protocol. You can disable Shared Memory protocol to preclude its use and change the order of the other protocols by completing the following steps:

1. Start SQL Server Configuration Manager. Expand SQL Native Client Configuration, and then click Client Protocols.

2. Right-click any of the protocols listed, and then select Order. The Client Protocols Properties dialog box opens.

3. In the Client Protocols Properties dialog box, you can

   ❑ Change the order of an enabled protocol. First click the name of the protocol you want to move, and then use the arrow buttons to the right of the Enabled Protocols list as appropriate until the protocol is positioned where you want it in the list.

❑ Disable or enable protocols. To disable an enabled protocol, select it, and then click the shift left button to move the name of the protocol to the Disabled Protocols list. To enable a disabled protocol, select it, and then click the shift right button to move the name of the protocol to the Enabled Protocols list.

❑ Enable or disable the Shared Memory protocol. To enable the Shared Memory protocol for local client connections, select Enable Shared Memory Protocol. To disable the Shared Memory protocol for local client connections, clear Enable Shared Memory Protocol.

4. Click OK.

## Configuring the Shared Memory Native Client Configuration

The Shared Memory protocol is used for local client connections only. You can enable or disable the Shared Memory protocol for clients by completing the following steps:

1. Start SQL Server Configuration Manager. Expand SQL Server Network Configuration, SQL Native Client Configuration, and then click Client Protocols.

2. Right-click Shared Memory and then select Properties.

3. You can now use the Enabled drop-down menu to enable or disable the protocol. Select Yes to allow the protocol to be used; select No to prevent the protocol from being used.

## Configuring the Named Pipes Native Client Configuration

The Named Pipes protocol is used primarily for local or remote connections by applications written for early versions of the Windows operating system. The default named pipes are \\.\pipe\sql\query for the default instance, and \\.\pipe\MSSQL$*instancename*\sql\query for a named instance. The default pipe for clients is set using an alias. The standard alias for clients is sql\query, which refers to the default pipe, such as \\.\pipe\sql\query or \\.\pipe\MSSQL$*instancename*\sql\query. If you changed the default pipe in the server's network configuration, you will need to change the default pipe in the client configuration (and for all clients that will connect to SQL Server in this way). For example, if SQL Server is using \\.\pipe\sqlserver\app1 as the default pipe, the client must use \sqlserver\app1 as the pipe name.

You can manage the Named Pipes client configuration by completing the following steps:

1. Start SQL Server Configuration Manager. Expand SQL Native Client Configuration, and then click Client Protocols.

2. Right-click Named Pipes and select Properties. You can now

❑ Use the Enabled drop-down menu to enable or disable the protocol. Select Yes to allow the protocol to be used; select No to prevent the protocol from being used.

❑  Set the default pipe. In the Named Pipes Properties dialog box, enter the default pipe for the client in the field provided, and then click OK.

## Configuring the TCP/IP Native Client Configuration

The TCP/IP protocol is the preferred protocol for local or remote connections to SQL Server. When connecting to a default instance of the Database Engine using TCP/IP, the client must know the TCP port value. Thus, if a default instance has been configured to listen on a different port, you must change the client TCP/IP configuration to that port number. When connecting to a named instance of the Database Engine, the client will attempt to obtain the port number from the SQL Browser service on the server to which it is connecting. If the SQL Browser service is not running, the TCP port number must be provided in the client configuration or as part of the connection string.

You can configure the TCP/IP client configuration by completing the following steps:

1. Start SQL Server Configuration Manager. Expand SQL Native Client Configuration, and then click Client Protocols.

2. If you want to enable or disable TCP/IP, right-click TCP/IP, and then select Enable or Disable as appropriate.

3. To view TCP/IP connection properties, right-click TCP/IP, and then select Properties.

4. To set the default port, select Properties. In the TCP/IP Properties dialog box, enter the default port for the client in the field provided.

5. You can also configure parameters that control whether and how the client tries to maintain idle TCP/IP connections. Two parameters are used:

   ❑  **Keep Alive**  Controls when a client first tries to verify that an idle connection is still valid and attempts to maintain the connection. By default, the client checks a connection after it has been idle for 30,000 milliseconds (30 seconds). In most cases, a value between 30 and 60 seconds will suffice. Depending on how busy the server is and the importance of client activity, you might want to verify and maintain idle connections more quickly, which can ensure that idle connections are not terminated. For example, you could use a smaller value, such as 15,000 or 20,000 milliseconds, to ensure that idle connections are validated faster.

   ❑  **Keep Alive Interval**  Controls how frequently a client rechecks an idle connection when there is no initial response to the KEEPALIVE transmission. By default, the client retransmits the KEEPALIVE request every 1,000 milliseconds (1 second). If many clients are connecting to a busy server, you might want to lengthen the Keep Alive interval to decrease the number of KEEPALIVE retransmissions.

6. Click OK.

# Chapter 4

# Configuring and Tuning Microsoft SQL Server 2008

Microsoft designed SQL Server 2008 to balance the workload dynamically and to self-tune configuration settings. For example, SQL Server can increase or decrease memory usage dynamically based on overall system memory requirements. SQL Server also manages memory efficiently, especially when it comes to queries and user connections—and memory is just one of dozens of areas in which the configuration is automatically adjusted.

Although the SQL Server self-tuning feature works well, there are times when you will need to configure SQL Server settings manually. For example, if you are running a large database with special constraints and the database is not working the way you expect it to perform, you might want to customize the configuration. You might also need to modify configuration settings for SQL Server accounts, authentication, and auditing. Key tools you will use to configure and tune SQL Server include the following:

- **System catalog queries** Provide a direct way to determine database configuration characteristics and their related settings.

- **Stored procedures** Let you view and manage configuration settings through stored procedures, such as sp_configure. Note that you can change some options of sp_configure only when Show Advanced Options is set to 1, as in the following example:

```
exec sp_configure "show advanced options" 1
```

- **SQL Server Management Studio** Provides an easy-to-use interface that updates the database and registry settings for you.

- **SQLServr.exe** Starts SQL Server from the command line, and you can use it to set configuration parameters at startup.

In this chapter, we will examine the structures available for configuring and tuning SQL Server. We start with a look at the SQL Server 2008 system catalog, and then continue with a discussion of catalog queries and stored procedures. This discussion provides the essential background for understanding how to configure and tune SQL Server 2008. The next chapter—Chapter 5, "Managing the Enterprise"—provides details about using SQL Server Management Studio and SQLServr.exe.

# Accessing SQL Server Configuration Data

SQL Server 2008 uses an object-based approach to representing servers, databases, and all of their configuration characteristics and data contents. At the heart of this object-based structure is the system catalog, which describes the objects in a particular instance of SQL Server along with their attributes. For example, attributes of a database describe

- The number and names of the tables and views

- The number and names of columns in a table or view

- The column data type, scale, and precision

- The triggers and constraints that are defined on a table

- The indexes and keys that are defined for a table

- The statistics used by the query optimizer for generating query plans

In queries, you can access this and other system catalog information using

- **Catalog views**   Provide access to metadata stored in a database, which includes database attributes and their values. Catalog views can be used to access all user-available metadata, except for replication, backup, database maintenance plan, and SQL Server Agent metadata.

- **Compatibility views**   Provide access to many of the system tables from earlier releases of SQL Server using SQL Server 2008 views. These views are meant for backward compatibility only, and they expose the same metadata that was available in SQL Server 2000. They do not expose metadata for new SQL Server 2008 features, such as database partitioning and mirroring.

- **Information Schema views**   Provide access to a subset of metadata stored in a database, which includes database attributes and their values. Information Schema views are based on catalog view definitions in the SQL-92 standard and do not contain metadata specific to SQL Server 2008. Applications that use these views are portable between heterogeneous SQL-92 compliant database systems.

- **ODBC catalog functions**   Provide an interface that Open Database Connectivity (ODBC) drivers can use to return result sets containing system catalog information. The result sets present catalog information in a way that is independent of the structure of the underlying catalog tables.

- **OLE DB schema rowsets**   Provide an IDBSchemaRowset interface that OLE DB providers can use to access system catalog information. The rowsets present catalog information independently from the structure of the underlying catalog tables.

- **System stored procedures and functions**   Provide Transact-SQL stored procedures and functions that return catalog information.

Catalog views and stored procedures are the methods recommended to access a database's metadata. This is primarily because catalog views present metadata in a format that is independent of any catalog table implementation, which means that the views are not affected by changes in the underlying catalog tables. When you want to configure or manage a server, you will typically use stored procedures to help you perform the necessary tasks. Stored procedures provide the necessary functionality to view and manage the configuration of SQL Server and related databases with ease.

## Working with the System Catalog and Catalog Views

Catalog views contain information used by the SQL Server 2008 Database Engine. They provide the most general interface to the catalog metadata and are the most direct way to access and work with this information. All user-available metadata in the system catalog is exposed through catalog views. Catalog views do not contain information about replication, backup, database maintenance plans, or SQL Server Agent.

Like all structures in SQL Server 2008 databases, catalog views follow an object-based hierarchy in which lower-level objects inherit attributes of higher-level objects. Some catalog views inherit rows from other catalog views. For example, the Tables catalog view inherits all the columns of the Objects catalog view. Thus, in addition to columns that are specific to the Tables catalog view itself, the Tables catalog view has all the columns from the Objects catalog view. Table 4-1 summarizes the SQL Server 2008 catalog views and their uses.

**Table 4-1   SQL Server 2008 Catalog Views**

| View Type | Description | Key Catalog Views |
|---|---|---|
| Change Tracking | Describes change tracking components and values in databases and tables | sys.change_tracking_databases<br>sys.change_tracking_tables |
| CLR Assembly | Describe Common Language Runtime (CLR) assemblies | sys.assemblies<br>sys.assembly_files<br>sys.assembly_references |
| Databases and Files | Describe databases, database files, and backup devices associated with a SQL Server instance | sys.backup_devices<br>sys.database_files<br>sys.databases<br>sys.database_recovery_status<br>sys.master_files |

Table 4-1   SQL Server 2008 Catalog Views

| View Type | Description | Key Catalog Views |
| --- | --- | --- |
| Database Mirroring | Describe witness roles that a server plays as a Database Mirroring partner | sys.database_mirroring<br>sys.database_mirroring_endpoints<br>sys.database_mirroring_witnesses |
| Data Spaces | Describe filegroups and partition schemes | sys.data_spaces<br>sys.destination_data_spaces<br>sys.filegroups<br>sys.partition_schemes |
| Endpoints | Describe endpoints used for mirroring, service broker messaging, and Web services | sys.endpoints<br>sys.endpoint_webmethods<br>sys.http_endpoints<br>sys.service_broker_endpoints<br>sys.soap_endpoints<br>sys.tcp_endpoints<br>sys.via_endpoints |
| Extended Properties | Describe extended properties and the class of objects from which they originate | sys.extended_properties |
| Linked Servers | Describe linked or remote servers and their related logins | sys.linked_logins<br>sys.remote_logins<br>sys.servers |
| Messages (for Errors) | Describe system-defined and user-defined error messages | sys.messages |
| Objects | Describe top-level database objects | sys.allocation_units<br>sys.assembly_modules<br>sys.check_constraints<br>sys.columns<br>sys.computed_columns<br>sys.default_constraints<br>sys.event_notifications<br>sys.events<br>sys.extended_procedures<br>sys.foreign_key_columns<br>sys.foreign_keys<br>sys.identity_columns<br>sys.index_columns<br>sys.indexes<br>sys.key_constraints<br>sys.numbered_procedure_parameters<br>sys.numbered_procedures<br>sys.objects<br>sys.parameters |

**Table 4-1**   SQL Server 2008 Catalog Views

| View Type | Description | Key Catalog Views |
| --- | --- | --- |
| Objects<br>*(continued)* | Describe top-level<br>database objects | sys.partitions<br>sys.procedures<br>sys.service_queues<br>sys.spatial_index_tessellations<br>sys.spatial_indexes<br>sys.sql_dependencies<br>sys.sql_modules<br>sys.stats<br>sys.stats_columns<br>sys.synonyms<br>sys.table_types<br>sys.tables<br>sys.trace_events<br>sys.traces<br>sys.trigger_event_types<br>sys.trigger_events<br>sys.triggers<br>sys.views |
| Partition<br>Function | Describe partition<br>functions, parameters, and<br>range values | sys.partition_functions<br>sys.partition_parameters<br>sys.partition_range_values |
| Resource<br>Governor | Describe workloads,<br>resource pools, and states<br>for managed resources | sys.resource_governor_configuration<br>sys.resource_governor_workload_groups<br>sys.resource_governor_resource_pools |
| Scalar Types | Describe user-defined<br>scalar types for CLR<br>assemblies as well as other<br>system-defined and user-<br>defined scalar types | sys.assembly_types<br>sys.types |
| Schemas | Describe database<br>schemas | sys.schemas |
| Security | Describe server-level,<br>database-level, and<br>encryption security<br>attributes and values | Database-Level Views<br>(sys.database_permissions,<br>sys.database_principals,<br>sys.database_role_members,<br>sys.master_key_passwords)<br><br>Server-Level Views (sys.server_permissions,<br>sys.server_principals,<br>sys.server_role_members, sys.sql_logins,<br>sys.system_components_surface_area_<br>configuration) |

Table 4-1   SQL Server 2008 Catalog Views

| View Type | Description | Key Catalog Views |
|---|---|---|
| Security (continued) | Describe server-level, database-level, and encryption security attributes and values | Encryption Views (sys.asymmetric_keys, sys.certificates, sys.credentials, sys.crypt_properties, sys.cryptographic_providers, sys.key_encryptions, sys.symmetric_keys) |
| | | Audit Views (sys.server_audits, sys.server_file_audits, sys.server_audit_specifications, sys.server_audit_specifications_details, sys.database_ audit_specifications, sys.database_audit_specification_details) |
| Service Broker | Describe Service Broker endpoints and messaging components | sys.conversation_endpoints sys.conversation_groups sys.conversation_priorities sys.remote_service_bindings sys.routes sys.service_contract_message_usages sys.service_contract_usages sys.service_contracts sys.service_message_types sys.service_queue_usages sys.services sys.transmission_queue |
| Server-Wide Configuration | Describe server-wide configuration option values | sys.configurations sys.trace_categories sys.trace_columns sys.trace_events sys.trace_event_bindings sys.trace_subclass_values sys.traces |
| XML Schemas (XML Type System) | Describe XML Schema components and values | sys.xml_indexes sys.xml_schema_attributes sys.xml_schema_collections sys.xml_schema_component_placements sys.xml_schema_components sys.xml_schema_elements sys.xml_schema_facets sys.xml_schema_model_groups sys.xml_schema_namespaces sys.xml_schema_types sys.xml_schema_wildcard_namespaces sys.xml_schema_wildcards |

Table 4-2 provides mapping between SQL Server 2000 system tables and SQL Server 2008 system views. The entries are organized by database and view type. Mappings for the *master* database are followed by mappings for all databases. When you want to map uses of the sysfulltextcatalogs stored procedure, you should use the following data definition language (DDL) statements instead of the available SQL Server stored procedures: CREATE FULLTEXT CATALOG, ALTER FULLTEXT CATALOG, and DROP FULLTEXT CATALOG. These statements provide additional functionality and will help ensure your applications are compatible with future editions of SQL Server.

**Table 4-2    Mapping SQL Server 2000 System Tables to SQL Server 2008 System Views**

| SQL Server 2000 System Table | SQL Server 2008 System View | SQL Server 2008 View Type |
|---|---|---|
| **Master Database** | | |
| sysaltfiles | sys.master_files | Catalog view |
| syscacheobjects | sys.dm_exec_cached_plans sys.dm_exec_plan_attributes sys.dm_exec_sql_text sys.dm_exec_cached_plans_ dependent_objects | Dynamic management view |
| syscharsets | sys.syscharsets | Compatibility view |
| sysconfigures | sys.configurations | Catalog view |
| syscurconfigs | sys.configurations | Catalog view |
| sysdatabases | sys.databases | Catalog view |
| sysdevices | sys.backup_devices | Catalog view |
| syslanguages | sys.languages | Compatibility view |
| syslockinfo | sys.dm_tran_locks | Dynamic management view |
| syslocks | sys.dm_tran_locks | Dynamic management view |
| syslogins | sys.server_principals sys.sql_logins | Catalog view |
| sysmessages | sys.messages | Catalog view |
| sysoledbusers | sys.linked_logins | Catalog view |
| sysopentapes | sys.dm_io_backup_tapes | Dynamic management view |
| sysperfinfo | sys.dm_os_performance_counters | Dynamic management view |
| sysprocesses | sys.dm_exec_connections sys.dm_exec_sessions sys.dm_exec_requests | Dynamic management view |
| sysremotelogins | sys.remote_logins | Catalog view |
| sysservers | sys.servers | Catalog view |

Table 4-2   Mapping SQL Server 2000 System Tables to SQL Server 2008 System Views

| SQL Server 2000 System Table | SQL Server 2008 System View | SQL Server 2008 View Type |
|---|---|---|
| **All Databases** | | |
| fn_virtualfilestats | sys.dm_io_virtual_file_stats | Dynamic management view |
| syscolumns | sys.columns | Catalog view |
| syscomments | sys.sql_modules | Catalog view |
| sysconstraints | sys.check_constraints<br>sys.default_constraints<br>sys.key_constraints<br>sys.foreign_keys | Catalog view |
| sysdepends | sys.sql_expression_dependencies | Catalog view |
| sysfilegroups | sys.filegroups | Catalog view |
| sysfiles | sys.database_files | Catalog view |
| sysforeignkeys | sys.foreign_key_columns<br>sys.foreign_keys | Catalog view |
| sysindexes | sys.indexes, sys.partitions,<br>sys.allocation_units | Catalog view |
| | sys.dm_db_partition_stats | Dynamic management view |
| sysindexkeys | sys.index_columns | Catalog view |
| sysmembers | sys.database_role_members | Catalog view |
| sysobjects | sys.objects | Catalog view |
| syspermissions | sys.database_permissions<br>sys.server_permissions | Catalog view |
| sysprotects | sys.database_permissions<br>sys.server_permissions | Catalog view |
| sysreferences | sys.foreign_keys | Catalog view |
| systypes | sys.types | Catalog view |
| sysusers | sys.database_principals | Catalog view |

## Working with System Stored Procedures

You can use system stored procedures to view SQL Server configuration details and to perform general administration. SQL Server 2008 has two main categories of system stored procedures:

- Those meant for administrators
- Those used to implement functionality for database application programming interfaces (APIs)

Naturally, you will want to work with system stored procedures meant for administration and not those that implement database API functions. System stored procedures are written using Transact-SQL (T-SQL). Most return a value of 0 to indicate success and a nonzero value to indicate failure. As an example, sp_dboption is a stored procedure for managing the configuration options of SQL Server databases (except for the master and tempdb databases). When you use sp_dboption to set a database configuration value, a return code of 0 indicates that the option was set as expected. A return code of 1 indicates that the stored procedure failed and the option was not set as expected.

The following example takes the Personnel database offline if there are no current users:

```
USE master;
GO
EXEC sp_dboption "Personnel", "offline", "TRUE";
GO
```

If the stored procedure returns 0, the database was successfully taken offline. A return value of 1 indicates that there was a problem taking the database offline, which means that the database is still online. For more information on using stored procedures, see "Configuring SQL Server with Stored Procedures" on page 99.

Table 4-3 provides a summary of stored procedures for administration. The table entries are organized by the type of administration activity for which the stored procedure is designed.

**Table 4-3  Key System Stored Procedures by Type**

| Stored Procedure Type | Description | Related System Stored Procedures |
|---|---|---|
| Active Directory Stored Procedures | Register instances of SQL Server and SQL Server databases in Active Directory. | sp_ActiveDirectory_Obj, sp_ActiveDirectory_SCP |
| Catalog Stored Procedures | Implement ODBC data dictionary functions. | sp_column_privileges, sp_columns, sp_databases, sp_fkeys, sp_pkeys, sp_server_info, sp_special_columns, sp_sproc_columns, sp_statistics, sp_stored_procedures, sp_table_privileges, sp_tables |
| Change Tracking Stored Procedures | Implement, manage, and monitor change tracking functionality. | sys.sp_cdc_add_job, sys.sp_cdc_change_job, sys.sp_cdc_cleanup_change_table, sys.sp_cdc_disable_db, sys.sp_cdc_disable_table, sys.sp_cdc_drop_job, sys.sp_cdc_enable_db, sys.sp_cdc_enable_table, sys.sp_cdc_generate_wrapper_function, |

Table 4-3   Key System Stored Procedures by Type

| Stored Procedure Type | Description | Related System Stored Procedures |
|---|---|---|
| Change Tracking Stored Procedures *(continued)* | Implement, manage, and monitor change tracking functionality. | sys.sp_cdc_get_captured_columns, sys.sp_cdc_get_ddl_history, sys.sp_cdc_help_change_data_capture, sys.sp_cdc_help_jobs, sys.sp_cdc_scan, sys.sp_cdc_start_job, sys.sp_cdc_stop_job |
| Cursor Stored Procedures | Implement cursor variable functionality. | sp_cursor_list, sp_describe_cursor, sp_describe_cursor_columns, sp_describe_cursor_tables |
| Database Engine Stored Procedures | Maintain SQL Server instances and perform general administration activities. | sp_add_data_file_recover_suspect_db, sp_add_log_file_recover_suspect_db, sp_addextendedproc, sp_addextendedproperty, sp_addmessage, sp_addtype, sp_addumpdevice, sp_altermessage, sp_attach_db, sp_attach_single_file_db, sp_autostats, sp_bindefault, sp_bindrule, sp_bindsession, sp_certify_removable, sp_configure, sp_control_plan_guide, sp_create_plan_guide, sp_create_plan_guide_from_cache, sp_create_removable, sp_createstats, sp_cycle_errorlog, sp_datatype_info, sp_dbcmptlevel, sp_dbmmonitoraddmonitoring, sp_dbmmonitorchangealert, sp_dbmmonitorchangemonitoring, sp_dbmmonitordropalert, sp_dbmmonitordropmonitoring, sp_dbmmonitorhelpalert, sp_dbmmonitorhelpmonitoring, sp_dbmmonitorresults, sp_dboption, sp_dbremove, sp_delete_backuphistory, sp_depends, sp_detach_db, sp_dropdevice, sp_dropextendedproc, sp_dropextendedproperty, sp_dropmessage, sp_droptype, sp_executesql, sp_filestream_configure, sp_getapplock, sp_getbindtoken, sp_help, sp_helpconstraint, sp_helpdb, sp_helpdevice, sp_helpextendedproc, sp_helpfile, sp_helpfilegroup, sp_helpindex, sp_helplanguage, sp_helpserver, sp_helpsort, sp_helpstats, sp_helptext, sp_helptrigger, sp_indexoption, sp_invalidate_textptr, sp_lock, sp_monitor, sp_procoption, sp_recompile, sp_refreshview, sp_releaseapplock, sp_rename, |

Table 4-3    Key System Stored Procedures by Type

| Stored Procedure Type | Description | Related System Stored Procedures |
|---|---|---|
| Database Engine Stored Procedures (continued) | Maintain SQL Server instances and perform general administration activities. | sp_renamedb, sp_resetstatus, sp_serveroption, sp_setnetname, sp_settriggerorder, sp_spaceused, sp_tableoption, sp_unbindefault, sp_unbindrule, sp_updateextendedproperty, sp_updatestats, sp_validname, sp_who |
| Database Mail Stored Procedures | Perform e-mail operations from within SQL Server. | sp_send_dbmail, sysmail_add_account_sp, sysmail_add_principalprofile_sp, sysmail_add_profile_sp, sysmail_add_profileaccount_sp, sysmail_configure_sp, sysmail_delete_account_sp, sysmail_delete_log_sp, sysmail_delete_mailitems_sp, sysmail_delete_principalprofile_sp, sysmail_delete_profile_sp, sysmail_delete_profileaccount_sp, sysmail_help_account_sp, sysmail_help_configure_sp, sysmail_help_principalprofile_sp, sysmail_help_profile_sp, sysmail_help_profileaccount_sp, sysmail_help_queue_sp, sysmail_start_sp, sysmail_stop_sp, sysmail_update_account_sp, sysmail_update_principalprofile_sp, sysmail_update_profile_sp, sysmail_update_profileaccount_sp |
| Database Maintenance Plan Stored Procedures | Configure and manage database maintenance plans and related tasks. | sp_add_maintenance_plan, sp_add_maintenance_plan_db, sp_add_maintenance_plan_job, sp_delete_maintenance_plan, sp_delete_maintenance_plan_db, sp_delete_maintenance_plan_job, sp_help_maintenance_plan |
| Distributed Queries Stored Procedures | Implement and manage distributed queries. | sp_addlinkedserver, sp_addlinkedsrvlogin, sp_catalogs, sp_column_privileges_ex, sp_columns_ex, sp_droplinkedsrvlogin, sp_dropserver, sp_foreignkeys, sp_indexes, sp_linkedservers, sp_primarykeys, sp_serveroption, sp_table_privileges_ex, sp_tables_ex, sp_testlinkedserver |

Table 4-3   Key System Stored Procedures by Type

| Stored Procedure Type | Description | Related System Stored Procedures |
|---|---|---|
| Full-Text Search Stored Procedures | Implement and query full-text indexes. | Deprecated. Use CREATE FULLTEXT CATALOG, ALTER FULLTEXT CATALOG, and DROP FULLTEXT CATALOG. |
| General Extended Stored Procedures | Provide an interface from SQL Server to external programs, primarily for server maintenance. | xp_cmdshell, xp_enumgroups, xp_findnextmsg, xp_grantlogin, xp_logevent, xp_loginconfig, xp_logininfo, xp_msver, xp_revokelogin, xp_sprintf, xp_sqlmaint, xp_sscanf |
| Log Shipping Stored Procedures | Implement, manage, and monitor log shipping configurations. | sp_add_log_shipping_alert_job, sp_add_log_shipping_primary_database, sp_add_log_shipping_primary_secondary, sp_add_log_shipping_secondary_database, sp_add_log_shipping_secondary_primary, sp_change_log_shipping_primary_database, sp_change_log_shipping_secondary_database, sp_change_log_shipping_secondary_primary, sp_cleanup_log_shipping_history, sp_delete_log_shipping_alert_job, sp_delete_log_shipping_primary_database, sp_delete_log_shipping_primary_secondary, sp_delete_log_shipping_secondary_database, sp_delete_log_shipping_secondary_primary, sp_help_log_shipping_alert_job, sp_help_log_shipping_monitor_primary, sp_help_log_shipping_monitor_secondary, sp_help_log_shipping_primary_database, sp_help_log_shipping_primary_secondary, sp_help_log_shipping_secondary_database, sp_help_log_shipping_secondary_primary, sp_refresh_log_shipping_monitor, sp_resolve_logins |
| OLE Automation Stored Procedures | Create and manage OLE automation objects. | sp_OACreate, sp_OADestroy, sp_OAGetErrorInfo, sp_OAGetProperty, sp_OAMethod, sp_OASetProperty, sp_OAStop |
| Security Stored Procedures | Manage server and database security. | sp_addapprole, sp_addlinkedsrvlogin, sp_addlogin, sp_addremotelogin, sp_addrole, sp_addrolemember, sp_addserver, sp_addsrvrolemember, sp_adduser, sp_approlepassword, sp_change_users_login, sp_changedbowner, sp_changeobjectowner, sp_dbfixedrolepermission, sp_defaultdb, |

Table 4-3    Key System Stored Procedures by Type

| Stored Procedure Type | Description | Related System Stored Procedures |
|---|---|---|
| Security Stored Procedures (continued) | Manage server and database security. | sp_defaultlanguage, sp_denylogin, sp_dropalias, sp_dropapprole, sp_droplinkedsrvlogin, sp_droplogin, sp_dropremotelogin, sp_droprolemember, sp_dropserver, sp_dropsrvrolemember, sp_dropuser, sp_grantdbaccess, sp_grantlogin, sp_helpdbfixedrole, sp_helplinkedsrvlogin, sp_helplogins, sp_helpntgroup, sp_helpremotelogin, sp_helprole, sp_helprolemember, sp_helpprotect, sp_helpsrvrole, sp_helpsrvrolemember, sp_helpuser, sp_MShasdbaccess, sp_password, sp_remoteoption, sp_revokedbaccess, sp_revokelogin, sp_setapprole, sp_srvrolepermission, sp_validatelogins |
| SQL Mail Stored Procedures | Perform e-mail operations from within SQL Server. (In SQL Server 2008, Database Mail is preferred over SQL Mail.) | sp_processmail, xp_deletemail, xp_findnextmsg, xp_readmail, xp_sendmail, xp_startmail, xp_stopmail |
| SQL Server Profiler Stored Procedures | Used by SQL Server Profiler to monitor performance and activity. | sp_trace_create, sp_trace_generateevent, sp_trace_setevent, sp_trace_setfilter, sp_trace_setstatus, |
| SQL Server Agent Stored Procedures | Manage scheduled alerts and other SQL Server Agent activities. | sp_add_alert, sp_add_category, sp_add_job, sp_add_jobschedule, sp_add_jobserver, sp_add_jobstep, sp_add_notification, sp_add_operator, sp_add_proxy, sp_add_schedule, sp_add_targetservergroup, sp_add_targetsvrgrp_member, sp_apply_job_to_targets, sp_attach_schedule, sp_cycle_agent_errorlog, sp_cycle_errorlog, sp_delete_alert, sp_delete_category, sp_delete_job, sp_delete_jobschedule, sp_delete_jobserver, sp_delete_jobstep, sp_delete_jobsteplog, sp_delete_notification, sp_delete_operator, sp_delete_proxy, sp_delete_schedule, sp_delete_targetserver, sp_delete_targetservergroup, sp_delete_targetsvrgrp_member, sp_detach_schedule, sp_enum_login_for_proxy, |

Table 4-3   Key System Stored Procedures by Type

| Stored Procedure Type | Description | Related System Stored Procedures |
|---|---|---|
| SQL Server Agent Stored Procedures (continued) | Manage scheduled alerts and other SQL Server Agent activities. | sp_enum_proxy_for_subsystem, sp_enum_sqlagent_subsystems, sp_grant_login_to_proxy, sp_grant_proxy_to_subsystem, sp_help_alert, sp_help_category, sp_help_downloadlist, sp_help_job, sp_help_jobactivity, sp_help_jobcount, sp_help_jobhistory, sp_help_jobs_in_schedule, sp_help_jobschedule, sp_help_jobserver, sp_help_jobstep, sp_help_jobsteplog, sp_help_notification, sp_help_operator, sp_help_proxy, sp_help_schedule, sp_help_targetserver, sp_help_targetservergroup, sp_manage_jobs_by_login, sp_msx_defect, sp_msx_enlist, sp_msx_get_account, sp_msx_set_account, sp_notify_operator, sp_post_msx_operation, sp_purge_jobhistory, sp_remove_job_from_targets, sp_resync_targetserver, sp_revoke_login_from_proxy, sp_revoke_proxy_from_subsystem, sp_start_job, sp_stop_job, sp_update_alert, sp_update_category, sp_update_job, sp_update_jobschedule, sp_update_jobstep, sp_update_notification, sp_update_operator, sp_update_proxy, sp_update_schedule, sp_update_targetservergroup |
| XML Stored Procedures | Manage Extensible Markup Language (XML) text. | sp_xml_preparedocument, sp_xml_removedocument |

# Techniques for Managing SQL Server Configuration Options

You can think of configuration options as a set of rules that define how SQL Server is configured and used. Individual server instances can have different configurations, as can the databases they support, the connections made by applications, and any statements or batch programs that are executed.

## Setting Configuration Options

Configuration options can be set for

- **A specific server instance**   Server options are also referred to as instance-wide options and are set by executing the sp_configure stored procedure.

- **A specific database**   Database options are also referred to as database-level options and are set by executing the ALTER DATABASE statement. The database compatibility level can be set by executing the sp_dbcmptlevel stored procedure.

- **A specific connection**   Connection options are set by the Microsoft OLE DB Provider for SQL Server or the SQL Server ODBC driver properties and by ANSI SET options when a connection is established.

- **A specific statement or batch**   Batch-level options are specified with SET statements. Statement-level options are specified in individual Transact-SQL statements.

Each of these configuration areas can be thought of as a level in the SQL Server configuration hierarchy. When an option is supported at more than one level, the applicable option setting is determined according to the following precedence order:

1. A server option

2. A database option

3. A connection (ANSI SET) or batch (SET) option

4. A specific statement (HINT) option

> **Note**   The stored procedure sp_configure provides the option *user options*, which allows you to change the default values of several SET options. Although *user options* appears to be an instance option, it is a SET option. In previous releases of SQL Server, batch-level options are called *connection-level options*. When you disable Multiple Active Result Sets (MARS), batch-level options are considered connection-level options as well.

You use ALTER DATABASE to change settings for a database, sp_configure to change server-level settings, and the SET statement to change settings that affect only the current session. If there are conflicts among configuration options, the options applied later have precedence over previously set options. For example, connection options have precedence over database and server options.

## Working with SET Options

Typically, SET options are configured by users within a batch or script and they apply until they are reset or the user's session with the server is terminated. SET options can also be configured within a stored procedure or trigger. In that case, the SET options apply until they are reset inside that stored procedure or trigger, or until control returns to the code that invoked the stored procedure or trigger.

SET options are applied at either parse time or execute time. The parse-time options are QUOTED_IDENTIFIER, PARSEONLY, OFFSETS, and FIPS_FLAGGER. All other SET options are execute-time options. Parse-time options are applied during parsing as they are encountered. Execute-time options are applied during the execution of the code in which they are specified.

Batch statements are parsed in their entirety prior to execution. This means that control flow statements do not affect parse-time settings. In contrast, both control flow and execution affect whether execute-time options are set. Execute-time options are set only if control is changed to a section of the batch containing execute-time options and the related statements are executed without error. If execution fails before an execute-time option is set or during the processing of the statement that sets the option, the option is not set.

When a user connects to a database, some options might be set to ON automatically. These options can be set through user options, server options, or the ODBC and OLE DB connection properties. If the user changes the SET options within a dynamic SQL batch or script, those changes apply only for the duration of that batch or script.

**Note**   MARS-enabled connections maintain a list of default SET option values. When a batch or script executes under that connection, the default SET option values are copied to the current request's environment. These values remain in effect unless they are reset within the connection. When the batch or script ends, the execution environment is copied back to the session's default. This ensures that multiple batches executing simultaneously under the same connection run in an isolated SET options environment. However, because the execution environment is copied back to the session default when batch or script execution completes, the current default environment for a connection depends on the last batch or script that completes execution.

Table 4-4 lists the batch/connection SET options available, providing the corresponding database and server options supported in SQL Server 2008 as well as the default setting (as applicable). The SET ANSI_DEFAULTS statement is provided as a shortcut for setting SQL-92 standard options to their default values. The options that reset when this statement is used are as follows: SET ANSI_NULLS, SET CURSOR_CLOSE_ON_COMMIT, SET ANSI_NULL_DFLT_ON, SET IMPLICIT_TRANSACTIONS, SET ANSI_PADDING, SET QUOTED_IDENTIFIER, and SET ANSI_WARNINGS.

**Note**   In a future edition of SQL Server, ANSI_PADDING will always be turned on and you will not be able to turn this setting off. ANSI_PADDING must be ON when you are creating or changing indexes on computer columns or indexed views. The SQL Server Native Client ODBC driver and SQL Server Native Client OLE DB Provider for SQL Server automatically set ANSI_PADDING to ON when connecting. For connections from DB-Library applications, however, the default for SET ANSI_PADDING is OFF.

Table 4-4    SET Options

| SET Option | Database Option | Server Option | Default Setting |
|---|---|---|---|
| ANSI_DEFAULTS | None | None | N/A |
| ANSI_NULL_DFLT_OFF ANSI_NULL_DFLT_ON | ANSI_NULL_DEFAULT | user options default | OFF |
| ANSI_NULLS | ANSI_NULLS | user options default | OFF |
| ANSI_PADDING | ANSI_PADDING | user options default | ON |
| ANSI_WARNINGS | ANSI_WARNINGS | user options default | OFF |
| ARITHABORT | ARITHABORT | user options default | OFF |
| ARITHIGNORE | None | user options default | OFF |
| CONCAT_NULL_YIELDS_NULL | CONCAT_NULL_YIELDS _NULL | None | OFF |
| CONTEXT_INFO | None | None | OFF |
| CURSOR_CLOSE_ON_COMMIT | CURSOR_CLOSE ON_ COMMIT | user options default | OFF |
| DATEFIRST | None | None | 7 |
| DATEFORMAT | None | None | mdy |
| DEADLOCK_PRIORITY | None | None | NORMAL |
| FIPS_FLAGGER | None | None | OFF |
| FMTONLY | None | None | OFF |
| FORCEPLAN | None | None | OFF |
| IDENTITY_INSERT | None | None | OFF |
| IMPLICIT_TRANSACTIONS | None | user options default | OFF |
| LANGUAGE | None | None | us_english |
| LOCK_TIMEOUT | None | None | No limit |
| NOCOUNT | None | user options default | OFF |
| NOEXEC | None | None | OFF |

Table 4-4   SET Options

| SET Option | Database Option | Server Option | Default Setting |
|---|---|---|---|
| NUMERIC_ROUNDABORT | NUMERIC_ROUNDABORT | None | OFF |
| OFFSETS | None | None | OFF |
| PARSEONLY | None | None | OFF |
| QUERY_GOVERNOR_COST_LIMIT | None | query governor cost limit | OFF |
| QUOTED_IDENTIFIER | quoted identifier | user options default | OFF |
| REMOTE_PROC_TRANSACTIONS | None | None | OFF |
| ROWCOUNT | None | None | OFF |
| SHOWPLAN_ALL | None | None | OFF |
| SHOWPLAN_TEXT | None | None | OFF |
| SHOWPLAN_XML | None | None | OFF |
| STATISTICS IO | None | None | OFF |
| STATISTICS PROFILE | None | None | OFF |
| STATISTICS TIME | None | None | OFF |
| STATISTICS XML | None | None | OFF |
| TEXTSIZE | None | None | OFF |
| TRANSACTION ISOLATION LEVEL | None | None | N/A |
| XACT_ABORT | None | None | OFF |

## Working with Server Options

Server options can be set using the properties dialog boxes in SQL Server Management Studio or the sp_configure stored procedure. The difference between the two methods is which options are available to set. Only the most commonly used server configuration options are available through SQL Server Management Studio, but all configuration options are accessible through sp_configure. Table 4-5 lists the server options available and provides the corresponding SET options and database options that are supported in SQL Server 2008, as well as the default setting (as applicable).

**Table 4-5    Server Options**

| Server Option | SET Option | Database Option | Default Setting |
|---|---|---|---|
| allow updates | None | None | 0 |
| backup compression default | None | None | 0 |
| clr enabled | None | None | 0 |
| cross db ownership chaining | None | None | 5 |
| default language | None | None | 0 |
| filestream access level | None | None | 0 |
| max text repl size | None | None | 65536 |
| nested triggers | None | None | 1 |
| remote access | None | None | 1 |
| remote admin connections | | | |
| remote login timeout | None | None | 20 |
| remote proc trans | None | None | 0 |
| remote query timeout | None | None | 600 |
| server trigger recursion | None | None | 0 |
| show advanced options | None | None | 0 |
| user options | ANSI_NULL_DFLT_ON ANSI_NULL_DFLT_OFF | ANSI_NULL_DEFAULT | OFF |
| | ANSI_NULLS | ANSI_NULLS | OFF |
| | ANSI_PADDING | ANSI_PADDING | ON |
| | ANSI_WARNINGS | ANSI_WARNINGS | OFF |
| | CURSOR_CLOSE_ON_ COMMIT | CURSOR_CLOSE_ON_ COMMIT | OFF |
| | IMPLICIT_TRANSACTIONS | None | OFF |

Table 4-5   Server Options

| Server Option | SET Option | Database Option | Default Setting |
|---|---|---|---|
| user options (continued) | QUOTED_IDENTIFIER | QUOTED_IDENTIFIER | OFF |
| | ARITHABORT | ARITHABORT | OFF |
| | ARITHIGNORE | None | OFF |
| | DISABLE_DEF_CNST_CHK | None | OFF |
| | NOCOUNT | None | OFF |

## Working with Database Options

Database options are set by executing the ALTER DATABASE statement. In new SQL Server installations, the settings in the model and master databases are the same. When you create new databases, the default database options for those databases are taken from the *model* database. Whenever you change a database option, the Database Engine recompiles everything in the database cache. Table 4-6 lists the database options available and provides the corresponding SET and server options supported in SQL Server 2008, as well as the default setting (as applicable).

**Note**   Microsoft recommends that ANSI_PADDING always be set to ON to avoid problems with future versions of SQL Server. Note that AUTO_UPDATE_STATISTICS_ASYNC has no effect unless you set AUTO_UPDATE_STATISTICS to ON.

Table 4-6   Database Options

| Database Option | SET Option | Server Option | Default Setting |
|---|---|---|---|
| ANSI_NULL_DEFAULT | ANSI_NULL_DFLT_ON ANSI_NULL_DFLT_OFF | user options default | OFF |
| ANSI_NULLS | ANSI_NULLS | user options default | OFF |
| ANSI_PADDING | ANSI_PADDING | user options default | ON |
| ANSI_WARNINGS | ANSI_WARNINGS | user options default | OFF |
| AUTO_CLOSE | None | None | OFF |
| AUTO_CREATE_STATISTICS | None | None | ON |
| AUTO_SHRINK | None | None | OFF |
| AUTO_UPDATE_STATISTICS | None | None | ON |
| AUTO_UPDATE_STATISTICS_ASYNC | None | None | OFF |

**Table 4-6    Database Options**

| Database Option | SET Option | Server Option | Default Setting |
|---|---|---|---|
| CONCAT_NULL_YIELDS_NULL | CONCAT_NULL_YIELDS_NULL | None | OFF |
| CURSOR_CLOSE_ON_COMMIT | CURSOR_CLOSE_ON_COMMIT | user options default | OFF |
| CURSOR_DEFAULT | None | None | GLOBAL |
| MERGE PUBLISH | None | None | FALSE |
| PUBLISHED | None | None | FALSE |
| QUOTED_IDENTIFIER | QUOTED_IDENTIFIER | user options default | ON |
| READ_ONLY | None | None | FALSE |
| RECOVERY BULK_LOGGED | None | None | FALSE |
| RECOVERY SIMPLE | None | None | TRUE |
| RECURSIVE_TRIGGERS | None | None | FALSE |
| RESTRICTED_USER | None | None | FALSE |
| SINGLE_USER | None | None | FALSE |
| SUBSCRIBED | None | None | TRUE |
| TORN_PAGE_DETECTION | None | None | TRUE |

## Managing Database Compatibility

By default, when you create a new database in SQL Server 2008, the default compatibility level is 100 (unless the *model* database has a lower compatibility level). When a database is upgraded to SQL Server 2008, pre-SQL Server 2000 databases are upgraded to compatibility level 80. All other databases retain their existing compatibility level:

- 80 for SQL Server 2000 compatibility level
- 90 for SQL Server 2005 compatibility level
- 100 for SQL Server 2008 compatibility level

Although the compatibility level of the *master* database cannot be modified, the compatibility level setting of the *model* database can be changed. This flexibility allows you to create new databases with a nondefault compatibility level. To change the compatibility level, you can use the ALTER DATABASE statement.

The ALTER DATABASE statement allows you to set the database compatibility level to use for a specific database. The ALTER DATABASE statement sets certain database behaviors to be compatible with the specified earlier version of SQL Server. The following example changes the compatibility level of the Personnel database to SQL Server 2008:

```
ALTER DATABASE Personnel
SET COMPATIBILITY_LEVEL = 100;
GO
```

When there are possible conflicts between compatibility (and other) settings, it is important to know which database context is being used. Generally speaking, the current database context is the database defined by the USE statement if it is in a batch/script, or it is the database that contains the stored procedure if it is in a stored procedure applied to that statement. When a stored procedure is executed from a batch or another stored procedure, it is executed under the option settings of the database in which it is stored. For example, when a stored procedure in the Support database calls a stored procedure in the Personnel database, the Support procedure is executed under the compatibility level setting of the Support database and the Personnel procedure is executed under the compatibility level setting of the Personnel database.

# Configuring SQL Server with Stored Procedures

You can configure many areas of SQL Server using the SQL Server Properties dialog box, which will be discussed in Chapter 5. As you have learned in this chapter, you can also configure SQL Server with stored procedures, such as sp_configure. You execute stored procedures and other queries in SQL Server Management Studio. SQL Server Management Studio has a built-in client tool that sends commands to a SQL Server instance, which in turn parses, compiles, and executes the commands.

The following sections explain how to configure SQL Server using SQL Server Management Studio and stored procedures. You will find more detailed coverage of SQL Server Management Studio in other chapters.

## Using SQL Server Management Studio for Queries

You can start SQL Server Management Studio and access the built-in query client by completing the following steps:

1. Select Start, Programs or All Programs, Microsoft SQL Server, SQL Server Management Studio. Or click Start, type **ssms** in the Search box, and then press Enter.

2. In the Connect To Server dialog box, shown in Figure 4-1, use the Server Type drop-down list to select the database component to which you want to connect, such as Database Engine.

**Figure 4-1** The Connect To Server dialog box.

3. In the Server Name field, type the name of the server on which SQL Server is running, such as CorpSvr04.

> **Note** You can only connect to registered servers. If the instance of SQL Server you want to work with is not registered, you will need to register the server before you can work with it. See "Managing Servers" on page 119 for details.

4. Use the Authentication selection menu to choose the authentication type as Windows Authentication or SQL Server Authentication (based on the allowed authentication types when you installed the server). Provide a Windows user name or SQL Server login ID and password as necessary.

   ❑ **Windows Authentication** Uses your current domain account and password to establish the database connection. This option works only if Windows authentication is enabled and you have appropriate privileges.

   ❑ **SQL Server Authentication** Allows you to specify a SQL Server login ID and password.

5. Click Connect. You connect to the default instance (unless you have configured another default previously). To change the instance to which you connect, click the Options button prior to clicking Connect, select the Connection Properties tab, and then use the Connect To Database drop-down list to select the instance to which you want to connect.

6. In SQL Server Management Studio, you can connect to the database instance you previously selected by clicking New Query on the tool bar and skip the remaining steps. To connect to a different database instance, click File, click New, and then select the query type, such as Database Engine Query.

7.  In the Connect To Server dialog box, specify the server name, or select Browse For More in the drop-down list to search for all computers that are running SQL Server within an entire Active Directory forest.

8.  Specify the authentication technique to use. Click Connect. As before, you connect to the default instance (unless you have configured another default previously). To change the instance to which you connect, click the Options button, select the Connection Properties tab, and then use the Connect To Database drop-down list to select the instance to which you want to connect.

If you are working with an active database in SQL Server Management Studio and have already authenticated the connection, you can automatically connect to the currently selected database server instance and use your current authentication information to log on. To do this, right-click the database in Object Explorer view in SQL Server Management Studio, and then select New Query.

## Executing Queries and Changing Settings

The query window in SQL Server Management Studio is normally divided into two panes. (See Figure 4-2.) The top pane allows you to enter queries. The lower pane displays results.

If you do not see a separate pane in the lower part of the window, don't worry. It appears automatically when you type a query. You can also set the pane to open by default. Select the Show Results Pane option on the Window menu.

**Figure 4-2**   Executing queries in SQL Server Management Studio.

As you know, you can use sp_configure to view and change SQL Server configuration settings. Two types of configuration settings are available: those that are dynamic and those that are not. In this instance, a dynamic setting is one that you can change without having to stop and restart SQL Server. To execute sp_configure or other types of queries, type a command in the top pane and then click the Execute Query button on the toolbar (the red exclamation point). You can also execute commands using these key sequences:

- F5

- Ctrl+E

- Alt+X

**Note**   By default, all users have execute permissions on sp_configure so that they can view settings. However, only users with the Alter Settings server-level permission can use sp_configure to change configuration options. By default, only members of the sysadmin and serveradmin fixed server roles have this permission. As with sp_configure, only users with Alter Settings server-level permission can execute the RECONFIGURE or RECONFIGURE WITH OVERRIDE command.

Whenever you use sp_configure to modify settings, the changes do not actually take place until you also execute the RECONFIGURE command. You can change some highly risky settings only with the RECONFIGURE WITH OVERRIDE command. Additionally, sp_configure settings are divided into two categories: standard and advanced. You can execute standard commands at any time, but you can execute advanced commands only when Show Advanced Options is set to 1. With this setting in effect, you can modify both standard and advanced settings. Follow this procedure to allow modification of advanced settings:

1. In SQL Server Management Studio, type the following:

   ```
   exec sp_configure 'show advanced options', 1
   go
   reconfigure
   go
   ```

   **Tip**   You can disable advanced options later by setting the value to 0.

2. Execute the commands by pressing Ctrl+E.

3. Clear the query window.

4. Now type one sp_configure command for each option you want to change.

5. Type **reconfigure** (or **reconfigure with override**).

6. Type **go**.

7. Execute the commands by pressing Ctrl+E.

8.  If you changed any nondynamic settings, stop and start the server. (See Table 4-7 and Table 4-8 for details.)

## Checking and Setting Configuration Parameters

Table 4-7 provides a summary of the standard configuration parameters. The parameters are listed in alphabetical order, with the minimum, maximum, and default values shown. The dynamic parameter column tells you if the setting is dynamic. If you see an "N" in this column, you will need to stop and restart the server to enforce changes.

**Table 4-7   Quick Reference Summary for Standard Configuration Parameters**

| Configuration Option | Minimum Value | Maximum Value | Default Value | Dynamic Yes/No |
|---|---|---|---|---|
| allow updates | 0 | 1 | 0 | Y |
| backup compression default | 0 | 1 | 0 | Y |
| clr enabled | 0 | 1 | 0 | Y |
| cross db ownership chaining | 0 | 1 | 0 | Y |
| default language | 0 | 9999 | 0 | Y |
| filestream access level | 0 | 2 | 0 | Y |
| max text repl size | −1 | 2147483647 | 65536 | Y |
| nested triggers | 0 | 1 | 1 | Y |
| remote access | 0 | 1 | 1 | N |
| remote admin connections | 0 | 1 | 0 | Y |
| remote login timeout | 0 | 2147483647 | 20 | Y |
| remote proc trans | 0 | 1 | 0 | Y |
| remote query timeout | 0 | 2147483647 | 600 | Y |
| server trigger recursion | 0 | 1 | 1 | Y |
| show advanced options | 0 | 1 | 0 | Y |
| user options | 0 | 32767 | 0 | Y |

Table 4-8 provides a summary of the advanced configuration parameters. To view or change these parameters, you have to set the parameter Show Advanced Options to 1. Self-configuring options have an asterisk (*) after the name. With max worker threads, 1024 is the maximum recommended for 32-bit operating systems. The default value zero (0) autoconfigures using the following formula: 256 + (number of processors − 4) * 8). Note also that you cannot change some advanced options (you can only view them).

Table 4-8   Quick Reference Summary for Advanced Configuration Parameters

| Configuration Option | Minimum Value | Maximum Value | Default Value | Dynamic Yes/No |
|---|---|---|---|---|
| Ad Hoc Distributed Queries | 0 | 1 | 0 | Y |
| access check cache bucket count | 0 | 655346 | 0 | Y |
| access check cache quota | 0 | 2147483647 | 0 | Y |
| affinity I/O mask | –2147483648 | 2147483647 | 0 | N |
| affinity64 I/O mask | –2147483648 | 2147483647 | 0 | Y |
| affinity mask | –2147483648 | 2147483647 | 0 | Y |
| affinity64 mask | –2147483648 | 2147483647 | 0 | Y |
| Agent XPs | 0 | 1 | 0 | Y |
| awe enabled | 0 | 1 | 0 | N |
| blocked process threshold | 0 | 86400 | 0 | Y |
| c2 audit mode | 0 | 1 | 0 | N |
| common criteria compliance enabled | 0 | 1 | 0 | N |
| cost threshold for parallelism | 0 | 32767 | 5 | Y |
| cursor threshold | –1 | 2147483647 | –1 | Y |
| Database Mail XPs | 0 | 1 | 0 | Y |
| default full-text language | 0 | 2147483647 | 1033 | Y |
| default trace enabled | 0 | 1 | 1 | Y |
| disallow results from triggers | 0 | 1 | 0 | Y |
| EKM provider enabled | 0 | 1 | 0 | |
| fill factor | 0 | 100 | 0 | N |
| ft crawl bandwidth max | 0 | 32767 | 100 | Y |
| ft crawl bandwidth min | 0 | 32767 | 0 | Y |
| ft notify bandwidth max | 0 | 32767 | 100 | Y |
| ft notify bandwidth min | 0 | 32767 | 0 | Y |
| index create memory* | 704 | 2147483647 | 0 | Y |
| in-doubt xact resolution | 0 | 2 | 0 | Y |
| lightweight pooling | 0 | 1 | 0 | N |
| locks* | 5000 | 2147483647 | 0 | N |

Table 4-8   Quick Reference Summary for Advanced Configuration Parameters

| Configuration Option | Minimum Value | Maximum Value | Default Value | Dynamic Yes/No |
|---|---|---|---|---|
| max degree of parallelism | 0 | 64 | 0 | Y |
| max full-text crawl range | 0 | 256 | 4 | Y |
| max server memory* | 16 | 2147483647 | 2147483647 | N |
| max text repl size | 0 | 2147483647 | 65536 | Y |
| max worker threads | 128 | 32767 | 0 | N |
| media retention | 0 | 365 | 0 | N |
| min memory per query | 512 | 2147483647 | 1024 | Y |
| min server memory* | 0 | 2147483647 | 0 | N |
| network packet size | 512 | 32767 | 4096 | Y |
| Ole Automation Procedures | 0 | 1 | 0 | Y |
| open objects | 0 | 2147483647 | 0 | N |
| optimize for ad hoc workloads | 0 | 1 | 0 | Y |
| ph_timeout | 1 | 3600 | 60 | Y |
| precompute rank | 0 | 1 | 0 | Y |
| priority boost | 0 | 1 | 0 | N |
| query governor cost limit | 0 | 2147483647 | 0 | Y |
| query wait | −1 | 2147483647 | −1 | Y |
| recovery interval* | 0 | 32767 | 0 | N |
| Replication XPs | 0 | 1 | 0 | Y |
| scan for startup procs | 0 | 1 | 0 | N |
| set working set size | 0 | 1 | 0 | N |
| SMO and DMO XPs | 0 | 1 | 1 | Y |
| SQL Mail XPs | 0 | 1 | 0 | Y |
| transform noise words | 0 | 1 | 0 | Y |
| two digit year cutoff | 1753 | 9999 | 2049 | Y |
| user connections* | 0 | 32767 | 0 | N |
| xp_cmdshell | 0 | 1 | 0 | Y |

You can view the current settings of all configuration options by executing the following query:

```
exec sp_configure
go
```

**Note**   Show Advanced Options must be set to 1 to see advanced options.

To view the current setting of a configuration option, execute the following query:

```
exec sp_configure 'optionName'
go
```

where *optionName* is the name of the option you want to examine, such as:

```
exec sp_configure 'allow updates'
go
```

To change the value of a setting, execute the following query:

```
exec sp_configure 'optionName' newValue
go
reconfigure with override
go
```

where *optionName* is the name of the option you want to examine, and *newValue* is the new value for this option, such as:

```
exec sp_configure 'allow updates' 1
go
reconfigure with override
go
```

**Note**   You do not always have to use RECONFIGURE WITH OVERRIDE. This value is required only when making ad hoc updates and setting an option to a value that is not generally recommended. Keep in mind that some setting changes are applied only when you restart the SQL Server instance.

## Changing Settings with ALTER DATABASE

For SQL Server 2008 and later, the ALTER DATABASE statement replaces the sp_dboption stored procedure as the preferred way to change database settings. To change database settings, you must be a member of a role granted the ALTER permission on the database or be explicitly assigned this permission. When you execute an ALTER DATABASE statement, a checkpoint occurs in the database for which the option was changed and this causes the change to take effect immediately. Table 4-9 provides an overview of the database options you can set with ALTER DATABASE.

Table 4-9    Quick Reference Summary for Database Options

| Option | When TRUE or Set to Value... | Accepted Values |
|---|---|---|
| ANSI_NULL_DEFAULT | CREATE TABLE uses SQL-92 rules to determine if a column allows null values. | ON \| OFF |
| ANSI_NULLS | All comparisons to a null value evaluate to UNKNOWN. (When OFF, non-UNICODE values evaluate to TRUE if both values are NULL.) | ON \| OFF |
| ANSI_PADDING | Trailing blanks are inserted into character values, and trailing zeros are inserted into binary values to pad to the length of the column. | ON \| OFF |
| ANSI_WARNINGS | Errors or warnings are issued when conditions such as "divide by zero" occur. | ON \| OFF |
| ARITHABORT | An overflow or divide-by-zero error causes the query or batch to terminate. If the error occurs in a transaction, the transaction is rolled back. (When OFF, a warning message is displayed, but execution continues as if no error occurred.) | ON \| OFF |
| AUTO_CLEANUP | Change tracking information is automatically removed after the retention period. | ON \| OFF |
| AUTO_CREATE_STATISTICS | Any missing statistics needed for query optimization are automatically generated. | ON \| OFF |
| AUTO_UPDATE_STATISTICS | Any out-of-date statistics needed for query optimization are automatically generated. | ON \| OFF |
| AUTOCLOSE | After the last user logs off, the database is shut down cleanly and its resources are freed. | ON \| OFF |
| AUTOSHRINK | Automatic periodic shrinking is enabled for the database. | ON \| OFF |
| CHANGE_RETENTION | When change tracking is ON, sets the retention period for change tracking information. | *RetPeriod* {DAYS \| HOURS \| MINUTES} |
| CHANGE_TRACKING | Turns on and enables change tracking. | ON \| OFF |

Table 4-9   Quick Reference Summary for Database Options

| Option | When TRUE or Set to Value... | Accepted Values |
|---|---|---|
| COMPATIBILITY_LEVEL | Sets the database compatibility level. | 80 \| 90 \| 100 |
| CONCAT_NULL_YIELDS_NULL | If either operand in a concatenation operation is NULL, the result is NULL. | ON \| OFF |
| CURSOR_CLOSE_ON_COMMIT | Any cursors that are open when a transaction is committed or rolled back are closed. (When OFF, cursors remain open when a transaction is committed. Rolling back a transaction closes any cursors except those defined as INSENSITIVE or STATIC.) | ON \| OFF |
| CURSOR_DEFAULT | Cursor declarations default to LOCAL. | LOCAL \| GLOBAL |
| DATE_CORRELATION_ OPTIMIZATION | SQL Server maintains correlation statistics between tables in a database that are linked by a foreign key constraint and have datetime columns. | ON \| OFF |
| DB_CHAINING | The database can be the source or target of a cross-database ownership chain. The instance of SQL Server will recognize this setting only when the cross db ownership chaining server option is 0 (OFF). Otherwise, all user databases can participate in cross-database ownership chains, regardless of the value of this option. | ON \| OFF |
| EMERGENCY | Marks the database as read-only, disables logging, and allows access only by members of the Sysadmin role. | EMERGENCY |
| ENCRYPTION | Transparent data encryption is turned on for the database. | ON \| OFF |
| MULTI_USER | Multiple users can access the database. | MULTI_USER |

**Table 4-9   Quick Reference Summary for Database Options**

| Option | When TRUE or Set to Value... | Accepted Values |
|---|---|---|
| NUMERIC_ROUNDABORT | An error is generated when loss of precision occurs in an expression. (When OFF, losses of precision do not generate error messages and the result is rounded to the precision of the column or variable storing the result.) | ON \| OFF |
| OFFLINE | The database is offline. (Otherwise, the database is online.) | OFFLINE |
| ONLINE | The database is online and available for use. | ONLINE |
| PAGE_VERIFY | SQL Server can discover damaged database pages. | CHECKSUM \| TORN_PAGE_ DETECTION \| NONE |
| PARAMETERIZATION | SQL Server parameterizes all queries in the database. | SIMPLE \| FORCED |
| QUOTED_IDENTIFIER | Double quotation marks can be used to enclose delimited identifiers. | ON \| OFF |
| READ_ONLY | The database is set to read-only (but can be deleted using the DROP DATABASE statement). The database cannot be in use when this option is set (except for *master*). | READ_ONLY |
| RECOVERY | Causes the recovery model to be reset. SIMPLE allows a checkpoint to truncate the inactive part of the log. | FULL \| BULK_LOGGED\| SIMPLE |
| RECURSIVE_TRIGGERS | Enables recursive firing of triggers. (When OFF, prevents direct recursion but not indirect recursion. To disable indirect recursion, set the nested triggers server option to 0 using sp_configure.) | ON \| OFF |
| RESTRICTED_USER | Only the database owner can use the database. | RESTRICTED_ USER |
| SINGLE_USER | Only one user at a time can access the database. | SINGLE_USER |

Table 4-9   Quick Reference Summary for Database Options

| Option | When TRUE or Set to Value... | Accepted Values |
|---|---|---|
| TORN_PAGE_DETECTION | Allows incomplete pages to be detected. (This option is being replaced by PAGE_VERIFY.) | ON \| OFF |
| TRUSTWORTHY | Database modules that use impersonation can access resources outside the database. | ON \| OFF |

Most of the listed options accept a value of ON or OFF, which is used to set the state of the option. For example, you could enable transparent data encryption on the CustomerSupport database using the following command:

```
USE master;
GO
ALTER DATABASE CustomerSupport
SET ENCRYPTION ON;
GO
```

Some options explicitly set a specific state. For example, if there were no current users connected to the CustomerSupport database, you could set the database to read-only using the following command:

```
USE master;
GO
ALTER DATABASE CustomerSupport
SET READ_ONLY;
GO
```

## Part II
# Microsoft SQL Server 2008 Administration

In Part II, you will learn about essential tasks for managing Microsoft SQL Server 2008. Chapter 5 introduces general management techniques for servers. In this chapter, you will also learn how to control processes and manage related server components. Chapter 6 presents information about how to use SQL Server Management Studio to configure SQL Server. Chapter 7 covers the core administration tasks for creating and managing databases. Chapter 8 discusses the essential techniques for managing full-text catalogs, full-text indexes, stopwords, stoplists, thesaurus files, and other components of full-text search. Chapter 9 focuses on SQL Server security. To manage server security, you'll create user logins, configure login permissions, and assign roles. The permissions and roles you assign determine the actions users can perform as well as what types of data they can access.

# Chapter 5
# Managing the Enterprise

Microsoft SQL Server Management Studio is the primary tool you will use to manage database servers. Other tools that are available to manage local and remote servers include SQL Server Configuration Manager, Reliability And Performance Monitor, and Event Viewer. You will use SQL Server Configuration Manager to manage SQL Server services, networking, and client configurations. Reliability And Performance Monitor is available to track SQL Server activity and performance, and Event Viewer provides a way to examine events generated by SQL Server, which can provide helpful details for troubleshooting. In this chapter, you will learn how to use SQL Server Management Studio. SQL Server Configuration Manager is discussed in Chapter 3, "Managing the Surface Security, Access, and Network Configuration." For details on Performance Monitor and Event Viewer, see Chapter 14, "Profiling and Monitoring Microsoft SQL Server 2008."

## Using SQL Server Management Studio

The SQL Server Management Studio graphical point-and-click interface makes server, database, and resource management easy to do. Using SQL Server Management Studio, you can manage both local and remote server instances by establishing a connection to SQL Server and then administering its resources. If you have disabled remote server connections to a particular server, however, you can work only with the server locally (by logging on to the system at the keyboard or by establishing a remote Terminal Server session in Microsoft Windows and then running the local management tools).

# Getting Started with SQL Server Management Studio

To run SQL Server Management Studio, click the Start button, point to All Programs, Microsoft SQL Server 2008, and then select SQL Server Management Studio. Then you must connect to the server with which you want to work. There are several ways to do this:

- Connect using a standard login to a server instance.

- Connect using a login to a specific database.

- Connect using server groups and registered servers.

Connecting to a server instance allows you to work with that particular server and its related components. Typically, you will want to connect to a server's Database Engine. As you can see in Figure 5-1, the Database Engine gives you access to the following components and features:

- **Databases**   Manage system databases, including *master* and *model*, as well as user databases and database snapshots. You can also access the ReportServer and Report ServerTempDB databases under this node.

- **Security**   Manage SQL logins, server roles, stored credentials, cryptographic providers, and auditing.

- **Server Objects**   Configure backup devices, HTTP endpoints, linked servers, and server triggers.

- **Replication**   Configure distribution, update replication passwords, and launch Replication Monitor.

- **Management**   Configure SQL Server logs, maintenance plans, Distributed Transaction Coordinator, and Database Mail. Configure data collection, Resource Governor, and Policy-Based Management policies. You can also configure legacy features, such as SQL Server 2000 database maintenance plans, SQL Mail, and DTS 2000 packages.

- **SQL Server Agent**   Configure SQL Server Agent jobs, alerts, operators, proxies, and error logs.

If you are not automatically connected or you exited the Connect To Server dialog box, you can connect to a server instance by clicking Connect in the Object Explorer view. You store server and login information using the registration feature. Registered servers can be organized using server groups and then can be accessed quickly in the Registered Servers view. Methods to manage server groups and register servers are discussed in "Managing SQL Server Groups" on page 116 and "Managing Servers" on page 119, respectively.

**Figure 5-1**    Use the Database Engine to access core SQL Server components and features.

## Connecting to a Specific Server Instance

To connect to a specific server instance using a standard logon, follow these steps:

1. Start SQL Server Management Studio by clicking the Start button, pointing to All Programs, Microsoft SQL Server 2008, and then selecting SQL Server Management Studio.

2. In the Connect To Server dialog box, use the Server Type drop-down list to select the database component to which you want to connect, such as Database Engine.

3. In the Server Name box, type the fully qualified or host name of the server on which SQL Server is running, such as **corpsvr04.cpandl.com** or **CorpSvr04**. Or select Browse For More on the related drop-down list. In the Browse For Server dialog box, select the Local Servers or Network Servers tab as appropriate. After the instance data has been retrieved, expand the nodes provided, select the server instance, and then click OK.

    **Note**    The list in the Browse For Servers dialog box is populated by the SQL Server Browser service running on the database servers. There are several reasons why a SQL Server instance you want to work with might not be listed. The SQL Server Browser service might not be running on the computer running SQL Server. A firewall might be blocking UDP port 1434, which is required for browsing. Or the HideInstance flag might be set on the SQL Server instance.

4. Use the Authentication drop-down list to choose the authentication type, either Windows Authentication or SQL Server Authentication (based on the authentication types selected when you installed the server). Provide a Windows user name or SQL Server login ID and password as necessary.

❑ **Windows Authentication**   Uses your current domain account and password to establish the database connection. This authentication type works only if Windows authentication is enabled and you have appropriate privileges.

❑ **SQL Server Authentication**   Allows you to specify a SQL Server login ID and password. To save the password so that you do not have to re-enter it each time you connect, select Remember Password.

5. Click Connect. You can now use the Object Explorer view to work with this server.

## Connecting to a Specific Database

To connect to a specific database using a standard login, follow these steps:

1. Start SQL Server Management Studio by clicking the Start button, pointing to All Programs, Microsoft SQL Server 2008, and then selecting SQL Server Management Studio. Or click Start, type **ssms.exe** in the Search box, and then press Enter.

2. In the Connect To Server dialog box, use the Server Type drop-down list to select the database component to which you want to connect, such as Database Engine, and then, in the Server Name box, type the fully qualified or host name of the server on which SQL Server is running, such as **corpsvr04.cpandl.com** or **CorpSvr04**.

3. Use the Authentication drop-down list to choose the authentication type, either Windows Authentication or SQL Server Authentication (based on the authentication types selected when you installed the server). Provide a Windows user name or SQL Server login ID and password as necessary.

4. Click Options to display the advanced view of the Connect To Server dialog box. Select the Connection Properties tab, as shown in Figure 5-2.

5. In the Connect To Database box, type the name of the database to which you want to connect, such as Personnel. Or select Browse Server in the related drop-down list. When prompted, click Yes to establish a connection to the previously designated server. In the Browse Server For Database dialog box, select the database you want to use, and then click OK.

6. Using the Network Protocol list, select the network protocol and any other connection properties if you are prompted to do so. Shared Memory is the default network protocol for local connections. TCP/IP is the default for remote connections. Optionally, establish a secure connection by selecting Encrypt Connection.

7. Click Connect. You will then be able to work with the specified database in the Object Explorer view.

Figure 5-2   The Connection Properties tab in the Connect To Server dialog box.

# Managing SQL Server Groups

You use SQL Server groups to organize sets of SQL servers. You define these server groups, and you can organize them by function, department, or any other criteria. Creating a server group is easy. You can even create subgroups within a group, and if you make a mistake, you can delete groups as well.

## Introducing SQL Server Groups

In SQL Server Management Studio, you use the Registered Servers view to work with server groups. To use this view, or to display it if it is hidden, press Ctrl+Alt+G.

The top-level groups are already created for you, based on the SQL Server instances. Use the Registered Servers toolbar to switch between the various top-level groups. These top-level groups are organized by SQL Server instance:

- Database Engine
- Analysis Services
- Reporting Services
- SQL Server Compact Edition
- Integration Services

Although you can add registered servers directly to the top-level groups (as explained in "Managing Servers" on page 119), in a large enterprise with many SQL Server instances, you will probably want to create additional levels in the server group hierarchy. These additional levels make it easier to access and work with your SQL servers. You can use the following types of organizational models:

- **Division or business unit model**   In this model, group names reflect the divisions or business units to which the SQL servers belong or in which they are located. For example, you could have Engineering, IS, Operations, and Support server groups.

- **Geographic location model**   In this model, group names reflect the geographic location of SQL servers, such as North America and Europe. You could have additional levels under North America for USA, Canada, and Mexico, for example, and levels under Europe could include UK, Germany, and Spain.

Figure 5-3 shows an example using server groups. As the figure shows, subgroups are organized under their primary group. Under Database Engine, you might have Corporate Customers, Engineering, and Enterprise Data groups. Within Engineering, you might have Dev, Test, and Core subgroups.

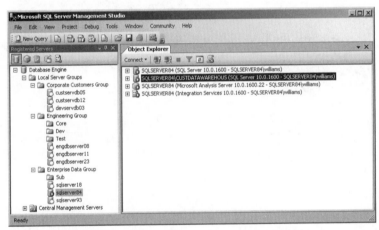

**Figure 5-3**   Use server groups to organize SQL Server deployments.

## Creating a Server Group

You can create a server group or a subgroup by completing the following steps:

1. In SQL Server Management Studio display the Registered Servers view by pressing Ctrl+Alt+G. If the view was previously hidden, this also displays the view.

2. Use the Registered Servers toolbar to select the top-level group. For example, if you want to create a second-level or third-level group for Database Engine instances, select Database Engine.

3. As necessary, expand the top-level group node and the Local Server Groups nodes by double-clicking each in turn. You will see the names of the top-level

server group and any second-level server groups that you created. You can now do the following:

- ❑ Add the server group to one of the top-level or second-level groups by right-clicking the group name and choosing New Server Group.

- ❑ Add the server group to a lower-level group by expanding the server group entries until the group you want to use is displayed. Then right-click the group name and choose New Server Group.

4. In the New Server Group Properties dialog box, shown in Figure 5-4, type a name and description for the new group in the boxes provided. Click OK.

**Figure 5-4** Enter a name and description in the New Server Group Properties dialog box.

## Deleting a Server Group

You can delete a group or subgroup by completing the following steps:

1. In SQL Server Management Studio, display the Registered Servers view by pressing Ctrl+Alt+G. If the view was previously hidden, this also displays the view.

2. Use the Registered Servers toolbar to select the top-level group in which the group you want to delete is located. For example, if you want to delete a second-level or third-level group for Database Engine instances, select Database Engine.

3. Click the plus sign (+) next to the group or subgroup you want to delete. If the group has servers registered in it, move them to a different group. (The steps involved in moving servers to a new group are explained in "Moving a Server to a New Group" on page 126.)

4. Select the group or subgroup entry.

5. Press Delete. When prompted to confirm the action, click Yes.

## Editing and Moving Server Groups

Server groups have several key properties you can edit: the name, the description, and the location in the Registered Server hierarchy. To edit a group's name or description, follow these steps:

1. Right-click the group in the Registered Servers view, and then select Properties.

2. In the Edit Server Group Properties dialog box, enter the new group name and description. Click OK.

To move a group (and all its associated subgroups and servers) to a new level in the server group hierarchy, follow these steps:

1. Right-click the group in the Registered Servers view, point to Tasks, and then select Move To.

2. In the Move Server Registration dialog box, you can now do the following:

   ❑ Move the group to the top-level group by selecting the top-level group. This will make the group a second-level group.

   ❑ Move the group to a different level by selecting a subgroup into which you want to place the group.

3. Click OK.

## Adding SQL Servers to a Group

When you register a SQL Server for use with SQL Server Management Studio, you can choose the group in which you want the server. You can even create a new group specifically for the server. The next section, "Managing Servers," covers the topic of server registration.

# Managing Servers

Servers and databases are the primary resources you manage in SQL Server Management Studio. When you select a top-level group in the Registered Servers view, you can see the available server groups. If you expand the view of these groups by double-clicking the group name, you can see the subgroups or servers assigned to a particular group. Local servers are registered automatically (in most cases). If a local server is not shown, you will need to update the local registration information. If the remote server you want to manage is not shown, you will need to register it.

Registration saves the current connection information and assigns the server to a group for easy future access using the Registered Servers view. Once you register a server, you can connect to the server to work with it and then disconnect when you are finished simply by double-clicking the server entry in the Registered Servers view. If you are not automatically connected, you can force a connection by right-clicking the server entry, and then selecting New Query (if you want to make a SQL query) or Object Explorer (if you want to view and manage the server).

You can start the registration process by using either of the following techniques:

- Register a server to which you are connected in Object Explorer.

- Register a new server in the Registered Servers view.

You can manage previous registrations in a variety of ways:

- Import registration information on previously registered SQL Server 2000 servers.

- Update registration information for local servers.

- Copy registration information from one computer to another using import and export.

## Registering a Connected Server

Any server to which you have connected in Object Explorer can be registered easily. Registration saves the current connection information and assigns the server to a group for easy future access using the Registered Servers view. To register a connected server, follow these steps:

1. Right-click any server to which you are currently connected in the Object Explorer view, and then choose Register to display the New Server Registration dialog box shown in Figure 5-5.

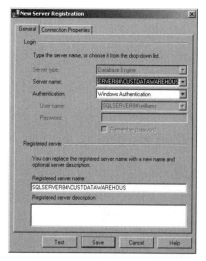

**Figure 5-5**   The New Server Registration dialog box.

2. On the General tab, the current values for the server name and authentication are filled in for you. Although the Registered Server Name option is set to the same value as the server name, you can modify this name and add a description if desired.

3. On the Connection Properties tab, you can specify the database to which you want to connect and set options for networking and connections. If you want to encrypt the connection, select the Encrypt Connection check box.

4. To test your settings before saving the registration settings, click Test. If the test was unsuccessful, verify the settings and then make changes as necessary. As discussed in Chapter 3, SQL Server doesn't allow remote connections by default and you must change the configuration settings to allow remote connections.

5. Click Save to save the server registration.

By default, the server is added to the top-level group. To move the server to a new level in the server group hierarchy, follow these steps:

1. Right-click the servers in the Registered Servers view, point to Tasks, and then select Move To.

2. In the Move Server Registration dialog box, you can move the server to a different level by selecting the subgroup into which you want to place the group.

3. Click OK.

## Registering a New Server in the Registered Servers View

You do not have to connect to a server in Object Explorer to register it. You can register new servers directly in the Registered Servers view by following these steps:

1. In the Registered Servers view, use the toolbar to select the type of server to which you want to connect, such as Database Engine.

2. After you expand the available groups as necessary, right-click the group into which you want to place the server in the Registered Servers view and then select New Server Registration to display the New Server Registration dialog box shown previously in Figure 5-5.

3. In the Server Name box, type the fully qualified domain name or host name of the server on which SQL Server is running, such as **corpsvr04.cpandl.com** or **CorpSvr04**.

4. Use the Authentication list to choose the authentication type, either Windows Authentication or SQL Server Authentication (based on the authentication types selected when you installed the server). Provide a Windows user name or SQL Server login ID and password as necessary.

   ❑ **Windows Authentication**   Uses your current domain account and password to establish the database connection. This authentication type works only if Windows authentication is enabled and you have appropriate privileges.

   ❑ **SQL Server Authentication**   Allows you to specify a SQL Server login ID and password. To save the password so that you do not have to re-enter it each time you connect, select Remember Password.

5. You can also set connection settings using the options on the Connection Properties tab. These options allow you to connect to a specific database instance and to set the network configuration. If you want to encrypt the connection, select the Encrypt Connection check box.

6. The registered server name is filled in for you based on the previously entered server name. Change the default name only if you want SQL Server Management Studio to use an alternate display name for the server.

7. To test the settings, click Test. If you successfully connect to the server, you will see a prompt confirming this. If the test fails, verify the information you provided, make changes as necessary, and then test the settings again.

8. Click Save.

## Registering Previously Registered SQL Server 2000 Servers

Registration details for servers registered by SQL Server 2000 can be imported into SQL Server Management Studio. This makes it easier to work with existing SQL Server 2000 installations. If the SQL Server 2000 installations were previously registered on the computer, you can import the registration details into a specific server group by completing the following steps:

1. In the Registered Servers view, use the toolbar to select the type of servers you are registering, such as Database Engine.

2. Right-click the Local Server Groups entry, point to Tasks, and then select Previously Registered Servers.

3. Available registration information for SQL Server 2000 servers will be imported. If an error prompt is displayed, you might not be logged on locally to the computer on which the servers were registered previously.

## Updating Registration for Local Servers

Local servers are registered automatically (in most cases). If you have added or removed SQL Server instances on the local computer and those instances are not displayed, you will need to update the local server registration. Updating the registration information ensures that all currently configured local server instances are shown in SQL Server Management Studio.

To update registration details for local servers, follow these steps:

1. In the Registered Servers view, use the toolbar to select the type of servers you are registering, such as Database Engine.

2. Right-click the Local Server Groups entry, point to Tasks, and then select Register Local Servers.

## Copying Server Groups and Registration Details from One Computer to Another

After you have registered servers in SQL Server Management Studio and placed the servers into a specific group hierarchy, you might find that you want to use the same registration information and server group structure on another computer. SQL Server Management Studio allows you to copy registration information from one computer to another using an import/export process. You can copy the registration details with or without the user names and passwords.

To export the registration and group information to a file on one computer and then import it onto another computer, complete the following steps:

1. Start SQL Server Management Studio on the computer with the registration and group structure details that you want to copy.

2. Select the Registered Servers view by pressing Ctrl+Alt+G.

3. In the Registered Servers view, use the toolbar to select the type of servers you want to work with, such as Database Engine.

4. Right-click the Local Server Groups entry, point to Tasks, and then select Export to display the Export Registered Servers dialog box shown in Figure 5-6.

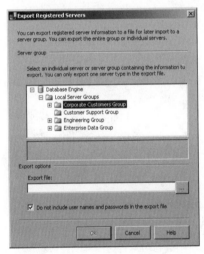

**Figure 5-6**   The Export Registered Servers dialog box.

5. Under Server Group, select the point from which the export process will begin. You can start copying registration information at any level in the group structure:

   ❑   To copy the structure for a top-level group, all its subgroups, and all registration details for all related servers, select the Local Server Groups entry.

❑  To copy the structure for a subgroup, its subgroups (if any), and all registration details for all related servers, select a subgroup.

❑  To copy the registration details for a single server, select the server.

6.  The server group structure and registration details are exported to a Registration Server File with the .regsrvr extension. By default, this file is created in the %SystemRoot%\System32 folder. Under Export Options, type a name for the registration server file, such as **CurrentDBConfig**.

> **Tip**  If you place the registration server file on a secure network share, you can access it on the computer to which you want to copy the registration information. Otherwise, you will need to copy this file to this computer later.

7.  By default, the current authentication details for server connections are not exported into the saved file. If you want to export user names and passwords, clear the Do Not Include User Names And Passwords In The Export File check box.

8.  Click OK. If the export was successful, you will see a dialog box confirming this. Click OK in the dialog box. If there was a problem, note and correct the problem.

9.  Start SQL Server Management Studio on the computer to which you want to copy the server group and registration details. If you did not place the registration server file on a secure network share, you will need to copy the file to this computer now.

10.  Select the Registered Servers view by pressing Ctrl+Alt+G.

11.  In the Registered Servers view, use the toolbar to select the type of servers you want to work with, such as Database Engine.

12.  Right-click the Local Server Groups entry, point to Tasks, and then select Import to display the Import Registered Servers dialog box shown in Figure 5-7.

13.  Click the button to the right of the Import File text box in the dialog box, and then use the Open dialog box that appears to select the registration server file you want to import.

14.  Under Server Group, select the server group under which you want the imported groups and servers to be created.

15.  Click OK. If the import was successful, you will see a dialog box confirming this. Click OK in the dialog box. If there was a problem, note and correct the problem.

**Figure 5-7**   The Import Registered Servers dialog box.

## Editing Registration Properties

You can change a server's registration properties at any time by right-clicking the server entry in the Registered Servers view in SQL Server Management Studio and then selecting Properties. Use the Edit Server Registration Properties dialog box to make necessary changes. The only property you cannot change is the server type. Be sure to test the settings before saving them.

## Connecting to a Server

Once you have registered a server, connecting to it is easy. Right-click the server entry in the Registered Servers view in SQL Server Management Studio, and then select New Query (if you want to make an SQL query) or Object Explorer (if you want to view and manage the server). Or you can double-click the server entry to establish a connection, and then work with the server in the Object Explorer view.

> **Note**   SQL Server Management Studio connects to other servers that are running SQL Server by using the network protocol set in the registration properties. If you have disabled the network protocol or remote access entirely for a server, however, you will not be able to connect to that server in SQL Server Management Studio. You will need to make the appropriate changes in the registration properties or in the surface area configuration. Chapter 3 discusses surface area configuration.

## Disconnecting from a Server

When you are finished working with a server, you might want to disconnect from it. This cuts down on the back-and-forth communications to the server. To disconnect, right-click the server's entry in the Object Explorer view in SQL Server Management Studio, and then select Disconnect from the shortcut menu.

### Moving a Server to a New Group

To move the server to a new group, complete the following steps:

1. Right-click the server in the Registered Servers view, point to Tasks, and then select Move To from the shortcut menu to display the Move Server Registration dialog box.

2. In the Move Server Registration dialog box, expand the Local Server Groups entry to see a list of subgroups. Expand subgroups as necessary. You can now do the following:

   ❑ Move the server to the top-level group by selecting the top-level group. This will make the server a member of the top-level group.

   ❑ Move the server to a different level by selecting a subgroup into which you want to place the server.

3. Click OK.

### Deleting a Server Registration

If you change a server name or remove a server, you might want to delete the server registration in SQL Server Management Studio so that SQL Server Management Studio no longer tries to connect to a server that cannot be accessed. Right-click the server entry in the Registered Servers view, and then select Delete. When prompted to confirm the action, click Yes to delete the server registration details.

## Starting, Stopping, and Configuring SQL Server Agent

SQL Server Agent runs as a service, and it is used to schedule jobs, alerts, and other automated tasks. After you have scheduled automated tasks, you will usually want SQL Server Agent to start automatically when the system starts. This configuration ensures that the scheduled tasks are performed as expected. Using SQL Server Service Manager, you can control the related SQL Server Agent (*InstanceName*) service just as you do the SQL Server service. For details, see "Configuring SQL Server Services" on page 56.

You use SQL Server Management Studio to configure SQL Server Agent. Chapter 16, "Database Automation and Maintenance," covers the agent configuration in detail, but the basic steps are as follows:

1. Connect to the Database Engine on the server you want to configure. You can do this in the Registered Servers view by double-clicking the server entry, or you can use the Object Explorer view. In the Object Explorer view, click Connect, and then select Database Engine to display the Connect To Server dialog box, which you can use to connect to the server.

2. Right-click the SQL Server Agent node, and then select Properties from the shortcut menu. You can now configure SQL Server Agent. Keep in mind that if the service is not running, you will need to start it before you can manage its properties.

3. The SQL Server Agent shortcut menu also lets you manage the SQL Server Agent service. Select Start, Stop, or Restart as appropriate.

# Starting, Stopping, and Configuring Microsoft Distributed Transaction Coordinator

Microsoft Distributed Transaction Coordinator (DTC) is a transaction manager that makes it possible for client applications to work with multiple sources of data in one transaction.

When a distributed transaction spans two or more servers, the servers coordinate the management of the transaction using DTC. When a distributed transaction spans multiple databases on a single server, SQL Server manages the transaction internally.

SQL Server applications can call DTC directly to start an explicit distributed transaction. Distributed transactions can also be started implicitly by using one of the following methods:

- Calling stored procedures on remote servers running SQL Server
- Updating data on multiple OLE DB data sources
- Enlisting remote servers in a transaction

If you work with transactions under any of these scenarios, you will want to have DTC running on the server, and you will probably also want DTC to start automatically when the server starts. As with SQL Server itself, DTC runs as a service. This service is named Distributed Transaction Coordinator. Unlike the SQL Server service, only one instance of the MS DTC service runs on a computer, regardless of how many database server instances are available. This means that all instances of SQL Server running on a computer use the same transaction coordinator.

You can view the current state of Distributed Transaction Coordinator in SQL Server Management Studio by connecting to the server's Database Engine. In Object Explorer, expand the server and Management nodes. If the service is running, you will see a green circle with a right-facing triangle in it (similar to a play button). If the service is stopped, you will see a red circle with a square in it (similar to a stop button). You can control the DTC service with Computer Management. Follow these steps:

1. Start Computer Management by clicking the Start button, pointing to All Programs, Administrative Tools, and then selecting Computer Management.

2. By default, you are connected to the local computer. To connect to a remote computer, right-click the Computer Management node and then select Connect To Another Computer. In the Select Computer dialog box, choose Another Computer, and then type the name of the computer. The name can be specified as a host name, such as **CorpSvr04**, or a fully qualified domain name, such as **corpsvr04.cpandl.com**.

3. Expand Services And Applications, and then select Services. Right-click Distributed Transaction Coordinator, and then choose Properties. You can now manage DTC.

# Managing SQL Server Startup

The SQL Server Database Engine has two modes of operation. It can run as a command-line application (SQLServr.exe) or as a service. Use the command-line application when you need to troubleshoot problems or modify configuration settings in single-user mode. Other than that, you will normally run SQL Server as a service.

## Enabling or Preventing Automatic SQL Server Startup

In Chapter 3, you learned that you can use SQL Server Configuration Manager to manage the SQL Server (MSSQLSERVER) service, related services for other Database Engine instances, and other SQL Server–related services. Any of these services can be configured for automatic startup or can be prevented from starting automatically. To enable or prevent automatic startup of a service, follow these steps:

1. Start SQL Server Configuration Manager using one of the following techniques:

   ❑ Log on to the database server through a local or remote login, and then start SQL Server Configuration Manager by clicking the Start button; pointing to All Programs, Microsoft SQL Server 2008, Configuration Tools; and then selecting SQL Server Configuration Manager.

   ❑ In SQL Server Management Studio, open the Registered Servers view by pressing Ctrl+Alt+G. Use the Registered Servers toolbar to select the top-level group, and then expand the group nodes by double-clicking them. Right-click the server entry and then select SQL Server Configuration Manager.

2. Select the SQL Server Services node. Right-click the SQL Server service that you want to start automatically, and then select Properties. You can now do the following:

   ❏ **Enable automatic startup**   On the Service tab, set the Start Mode to Automatic. If the server state is Stopped, click Start on the Log On tab to start the service.

   ❏ **Prevent automatic startup**   On the Service tab, set the Start Mode to Manual.

3. Click OK.

You can also use Computer Management to configure services. To configure automatic startup of a service using Computer Management, follow these steps:

1. Click the Start button, point to All Programs, and then select Administrative Tools, Computer Management.

2. By default, you are connected to the local computer. To connect to a remote computer, right-click the Computer Management node and select Connect To Another Computer. In the Select Computer dialog box, select Another Computer and then type the name of the computer. The name can be specified as a host name, such as **CorpSvr04**, or a fully qualified domain name, such as **corpsvr04.cpandl.com**.

3. Expand Services And Applications, and then select Services.

4. Right-click the SQL Server service that you want to start automatically, and then select Properties.

5. You can now do the following:

   ❏ **Enable automatic startup**   On the General tab, set the Startup Type to Automatic. If the Service Status reads Stopped, click Start.

   ❏ **Prevent automatic startup**   On the General tab, set the Startup Type to Manual.

6. Click OK.

## Setting Database Engine Startup Parameters

Startup parameters control how the SQL Server Database Engine starts and which options are set when it does. You can configure startup options using SQL Server Configuration Manager or Computer Management. SQL Server Configuration Manager is the recommended tool for this task because it provides the current default settings and allows you to easily make modifications.

**Tip**   You can pass startup parameters to the command-line utility SQLServr.exe as well. Passing the –c option to this utility starts SQL Server without using a service. You must run SQLServr.exe from the Binn directory that corresponds to the instance of the SQL Server Database Engine that you want to start. For the default instance, the utility is located in MSSQL10.MSSQLSERVER\MSSQL\Binn. For named instances, the utility is located in MSSQL10.*InstanceName*\MSSQL\Binn.

### Adding Startup Parameters

You can add startup parameters by completing the following steps:

1. Start SQL Server Configuration Manager using one of the following techniques:

   ❑ Log on to the database server through a local or remote login, and then start SQL Server Configuration Manager by clicking the Start button; pointing to All Programs, Microsoft SQL Server 2008, Configuration Tools; and then selecting SQL Server Configuration Manager.

   ❑ In SQL Server Management Studio, open the Registered Servers view by pressing Ctrl+Alt+G. Use the Registered Servers toolbar to select the top-level group, and then expand the group nodes by double-clicking them. Right-click the server entry and then select SQL Server Configuration Manager.

2. Select the SQL Server Services node. Right-click the SQL Server service that you want to modify, and then select Properties.

3. On the Advanced tab, click in the Startup Parameters box, and then press End to go to the end of the currently entered parameters. The –d, –e, and –l parameters are set by default. Be careful not to modify these or other existing parameters accidentally.

4. Each parameter is separated by a semicolon. Type a semicolon and then a hyphen followed by the letter and value of the parameter you are adding, such as **;–g512**.

5. Repeat step 3 and step 4 as necessary to specify additional parameters and values.

6. Click Apply to save the changes. The parameters are applied the next time the SQL Server instance is started. To apply the parameters right away, you must stop and then start the service by clicking Restart on the Log On tab.

### Removing Startup Parameters

You can remove startup parameters by completing the following steps:

1. Start SQL Server Configuration Manager using one of the following techniques:

   ❑ Log on to the database server through a local or remote login, and then start SQL Server Configuration Manager by clicking the Start button;

pointing to All Programs, Microsoft SQL Server 2008, Configuration Tools; and then selecting SQL Server Configuration Manager.

❑ In SQL Server Management Studio, open the Registered Servers view by pressing Ctrl+Alt+G. Use the Registered Servers toolbar to select the top-level group, and then expand the group nodes by double-clicking them. Right-click the server entry and then select SQL Server Configuration Manager.

2. Select the SQL Server Services node. Right-click the SQL Server service that you want to modify, and then select Properties.

3. On the Advanced tab, click in the Startup Parameters box. Each parameter is specified with a hyphen, parameter letter, and parameter value. A semicolon is used to separate parameter values, as shown in the following example:

```
-g512;
```

4. Remove the parameter by deleting its related parameter entry.

5. The change is applied the next time the SQL Server instance is started. To apply the parameters right away, you must stop and then start the service by clicking Restart on the Log On tab.

## Common Startup Parameters

Table 5-1 shows startup parameters and how they are used. The first three parameters (–d, –e, and –l) are the defaults for SQL Server. The remaining parameters allow you to configure additional settings.

**Table 5-1   Startup Parameters for SQL Server**

| Parameter | Description |
| --- | --- |
| –d*<path>* | Sets the full path for the *master* database. If this parameter is omitted, the registry values are used.<br>**Example**: –dC:\Program Files\Microsoft SQL Server\<br>MSSQL10.MSSQLSERVER\MSSQL\DATA\master.mdf |
| –e*<path>* | Sets the full path for the error log. If this parameter is omitted, the registry values are used.<br>**Example**: –eC:\Program Files\Microsoft SQL Server\<br>MSSQL10.MSSQLSERVER\MSSQL\LOG\ERRORLOG |
| –l*<path>* | Sets the full path for the *master* database transaction log. If this parameter is omitted, the registry values are used.<br>**Example**: –lC:\Program Files\Microsoft SQL Server\<br>MSSQL10.MSSQLSERVER\MSSQL\DATA\mastlog.ldf |
| –B | Sets a breakpoint on error; used with the –y option when debugging. |
| –c | Prevents SQL Server from running as a service. This setting makes startup faster when you are running SQL Server from the command line. |

Table 5-1 Startup Parameters for SQL Server

| Parameter | Description |
|---|---|
| –f | Starts SQL Server with minimal configuration. This setting is useful if a configuration value has prevented SQL Server from starting. |
| –g *number* | Specifies the amount of virtual address space memory in megabytes to reserve for SQL Server. This memory is outside the SQL Server memory pool and is used by the extended procedure .dlls, OLE DB providers referenced in distributed queries, and the automation object referenced in Transact-SQL (T-SQL). The default value is 256.<br>**Example:** –g256 |
| –h | Reserves virtual address space for Hot-Add Memory metadata when Address Windowing Extensions (AWE) is enabled with 32-bit editions of SQL Server. Although this is required for using Hot-Add Memory with 32-bit AWE, it uses approximately 500 MB of virtual address space and makes memory tuning more difficult. This setting is not required for using Hot-Add Memory with 64-bit editions of SQL Server. Hot-Add Memory is available only for Enterprise and Datacenter Editions of Windows Server and must also be supported by the server hardware. |
| –K | Forces regeneration of the service master key if it exists. |
| –k *number* | Sets the checkpoint speed in MB per second. Use a decimal value.<br>**Example:** –k25 |
| –m | Starts SQL Server in single-user mode. Only a single user can connect, and the checkpoint process is not started. Enables the *Sp_Configure* Allow Updates option, which is disabled by default. |
| –n | Tells SQL Server not to log errors in the application event log. Use with –e. |
| –s *instance* | Starts the named instance of SQL Server. You must be in the relevant Binn directory for the instance.<br>**Example:** –sdevapps |
| –T*<tnum>* | Sets a trace flag. Trace flags set nonstandard behavior and are often used in debugging or diagnosing performance issues.<br>**Example:** –T237 |
| –t*<tnum>* | Sets an internal trace flag for SQL Server. Used only by SQL Server support engineers.<br>**Example:** –t8837 |
| –x | Disables statistics tracking for CPU time and cache-hit ratio. Allows maximum performance. |
| –y *number* | Sets an error number that causes SQL Server to dump the stack.<br>**Example:** –y1803 |

## Managing Services from the Command Line

You can start, stop, and pause SQL Server as you would any other service. On a local system, you can type the necessary command at a standard command prompt. On a remote system, you can connect to the system remotely and then issue the necessary command. To manage the default database server instance, use these commands:

- **NET START MSSQLSERVER**   Starts SQL Server as a service.

- **NET STOP MSSQLSERVER**   Stops SQL Server when running as a service.

- **NET PAUSE MSSQLSERVER**   Pauses SQL Server when running as a service.

- **NET CONTINUE MSSQLSERVER**   Resumes SQL Server when running as a service.

To manage named instances of SQL Server, use the following commands:

- **NET START MSSQL$*instancename***   Starts SQL Server as a service, where *instancename* is the actual name of the database server instance.

- **NET STOP MSSQL$*instancename***   Stops SQL Server when running as a service, where *instancename* is the actual name of the database server instance.

- **NET PAUSE MSSQL$*instancename***   Pauses SQL Server when running as a service, where *instancename* is the actual name of the database server instance.

- **NET CONTINUE MSSQL$*instancename***   Resumes SQL Server when running as a service, where *instancename* is the actual name of the database server instance.

You can add startup options to the end of net start MSSQLSERVER or net start MSSQL$*instancename* commands. Use a slash (/) instead of a hyphen (–) as shown in these examples:

```
net start MSSQLSERVER /f /m
net start MSSQL$CUSTDATAWAREHOUS /f /m
```

**Real World**   Instead of referencing MSSQLSERVER or MSSQL$*instancename*, you also can reference the service by its display name. For the default instance, you use "SQL Server (MSSQLSERVER)" with net start, net stop, net pause, and net continue. For a named instance, you use net start "SQL Server (*InstanceName*)", where *InstanceName* is the name of the instance, such as net start "SQL Server (CUST-DATAWAREHOUS)". In both usages, the quotation marks are required as part of the command text.

## Managing the SQL Server Command-Line Executable File

The SQL Server command-line executable file (SQLServr.exe) provides an alternative to the SQL Server service. You must run SQLServr.exe from the Binn directory that corresponds to the instance of the SQL Server Database Engine that you want to start. For the default instance, the utility is located in MSSQL10.MSSQLSERVER\MSSQL\Binn. For named instances, the utility is located in MSSQL10.*InstanceName*\MSSQL\Binn.

When SQL Server is installed on a local system, start SQL Server by changing to the directory where the instance of SQL Server you want to start is located, and then type **sqlservr** at the command line. On a remote system, connect to the system remotely, change to the appropriate directory, and then issue the startup command. Either way, SQL Server reads the default startup parameters from the registry and starts execution.

You can also enter startup parameters and switches that override the default settings. (The available parameters were summarized in Table 5-1.) You can still connect SQL Server Management Studio and SQL Configuration Manager to the server. However, when you do, these programs will show an icon indicating that the SQL Server service is stopped because you aren't running SQL Server via the related service. You also will be unable to pause, stop, or resume the instance of SQL Server as a Microsoft Windows service.

When you are running SQL Server from the command line, SQL Server runs in the security context of the user, not the security context of the account assigned to the SQL Server service. You should not minimize the command console in which SQL Server is running because doing so will cause Windows to remove nearly all resources from SQL Server.

Additionally, when you are running SQL Server from the command line, you can make configuration changes that might be necessary for diagnosing and resolving problems as well as tasks that you can accomplish only when SQL Server is running in single-user mode. However, you should be careful when creating databases, changing data file locations, or making other similar types of changes. If you are logged in as an administrator and create a new database or change the location of a data file, SQL Server might not be able to access the database or data file when running later under the default account for the SQL Server service.

You must shut down the instance of SQL Server before logging off Windows. To stop an instance of SQL Server started from the command line, complete the following steps:

1. Press Ctrl+C to break into the execution stream.

2. When prompted, press Y to stop SQL Server.

# Managing Server Activity

As a database administrator, it is your job to make sure that SQL Server runs smoothly. To ensure that SQL Server is running optimally, you can actively monitor the server to

- Keep track of user connections and locks

- View processes and commands that active users are running

- Check the status of locks on processes and objects

- See blocked or blocking transactions

- Ensure that processes complete successfully, and detect errors if they do not

When problems arise, you can terminate a process, if necessary.

> **Note**   For more coverage of monitoring SQL Server, see Chapter 14. In that chapter, you will learn how to use Performance Monitor and SQL Server Profiler to keep track of SQL Server activity, performance, and errors.

## Examining Process Information

Process information provides detailed information about the status of processes, current user connections, and other server activity. You can view process information by completing the following steps:

1. Start SQL Server Management Studio, and then connect to a server.

2. Use the Object Explorer view to access an instance of the Database Engine.

3. Right-click the Database Engine instance and then select Activity Monitor.

In Activity Monitor, shown in Figure 5-8, you should see a graphical overview of activity as well as an activity summary by processes, resource waits, data file I/O, and recent expensive queries. The overview and the summaries are provided in separate panels that you can expand to display or shrink to hide.

Figure 5-8   Working with Activity Monitor.

The Overview panel has graphs depicting processor time, waiting tasks, database I/O, and batch requests. The graphs are updated automatically every 10 seconds by default. You can specify a different refresh interval by right-clicking in the panel, pointing to Refresh Interval, and then selecting the desired interval, such as 30 seconds.

In the Processes panel, processes are sorted by process ID by default, but you can arrange them by any of the available information categories summarized in Table 5-2. Click a category header to sort processes based on that category. Click the same category header again to perform a reverse sort on the category.

**Table 5-2   Process Information Used in Database Administration**

| Category | Description |
|---|---|
| Session ID | Provides the session ID of the process on the server. |
| User Process | Provides the user ID of the process on the server. |
| Login | Shows which user is running the process by SQL Server ID or domain account, depending on the authentication technique used. |
| Database | Indicates the database with which the process is associated. |
| Task Status | Shows the status of the process. A running process is active and currently performing work. A runnable process has a connection but currently has no work to perform. A sleeping process is waiting for something such as user input or a lock. A background process is running in the background and periodically performing tasks. A suspended process has work to perform but has stopped. |
| Command | Displays the command being executed or the last command executed. |
| Application | Shows the application or SQL Server component connecting to the server and running the process, such as a report server. |
| Wait Time | Indicates the elapsed wait time in milliseconds. |
| Wait Type | Specifies whether the process is waiting or not waiting. |
| Wait Resource | Displays the resource that the process is waiting for (if any). |
| Blocked By | Displays the process ID blocking this process. |
| Head Blocker | Shows 1 if the session ID is the head blocker in the blocking chain. Otherwise shows 0. |
| Memory Use | Displays the amount of memory the process is using (in KB). |
| Host Name | Displays the host from which the connection originated. |
| Workload Group | Displays the name of the Resource Governor workload group for the query. |

## Tracking Resource Waits and Blocks

When you are diagnosing performance issues, you'll want to look closely at the Wait Time, Wait Type, Wait Resource, and Blocked By values for each process. Most of the process information is gathered from data columns returned by various dynamic management views, including the following:

- **sys.dm_os_tasks**   Returns information about each task that is active in the instance of SQL Server.

- **sys.dm_os_waiting_tasks**   Returns information about each task that is waiting on some resource.

- **sys.dm_exec_requests**   Returns information about each request that is executing within SQL Server.

- **sys.dm_exec_sessions**   Returns information about each authentication session within SQL Server.

- **sys.dm_resource_governor_workload_group**   Returns information about workload groups configured for Resource Governor.

Although Activity Monitor provides a good overview, you might need to use these dynamic management views to get more detailed information about processes, resource waits, and resource blocks.

The Resource Waits panel provides additional information about resource waits. Each wait category combines the wait time for closely related wait types, such as buffer I/O or network I/O. Keep the following in mind:

- **Wait Time**   Shows the accumulated wait time per second. Here, a rate of 3000 ms per second indicates three tasks on average were waiting with this wait category.

- **Recent Wait Time**   Shows the wait average of accumulated wait time per second. This combines all the wait times over the last several minutes and averages them for this wait category.

- **Average Waiter Count**   Shows the average number of waiting tasks per second for this wait category.

- **Cumulative Wait Time**   Shows the total amount of wait time for this wait category since SQL Server was started or the wait statistics were reset.

   **Tip**   You can reset wait statistics using DBCC SQLPERF.

To get a clearer picture of resource waits and blocks, you can use the sys.dm_tran_locks view. Table 5-3 summarizes the information returned with this view with actual values in parentheses preceded by a general category name.

**Table 5-3   Lock-Related Information Used in Database Administration**

| Category | Type | Description |
|----------|------|-------------|
| Process ID (request_session_id) | | The process ID of the related user process within SQL Server. |
| Object ID (resource_associated_entity_id) | | The ID of the entity with which a resource is associated. |
| Context (request_exec_context_id) | | The ID of the thread associated with the process ID. |
| Batch ID (request_request_id) | | The batch ID associated with the process ID. |
| Type (resource_type) | RID | Row identifier; used to lock a single row within a table. |
| | KEY | A row lock within an index; used to protect key ranges. |
| | PAGE | A lock on a data or index page. |
| | EXTENT | A lock on a contiguous group of eight data or index pages. |
| | TABLE | A lock on an entire table, including all data and indexes. |
| | DATABASE | A lock on an entire database. |
| | METADATA | A lock on descriptive information about the object. |
| | ALLOCATION_UNIT | A lock on allocation unit page count statistics during deferred drop operations. |
| | HOBT | A lock on basic access path structures for heap or index reorganization operations or heap-optimized bulk loads. |
| Subtype (resource_subtype) | | The lock subtype, frequently used with METADATA locks to identify metadata lock activity. |
| Description (resource_description) | | Optional descriptive information. |

Table 5-3   Lock-Related Information Used in Database Administration

| Category | Type | Description |
| --- | --- | --- |
| Request Mode (request_mode) | S | Shared; used for read-only operations, such as a *select* statement. |
| | U | Update; used when reading/locking an updatable resource; prevents some deadlock situations. |
| | X | Exclusive; allows only one session to update the data; used with the modification operations, such as INSERT, DELETE, and UPDATE. |
| | I | Intent; used to establish a lock hierarchy. |
| | Sch-S | Schema stability; used when checking a table's schema. |
| | Sch-M | Schema modification; used when modifying a table's schema. |
| | BU | Bulk update; used when bulk copying data into a table and the TABLOCK hint is specified. |
| | RangeS_S | Serializable range scan; used with shared resource locks on shared ranges. |
| | RangeS_U | Serializable update; used for updating resource locks on shared ranges. |
| | RangeI_N | Insert range with a null resource lock; used to test ranges before inserting a new key into an index. |
| | RangeX_X | Exclusive range with an exclusive lock; used when updating a key in a range. |
| Request Type (request_type) | | The type of object requested. |

**Table 5-3**    Lock-Related Information Used in Database Administration

| Category | Type | Description |
| --- | --- | --- |
| Request Status (request_status) | GRANT | The lock was obtained. |
| | WAIT | The lock is blocked by another process. |
| | CNVT | The lock is being converted—that is, it is held in one mode but waiting to acquire a stronger lock mode. |
| Owner Type (request_owner_type) | CURSOR | The lock owner is a cursor. |
| | SESSION | The lock owner is a user session. |
| | TRANSACTION | The lock owner is a transaction. |
| | SHARED_TRANSACTION_WORKSPACE | The lock owner is the shared portion of the transaction workspace. |
| | EXCLUSIVE_TRANSACTION_WORKSPACE | The lock owner is the exclusive portion of the transaction workspace. |
| Owner ID (request_owner_id) | | The owner ID associated with the lock. |
| Owner GUID (request_owner_guid) | | The GUID of the owner associated with the lock. |
| Database (resource_database_id) | | The database containing the lock. |
| Object (resource_associated_entity_id) | | The name of the object being locked. |

# Troubleshooting Deadlocks and Blocking Connections

Two common problems you might encounter are deadlocks and blocking connections. Deadlocks and blocking connections, as described in the following list, can occur in almost any database environment, especially when many users are making connections to databases:

- Deadlocks occur when two users have locks on separate objects and each wants a lock on the other's object. Each user waits for the other user to release the lock, but this does not happen.

- Blocking connections occur when one connection holds a lock and a second connection wants a conflicting lock type. This forces the second connection either to wait or to block the first.

Both deadlocks and blocking connections can degrade server performance.

Although SQL Server can detect and correct deadlock and blocking situations, you can help speed up this process by identifying potential problems and taking action, if necessary. Process information can tell you when deadlocks or blocking occur. Examine these process information columns: Wait Time, Wait Type, Resource, Blocking, and Blocked By. When you have a deadlock or blocking situation, take a closer look at the locks on the objects that are causing problems. Refer to "Tracking Resource Waits and Blocks" on page 137 for details. You might also want to stop the offending processes, and you can do this by following the steps described in "Killing Server Processes" on page 143.

You can also use the sys.dm_tran_locks view to obtain information about active locks. Each row in the results returned by this view represent a currently active request to the lock manager for a lock that has been granted or is waiting to be granted. The following example returns a list of locks in the Customer database:

```
USE customer;
GO
SELECT * FROM sys.dm_tran_locks
```

In the result set, the results are organized in two main groups. Columns that begin with *resource_* describe the resource on which the lock request is being made. Columns that begin with *request_* describe the lock request itself. Earlier, Table 5-3 listed the correlation between the columns in the results and the categories listed in Activity Monitor. While Activity Monitor returns the actual database name, the resource_ database_id column returns the database_id as set in the sys.databases view. In SQL Server, database IDs are set on a per-server basis. You can determine the database name for a particular database ID on a particular server using the following statement:

```
SELECT name, database_id FROM sys.databases
```

In the results returned by sys.dm_tran_locks, the request_session_id tracks process IDs. Process IDs as tracked internally by SQL Server do not correspond to process IDs tracked by the operating system. You can determine the association between the SQL Server process IDs and Windows thread IDs using the following query:

```
SELECT ServerTasks.session_id, ServerThreads.os_thread_id
    FROM sys.dm_os_tasks AS ServerTasks
    INNER JOIN sys.dm_os_threads AS ServerThreads
        ON ServerTasks.worker_address = ServerThreads.worker_address
    WHERE ServerTasks.session_id IS NOT NULL
    ORDER BY ServerTasks.session_id;
GO
```

While you are connected to the database that contains the locking object, you get more information about the locking object and blocking information. Use the following query, where *<resource_associated_entity_id>* is the value in the related column, to get information about the locking object:

```
SELECT object_name(object_id), *
    FROM sys.partitions
    WHERE hobt_id=<resource_associated_entity_id>
```

Use the following query to get blocking information:

```
SELECT
        tr1.resource_type,
        tr1.resource_subtype,
        tr1.resource_database_id,
        tr1.resource_associated_entity_id,
        tr1.request_mode,
        tr1.request_type,
        tr1.request_status,
        tr1.request_session_id,
        tr1.request_owner_type,
        tr2.blocking_session_id
    FROM sys.dm_tran_locks as tr1
    INNER JOIN sys.dm_os_waiting_tasks as tr2
        ON tr1.lock_owner_address = tr2.resource_address;
```

## Tracking Command Execution in SQL Server

Sometimes you will want to track the commands that users are executing. You can do this by using Activity Monitor:

1. In SQL Server Management Studio, use the Object Explorer view to access an instance of the Database Engine.

2. Right-click the Database Engine instance and then select Activity Monitor.

3. Expand the Processes panel by clicking the Options button. The entries in the Session ID, User Process, and Login columns can help you track user sessions and the processes they are using.

4. Right-click a process and then select Details to display the dialog box shown in Figure 5-9. This dialog box shows the last command batch executed by the user.

5. To track current commands being executed by the user, click Refresh periodically.

6. To kill the process, click Kill Process. Then, when prompted, choose Yes.

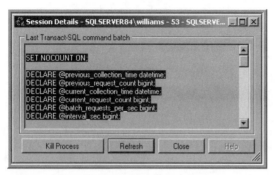

**Figure 5-9**   The Session Details dialog box.

## Killing Server Processes

You might need to stop processes that are blocking connections or using too much CPU time. To do this, complete the following steps:

1. In SQL Server Management Studio, use the Object Explorer view to access an instance of the Database Engine.

2. Right-click the Database Engine instance and then select Activity Monitor.

3. Expand the Processes panel by clicking the Options button.

4. Right-click the process you want to stop and then choose Kill Process. When prompted to confirm, click Yes.

> **Note**   Usually, you will not want to kill processes that SQL Server is running. If you are concerned about a process, stop it and then restart the related service instead of trying to kill the process.

Chapter 6

# Configuring Microsoft SQL Server with SQL Server Management Studio

**In this chapter:**

SQL Server 2008 replaces Enterprise Manager with SQL Server Management Studio to complement the expanding role of SQL Server administrators and developers. SQL Server Management Studio provides the easiest way to configure SQL Server. In SQL Server Management Studio, you can access the properties of a registered server easily, and then use the pages and options provided to configure the server.

**Note**  Policy-Based Management settings can affect your ability to configure SQL Server 2008. See Chapter 18, "Implementing Policy-Based Management," for more information.

# Managing the Configuration with SQL Server Management Studio

After you connect to a registered server in SQL Server Management Studio, you can view and manage its configuration properties using the Server Properties dialog box. To access this dialog box, complete the following steps:

1. Click the Start button; point to All Programs, Microsoft SQL Server 2008; and then select SQL Server Management Studio.

2. In the Connect To Server dialog box, use the Server Type drop-down list to select the server instance to which you want to connect, such as Database Engine.

3. Select or type the name of the server on which SQL Server is running in the Server Name box, such as **DBSvr18**.

   > **Note**   You can connect to registered servers only. If you want to work with a SQL Server that is not registered, you must register the server before you can use SQL Server Management Studio to configure it. See "Managing Server Settings" on page 165 for details.

4. Use the Authentication drop-down list to choose the authentication type, either Windows Authentication or SQL Server Authentication (based on the authentication types selected when you installed the server). Provide a Microsoft Windows user name or SQL Server login ID and password as necessary.

   ❑ **Windows Authentication**   Uses your current domain account and password to establish the database connection. This authentication type works only if Windows authentication is enabled and you have appropriate privileges.

   ❑ **SQL Server Authentication**   Allows you to specify a SQL Server login ID and password.

5. Click Connect. You connect to the default instance (unless you have configured another default previously). To change the instance to which you connect, click Options, select the Connection Properties tab, and then use the Connect To Database drop-down list to select the instance to which you want to connect.

6. Right-click the server name in the SQL Server Management Studio Object Explorer view, and choose Properties from the shortcut menu to open the dialog box shown in Figure 6-1.

You can now manage common SQL Server configuration settings. For more advanced settings, you need to use a stored procedure, such as sp_configure, as discussed in Chapter 4, "Configuring and Tuning Microsoft SQL Server 2008."

The Server Properties dialog box has many pages, which are listed at the top of the left pane in Figure 6-1. The rest of the sections in this chapter explain how to use the configuration options provided on these Server Properties pages. Permissions are discussed in Chapter 9, "Managing Microsoft SQL Server 2008 Security."

**Figure 6-1**   The General page of the Server Properties dialog box.

If you want to view a summary of current settings, run the following query in Query view:

```
USE master
GO
EXEC sp_configure
GO
```

> **Note**   Show Advanced Options must be set to 1 to see advanced options, as discussed in Chapter 4.

## Determining System and Server Information

General system and server information is available on the General page of the Server Properties dialog box. (See Figure 6-1.) The information on the General page helps you determine the following:

- SQL Server edition
- Operating system version
- SQL Server version

- Platform and chip architecture

- Default language

- Amount of RAM installed on the system

- Number of CPUs

- Root directory location for the selected instance

- Default server collation

You also can obtain similar information using the extended stored procedure xp_msver. Execute the following command:

```
exec xp_msver "ProductName", "ProductVersion", "Language", "Platform",
   "WindowsVersion", "PhysicalMemory", "ProcessorCount"
```

**Tip**   You can use Query view to execute the command shown. Basic techniques for using this utility are covered in "Configuring SQL Server with Stored Procedures" on page 99.

# Configuring Authentication and Auditing

You configure authentication and auditing options with the Security page of the Server Properties dialog box. This page is shown in Figure 6-2.

**Figure 6-2**   The Security page options.

## Setting the Authentication Mode

SQL Server security is completely integrated with Windows domain security, allowing for authentication based on user and group memberships as well as standard SQL Server user accounts.

In the Server Properties dialog box, go to the Security page. The Server Authentication options on the Security page allow you to configure authentication. To use combined authentication, select the SQL Server And Windows Authentication Mode option. Now users in Windows domains can access the server using a domain account, and other users can be logged on using a SQL Server login ID.

To use domain authentication only, select the Windows Authentication Mode option. Now only users with a domain account can access the server.

> **Tip**    If you change the authentication settings, you must restart all SQL Server instance services. With combined authentication, SQL Server first checks to see if a new login is a SQL Server login. If the login exists, SQL Server then uses the password provided to authenticate the user. If the login does not exist, it uses Windows authentication.

## Setting the Auditing Level

Auditing allows you to track user access to SQL Server. You can use auditing with both authentication modes as well as with trusted and untrusted connections.

The Login Auditing options on the Security page allow you to configure auditing. When auditing is enabled, user logins are recorded in the Windows application log, the SQL Server error log, or both, depending on how you configure logging for SQL Server. The available auditing options include the following:

- **None**    Disables auditing
- **Failed Logins Only**    Audits only failed login attempts (the default setting)
- **Successful Logins Only**    Audits only successful login attempts
- **Both Failed And Successful Logins**    Audits both successful and failed login attempts

To manage the auditing level, complete the following steps:

1. In the Server Properties dialog box, go to the Security page.
2. Select the desired auditing level and then click OK.
3. If you change the auditing settings, you must restart all SQL Server instance services.

## Enabling or Disabling C2 Audit Logging

Standards organizations have created many security standards. The Department of Defense (DOD) in the United States created the Trusted Computer System Evaluation

Criteria standard as a means of evaluating the security of computer systems. The criteria define the security divisions from D (the lowest) to A (the highest), and it specifies the criteria against which computer systems can be evaluated for each of these classifications. Within divisions C and B, there are subdivisions known as classes. Criteria for classes C2 through A1 require that a user's actions be open to auditing and that there be personnel designated as responsible for audit procedures. C2 audit requirements define specific events and auditable information. B1 and higher classes add further requirements.

On your SQL Server implementation, you can enable C2 audit tracing to meet C2 compliance requirements. When you enable C2 audit tracing, SQL Server audits all attempts to access statements and objects and records them to a file in the \MSSQL\Data directory. If the audit log file reaches its size limit of 200 megabytes (MB), SQL Server will create a new file, close the old file, and write all new audit records to the new file. This process will continue until the audit data directory fills up or auditing is turned off. You can determine the status of a C2 trace by querying the sys.traces view.

C2 auditing saves a large amount of event information to the audit log file. If the log directory runs out of space, SQL Server will shut itself down. To restart SQL Server after a forced shutdown, you need to use the −f flag to bypass auditing or free up additional disk space for the audit logs.

In the Server Properties dialog box, go to the Security page. You can enable C2 audit logging by selecting the Enable C2 Audit Tracing check box on the Security page. With sp_configure, the related Transact-SQL statement is

```
exec sp_configure "c2 audit mode", <0 or 1>
GO
RECONFIGURE
GO
```

You use 0 to disable and 1 to enable C2 audit mode.

## Enabling or Disabling Common Criteria Compliance

Beginning with SQL Server 2005 Service Pack 2 (SP2), a set of common criteria could be enabled to enhance security and comply with Common Criteria Evaluation Level 4 (EAL4+) security requirements. Common Criteria (CC) is an international security standard meant to be used as the basis for evaluation of the security properties of applications and servers. Enabling compliance with these security requirements enforces the following common criteria:

- **Column GRANT should not override table DENY**   Ensures a table-level DENY takes precedence over a column-level GRANT. Without this criteria, a column-level GRANT takes precedence over a table-level DENY.

■ **View login statistics capability** Ensures login auditing is enabled so that each time a user logs in to SQL Server information is made available about the last successful login time, the last unsuccessful login time, and the number of attempts between the last successful and current login times. You can view these statistics by querying the sys.dm_exec_sessions view.

■ **Residual Information Protection (RIP) compliance** Requires previously allocated memory to be overwritten with a known pattern of bits before SQL Server reallocates the memory to a new resource. Although this technique can improve security, overwriting previously allocated memory can slow performance.

From the Server Properties dialog box, go to the Security page. You can enable common criteria compliance by selecting the Enable Common Criteria Compliance check box on the Security page. With sp_configure, the related Transact-SQL statement is

```
exec sp_configure "common criteria compliance", <0 or 1>
GO
RECONFIGURE
GO
```

You use 0 to disable and 1 to enable common criteria compliance.

## Tuning Memory Usage

SQL Server is designed to manage memory needs dynamically, and it does an excellent job in most cases. Using dynamic memory allocation, SQL Server can add memory to handle incoming queries, release memory for another application you are starting, or reserve memory for possible needs. The default memory settings are the following:

■ Dynamically configure SQL Server memory

■ Minimum memory allocation set at 0 MB

■ Maximum memory allocation set to allow SQL Server to use virtual memory on disk as well as physical RAM

■ No memory reserved specifically for SQL Server

■ Address Windowing Extensions (AWE) not enabled

■ Minimum memory for query execution set at 1024 KB

You can change these settings, but you need to be careful about allocating too little or too much memory to SQL Server. Too little memory might prevent SQL Server from handling tasks in a timely manner. Too much memory might cause SQL Server to take essential resources from other applications or the operating system, which might result in excessive paging and a drain on overall server performance.

**Tip**   Some statistics can help you allocate memory correctly, such as the number of page faults per second and the cache-hit ratio. Page faults per second can track paging to and from virtual memory. The cache-hit ratio can determine if data being retrieved is in memory. You will learn more about using these types of statistics in Chapter 14, "Profiling and Monitoring Microsoft SQL Server 2008."

This section examines important areas of memory management. The primary method to configure memory usage is by selecting options on the Memory page of the Server Properties dialog box, shown in Figure 6-3. You will also learn a better way to configure Windows memory usage for SQL Server.

**Figure 6-3**   The Memory page of the Server Properties dialog box.

**Real World**   With Windows Server 2003, do not use the Maximize Data Throughput For Network Applications setting with SQL Server 2008. This setting gives priority to applications that perform buffered I/O by caching their I/O pages in file system cache. Using this option might limit the amount of memory available to SQL Server 2008. To view and change this setting, complete the following steps:

1. Access Network Connections in Control Panel.

2. Right-click Local Area Connection, and then select Properties.

3. Select File And Printer Sharing For Microsoft Networks, and then choose Properties.

4. On the Server Optimization tab, choose an appropriate setting other than Maximize Data Throughput For Network Applications.

5. Restart the server to apply the setting change.

## Working with Dynamically Configured Memory

With dynamically configured memory, SQL Server configures memory usage automatically, based on workload and available resources. Total memory usage varies between the minimum and maximum values that you set. The minimum server memory sets the baseline usage for SQL Server, but this memory is not allocated at startup. Memory is allocated as needed based on the database workload. When the minimum server memory threshold is reached, this threshold becomes the baseline, and memory is not released if it would leave SQL Server with less than the minimum server memory threshold.

To use dynamically configured memory, complete the following steps:

1. In the Server Properties dialog box, go to the Memory page.

2. Set the memory usage values to different values with the Minimum Server Memory and Maximum Server Memory boxes, respectively. The recommended maximum value for standalone servers is at or near total RAM (physical memory + virtual memory). However, if multiple instances of SQL Server are running on a computer, you should consider setting the maximum server memory so that the instances are not competing for memory.

3. Click OK.

You can use the stored procedure sp_configure to change the minimum and maximum settings. Use the following Transact-SQL commands:

```
exec sp_configure "min server memory", <number of megabytes>
exec sp_configure "max server memory", <number of megabytes>
```

**Best Practices** With dynamically configured memory, you usually do not need to set minimum and maximum memory usage values. On a dedicated system running only SQL Server, however, you might achieve smoother operation by setting minimum memory to 8 MB + (24 KB * *NumUsers*), where *NumUsers* is the average number of users simultaneously connected to the server. You might also want to reserve physical memory for SQL Server. SQL Server uses about 8 MB for its code and internal structures. Additional memory is used as follows: 96 bytes for locks, 2880 bytes for open databases, and 276 bytes for open objects, which include all tables, views, stored procedures, extended stored procedures, triggers, rules, constraints, and defaults.

You can check the baseline memory usage using the SQLServer:Memory Manager performance object. Select all counters for monitoring, and use the Report view to examine the memory usage. Pay particular attention to the Total Server Memory counter. See Chapter 14 for more details on monitoring SQL Server performance.

## Using Fixed Memory

If you want to override the dynamic memory management features, you can do this by reserving memory specifically for SQL Server. When you reserve physical memory for SQL Server, the operating system does not swap out SQL Server memory pages even if that memory could be allocated to other processes when SQL Server is idle. This means SQL Server has a fixed memory set. On a dedicated system, reserving memory can improve SQL Server performance by cutting down on paging and cache hits.

To reserve physical memory for SQL Server, complete the following steps:

1. In the Server Properties dialog box, go to the Memory page.

2. Set the Minimum Server Memory and Maximum Server Memory fields to the desired working set memory size. Use the same value for both fields.

3. Click OK.

You can also use the stored procedure sp_configure to reserve physical memory. The Transact-SQL command you use to do this is

```
exec sp_configure "set working set size", 1
go
exec sp_configure "min server memory", <number of megabytes>
go
exec sp_configure "max server memory", <number of megabytes>
go
reconfigure with override
go
```

> **Caution**   Setting fixed working set memory incorrectly can cause serious perfor-
> mance problems on SQL Server. Use fixed working set memory only in circum-
> stances in which you need to ensure that an exact amount of memory is available
> for SQL Server.

## Enabling AWE Memory Support

Address Windowing Extensions (AWE) memory allows Windows to support up to 64 gigabytes (GB) of physical memory. AWE support is required only on 32-bit operating systems. SQL Server 2008 Enterprise, Standard, and Developer Editions include AWE memory support. Analysis Services cannot take advantage of AWE mapped memory. Additionally, if the available physical memory is less than the user mode virtual address space, AWE cannot be enabled.

When AWE memory support is enabled, SQL Server 2008 dynamically allocates AWE memory at startup and allocates or deallocates AWE-mapped memory as required within the constraints of the minimum server memory and maximum server memory options. The goal is to balance SQL Server memory use with the overall system require-ments. SQL Server always attempts to use AWE-mapped memory, even on computers configured to provide applications with less than 3 GB of user mode address space.

> **Note**   The Hot-Add Memory feature requires AWE to be enabled during SQL
> Server startup. Additionally, note that SQL Server can dynamically release AWE-
> mapped memory, but the current amount of allocated AWE-mapped memory can-
> not be swapped out to the page file.

**Tip** If you enable AWE support, the user or system account under which the instance runs must have the Lock Pages In Memory user privilege. This privilege can be assigned to the account using Group Policy. See Chapters 9 and 10 of *Windows Server 2008 Administrator's Pocket Consultant* (Microsoft Press, 2008) for details.

To enable AWE support, complete the following steps:

1. In the Server Properties dialog box, go to the Memory page and select the Use AWE To Allocate Memory option.

2. Consider setting a specific maximum server memory for SQL Server to ensure other applications have additional memory. For example, you might want to set minimum server memory to 2 GB (2048 MB) and maximum server memory to 8 GB (8192 MB) to limit the amount of memory SQL Server 2008 can use.

3. Click OK.

You can also use the stored procedure sp_configure to enable AWE support. The Transact-SQL command you use to do this is

```
exec sp_configure "awe enabled", 1
reconfigure
go
```

## Optimizing Memory for Indexing

By default, SQL Server 2008 dynamically manages the amount of memory allocated for index creation operations. If additional memory is needed for creating indexes, and the memory is available based on the server memory configuration settings, the server will allocate additional memory for index creation operations. If additional memory is needed but not available, the index creation will use the memory already allocated to perform index creation.

Normally, the self-tuning works very well with this feature. The main exception is in cases in which you use partitioned tables and indexes, and have nonaligned partitioned indexes. In these cases, if there is a high degree of parallelism (lots of simultaneous index creation operations), you might encounter problems creating indexes. If this happens, you can allocate a specific amount of index creation memory.

To use a specific index creation memory allocation, complete the following steps:

1. In the Server Properties dialog box, go to the Memory page and set a value in the Index Creation Memory box. This value is set in kilobytes.

2. Click OK.

You can also use the stored procedure sp_configure to set the index creation memory size. The related command is

```
exec sp_configure "index create memory", <number of kilobytes>
```

**Note**   The amount of memory allocated to index creation operations should be at least as large as the minimum memory per query. If it is not, SQL Server will use the amount of memory specified as the minimum memory per query and display a warning about this.

## Allocating Memory for Queries

By default, SQL Server allocates a minimum of 1024 KB of memory for query execution. This memory allocation is guaranteed per user, and you can set it anywhere from 512 KB to 2 GB. If you increase the minimum query size, you can improve the performance of queries that perform processor-intensive operations, such as sorting or hashing. If you set the value too high, however, you can degrade the overall system performance. Because of this, adjust the minimum query size only when you are having trouble executing queries quickly.

**Best Practices**   The default setting of 1024 KB of RAM works in most cases. However, you might want to consider changing this value if the server operates in an extremely busy environment, with lots of simultaneous queries running in separate user connections, or in a relatively slow environment, with few (but large or complex) queries. In this case, four factors should determine your decision to adjust the minimum query size:

- The total amount of free memory (when the system is idle and SQL Server is running)
- The average number of simultaneous queries running in separate user connections
- The average query size
- The query response time you hope to achieve

Often a compromise is necessary with these values. You cannot always get an instant response, but you can optimize performance based on available resources. Use the following equation to get a starting point for the optimization:

*FreeMemory / (AvgQuerySize \* AvgNumSimulQueries)*

For example, if the system has 2200 MB of free memory, the average query size is 2 MB, and the average number of simultaneous queries is 50, then the optimal value for the query size is 2200 MB / (2 \* 50), or 22 MB. Generally, this value represents the maximum you should assign given the current environment, and you will want to lower this value if possible.

To allocate memory for queries, complete the following steps:

1. In the Server Properties dialog box, go to the Memory page and set a value for the Minimum Memory Per Query box. This value is set in kilobytes.

2. Click OK.

You can also use the stored procedure sp_configure to set the minimum query size. The related command is

```
exec sp_configure "min memory per query", <number of kilobytes>
```

# Configuring Processors and Parallel Processing

Systems that use multiprocessors can take advantage of the enhancements provided by SQL Server for parallel and symmetric multiprocessing. You can control how and when processors are used by SQL Server as well as when queries are processed in parallel.

## Optimizing CPU Usage

Multitasking is an important part of the operating system. Often the operating system will need to move threads of execution among different processors. On a system with a light load, moving threads of execution allows the server to improve performance by balancing the workload. On a system with a heavy load, however, this shuffling of threads can reduce performance because processor cache has to be reloaded repeatedly.

SQL Server 2008 supports processor affinity and I/O affinity to optimize how processors are used. Processor affinity assigns processors to specific threads of execution to eliminate processor reloads and reduce thread migration across processors. I/O affinity specifies which processors are eligible to process SQL Server–related disk I/O operations. If you decide to manage affinity manually, you will want some processors to have priority for threading and some processors to have priority for disk I/O, with no overlap between the two. For example, on a 32-processor system running SQL Server 2008 Enterprise Edition, you might want processors 0 through 15 to have processor affinity (which means they will manage threads of execution) and processors 16 through 31 to have I/O affinity (which means they will manage disk I/O operations).

> **Note**   There is no specific formula for allocation. You do not need to allocate half of the CPUs to processor affinity and half to I/O affinity. The actual configuration will depend on server usage and load.

Affinity settings are automatically configured and optimized when you install SQL Server. If you are trying to optimize performance for a server under a heavy load, you might want to try to optimize the affinity settings. Keep the following guidelines in mind before reconfiguring affinity settings:

- Do not change these settings without careful forethought. You can reduce performance by incorrectly managing affinity settings.

- Do not configure CPU affinity in both the operating system and in SQL Server. Both techniques have the same goal. Use one technique or the other.

- Do not enable the same CPU for both processor and I/O affinity. Each processor can have only one affinity. This means that there are three possible affinity states: processor affinity enabled, I/O affinity enabled, or no affinity enabled.

You can manually configure processor usage by completing the following steps:

1. Start SQL Server Management Studio, and then connect to the server you want to configure.

2. Right-click the server name in the SQL Server Management Studio Object Explorer view, and then choose Properties from the shortcut menu.

3. In the Server Properties dialog box, go to the Processors page, as shown in Figure 6-4.

**Figure 6-4**   The Processors page of the Server Properties dialog box.

4. By default, the processor affinity is set automatically and you are unable to change the processor affinity settings. When you clear the Automatically Set Processor Affinity Mask For All Processors check box, the fixed option will change to check boxes that you can select or clear. Use the Processor Affinity check boxes in the Processor list to determine which processors SQL Server uses. Select the check box for processors you want to use, and clear the check box for processors you do not want to use. The first CPU on the system is identified as CPU 0, the second as CPU 1, and so on.

> **Best Practices**   If the system has more processors than SQL Server sup-
> ports, SQL Server does not use all of them. For example, on an eight-way
> symmetric multiprocessing (SMP) system, SQL Server Standard Edition can
> use only four processors. This leaves four processors for other applications
> and system-level tasks.
>
> You might be tempted to assign SQL Server to the higher numbered proces-
> sors (5, 6, 7, and 8), but this is not a good idea. Windows assigns deferred
> process calls associated with network interface cards (NICs) to the highest
> numbered processors. So, if the system described in the example had two
> NICs, these calls would be directed to CPU 8 and CPU 7. Be sure to consult the
> equipment documentation before changing these values.

5. By default, the I/O affinity is set automatically and you are unable to change the processor affinity settings. When you clear the Automatically Set I/O Affinity Mask For All Processors check box, the fixed option will change to check boxes that you can select or clear. Use the I/O Affinity check boxes in the Processor list to determine which processors SQL Server uses.

6. Click OK. The new settings will apply when the SQL Server instance has been stopped and then started.

You can also use the stored procedure sp_configure to set the affinity mask. The related command is

```
exec sp_configure "affinity mask", <integer value>
exec sp_configure "affinity i/o mask", <integer value>
```

SQL Server interprets the integer value as a bit mask representing the processors you want to use. In this bit mask, CPU 0 is represented by bit 0, CPU 1 with bit 1, and so on. A bit value of 1 tells SQL Server to use the CPU. A bit value of 0 tells SQL Server not to use the CPU. For example, if you wanted to turn on support for processors 1, 2, and 5, you would have a binary value of

*000100110*

The corresponding integer value is 38:

*32 + 4 + 2 = 38*

## Setting Parallel Processing

A lot of calculations are required to determine whether parallel processing should be used. Generally, SQL Server processes queries in parallel in the following cases:

- When the number of CPUs is greater than the number of active connections

- When the estimated cost for the serial execution of a query is higher than the query plan threshold (The estimated cost refers to the elapsed time in seconds required to execute the query serially.)

Certain types of statements cannot be processed in parallel unless they contain clauses, however. For example, UPDATE, INSERT, and DELETE are not normally processed in parallel even if the related query meets the criteria. But if the UPDATE or DELETE statements contain a WHERE clause, or an INSERT statement contains a SELECT clause, WHERE and SELECT can be executed in parallel. Changes are applied serially to the database in these cases.

You can configure parallel processing by completing the following steps:

1. In the Server Properties dialog box, go to the Advanced page.

2. By default, the Max Degree Of Parallelism setting has a value of 0, which means that the maximum number of processors used for parallel processing is controlled automatically. Essentially, SQL Server uses the actual number of available

processors, depending on the workload. To limit the number of processors used for parallel processing to a set amount (up to the maximum supported by SQL Server), change the Max Degree Of Parallelism setting to a value greater than 1. A value of 1 tells SQL Server not to use parallel processing.

3. Large, complex queries usually can benefit from parallel execution. However, SQL Server performs parallel processing only when the estimated number of seconds required to run a serial plan for the same query is higher than the value set in the cost threshold for parallelism. Set the cost estimate threshold using the Cost Threshold For Parallelism box on the Advanced page of the Server Properties dialog box. You can use any value from 0 through 32,767. On a single CPU, the cost threshold is ignored.

4. Click OK. These changes are applied immediately. You do not need to restart the server.

You can use the stored procedure sp_configure to configure parallel processing. The Transact-SQL commands are

```
exec sp_configure "max degree of parallelism", <integer value>
exec sp_configure "cost threshold for parallelism", <integer value>
```

# Configuring Threading, Priority, and Fibers

Threads are an important part of a multitasking operating system, and they enable SQL Server to do many things at once. Threads are not processes, however. They are concurrent execution paths that allow applications to use the CPU more effectively.

SQL Server tries to match threads to user connections. When the number of threads that are available is greater than the number of user connections, at least a one-to-one ratio of threads to user connections exists, which allows each user connection to be handled uniquely. When the number of threads available is less than the number of user connections, SQL Server must pool threads; as a result, the same thread might serve multiple user connections, which can reduce performance and response time if additional resources are available and are not being used.

Normally, the operating system handles threads in kernel mode, but it handles applications and user-related tasks in user mode. Switching between modes, such as when the kernel needs to handle a new thread, requires CPU cycles and resources. To allow the application to handle threading directly, you can use fibers. Switching fibers does not require changing modes and therefore can sometimes improve performance.

Another way to improve performance is by increasing the priority of SQL Server threads. Normally, threads have a priority of 1 through 31, and higher priority threads get more CPU time than lower priority threads. Higher priority threads can also preempt lower priority threads, forcing threads to wait until higher priority threads finish executing. By increasing thread priority, you can give the threads a higher preference for CPU time and ensure that other threads do not preempt them.

**Note**   The complete range for thread priority is 0 through 31. Thread priority 0 is reserved for operating system use.

You configure worker threads, fibers, and thread priority using the Server Properties dialog box. Go to the Processors page and use these options:

- **Maximum Worker Threads**   Sets the maximum number of threads. By default, the value is set to 0, which allows SQL Server to configure the number of worker threads as shown in Table 6-1. However, you can use any value from 10 through 32,767. On a busy server with many user connections, you might want to increase this value. On a slow server with few connections, you might want to decrease this value. Computers with multiple processors can concurrently execute one thread per CPU. Microsoft recommends a maximum setting of 1024 on 32-bit systems and 2048 on 64-bit systems.

- **Boost SQL Server Priority**   Increases the priority of SQL Server threads. Without boosting, SQL Server threads have a priority of 7 (normal priority). With boosting, SQL Server threads have a priority of 13 (high priority). On a dedicated system running only SQL Server, this option can improve performance. However, if the server runs other applications, the performance of those applications might be degraded.

- **Use Windows Fibers (Lightweight Pooling)**   Configures SQL Server to use fibers, which it can handle directly. SQL Server still needs threads to carry out tasks. SQL Server allocates one thread per CPU, and then allocates one fiber per concurrent user connection up to the Maximum Worker Threads value. You must restart the server to apply this option.

**Tip**   Fibers work best when the server has multiple CPUs and a relatively low user-to-CPU ratio. For example, on an Enterprise Edition installation with 32 CPUs and 250 users, you might see a noticeable performance boost with fibers. But if you have a system with eight CPUs and 5000 users, you might see performance decrease with fibers.

**Table 6-1   The Default Maximum Worker Threads Used by SQL Server**

| Number of CPUs | 32-Bit Operating System | 64-Bit Operating System |
| --- | --- | --- |
| 1–4 | 256 | 512 |
| 5–8 | 288 | 576 |
| 9–16 | 352 | 704 |
| 17–32 | 480 | 960 |

You can use sp_configure to set fibers, maximum worker threads, and priority boost using the following commands:

```
exec sp_configure "lightweight pooling", <0 or 1>
exec sp_configure "max worker threads", <integer value>
exec sp_configure "priority boost", <0 or 1>
```

When setting lightweight pooling (fibers) and priority boost, you use 0 to disable and 1 to enable.

# Configuring User and Remote Connections

Requests for data are handled through user connections to client systems. The client opens a connection to SQL Server, makes a request, and waits for a response from SQL Server. When the client is finished with its request, it closes the connection. Other servers and applications can also connect to SQL Server remotely. To configure client connections and remote server connections, you can use the Connections page in the Server Properties dialog box.

Many settings are associated with client and server connections, as you can see in Figure 6-5, which shows the default configuration. This section examines connection settings and cases in which you might want to change these settings.

**Figure 6-5**   The default connection settings on the Connections page of the Server Properties dialog box.

## Setting Maximum User Connections

On the Connections page, the Maximum Number Of Concurrent Connections box provides you with the ability to set the maximum number of connections to SQL

Server at any one time. You can set this value from 0 through 32,767. By default, the value is set to 0, which means that an unlimited number of connections can be made to SQL Server. However, the actual number of possible user connections really depends on hardware, application, and other server limitations. You can determine the number of user connections your system can handle by executing the following command in Query view:

```
select @@max_connections
```

To set the maximum number of user connections, complete the following steps:

1. In the Server Properties dialog box, go to the Connections page.

2. Type a new value in the Maximum Number Of Concurrent Connections box, and then click OK. The new settings will apply when the SQL Server instance has been stopped and then started.

You can also set the maximum number of concurrent connections by using the following command:

```
exec sp_configure "user connections", <integer value>
```

> **Note**   You should not need to change the Maximum Number Of Concurrent Connections value. If you do change the setting, be careful. When the server reaches the maximum number of connections, users receive an error message and are not able to connect to the server until another user disconnects and a connection becomes available. The only time you would need to set this option is in a situation with a large number of users in which you need to limit the number of active connections to ensure that requests for connected users are handled in a timely manner. A better alternative is to add sufficient memory to the system, or configure a cluster to balance the workload, or both. If you administer a system with a large numbers of users, you should also ensure that SQL applications connect and then disconnect promptly when finished to reallocate resources quickly to other users.

## Setting Default Connection Options

On the Connections page, you will see a list box labeled Default Connection Options. (See Figure 6-5.) Use the list box options to set default query-processing options for user connections. Select an option by selecting its check box. Cancel an option by clearing the check box. Any changes you make will affect new logins only; current logins are not affected. Furthermore, users can override the defaults by using SET statements, if necessary.

Table 6-2 provides a summary of the connection options, as well as the default state for ODBC (open database connectivity) and OLE DB (object linking and embedding database, which might be different from the SQL Server default). The table also includes a list of commands you can use with sp_configure, the corresponding value for the configuration bit mask, and the SET commands that can override the default settings in a user session.

Table 6-2    Configuring Connection Options

| Connection Option | When On... | Default State | Bit Mask Value | SET Command |
|---|---|---|---|---|
| Implicit Transactions | Uses transactions implicitly whenever statements are executed. | OFF | 2 | IMPLICIT_ TRANSACTIONS |
| Cursor Close On COMMIT | Automatically closes a cursor at the end of a transaction. | OFF | 4 | CURSOR_CLOSE_ ON_COMMIT |
| ANSI Warnings | SQL Server displays null, overflow, and divide-by-zero warnings. Otherwise, no error or NULL might be returned. | OFF | 8 | ANSI_ WARNINGS |
| ANSI Padding | Data in fixed-length fields are padded with trailing spaces to fill out the width of the column. | OFF | 16 | ANSI_PADDING |
| ANSI Nulls | Comparing anything with NULL gives an unknown result. | OFF | 32 | ANSI_NULLS |
| Arithmetic Abort | Causes a query to terminate when an overflow or divide-by-zero error occurs. | OFF | 64 | ARITHABORT |
| Arithmetic Ignore | Returns NULL when an overflow or divide-by-zero error occurs during a query. | OFF | 128 | ARITHIGNORE |
| Quoted Identifier | SQL Server interprets double quotation marks as indicating an identifier rather than as delimiting a string. | OFF | 256 | QUOTED_ IDENTIFIER |
| No Count | Turns off the display of the number of rows returned in a query. | OFF | 512 | NOCOUNT |
| ANSI Null Default ON | New columns are defined to allow nulls (if you do not explicitly allow or disallow nulls). | OFF | 1024 | ANSI_NULL_ DFLT_ON |
| ANSI Null Default OFF | New columns are defined not to allow nulls (if you don't explicitly allow or disallow nulls). | OFF | 2048 | ANSI_NULL_ DFLT_OFF |
| Concat Null Yields Null | Returns NULL when concatenating a NULL value within a string. | OFF | 4096 | CONCAT_NULL_ YIELDS_NULL |
| Numeric Round Abort | Generates an error when a loss of precision occurs. | OFF | 8192 | NUMERIC_ ROUNDABORT |

Table 6-2  Configuring Connection Options

| Connection Option | When On... | Default State | Bit Mask Value | SET Command |
|---|---|---|---|---|
| Xact Abort | Rolls back a transaction if a T-SQL statement raises a runtime error. | OFF | 16384 | XACT_ABORT |

For sp_configure, the default options are set with the following user options parameter:

```
exec sp_configure "user options", <integer bit mask value>
```

In this case, the bit mask value is the sum of the numeric values for all the options you want to use. Each option has a corresponding SET command as well. When you make a connection, you can use the SET command to override the default setting for the session. For example, if you want to turn on ANSI padding, ANSI nulls, and ANSI warnings, use the bit mask value 56, such as in the following line of code:

```
exec sp_configure "user options", 56
```

In a user session, you can later turn these options on or off by using a line of code such as the following:

```
set ansi_padding on set ansi_nulls off
```

## Configuring Remote Server Connections

Connections from other servers are handled differently than user connections. You can determine whether or not servers can connect to this server, how long it takes for remote queries to time out, and if distributed transactions are used. To configure remote connections, complete these steps:

1.  In the Server Properties dialog box, go to the Connections page.

2.  To allow servers to connect to this server, select the option Allow Remote Connections To This Server. Remote servers can then log on to the server to execute stored procedures remotely. You must stop and then start the SQL Server instance to apply the change if you select this option.

    > **Caution**  Remote procedure call (RPC) connections are allowed by default. If you change this behavior, remote servers cannot log on to SQL Server. This setting change keeps SQL Server secure from remote server access.

3.  By default, queries executed by remote servers time out in 600 seconds. To change this behavior, type a time-out value in the Remote Query Timeout box on the Connections page. Time-out values are set in seconds, and the acceptable range of values is from 0 through 2,147,483,647. A value of 0 means that there is no query time-out for remote server connections.

4. Stored procedures and queries executed on the server can be handled as distributed transactions by using Distributed Transaction Coordinator (DTC). If you want to execute procedures this way, select the Require Distributed Transactions For Server-To-Server Communication check box. If you change this option, you must stop and then start the SQL Server instance.

5. Click OK.

These options can also be set with sp_configure. The related Transact-SQL statements are

```
exec sp_configure "remote access", <0 or 1>
exec sp_configure "remote query timeout", <number of seconds>
exec sp_configure "remote proc trans", <0 or 1>
```

**Note**   A value of 0 turns a remote server connection option off, and a value of 1 turns an option on.

# Managing Server Settings

You use the Advanced page of the Server Properties dialog box to configure many server settings. As shown in Figure 6-6, you can set the default language, general server behavior, and other options on this page.

**Figure 6-6**   General server settings options on the Advanced page.

## Enabling or Disabling File Streaming Support

When file streaming is enabled, SQL Server Database Engine can work with binary large objects (BLOBs) that are stored outside the database. At the server level, you control whether and how file streaming can be used using the Filestream Access Level setting, which by default is set to Disabled. When file streaming is disabled, BLOB databases cannot be stored on the file system. If you want to enable file streaming, you can do the following on the Advanced page:

- **Enable Transact-SQL access** Enabling Transact-SQL access allows you to use Transact-SQL statements to insert, update, query, search, and delete file-stream data.

- **Enable Full access** Enabling Full access allows you to use the OpenSql-Filestream application programming interface (API) to obtain a file handle and operate on the BLOB via the file system.

On the Advanced page of the Server Properties dialog box, use the Filestream Access Level drop-down list box to set the desired access level for file streaming, and then click OK. The first time you enable file streaming, you might need to restart the computer to allow Windows to reconfigure drivers. With sp_configure, the related Transact-SQL statement is

```
exec sp_configure "filestream access level", <0 or 1 or 2>
```

Use 0 for disabled, 1 for Transact-SQL access, or 2 for Full access. To complete the file-streaming configuration, you must also configure the settings discussed in "Configuring File Streaming" on page 64.

## Setting the Default Language for SQL Server

The default language determines default display formats for dates as well as the names of months and days. All output is in U.S. English unless you are running a localized version of SQL Server. Localized versions of SQL Server are available for French, German, Japanese, Spanish, and other languages. On a localized server, two sets of system messages are available, one in U.S. English and one in the local language. If the default language is set to the local language, SQL Server messages are displayed in the local language. Otherwise, they are displayed in U.S. English.

On the Advanced page of the Server Properties dialog box, use the Default Language drop-down list box to select the default language, and then click OK. You must stop and then start the SQL Server instance to apply a new default language setting. With sp_configure, the related Transact-SQL statement is

```
exec sp_configure "default language", <language id number>
```

The language ID number for U.S. English is always 0. The sys.languages system view contains one row for each language present on a server.

## Allowing and Disallowing Nested Triggers

By default, SQL Server allows you to nest up to 32 levels of triggers. Nested triggers are useful for executing a series of tasks within a single transaction. For example, an action can initiate a trigger that starts another trigger, which in turn can start another trigger, and so on. Because the trigger is handled within a transaction, a failure at any level causes the entire transaction to roll back, which reverses all changes to the database. As a fail-safe measure, triggers are terminated when the maximum nesting level is exceeded. This protects against an infinite loop.

An option on the Advanced page allows you to configure SQL Server to use nested triggers. To do so, complete the following steps:

1. In the Server Properties dialog box, go to the Advanced page.

2. Set Allow Triggers To Fire Others to True or False as appropriate.

3. Click OK.

With sp_configure, the related Transact-SQL statement is

```
exec sp_configure "nested triggers", <0 or 1>
```

You use 0 to set this option to false and 1 to set it to true.

## Controlling Query Execution

The query governor does not allow the execution of any query that has a running time that exceeds a specified query cost. The query cost is the estimated time, in seconds, required to execute a query, and it is estimated prior to execution based on an analysis by the query engine. By default, the query governor is turned off, meaning there is no maximum cost. To activate the query governor, complete the following steps:

1. In the Server Properties dialog box, go to the Connections page.

2. Select the option Use Query Governor To Prevent Long-Running Queries.

3. In the box below the option, type a maximum query cost limit. The valid range is 0 through 2,147,483,647. A value of 0 disables the query governor; any other value sets a maximum query cost limit.

4. Click OK.

With sp_configure, the following Transact-SQL statement will activate the query governor:

```
exec sp_configure "query governor cost limit", <limit>
```

You can also set a per-connection query cost limit in Transact-SQL using the following statement:

```
set query_governor_cost_limit <limit>
```

**Note**    Before you activate the query governor, you should use the Query view to estimate the cost of current queries you are running on the server. This will give you a good idea of a value to use for the maximum query cost. You can also use the Query view to optimize queries.

## Configuring Year 2000 Support

SQL Server allows you to insert or modify dates without specifying the century part of the date. However, to be Year 2000–compliant, SQL Server interprets two-digit dates within a certain time span. By default, this time span includes the years 1950 through 2049. Using this default setting, all two-digit dates from 50 through 99 are read as years beginning with 19, and all two-digit dates from 00 through 49 are read as years beginning with 20. Thus, SQL Server would interpret a two-digit year of 99 as 1999 and a two-digit year of 02 as 2002.

To maintain backward compatibility, Microsoft recommends that you leave the setting at the default value. You can, however, change this value by completing the following steps:

1. In the Server Properties dialog box, go to the Advanced page.

2. Set Two Digit Year Cutoff to a value that is the ending year of the time span you want to use. The valid range for the ending year is 1753 through 9999.

3. Click OK.

**Note**    The time span you select will affect all databases on the current server. Also, some older OLE clients only support dates in a range of years from 1931 through 2030. To maintain compatibility with these clients, you might want to use 2030 as the ending year for the time span.

With sp_configure, the related Transact-SQL statement is

```
exec sp_configure "two digit year cutoff", <ending year>
```

# Managing Database Settings

You use the Database Settings page of the Server Properties dialog box to configure serverwide database settings. As shown in Figure 6-7, you can use this page to set index fill, backup and restore options, and recovery intervals for checkpoint execution.

## Setting the Index Fill

The default index fill determines how much space SQL Server should reserve when it creates a new index using existing data. Setting the fill factor involves a tradeoff—if you set the fill factor too high, SQL Server will slow down when you add data to a table. However, if you set the fill factor too low, read performance can be affected by an amount inversely proportional to the fill factor. For example, a fill factor of 25 percent can degrade read performance by a factor of 4 (or 4 times normal), but the setting makes it possible to perform large updates faster initially. Ideally, you should balance the need to make updates quickly with the need to have good read performance, and then select a fill factor that makes sense for your situation.

**Figure 6-7**   The Database Settings page of the Server Properties dialog box.

**Best Practices**   The fill factor is used only when an index is created; it is not maintained afterward. This allows you to add, delete, or update data in a table without worrying about maintaining a specific fill factor.

Therefore, the empty space in the data pages can fill up if you make extensive additions or modifications to the data. To redistribute the data, re-create the index and specify a fill factor when you do so. Indexes are discussed more completely in Chapter 10, "Manipulating Schemas, Tables, Indexes, and Views."

By default, the index fill is set at 0, but the valid range is 0 through 100. The setting of zero is the optimized index fill setting; any other value is an actual fill percentage.

SQL Server handles the optimized setting in much the same way as a fill percentage of 100—SQL Server creates clustered indexes with full data pages and nonclustered indexes with full leaf pages. But the optimized setting of 0 leaves space for growth in the upper level of the index tree, which an index fill setting of 100 does not do. This is the reason why you should use this value only with read-only tables in which you never plan to add data.

If necessary, you can override the default setting when you create indexes, but you have to remember to do this. You can also set a fixed index fill as the default by completing the following steps:

1. In the Server Properties dialog box, go to the Database Settings page.

2. Use the Default Index Fill Factor box to set a fill percentage. A low fill factor provides more room for insertions without requiring page splits, but the index takes up more space. A high fill factor provides less room for insertions that do not require page splits, but the index uses less space.

3. Click OK.

With sp_configure, the related Transact-SQL statement is

```
exec sp_configure "fill factor (%)", <integer percentage>
```

## Configuring Backup and Restore Time-Out Options

You can make SQL Server backups to tape devices. When working with tape devices and DB-Library (which supports connections from older applications as long as a related DLL is available), you might want to control whether or not you want to enforce a read/write time-out to wait for a new tape. The options you can use include the following:

- **Wait Indefinitely**   DB-Library waits until a new tape is found. If you select this option, however, you will not necessarily receive an error message to let you know that you are having backup problems.

- **Try Once**   DB-Library tries once for a response from SQL Server. If there is no response or no tape is available, it quits and typically generates an error.

- **Try For**   DB-Library tries to get a response from SQL Server for a specified number of minutes. If there is no response or no tape is available within the wait time, DB-Library quits and typically generates an error.

You set the time-out period by completing the following steps:

1. In the Server Properties dialog box, go to the Database Settings page.

2. To set an indefinite time-out, select the Wait Indefinitely option.

3. To set the backup process to try once and then quit, select the Try Once option.

4. To set the backup process to try for a specified amount of time, select the Try For *n* Minute(s) option, and then enter the time-out period in the box provided.

5. Click OK.

## Configuring Backup and Restore Retention Options

As you will learn in Chapter 15, "Backing Up and Recovering Microsoft SQL Server 2008," SQL Server has many features to help you back up and restore data. When you write data to tapes using DB-Library, you can specify the number of days to maintain old files. This value is called the *retention period*, and you set it by completing the following steps:

1. In the Server Properties dialog box, go to the Database Settings page.

2. Enter the number of days you want to maintain old files in the Default Backup Media Retention (In Days) box. The minimum value is 0, which specifies that old files are always overwritten. The valid range is 0 through 365.

3. Click OK.

With sp_configure, the related Transact-SQL statement to set the retention period for backup files is

```
exec sp_configure "media retention", <number of days>
```

## Flushing the Cache with Checkpoints

Database checkpoints flush all cached data pages to the disk, and these checkpoints are done on a per-database basis. In SQL Server, you control how often checkpoints occur using the Recovery Interval setting on the Database Settings page. By default, the recovery interval is set to 0, which allows SQL Server to control when checkpoints occur dynamically. This usually means that checkpoints occur about once a minute on active databases. Unless you are experiencing performance problems that are related to checkpoints, you should not change this option.

If you need to set the checkpoint interval manually, you must complete the following steps:

1. In the Server Properties dialog box, go to the Database Settings page.

2. Enter the checkpoint time in minutes in the Recovery Interval (Minutes) box. The valid range is 0 through 32,767, and this is a serverwide setting.

3. Click OK.

With sp_configure, the related Transact-SQL statement is

```
exec sp_configure "recovery interval", <number of minutes>
```

## Compressing the Backup Media

Backup compression reduces the amount of data SQL Server 2008 has to write and the size of your SQL backups. Although using compression can significantly speed up the backup and restore process when working over a network, compression significantly increases CPU usage. To reduce the impact on SQL Server performance, you can configure backup to run under a user login whose CPU usage is limited by Resource Governor whenever CPU contention occurs.

To enable backup media compression, complete the following steps:

1. In the Server Properties dialog box, go to the Database Settings page.

2. Select the Compress Backup check box and then click OK.

With sp_configure, the related Transact-SQL statement is

```
exec sp_configure "backup compression default", <0 or 1>
```

You use 0 to disable backup compression and 1 to enable it.

# Adding and Removing Active Directory Information

For servers that are part of an Active Directory domain, you use the Active Directory page of the Server Properties dialog box to manage SQL Server information published in Active Directory services. The page has the following three buttons:

- **Add** Publishes information about a SQL Server instance in Active Directory.

- **Refresh** Updates information related to a SQL Server instance in Active Directory. This option is useful when you create databases, server cubes, or data-mining models, and you want the updates reflected throughout the directory before normal replication.

- **Remove** Removes information about a SQL Server instance from Active Directory.

# Troubleshooting Configuration Problems

There are two specific techniques that you can use to resolve SQL Server configuration problems. In this section, you will learn how to recover from a bad configuration and how to rebuild the *master* database.

## Recovering from a Bad Configuration

Although SQL Server 2008 has many safeguards that help you avoid configuration settings that keep SQL Server from starting, you might occasionally find that a configuration change prevents SQL Server from starting. If you encounter this situation, you can recover the server instance by completing the following steps:

1. Log on to the affected server locally, or log on remotely through Telnet or Terminal Server. You must log on using a local administrator account or the account used by the database server instance.

2. Make sure that the MSSQLServer or MSSQL$*instancename* service is stopped. If it is not, stop the service using one of the following methods:

   ❑ SQL Server Configuration Manager

   ❑ Computer Management

   ❑ Services

   If the instance of SQL Server was installed as a default installation, you can stop the service by using the following command:

   ```
   net stop MSSQLSERVER
   ```

3. From the command prompt, switch to the directory of the associated SQL Server instance (either MSSQL10.MSSQLSERVER\MSSQL\Binn or MSSQL10.*InstanceName*\MSSQL\Binn.). You must be in this directory to use the Sqlservr utility.

4. Start SQL Server from the command line with the following option:

   ```
   sqlservr -s(instancename) -f
   ```

5. You must use the −s option to specify the instance of SQL Server if multiple instances of SQL Server are installed. The −f option starts SQL Server in single-user mode with a minimum configuration. This ensures that the bad configuration is not loaded.

6. Wait for the server to start up. SQL Server should write a few pages of output to the screen. Leave the server running.

7. In another command prompt window or Telnet session, start SQLCMD with the user name of a SQL Server account with administrator privileges and password:

   ```
   sqlcmd -U username -P password
   ```

   > **Note**   You must specify the instance to which you are connecting (sqlcmd −U username −P password −S*computername*\*instancename*) if multiple instances of SQL Server 2008 are installed.

8. If you have accessed SQLCMD properly, you should see the prompt change to >.

9. Reverse the changes made to the configuration by entering commands as you would in SQL Server Management Studio. The main difference is that you follow the commands with GO, as shown in the following example:

   ```
   exec sp_configure "max server memory", 128
   go
   reconfigure
   go
   ```

10. When you are finished, exit SQLCMD by typing **exit**.

11. From the command line in the window running SQL Server, press Ctrl+C.

12. When prompted, type **Y** for Yes. This stops SQL Server.

13. Restart SQL Server as you normally would. If you have made the appropriate changes, the server should start normally. Otherwise, repeat this procedure.

## Changing Collation and Rebuilding the *master* Database

Rebuilding the *master* database restores all system databases to their original contents and attributes. The main reasons for rebuilding the *master* database are as follows:

■ To set a new default collation for a database server instance

> **Tip**   In SQL Server 2000 and later, collation can be set separately for each database—as well as for tables, parameters, and literal strings—without having to rebuild the *master* database.

■ To repair a corrupted *master* database when no backup of the master is available

■ To repair a corrupted *master* database when the SQL Server instance cannot be started

The Rebuildm utility is no longer used for rebuilding the *master* database. Instead, run the SQL Server 2008 Setup program again to rebuild the *master* database. If you choose to rebuild the *master* database, keep the following guidelines in mind:

■ After you rebuild the *master* database, you should restore the most recent *master*, *model*, and *msdb* databases. If the server was configured for replication, you must restore the most recent *distribution* database. Any data that cannot be restored must be manually created.

■ After you rebuild the *master* database, all user databases are detached and unreadable. To recover them, you must re-create all your user databases. You cannot restore the user databases from backup—the restore maintains the information that was set when you created the backup, and you might instead want to move the databases to another server by means of import and export, covered in Chapter 11, "Importing, Exporting, and Transforming Data."

■ You must reapply any SQL Server updates to bring the Resource database up to date. The Resource database is updated whenever patches, hot fixes, or service packs are applied to SQL Server.

To rebuild the *master* database, follow these steps:

1. Log on to the server using an account with administrator privileges. With Windows Server 2003, double-click Add Or Remove Programs in Control Panel. With Windows Server 2008, click the Uninstall A Program link under Programs in Control Panel.

2. Select Microsoft SQL Server 2008, and then click Change. When the SQL Server 2008 Maintenance Wizard starts, select the SQL Server instance to maintain and then click Next.

3. On the Feature Maintenance page, select the component you want to work with, such as Analysis Services or Database Engine and then click Next.

4. The SQL Server Installation Wizard is started. Click Next to allow Setup to perform a system configuration check. When the system configuration check is completed, note any issues and correct problems as necessary. Click Next.

5. Setup will then review the installed components. On the Change Or Remove Instance page, click Change.

6. On the Feature Selection page, double-click the entry for the component. This will expand the component details so that you can see subcomponents. Click the icon for the subcomponent to specify its availability.

7. Click Next and then click Install. SQL Server will then verify the installation and rebuild a damaged installation as necessary. When this process completes, click Next and then click Finish.

You can also use the following command line to rebuild the *master* database:

```
start /wait setup.exe /qb INSTANCENAME=MSSQLSERVER REINSTALL=SQL_Engine
    REBUILDDATABASE=1 SAPWD=Password SQLCOLLATION=DesiredCollation
```

where *Password* is the new SA password and *DesiredCollation* is the collation desired, such as

```
start /wait setup.exe /qb INSTANCENAME=MSSQLSERVER REINSTALL=SQL_Engine
    REBUILDDATABASE=1 SAPWD=Quirky345
    SQLCOLLATION=SQL_Latin1_General_CP1_CI_AI
```

# Chapter 7
# Core Database Administration

Core database administration tasks involve creating, manipulating, and supporting databases. In Microsoft SQL Server 2008, a database is a collection of data and the objects that represent and interact with that data. Tables, views, stored procedures, triggers, and constraints are typical database objects.

A single database server instance can have up to 32,767 databases, and each database can have more than 2 billion objects. These are theoretical limits, of course, but they demonstrate that SQL Server can handle just about any job. To perform most administration tasks, you must log on to the database using an account that has the Sysadmin fixed server role, such as the local sysadmin account (sa). Detailed information on roles and SQL Server security is found in Chapter 9, "Managing Microsoft SQL Server 2008 Security."

## Database Files and Logs

Each SQL Server database has a transaction log associated with it. A *transaction log* is a history of modifications to the database, and SQL Server uses it to ensure database integrity. All changes to the database are first written to the transaction log and then applied to the database. If the database update is successful, the transaction is completed and recorded as successful. If the database update fails, SQL Server uses the transaction log to restore the database to its original state (which is called *rolling back* the transaction). This two-phase commit process makes it possible for SQL Server to restore a database automatically in case of power failure, server outage, or other problems that occur when you enter a transaction.

SQL Server databases and transaction logs are contained in separate database files. This means that each database always has at least two files associated with it—a data file and a log file. Databases also can have secondary data files. SQL Server uses three types of database files:

- **Primary data files**   Every database has one primary data file. These files store data and maintain records of other files used in a database. By default, these files end with the .mdf extension.

- **Secondary data files**   These files store additional data for a database. Though not all databases have secondary databases, a single database can have multiple secondary data files. By default, these files end with the .ndf extension.

- **Transaction log files**   Every database has at least one transaction log file. This file contains information necessary to restore the database. By default, log files end with the .ldf extension.

**Note**   SQL Server also uses backup devices. Backup devices can be physical devices, such as tape drives, or files that are stored on a local drive or a network share. SQL Server data and log files can be stored on either FAT or NTFS partitions, but they cannot be stored on any compressed file system.

**Tip**   In SQL Server 2008, full-text catalogs are represented logically as virtual objects that refer to groups of full-text indexes rather than as separate database files with physical paths. This is a significant change over earlier releases. See Chapter 8, "Full-Text Search Administration," for more information.

Database files are set when you create or modify the database. Because multiple database files are allowed, SQL Server can create databases that span multiple disk drives and that can grow in size as needed. Although the size of a SQL Server database is often measured in gigabytes, with all editions of SQL Server except the Express Edition, databases can range in size from 1 MB to a theoretical limit of 1,048,516 terabytes. With the Express Edition, databases have a maximum size limit of 4 GB.

As you work with databases, keep in mind that SQL Server is designed to expand databases automatically as necessary. This means that *master*, *tempdb*, *msdb*, and other critical databases will not run out of space under normal conditions—provided, of course, that there is file space on the configured drives and that you have not set a maximum database size manually.

System databases are the most important databases on the server. You should never directly update tables in system databases. Instead, use the appropriate management tools or stored procedures to modify the system databases if necessary. The only exception is the *model* database, which you can update with settings for new databases.

Table 7-1 provides a summary of other size and number constraints for SQL Server 2008. These constraints apply to both 32-bit and 64-bit editions, unless otherwise noted.

Table 7-1   Size and Number Constraints for the Database Engine

| Database Engine Object | Maximum Value |
|---|---|
| Batch size | 65,536 * network packet size (The default is 4 KB.) |
| Bytes in source text of a stored procedure | Lesser of batch size or 250 MB |
| Bytes per foreign key | 900 |
| Bytes per GROUP BY, ORDER BY | 8060 |
| Bytes per index key | 900 |
| Bytes per primary key | 900 |
| Bytes per row | 8060 (except for varchar, nvarchar, varbinary, sql_variant, or CLR user-defined type columns) |
| Bytes per short string column | 8000 |
| Bytes per varchar(max), varbinary(max), xml, text, or image column | $2^{31} - 1$ |
| Characters per ntext or nvarchar(max) column | $2^{30} - 1$ |
| Clustered indexes per table | 1 |
| Columns in GROUP BY, ORDER BY | Limited only by number of bytes |
| Columns or expressions in a GROUP BY WITH CUBE or WITH ROLLUP statement | 10 |
| Columns per nonwide table | 1024 |
| Columns per wide table | 30000 |
| Columns per foreign key | 16 |
| Columns per index key | 16 (15 when you use XML indexes) |
| Columns per INSERT statement | 1024 |
| Columns per primary key | 16 |
| Columns per SELECT statement | 4096 |
| Connections per client | Maximum value of configured connections |
| Database size | 524,272 terabytes |
| Databases per instance of SQL Server | 32,767 |
| File size (data) | 16 terabytes |
| File size (log) | 2 terabytes |
| Filegroups per database | 32,767 |
| Files per database | 32,767 |

**Table 7-1   Size and Number Constraints for the Database Engine**

| Database Engine Object | Maximum Value |
| --- | --- |
| Foreign key table references per table | Unlimited; recommended maximum is 253 to maintain expected performance levels. |
| Identifier length (in characters) | 128 |
| Instances per computer (no clustering) | 50 instances for Standard, Developer, and Enterprise Editions. 16 instances for Workgroup Edition. |
| Instances per computer (with clustering) | 25 instances for clustered Standard, Developer, and Enterprise Editions. 16 instances for Workgroup Edition. |
| Length of a string containing SQL statements (batch size) | 65,536 * network packet size (The default is 4 KB.) |
| Locks per connection | Maximum locks per server |
| Locks per instance of SQL Server | Up to 2,147,483,647 on 32-bit for static locks. Otherwise, limited only by memory. |
| Nested stored procedure levels | 32, but limited to 8 databases or 2 databases with interleaving. |
| Nested subqueries | 32 |
| Nested trigger levels | 32 |
| Nonclustered indexes per table | 999 |
| Number of distinct expressions in the GROUP BY clause using CUBE, ROLLUP, GROUPING SETS, WITH CUBE, WITH ROLLUP | 32 |
| Number of grouping sets generated by operators in the GROUP BY clause | 4096 |
| Parameters per stored procedure | 2100 |
| Parameters per user-defined function | 2100 |
| Partitions per partitioned table or index | 1000 |
| REFERENCES per table | 253 |
| Rows per table | Limited by available storage |
| Statistics on nonindexed columns | 30000 |
| Tables per database | The sum of the number of all objects in a database cannot exceed 2,147,483,647. |
| Tables per SELECT statement | 256 |

**Table 7-1    Size and Number Constraints for the Database Engine**

| Database Engine Object | Maximum Value |
|---|---|
| Triggers per table | The sum of the number of all objects in a database cannot exceed 2,147,483,647. |
| UNIQUE indexes or constraints per table | 249 nonclustered and 1 clustered. |
| User connections | 32,767 |
| XML indexes | 249 |

SQL Server 2008 supports row-overflow storage, which enables variable length columns to be pushed off-row and to exceed the maximum allowed size of 8060 bytes per row. Row-overflow storage applies only to varchar, nvarchar, varbinary, sql_variant, or Common Language Runtime (CLR) user-defined type columns. It does not apply to varchar(max), nvarchar(max), varbinary(max), text, image, or xml columns, which have a maximum size of $2^{31} - 1$ bytes.

When the Database Engine uses row-overflow storage, it moves the record column with the largest width to another page in the ROW_OVERFLOW_DATA allocation unit, while maintaining a 24-byte pointer on the original page. As part of ongoing operations, the Database Engine moves large records to another page dynamically as records are lengthened based on update operations. Update operations that shorten records might cause records to be moved back to the original page in the IN_ROW_DATA allocation unit. Using the sys.dm_db_index_physical_stats object, you can obtain information about tables or indexes that might contain row-overflow data.

Because records that contain row-overflow data are processed synchronously instead of asynchronously, querying and performing other select operations, such as sorts or joins, slows processing time and this might have an impact on the server's performance. To reduce the performance impact, consider the frequency with which this overflow data is likely to be queried and the percentage of rows that are likely to overflow. If users or applications are likely to perform frequent queries on many rows of row-overflow data, you should consider normalizing tables so that some columns are moved to another table. You can then make queries against the data using an asynchronous JOIN operation.

> **Note**    The length of individual columns must still fall within the limit of 8000 bytes for varchar, nvarchar, varbinary, sql_variant, and CLR user-defined type columns. Only their combined lengths can exceed the 8060-byte row limit of a table.

You can include columns that contain row-overflow data as key or nonkey columns of a nonclustered index. However, the index key of a clustered index cannot contain varchar columns that have existing data in the ROW_OVERFLOW_DATA allocation unit. If a clustered index is created on a varchar column and the existing data is in the IN_ROW_DATA allocation unit, subsequent insert or update actions on the column that would push the data off-row will fail.

# Database Administration Basics

You perform most database administration work through SQL Server Management Studio. Use SQL Server Management Studio to carry out many common database administration tasks, including

- Viewing database information
- Checking user and system databases
- Examining database objects

This section examines each of these tasks.

## Viewing Database Information in SQL Server Management Studio

SQL Server organizes information using a top-down hierarchy that starts with server groups at the highest level and then moves down to servers, and then to databases, and then to objects. Therefore, you must work your way down to the database level to view the databases installed on a particular server instance. If you have registered a server instance and have connected to it previously, you can view its databases by completing the following steps:

1. In SQL Server Management Studio, use the Registered Servers view to select a type of server, such as Database Engine. If you need to expand a server group to see the servers listed in the group, click the plus sign (+) next to the name of the group.

2. In the Registered Servers view, select a server by double-clicking its name in the list. This connects you to the server in the Object Explorer view.

   **Note**   If the SQL Server service is stopped, you must restart it before accessing the server. Additionally, if you have not authenticated the server connection, you might need to provide a SQL login account and password. You might also need to reestablish a connection with the server. In either case, enter any necessary information and then click OK or Yes to continue.

3. In the Object Explorer view, click the plus sign (+) next to the server's Databases folder to see a list of the databases available on the server.

4. Right-click the database you want to work with, and then select Properties. This displays the Database Properties dialog box shown in Figure 7-1.

**Figure 7-1**    The General page of the Database Properties dialog box.

The Database Properties dialog box includes several different properties pages:

- **General**    Provides general database information, such as status, owner, date created, size, and space available. This page also details the last backup date and collation setting.

- **Files**    Provides details on the data and log files associated with the database. If the database has been configured for full-text search, the Use Full-Text Indexing check box is selected. However, catalog files associated with the database are not listed.

- **Filegroups**    Lists the filegroups associated with the database, and allows you to add or remove filegroups.

- **Options**    Provides boxes for viewing and managing standard database options and settings.

- **Change Tracking**    Provides boxes for viewing and managing change-tracking settings.

- **Permissions**    Lists users or roles that have specific permissions allowed or denied in the database, and allows you to set database permissions for users or roles.

- **Extended Properties**   Provides boxes for viewing and managing extended database properties.

- **Mirroring**   Provides boxes for viewing and managing database mirroring settings.

- **Transaction Log Shipping**   Details the current log shipping configuration (if any), and allows you to manage log shipping.

## Viewing Database Information Using T-SQL

You can also use Transact-SQL (T-SQL) to examine database information. Transact-SQL is an enhanced version of the standard structured query language that SQL Server uses. In SQL Server Management Studio, access the Query view. You can do this by right-clicking the name of a server to which you have already connected in the Object Explorer view and then selecting New Query. Alternatively, click New Query on the main toolbar, select Database Engine Query, and then establish a connection to the Database Engine on a specific server.

After you have accessed the Query view, use the following command, where *dbname* is the name of the database you want to examine, to view database information:

```
sp_helpdb <dbname>
go
```

When you view database information in this way, you get an overview of the database as well as a listing of current data and log files. Table 7-2 summarizes the information available when you view database properties using T-SQL. This data is returned in two different result sets; you will need to scroll down in the Results pane to see the additional result set.

**Table 7-2   Database Properties Viewable Using T-SQL**

| Column Name | Description |
| --- | --- |
| compatibility_level | The current compatibility level of the database. The level 90 indicates SQL Server 2008 compatibility. |
| created | The date the database was created. |
| db_size | The total size of the database, including all data and log files. |
| dbid | The unique identifier for the database on the current server. |
| filegroup | The filegroup associated with the database file. Filegroups allow you to group sets of database files together. |
| fileid | The unique identifier for the file in the current database. |
| filename | The full file name and path. |
| growth | The number of megabytes or percent by which the file grows. |
| maxsize | The maximum file size. *Unlimited* means there is no limit. |
| name | The name of the database or file (without a file extension). |

**Table 7-2** Database Properties Viewable Using T-SQL

| Column Name | Description |
|---|---|
| owner | The database owner. |
| size | The current size of a file. |
| status | The database status. |
| usage | The way the file is used, such as data only or log only. |

## Checking System and Sample Databases

A new SQL Server installation includes the system databases listed in Table 7-3. System databases are critical to the proper operation of SQL Server, and an important aspect of the administration process is backing up and maintaining these databases. Sample databases can also be installed, but they are meant only to provide examples and do not need regular maintenance. You can locate and download the examples and sample databases from the Microsoft SQL Server Community & Samples Web site at *http://www.codeplex.com/sqlserversamples*. In the Microsoft Product Samples section, you'll find links to samples for the SQL Server components and to the official SQL Server sample databases. If you install the samples, the sample files are installed by default in a component-specific subfolder of C:\Program Files\Microsoft SQL Server\100\Samples.

**Table 7-3** Summary of System Databases

| Database Name | Database Type | Description |
|---|---|---|
| *master* | System | Maintains information on all databases installed on the server. This database is modified anytime you create databases, manage accounts, or change configuration settings. Back up the *master* database regularly. |
| *model* | System | Provides a template for all new databases. If you want new databases to have certain properties or permissions, put these changes in the *model* database, and then all new databases will inherit the changes. |
| *tempdb* | System | Provides a temporary workspace for processing queries and handling other tasks. This database is re-created each time SQL Server is started, and it is based on the *model* database. |
| *msdb* | System | Used by the SQL Server Agent services when handling alerts, notifications, and scheduled tasks. You can access all the information in this database using SQL Server Management Studio options. |
| *distribution* | System/Replication | Used by Replication Services when you configure a server as a publisher, distributor, or both. This database is created when you configure replication, and it is not created automatically with a new installation. |

## Examining Database Objects

The main elements of a SQL Server database are referred to as *objects*. The objects you can associate with a database include

- Certificates
- Constraints
- Defaults
- Indexes
- Keys
- Stored procedures
- Extended stored procedures
- Tables
- Triggers
- User-defined data types
- User-defined functions
- Views

You can also associate users, roles, rules, and full-text catalogs with databases.

To examine objects within a database, complete the following steps:

1. In SQL Server Management Studio, use the Registered Servers view to select a type of server, such as Database Engine. If you need to expand a server group to see the servers available in the group, click the plus sign (+) next to the name of a group.

2. In the Registered Servers view, select a server by double-clicking its name in the list. This connects you to the server in the Object Explorer view.

   **Note**   If you have not authenticated the server connection, you might need to provide a SQL login account and password. You might also need to reestablish a connection with the server. In either case, enter any necessary information and then click Connect to continue.

3. In the Object Explorer view, work your way down to the database level. Expand the Databases folder, and then expand the entry for a specific database to see a list of nodes for database objects, including the following ones:

   - **Database Diagrams**   Contains database diagrams, which are visual diagrams of a database and the information it contains. Use Database Designer to create and manage diagrams.

❑ **Tables**   Contains system and user tables. System tables are used for many purposes, including database mail, database maintenance plans, replication, backup and restore, and log shipping. System tables should not be modified directly.

❑ **Views**   Contains system and user views. Standard views combine data from one or more tables to make it easier to work with the data. Indexed views have unique clusters to improve query performance. Partitioned views join horizontally partitioned data from tables on one or more servers.

❑ **Synonyms**   Contains synonyms, which are alternate names for schema scoped objects. Applications can use synonyms to refer to objects in the database abstractly. You can then change the underlying name of the object without having to modify the application programming.

❑ **Programmability**   Contains nodes used to represent most programmable object types and subtypes, including stored procedures, functions, triggers, assemblies, data types, rules, and defaults. This node also contains plan guides.

❑ **Service Broker**   Contains Service Broker–related objects, including message types, contracts, queues, services, routes, and remote service bindings. This node also contains broker priorities.

❑ **Storage**   Contains storage-related objects, including full-text catalogs, partition schemes, and partition functions. This node also contains full-text stoplists.

❑ **Security**   Contains security-related objects, including users, roles, schemas, keys, and certificates. It also contains database audit specifications.

**Note**   Database objects are covered in detail in the chapters in Part III, "Microsoft SQL Server 2008 Data Administration." For example, you will find more information on tables, indexes, and views in Chapter 10, "Manipulating Schemas, Tables, Indexes, and Views."

Plan guides, broker priorities, and full-text stoplists deserve additional discussion. Broker priorities define a priority level and the set of criteria for determining which Service Broker conversations to assign the priority level. Servicer Broker assigns the priority level to any conversation endpoint that uses the same combination of contracts and services that are specified in the conversation priority. Priorities range in value from 1 (low) through 10 (high). The default is 5.

You can create plan guides to help optimize queries when a small subset of queries in a database application deployed from a third-party vendor are not performing as expected. In a plan guide, you can specify the Transact-SQL statement that you want optimized and either an OPTION clause that contains the query hints you want to use or a specific query plan you want to use to optimize the query. When the query executes, the query optimizer matches the Transact-SQL statement to the plan guide and either attaches the OPTION clause to the query at run time or uses the specified query plan.

You can create three types of plan guides:

- **OBJECT plan guide**   Matches queries that execute in the context of Transact-SQL stored procedures, scalar user-defined functions, multistatement table-valued user-defined functions, and DML triggers.

- **SQL plan guide**   Matches queries that parameterize to a specified form, execute in the context of standalone Transact-SQL statements, or execute in batches that are not part of a database object.

- **TEMPLATE plan guide**   Matches standalone queries that parameterize to a specified form and override the current PARAMETERIZATION database SET option of a database for a class of queries.

If you've used plan guides with earlier releases of SQL Server, your plan guides will remain intact after the upgrade, but they should be validated. You can validate existing plan guides using the sys.fn_validate_plan_guide function. You also can use SQL Server Profiler to monitor SQL Server for Plan Guide Unsuccessful events, which indicate problems with a plan guide.

SQL Server discards commonly occurring strings, called *stopwords*, that do not help with searches. During index creation, the Full-Text Engine omits stopwords from the full-text index and, as a result, full-text queries will not search on stopwords. SQL Server 2008 stopwords replace SQL Server 2005 noise words.

In SQL Server 2008, you can create and use lists of stopwords. You associate these stoplists with full-text indexes, and then SQL Server applies the list when it builds indexes and applies queries. You create stoplists by uploading the system-supplied stoplist to the database, by creating your own stopwords and lists, or by combining these techniques. The system stoplist includes common stopwords for all supported languages. You can tailor the system-supplied stoplist by adding and removing stopwords.

# Creating Databases

SQL Server uses the *model* database as the prototype for new databases. If you want new databases to have a particular setup, first modify the *model* database, and then create the new databases. Otherwise, you will have to modify the settings of each new database manually.

The easiest way to create a new database is by using SQL Server Management Studio. You can also create databases using Transact-SQL.

## Creating Databases in SQL Server Management Studio

In SQL Server Management Studio, you set database properties with buttons and input boxes and let SQL Server do all the SQL detail work. Create a database with the default options by completing these steps:

1.  In SQL Server Management Studio, use the Registered Servers view to select a type of server, such as Database Engine. If you need to expand a server group to see the servers available in a group, click the plus sign (+) next to the name of a group.

2.  In the Registered Servers view, select a server by double-clicking its name in the list. This connects you to the server in the Object Explorer view.

3.  Right-click the Databases folder, and then from the shortcut menu, choose New Database to display the dialog box shown in Figure 7-2.

4.  On the General page, type a name for the database in the Database Name box. Although database names can have up to 128 characters, it is a good idea to give a new database a short but descriptive name to make it easier to track.

**Figure 7-2**    The New Database dialog box.

> **Note**   The names of database objects are referred to as *identifiers*. Identifiers can contain from 1 to 128 characters (except for local temporary tables, which can have from 1 to 116 characters), and they must follow the specific naming conventions for the identifier class to which they belong. Generally, if the identifier name uses spaces or if it begins with a number, you must use brackets ([ ]) or double quotation marks (" ") to delimit the name when referencing it in Transact-SQL commands.

5. Click OK. SQL Server creates the database.

To customize the creation process, follow steps 1 through 4 (but not 5) in the previous example, and then continue with these steps:

1. On the General page, set the database owner by clicking the button to the right of the Owner box to display the Select Database Owner dialog box.

2. In the Select Database Owner dialog box, click Browse, and then in the Browse For Objects dialog box that opens, select the login that will be the owner of the database. Click OK twice.

3. By default, SQL Server bases the data file name on the database name. For example, if you type **Projects** as the database name, the data file is named Projects. You can change the default name by typing a new value.

4. The File Group box shows which filegroup the data file belongs to. By default, all files are placed in the primary group. Although the primary data file must be in the primary group, you can create other data files and place them in different filegroups. Filegroups provide additional options for determining where data is stored and how it is used, as well as how data is backed up and restored.

> **Tip**   Filegroups are designed primarily for large databases and advanced administration. If your database might grow to 1 GB or larger, consider using multiple filegroups. Otherwise, you really do not need to use multiple filegroups. The primary reason to use filegroups is to improve database response time. You do this by allowing database files to be created across multiple disks or to be accessed by multiple disk controllers, or both.

5. In the Initial Size box, type an initial size for the database in megabytes. Use a size that makes sense for the amount of data that the database will store. By default, new databases have the same size as the *model* database. The size range for databases is 1 MB to many terabytes.

> **Tip**   Setting the initial database size to a reasonable value cuts down on the overhead that might be associated with growing the database. Whether you grow the database manually or SQL Server grows it automatically, the database is locked until the growth is complete. This can cause delays in processing queries and handling transactions.

**Note**   Keep in mind that you cannot shrink a database to make it smaller than it was when you created it. However, you can shrink individual data and log files to make them smaller than their original sizes by using the DBCC SHRINKFILE statement. With DBCC SHRINKFILE, you must shrink each file individually; you cannot shrink the entire database.

6. By default, new databases are set to auto grow each time a data file needs to be expanded. Click the button to the right of the Autogrowth box to adjust the settings. As Figure 7-3 shows, the Autogrowth feature can be set to grow using a percentage or an amount in megabytes, and you can either restrict the maximum file growth to a specific size or allow unrestricted file growth.

**Real World**   The Autogrowth feature is a good tool to use to ensure that databases do not run out of space. Be careful when configuring the database to enable growth by a certain percentage, however. Setting a 10-percent growth rate, for example, will cause a database that is 5 GB in size to grow by a whopping 500 MB each time a data file needs to be expanded, and a server with multiple databases might run out of space as a result of the growth factor. If you set the growth in megabytes, with 1 MB as a minimum growth size, you will know exactly how much the database will grow each time the data file expands. You might also want to configure an alert to notify you when the database grows to a certain size. You will learn how to configure an alert in Chapter 16, "Database Automation and Maintenance."

**Figure 7-3**   Configuring the Autogrowth feature.

7. In the Path box, type the full path to the data file. The primary data file name should end with the .mdf file extension. By default, SQL Server uses the default data location you selected when you installed the server. Click the button to the right of the Path box to find a new path, or you can enter a new path directly.

8.  Secondary data files provide an additional location for data. If you want to configure secondary data files, click Add to start on a new line, and then repeat steps 5 through 9. Secondary data file names should end with the .ndf file extension.

9.  Transaction logs are listed with the Log file type. After you configure data files, you can configure one or more transaction log files in much the same way that you configured the data files. Type the file name, filegroup, initial size, and path information. Configure Autogrowth as necessary. Be sure to name the log files with the .ldf file extension.

> **Note**   Setting a size for the transaction log can be tricky. You do not want to rob the system of needed space for data, but you do want to avoid a situation in which the transaction logs are resized again and again, because a file is locked when it is being expanded. I recommend 2 MB to 3 MB as a minimum for most databases, and 25 percent of total data file size on a moderately active database. Note also that placing transaction logs on separate drives from data files can usually improve database performance.

10.  On the Options page, use the Collation drop-down list to choose a collation for the database. Microsoft Windows collation names have two components: a collation designator and a comparison style. The collation designator specifies the alphabet or language whose sorting rules are applied with dictionary sorting and the code page to use when storing non-Unicode character data. The comparison style specifies additional collation styles as identified by the following abbreviations:

- ❏ **90**   Code-point sorting (updated collation to include code-point sorting)
- ❏ **CI**   Case insensitive
- ❏ **CS**   Case sensitive
- ❏ **AI**   Accent insensitive
- ❏ **AS**   Accent sensitive
- ❏ **KS**   Kanatype sensitive
- ❏ **WS**   Width sensitive
- ❏ **BIN**   Binary sort order
- ❏ **BIN2**   Code-point binary sort (for pure code-point comparison collations)

11.  Click OK to complete the creation process.

After you finish creating a new database, you should set options and permissions for that database. You will learn about setting options in "Setting Database Options in SQL Server Management Studio" on page 193. Setting permissions is covered in Chapter 9.

## Creating Databases Using T-SQL

You can also create a database by using the CREATE DATABASE command. This command has options that are similar to those on the Database Properties tab, and the best way to learn how the command works is by creating databases in SQL Server Management Studio first, and then trying the CREATE DATABASE command.

The syntax and usage for CREATE DATABASE are shown in Sample 7-1.

**Sample 7-1**   CREATE DATABASE Command Syntax and Usage

```
Syntax
CREATE DATABASE database_name
    [ ON
        [ <filespec> [ ,...n ] ]
        [ , <filegroup> [ ,...n ] ]
    ]
[
    [ LOG ON { <filespec> [ ,...n ] } ]
    [ COLLATE collation_name ]
    [ WITH <external_access_option> ]
]
[;]

<filespec> ::=
{
[ PRIMARY ]
(    NAME = logical_file_name ,
    FILENAME = "os_file_name"
        [ , SIZE = size [ KB | MB | GB | TB ] ]
        [ , MAXSIZE = { max_size [ KB | MB | GB | TB ] | UNLIMITED } ]
]
        [ , FILEGROWTH = growth_increment [ KB | MB | % ] ]
) [ ,...n ] }

<filegroup> ::=
{ FILEGROUP filegroup_name [ CONTAINS FILESTREAM ] [ DEFAULT ]
        <filespec> [ ,...n ]  }

<external_access_option> ::=
{ DB_CHAINING { ON | OFF }
  | TRUSTWORTHY { ON | OFF } }

Usage
USE MASTER
GO
CREATE DATABASE Sample
ON
PRIMARY
```

```
( NAME = Sample1,
FILENAME = "c:\data\sampledat1.mdf",
SIZE = 100MB,
MAXSIZE = UNLIMITED,
FILEGROWTH = 10%),
( NAME = Sample2,
FILENAME = "c:\data\sampledat2.ndf",
SIZE = 100MB,
MAXSIZE = UNLIMITED,
FILEGROWTH = 10%)
LOG ON
( NAME = SampleLog1,
FILENAME = "c:\data\samplelog1.ldf",
SIZE = 3MB,
MAXSIZE = UNLIMITED,
FILEGROWTH = 5MB)
GO
```

# Altering Databases and Their Options

New databases inherit options from the *model* database. After you create a database, you can modify these settings at any time by using SQL Server Management Studio, the ALTER DATABASE statement, and other SQL commands. In most SQL Server editions, many standard options can be set to TRUE (ON) or FALSE (OFF) states. Other options accept specific values that specify their configured state, such as GLOBAL or LOCAL.

## Setting Database Options in SQL Server Management Studio

To set database options in SQL Server Management Studio, complete the following steps:

1.  In SQL Server Management Studio, use the Registered Servers view to select a type of server, such as Database Engine. If you need to expand a server group to see the servers listed in the group, click the plus sign (+) next to the name of a group.

2.  In the Registered Servers view, select a server by double-clicking its name in the list. This connects you to the server in the Object Explorer view.

3.  Click the plus sign (+) next to the Databases folder. Right-click the name of a database, and then choose Properties from the shortcut menu to display the Database Properties dialog box.

4.  In the Database Properties dialog box, select Options from the Select A Page list as shown in Figure 7-4. You can now configure options for the database using the

drop-down lists provided. Most options can be turned off using a value of False or turned on using a value of True.

**Figure 7-4** The Options page of the Database Properties dialog box.

5. Click OK when you are finished selecting options. Your changes take effect immediately, and you do not need to restart the server.

## Modifying Databases Using ALTER DATABASE

SQL Server Management Studio gives you one easy way to modify the configuration of a database. Another way to modify a database is to use ALTER DATABASE. You can use the ALTER DATABASE command to perform the following tasks:

- Set database options. You can use the ALTER DATABASE command instead of the sp_dboption stored procedure.

- Add new data and log files to a database. All the files must be placed in the same filegroup.

- Modify properties of data and log files, such as increasing file size, changing the maximum size, or setting file growth rules.

- Add a new filegroup to a database.

- Modify the properties of an existing filegroup, such as designating whether the filegroup is read-only or read-write, and which filegroup is the default.

- Remove files and filegroups from a database. These elements can be removed only when they do not contain data.

The ALTER DATABASE command is designed to make one database change at a time, and it uses the syntax shown in Sample 7-2. The examples in the listing show how you can use ALTER DATABASE to perform important administrative tasks. You can use the Query view in SQL Server Management Studio or SQLCMD. Execute commands with either the Execute Command button or the GO statement, respectively.

**Sample 7-2**   ALTER DATABASE Syntax and Usage

```
Syntax
ALTER DATABASE database_name
{ <add_or_modify_files>
  | <add_or_modify_filegroups>
  | <set_database_options>
  | MODIFY NAME = new_database_name
  | COLLATE collation_name }
[;]
<add_or_modify_files>::=
{ ADD FILE <filespec> [ ,...n ]
       [ TO FILEGROUP { filegroup_name | DEFAULT } ]
  | ADD LOG FILE <filespec> [ ,...n ]
  | REMOVE FILE logical_file_name
  | MODIFY FILE <filespec>
}
<filespec>::=
(   NAME = logical_file_name
    [ , NEWNAME = new_logical_name ]
    [ , FILENAME = 'os_file_name' ]
    [ , SIZE = size [ KB | MB | GB | TB ] ]
    [ , MAXSIZE = { max_size [ KB | MB | GB | TB ] | UNLIMITED } ]
    [ , FILEGROWTH = growth_increment [ KB | MB | % ] ]
    [ , OFFLINE ]
)
<add_or_modify_filegroups>::=
{   | ADD FILEGROUP filegroup_name
    | REMOVE FILEGROUP filegroup_name
    | MODIFY FILEGROUP filegroup_name
         { <filegroup_updatability_option>
         | DEFAULT
         | NAME = new_filegroup_name
         }
}
<filegroup_updatability_option>::=
{   { READONLY | READWRITE }
    | { READ_ONLY | READ_WRITE }
}
```

```
<set_database_options>::=
SET {
    { <optionspec> [ ,...n ] [ WITH <termination> ] }
    | ALLOW_SNAPSHOT_ISOLATION {ON | OFF }
    | READ_COMMITTED_SNAPSHOT {ON | OFF } [ WITH <termination> ]
}
<optionspec>::=
{ <auto_option>
  | <change_tracking_option>
  | <cursor_option>
  | <database_mirroring_option>
  | <date_correlation_optimization_option>
    | <db_encryption_option>
  | <db_state_option>
  | <db_update_option>
  | <db_user_access_option>
  | <external_access_option>
  | <parameterization_option>
  | <recovery_option>
  | <service_broker_option>
  | <snapshot_option>
  | <sql_option>
}

<auto_option> ::=
{ AUTO_CLOSE { ON | OFF }
  | AUTO_CREATE_STATISTICS { ON | OFF }
  | AUTO_SHRINK { ON | OFF }
  | AUTO_UPDATE_STATISTICS { ON | OFF }
  | AUTO_UPDATE_STATISTICS_ASYNC { ON | OFF }
}

<change_tracking_option> ::=
{ CHANGE_TRACKING {
        = ON [ <change_tracking_settings> ]
  | <change_tracking_settings>
    | = OFF
  }
}
<change_tracking_settings> ::=
{ [ AUTO_CLEANUP = { ON | OFF } [ , ] ]
[ CHANGE_RETENTION = retention_period { DAYS | HOURS | MINUTES } ] ] }


<cursor_option> ::=
{ CURSOR_CLOSE_ON_COMMIT { ON | OFF }
  | CURSOR_DEFAULT { LOCAL | GLOBAL }
}
```

```
<partner_option> ::=
{ PARTNER { = 'partner_server'
            | FAILOVER
            | FORCE_SERVICE_ALLOW_DATA_LOSS
            | OFF
            | RESUME
            | SAFETY { FULL | OFF }
            | SUSPEND
            | TIMEOUT integer
            }
    <witness_option> ::=
    WITNESS { = 'witness_server'
            | OFF
            }
}
<date_correlation_optimization_option> ::=
{ DATE_CORRELATION_OPTIMIZATION { ON | OFF }
}
<db_encryption_option> ::=
{        ENCRYPTION { ON | OFF }
}
<db_state_option> ::=
    { ONLINE | OFFLINE | EMERGENCY }
<db_update_option> ::=
    { READ_ONLY | READ_WRITE }
<db_user_access_option> ::=
    { SINGLE_USER | RESTRICTED_USER | MULTI_USER }
<external_access_option> ::=
{ DB_CHAINING { ON | OFF }
 | TRUSTWORTHY { ON | OFF }
}
<parameterization_option> ::=
{ PARAMETERIZATION { SIMPLE | FORCED }
}
<recovery_option> ::=
{ RECOVERY { FULL | BULK_LOGGED | SIMPLE }
 | TORN_PAGE_DETECTION { ON | OFF }
 | PAGE_VERIFY { CHECKSUM | TORN_PAGE_DETECTION | NONE }
}
<service_broker_option> ::=
{ ENABLE_BROKER
 | DISABLE_BROKER
 | NEW_BROKER
 | ERROR_BROKER_CONVERSATIONS
 | HONOR_BROKER_PRIORITY { ON | OFF}
}
```

```
<snapshot_option> ::=
{ ALLOW_SNAPSHOT_ISOLATION { ON | OFF }
  | READ_COMMITTED_SNAPSHOT {ON | OFF }
}
<sql_option> ::=
{ ANSI_NULL_DEFAULT { ON | OFF }
  | ANSI_NULLS { ON | OFF }
  | ANSI_PADDING { ON | OFF }
  | ANSI_WARNINGS { ON | OFF }
  | ARITHABORT { ON | OFF }
  | COMPATIBLITY_LEVEL = { 80 | 90 | 100 }
  | CONCAT_NULL_YIELDS_NULL { ON | OFF }
  | NUMERIC_ROUNDABORT { ON | OFF }
  | QUOTED_IDENTIFIER { ON | OFF }
  | RECURSIVE_TRIGGERS { ON | OFF }
}
<termination> ::=
{ ROLLBACK AFTER integer [ SECONDS ]
  | ROLLBACK IMMEDIATE
  | NO_WAIT
}
```

**Usage: Adding a File to a Database**
```
ALTER DATABASE Customer
ADD FILE
( NAME = Customerdata2,
    FILENAME = "c:\data\customerdat2.ndf",
    SIZE = 10MB,
    MAXSIZE = 500MB,
    FILEGROWTH = 5MB )
```

**Usage: Adding a Filegroup**
```
ALTER DATABASE Customer
ADD FILEGROUP Secondary
```

**Usage: Adding Files and Placing Them in a Filegroup**
```
ALTER DATABASE Customer
ADD FILE
( NAME = Customerdata3,
    FILENAME = "c:\data\customerdat3.ndf",
    SIZE = 10MB,
    MAXSIZE = UNLIMITED,
    FILEGROWTH = 5MB),
( NAME = Customerdata4,
    FILENAME = "c:\data\customerdat4.ndf",
    SIZE = 10MB,
    MAXSIZE = UNLIMITED,
    FILEGROWTH = 5MB)
TO FILEGROUP Secondary
```

**Usage: Setting the Default Filegroup**
```
ALTER DATABASE Customer
MODIFY FILEGROUP Secondary DEFAULT
```

**Usage: Modifying a File**
```
ALTER DATABASE Customer
MODIFY FILE
(NAME = Customerdata3,
   SIZE = 20MB)
```

**Usage: Removing a File from a Database**
```
USE Customer
DBCC SHRINKFILE (Customerdata3, EMPTYFILE)
ALTER DATABASE Customer
REMOVE FILE Customerdata3
```

**Usage: Setting the Recovery Model Option**
```
ALTER DATABASE Customer
SET RECOVERY FULL
GO
```

**Usage: Setting Single User with Rollback of Incomplete Transactions**
```
ALTER DATABASE Customer
SET SINGLE_USER
WITH ROLLBACK IMMEDIATE
GO
```

**Note**    The EMPTYFILE option of DBCC SHRINKFILE empties a file by moving its data to other files in the same filegroup. Then you can use the REMOVE FILE option of the ALTER DATABASE command to delete the file.

## Configuring Automatic Options

SQL Server 2008 has several important features that can be managed automatically. You will find the automatic options on the Options page of the Database Properties dialog box. These options are shown as TRUE when they are set to ON and FALSE when they are set to OFF. In the following list, Database Properties dialog box options are listed first, with the related ALTER DATABASE keyword following in parentheses. Automatic options include the following:

■ **Auto Close (auto_close)**    When this option is set to TRUE, the database closes and resources become available again when the last user connection ends and all database processes are completed. The database reopens automatically when a user connects to the database again. In the SQL Server 2008 Express Edition, this option is set to TRUE by default. All other editions set this option to FALSE by default, which can improve database performance because the overhead of opening and closing databases is eliminated. When this option is set to FALSE, the database remains open even if no users are currently using it.

> **Tip** In the Express Edition, Auto Close is a useful feature that allows databases to be treated like any other files. When the database is closed, you can move, copy, or change it.

- **Auto Create Statistics (auto_create_statistics)** When this option is set to TRUE (the default), statistics are automatically created by SQL Server for columns used in a WHERE clause and as otherwise needed. These statistics are used to determine the best way to evaluate a query, which in turn can improve query performance.

- **Auto Shrink (auto_shrink)** When this option is set to TRUE, data and log files are reduced in size and compacted automatically. When records are deleted or purged, SQL Server automatically reduces the size of data or log files, or both. However, log files are reduced in size only when you back up the transaction log or set the Recovery Model to Simple.

> **Note** Several caveats apply to Auto Shrink. The Auto Shrink option is applied only when more than 25 percent of a file contains unused space. This causes SQL Server to reduce the file size so that only 25 percent of file space is free, or to set the file size to its original size setting, whichever is greater. The process that shrinks the database checks the database size at 30-minute intervals. As with the Autogrowth feature discussed earlier, the database is locked when SQL Server shrinks files, which can reduce query response time. Because of this, it is usually a better choice to run the DBCC SHRINK-DATA-BASE command periodically or to schedule this task on a recurring basis, as explained in "Compressing and Shrinking a Database Manually" on page 214.

- **Auto Update Statistics (auto_update_statistics)** When this option is set to TRUE (the default), existing statistics are updated automatically if data in the related tables changes. Otherwise, existing statistics are not updated automatically; you can only update them manually. The UPDATE STATISTICS statement reenables automatic statistical updating unless the NORECOMPUTE clause is specified.

- **Auto Update Statistics Asynchronously (auto_update_statistics_async)** When this option is set to TRUE, queries that initiate an automatic update of out-of-date statistics will not wait for the statistics to be updated before compiling. Otherwise, queries that initiate an automatic update of out-of-date statistics wait for the statistics to be updated before compiling.

To manage the automatic features using SQL Server Management Studio, follow these steps:

1.  In the Object Explorer view in SQL Server Management Studio, right-click the database you want to configure, and then select Properties from the shortcut menu.

2.  In the Database Properties dialog box, select Options from the Select A Page list.

3.  Set the individual Automatic options to True or False as necessary. Click OK when you are finished setting options. Your changes take effect immediately without restarting the server.

To manage the automatic features using T-SQL, follow these steps:

1.  In the Object Explorer view in SQL Server Management Studio, right-click the database you want to configure, and then select New Query from the shortcut menu.

2.  In the Query view, type **ALTER DATABASE <dbname> SET <option> <option_value> GO**, where *dbname* is the name of the database you want to examine, *option* is the name of the option to set, and *option_value* is the value for the specified option. The following example shows the commands required to turn on the auto_shrink option for the Personnel database:

```
ALTER DATABASE Personnel
SET auto_shrink ON
GO
```

3.  Execute the query by clicking Execute or by pressing F5. If the option is set properly, the command should complete successfully.

## Controlling ANSI Compliance at the Database Level

ANSI compliance can be controlled at the database level using database options. You will find these options listed under the Miscellaneous heading on the Options page of the Database Properties dialog box. The settings for these options are shown as TRUE when they are set to ON and FALSE when they are set to OFF. In the following list, Database Properties dialog box options are listed first, followed by the related ALTER DATABASE keyword in parentheses:

- **ANSI NULL Default (ansi_null_default)**   When this option is set to TRUE, it changes the database default to NULL when no value is specified. You can override this setting by explicitly stating NULL or NOT NULL when you create user-defined data types or column definitions.

- **ANSI NULLS Enabled (ansi_nulls)**   When this option is set to TRUE, any comparison to a null value evaluates to NULL. Otherwise, comparisons of non-Unicode values evaluate to TRUE only when both values are NULL.

- **ANSI Padding Enabled (ansi_padding)**    When this option is set to TRUE, non-null values shorter than the defined column size are padded to fill the length of the column. Values are padded as appropriate for the relevant data type; for example, char columns are padded with trailing blanks, and binary columns are padded with trailing zeroes. When this option is set to FALSE, trailing blanks are trimmed.

- **ANSI Warnings Enabled (ansi_warnings)**    When this option is set to TRUE, SQL Server issues certain warnings that would otherwise not be displayed. For example, if this option is set to TRUE, divide-by-zero errors are displayed; if this option is set to FALSE, these errors are not displayed.

- **Arithmetic Abort Enabled (arithabort)**    When this option is set to TRUE, it terminates a query when an overflow or divide-by-zero error occurs. If the error occurs in a transaction, the transaction is rolled back. When the option is set to FALSE, a warning message might be displayed, but queries and transactions continue as if no error occurred.

- **Concatenate Null Yields Null (concat_null_yields_null)**    When this option is set to TRUE, concatenating a string containing NULL with other strings results in NULL. If this option is set to FALSE, the null value is treated as an empty string.

- **Numeric Round-Abort (numeric_roundabort)**    When this option is set to TRUE, an error is generated when a loss of precision occurs in an expression. When it is set to FALSE, losses of precision do not generate error messages, and the result is rounded to the precision of the column or variable storing the result.

- **Quoted Identifiers Enabled (quoted_identifier)**    When this option is set to TRUE, identifiers must be delimited by double quotation marks ("...") and literals must be delimited by single quotation marks ('...'). All strings that are delimited by double quotation marks are interpreted as object identifiers and do not have to follow the Transact-SQL rules for identifiers. When this option is set to FALSE, you need to use quoted identifiers only if names contain spaces.

- **Recursive Triggers Enabled (recursive_triggers)**    When this option is set to TRUE, a trigger can execute recursively. Triggers can be executed directly or indirectly. If a trigger is direct, a trigger in Table A1 modifies Table A1, which in turn causes the trigger to fire again. If a trigger is indirect, a trigger in Table A1 could modify data in Table A2, which in turn has a trigger that modifies data in Table A1, and this causes the original trigger to fire again. When this option is set to FALSE, only indirect triggers are allowed.

To manage the ANSI compliance features using SQL Server Management Studio, follow these steps:

1. In the Object Explorer view in SQL Server Management Studio, right-click the database you want to configure, and then select Properties from the shortcut menu.

2. In the Database Properties dialog box, select Options from the Select A Page list.

3. Set the ANSI compliance options to True or False as necessary. Click OK when you have finished setting these options. Your changes take effect immediately without restarting the server.

To manage the ANSI compliance features using T-SQL, follow these steps:

1. In the Object Explorer view in SQL Server Management Studio, right-click the database you want to configure, and then select New Query from the shortcut menu.

2. In the Query view, type **ALTER DATABASE** *<dbname>* **SET** *<option>* *<option_value>* **GO**, where *dbname* is the name of the database you want to examine, *option* is the name of the option to set, and *option_value* is the value for the specified option. The following example shows the commands required to turn on the numeric_roundabort option for the Personnel database:

```
ALTER DATABASE Personnel
SET numeric_roundabort ON
GO
```

3. Execute the query by clicking Execute or by pressing F5. If the option is set properly, the command should complete successfully.

## Configuring Parameterization

SQL Server can use parameters in Transact-SQL statements to increase the ability of the relational engine to match new SQL statements with existing, previously-compiled execution plans. The PARAMETERIZATION option controls how parameterization works.

When this option is set to SIMPLE, SQL Server parameterizes very few classes of queries and disables forced parameterization. When this option is set to FORCED, any literal value that appears in a SELECT, INSERT, UPDATE, or DELETE statement, submitted in any form, is converted to a parameter during query compilation. The exceptions are literals that appear in many types of query constructs.

With forced parameterization, individual statements in a batch are always parameterized. After compiling, a parameterized query is executed in the context of the batch in which it was originally submitted. When an execution plan for a query is cached, you can determine whether the query was parameterized by referencing the sql column of the sys.syscacheobjects view. With parameterized queries, the names and data types of parameters come before the text of the submitted batch in this column, such as (@1 tinyint). Only experienced database administrators should use forced parameterization, and they should do so only after determining whether and how this affects performance.

You can override the parameterization behavior for a query, and any others that are syntactically equivalent but differ only in their parameter values. When SQL Server parameterizes literals, the parameters are converted to the following data types:

- Money type literals parameterize to money.

- Integer literals whose size would otherwise fit within the int data type parameterize to int.

- Large integer literals that are not parts of predicates that involve comparison operators parameterize to numeric data types whose precision is just large enough to support its size and whose scale is 0.

- Large integer literals that are parts of predicates that involve any comparison operator (includes <, <=, =, !=, >, >=, !<, !>, <>, ALL, ANY, SOME, BETWEEN, and IN) parameterize to numeric(38,0).

- Fixed-point numeric literals that are not parts of predicates that involve comparison operators parameterize to numeric data types whose precision and scale are just large enough to support its size.

- Fixed-point numeric literals that are parts of predicates that involve comparison operators parameterize to numeric data types whose precision is 38 and whose scale is just large enough to support its size.

- Binary literals parameterize to varbinary(8000) if the literal fits within 8000 bytes. If it is larger than 8000 bytes, it is converted to varbinary(max).

- Non-Unicode string literals parameterize to varchar(8000) if the literal fits within 8000 characters and to varchar(max) if it is larger than 8000 characters.

- Unicode string literals parameterize to nvarchar(4000) if the literal fits within 4000 Unicode characters and to nvarchar(max) if the literal is larger than 4000 characters.

- Floating point numeric literals parameterize to float(53).

**Note** When arithmetic operators (including the +, −, *, /, or %) are used to perform implicit or explicit conversion of int, smallint, tinyint, or bigint constant values to the float, real, decimal, or numeric data types, SQL Server applies different rules of parameterized and nonparameterized values to calculate the type and precision of the expression results.

SQL Server uses simple parameterization by default. When you change the PARAME-TERIZATION option from SIMPLE to FORCED, SQL Server flushes all query plans from the plan cache of a database, except those that currently are compiling, recompiling, or running. Plans for queries that are actively compiling, recompiling, or running are parameterized the next time they are executed. SQL Server preserves the current setting of the PARAMETERIZATION option when reattaching or restoring a database.

To manage parameterization using SQL Server Management Studio, follow these steps:

1. In the Object Explorer view in SQL Server Management Studio, right-click the database you want to configure, and then select Properties from the shortcut menu.

2. In the Database Properties dialog box, select Options from the Select A Page list.

3. Set the Parameterization option to Simple or Forced as necessary. Click OK when you have finished setting this option. Your changes take effect immediately without restarting the server.

To manage parameterization using T-SQL, follow these steps:

1. In the Object Explorer view in SQL Server Management Studio, right-click the database you want to configure, and then select New Query from the shortcut menu.

2. In the Query view, type **ALTER DATABASE** *<dbname>* **SET PARAMETERIZA-TION <SIMPLE | FORCED> GO**, where *dbname* is the name of the database you want to examine and the parameterization option is set to a value of SIMPLE or FORCED. The following example shows the commands required to set the parameterization option for the Personnel database:

```
ALTER DATABASE Personnel
SET PARAMETERIZATION FORCED
GO
```

3. Execute the query by clicking Execute or by pressing F5. If the option is set properly, the command should complete successfully.

## Configuring Cursor Options

Cursors are used with stored procedures, with triggers, and in batch scripts to make the contents of a result set available to other statements. You have limited control over cursor behavior using the options listed under the Cursor heading on the Options page of the Database Properties dialog box. These options are shown as TRUE when they are set to ON and FALSE when they are set to OFF. In the following list, Database Properties dialog box options are listed first, with the related ALTER DATABASE keyword following in parentheses:

- **Close Cursor On Commit Enabled (cursor_close_on_commit)**   When this option is set to TRUE, open cursors are closed automatically when a transaction is committed or rolled back. This behavior is in compliance with SQL-92, but the option is not set to TRUE by default. As a result, cursors remain open across transaction boundaries, and they close only when the related connection is closed or when the cursor is explicitly closed.

> **Note**   SQL-92 is the most widely used version of the SQL standard and is sometimes referred to as ANSI SQL.

- **Default Cursor (cursor_default)**   When this option is set to LOCAL, cursors are created with local scope unless otherwise specified, and as a result, the cursor name is valid only within this scope. When the option is set to GLOBAL, cursors not explicitly set to LOCAL are created with a global scope and can be referenced in any stored procedure, batch, or trigger that the connection executes.

To manage the cursor settings using SQL Server Management Studio, follow these steps:

1. In the Object Explorer view in SQL Server Management Studio, right-click the database you want to configure, and then select Properties from the shortcut menu.

2. In the Database Properties dialog box, select Options from the Select A Page list.

3. Set the Cursor options as necessary. Click OK when you have finished setting options. Your changes take effect immediately without restarting the server.

To manage the cursor settings using T-SQL, follow these steps:

1. In the Object Explorer view in SQL Server Management Studio, right-click the database you want to configure, and then select New Query from the shortcut menu.

2. In the Query view, type **ALTER DATABASE** *<dbname>* **SET** *<option>* *<option_value>* **GO**, where *dbname* is the name of the database you want to examine, *option* is the name of the option to set, and *option_value* is the value for the specified option. The following example shows the commands required to set cursor_default to GLOBAL for the Personnel database:

```
ALTER DATABASE Personnel
SET cursor_default GLOBAL
GO
```

3. Execute the query by clicking Execute or by pressing F5. If the option is set properly, the command should complete successfully.

## Controlling User Access and Database State

As you might expect, managing user access and database state is a complex process. In SQL Server Management Studio, you can control the general state of the database, including whether the database is read-only or read-write, and who has access to the database.

When a database is set to READ_ONLY, you can read data but not modify it. You use this option to prevent users from changing data and modifying database configuration settings. Several caveats apply when a database is read-only: automatic recovery is skipped at system startup, locking does not take place, and the database will not shrink. The normal mode is READ_WRITE, which allows the database to be read and modified.

When a database is set to SINGLE_USER, only the database owner can access the database. You use this option when you are modifying a database and temporarily want to block access to it. When a database is set to RESTRICTED_USER, only members of the db_owner, dbcreator, or sysadmin roles can use the database. When a database is set to MULTI_USER, all users with the appropriate permissions to connect to the database are permitted to use it.

To manage the database state using SQL Server Management Studio, follow these steps:

1. In the Object Explorer view in SQL Server Management Studio, right-click the database you want to configure, and then select Properties from the shortcut menu.

2. In the Database Properties dialog box, select Options from the Select A Page list. You can now manage the database state:

   ❑ To set the database to the READ_WRITE state, set the Database Read-Only option to False.

   ❑ To set the database to the READ_ONLY state, set the Database Read-Only option to True.

   ❑ To allow access only to the database owner, set the Restrict Access option to Single_User.

   ❑ To allow access to the members of the db_owner, dbcreator, or sysadmin roles, set the Restrict Access option to Restricted_User.

   ❑ To allow all users with the appropriate permissions to connect to the database, set the Restrict Access option to Multiple_User.

3. Click OK when you have finished setting the options. Your changes take effect immediately without restarting the server.

To manage the state settings using T-SQL, follow these steps:

1. In the Object Explorer view in SQL Server Management Studio, right-click the database you want to configure, and then select New Query from the shortcut menu.

2. In the Query view, type **ALTER DATABASE** *<dbname>* **SET** *<keyword>* **GO**, where *dbname* is the name of the database you want to examine, and *keyword* is

one of the following states: READ_ONLY, READ_WRITE, SINGLE_USER, RESTRICTED_USER, or MULTI_USER. The following example shows the commands required to set the Personnel database for multiple user access:

```
ALTER DATABASE Personnel
SET MULTI_USER
GO
```

3. Execute the query by clicking Execute or by pressing F5. If the option is set properly, the command should complete successfully.

## Setting Online, Offline, or Emergency Mode

In SQL Server 2008, you can put an individual database online or offline, or you can set an emergency state that allows you to troubleshoot for database problems. When the option is set to ONLINE, the database is open and available for use. When it is set to OFFLINE, the database is offline, and you can mount or dismount it as necessary. When it is set to EMERGENCY, the database is marked READ_ONLY, logging is disabled, and access is limited to members of the sysadmin fixed server role.

> **Note**    In SQL Server 2008, the offline or online state of a database file is maintained independently from the state of the database. For a filegroup to be available, all files in the filegroup must be online. If a filegroup is offline, you cannot query the related data using SQL statements. The query optimizer does not consider the filegroup state when selecting a query plan.

To put a database in the online, offline, or emergency state, follow these steps:

1. In the Object Explorer view in SQL Server Management Studio, right-click the database you want to configure, and then select New Query from the shortcut menu.

2. In the Query view, type **ALTER DATABASE <*dbname*> SET <*keyword*> GO**, where *dbname* is the name of the database you want to examine, and *keyword* is one of the following states: ONLINE, OFFLINE, or EMERGENCY. The following example shows the commands required to put the Personnel database in the emergency state for troubleshooting:

```
ALTER DATABASE Personnel
SET EMERGENCY
GO
```

3. Execute the query by clicking Execute or by pressing F5. If the option is set properly, the command should complete successfully.

## Managing Cross-Database Chaining and External Access Options

Ownership chaining is used to determine how multiple objects access each other sequentially. When chaining is allowed, SQL Server compares ownership of a calling object to the owner of the object being called. If both objects have the same owner, the object being called is considered to have the same object permissions as the calling object. In this case, you can achieve a cascade effect if the initial permissions on a view are used when the view needs access to other objects and the owners of these objects are the same.

In some limited circumstances, you might need to configure cross-database ownership chaining between specific databases and across all databases in a single instance. Although this feature is disabled by default, you can enable it using ALTER DATABASE SET DB_CHAINING ON. When DB_CHAINING is TRUE (ON), the database can be the source or target of a cross-database ownership chain. You cannot set DB_CHAINING on *master*, *model*, or *tempdb*, and you must log on as a member of the sysadmin fixed server role to set this option.

A related option is TRUSTWORTHY. When TRUSTWORTHY is TRUE (ON), database modules that use an impersonation context can access resources outside of the database. For example, user-defined functions and stored procedures can access resources outside of the database. By default, the *master* database has TRUSTWORTHY set to ON. The *model* and *tempdb* databases always have TRUSTWORTHY set to OFF, however, and the value cannot be changed for these databases. If you want to permit another database to access outside resources, you must set TRUSTWORTHY to TRUE (ON). You must be logged on as a member of the sysadmin fixed server role to set this option.

To configure chaining or trustworthiness, follow these steps:

1. In the Object Explorer view in SQL Server Management Studio, right-click the database you want to configure, and then select New Query from the shortcut menu.

2. In the Query view, type **ALTER DATABASE** *<dbname>* **SET** *<option>* *<option_value>* **GO**, where *dbname* is the name of the database you want to examine, *option* is the name of the option to set, and *option_value* is the value for the specified option. The following example shows the commands required to turn on cross-database chaining for the Personnel database:

```
ALTER DATABASE Personnel
SET db_chaining ON
GO
```

3. Execute the query by clicking Execute or by pressing F5. If the option is set properly, the command should complete successfully.

## Configuring Recovery, Logging, and Disk I/O Error Checking Options

SQL Server 2008 has several options for managing recovery, logging, and I/O error checking. In SQL Server Management Studio, you manage recovery settings using the Recovery Model and Page Verify settings on the Options page. In T-SQL, you manage these options using the ALTER DATABASE SET RECOVERY and ALTER DATABASE SET PAGE_VERIFY commands.

Three recovery options are available:

- **FULL**   When recovery is set to FULL, transactions are fully logged, and the database can be recovered to the point of failure or to a specific point in time using the transaction logs.

- **BULK_LOGGED**   When recovery is set to BULK_LOGGED (previously managed using select into/bulk copy), certain SQL commands are not logged in the transaction log. These commands include using SELECT INTO and BULK INSERT with a permanent table, running fast bulk copy, using UPDATETEXT or WRITETEXT without logging, and using a table load. If you set this option and execute any command that bypasses the transaction log, you cannot recover the database from transaction logs and BACKUP LOG commands are prohibited. Instead, use BACKUP DATABASE to back up the entire database, and then later you can back up from the log (provided that you do not run any more commands that bypass the transaction log).

- **SIMPLE**   When recovery is set to SIMPLE (previously managed using trunc. log on chkpt), the transaction log can be automatically truncated. This setting allows the log to be cleared out after transactions have been committed. After the transaction log has been cleared out, you can perform BACKUP/RESTORE only at the database level (and not with the transaction log).

**Note**   Checkpoints occur at various times. A checkpoint is issued for each database when the SQL Server service shuts down normally. Checkpoints do not occur when the SHUTDOWN WITH NOWAIT statement is used. A checkpoint is executed in a single database when a database is changed with sp_dboption. SQL Server also automatically issues a checkpoint on a database as necessary to ensure that the designated recovery interval can be achieved and when the log becomes 70 percent full.

**Note**   The transaction log must be large enough to store all active transactions. Otherwise, you cannot roll back transactions. In a deployment environment, you should use this option only when you can rely solely on database backups and do not supplement with transaction log backups. Note also that the *tempdb* database is always truncated at a checkpoint, regardless of the setting of this option.

Disk I/O errors can cause database corruption problems and are usually the result of power failures or disk hardware failures that occur at the time a page is written to disk. There are three page verification options to help identify incomplete I/O transactions caused by disk I/O errors:

- **CHECKSUM**   When PAGE_VERIFY is set to CHECKSUM, checksums are used to find incomplete I/O transactions caused by disk I/O errors. The checksum is computed over the contents of the entire page and stored in the page header when a page is written to disk. When the page is read from disk, the checksum is recomputed and compared to the checksum value stored in the page header. When there are mismatches, error message 824 is reported to both the SQL Server error log and the Windows Event Viewer. Any I/O errors detected by the operating system are logged with error message 823.

- **TORN_PAGE_DETECTION**   When PAGE_VERIFY is set to TORN_PAGE_DETECTION, a bit is reversed for each 512-byte sector in an 8-KB database page when the page is written to disk. If a bit is in the wrong state when the page is later read, the page was written incorrectly and a torn page is detected. If SQL Server detects a torn page during a user connection, it sends an I/O error message 824 indicating a torn page error and terminates the user connection. If it detects a torn page during recovery, it marks the database as suspect. In either case, you might want to restore the database from backup and apply any backup transaction logs.

  **Tip**   You can use battery-backed disk caches to ensure that data is successfully written to disk or not written at all. But in this case, do not set torn page detection to TRUE.

- **NONE**   When PAGE_VERIFY is set to NONE (OFF), future data page writes will not contain a checksum or torn page bit, and pages will not be verified at read time, even for previously written pages that contain a checksum or torn page bit.

  **Note**   Early versions of SQL Server used the TORN_PAGE_DETECTION option to help detect I/O errors. This option is still supported, but its use is usually rejected in favor of PAGE_VERIFY. When TORN_PAGE_DETECTION is set to TRUE (ON), SQL Server automatically detects incomplete I/O operations known as torn pages.

SQL Server 2008 also supports supplemental logging, which adds information to the logs for third-party products. You can enable logging of additional information by setting the SUPPLEMENTAL_LOGGING option to TRUE (ON). Using this option adds a lot of information to the logs, however, and can have an impact on overall performance.

## Viewing, Changing, and Overriding Database Options

Although SQL Server Management Studio makes it easy to set database options, you will often want to view or change options using SQL commands. To do this, you can use the sp_dboption stored procedure, individual SET commands, or the ALTER DATABASE command. Tasks you can perform with the sp_dboption and SET commands include

- **Displaying an options list**    To display a list of available options, type **EXEC sp_dboption**.

- **Viewing database option settings**    To view the current option settings for a database, type **EXEC sp_dboption <*dbname*>**, where *dbname* is the name of the database you want to examine, such as **EXEC sp_dboption Subs**.

- **Enabling database options**    To turn on a database option, type **ALTER DATABASE <*dbname*> SET <*option*>**, where *dbname* is the name of the database you want to examine and *option* is the name of the option flag to set to the TRUE (ON) state.

- **Setting specific database option values**    To set a specific database option value, type **ALTER DATABASE <*dbname*> SET <*option*> <*option_value*>**, where *dbname* is the name of the database you want to examine, *option* is the name of the option to set, and *option_value* is the value for the specified option.

- **Overriding database options**    Use SET options for individual sessions or database drivers to override default settings. You can also check options using properties of the Databaseproperty function. See "Working with SET Options" on page 92 for more information.

> **Note**    The sp_dboption stored procedure should not be used to modify the *master* and *tempdb* databases. It is supported only for backward compatibility, and it should be used primarily to display database options. Whenever possible, use the ALTER DATABASE command to modify database options instead.

# Managing Database and Log Size

With SQL Server 2008, you can manage database and log size either automatically or manually. You can use SQL Server Management Studio or Transact-SQL to configure database or log size. This section looks primarily at configuration through SQL Server Management Studio.

## Configuring SQL Server to Automatically Manage File Size

To configure automatic management of database and log size in SQL Server Management Studio, complete the following steps:

1. Start SQL Server Management Studio. In the Object Explorer view, connect to the appropriate server, and then work your way down to the Databases folder.

2. Right-click the database you want to configure, and then select Properties from the shortcut menu.

3. Select Files from the Select A Page list in the Database Properties dialog box. Each data and log file associated with the database is listed under Database Files. For each data and log file, do the following:

   a. Click the button to the right of the file's Autogrowth box to adjust the related settings. This will display the Change Autogrowth For dialog box.

   b. Set the file to grow using a percentage or an amount in megabytes, and then either restrict the maximum file growth to a specific size or allow unrestricted file growth.

   c. Click OK.

4. Optionally, access the Options page and set Auto Shrink to True. Auto Shrink compacts and shrinks the database periodically.

5. Click OK when you have finished. Your changes take effect immediately without restarting the server.

**Note**    See "Creating Databases in SQL Server Management Studio" on page 188 for tips and advice on sizing databases and transaction logs.

## Expanding Databases and Logs Manually

Sometimes you might want to increase the size of a database or log file manually. You can do this by completing the following steps:

1. Start SQL Server Management Studio. In the Object Explorer view, connect to the appropriate server, and then work your way down to the Databases folder.

2. Right-click the database you want to configure, and then select Properties from the shortcut menu.

3. Select Files from the Select A Page list in the Database Properties dialog box. Each data and log file associated with the database is listed under Database Files.

4. To expand a data file, click in the related Initial Size box, and then enter a larger file size. (You can also create and size a new secondary file for the database. The advantage provided by using a new file rather than an existing file is that SQL Server does not need to lock what might be an active database file in order to expand the database.)

5.  To expand a log file, click in the appropriate Initial Size box, and then enter a larger file size in the text box that becomes available. (You can also create and size a new transaction log file.)

> **Tip**   With data and log files, the new file size must be larger than the current size. If it is not, you will get an error. The reason for this is that shrinking the database is handled in a different way. See "Compressing and Shrinking a Database Manually" below for details.

6.  Click OK to make the changes. SQL Server locks the database while expanding it, which blocks access.

> **Tip**   You can add files using Transact-SQL as well. The command you use is ALTER DATABASE. For more information about using this command, see "Altering Databases and Their Options" on page 193.

## Compressing and Shrinking a Database Manually

Compressing and shrinking a database is a bit different from expanding it, and in many cases, you will want finer control over the process than you get with the Auto Shrink option. Fortunately, you can manage this process manually, and you can also schedule this process on a recurring basis.

To compress or shrink all database files (both data and log files) manually in SQL Server Management Studio, complete the following steps:

1.  Start SQL Server Management Studio. In the Object Explorer view, connect to the appropriate server, and then work your way down to the Databases folder.

2.  Right-click the database you want to configure. Select Tasks from the shortcut menu, choose Shrink, and then choose Database to display the Shrink Database dialog box shown in Figure 7-5.

3.  The Database Size area in the dialog box shows the total amount of space allocated to all database files and the amount of free space. Use this information to decide if you really want to shrink the database.

4.  To reorganize data pages and move them to the beginning of the data files, select the Reorganize Files Before Releasing Unused Space check box. This compresses the data pages but does not remove empty data pages.

> **Note**   Selecting the Reorganize Files Before Releasing Unused Space option performs the same task accomplished by using DBCC SHRINKDATABASE and specifying the amount of free space that you want left in the database after shrinking. If you clear the check box for this option, the database files are compressed in the same way as when you use DBCC SHRINKDATABASE with TRUNCATEONLY, which means that the file size is reduced without moving any data or reallocating rows to unallocated pages.

**Note**   Log files are not reduced in size immediately. Instead, the size is reduced when the transaction log is backed up or the log is truncated, whichever occurs first. Also, you normally cannot shrink a database smaller than the *model* database (which is the database template).

5. Set the percentage of free space in the database in the Maximum Free Space In Files After Shrinking box. To squeeze all the extra space out of the database, use a value of 0 percent, but be aware that the next write operation might cause the database to grow automatically.

6. Click OK to begin. Although other users can be working in the database as it is shrunk, you cannot shrink a database while the database is being backed up.

**Figure 7-5**   The Shrink Database dialog box.

To compress or shrink individual database files manually in SQL Server Management Studio, complete the following steps:

1. Start SQL Server Management Studio. In the Object Explorer view, connect to the appropriate server, and then work your way down to the Databases folder.

2. Right-click the database you want to configure. Select Tasks from the shortcut menu, choose Shrink, and then choose Files to display the Shrink File dialog box shown in Figure 7-6.

**Figure 7-6**   The Shrink File dialog box.

3.  Use the File Type, Filegroup, and File Name selection menus to choose the data or log file that you want to shrink. When you select a specific file, the total amount of space allocated and the amount of free space are shown. Use this information to decide if you really want to shrink the file.

4.  Choose a shrink action:

    ❑ **Release Unused Space**   Truncates free space from the end of the file. Unused space is released, and the file is reduced in size to the last allocated extent. The file size is reduced without moving any data or reallocating rows to unallocated pages. You can accomplish the same task by using DBCC SHRINKDATABASE with TRUNCATEONLY and specifying the target file.

    ❑ **Reorganize Pages Before Releasing Unused Space**   Reorganizes data pages, and moves them to the beginning of the data files. This compresses the data pages but does not remove empty data pages. You can accomplish the same task by using DBCC SHRINKDATABASE and specifying the amount of free space that you want left in a target file after shrinking. After you select this option, set the file size by selecting a value in the Shrink File To box. The size cannot be less than the current allocated space or more than the total extents allocated.

❏ **Empty File By Migrating The Data**   Migrates the data in this file to other files in the same filegroup. This option is equivalent to executing DBCC SHRINKFILE with the EMPTYFILE option, and it allows the file to be dropped later using the ALTER DATABASE command.

5. Click OK. Other users can be working in the database as a file is shrunk.

Another way to shrink a database is to use Transact-SQL. Two commands are provided as shown in Sample 7-3.

**Sample 7-3**   DBCC SHRINKDATABASE and DBCC SHRINKFILE Syntax

```
DBCC SHRINKDATABASE Syntax
( "database_name" | database_id | 0
    [ ,target_percent ]
    [ , { NOTRUNCATE | TRUNCATEONLY } ] )
[ WITH NO_INFOMSGS ]


DBCC SHRINKFILE Syntax
(    { " file_name " | file_id }
    { [ , EMPTYFILE]
    | [ [ , target_size ] [ , { NOTRUNCATE | TRUNCATEONLY } ] ]
    } )
[ WITH NO_INFOMSGS ]
```

You use DBCC SHRINKDATABASE to shrink all data files in the database and DBCC SHRINKFILE to shrink a specific data file. By default, these commands also compress the database. You can override this option with TRUNCATEONLY or specify that you only want to compress the database with NOTRUNCATE. To suppress informational messages, use WITH NO_INFOMSGS.

The following command compresses and then shrinks the Customer database to 30-percent free space:

```
DBCC SHRINKDATABASE ( Customer, 30 )
```

The following commands compress and then shrink an individual file in the Customer database to 5 MB of free space:

```
USE Customer
DBCC SHRINKFILE ( Customer_Data, 5 )
```

> **Note**   The DBCC SHRINKFILE command is the only method you can use to shrink individual data and log files to make them smaller than their original size. With DBCC SHRINKFILE, you must shrink each file individually, rather than trying to shrink the entire database. Additionally, the truncation options for DBCC SHRINKDATABASE and DBCC SHRINKFILE apply only to data files; they are ignored for log files. You cannot truncate transaction logs with these commands.

# Manipulating Databases

Other core administration tasks include renaming, dropping, deleting, detaching, and attaching databases. These tasks are examined in this section.

## Renaming a Database

Although you cannot rename system databases, you can rename user databases using either SQL Server Management Studio or the ALTER DATABASE MODIFY NAME statement. With the database in single-user or offline mode, right-click the database name in SQL Server Management Studio and select Rename from the shortcut menu. Then type the database name and press Tab.

To use T-SQL to put the database in single-user mode and change the name, complete the following steps:

1. Ask all users to disconnect from the database. Make sure that all SQL Server Management Studio connections to the database are closed. If necessary, kill the user processes, as explained in Chapter 5, "Managing the Enterprise."

2. Access the Query view in SQL Server Management Studio, and then put the database in single-user mode. The following example puts a database called Customer in single-user mode:

```
use master
ALTER DATABASE Customer
SET single_user
GO
```

> **Tip**   You execute commands in the Query view by clicking Execute or by pressing F5. With SQLCMD, you can execute commands by entering the GO statement.

3. Rename the database using the ALTER DATABASE statement. In the following example, the Customer database is renamed cust:

```
ALTER DATABASE Customer
MODIFY NAME = cust
GO
```

4. After you run the SQL commands, set the renamed database back to multiuser mode. The following example sets the cust database to multiuser mode:

```
ALTER DATABASE cust
SET multi_user
GO
```

5. Be sure that all commands, applications, and processes that use the old database name are pointed to the new database name. If you do not do this, you will have problems using the database.

## Dropping and Deleting a Database

In SQL Server 2008, dropping and deleting a database are the same thing. When you drop a database, you remove the database and its associated files from the server. After you drop a database, it is permanently deleted, and you cannot restore it without using a backup. To delete references to a database without removing the database files, use sp_detach_db, as described later in this section.

You cannot drop system databases, and you cannot drop databases that are currently in use by SQL Server or other users. A database can be dropped regardless of its state. However, any replication or database snapshots on a database must be stopped or dropped before the database can be deleted. Furthermore, if the database is configured for log shipping, you should remove log shipping before dropping the database. Also note that a dropped database can be re-created only by restoring a backup. After you drop a database, you should back up the *master* database.

You can drop a database by completing the following steps:

1. In SQL Server Management Studio, right-click the database you want to drop, and then select Delete from the shortcut menu to display the Delete Object dialog box.

2. To delete backup and history information from the *msdb* database, select Delete Backup And Restore History Information For Databases.

3. To close existing connections to the database before deleting it, select Close Existing Connections.

   **Note**   You cannot drop a database that is being used by SQL Server or by other users. For example, if you are restoring the database, or the database is published for replication, you cannot delete it. You also cannot delete the database if there are any active user sessions.

4. Click OK. Optionally, back up the *master* database as explained in Chapter 15, "Backing Up and Recovering Microsoft SQL Server 2008." You back up the *master* database to ensure that the most current system information is stored and that information from the old database will not be restored accidentally with the *master* database.

You can also delete a database with the DROP DATABASE command. The syntax and usage for this command are shown in Sample 7-4.

Sample 7-4   DROP DATABASE Syntax and Usage

```
Syntax
DROP DATABASE { database_name | database_snapshot_name} [,...n]

Usage
use master
ALTER DATABASE Customer
SET single_user
GO
DROP DATABASE "Customer"
GO
```

## Attaching and Detaching Databases

The attach and detach operations are designed primarily to move database files or disable databases without deleting their files. When you detach a database, you remove references to the server in the *master* database, but you do not delete the related database files. Detached databases are not displayed in SQL Server Management Studio, and they are not accessible to users. If you want to use the database again, you can reattach it. Attaching a database creates a new database that references data stored in existing data and log files.

Before you can detach a database, you must ensure that none of the following conditions are true:

- A database snapshot exists on the database. You must drop all of the database's snapshots before you can detach it. Snapshots can be deleted, but they cannot be detached or attached.

- The database is being mirrored. You must stop database mirroring and end the mirror session.

- The database is replicated and published. If it is replicated, the database must be unpublished. Before you can detach it, you need to disable publishing by running sp_replicationdboption or sp_removedbreplication.

- The database is suspect. You must put the database into EMERGENCY mode and then detach it.

Usually, attaching a database places it in the same state that it was in when it was detached. However, SQL Server 2008 disables cross-database ownership chaining and sets the TRUSTWORTHY option to OFF when a database is attached. You can re-enable these features if necessary as discussed in "Managing Cross-Database Chaining and External Access Options" on page 209.

When you attach a database, all primary and secondary data files must be available. If any data file has a different path than it had when the database was first created or last attached, you must specify the file's current path.

### Detaching a Database

When you detach a database, you can specify if you want to update the statistics before the database is detached. Updating statistics makes the database easier to use with read-only media; otherwise, you really do not need the update. To update statistics, set the skipchecks flag to FALSE.

Because full-text catalogs are associated with databases in SQL Server 2008, you can also control whether they are maintained or dropped during the detach operation. By default, full-text catalogs are maintained as part of the database. To drop catalogs, set the KeepFullTextIndexFile flag to FALSE.

You detach a database using sp_detach_db, as shown in Sample 7-5.

**Sample 7-5**   sp_detach_db Syntax and Usage

```
Syntax
sp_detach_db [ @dbname= ] "dbname"
    [ , [ @skipchecks= ] "skipchecks" ]
    [ , [ @KeepFulltextIndexFile= ] "KeepFulltextIndexFile" ]


Usage
exec sp_detach_db "sample", "true"
```

**Tip**   You cannot detach system databases, and you can detach user databases only when they are not in use. Furthermore, before detaching a user database, you might want to close all current connections, put the database in single-user mode, and then run the detach operation.

### Attaching a Database with Multiple Files

When you reattach a database, use the CREATE DATABASE statement with FOR ATTACH. For this statement to work, all primary and secondary data files must be available. If the database has multiple log files, all the log files must be available. The only exception is for a read-write database with a single log file that is currently unavailable. If the database was shut down with no users or open transactions before it was detached, FOR ATTACH automatically rebuilds the log file and updates the primary data file as appropriate. The log file for a read-only database cannot be rebuilt, because the primary data file cannot be updated; you must provide the log file or files in the FOR ATTACH clause.

Any full-text catalogs that are part of the database being attached will be attached with the database. To specify a new path to the full-text catalog, you can specify the catalog file by supplying a directory name without a file name.

When you use the CREATE DATABASE statement with FOR ATTACH, you can specify only the primary file name. This file contains pointers to the original locations of all other database files. If the other files have not changed location, you can specify only the primary file name, and then let the Database Engine use the primary file to find the rest of the files.

Sample 7-6 shows the code required to attach the database using the CREATE DATABASE statement with FOR ATTACH.

**Sample 7-6** The CREATE DATABASE Statement with FOR ATTACH Syntax and Usage

```
Syntax
CREATE DATABASE database_name
    ON <filespec> [ ,...n ]
    FOR { ATTACH [ WITH <service_broker_option> ]
        | ATTACH_REBUILD_LOG }
[;]

<filespec> ::=
{
[ PRIMARY ]
(
    [ NAME = logical_file_name , ]
    FILENAME = "os_file_name"
        [ , SIZE = size [ KB | MB | GB | TB ] ]
        [ , MAXSIZE = { max_size [ KB | MB | GB | TB ] | UNLIMITED }]
        [ , FILEGROWTH = growth_increment [ KB | MB | % ] ]
) [ ,...n ]
}

Usage
CREATE DATABASE Customer
ON (FILENAME = "c:\data\customer_data.mdf")
FOR ATTACH
GO
```

### Attaching a Database with Only Data Files

You might not need old transaction logs in a new database. If this is the case, you might want only to restore data files and let SQL Server create new log files for you. To do this, use the CREATE DATABASE statement with FOR ATTACH_REBUILD_LOG, as shown in Sample 7-7.

**Sample 7-7**    The CREATE DATABASE Statement with FOR ATTACH_REBUILD_LOG Syntax and Usage

```
Syntax
CREATE DATABASE database_name
    ON <filespec> [ ,...n ]
    FOR ATTACH_REBUILD_LOG }
[;]

<filespec> ::=
{
[ PRIMARY ]
(
    [ NAME = logical_file_name , ]
    FILENAME = "os_file_name"
        [ , SIZE = size [ KB | MB | GB | TB ] ]
        [ , MAXSIZE = { max_size [ KB | MB | GB | TB ] | UNLIMITED }]
        [ , FILEGROWTH = growth_increment [ KB | MB | % ] ]
) [ ,...n ]
}

Usage
CREATE DATABASE Customer
ON (FILENAME = "c:\data\customer_data.mdf")
FOR ATTACH_REBUILD_LOG
GO
```

# Tips and Techniques

All great administrators know a few tricks to help manage databases more efficiently and to keep things running smoothly. Here are a few tips to help you with database administration.

## Copying and Moving Databases

All databases except *model*, *msdb*, and *master* can be copied or moved using the Copy Database Wizard. You can also use this wizard to create a copy of a database, to copy or move databases between different instances of Microsoft SQL Server, and to upgrade databases from SQL Server 2000 or SQL Server 2005 to SQL Server 2008. The Copy Database Wizard uses one of two techniques for copy and move operations:

- **Detach and Attach**    This method is the fastest way to copy a database, but it requires the source database to be offline so that it can be detached and copied/ moved. The database is then reattached when the copy/move operation is complete. To use this technique, you must be a member of the sysadmin fixed server role on both the source and destination servers. Also, you should place the database in single-user mode before starting the copy operation to ensure that there are no active sessions. If there are active sessions, the Copy Database Wizard will not execute the move or copy operation.

- **SQL Management Object** This method is slower, but it does not require the source database to be offline. To use this technique, you must be a database owner for the source database and you must have the CREATE DATABASE permission or be a member of the dbcreator fixed server role on the destination database. You do not have to place the database in single-user mode prior to starting the copy/move operation. Active connections are allowed during the operation because the database is never taken offline.

**Note** The copy/move operation preserves full-text catalogs if both the source and destination servers are SQL Server 2008 servers. However, if the source server is a SQL Server 2000 or SQL Server 2005 server, the full-text catalogs must be rebuilt and fully populated again after the copy/move is completed.

When you move databases between different servers or disk drives, the Copy Database Wizard copies the database to the destination server and verifies that it is online. When you move databases between two instances on the same server, a file system move operation is performed. If you elect to move a database, the Copy Database Wizard deletes the source database automatically after the move is completed. However, the Copy Database Wizard does not delete the source database when you perform a copy operation.

You can copy or move a database by completing the following steps:

1. In SQL Server Management Studio, right-click a database in the Object Explorer view, point to Tasks, and then select Copy Database.

   **Note** To use the detach-and-attach method, the SQL Server Agent service must be running and the SQL Server Agent job must be running under an Integration Services Proxy account that can access the file system of both the source and destination servers. For this reason, you should ensure that the SQL Server Agent is running on the destination server before you begin. In SQL Server Management Studio, you can start the SQL Server Agent service, by right-clicking the related node and then selecting Start.

2. When the Copy Database Wizard starts, click Next.

3. On the Select A Source Server page, specify the server that has the database you want to copy or move. Type the DNS or host name of the source server, such as CORPSVR09. (See Figure 7-7.) Alternatively, you can click the button to the right of the Source Server box to browse for available source servers.

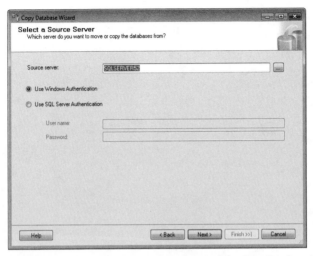

**Figure 7-7**    The Select A Source Server page of the Copy Database Wizard.

4. Windows authentication is used by default, which means that your current login credentials are used to determine if you have appropriate permissions. If you want to use SQL Server authentication, select Use SQL Server Authentication, and then enter your SQL Server user name and password in the text boxes provided. Click Next.

5. On the Select A Destination Server page, specify the server to which you are copying or moving the selected database, and then specify the authentication technique to use. Click Next.

   **Note**    SQL Server Agent must be running on the destination server.

6. Select the transfer method—either Use The Detach And Attach Method or Use The SQL Management Object Method. If you choose to detach and attach the database, the source database is reattached automatically by default if failure occurs. To prevent this, clear the If A Failure Occurs, Reattach The Database check box. Click Next.

7. As shown in Figure 7-8, you can now select the database you want to copy or move. Click Next.

**Figure 7-8**    The Select Databases page of the Copy Database Wizard.

8. Use the Configure Destination Database page shown in Figure 7-9 to define the destination configuration of each database you are copying or moving, one at a time. Pay particular attention to the Source Database and Destination Database boxes. The Source Database box shows the current name of the database on the source. Use the Destination Database box to set the name that will be used on the destination server.

**Figure 7-9**    The Configure Destination page of the Copy Database Wizard.

9. Any data and log files associated with the database are shown with their destination file name and folder. You can change the default locations by typing new values. If you are creating a copy of a database on the same source and destination instance, be sure to change the database name and file names.

10. If the destination database already exists, the default option is to stop the transfer. You can drop the existing database and force the transfer by selecting the Drop Any Database... option.

11. Click Next. If you are copying or moving multiple databases, you will see a Configure Destination Database page for each database.

12. When you have configured all destination databases, the next page you will see is the Configure The Package page. Set the package name and logging options you prefer, and then click Next.

13. You can run the wizard now or schedule the wizard to run at a later time. To run the wizard immediately and perform the copy/move operations, select Run Immediately. To schedule the wizard to run at a later time, select Schedule and then click Change Schedule. You will then be able to schedule this task as a new job. See Chapter 16 for details on scheduling.

14. Click Next. Review your choices, and then click Finish. The wizard will perform the necessary tasks to prepare and create the copy/move package. If a critical error occurs during these tasks, the operation will fail, and you should view the report to determine what error occurred and then resolve it.

## Moving Databases

You can move any system or user-defined database files except for Resource database files using the ALTER DATABASE statement. To move files, you specify the current logical name of the file and the new file path, which includes the new file name. You can move only one file at a time in this manner.

To move data or log files to a new location, follow these steps:

1. Get the logical name of the data and log files associated with the database by typing

```
USE master
SELECT name, physical_name
FROM sys.master_files
WHERE database_id = DB_ID("Personnel");
```

2. Take the database you want to work with offline by typing

```
ALTER DATABASE Personnel
SET offline
GO
```

3. Move one file at a time to the new location by typing

```
ALTER DATABASE Personnel
MODIFY FILE ( NAME = Personnel_Data, FILENAME = "C:\Data\
Personnel_Data.mdf")
GO
```

4. Repeat the previous step to move other data and log files.

5. Put the database online by typing

```
ALTER DATABASE Personnel
SET online
GO
```

You can verify the change or changes by typing

```
USE master
SELECT name, physical_name
FROM sys.master_files
WHERE database_id = DB_ID("Personnel");
```

You can move full-text catalogs by their logical name as well. However, when specifying the new catalog location, you specify only the new_path rather than new_path/file_name. To move a full-text catalog file to a new location, follow these steps:

1. Take the database you want to work with offline by typing

```
ALTER DATABASE database_name
SET offline
GO
```

2. Move one file at a time to the new location by typing

```
ALTER DATABASE database_name
MODIFY FILE ( NAME = logical_name, FILENAME = "new_path".
GO
```

3. Repeat the previous step to move other full-text catalog files as necessary.

4. Put the database online by typing

```
ALTER DATABASE database_name
SET online
GO
```

## Moving and Resizing *tempdb*

The *tempdb* database contains temporary tables created by users, by SQL Server, or by both. SQL Server 2008 does not store complete transactions for temporary tables in *tempdb*. With temporary tables, SQL Server 2008 stores only enough information to roll back a transaction and not enough to redo a transaction.

The *tempdb* database is created each time you start the SQL Server service, which ensures that the database starts clean. As with other databases, the default structure of *tempdb* is based on the *model* database. This means that each time you start SQL Server, a snapshot is taken of the current *model* database and applied to *tempdb*.

By default, the *tempdb* primary data file has a size of 8 MB and is set to automatically grow the database by 10 percent when necessary. On a busy server, this 8 MB can fill up quickly, and as a result the server might need to frequently expand *tempdb*. Unfortunately, while *tempdb* expands, SQL Server locks the database. This can slow down queries and make the server seem unresponsive. Following are some ways you can improve the performance of *tempdb*:

- Permanently expand *tempdb* to accommodate space needs during busy periods. To do this, follow the steps described in "Expanding Databases and Logs Manually" on page 213. Even if the *model* database is smaller, *tempdb* will retain this new size.

- By default, *tempdb* is stored in the same location as other data. To resolve any performance issues, you can create a secondary data file for *tempdb* and put this file on its own drive. Or you can move *tempdb* and all its associated files to a new location.

You can move individual *tempdb* files or all *tempdb* files by completing the following steps:

1. Get the logical name of the data and log files associated with *tempdb* by typing

   ```
   Use Master
   SELECT name, physical_name
   FROM sys.master_files
   WHERE database_id = DB_ID("tempdb");
   GO
   ```

2. Move each data and log file to a new location one at a time by typing

   ```
   USE master
   GO
   ALTER DATABASE tempdb
   MODIFY FILE (NAME = logical_name, FILENAME = "new_path/file_name")
   GO
   ```

3. Repeat the previous step to move other data and log files as necessary.

4. Stop and restart SQL Server.

You can verify the change or changes by typing

```
USE master
SELECT name, physical_name
FROM sys.master_files
WHERE database_id = DB_ID("tempdb");
```

## Creating Secondary Data and Log Files

Secondary data and log files can improve the performance of busy databases and can help make large databases easier to manage. You might want to create secondary files to distribute the load over several drives. For example, you could place the primary file on drive D, secondary files on drive E, and transaction logs on drive F. See "SQL Server 2008 and Your Hardware" on page 3 for more tips on drives and RAID arrays.

Another reason you might want to create secondary files is to make it easier to restore a large database. For example, if you have a 10-GB database in a single file, you can restore the database only on a 10-GB drive, which you might not have at 3:00 A.M. on a Sunday if a drive fails. Instead, create several smaller files for the database, such as five 2-GB files, and then you can restore these files to several smaller drives if necessary.

You can create secondary data or log files by completing the following steps:

1. Start SQL Server Management Studio. In the Object Explorer view, connect to the appropriate server, and then work your way down to the Databases folder.

2. Right-click the database you want to manage, and then select Properties from the shortcut menu to open the Database Properties dialog box.

3. Select the Files page from the Select A Page list in the Database Properties dialog box.

4. On the Files page, click Add to set a secondary data file. Then, in the Database Files area, type a new file name, such as Personnel_Data2 or Personnel_Log2.

5. Set the file type:

   ❑ To create the new file as a data file, select Data under File Type.

   ❑ To create the new file as a log file, select Log under File Type.

6. Set the initial size of the file, and then click the button to the right of the Autogrowth box. Then you can set Autogrowth options for the new data or log file.

7. Click the button to the right of the Path box to find a new path, or you can enter a new path directly. The file name is set based on the logical name and file type.

8. Click OK to make the changes.

## Preventing Transaction Log Errors

The transaction log is essential to the smooth running of SQL Server. If the log fills up or otherwise fails, SQL Server cannot process most types of queries. To ensure that the transaction log runs smoothly, you might want to use these techniques:

- To reduce the load on the transaction log, use SQL commands that are not logged. This invalidates the transaction logs, as explained in Chapter 16.

- To ensure that the log is cleaned out periodically, set the database Recovery Model to Simple. This invalidates the transaction logs, as explained in Chapter 16.

- To prevent the log from running out of space, do not set a maximum file size, but do increase the frequency of the log backup and watch the amount of free drive space closely.

- To make sure you can recover transactions, increase the permanent size of the log and increase the frequency of the log backup.

## Preventing a Filegroup Is Full Error

When you encounter a situation in which it is not possible to write to a data file, you will see a Filegroup Is Full error. This error usually occurs when the data file has reached its maximum size or you have run out of file space. To reduce the chances of this error reoccurring, you can use the following techniques:

- Do not set a maximum file size.

- Watch the amount of free drive space closely.

- Schedule data files to be compacted periodically.

- Remove unused tables, indexes, or objects.

## Creating a New Database Template

The *model* database is used as the template for all new databases. You can avoid repetitive work by modifying the options and properties of the *model* database; then any new databases created on the server will inherit these options and properties.

## Configuring Database Encryption

SQL Server 2008 provides Transparent Data Encryption (TDE) as a database encryption solution. When enabled, TDE performs real-time I/O encryption and decryption of data and log files. TDE relies on a database encryption key (DEK) stored as a certificate in the *master* database or an asymmetric key protected by an encryption module. Encrypting a database with TDE provides physical protection for the data and log files but does not provide encryption across communication channels. You can encrypt communication channels as discussed in "Configuring Security for Native Client Configurations" on page 75. Also keep in mind that when you use TDE, FILESTREAM data is not encrypted.

Before you can use TDE, you must create a master key, create or obtain a certificate protected by the master key, and create a database encryption key and protect it by the certificate. Afterward, you must enable encryption for the database. Sample 7-8 provides the syntax and usage for the related Transact-SQL commands.

**Sample 7-8**  Sample 7-8 Configuring Database Encrypt

```
Syntax
USE master;
GO
CREATE MASTER KEY ENCRYPTION BY PASSWORD = 'Password';
GO
CREATE CERTIFICATE CertificateName WITH SUBJECT =
    'CertificateSubject'
GO
USE DatabaseName
GO
CREATE DATABASE ENCRYPTION KEY
    WITH ALGORITHM = { AES_128 | AES_192 | AES_256
        | TRIPLE_DES_3KEY }
    ENCRYPTION BY SERVER CERTIFICATE CertificateName
GO
ALTER DATABASE DatabaseName
SET ENCRYPTION ON
GO


Usage
USE master;
GO
CREATE MASTER KEY ENCRYPTION BY PASSWORD = 'ObyGoxDandy2974728';
GO
CREATE CERTIFICATE PersDBCert WITH SUBJECT = 'Certificate for
    Personnel DB'
GO
USE Personnel
GO
CREATE DATABASE ENCRYPTION KEY WITH ALGORITHM = TRIPLE_DES_3KEY
    ENCRYPTION BY SERVER CERTIFICATE PersDBCert
GO
ALTER DATABASE Personnel
SET ENCRYPTION ON
GO
```

To manage the encryption state of the database using SQL Server Management Studio, follow these steps:

1. In the Object Explorer view in SQL Server Management Studio, right-click the database you want to configure, and then select Properties from the shortcut menu.

2. In the Database Properties dialog box, select Options from the Select A Page list. You can now

- ❑ Turn on database encryption by setting Encryption Enabled to True.

- ❑ Turn off database encryption by setting Encryption Enabled to False.

3. Click OK when you have finished setting the options. Your changes take effect immediately without restarting the server.

You can determine the state of the database encryption using the sys.dm_database_encryption_keys view. Once you enable TDE, all files and filegroups in the database are encrypted. If any filegroups in a database are marked READ ONLY, the database encryption operation will fail. With database mirroring or log shipping, both databases will be encrypted and the log transactions will be encrypted when sent between the database servers.

When you enable encryption, the Database Engine closes out the virtual transaction log and starts the next virtual transaction log to ensure that no clear text is left after the database is set for encryption. The *tempdb* system database is encrypted for similar reasons. Additionally, any new full-text indexes will be encrypted when a database is set for encryption.

> **Tip**   As part of the encryption process, the Database Engine also compresses the data, though not as much as when you use compression separately. As the encrypted data is compressed, you will not be able to significantly compress the backup storage. Because of this, Microsoft recommends that you do not use data encryption and backup compression together.

Backup files of encrypted databases also are encrypted by using the database encryption key. When you restore encrypted backups, the certificate protecting the database encryption key must be available. Thus, in addition to backing up databases, you must maintain backups of the server certificates to prevent data loss. If you lose a certificate, you will lose your data.

The Database Engine doesn't automatically replicate data from TDE-enabled databases in an encrypted form. You must separately enable TDE if you want to protect the distribution and subscriber databases.

# Chapter 8
# Full-Text Search Administration

Full-text search allows extensive word searches of textual data, and it is an additional component that you can add to the Microsoft SQL Server 2008 installation. (For details, see "Installing a SQL Server Instance" on page 39.) After you install the Full-Text Search component, you can manage full-text searches by using the methods described in this chapter.

Full-text search for SQL Server 2008 is significantly different from full-text search for earlier releases of SQL Server, where full-text indexes resided in full-text catalogs that belonged to filegroups, had physical paths, and were treated as database files. In SQL Server 2008, a full-text catalog is represented logically as a virtual object that refers to a group of full-text indexes rather than as a database file with a physical path.

## Full-Text Catalogs and Indexes

Unlike earlier releases of SQL Server, SQL Server 2008 does not use Microsoft Search Service (MSFTESQL) for full-text search. In SQL Server 2008, full-text search is provided by the Microsoft Full-Text Engine for SQL Server, which handles all indexing and query functions and is fully integrated with the query processor. Additionally, in SQL Server 2008, user databases are always enabled for full-text search and cannot be disabled. SQL Server 2008 Setup upgrades database files and full-text catalogs from a previous version of SQL Server during the installation process. Any database you attach, restore, or copy using the Copy Database Wizard will be upgraded to SQL Server 2008 Full-Text Search.

The filter daemon host (fdhost.exe) replaces the filter daemon process (mstfefd.exe) used in earlier versions of SQL Server. The filter daemon host loads the components used for index and query, including word breakers that help find word boundaries, stemmers that help conjugate verbs, and document filters that help extract textual information. In SQL Server 2008, each instance uses its own set of word breakers, stemmers, and filters, no longer relying on the operating system versions of these components. SQL Server 2008 includes word breakers for over 40 languages.

You can view a list of the languages supported by Full-Text Search by using the following Transact-SQL (T-SQL) statement: SELECT * FROM sys.fulltext_languages. The language of the full-text indexed column you are querying determines the way the text is analyzed. All columns listed in a single full-text query function clause must use the same language, unless you've specified the LANGUAGE option in the query.

If you haven't specified a language for a column, the default language is the value of the configuration option default full-text language. For localized versions of SQL Server, SQL Server Setup sets the default full-text language so that it matches the default language of the operating system. For nonlocalized versions of SQL Server, the default full-text language is English.

Document filters help SQL Server extract textual data from binary data. As you can store many document types in a single varbinary(max) or image column, SQL Server chooses the correct filter based on the file extension. Because the file extension is not visible when the file is stored in a varbinary(max) or image column, the file extension must be stored in a separate column in the table, called a *type column*. The type column can be of any character-based data type and contains the document file extension, such as .doc for a Microsoft Office Word document.

You can view a list of document filters supported by Full-Text Search by using the following Transact-SQL (T-SQL) statement: SELECT * FROM sys.fulltext_document_types. Each document type supported is listed according to its file extension and the path to the related filter. Generally, filters are implemented as dynamic-link libraries (DLLs).

When upgrading to SQL Server 2008, Setup allows you to choose one of the following full-text upgrade options:

- **Import**   Imports the full-text indexes. If a full-text catalog is not available, the associated full-text indexes are rebuilt. This option is the default for SQL Server 2005 databases. However, don't use this option if you are at all concerned about recall accuracy.

- **Rebuild**   Rebuilds the full-text indexes. Rebuilding indexes can take a long time and takes longer than if the indexes are imported or reset. This option is the default for SQL Server 2000 databases.

- **Reset**   Resets full-text indexes and removes full-text catalogs. After Setup finishes the upgrade, it disables all full-text indexes and sets crawls so that they are not started automatically. The catalog will remain empty until you manually issue a full population, after the upgrade completes.

**Note**   During an upgrade of any full-text catalog that contains data files, the setup process creates a new filegroup on the same disk and any full-text index from that catalog is placed in the new filegroup if the root path exists. If the old full-text catalog path is invalid, the setup process keeps the full-text index in the same filegroup as the base table or, for a partitioned table, in the primary filegroup.

In addition to upgrades during setup, you can upgrade database files and full-text catalogs by attaching or restoring a database or full-text index from an earlier release of SQL Server to a server running SQL Server 2008. You also can upgrade using the Copy Database Wizard. For these types of upgrades, the upgrade_option server property controls the full-text upgrade technique that SQL Server uses. You can set this property using the Server Properties dialog box in SQL Server Management Studio or the sp_fulltext_service stored procedure.

To manage the full-text upgrade options using SQL Server Management Studio, follow these steps:

1. In the Object Explorer view in SQL Server Management Studio, right-click the server you want to configure, and then select Properties from the shortcut menu.

2. In the Server Properties dialog box, select Advanced from the Select A Page list.

3. Set the Full-Text Catalog Upgrade Option to Import, Rebuild, or Reset as necessary. Click OK when you are finished setting options. Your changes take effect immediately without restarting the server.

To manage the full-text upgrade options using the sp_fulltext_service stored procedure, follow these steps:

1. In the Object Explorer view in SQL Server Management Studio, right-click the server you want to configure, and then select New Query from the shortcut menu.

2. In the Query view, type the following commands:

```
USE master
GO
EXEC sp_fulltext_service @action='upgrade_option',
    @value=<option_value>
GO
```

where *option_value* is 0 for Rebuild, 1 for Reset, or 2 for Import. The following example shows the commands required to use the import technique during upgrades:

```
USE master
GO
EXEC sp_fulltext_service @action='upgrade_option', @value=2
GO
```

3. Execute the query by clicking Execute or by pressing F5. If the option is set properly, the command should complete successfully.

Several administration tasks are required to use full-text search. You must do the following:

- Install the Full-Text Search component using SQL Server 2008 Setup.

- Create a full-text catalog for the database.

- Have a unique index.

- Create a full-text index on specific tables and views.

**Real World**    You can use CREATE FULLTEXT CATALOG to create full-text catalogs. Because catalogs are now a part of the database, you no longer need to use the IN PATH clause to set the file location.

Before you create a searchable full-text index from a catalog, you must ensure the table or view has a unique, single-column, non-nullable index. The full-text search engine uses this unique index to map rows in the tables to unique keys. You can create a unique index using CREATE UNIQUE INDEX. The syntax is

```
CREATE UNIQUE INDEX indexname on table(uniquecolumn)
```

The following example creates an index called ui_per on the Employee table in the Personnel database using the EmpID column:

```
use Personnel
go
CREATE UNIQUE INDEX ui_per on dbo.Employee(EmpID)
go
```

After you have a unique key, you can create a full-text index on the database table using CREATE FULLTEXT INDEX or Object Explorer view. A table is automatically enabled for full-text indexing as soon as a full-text index is created on it and a column is added to the index. A table is automatically disabled for full-text indexing when the last column is dropped from its full-text index.

When you create a full-text catalog, the Database Engine creates full-text indexes of textual data contained in the database. Then the Database Engine manages the indexes and provides the primary mechanism for examining the data they contain. The concept of a full-text index in SQL Server might be a bit different than you have encountered elsewhere. In SQL Server, a full-text index stores information about keywords and their location within a specific column. These text indexes are created for each table in the database, and groups of indexes are contained in catalogs. Each full-text catalog is treated as part of the database, and it is included in the database to facilitate backup and restore utilities so that you can back up and restore full-text catalogs with other SQL Server data, eliminating the need to repopulate catalogs completely after a database restore.

**Note**    Full-text catalogs are also attached and detached with the database, so full-text catalogs are preserved when you move databases to new locations. You no longer have to delete and rebuild the full-text catalog. You simply detach the database, copy it to a new location, and then reattach it. The full-text catalog is preserved.

The all-table column text is indexed, including the columns containing the XML data type. This allows you to perform full-text searches on column values that contain XML data as well as any other type of textual data. In early versions of SQL Server, you could query linked servers, but you could not perform full-text queries against linked servers.

When searching tables in early versions, you were limited to searching one column or all columns, but now you can search any number of columns. SQL Server 2008 allows you to issue full-text queries referencing a remote linked server and to search across multiple columns.

Full-text indexes are defined on base tables and views that have one or more full-text indexed base tables. They are not defined on views, system tables, or temporary tables. The ability to search on views is an important new change for SQL Server 2008. Indexes are populated with key values that have information about the significant words in a table, such as the column they are in and their location in the column. You can create, modify, and implement full-text catalogs and indexes using both stored procedures and data definition language (DDL) statements. In Transact-SQL, you can test rows against a full-text search condition using the functions *contains* and *freetext*. You can also return the set of rows that match a full-text search condition using the functions *containstable* and *freetexttable*.

# Managing Full-Text Catalogs

Each database that you want to search must have its own full-text catalog. When you create a catalog, you can set a schedule for populating the catalog on a regular basis, or you can elect to manually populate the catalog as necessary. Populating the catalog updates the full-text indexes for the catalog and ensures that the search results are accurate. SQL Server supports several methods for populating catalogs:

- **Full population**   The Database Engine builds index entries for all rows in all the tables or views covered by the full-text catalog. In most cases, you perform a full population only when you create a catalog or need to refresh the entire contents of a catalog.

- **Incremental population**   The Database Engine changes index entries only for rows that have been added, deleted, or modified since the last population. You can perform incremental population only on tables or views that have a time-stamp column. If a table or view does not have a time-stamp column, full populations are always performed.

- **Update population**   The Database Engine uses update population in conjunction with change tracking. Change tracking of tables and views allows Full-Text Search to track changes in the catalog or views and update the catalog either automatically or manually. If you disable change tracking, you can perform incremental population only on tables or views that have a time-stamp column (and if a table or view does not have a time-stamp column, full populations are always performed).

Creating a catalog is only one part of the indexing process. After you create the catalog, you must select individual tables or views for indexing and associate these with the catalog. You also need to specify the individual table or view columns that should be indexed. Periodically, you might also need to clean up old catalogs. Use sys.fulltext_catalogs to obtain a list of all the full-text catalogs associated with a database. Use sys.fulltext_indexes to obtain a list of all the tables and views in a database that have been enabled for full-text processing.

## Viewing Catalog Properties

Catalogs are stored separately from the databases themselves. You can set the catalog file location when you create the catalog. You cannot change or view the file location after the catalog is created. To examine other catalog configuration properties on a database for which you have configured full-text search, complete the following steps:

1. Start SQL Server Management Studio, and then connect to a server of your choice.

2. Use the Object Explorer view to access a database. Expand the server node and the Databases node.

3. Under the Databases node, expand the Storage and Full Text Catalogs nodes to display the catalog or catalogs for the selected database.

4. Right-click the catalog, and then choose Properties to open the Full-Text Catalog Properties dialog box shown in Figure 8-1.

**Figure 8-1**   The General page of the Full-Text Catalog Properties dialog box.

5. The General page provides the following information:

   ❑ **Unique Key Count**   Specifies the number of unique keys cataloged.

   ❑ **Item Count**   Specifies the number of items cataloged.

❑ **Owner** Specifies the catalog owner. If no owner was set when the catalog was created, the owner is set as dbo.

❑ **Accent Sensitive** Indicates if the catalog is accent sensitive. The default sensitivity is set the same as the database.

❑ **Catalog Size** Specifies the total size of the catalog on disk.

❑ **Default Catalog** Indicates if the catalog is the default for the database.

❑ **Name** Specifies the name of the catalog.

❑ **Population Status** Indicates whether the catalog is being built or updated (referred to as populating).

❑ **Last Population Date** Specifies the date the catalog was last populated. For new catalogs, this will be blank.

## Creating Catalogs

You need catalogs to perform full-text searches of databases. A single database can have multiple catalogs associated with it, and you can use these catalogs to perform different types of searches. For example, in a customer database, you can create one catalog for searching company contact information and another for searching account history.

You cannot create full-text catalogs in the *master*, *model*, or *tempdb* databases. Although a full-text catalog can have several full-text indexes, a full-text index can be part of only one full-text catalog. To create a catalog for a database, complete the following steps:

1. Start SQL Server Management Studio, and then connect to a server.

2. Use the Object Explorer view to access a database. Expand the server node and the Databases node.

3. Under the Databases node, expand the Storage and Full Text Catalogs nodes to display the catalog or catalogs for the selected database.

4. Right-click Full-Text Catalogs, and then select New Full-Text Catalog to display the New Full-Text Catalog properties dialog box shown in Figure 8-2.

5. Type a descriptive name for the catalog in the Full-Text Catalog Name box.

6. Use the Owner box to set the catalog owner. The default catalog owner is dbo. If you do not want to use the default, type a new user or database role name in the text box provided or click the Options button (. . .) to browse for a user or database role to use.

7. If you want to make the catalog the default for the selected database, select Set As Default Catalog.

**Figure 8-2**   New Full-Text Catalog dialog box.

8. By default, catalog accent sensitivity is set the same as the selected database. If you want to allow accent-sensitive searches, select the Sensitive option. Otherwise, select Insensitive to allow searches to match characters without regard to accents.

9. Click OK to create the catalog.

Next, you will need to enable indexing and populate the catalog.

## Enabling Indexing of Tables and Views

You can enable indexing of a table or view by completing the following steps:

1. Start SQL Server Management Studio, and then connect to a server.

2. Use the Object Explorer view to access a database. Expand the server node and the Databases node.

3. Under the Databases node, expand Tables or Views as appropriate. Right-click the table or view, point to Full-Text Index, and then select Define Full-Text Index to start the Full-Text Indexing Wizard. Click Next.

4. Select a unique index for the table or view, and then click Next. The index is used as a unique constraint on a single column in the table and can be used in joins. If the table or view does not have a unique index, you must exit the wizard, create

an index (as discussed in "Full-Text Catalogs and Indexes" on page 234), and then restart this process.

5. As shown in Figure 8-3, select the character-based or image-based columns that you want to index. Each column can be set with a language constraint that identifies the natural language of the column. With text and binary data, you can also specify a document type. Click Next.

> **Tip**   Type the first letter of the language to find it more quickly in the drop-down list.

**Figure 8-3**   Select table columns.

6. Specify if you want the changes to the tables and views to be tracked for the purpose of updating the full-text catalog. When you make a decision about automatically tracking changes, keep the following information in mind:

   ❑ If you elect to automatically track changes, the wizard will fully populate the catalog with the index for this table before exiting. The catalog will also be configured so that changes are tracked as they occur, and the changes will be applied automatically to keep the catalog up to date with regard to the current table or view.

   ❑ If you elect to manually track changes, the wizard will fully populate the catalog with the index for this table before exiting. Then you can apply tracked changes manually to keep the catalog up to date with regard to the current table or view.

❑    If you do not want to track changes and do not want the catalog to be populated at this time, select Do Not Track Changes and clear Start Full Population When Index Is Created.

7.    Click Next. As shown in Figure 8-4, use the Select Full-Text Catalog drop-down list to choose an existing catalog, or select Create A New Catalog, and then configure the new catalog options.

**Figure 8-4**    Select a catalog, index filegroup, and stoplist.

8.    Use the Select Index Filegroup list to specify the filegroup in which the index should be created. If you don't specify a filegroup, the index will be part of the default filegroup used for all full-text indexes. The default full-text indexing filegroup is the primary filegroup for the database. You might want to store full-text indexes in secondary filegroups because this can give you additional recovery options.

9.    By default, full-text indexes use the system stoplist. If you don't want to use the system stoplist, select Off under Select Full-Text Stoplist.

10.    Click Next. You can now select or create population schedules for the catalog. You can also select or create a population schedule for the currently selected table.

**Real World**    In most cases, you will want to create schedules for populating an entire catalog rather than an individual table. However, in some cases, populating individual tables makes sense, especially if the contents of a particular table change frequently and contents of other tables change rarely.

11. Click Next, and then click Finish. SQL Server Management Studio defines the full-text index for the table. If you selected the Do Not Track Changes option and cleared Start Full Population When Index Is Created, you must populate the index manually or create a schedule for performing this task. Otherwise, the index is populated in the catalog.

## Editing Indexing of Tables and Views

To change the indexing settings of a table, complete the following steps:

1. Start SQL Server Management Studio, and then connect to a server.

2. Use the Object Explorer view to access a database. Expand the server node and the Databases node.

3. Under the Databases node, expand Tables or Views as appropriate. Right-click the table or view, point to Full-Text Index, and then select Properties to display the Full-Text Indexing Properties dialog box for the table or view. Then use the dialog box options to edit the settings you want to change.

The Full-Text Indexing Properties dialog box has three pages:

- **General**   Shows the current configuration. Properties that are dimmed cannot be changed. Select System or Off for the Full-Text Index Stoplist option to enable or disable the system stoplist. Select or clear the Full-Text Indexing Enabled option to enable or disable indexing. Use the Change Tracking option to configure manual or automatic change tracking, or to turn change tracking off.

- **Columns**   Shows the unique index and index columns. You can change the unique index and the index column settings using the options provided.

- **Schedule**   Shows currently defined schedules for populating the full-text index. You can add and modify schedules using the options provided.

## Disabling and Removing Full-Text Indexing from Tables and Views

If you want to stop full-text indexing of a table or view temporarily, you can disable the related full-text index. It is useful to disable full-text indexing if you are making a lot of updates to a table or view, to avoid triggering an update, or to prevent a scheduled incremental or full population of the database.

If you decide that you do not want to index a table or view any more, you can remove full-text indexing completely. Removing full-text indexing removes all references to the table or view in the related catalog. This data must be re-created if you later decide to restore full-text indexing.

To disable or remove full-text indexing from a table or view, complete the following steps:

1. Start SQL Server Management Studio, and then connect to a server.

2. Use the Object Explorer view to access a database. Expand the server node and the Databases node.

3. Under the Databases node, expand Tables or Views as appropriate. You can now do the following:

    ❑ Disable the full-text index. To do so, right-click the table or view, point to Full-Text Index, and then select Disable Full-Text Index.

    ❑ Delete the full-text index. To do so, right-click the table or view, point to Full-Text Index, and then select Delete Full-Text Index. When prompted to confirm the action, click OK.

## Populating Full-Text Catalogs

After you select the tables and views you want to index, you can fully populate the catalog so that the table or view can be searched in connection with the related catalog. After the catalog is populated with this data, you can maintain the catalog related to a table or view manually, according to a schedule, or through change tracking. With scheduled jobs, you set a schedule that instructs SQL Server Agent to run a one-time or recurring job that populates the catalog. You can populate catalogs at the database level or at the table level. In most cases, you will want to create schedules for populating an entire catalog rather than an individual table. However, there are times when populating individual tables makes sense, especially if the contents of a particular table change frequently and the contents of other tables change rarely.

### Populating Catalogs Manually for All Selected Tables and Views

To populate a catalog manually with text for all tables and views selected for indexing, complete the following steps:

1. Start SQL Server Management Studio, and then connect to a server.

2. Use the Object Explorer view to access a database. Expand the server node and the Databases node.

3. Under the Databases node, expand the Storage and Full Text Catalogs nodes to display the catalog or catalogs for the selected database.

4. Right-click Full Text Catalogs, and then select Rebuild All to rebuild the entire full-text index. To rebuild only a catalog of interest, right-click the catalog and select Rebuild.

## Using Scheduled Jobs to Populate Catalogs for All Selected Tables and Views

To set a schedule for populating a catalog with text for all tables and views selected for indexing, complete the following steps:

1. Start SQL Server Management Studio, and then connect to a server.

2. Use the Object Explorer view to access a database. Expand the server node and the Databases node.

3. Under the Databases node, expand the Storage and Full Text Catalogs nodes to display the catalog or catalogs for the selected database.

4. Right-click the catalog you want to work with, and then select Properties to display the Full-Text Catalog Properties dialog box.

5. Select the Schedule page under Select A Page. Any currently scheduled jobs are listed by name and population type. You can edit or delete existing jobs, enable or disable existing jobs, or click New to create a new schedule for populating the catalog.

6. In the New Full-Text Indexing Catalog Schedule dialog box, shown in Figure 8-5, type a descriptive name for the job used to schedule the catalog population.

**Figure 8-5**  Creating a new full-text indexing schedule for a full-text catalog.

7. Set the schedule type. Typically, you will want to select either One Time or Recurring.

8. Use the remaining options to determine when the job runs. One-time jobs run at a specific date and time. Recurring jobs run daily, weekly, or monthly at a specific date and time.

> **Tip**    In most cases, you will want to create a recurring job. The first time the job is run, it will perform a full population of the catalog if this task has not been performed previously. On successive runs, the job will perform the population according to the population type. SQL Server Agent runs scheduled tasks. The agent identifies scheduled tasks by the unique job name you specify. You will learn more about SQL Server Agent in Chapter 16, "Database Automation and Maintenance."

9. Click OK to close the New Full-Text Indexing Catalog Schedule dialog box.

10. In the Full-Text Catalog Properties dialog box, click in the Population Type column for the scheduled job you just created. The options depend on the state of the catalog and include the following:

   ❑ **Catalog – Full**    Performs a full population of the catalog, which essentially rebuilds the catalog. This is a task that you will select only occasionally. For example, you might rebuild a catalog once a quarter.

   ❑ **Catalog – Incremental**    Performs an incremental population of the catalog based on time-stamp changes. With change tracking, an incremental build updates the catalog for tracked changes as well. You can also apply tracked changes manually.

   ❑ **Catalog – Optimize**    Performs an optimized build of the catalog to improve performance. This is a task you might want to schedule periodically to enhance search performance. However, optimization, like a rebuild, can be a time-consuming and resource-intensive process, so you will want to schedule this task when activity levels are low.

11. Click OK.

### Populating Catalogs Manually for a Specific Table or View

To manually populate a catalog with text for a single table or view, complete the following steps:

1. Start SQL Server Management Studio, and then connect to a server.

2. Use the Object Explorer view to access a database. Expand the server node and the Databases node.

3. Under the Databases node, expand Tables or Views as appropriate. Right-click the table or view, point to Full-Text Index, and then select Start Full Population or Start Incremental Population. If you want to stop the population, right-click the table or view, select Full-Text Index, and then select Stop Population.

### Using Scheduled Jobs to Populate Catalogs for a Specific Table or View

To set a schedule for populating a catalog with text for a single table, complete the following steps:

1. Start SQL Server Management Studio, and then connect to a server.

2. Use the Object Explorer view to access a database. Expand the server node and the Databases node.

3. Under the Databases node, expand Tables or Views as appropriate. Right-click the table or view, point to Full-Text Index, and then select Properties.

4. Select the Schedule page under Select A Page. Any current scheduled jobs are listed by name and population type. You can edit or delete existing jobs, enable or disable existing jobs, or click New to create a new schedule for populating the catalog with text for the table or index.

5. In the New Full-Text Indexing Table Schedule dialog box, shown in Figure 8-6, type a descriptive name for the job used to schedule the catalog population.

**Figure 8-6**   Creating a new full-text indexing schedule for a table or view.

6. Set the schedule type. Typically, you will want to use One Time or Recurring.

7. Use the remaining options to determine when the job runs. One-time jobs run at a specific date and time. Recurring jobs run daily, weekly, or monthly at a specific date and time.

**Note**  In most cases, you will want to create a recurring job. The first time the job is run, it will perform a full population of the catalog if this task has not been performed previously. On successive runs, the job will perform the population according to the population type. SQL Server Agent runs scheduled tasks. The agent identifies scheduled tasks by the unique job name you specify. You will learn more about SQL Server Agent in Chapter 16.

8. Click OK to close the New Full-Text Indexing Table Schedule dialog box.

9. In the Full-Text Index Properties dialog box, click in the Population Type column for the scheduled job you just created. The options are as follows:

   ❏ **Table – Full**   Performs a full population of the catalog, which essentially rebuilds the index for the table in the catalog. This is a task that you will select only occasionally.

   ❏ **Table – Incremental**   Performs an incremental population of the catalog based on time-stamp changes to the table or index.

   ❏ **Table – Update**   Performs an update population of the catalog based on tracked changes. You can also apply tracked changes manually.

10. Click OK.

## Rebuilding Current Catalogs

When you make frequent changes to a database, catalogs can sometimes become inconsistent with the contents of a database. Over an extended period of time, catalogs also can become quite large. To resynchronize the catalog with the contents of the database or to compress a large catalog so that it does not waste space, you must rebuild the catalog.

You can rebuild catalogs individually or you can rebuild all the catalogs used by a database. When you rebuild a catalog, you delete the existing catalog and re-create it. To rebuild a single catalog, complete the following steps:

1. Start SQL Server Management Studio, and then connect to a server.

2. Use the Object Explorer view to access a database. Expand the server node and the Databases node.

3. Under the Databases node, expand the Storage and Full Text Catalogs nodes to display the catalog or catalogs for the selected database.

4. Right-click the catalog, and then select Rebuild. When prompted to confirm the action, click OK to allow the Database Engine to delete the existing catalog and then rebuild it.

5. Use the Rebuild Full-Text Catalog dialog box to track the rebuild status, stop the rebuild, and display a rebuild report. Note any errors or warnings, and read the related details in the report carefully. Click Close.

To rebuild all catalogs associated with a database, complete the following steps:

1. Start SQL Server Management Studio, and then connect to a server.

2. Use the Object Explorer view to access a database. Expand the server node and the Databases node.

3. Under the Databases node, expand the Storage and Full Text Catalogs nodes to display the catalog or catalogs for the selected database.

4. Right-click Full Text Catalogs, and then select Rebuild All. When prompted to confirm the action, click OK to allow the Database Engine to delete all existing catalogs on the database and then rebuild them.

5. Use the Rebuild All Full-Text Catalogs dialog box to track the rebuild status, stop the rebuild, and display a rebuild report. Note any errors or warnings, and read the related details in the report carefully. Click Close.

**Caution**   Rebuilding catalogs can be a time-consuming and resource-intensive process. In a production environment, you should rebuild catalogs only during off-peak hours.

## Cleaning Up Old Catalogs

Although the Full-Text Search components do a good job of maintaining indexes and cleaning up after themselves, you will want to monitor the number and size of catalog files. You should also regularly clean up old catalogs to eliminate wasted storage space. You do this by completing the following steps:

1. Start SQL Server Management Studio, and then connect to a server.

2. Use the Object Explorer view to access a database. Expand the server node and the Databases node.

3. Under the Databases node, expand the Storage and Full Text Catalogs nodes to display the catalog or catalogs for the selected database.

4. Right-click the catalog, and then select Properties to display the Full-Text Catalog Properties dialog box.

5. On the General page, select Optimize Catalog, and then click OK.

## Removing Catalogs

To remove a single catalog, complete the following steps:

1. Start SQL Server Management Studio, and then connect to a server.

2. Use the Object Explorer view to access a database. Expand the server node and the Databases node.

3. Under the Databases node, expand the Storage and Full Text Catalogs nodes to display the catalog or catalogs for the selected database.

4. Right-click the catalog, and then select Delete.

5. The Delete Object dialog box shows you which catalog you are deleting. Click OK to remove the catalog.

# Managing Full-Text Search

SQL Server supports all languages that are supported by Microsoft Windows operating systems. To help the Database Engine perform searches efficiently, you should set the default language for full-text searches, manage stopwords and stoplists, and configure the thesaurus file.

## Setting the Default Full-Text Language

When you select a default full-text language, the Database Engine uses that language to index data stored in char, nchar, varchar, nvarchar, text, and ntext columns. This language is also the default language used at query time if the language_term clause is not specified as part of a full-text search. If you don't set a default full-text language, this option is set the same as the default language for the SQL Server instance.

You can determine the languages supported and the related language codes using the sys.fulltext_languages view. Enter the following query in the Query view:

```
use master
go
select * from sys.fulltext_languages
go
```

To manage the default full-text language option for a server using SQL Server Management Studio, follow these steps:

1. In the Object Explorer view in SQL Server Management Studio, right-click the server you want to configure, and then select Properties from the shortcut menu.

2. In the Server Properties dialog box, select Advanced from the Select A Page list.

3. Set the Default Full-Text Language option to the desired default language using the appropriate language code as specified in the sys.fulltext_languages view. Click OK when you are finished setting options. Your changes take effect immediately without restarting the server.

To manage the full-text upgrade options using the sp_configure procedure, follow these steps:

1. In the Object Explorer view in SQL Server Management Studio, right-click the server you want to configure, and then select New Query from the shortcut menu.

2. In the Query view, where *language_id* is a language code defined in the sys.fulltext_languages view, type the following commands:

```
EXEC sys.sp_configure 'default full-text language', <language_id>
GO
RECONFIGURE WITH OVERRIDE
GO
```

The following example shows the commands required to set British English as the default language:

```
USE master
GO
EXEC sys.sp_configure 'default full-text language', '2057'
GO
RECONFIGURE WITH OVERRIDE
GO
```

3. Execute the query by clicking Execute or by pressing F5. If the option is set properly, the command should complete successfully.

## Working with Stoplists

During full-text index creation, SQL Server discards stopwords because they do not help with searches. A stopword is a commonly occurring character string, such as *the, a,* or *an.* SQL Server 2008 stopwords replace SQL Server 2005 noise words. A grouping of stopwords is referred to as a *stoplist.* To help in the indexing process, you can create stoplists and associate them with full-text indexes. You create stoplists by uploading the system-supplied stoplist to the database, by creating your own stopwords and lists, or by combining these techniques. The system stoplist includes common stopwords for all supported languages. You can tailor the system-supplied stoplist by adding and removing stopwords.

As you create stoplists on a per-database basis, each database can have a separate stoplist configuration. You can view the stopwords in the System stoplist for a database using the sys.fulltext_system_stopwords view. Stopwords are listed by their character string and language identifier as specified in the sys.fulltext_languages view. The following example shows the stopwords in the System stoplist for the Personnel database:

```
use Personnel
go
select * from sys.fulltext_system_stopwords
go
```

You can view the stoplists associated with a database using the sys.fulltext_stoplists view. The following example shows the available stoplists for the Personnel database:

```
use Personnel
go
select * from sys.fulltext_stoplists
go
```

Stoplists are listed by the following values:

- **stoplist_id**   ID of the stoplist, which is unique within the database

- **name**   Name of the stoplist

- **create_date**   Date that the stoplist was created

- **modify_date**   Date that the stoplist was last modified

Knowing the stoplist_id and name will help you when you view a list of all stopwords configured for a database. You can view all configured stopwords using the sys.fulltext_stopwords view. The following example shows all configured stopwords for the Personnel database:

```
use Personnel
go
select * from sys.fulltext_stopwords
go
```

Stopwords are listed by the following values:

- **stoplist_id**   ID of the stoplist to which the stopword belongs

- **stopword**   Character string definition

- **language**   Language alias as specified in the sys.fulltext_languages view

- **language_id**   Language identifier as specified in the sys.fulltext_languages view

## Creating Stoplists

In SQL Server Management Studio, you can create and manage stoplists using the Full-Text Stoplists entry under the Storage node. To create a stoplist for a database, complete the following steps:

1. Start SQL Server Management Studio, and then connect to a server.

2. Use the Object Explorer view to access a database. Expand the server node and the Databases node.

3. Under the Databases node, expand the Storage and Full Text Catalogs nodes to display the catalog or catalogs for the selected database.

4. Right-click Full-Text Stoplists, and then select New Full-Text Stoplist to display the New Full-Text Stoplist dialog box shown in Figure 8-7.

**Figure 8-7** New Full-Text Stoplist dialog box.

5. Type a descriptive name for the stoplist in the Full-Text Stoplist Name box.

6. Use the Owner box to set the stoplist owner. The default stoplist owner is dbo. If you do not want to use the default, type a new user or database role name in the text box provided or click the Options button (. . .) to browse for a user or database role to use.

7. Do one of the following to specify how the stoplist will be created:

   ❑ **Choose Create An Empty Stoplist** Creates a stoplist containing no stopwords. You will need to specify all the stopwords.

   ❑ **Choose Create From The System Stoplist** Creates a new stoplist using the System stoplist as defined in the *master* database. If you base a stoplist on the System stoplist, you can then modify this new stoplist to optimize searches for a subset of languages rather than all supported languages. This can increase index and query performance.

   ❑ **Choose Create From An Existing Full-Text Stoplist** Creates a new stoplist by copying a specified stoplist from a specified database. Use the drop-down lists provided to choose the source database and source stoplist.

**Note**   When you use a stoplist from another database, all languages specified in the stopwords of the source stoplist need to be registered and available in the current database. If they aren't, the CREATE FULLTEXT STOPLIST
operation succeeds, but SQL Server Management Studio displays a warning.

8.  Click OK to create the stoplist.

You can also create a stoplist by using the CREATE FULLTEXT STOPLIST command.
The syntax and usage for CREATE FULLTEXT STOPLIST are shown in Sample 8-1.

**Sample 8-1**   CREATE FULLTEXT STOPLIST Command Syntax and Usage

```
Syntax
CREATE FULLTEXT STOPLIST stoplist_name
    [ FROM { [ database_name. ] source_stoplist_name }
    | SYSTEM STOPLIST] [ AUTHORIZATION owner_name ]


Creating an Empty Stoplist
CREATE FULLTEXT STOPLIST primaryStopList;


Creating a Stoplist from the System Stoplist
CREATE FULLTEXT STOPLIST primaryStopList FROM SYSTEM STOPLIST;


Creating a Stoplist from an Existing Stoplist
CREATE FULLTEXT STOPLIST primaryStopList FROM Personnel.mainStoplist;
```

## Managing Stoplists

After you create stoplists for a database, you can manage individual stoplists in SQL
Server Management Studio using the following techniques:

**Add a Stopword**

1.  Right-click the stoplist, and then select Properties to display the Full-Text
    Stoplist Properties dialog box.

2.  Select Add Stop Word in the Action list, and then type the stopword in the Stop
    Word box.

3.  Use the Full-Text Language list to specify the language for the stopword.

4.  Click OK.

**Delete a Stopword**

1.  Right-click the stoplist, and then select Properties to display the Full-Text
    Stoplist Properties dialog box.

2.  Select Delete Stop Word in the Action list, and then type the stopword that you
    want to remove in the Stop Word box.

3. Use the Full-Text Language list to specify the language associated with the stop-word when you added it previously.

4. Click OK. If the stopword for the language you specified does not exist, you'll see an error. Click OK. Modify the stopword, language, or both as necessary, and then click OK again.

### Delete All Stopwords for a Specific Language

1. Right-click the stoplist, and then select Properties to display the Full-Text Stoplist Properties dialog box.

2. Select Delete All Stop Words in the Action list.

3. Use the Full-Text Language list to specify the language for which all stopwords should be removed.

4. Click OK. If the stopwords for the language you specified do not exist, you'll see an error. Click OK. Modify the stopwords, language, or both as necessary, and then click OK again.

### Clear the Stoplist of All Stopwords

1. Right-click the stoplist, and then select Properties to display the Full-Text Stoplist Properties dialog box.

2. Select Clear Stoplist.

3. Click OK.

Using Transact-SQL, you can also modify a stoplist by using the ALTER FULLTEXT STOPLIST command. The syntax and usage for ALTER FULLTEXT STOPLIST are shown in Sample 8-2.

**Sample 8-2**  ALTER FULLTEXT STOPLIST Command Syntax and Usage

```
Syntax
ALTER FULLTEXT STOPLIST stoplist_name
{
    ADD 'stopword' LANGUAGE language_id
  | DROP
    {
                'stopword' LANGUAGE language_id
      | ALL LANGUAGE language_id
          | ALL
    };


Adding a Stopword
ALTER FULLTEXT STOPLIST primaryStopList
{ ADD 'theat' LANGUAGE 1033 };
```

**Deleting a Stopword**
```
ALTER FULLTEXT STOPLIST primaryStopList
{ DROP 'theat' LANGUAGE '1033' };
```

**Deleting All Stopwords for a Specified Language**
```
ALTER FULLTEXT STOPLIST primaryStopList
{ DROP ALL LANGUAGE '1033' };
```

**Clearing the Stoplist of All Stopwords**
```
ALTER FULLTEXT STOPLIST primaryStopList
{ DROP ALL };
```

## Creating and Using Thesaurus Files

Full-text queries can also search for synonyms of search terms by using a thesaurus. SQL Server uses a thesaurus only for CONTAINS and CONTAINSTABLE queries that specify the FORMSOF THESAURUS clause and for FREETEXT and FREETEXTABLE queries. Within the context of a specified thesaurus, search patterns are either accent sensitive or accent insensitive. With an accent-sensitive setting, the word résumé is matched only when the user queries for résumé. With an accent-insensitive setting, the word résumé is matched when the user queries for résumé, resume, or resumé. By default, a thesaurus is accent insensitive.

SQL Server 2008 defines synonyms on a per-language basis. Synonyms are either of the following sets:

- **Expansion sets**   Contain a group of synonyms that are substituted for one another by a full-text query. Queries that contain a match for any synonym in an expansion set are expanded to include every other synonym in the expansion set.

- **Replacement sets**   Contain a text pattern to be replaced by a substitution set. Queries that contain a match for any synonym in a replacement set are replaced with the substitution value defined in the substitution set.

SQL Server provides a default set of XML thesaurus files for each supported language. These files contain only the top-level XML structure that is common to all SQL Server thesaurus files and a sample thesaurus, such as

```
<XML ID="Microsoft Search Thesaurus">
<!-- Commented out
    <thesaurus xmlns="x-schema:tsSchema.xml">
        <diacritics_sensitive>0</diacritics_sensitive>
        <expansion>
            <sub>Internet Explorer</sub>
            <sub>IE</sub>
```

```
            <sub>IE8</sub>
        </expansion>
        <replacement>
            <pat>NT6.1</pat>
            <pat>W08</pat>
            <pat>WS08</pat>
            <sub>Windows Server 2008</sub>
        </replacement>
        <expansion>
            <sub>run</sub>
            <sub>jog</sub>
        </expansion>
    </thesaurus>
-->
</XML>
```

The sample thesaurus is not used because its elements are enclosed in an XML comment:

```
<!--
    Not included text and elements.
-->
```

All text and elements within comments are ignored. By default, thesaurus files are stored under Microsoft SQL Server\MSSQL10.*InstanceName*\MSSQL\FTDATA\. The global thesaurus file is used with language-neutral searches. A neutral language is identified with the language ID 0 (zero). The global thesaurus file is named tsGlobal.xml. Other thesaurus files are named using the following format:

```
'ts' + <three-letter language-abbreviation> + '.xml'
```

such as tseng.xml for the U.S. English language thesaurus file.

If you want a SQL Server instance to use synonyms, you need to modify the thesaurus file for the appropriate languages. The basic elements in a thesaurus file are the following:

```
<XML ID="Microsoft Search Thesaurus">
    <thesaurus xmlns="x-schema:tsSchema.xml">
        <diacritics_sensitive>0</diacritics_sensitive>
    </thesaurus>
</XML>
```

The XML element is the top-level element. Its ID attribute specifies that the file is a thesaurus file. The THESAURUS element is a top-level container for all DIACTRICS_ SENSITIVE, EXPANSION, and REPLACEMENT elements. Its XMLNS attributes set the XML namespace to be used. The DIACTRICS_SENSITIVE element specifies whether thesaurus searches for the language are case sensitive or case insensitive. For accent-insensitive searches, use

```
<diacritics_sensitive>0</diacritics_sensitive>
```

For accent-sensitive searches, use

```
<diacritics_sensitive>1</diacritics_sensitive>
```

Within the THESAURUS element, you can insert one or more EXPANSION and REPLACEMENT elements. EXPANSION elements define the substituted values for expansion sets. In the following example, queries that contain a match for any synonym in an expansion set are expanded to include every other synonym in the expansion set:

```
<expansion>
    <sub>Internet Explorer</sub>
    <sub>IE</sub>
    <sub>IE8</sub>
</expansion>
```

Therefore, when a user queries on IE, Full-Text Search also returns results containing "Internet Explorer" and "IE8."

REPLACEMENT elements define replaced values. Patterns to match are defined using PAT elements. Replacement values are defined using SUB elements. In the following example, queries that contain a match for any synonym in the replacement set are replaced by the substitution value:

```
<expansion>
    <pat>NT6.1</pat>
    <pat>W08</pat>
    <pat>WS08</pat>
    <sub>Windows Server 2008</sub>
<expansion>
```

Therefore, when a user queries on NT6.1, Full-Text Search returns results containing "Windows Server 2008" rather than "NT6.1." You can also define multiple substitution values. When you do this, Full-Text Search returns results for both substitution values. In this example, when a user searches for NT6.1, W08, or WS08, Full-Text Search returns results for both Windows Server and Windows Server 2008:

```
<expansion>
    <pat>NT6.1</pat>
    <pat>W08</pat>
    <pat>WS08</pat>
    <sub>Windows Server</sub>
    <sub>Windows Server 2008</sub>
<expansion>
```

When multiple replacement sets have similar patterns being matched, the longest form takes precedence. For example, suppose that a user searches on "Windows Server support" and you've defined the following replacement sets:

```
<expansion>
    <pat>Windows</pat>
    <sub>Broken Windows</sub>
<expansion>
<expansion>
    <pat>Windows Server</pat>
    <sub>Windows Server 2008</sub>
<expansion>
```

Full-Text Search returns results for "Windows Server 2008 support" because "Windows Server" is the longest matching form.

SQL Server automatically loads thesaurus files for full-text queries that use the thesaurus. If a thesaurus file has been modified since it was last used, SQL Server also parses and processes the file. To have SQL Server process thesaurus files ahead of time and avoid the first-use performance impact, use the sp_fulltext_load_thesaurus_file procedure.

The syntax and usage for sp_fulltext_load_thesaurus_file are shown in Sample 8-3. Here, *language_id* is a language code defined in the sys.fulltext_languages view.

**Sample 8-3**   sp_fulltext_load_thesaurus_file Syntax and Usage

**Syntax**
```
sys.sp_fulltext_load_thesaurus_file language_id
```

**Usage**
```
sys.sp_fulltext_load_thesaurus_file 1033
```

You can view the query results of combining word breakers, thesaurus files, and stoplists as part of a search using the sys.dm_fts_parser function. The syntax and usage for this function are shown in Sample 8-4.

**Sample 8-4**   sys.dm_fts_parser Syntax and Usage

**Syntax**
```
sys.dm_fts_parser('query_string', language_id, stoplist_id,
    accent_sensitivity)
```

**Usage**
```
SELECT * FROM sys.dm_fts_parser (' "Windows Server" ', 1033, 0, 0)

SELECT * FROM sys.dm_fts_parser (' "Windows Server" ', 1033, 124, 0)
```

Use 0 (zero) for the stoplist ID to specify that you don't want to use a stoplist. Otherwise, specify an actual stoplist ID as returned by sys.fulltext_stoplists.

# Managing SQL Server 2008 Security

Microsoft SQL Server 2008 is being used more frequently both within organizations and for external access to information. Whether employees, contractors, or outside users access your databases, your job as an administrator is to manage that database access efficiently. You do this by creating user logins, configuring login permissions, and assigning roles. The permissions and roles you assign determine which actions users can perform as well as what kinds of data they can access.

Your primary goals in managing security should be to

- Balance the user's need for access to data against your need for protection from unauthorized access to data.

- Restrict database permissions so that users are less likely to execute harmful commands and procedures (maliciously or accidentally).

- Close off other security holes, such as those that might be caused by ordinary users with membership in administrator-related groups.

## Overview of SQL Server 2008 Security

In SQL Server 2008, all objects in a database are located in *schemas*. Each schema is owned by roles rather than individual users, allowing multiple users to administer database objects. This arrangement resolves an issue in earlier versions of SQL Server, in which users could not be dropped from a database without having to reassign the ownership of every object they owned. Now you need to change ownership only for the schema, not for each object.

## Working with Security Principals and Securables

SQL Server 2008 makes extensive uses of security principals and securables. An entity that can request a server, database, or schema resource is referred to as a security principal. Each security principal has a unique security identifier (SID). Security principals are managed at three levels: Windows, SQL Server, and database. The level at which the security principal is defined sets its scope of influence. Generally, Windows-level and SQL Server–level security principals have an instance-wide scope, and database-level principals have a scope of influence within a specific database.

Table 9-1 lists the security principals at each level. Some security principals, including Windows groups, database roles, and application roles, can include other security principals. These security principals are also referred to as *collections*. Every database user belongs to the public database role. When a user has not been granted or denied specific permissions on a securable, the user inherits the permissions granted to the public role on that securable.

**Table 9-1    SQL Server Principal Levels and the Included Principals**

| Principal Level | Principals Included |
| --- | --- |
| Windows level | Windows domain login |
| | Windows local login |
| | Windows group |
| SQL Server level | Server role |
| | SQL Server login |
| | SQL Server login mapped to an asymmetric key |
| | SQL Server login mapped to a certificate |
| | SQL Server login mapped to a Windows login |
| Database level | Database user |
| | Database user mapped to an asymmetric key |
| | Database user mapped to a certificate |
| | Database user mapped to a Windows login |
| | Application role |
| | Database role |
| | Public database role |

Security principals can be assigned specific permissions on hierarchical collections of entities referred to as *securables*. As Table 9-2 shows, the three top-level securables are server, database, and schema. Each of these securables contains other securables, which in turn can contain other securables. These nested hierarchies are referred to as *scopes*. Thus, you can also say that the main securable scopes in SQL Server are server, database, and schema.

**Table 9-2   SQL Server Securable Scopes and the Securables They Contain**

| Securable Scope | Securable Contained |
| --- | --- |
| Server | Servers/current instance |
| | Database |
| | Endpoint |
| | Login |
| | Server role |
| Database | Application role |
| | Assembly |
| | Asymmetric key |
| | Certificate |
| | Contract |
| | Database role |
| | Full-text catalog |
| | Message type |
| | Remote service binding |
| | Route |
| | Schema |
| | Service |
| | Symmetric key |
| | User |
| Schema | Aggregate |
| | Constraint |
| | Function |
| | Procedure |
| | Queue |
| | Statistic |
| | Synonym |

Table 9-2    SQL Server Securable Scopes and the Securables They Contain

| Securable Scope | Securable Contained |
|---|---|
| Schema *(continued)* | Table |
| | Type |
| | View |
| | XML schema collection |

## Understanding Permissions of Securables

Each SQL Server 2008 securable has permissions that can be granted to a security principal. These permissions begin with a keyword or keywords that identify the permission being granted, and these are summarized in Table 9-3.

Table 9-3    Permission Keywords and How They Work

| Permission Keyword(s) | Permission Granted | Primarily Applies To... |
|---|---|---|
| ALTER ANY *<Database>* | Grants the ability to CREATE, ALTER, or DROP individual securables for the database. For example, granting a principal ALTER ANY SCHEMA for a database gives the principal the ability to CREATE, ALTER, or DROP any schema in the database. | Database instance |
| ALTER ANY *<Server>* | Grants the ability to CREATE, ALTER, or DROP individual securables for the server. For example, granting a principal ALTER ANY LOGIN for a server gives that principal the ability to CREATE, ALTER, and DROP any login in that server instance. | Server instance |
| ALTER | Grants the ability to alter properties of a particular securable except for ownership. When a principal is granted on a scope, the principal has the ability to ALTER, CREATE, or DROP any securable contained within that scope. For example, granting a principal ALTER on a schema gives that principal the ability to CREATE, ALTER, and DROP objects from the schema. | Stored procedures, Service Broker queues, functions, synonyms, tables, and views |
| BACKUP/ DUMP | Grants permission to back up (dump). | Database instance |

Table 9-3   Permission Keywords and How They Work

| Permission Keyword(s) | Permission Granted | Primarily Applies To... |
| --- | --- | --- |
| CONTROL | Grants ownership-like capabilities. The principal has all defined permissions on the securable and can grant permissions on the securable as well. When you assign CONTROL permissions, consider the security model's hierarchy. Granting CONTROL at a particular scope implicitly includes CONTROL on all the securables under that scope. For example, CONTROL on a database implies all permissions on the database, including all assemblies and schemas in the database and all objects within all schemas. | Stored procedures, functions, synonyms, Service Broker queues, tables, and views |
| CREATE <Database Securable> | Grants permission to create the database securable. | Database instance |
| CREATE <Schema-Contained Securable> | Grants permission to create the schema-contained securable. Remember that ALTER permissions on the schema are needed to create the securable in a particular schema. | Database instance |
| CREATE <Server Securable> | Grants permission to create the server securable. | Server instance |
| DELETE | Grants permission to delete the securable. | Synonyms, tables, and views |
| EXECUTE | Grants permission to execute the securable. | Stored procedures, functions, and synonyms |
| IMPERSONATE <Login> | Grants the ability to impersonate the login. | |
| IMPERSONATE <User> | Grants the ability to impersonate the user. | |
| INSERT | Grants permission to insert data into the securable. | Synonyms, tables, and views |
| RECEIVE | Grants permission to receive Service Broker messages. | Service Broker queues |
| REFERENCES | Grants permission to reference the securable. | Functions, Service Broker queues, tables, and views |

Table 9-3 Permission Keywords and How They Work

| Permission Keyword(s) | Permission Granted | Primarily Applies To... |
|---|---|---|
| RESTORE/ LOAD | Grants permission to restore (load). | |
| SELECT | Grants permission to view data stored in the securable. | Synonyms, tables, table-valued functions, and views |
| TAKE OWNERSHIP | Grants the ability to take ownership of the securable. | Stored procedures, functions, synonyms, tables, and views |
| UPDATE | Grants permission to change data stored in the securable. | Synonyms, tables, and views |
| VIEW DEFINITION | Grants permission to view the securable definition in the related metadata. | Stored procedures, Service Broker queues, functions, synonyms, tables, and views |

## Examining Permissions Granted to Securables

SQL Server functions that you will find helpful for examining permissions granted to securables include the following:

- sys.fn_builtin_permissions
- Has_perms_by_name

You will learn more about how these functions are used in the sections that follow.

### Examining Built-in Permissions

Each object class from the server scope down has a specific set of grantable permissions. The sys.fn_builtin_permissions function returns a description of the server's built-in permissions hierarchy:

```
sys.fn_builtin_permissions( [ DEFAULT | NULL
    | empty_string | '< securable_class >' } )

< securable_class >::= APPLICATION ROLE | ASSEMBLY | ASYMMETRIC KEY
    | CERTIFICATE | CONTRACT | DATABASE | ENDPOINT | FULLTEXT CATALOG
    | LOGIN | MESSAGE TYPE | OBJECT | REMOTE SERVICE BINDING | ROLE
    | ROUTE | SCHEMA | SERVER | SERVICE | SYMMETRIC KEY | TYPE
    | USER | XML SCHEMA COLLECTION
```

In the preceding code segment, DEFAULT, NULL, or an empty string return a complete list of built-in permissions, or you can specify the name of a specific securable class to return all permissions that apply to the class.

The sys.fn_builtin_permissions function is accessible to the public role. You can view the grantable permissions for all objects by using the following query:

```
USE master
GO
SELECT * FROM sys.fn_builtin_permissions(default)
GO
```

If you want to view the grantable permissions for a specific object class, you can use the following query:

```
USE master
GO
SELECT * FROM sys.fn_builtin_permissions('object_class')
GO
```

where *object_class* is the object class you want to work with. The following example examines the grantable permissions for the LOGIN class:

```
SELECT * FROM sys.fn_builtin_permissions('login')
```

You can also list object classes for which a specific permission has been granted. In the following example, you list object classes that have the SELECT permission:

```
USE master
GO
SELECT * FROM sys.fn_builtin_permissions(DEFAULT)
        WHERE permission_name = 'SELECT';
GO
```

### Examining Effective Permissions

The Has_perms_by_name built-in function returns the effective permission on a securable. Effective permissions include

- Permissions granted directly to the user, and not denied

- Permissions implied by a higher-level permission held by the user, and not denied

- Permissions granted to a role of which the user is a member, and not denied

- Permissions held by a role of which the user is a member, and not denied

The Has_perms_by_name function is accessible to the public role. However, you cannot use Has_perms_by_name to check permissions on a linked server. The basic syntax of the Has_perms_by_name function follows:

```
Has_perms_by_name (
                securable ,
                securable_class ,
                permission
                [, sub-securable ]
                [, sub-securable_class ]
                )
```

In the preceding code segment, *securable* sets the name of the securable or NULL if the securable is the server itself, *securable_class* sets the name of the securable class or NULL if the securable is the server itself, and *permission* is a non-NULL value representing the permission name to be checked. You can use the permission name ANY as a wildcard to determine if the securable has any effective permissions. The optional *sub-securable* and *sub-securable_class* values specify the name of the securable subentity and the class of securable subentity against which the permission is tested. Both of these optional values default to NULL. If the function returns true (1), the securable has the effective permission. If the function returns false (0), the securable does not have the effective permission. A return value of NULL indicates that the query failed.

You can determine if the currently logged-on user has a specific permission on the server by executing the following query:

```
USE master
GO
SELECT has_perms_by_name(null, null, 'permission_name');
GO
```

In this code segment, *permission_name* is the name of the permission to examine.

The following example checks to see if the current user has the VIEW SERVER STATE permission:

```
select has_perms_by_name(null, null, 'VIEW SERVER STATE');
```

A true (1) or false (0) value is returned to indicate whether or not the user is granted the permission.

To determine if the current user has any permissions in a specific database, you can execute the following query:

```
USE master
GO
SELECT has_perms_by_name('database_name', 'DATABASE', 'ANY')
GO
```

In this code segment, *database_name* is the name of the database for which you are determining permissions.

The following example determines if the current user has any permissions in the Personnel database:

```
SELECT has_perms_by_name('Personnel', 'DATABASE', 'ANY')
```

If the query returns 1, the current user has some permissions for the specific database. You can indicate the current database with the db_name() function, such as:

```
SELECT has_perms_by_name(db_name(),'DATABASE', 'ANY')
```

You can determine the permissions of a specific user by using EXECUTE AS. In the following example, you check to see if EdwardM has any permissions in the Personnel database:

```
EXECUTE AS user = 'EdwardM'
GO
SELECT has_perms_by_name('Personnel', 'DATABASE', 'ANY')
GO
REVERT
GO
```

Permissions on schema objects, such as Tables and Views, can be examined as well. To do this, set the securable to the database name, the securable class to the literal value 'OBJECT', and permission to the permission you want to examine. To determine which tables the current user has SELECT permission on in the current database, you use the following query:

```
USE Personnel
GO
SELECT has_perms_by_name(dbname(), 'OBJECT', 'SELECT') as Have_Select,
    * from sys.tables;
go
```

The current user has SELECT permission on tables with a 1 in the Have_Select column. By specifying the two-part or three-part name, you can examine permissions on a specific table as well. For example, to determine if the current user has INSERT permission on the Address table in the current database, you use a two-part name:

```
select has_perms_by_name('Employee.Address', 'OBJECT', 'INSERT')
    as Have_Select, * from sys.tables;
```

Or you use a three-part name:

```
select has_perms_by_name('Personnel.Employee.Address', 'OBJECT', 'INSERT')
    as Have_Select, * from sys.tables;
```

# SQL Server 2008 Authentication Modes

The SQL Server security model has two authentication modes:

- **Windows authentication only**   Works best when the database is accessed within the organization only

- **Mixed security**   Works best when outside users need to access the database or when you do not use Windows domains

You configure these security modes at the server level, and they apply to all databases on the server. Note, however, that each database server instance has a separate security architecture. This means that different database server instances can have different security modes.

# Windows Authentication

If you use the Windows authentication mode, you can use the user and group accounts available in the Windows domain for authentication. This lets authenticated users access databases without a separate SQL Server login ID and password. This is beneficial because domain users do not have to keep track of multiple passwords, and if they update their domain password, they will not have to change SQL Server passwords as well. However, users are still subject to all the rules of the Windows security model, and you can use this model to lock accounts, audit logins, and force users to change their passwords periodically.

When you use Windows authentication, SQL Server automatically authenticates users based on their user account names or their group membership. If you have granted the user or the user's group access to a database, the user is automatically granted access to that database. By default, several local accounts are configured to use SQL Server. These accounts are the local Administrators group account and the local Administrator user account. (Administrator is included because it is a member of the Administrators group by default.) Local accounts are displayed as BUILTIN\*<AccountName>* or *COMPUTERNAME\<AccountName>* in SQL Server Management Studio. For example, Administrators is displayed as *BUILTIN\Administrators*.

> **Real World**   Domain accounts are the best way to manage users who access the database from within the organization. Also, if you assign users to security groups and then configure access for these groups in SQL Server, you cut down on the amount of administration you have to do. For example, if you assign users in the marketing department to a marketing group and then configure this group in SQL Server, you have only one account to manage instead of 10, 20, 50, or more. When employees leave the organization or change departments, you do not have to delete user accounts. When new employees are hired, you do not have to create new accounts either—you only need to make sure that they are added to the correct security group.

# Mixed Security and SQL Server Logins

With mixed security, you use both Windows authentication and SQL Server logins. SQL Server logins are primarily used by users outside the company, such as those who might access the database from the Internet. You can configure applications that access SQL Server from the Internet to use specific accounts automatically or to prompt the user for a SQL Server login ID and password.

With mixed security, SQL Server first determines if the user is connecting using a valid SQL Server login. If the user has a valid login and has the proper password, the user connection is accepted. If the user has a valid login but has an improper password, the user connection is refused. SQL Server checks the Windows account information only if the user does not have a valid login. In this case, SQL Server determines whether or not the Windows account has permission to connect to the server. If the account has permission, the connection is accepted. Otherwise, the connection is refused.

All SQL Server servers have the built-in sa login and might also have NETWORK SER-VICE and SYSTEM logins (depending on the server instance configuration). All data-bases have built-in SQL Server users known as dbo, guest, INFORMATION_SCHEMA, and sys. These logins and users that are provided for special purposes are discussed in the following section.

# Special-Purpose Logins and Users

You configure access to SQL Server using server logins. You can configure various lev-els of access for these logins in the following ways:

- By the roles to which those logins belong
- By permitting access to specific databases
- By allowing or denying object permissions

Just as there are two authentication modes, there are also two kinds of server logins. You create domain logins using domain accounts, which can be domain or local user accounts, local group accounts, or universal and global domain group accounts. You create SQL Server logins by specifying a unique login ID and password. Several logins are configured by default, and these include local Administrators, local Administrator, sa, NETWORK SERVICE, and SYSTEM.

To narrow the scope of access to a specific database, you use database user accounts. Several database users are configured by default, including the dbo user (a special database user), the guest user (a special database user with limited access), the INFORMATION_SCHEMA user, and the sys user.

In this section, you will learn more about these special-purpose logins.

## Working with the Administrators Group

The Administrators group is a local group on the database server. This group's mem-bers normally include the local Administrator user account and any other users set to administer the system locally. In SQL Server, this group is granted the sysadmin server role by default.

## Working with the Administrator User Account

Administrator is a local user account on the server. This account provides administra-tor privileges on the local system, and you use it primarily when you install a system. If the host computer is part of a Windows domain, the Administrator account usually has domain-wide privileges as well. In SQL Server, this account is granted the sysad-min server role by default.

## Working with the sa Login

The sa login is the system administrator's account for SQL Server. With the new integrated and expanded security model, sa is no longer needed, and it is primarily provided for backward compatibility with previous SQL Server versions. As with other administrator logins, sa is granted the sysadmin server role by default. When you install SQL Server, the sa login is not assigned a password.

To prevent unauthorized access to the server, you should set a strong password for this account, and you should also change the password periodically as you would the passwords for Windows accounts.

> **Best Practices**   Because the sa login is widely known to malicious users, you might want to delete or disable this account if possible. Instead of using the sa login, make system administrators members of the sysadmin server role and have them log on using their own logins. Anyone with the sysadmin server role can then log on and administer the server. If you ever get locked out of the server, you can log on to the server locally using an account with local administrator privileges, and then reset passwords or assign privileges as necessary.

## Working with the NETWORK SERVICE and SYSTEM Logins

NETWORK SERVICE and SYSTEM are built-in local accounts on the server. Whether or not server logins are created for these accounts depends on the server configuration. For example, if you have configured the server as a report server, you will have a login for the NETWORK SERVICE account, and this login will be a member of the special database role RSExecRole on the *master*, *msdb*, *ReportServer*, and *ReportServerTempDB* databases. RSExecRole is used primarily to manage the Report Server schema, and the service account for the server instance will also be a member of this role.

During setup of the server instance, the NETWORK SERVICE and SYSTEM accounts can be the selected service account for SQL Server, SQL Server Agent, SQL Server 2008 Analysis Services, and the report server. In this case, the SYSTEM account will typically have the sysadmin server role, giving it full access for administration of the server instance.

## Working with the Guest User

The guest user is a special user that you can add to a database to allow anyone with a valid SQL Server login to access the database. Users who access a database with the guest account assume the identity of the guest user and inherit all the privileges and permissions of the guest account. For example, if you configure the domain account GOTEAM to access SQL Server, GOTEAM can access any database with a guest login, and when GOTEAM does so, that person is granted all the permissions of the guest account. If you were to configure the Windows group DEVGROUP with guest access, you could simplify administration because any user that is a member of the group would be able to access any database as a guest.

By default, the guest user exists in the *model* database and is granted guest permissions. Because *model* is the template for all databases you create, all new databases will include the guest account, and this account will be granted guest permissions. You can add or delete a guest from all databases except *master* and *tempdb*. Most users access *master* and *tempdb* as guests, and for this reason, you cannot remove the guest account from these databases. This is not a problem, however, because a guest has limited permissions and privileges in *master* and *tempdb*.

Before using the guest user, you should note the following information about the account:

- The guest user is a member of the public server role and inherits the permissions of this role.

- The guest user must exist in a database before anyone can access it as a guest.

- The guest user is used only when a user account has access to SQL Server but does not have access to the database through this user account.

## Working with the dbo User

The database owner, or dbo, is a special type of database user and is granted special privileges. Generally speaking, the user who created a database is the database owner. The dbo is implicitly granted all permissions on the database and can grant these permissions to other users. Because members of the sysadmin server role are mapped automatically to the special user dbo, logins with the sysadmin role can perform any tasks that a dbo can perform.

Objects created in SQL Server databases also have owners. These owners are referred to as the *database object owners*. Objects created by a member of the sysadmin server role belong to the dbo user automatically. Objects created by users who are not members of the sysadmin server role belong to the user creating the object and must be qualified with the name of that user when other users reference them. For example, if GOTEAM is a member of the sysadmin server role and creates a table called Sales, Sales belongs to dbo and is qualified as dbo.Sales, or simply Sales. However, if GOTEAM is not a member of the sysadmin server role and creates a table called Sales, Sales belongs to GOTEAM and must be qualified as GOTEAM.Sales.

**Note**    Technically, dbo is a special user account and not a special-purpose login. However, you might see it referred to as a login. You cannot log in to a server or database as dbo, but you might be the person who created the database or a set of objects in it.

## Working with the sys and INFORMATION_SCHEMA Users

All system objects are contained in the schemas named sys or INFORMATION_
SCHEMA. These are two special schemas that are created in each database, but they are
visible only in the *master* database. The related sys and information schema views provide an internal system view of the metadata for all data objects stored in a database.
The sys and INFORMATION_SCHEMA users are used to reference into these views.

# Permissions

Permissions determine the actions that users can perform on SQL Server or in a database. Permissions are granted according to the login ID, group memberships, and role
memberships. Users must have appropriate permissions before they can perform any
action that changes database definitions or accesses data. Three types of permissions
are used in SQL Server:

- Object permissions
- Statement permissions
- Implicit permissions

## Object Permissions

In SQL Server 2008, all object permissions are grantable. You can manage permissions
for specific objects, all objects of particular types, and all objects belonging to a specific
schema. The objects for which you can manage permissions depend on the scope. At
the server level, you can grant object permissions for servers, endpoints, logins, and
server roles. You can also manage permissions for the current server instance.

At the database level, you can manage object permissions for application roles, assemblies, asymmetric keys, certificates, database roles, databases, full-text catalogs, functions, schemas, stored procedures, symmetric keys, synonyms, tables, user-defined
data types, users, views, and XML schema collections.

You control access to these objects by granting, denying, or revoking the ability to execute particular statements or stored procedures. For example, you can grant a user the
right to SELECT information from a table, but deny the right to INSERT, UPDATE, or
DELETE information in the table. Table 9-4 provides a summary of object permissions.

Table 9-4   Object Permissions

| Base Securable | Configurable Permissions | Highest Permission | Contained In | Implied Permission from Parent |
|---|---|---|---|---|
| APPLICA- TION ROLE | ALTER, CONTROL, VIEW DEFINITION | CONTROL | DATABASE | ALTER ANY APPLICA- TION ROLE, CONTROL, VIEW DEFINITION |
| ASSEMBLY | ALTER, CONTROL, EXECUTE, REFERENCES, TAKE OWNERSHIP, VIEW DEFINITION | CONTROL | DATABASE | ALTER ANY ASSEMBLY, CONTROL, EXECUTE, REFERENCES, VIEW DEFINITION |
| ASYMMET- RIC KEY | ALTER, CONTROL, REFERENCES, TAKE OWNERSHIP, VIEW DEFINITION | CONTROL | DATABASE | ALTER ANY ASYMMET- RIC KEY, CONTROL, REFERENCES, VIEW DEFINITION |
| CERTIFI- CATE | ALTER, CONTROL, REFERENCES, TAKE OWNERSHIP, VIEW DEFINITION | CONTROL | DATABASE | ALTER ANY CERTIFICATE, CONTROL, REFERENCES, VIEW DEFINITION |
| CONTRACT | ALTER, CONTROL, REFERENCES, TAKE OWNERSHIP, VIEW DEFINITION | CONTROL | DATABASE | ALTER ANY CONTRACT, CONTROL, REFERENCES, VIEW DEFINITION |

Table 9-4 Object Permissions

| Base Securable | Configurable Permissions | Highest Permission | Contained In | Implied Permission from Parent |
|---|---|---|---|---|
| DATABASE | ALTER, ALTER ANY APPLICATION ROLE, ALTER ANY ASSEMBLY, ALTER ANY ASYMMETRIC KEY, ALTER ANY CERTIFICATE, ALTER ANY CONTRACT, ALTER ANY DATABASE DDL TRIGGER, ALTER ANY DATABASE EVENT NOTIFICATION, ALTER ANY DATASPACE, ALTER ANY FULL-TEXT CATALOG, ALTER ANY MESSAGE TYPE, ALTER ANY REMOTE SERVICE BINDING, ALTER ANY ROLE, ALTER ANY ROUTE, ALTER ANY SCHEMA, ALTER ANY SERVICE, ALTER ANY SYMMETRIC KEY, ALTER ANY USER, AUTHENTICATE, BACKUP DATABASE, BACKUP LOG, CHECKPOINT, CONNECT, CONNECT REPLICATION, CONTROL, CREATE AGGREGATE, CREATE ASSEMBLY, CREATE ASYMMETRIC KEY, CREATE CERTIFICATE, CREATE CONTRACT, CREATE DATABASE, CREATE DATABASE DDL EVENT NOTIFICATION, CREATE DEFAULT, CREATE FULL-TEXT CATALOG, CREATE FUNCTION, CREATE MESSAGE TYPE, CREATE PROCEDURE, CREATE QUEUE, CREATE REMOTE SERVICE BINDING, CREATE ROLE, CREATE ROUTE, CREATE RULE, CREATE SCHEMA, CREATE SERVICE, CREATE SYMMETRIC KEY, CREATE SYNONYM, CREATE TABLE, CREATE TYPE, CREATE VIEW, CREATE XML SCHEMA COLLECTION, DELETE, EXECUTE, INSERT, REFERENCES, SELECT, SHOWPLAN, SUBSCRIBE QUERY NOTIFICATIONS, TAKE OWNERSHIP, UPDATE, VIEW DATABASE STATE, VIEW DEFINITION | ALTER ANY ASSEMBLY, ALTER ANY CERTIFICATE, ALTER ANY CONTRACT, ALTER ANY DATABASE EVENT NOTIFICATION, ALTER ANY FULLTEXT CATALOG, ALTER ANY MESSAGE TYPE, ALTER ANY REMOTE SERVICE BINDING, ALTER ANY ROLE, ALTER ANY ROUTE, ALTER ANY SCHEMA, ALTER ANY SERVICE, ALTER ANY SYMMETRIC KEY, CONNECT REPLICATION, CONTROL | SERVER | ALTER ANY DATABASE, ALTER ANY EVENT NOTIFICATION, ALTER TRACE, AUTHENTICATE SERVER, CONTROL SERVER, CREATE ANY DATABASE, CREATE DDL EVENT NOTIFICATION, EXTERNAL ACCESS, VIEW ANY DEFINITION, VIEW SERVER STATE |

Table 9-4   Object Permissions

| Base Securable | Configurable Permissions | Highest Permission | Contained In | Implied Permission from Parent |
|---|---|---|---|---|
| ENDPOINT | ALTER, CONNECT, CONTROL, TAKE OWNERSHIP, VIEW DEFINITION | CONTROL | SERVER | ALTER ANY ENDPOINT, CONTROL SERVER, VIEW ANY DEFINITION |
| FULLTEXT CATALOG | ALTER, CONTROL, REFERENCES, TAKE OWNERSHIP, VIEW DEFINITION | CONTROL | DATABASE | ALTER ANY FULLTEXT CATALOG, CONTROL, REFERENCES, VIEW DEFINITION |
| LOGIN | ALTER, CONTROL, IMPERSONATE, VIEW DEFINITION | CONTROL | SERVER | ALTER ANY LOGIN, CONTROL SERVER, VIEW ANY DEFINITION |
| MESSAGE TYPE | ALTER, CONTROL, REFERENCES, TAKE OWNERSHIP, VIEW DEFINITION | CONTROL | DATABASE | ALTER ANY MESSAGE TYPE, CONTROL, REFERENCES, VIEW DEFINITION |
| OBJECT | ALTER, CONTROL, DELETE, EXECUTE, INSERT, REFERENCES, SELECT, TAKE OWNERSHIP, UPDATE, VIEW CHANGE TRACKING, VIEW DEFINITION | CONTROL | SCHEMA | ALTER, CONTROL, DELETE, EXECUTE, INSERT, REFERENCES, SELECT, UPDATE, VIEW CHANGE TRACKING, VIEW DEFINITION |

Table 9-4 Object Permissions

| Base Securable | Configurable Permissions | Highest Permission | Contained In | Implied Permission from Parent |
|---|---|---|---|---|
| REMOTE SERVICE BINDING | ALTER, CONTROL, TAKE OWNERSHIP, VIEW DEFINITION | CONTROL | DATABASE | ALTER ANY REMOTE SERVICE BINDING, CONTROL, VIEW DEFINITION |
| ROLE | ALTER, CONTROL, TAKE OWNERSHIP, VIEW DEFINITION | CONTROL | DATABASE | ALTER ANY ROLE, CONTROL, VIEW DEFINITION |
| ROUTE | ALTER, CONTROL, TAKE OWNERSHIP, VIEW DEFINITION | CONTROL | DATABASE | ALTER ANY ROUTE, CONTROL, VIEW DEFINITION |
| SCHEMA | ALTER, CONTROL, DELETE, EXECUTE, INSERT, REFERENCES, SELECT, TAKE OWNERSHIP, UPDATE, VIEW CHANGE TRACKING, VIEW DEFINITION | CONTROL | DATABASE | ALTER ANY SCHEMA, CONTROL, DELETE, EXECUTE, INSERT, REFERENCES, SELECT, UPDATE, VIEW CHANGE TRACKING, VIEW DEFINITION |

**Table 9-4**   Object Permissions

| Base Securable | Configurable Permissions | Highest Permission | Contained In | Implied Permission from Parent |
|---|---|---|---|---|
| SERVER | ADMINISTER BULK OPERATIONS, ALTER ANY CONNECTION, ALTER ANY CREDENTIAL, ALTER ANY DATABASE, ALTER ANY ENDPOINT, ALTER ANY EVENT NOTIFICATION, ALTER ANY LINKED SERVER, ALTER ANY LOGIN, ALTER RESOURCES, ALTER SERVER STATE, ALTER SETTINGS, ALTER TRACE, AUTHENTICATE SERVER, CONNECT SQL, CONTROL SERVER, CREATE ANY DATABASE, CREATE DDL EVENT NOTIFICATION, CREATE ENDPOINT, CREATE TRACE EVENT NOTIFICATION, EXTERNAL ACCESS ASSEMBLY, SHUTDOWN, UNSAFE ASSEMBLY, VIEW ANY DATABASE, VIEW ANY DEFINITION, VIEW SERVER STATE | CONTROL SERVER, ALTER ANY DATABASE, ALTER ANY EVENT NOTIFICATION, ALTER ANY ENDPOINT, ALTER SERVER STATE | Not applicable | Not applicable |
| SERVICE | ALTER, CONTROL, SEND, TAKE OWNERSHIP, VIEW DEFINITION | CONTROL | DATABASE | ALTER ANY SERVICE, CONTROL, VIEW DEFINITION |
| SYMMETRIC KEY | ALTER, CONTROL, REFERENCES, TAKE OWNERSHIP, VIEW DEFINITION | CONTROL | DATABASE | ALTER ANY SYMMETRIC KEY, CONTROL, REFERENCES, VIEW DEFINITION |
| TYPE | CONTROL, EXECUTE, REFERENCES, TAKE OWNERSHIP, VIEW DEFINITION | CONTROL | SCHEMA | CONTROL, EXECUTE, REFERENCES, VIEW DEFINITION |
| USER | ALTER, CONTROL, IMPERSONATE, VIEW DEFINITION | CONTROL | DATABASE | ALTER ANY USER, CONTROL, VIEW DEFINITION |

Table 9-4   Object Permissions

| Base Securable | Configurable Permissions | Highest Permission | Contained In | Implied Permission from Parent |
|---|---|---|---|---|
| XML SCHEMA COLLEC- TION | ALTER, CONTROL, EXECUTE, REFERENCES, TAKE OWNERSHIP, VIEW DEFINITION | CONTROL | SCHEMA | ALTER, CONTROL, EXECUTE, REFERENCES, VIEW DEFINITION |

## Statement Permissions

Statement permissions control administration actions, such as creating a database or adding objects to a database. Only members of the sysadmin role and database owners can assign statement permissions. By default, normal logins are not granted statement permissions, and you must specifically grant these permissions to logins that are not administrators. For example, if a user needs to be able to create views in a database, you would assign permission to execute CREATE VIEW. Table 9-5 provides a summary of statement permissions that you can grant, deny, or revoke.

Table 9-5   Statement Permissions

| Statement Permission | Description |
|---|---|
| CREATE DATABASE | Determines if the login can create databases. The user must be in the *master* database or must be a member of the sysadmin server role. |
| CREATE DEFAULT | Determines if the user can create a default value for a table column. |
| CREATE FUNCTION | Determines if the user can create a user-defined function in the database. |
| CREATE PROCEDURE | Determines if the user can create a stored procedure. |
| CREATE RULE | Determines if the user can create a table column rule. |
| CREATE TABLE | Determines if the user can create a table. |
| CREATE VIEW | Determines if the user can create a view. |
| BACKUP DATABASE | Determines if the user can back up the database. |
| BACKUP LOG | Determines if the user can back up the transaction log. |

## Implied Permissions

Only members of predefined system roles or database/database object owners have implied permissions. Implied permissions for a role cannot be changed. You make other accounts members of the role to give the accounts the related implied permissions. For example, members of the sysadmin server role can perform any activity in SQL Server. They can extend databases, kill processes, and so on. Any account you add to the sysadmin role can perform these tasks as well.

Database and database object owners also have implied permissions. These permissions allow them to perform all activities with either the database or the object they own, or with both. For example, a user who owns a table can view, add, change, and delete data. That user can also alter the table's definition and control the table's permissions.

# Roles

Roles are a lot like Windows security groups—they allow you to assign permissions to a group of users easily and they can have built-in permissions (implicit permissions) that cannot be changed. Two types of roles are available:

- **Server roles**   Applied at the server level
- **Database roles**   Applied at the database level

## Server Roles

You use server roles to grant server administration capabilities. If you make a login a member of a role, users who use this login can perform any tasks permitted by the role. For example, members of the sysadmin role have the highest level of permissions on SQL Server and can perform any type of task.

You set server roles at the server level, and you predefine them. This means that these permissions affect the entire server and you cannot change the permission set. The following list provides a summary of each server role, from the lowest-level role (bulkadmin) to the highest-level role (sysadmin):

- **bulkadmin**   Designed for domain accounts that need to perform bulk inserts into the database. Members of this role can add members to bulkadmin and can execute the BULK INSERT statements.

- **dbcreator**   Designed for users who need to create, modify, drop, and restore databases. Members of this role can add members to dbcreator and perform these tasks: ALTER DATABASE, CREATE DATABASE, DROP DATABASE, EXTEND DATABASE, RESTORE DATABASE, and RESTORE LOG.

- **diskadmin**   Designed for users who need to manage disk files. Members of this role can add members to diskadmin and can use sp_addumpdevice and sp_dropdevice.

- **processadmin**   Designed for users who need to control SQL Server processes. Members of this role can add members to processadmin and can kill processes.

- **securityadmin**   Designed for users who need to manage logins, create database permissions, and read error logs. Members of this role can add members to securityadmin; grant, deny, and revoke server-level and database-level permissions; reset passwords; and read the error logs. In addition, they can also perform these tasks: sp_addlinkedsrvlogin, CREATE LOGIN, ALTER LOGIN, DROP LOGIN, sp_droplinkedsrvlogin, GRANT CONNECT, DENY CONNECT, sp_helplogins, and sp_remoteoption.

- **serveradmin**   Designed for users who need to set server-wide configuration options and shut down the server. Members of this role can add members to serveradmin and can perform these other tasks: DBCC FREEPROCCACHE, RECONFIGURE, SHUTDOWN, sp_configure, sp_fulltext_service, and sp_tableoption.

- **setupadmin**   Designed for users who need to manage linked servers and control startup procedures. Members of this role can add members to setupadmin; can add, drop, and configure linked servers; and can control startup procedures.

- **sysadmin**   Designed for users who need complete control over SQL Server and installed databases. Members of this role can perform any activity in SQL Server.

Fixed server roles can be mapped to the more granular permissions for SQL Server 2008, as shown in Table 9-6.

**Table 9-6   Granular Permissions Associated with Fixed Server Roles**

| Fixed Server Role | Permissions Granted with This Role |
| --- | --- |
| bulkadmin | ADMINISTER BULK OPERATIONS |
| dbcreator | CREATE DATABASE |
| diskadmin | ALTER RESOURCES |
| processadmin | ALTER ANY CONNECTION, ALTER SERVER STATE |
| securityadmin | ALTER ANY LOGIN |
| serveradmin | ALTER ANY ENDPOINT, ALTER RESOURCES, ALTER SERVER STATE, ALTER SETTINGS, SHUTDOWN, VIEW SERVER STATE |
| setupadmin | ALTER ANY LINKED SERVER |
| sysadmin | CONTROL SERVER |

## Database Roles

When you want to assign permissions at the database level, you can use database roles. You set database roles on a per-database basis, which means that each database has its own set of roles. SQL Server 2008 supports three types of database roles:

- User-defined standard roles

- User-defined application roles

- Predefined (or fixed) database roles

Standard roles allow you to create roles with unique permissions and privileges. You can use standard roles to logically group users together and then assign a single permission to the role rather than having to assign permissions to each user separately. For example, you could create a role called Users that allows users to SELECT, INSERT, and UPDATE specific tables in the database but does not allow them to perform any other tasks.

Application roles allow you to create password-protected roles for specific applications. For example, a user could connect through a Web-based application called NetReady; this application would activate the role, and the user would then gain the role's permissions and privileges. Standard database roles or other roles cannot be assigned to an application role. Instead, the application role is activated when the application connects to the database.

SQL Server also has predefined database roles. Predefined roles are built in, and they have permissions that cannot be changed. You use predefined roles to assign database administration privileges, and you can assign a single login to multiple roles. These privileges are summarized in the following list:

- **public**   The default role for all database users. Users inherit the permissions and privileges of the public role, and this role provides the minimum permissions and privileges. Any roles that you assign to a user beyond the public role can add permissions and privileges. If you want all database users to have specific permissions, assign the permissions to the public role.

- **db_accessadmin**   Designed for users who need to add or remove logins in a database.

- **db_backupoperator**   Designed for users who need to back up a database.

- **db_datareader**   Designed for users who need to view data in a database. Members of this role can select all data from any user table in the database.

- **db_datawriter**   Designed for users who need to add or modify any data in any user table in the database. Members of this role can perform the following tasks on any objects in the selected database: DELETE, INSERT, and UPDATE.

- **db_ddladmin**   Designed for users who need to perform tasks related to the data definition language (DDL) for SQL Server. Members of this role can issue any DDL statement except GRANT, REVOKE, or DENY.

- **db_denydatareader**   Designed to restrict access to data in a database by login. Members of this role cannot read any data in user tables within a database.

- **db_denydatawriter** Designed to restrict modification permissions in a database by login. Members of this role cannot add, modify, or delete any data in user tables within a database.

- **db_owner** Designed for users who need complete control over all aspects of the database. Members of this role can assign permissions, modify database settings, perform database maintenance, and perform any other administration task on the database, including dropping the database.

- **db_securityadmin** Designed for users who need to manage permissions, object ownership, and roles.

- **dbm_monitor** Designed for users who need to monitor the current status of database mirroring.

Fixed database roles can be mapped to the more granular permissions for SQL Server 2008, as shown in Table 9-7.

**Table 9-7** Granular Permissions Associated with Fixed Database Roles

| Fixed Database Role | Permissions Denied with This Role |
|---|---|
| db_denydatareader | SELECT |
| db_denydatawriter | DELETE, INSERT, UPDATE |

| Fixed Database Role | Permissions Granted with This Role |
|---|---|
| db_accessadmin | ALTER ANY USER, CONNECT with GRANT option, CREATE SCHEMA, VIEW ANY DATABASE |
| db_backupoperator | BACKUP DATABASE, BACKUP LOG, CHECKPOINT, VIEW ANY DATABASE |
| db_datareader | SELECT, VIEW ANY DATABASE |
| db_datawriter | DELETE, INSERT, UPDATE, VIEW ANY DATABASE |
| db_ddladmin | ALTER ANY ASSEMBLY, ALTER ANY ASYMMETRIC KEY, ALTER ANY CERTIFICATE, ALTER ANY CONTRACT, ALTER ANY DATABASE DDL TRIGGER, ALTER ANY DATABASE EVENT NOTIFICATION, ALTER ANY DATASPACE, ALTER ANY FULLTEXT CATALOG, ALTER ANY MESSAGE TYPE, ALTER ANY REMOTE SERVICE BINDING, ALTER ANY ROUTE, ALTER ANY SCHEMA, ALTER ANY SERVICE, ALTER ANY SYMMETRIC KEY, CHECKPOINT, CREATE AGGREGATE, CREATE DEFAULT, CREATE FUNCTION, CREATE PROCEDURE, CREATE QUEUE, CREATE RULE, CREATE SYNONYM, CREATE TABLE, CREATE TYPE, CREATE VIEW, CREATE XML SCHEMA COLLECTION, REFERENCES, VIEW ANY DATABASE |
| db_owner | CONTROL with GRANT option, VIEW ANY DATABASE |
| db_securityadmin | ALTER ANY APPLICATION ROLE, ALTER ANY ROLE, CREATE SCHEMA, VIEW DEFINITION, VIEW ANY DATABASE |
| dbm_monitor | VIEW status of database mirroring, VIEW ANY DATABASE |

**Real World**   The *msdb* database contains a number of special-purpose roles. When users work with SQL Server Integration Services (SSIS), you'll want to assign the db_ssisadmin role to SSIS administrators, the db_ssisoperator role to SSIS operators, and the db_ssisltduser role to limited users. When you use data collectors, you'll want to assign the dc_admin role to DC administrators, the dc_operator role to DC operators, and the dc_proxy role to DC proxy accounts.

Other important special-purpose roles include: PolicyAdministratorRole for administrators who perform configuration and maintenance activities for Policy-Based Management, ServerGroupAdministratorRole for administrators who manage and work with registered servers, and ServerGroupReaderRole for those who need to see what server groups are available.

# Managing Server Logins

SQL Server can use Windows logins as well as logins for SQL Server. If you have configured the server for mixed security, you can use both login types. Otherwise, you can use only Windows logins. You manage logins at the server level.

## Viewing and Editing Existing Logins

To view or edit an existing login, follow these steps:

1. Start SQL Server Management Studio. In the Object Explorer view, connect to the appropriate server, and then work your way down to the Security folder.

2. Expand the Security folder at the server level and the Logins folder to list the current logins. Right-click a login, and then select Properties to view the properties of the login.

3. The Login Properties dialog box, shown in Figure 9-1, has five pages:

    a. **General**   Provides an overview of the login configuration, including the authentication mode (which cannot be changed), the default database and language (which can be changed), and any mapped credentials (which can be added or removed).

    b. **Server Roles**   Lists the server roles, and allows you to add or remove the login's server roles.

    c. **User Mappings**   Lists databases accessible by the login, and allows you to manage, on a per-database basis, the default schema, the user identity for the database, and the assigned database roles.

    d. **Securables**   Shows current object permissions, and allows you to manage object permissions for the login.

    e. **Status**   Shows current status of the login, including whether the login is enabled, locked out, or denied permission to connect to the Database Engine.

**Note**  In the Connection area of any page, you can click the View Connection Properties link to see detailed information about the user's current connection properties. This information is helpful for trouble-shooting connection issues.

4. When you are finished working with the account, click OK.

**Figure 9-1**  Login Properties dialog box.

To view information about a login with Transact-SQL, use sp_helplogins. Sample 9-1 shows the syntax and usage for this command.

**Sample 9-1**  sp_helplogins Syntax and Usage

```
Syntax
sp_helplogins [[@LoginNamePattern =] 'login']


Usage
EXEC sp_helplogins 'goteam'
```

The output provided by sp_helplogins includes the login name, security identifier, default database, and default language. To determine the server roles and Windows groups to which the currently logged-on user belongs either implicitly or expressly, you can execute the following query:

```
USE master
GO
SELECT * FROM sys.login_token;
GO
```

## Creating Logins

You create new logins in SQL Server Management Studio by using the Login – New dialog box. If you want to use Windows user or group accounts, you must create these accounts on the local machine or in the Windows domain, and then create the related SQL Server logins. Ask a network administrator to set up the necessary accounts.

To create a SQL Server login, follow these steps:

1. Start SQL Server Management Studio. In the Object Explorer view, connect to the appropriate server, and then work your way down to the Security folder at the server level.

2. Right-click Logins, and then select New Login to display the Login – New dialog box shown in Figure 9-2.

**Figure 9-2**   The Login – New dialog box.

3. If you are creating a login for a Windows account, select the Windows Authentication option, and then type the user name in *DOMAIN\username* format, such as **CPANDL\wrstanek**. If you want to search Active Directory for the domain

and user information, click Search, and then use the Select User Or Group dialog box to select the user for which you are creating the SQL Server account. Password policy and expiration enforcement are handled by the local Windows password policy automatically.

4. If you want to create a new SQL Server login, select the SQL Server Authentication option, and then type the name of the account you want to use, such as **Sales** or **WRSTANEK**. Then enter and confirm the password for the account. To enforce the local Windows password expiration policy on the SQL Server login, select Enforce Password Policy. If you elect to enforce password policy, you can also elect to enforce password expiration. To do this, select Enforce Password Expiration.

5. Specify the default database and default language for the login. Assigning a default database does not give the login permission to access the database. Instead, it merely specifies the database that is used when no database is specified in a command.

6. Click OK to create the login. If you are creating a SQL Server login and an identically named login already exists on the server, you will see an error. Click OK and change the login, or click Cancel if you determine that the new login is not needed.

7. You have not yet assigned any roles or access permissions. Refer to "Configuring Server Roles" on page 294 and "Controlling Database Access and Administration" on page 297 to learn how to configure these options.

You can also create logins with Transact-SQL. Use CREATE LOGIN as shown in Sample 9-2. To use this statement, you need ALTER ANY LOGIN permission on the server (and if using credentials, you need ALTER ANY CREDENTIAL permission).

**Sample 9-2** CREATE LOGIN Syntax and Usage

```
Syntax
CREATE LOGIN login_name { WITH < option_list1 > | FROM < sources > }

< sources >::=
    WINDOWS [ WITH windows_options [,...] ]
    | CERTIFICATE certificate_name
    | ASYMMETRIC KEY asym_key_name

< option_list1 >::=
    PASSWORD = 'password' [ HASHED ] [ MUST_CHANGE ]
    [ , option_list2 [ ,... ] ]

< option_list2 >::=
    SID = sid
    | DEFAULT_DATABASE = database
```

```
| DEFAULT_LANGUAGE = language
| CHECK_EXPIRATION = { ON | OFF}
| CHECK_POLICY = { ON | OFF}
[ CREDENTIAL = credential_name ]

< windows_options >::=
   DEFAULT_DATABASE = database
   | DEFAULT_LANGUAGE = language
```

**Usage for SQL Logins**
```
create login wrstanek WITH PASSWORD = 'MZ82$!408765RTM'
```

**Usage for SQL Logins Mapped to Credentials**
```
create login wrstanek WITH PASSWORD = 'MZ82$!408765RTM',
    CREDENTIAL = StanekWR
```

**Usage for Logins from a Domain Account**
```
CREATE LOGIN [CPANDL\wrstanek] FROM WINDOWS;
```

## Editing Logins with T-SQL

You can edit logins in SQL Server Management Studio as explained in "Viewing and Editing Existing Logins" on page 285. Editing logins with T-SQL is more work, however, and requires you to use the ALTER LOGIN statement. You need ALTER ANY LOGIN permission to alter logins (and if working with credentials, ALTER ANY CREDENTIAL permission). When a login is a member of the sysadmin server role, only another member of this role can make the following changes:

- Reset the password without supplying the old password.

- Require a user to change the login password.

- Change the login name.

- Enable or disable the login.

- Change the login credential.

- Force SQL Server to check a password for compliance with Group Policy.

- Force SQL Server to enforce password expiration settings in Group Policy.

Sample 9-3 shows the syntax and usage for ALTER LOGIN.

**Sample 9-3**   ALTER LOGIN Syntax and Usage

```
Syntax
ALTER LOGIN login_name
    {
    < status_option >
    | WITH set_option [ ,... ]
    | <cryptographic_credential_option>
    }

< status_option >::=
        ENABLE | DISABLE

< set_option >::=
    PASSWORD = 'password' | hashed_password HASHED
    [
            OLD_PASSWORD = 'oldpassword'
      | secadmin_pwd_option [ secadmin_pwd_option ]
    ]
    | DEFAULT_DATABASE = database
    | DEFAULT_LANGUAGE = language
    | NAME = login_name
    | CHECK_POLICY = { ON | OFF }
    | CHECK_EXPIRATION = { ON | OFF }
    | CREDENTIAL = credential_name
    | NO CREDENTIAL

< secadmin_pwd_opt >::=
        MUST_CHANGE | UNLOCK

<cryptographic_credentials_option> ::=
    ADD CREDENTIAL credential_name
    | DROP CREDENTIAL credential_name

Usage for Changing the Login Name
ALTER LOGIN wrstanek WITH NAME = stanekwr

Usage for Changing the Login Password
ALTER LOGIN wrstanek WITH PASSWORD = '3948wJ698FFF7';

Usage for Requiring User to Change Password
ALTER LOGIN wrstanek MUST_CHANGE

Usage for Enforcing Password Policy
ALTER LOGIN wrstanek CHECK_POLICY=ON

Usage for Enforcing Password Expiration
ALTER LOGIN wrstanek CHECK_EXPIRATION=ON
```

## Granting or Denying Server Access

When you create a new login or modify an existing login based on a Windows account, you can explicitly grant or deny access to the server's Database Engine for this login. Explicitly denying access to the server is useful when a particular Windows account should be temporarily restricted from accessing the server.

To grant or deny access for an existing login, complete the following steps:

1. Start SQL Server Management Studio. In the Object Explorer view, connect to the appropriate server, and then work your way down to the Security folder at the server level.

2. Expand the Security folder and the Logins folder to list the current logins. Right-click a login, and then select Properties to view the properties of that login. This opens the Login Properties dialog box (shown previously in Figure 9-1).

3. Under Select A Page, select Status to display the Status page.

4. To grant access to the server, select the Grant option.

5. To deny access to the server, select the Deny option.

   **Note**   Denying access to the server does not prevent users from logging on to SQL Server. Instead, it prevents them from using their Windows domain account to log on to SQL Server. Users can still log on if they have a valid SQL Server login ID and password.

6. Click OK.

You can also grant or deny logins with Transact-SQL. To grant a login for a domain account, use GRANT CONNECT, as shown in Sample 9-4.

**Note**   Only members of the sysadmin or securityadmin fixed server roles can execute GRANT CONNECT and DENY CONNECT.

**Sample 9-4**   GRANT CONNECT Syntax and Usage

```
Syntax
USE [master]
GO
GRANT CONNECT SQL TO 'login'
GO


Usage
USE [master]
GO
GRANT CONNECT SQL TO 'GALAXY\WRSTANEK'
GO
```

To deny access to the server for the account, use DENY CONNECT as shown in Sample 9-5.

**Sample 9-5**  DENY CONNECT Syntax and Usage

```
Syntax
USE [master]
GO
DENY CONNECT SQL TO 'login'
GO


Usage
USE [master]
GO
DENY CONNECT SQL TO 'GALAXY\WRSTANEK'
GO
```

# Enabling, Disabling, and Unlocking Logins

Similar to Windows accounts, SQL Server logins can be enabled and disabled by administrators. Logins can also become locked based on policy settings and might need to be unlocked. For example, if a login's password expires, the login might become locked.

> **Tip**  You can determine whether a login is disabled or locked by selecting the server's Logins node in SQL Server Management Studio. The icon for the login is updated to show the status as locked or disabled.

To enable, disable, or unlock a login, complete the following steps:

1. Start SQL Server Management Studio. In the Object Explorer view, connect to the appropriate server, and then work your way down to the Security folder at the server level.

2. Expand the Security folder and the Logins folder to list the current logins. Right-click a login, and then select Properties to view the properties of that login. This opens the Login Properties dialog box.

3. Under Select A Page, select Status to display the Status page.

4. You can now do the following:

   ❑ Enable the login by selecting Enabled under Login.

   ❑ Disable the login by selecting Disabled under Login.

   ❑ Unlock the login by clearing Login Is Locked Out.

5. Click OK.

You can also enable, disable, or unlock a login with Transact-SQL. To grant a login for a domain account, use ALTER LOGIN, as shown in Sample 9-6.

> **Note**   Only members of the sysadmin or securityadmin fixed server roles can execute ALTER LOGIN.

**Sample 9-6**   Enabling, Disabling, and Unlocking Accounts

```
Syntax
USE [master]
GO
ALTER LOGIN 'login' DISABLE | ENABLE | UNLOCK
GO


Usage for Disabling Logins
USE [master]
GO
ALTER LOGIN 'GALAXY\WRSTANEK' DISABLE
GO


Usage for Enabling Logins
USE [master]
GO
ALTER LOGIN 'GALAXY\WRSTANEK' ENABLE
GO


Usage for Unlocking Logins
USE [master]
GO
ALTER LOGIN 'GALAXY\WRSTANEK' UNLOCK
GO
```

## Removing Logins

When a user leaves the organization or a login is no longer needed for another reason, you should remove the login from SQL Server. To remove a login, complete the following steps:

1. Start SQL Server Management Studio, and then access the appropriate server.

2. In the server's Security folder, expand the Logins folder.

3. Right-click the login you want to remove, and then select Delete from the shortcut menu.

4. The Delete Object dialog box shows you which account you are deleting. Click OK to remove the account. Remember that you might also need to delete users in each database.

Use DROP LOGIN to delete Windows user and group accounts, as shown in Sample 9-7.

**Sample 9-7** DROP LOGIN Syntax and Usage

```
Syntax
DROP LOGIN 'login'


Usage
DROP LOGIN 'GALAXY\WRSTANEK'
```

## Changing Passwords

You manage Windows user and group accounts in the Windows domain or on the local machine. Users can change their own passwords or ask the Windows administrator to reset their passwords, if necessary. For SQL Server logins, you change passwords through SQL Server Management Studio using the following steps:

1. Start SQL Server Management Studio and then access the appropriate server.

2. In the server's Security folder, expand the Logins folder.

3. Right-click the login you want to change, and then select Properties to display the Login Properties dialog box.

4. Type and then confirm the new password in the boxes provided.

5. Click OK.

To change passwords with Transact-SQL, you can use ALTER LOGIN as discussed previously.

# Configuring Server Roles

Server roles set server-wide administrator privileges for SQL Server logins. You can manage server roles by role or by individual logins.

## Assigning Roles by Login

To assign or change server roles for a login, follow these steps:

1. Start SQL Server Management Studio. In the Object Explorer view, connect to the appropriate server, and then work your way down to the Security folder at the server level.

2. Expand the Security folder and the Logins folder to list the current logins. Right-click a login, and then select Properties to display the Login Properties dialog box and view the properties of the login.

3. Select the Server Roles page, as shown in Figure 9-3.

4. Grant server roles by selecting the check boxes next to the roles you want to use. You learned about server roles in "Server Roles" on page 281.

5. When you have finished configuring server roles, click OK.

**Figure 9-3**    The Server Roles page of the Login Properties dialog box.

You can also configure server roles with Transact-SQL. The sp_addsrvrolemember stored procedure adds a login to a server role, and you can use it as shown in Sample 9-8.

> **Note**    To use sp_addsrvrolemember or sp_dropsrvrolemember, you must have ALTER ANY LOGIN permission on the server and membership in the role to which you are adding the new member.

**Sample 9-8**    sp_addsrvrolemember Syntax and Usage

```
Syntax
sp_addsrvrolemember [@loginame =] 'login', [@rolename =] 'role'


Usage
EXEC sp_addsrvrolemember 'GALAXY\WRSTANEK', 'sysadmin'
```

The sp_dropsrvrolemember stored procedure removes a login from a role, and you can use it as shown in Sample 9-9.

**Sample 9-9** sp_dropsrvrolemember Syntax and Usage

```
Syntax
sp_dropsrvrolemember [@loginame =] 'login', [@rolename =] 'role'


Usage
EXEC sp_dropsrvrolemember 'GALAXY\WRSTANEK', 'sysadmin'
```

## Assigning Roles to Multiple Logins

The easiest way to assign roles to multiple logins is to use the Server Role Properties dialog box. To access this dialog box and configure multiple logins, follow these steps:

1. Start SQL Server Management Studio. In the Object Explorer view, connect to the appropriate server, and then work your way down to the Security folder at the server level.

2. Expand the Server Roles node, right-click the role you want to configure, and then select Properties. This opens the Server Role Properties dialog box shown in Figure 9-4.

**Figure 9-4** The Server Role Properties dialog box.

3. To add logins, click Add, and then use the Select Logins dialog box to select the logins to add. You can enter partial names, and then click Check Names to expand the name. To search for names, click Browse.

4. To remove a login, select it, and then click Remove.

5. When you have finished configuring server roles, click OK.

### Revoking Access Rights and Roles by Server Login

To revoke access rights or to remove a user from a role in a database, complete the following steps:

1. Start SQL Server Management Studio. In the Object Explorer view, connect to the appropriate server.

2. Expand the server's Security folder, and then expand the related Logins folder.

3. Double-click the login that you want to configure to display the Login Properties dialog box.

4. Select the Server Roles page. Clear the check box next to the server roles that you want to remove from this login.

5. Select the User Mapping page. Clear the check box next to the databases to which this user should not have access. Alternatively, select a database to which access is permitted, and then modify the granted roles by clearing options under Database Role Membership For.

6. When you have finished, click OK.

# Controlling Database Access and Administration

You control database access and administration with database users and roles. Database users are the logins that have the right to access the database. Database access roles set administration privileges and other database permissions.

### Assigning Access and Roles by Login

For individual logins, you can grant access to databases and assign roles by completing the following steps:

1. Start SQL Server Management Studio. In the Object Explorer view, connect to the appropriate server, and then work your way down to the Security folder.

2. Expand the Security folder and the Logins folder to list the current logins. Right-click the login you want to configure, and then select Properties. This opens the Login Properties dialog box.

3. Select the User Mapping page, as shown in Figure 9-5.

**Figure 9-5**    The User Mapping page of the Login Properties dialog box.

4.  Select the check box for a database that you want the login to be able to access. Then, in the Database Role Membership For list box, select the check boxes next to the database roles that this login should have on the currently selected database.

> **Tip**    If you select the *msdb* database, as shown in Figure 9-5, you can assign special-purpose roles for SSIS, Policy-Based Management, and server groups.

5.  Repeat step 4 for other databases that you want the login to be able to access.

6.  When you have finished configuring database roles, click OK.

## Assigning Roles for Multiple Logins

At the database level, you can assign database roles to multiple logins. To do this, complete the following steps:

1.  Start SQL Server Management Studio. In the Object Explorer view, connect to the appropriate server.

2.  Expand the Databases folder, and then expand the node for the database you want to configure.

3.  Expand the database's Security, Roles, and Database Roles folders. Double-click the role you want to configure. This opens the Database Role Properties dialog box shown in Figure 9-6.

4. To add role members, click Add to display the Select Database User Or Role dialog box.

5. In the dialog box, enter the name of the user or role to add. Separate names with semicolons. You can enter partial names, and then click Check Names to expand the names. To search for names, click Browse.

6. To remove a role member, select a database user or other role, and then click Remove.

7. When you have finished configuring database roles, click OK.

**Figure 9-6**    The Database Role Properties dialog box.

## Creating Standard Database Roles

Although predefined roles have a specific set of permissions that you cannot change, you can set permissions for roles you create for a particular database. For example, suppose that a database has three different types of users: normal users who need to view data, managers who need to be able to modify data, and developers who need to be able to modify database objects. In this situation, you can create three roles to handle these user types. Then you need to manage only these roles and not the many different user accounts.

To create a standard database role, complete the following steps:

1. Start SQL Server Management Studio. In the Object Explorer view, connect to the appropriate server.

2. Expand the Databases folder, and then select a database and expand the node for it.

3. Expand the database's Security and Roles folders. Right-click Roles, point to New, and then choose New Database Role. This opens the Database Role – New dialog box shown in Figure 9-7.

4. Type a name for the role in the Role Name box.

> **Tip**   Use a name for the role that is short but descriptive, such as Normal Users, Editors, Testers, or Developers.

**Figure 9-7**   The Database Role – New dialog box.

5. The default owner of the role is dbo. To set a different owner, click the button to the right of the Owner box to display the Select Database User Or Role dialog box.

6. In the dialog box, enter the name of the users, the roles, or both that should be the owners of this role. Separate names with semicolons. You can enter partial names, and then click Check Names to expand the names. To search for names, click Browse.

7. To add role members, click Add to display the Select Database User Or Role dialog box.

8. In the dialog box, enter the names of the users or roles to add. Separate names with semicolons. You can enter partial names, and then click Check Names to expand the names. To search for names, click Browse. Click OK.

9. Choose Securables from the Select A Page list in the dialog box, and then use the Securables page options to configure database access permissions for this role. For more information about configuring database access permissions, see "Managing Database Permissions" on page 304.

10. Click OK.

## Creating Application Database Roles

Application roles are designed to be used by applications that access the database and do not have logins associated with them. You can configure an application role by completing the following steps:

1. Start SQL Server Management Studio. In the Object Explorer view, connect to the appropriate server.

2. Expand the Databases folder, and then select a database and expand the node for it.

3. Expand the database's Security and Roles folders. Right-click Roles, point to New, and then choose New Application Role. This opens the Application Role – New dialog box shown in Figure 9-8.

**Figure 9-8**   The Application Role – New dialog box.

4. Type a name for the role in the Role Name box.

5. The default schema for the role is dbo. The default (or base) schema sets the base permissions for the new role. To set a different default schema, click the button to the right of the Default Schema box to display the Locate Schema dialog box.

6. In the dialog box, enter the name of the default schema. You can enter a partial name, and then click Check Names to expand the name. To search for a schema to use, click Browse. Click OK.

7. Choose Securables from the Select A Page list, and then use the Securables page options to configure database access permissions for this role. For more information about configuring database access permissions, see "Managing Database Permissions" on page 304.

8. Click OK.

## Removing Role Memberships for Database Users

To revoke access rights or to remove a user from a role in a database, complete the following steps:

1. Start SQL Server Management Studio. In the Object Explorer view, connect to the appropriate server.

2. Expand the Databases folder, and then select a database and expand the node for it.

3. Expand the database's Security and Users folders. Double-click the user name. This opens the Database User dialog box.

4. On the General page, clear the check box next to the database roles that this user should not have on the currently selected database.

5. When you have finished removing roles for the database user, click OK.

## Deleting User-Defined Roles

To delete a user-defined role, complete the following steps:

1. Start SQL Server Management Studio. In the Object Explorer view, connect to the appropriate server.

2. Expand the Databases folder, and then select a database and expand the node for it.

3. Expand the database's Security and Roles folders.

4. If the role you want to remove is a database role, expand Database Roles. If the role you want to remove is an application role, expand Application Roles.

5. Select the role you want to delete, and then press the Delete key.

6. The Delete Object dialog box shows you which role you are deleting. Click OK to remove the role.

**Note**   User-defined roles cannot be deleted if they have members. First edit the properties for the role, deleting any currently listed members, and then delete the role.

## Transact-SQL Commands for Managing Access and Roles

SQL Server provides different commands for managing database access and roles. These commands are summarized in Sample 9-10.

**Sample 9-10**   Commands for Managing Database Access and Roles

```
Adding a User to the Current Database
CREATE USER user_name
    [ { { FOR | FROM }
        { LOGIN login_name
        | CERTIFICATE certificate_name
        | ASYMMETRIC KEY asym_key_name
        }
    ]
    [ WITH DEFAULT_SCHEMA = schema_name ]


Renaming a User or Changing Default Schema
ALTER USER user_name
    WITH < set_item > [ ,...n ]

< set_item > ::=
    NAME = new_user_name
    | DEFAULT_SCHEMA = schema_name


Removing a User from a Database
DROP USER user_name


Listing Server Role Members
sp_helpsrvrolemember [[@rolename =] 'role']


Managing Database Standard Roles
CREATE ROLE role_name [ AUTHORIZATION owner_name ]
ALTER ROLE role_name WITH NAME = new_name
DROP ROLE role_name
sp_helprole [[@rolename =] 'role']
```

```
Managing Database Role Members
sp_addrolemember [@rolename =] 'role',
    [@membername =] 'security_account'
sp_droprolemember [@rolename =] 'role',
    [@membername =] 'security_account'
sp_helprolemember [[@rolename =] 'role']


Managing Application Roles
CREATE APPLICATION ROLE application_role_name
    WITH PASSWORD = 'password' [ , DEFAULT_SCHEMA = schema_name ]

ALTER APPLICATION ROLE application_role_name
        WITH <set_item> [ ,...n ]

<set_item> ::=
    NAME = new_application_role_name
    | PASSWORD = 'password'
    | DEFAULT_SCHEMA = schema_name

DROP APPLICATION ROLE rolename
```

# Managing Database Permissions

The database owner, members of sysadmin, and members of securityadmin can assign database permissions. The available permissions include the following:

- **GRANT**  Gives permission to perform the related task. With roles, all members of the role inherit the permission.

- **REVOKE**  Removes prior GRANT permission, but does not explicitly prevent a user or role from performing a task. A user or role could still inherit GRANT permission from another role.

- **DENY**  Explicitly denies permission to perform a task, and prevents the user or role from inheriting the permission. DENY takes precedence over all other GRANT permissions.

    **Note**  DENY is a Transact-SQL command and is not part of the ANSI SQL-92 standard.

You can grant, deny, and revoke permissions at the database level or the object level. You can also assign permissions using database roles. For more information, see "Controlling Database Access and Administration" on page 297.

## Assigning Database Permissions for Statements

At the database level, you can grant, revoke, or deny permission to execute data definition language statements, such as CREATE TABLE or BACKUP DATABASE. These statements were summarized in Table 9-5 on page 280.

In SQL Server Management Studio, you grant, revoke, or deny database permissions for statements by completing the following steps:

1. Start SQL Server Management Studio. In the Object Explorer view, connect to the appropriate server.

2. Work your way down to the Databases folder using the entries in the left pane.

3. Select a database, right-click the database name, and then select Properties from the shortcut menu to display the Database Properties dialog box.

4. Select the Permissions page from the Select A Page list, as shown in Figure 9-9.

**Figure 9-9**   The Permissions page of the Database Properties dialog box.

5. To assign default permissions for all users, assign permissions to the public role. To add users or roles, click Search, and then use the Select User Or Group dialog box to select the user or role you want to add. To assign permissions for individual users or roles, select the user or role, and then use the Permissions For list

box to Grant or Deny permissions as appropriate. Clear both check boxes to revoke a previously granted or denied permission.

6. Click OK to assign the permissions.

With Transact-SQL, you use the GRANT, REVOKE, and DENY commands to assign permissions. Sample 9-11 shows the syntax and usage for GRANT; Sample 9-12 shows the syntax and usage for REVOKE; and Sample 9-13 shows the syntax and usage for DENY.

**Sample 9-11**   GRANT Syntax and Usage

```
Syntax for Permissions on Servers and Databases
GRANT < permission > [ ,...n ]
    TO < principal > [ ,...n ] [ WITH GRANT OPTION ]
    [ AS
        {
                Windows_group | SQL_Server_login | database_user
        | database_role | application_role
        }
    ]
< permission >::=  ALL [ PRIVILEGES ] | permission_name
    [ ( column [ ,...n ] ) ]
< principal >::= Windows_login | SQL_Server_login
    | SQL_Server_login_mapped_to_certificate
    | SQL_Server_login_mapped_to_asymmetric_key
    | Database_user | Database_role | Application_role
    | Database_user_mapped_to_certificate
    | Database_user_mapped_to_asymmetric_key


Syntax for Permissions on Members of the Object Class
GRANT < permission > [ ,...n ] ON [ OBJECT ::]  < securable_name >
    TO < principal > [ ,...n ] [ WITH GRANT OPTION ]
    [ AS
        {
                Windows_group | SQL_Server_login | database_user
        | database_role | application_role
        }
    ]
< permission >::=  ALL [ PRIVILEGES ] | permission_name
    [ ( column [ ,...n ] ) ]
< principal >::= Windows_login | SQL_Server_login
    | SQL_Server_login_mapped_to_certificate
    | SQL_Server_login_mapped_to_asymmetric_key
    | Database_user | Database_role | Application_role
    | Database_user_mapped_to_certificate
    | Database_user_mapped_to_asymmetric_key
```

**Syntax for Permissions on All Other Securables**

```
GRANT < permission > [ ,...n ] ON < scope >
    TO < principal > [ ,...n ] [ WITH GRANT OPTION ]
    [ AS
        {
                Windows_group | SQL_Server_login | database_user
            | database_role | application_role
        }
    ]
< permission >::=  ALL [ PRIVILEGES ] | permission_name
    [ ( column [ ,...n ] ) ]
< scope >::= [ securable_class :: ] securable_name
< securable_class >::= APPLICATION ROLE | ASSEMBLY | ASYMMETRIC KEY
    | CERTIFICATE | CONTRACT | ENDPOINT | FULLTEXT CATALOG
    | LOGIN | MESSAGE TYPE | REMOTE SERVICE BINDING | ROLE
    | ROUTE | SCHEMA | SERVICE | SYMMETRIC KEY | TYPE
    | USER | XML SCHEMA COLLECTION
< principal >::= Windows_login | SQL_Server_login
    | SQL_Server_login_mapped_to_certificate
    | SQL_Server_login_mapped_to_asymmetric_key
    | Database_user | Database_role | Application_role
    | Database_user_mapped_to_certificate
    | Database_user_mapped_to_asymmetric_key
```

**Usage**

```
GRANT CREATE DATABASE, CREATE TABLE
TO Users, [GALAXY\Sales]
GRANT SELECT
ON customer..customers
TO public
GRANT INSERT, UPDATE, DELETE
ON customer..customers
TO Devs, Testers
```

**Sample 9-12**   REVOKE Syntax and Usage

**Syntax for Permission on Servers and Databases**

```
REVOKE [ GRANT OPTION FOR ] < permission > [ ,...n ]
    { TO | FROM } < principal > [ ,...n ] [ CASCADE ]
    [ AS
        {
                Windows_group | SQL_Server_login
            | database_role | application_role
        }
    ]
< permission >::=  ALL [ PRIVILEGES ] | permission_name
    [ ( column [ ,...n ] ) ]
```

```
< principal >::= Windows_login | SQL_Server_login
    | SQL_Server_login_mapped_to_certificate
    | SQL_Server_login_mapped_to_asymmetric_key
    | Database_user | Database_role | Application_role
    | Database_user_mapped_to_certificate
    | Database_user_mapped_to_asymmetric_key
```

**Syntax for Permissions on Members of the Object Class**

```
REVOKE [ GRANT OPTION FOR ] < permission > [ ,...n ]
    ON [ OBJECT ::] < securable_name >
    { TO | FROM } < principal > [ ,...n ] [ CASCADE ]
    [ AS
        {
                Windows_group | SQL_Server_login
        | database_role | application_role
        }
    ]
< permission >::=  ALL [ PRIVILEGES ] | permission_name
    [ ( column [ ,...n ] ) ]
< principal >::= Windows_login | SQL_Server_login
    | SQL_Server_login_mapped_to_certificate
    | SQL_Server_login_mapped_to_asymmetric_key
    | Database_user | Database_role | Application_role
    | Database_user_mapped_to_certificate
    | Database_user_mapped_to_asymmetric_key
```

**Syntax for Permissions on All Other Securables**

```
REVOKE [ GRANT OPTION FOR ] < permission > [ ,...n ] [ ON < scope > ]
    { TO | FROM } < principal > [ ,...n ] [ CASCADE ]
    [ AS
        {
                Windows_group | SQL_Server_login
        | database_role | application_role
        }
    ]
< permission >::=  ALL [ PRIVILEGES ] | permission_name
    [ ( column [ ,...n ] ) ]
< scope >::= [ < securable_class > :: ] securable_name
< securable_class >::= APPLICATION ROLE | ASSEMBLY | ASYMMETRIC KEY
    | CERTIFICATE | CONTRACT | ENDPOINT | FULLTEXT CATALOG
    | LOGIN | MESSAGE TYPE | REMOTE SERVICE BINDING | ROLE
    | ROUTE | SCHEMA | SERVICE | SYMMETRIC KEY | TYPE
    | USER | XML SCHEMA COLLECTION
< principal >::= Windows_login | SQL_Server_login
    | SQL_Server_login_mapped_to_certificate
    | SQL_Server_login_mapped_to_asymmetric_key
    | Database_user | Database_role | Application_role
    | Database_user_mapped_to_certificate
    | Database_user_mapped_to_asymmetric_key
```

**Usage**
```
REVOKE CREATE TABLE, CREATE DEFAULT
FROM Devs, Testers
REVOKE INSERT, UPDATE, DELETE
FROM Users, [GALAXY\Sales]
```

**Sample 9-13**   DENY Syntax and Usage

**Syntax for Permission on Servers and Databases**
```
DENY < permission > [ ,...n ]
    TO < principal > [ ,...n ] [ CASCADE ]
    [ AS
      {
              Windows_group | SQL_Server_login | database_user
          | database_role | application_role
      }
    ]
< permission >::=  ALL [ PRIVILEGES ] | permission_name
    [ ( column [ ,...n ] ) ]
< principal >::= Windows_login | SQL_Server_login
    | SQL_Server_login_mapped_to_certificate
    | SQL_Server_login_mapped_to_asymmetric_key
    | Database_user | Database_role | Application_role
    | Database_user_mapped_to_certificate
    | Database_user_mapped_to_asymmetric_key
```

**Syntax for Permissions on Members of the Object Class**
```
DENY < permission > [ ,...n ] ON [ OBJECT ::] < securable_name >
        TO < principal > [ ,...n ] [ CASCADE ]
    [ AS
      {
              Windows_group | SQL_Server_login | database_user
          | database_role | application_role
      }
    ]
< permission >::=  ALL [ PRIVILEGES ] | permission_name
    [ ( column [ ,...n ] ) ]
< principal >::= Windows_login | SQL_Server_login
    | SQL_Server_login_mapped_to_certificate
    | SQL_Server_login_mapped_to_asymmetric_key
    | Database_user | Database_role | Application_role
    | Database_user_mapped_to_certificate
    | Database_user_mapped_to_asymmetric_key
```

```
Syntax for Permissions on All Other Securables
DENY < permission > [ ,...n ] ON < scope >
    TO < principal > [ ,...n ] [ CASCADE ]
        [ AS
        {
                Windows_group | SQL_Server_login | database_user
            | database_role | application_role
        }
    ]
< permission >::=  ALL [ PRIVILEGES ] | permission_name
    [ ( column [ ,...n ] ) ]
< scope >::= [ securable_class :: ] securable_name
< securable_class >::= APPLICATION ROLE | ASSEMBLY | ASYMMETRIC KEY
    | CERTIFICATE | CONTRACT | ENDPOINT | FULLTEXT CATALOG
    | LOGIN | MESSAGE TYPE | REMOTE SERVICE BINDING | ROLE
    | ROUTE | SCHEMA | SERVICE | SYMMETRIC KEY | TYPE
    | USER | XML SCHEMA COLLECTION
< principal >::= Windows_login | SQL_Server_login
    | SQL_Server_login_mapped_to_certificate
    | SQL_Server_login_mapped_to_asymmetric_key
    | Database_user | Database_role | Application_role
    | Database_user_mapped_to_certificate
    | Database_user_mapped_to_asymmetric_key

Usage
DENY CREATE TABLE
    TO Devs, Testers
DENY INSERT, UPDATE, DELETE
    ON customer..customers
    TO Users, [GALAXY\Sales]
```

## Object Permissions by Login

Object permissions apply to tables, views, and stored procedures. Permissions you assign to these objects include SELECT, INSERT, UPDATE, and DELETE. A summary of permitted actions by object was provided in Table 9-4 on page 275.

In SQL Server Management Studio, you grant, revoke, or deny object permissions by completing the following steps:

1. Start SQL Server Management Studio. In the Object Explorer view, connect to the appropriate server.

2. Work your way down to the Databases folder using the entries in the left pane.

3. Expand the Databases folder, and then select a database and expand the node for it.

4. Expand the Security and Users folders.

5. Double-click the user you want to configure to display the Database User dialog box.

6. Select the Securables page from the Select A Page list as shown in Figure 9-10.

**Figure 9-10**   The Securables page of the Database User dialog box.

7. To assign object permissions, click Search to display the Add Objects dialog box.

8. In the Add Objects dialog box, select the type of objects for which you want to manage permissions:

   ❑ Select Specific Objects if you know the name of the objects for which you want to manage permissions, and then click OK. In the Select Objects dialog box, click Object Types. Next, in the Select Object Types dialog box, select the type of objects to find, such as Tables And Views, and then click OK. In the Select Objects dialog box, enter the object names. Separate multiple names with a semicolon, and click Check Names to expand any partial name you enter to full names. To browse for objects of the previously selected type, click Browse. When you are finished selecting objects, click OK. The selected objects then will be listed in the Database User dialog box.

❏ Select All Objects Of The Types if you want to manage permissions for all objects of a specific type, such as all tables and views, and then click OK. In the Select Objects dialog box, click Object Types. Next, in the Select Object Types dialog box, select the type of objects to find, such as Tables And Views, and then click OK. In the Select Object Types dialog box, select the object types you want to manage, and then click OK. All objects of the selected types then will be listed in the Database User dialog box.

❏ Select All Objects Belonging To The Schema if you want to manage permissions for all objects owned by a particular schema. In the Add Objects dialog box, use the Schema Name selection menu to choose the schema whose objects you want to manage, and then click OK. All objects belonging to the schema will then be listed in the Database User dialog box.

9. In the Database User dialog box, you'll see a list of securables that match your criteria. Select a securable in the upper panel to display related permissions in the Permissions For panel. You can now do the following:

❏ Click the Effective tab to see the effective permissions a user is granted on a selected securable.

❏ Click the Explicit tab to set permissions. Grant or Deny permissions as appropriate. If you grant a permission and also want the user to be able to grant the permission, select the With Grant option. Clear both check boxes to revoke a previously granted or denied permission.

10. When you are finished, click OK to assign the permissions.

## Object Permissions for Multiple Logins

You can also assign permissions by object, and in this way assign object permissions for multiple logins. To do this, complete the following steps:

1. Work your way down to the Databases folder using the entries in the left pane.

2. Expand the Databases folder, and then select the folder for the type of objects you want to work with, such as Tables, Views, or Stored Procedures.

3. Double-click the object you want to configure to display a Properties dialog box. Or right-click and select Properties.

4. In the Properties dialog box, select the Permissions page from the Select A Page list as shown in Figure 9-11. Any users or roles directly assigned permissions on the object are listed in the Users Or Roles list box.

**Figure 9-11**   Permissions for an object.

5. To add specific permissions for users, roles, or both, click Search to open the Select Users Or Roles dialog box. Enter the names of the users or roles to add. Separate names with semicolons. You can enter partial names, and then click Check Names to expand the names. To search for names, click Browse.

6. To set permissions for the object, select a user or role in the Users Or Roles list box. You can now do the following:

   ❑ Click the Effective tab to see the effective permissions for the user or role.

   ❑ Click the Explicit tab to set permissions. Grant or Deny permissions as appropriate. If you grant a permission and also want the user or role to be able to grant the permission, select the With Grant option. Clear both check boxes to revoke a previously granted or denied permission.

7. When you are finished, click OK to assign the permissions.

More information about Transact-SQL commands for assigning permissions can be found in "Assigning Database Permissions for Statements" on page 305.

Part III

# Microsoft SQL Server 2008 Data Administration

This part of the book covers Microsoft SQL Server 2008 data administration. Chapter 10 discusses techniques for managing schemas, tables, indexes, and views. You'll also find tips for working with constraints and rules. In Chapter 11 you'll learn about importing, exporting, and transforming data. Chapter 12 focuses on integrating SQL Server databases with other SQL Server databases and with other data sources. You'll find detailed discussions on distributed queries, distributed transactions, Distributed Transaction Coordinator, and linking remote servers. Chapter 13 explores data replication. You'll learn all about the latest replication techniques, including merge replication and immediately updating subscribers.

# Chapter 10
# Manipulating Schemas, Tables, Indexes, and Views

Objects are the fundamental units of data storage within databases. All data within a database is contained within a Database object. Each Database object contains Schema objects and those Schema objects contain the tables, indexes, views, and other objects that make up the database. The three basic levels of scoping and ownership are as follows:

- **Database**  Includes all objects defined within a database and is owned by a specific user

- **Schema**  Includes all objects defined within a schema, and is owned by a database-level security principal

- **Schema-contained object**  Refers to any individual table, view, or so forth that is defined in the database, and is owned by a specific schema

When you move databases designed for early versions of Microsoft SQL Server to SQL Server 2008, this model still applies. In these databases, the *dbo* schema is the owner of tables, views, and other related objects, and you can extend the database structure by creating and using other schemas as necessary.

**Note**   Policy-Based Management settings can affect your ability to name objects. For more information, see Chapter 18, "Implementing Policy-Based Management."

# Working with Schemas

Schemas are containers of objects that are used to define the namespaces for objects within databases. They are used to simplify management and create object subsets that can be managed collectively. Schemas are separate from users. Users own schemas and always have a default schema that the server uses when it resolves unqualified objects in queries. This means that the schema name does not need to be specified when accessing objects in the default schema. To access objects in other schemas, a two-part or three-part identifier is required. A two-part identifier specifies the schema name and the object name in *schema_name.object_name* format. A three-part identifier specifies the database name, schema name, and object name in *database_name.schema_name.object_name* format.

Database synonyms can be used to create alternate names so that a user's default schema contains references to other schema. For example, if you create a synonym for the *Customers.Contact* table as *dbo.Contact*, any user with *dbo* as the default schema can access the table using only the table name. Although synonyms can refer to objects in other databases, including remote instances of SQL Server, synonyms are valid only within the scope of the database in which they are defined. This means that each database can have identically named synonyms, and these synonyms can possibly refer to different objects.

Schemas have many benefits. Because users are no longer the direct owners of objects, removing users from a database is a simpler task; you no longer need to rename objects before dropping the user that created them. Multiple users can own a single schema through membership in a role or Windows group, which makes it easier to manage tables, views, and other database-defined objects. Multiple users can share a single default schema, which makes it easier to grant access to shared objects.

Schemas can be used to scope database access by function, role, or purpose to make it easier to access objects contained in a database. For example, you can have schemas named for each application that accesses the database. In this way, when users of a particular application access the database, their namespace is set appropriately for the objects they routinely access.

## Creating Schemas

Before you create a table, you should carefully consider the schema name. Schema names can be up to 128 characters long. Schema names must begin with an alphabetic character, but they can also contain underscores (_), "at" symbols (@), pound signs (#), and numerals. Schema names must be unique within each database. Different databases, however, can contain like-named schemas; for example, two different databases could each have an *Employees* schema.

In SQL Server Management Studio, you create a new schema by completing the following steps:

1. In SQL Server Management Studio, connect to the server instance that contains the database in which you want to work.

2. In Object Explorer, expand the Databases node, and then select a database and expand the view to show its resource nodes.

3. Expand the database's Security node, and then right-click the Schemas node. From the shortcut menu, choose New Schema to display the Schema – New dialog box shown in Figure 10-1.

**Figure 10-1** The Schema – New dialog box.

4. On the General page, specify the name of the schema and set the schema owner. To search for an available database-level security principal to use as the owner, click Search to display the Search Roles And Users dialog box, and then click Browse to open the Browse For Objects dialog box. Select the user or role to act as the schema owner, and then click OK twice.

**Note**   The schema owner can be any database-level security principal (database user, database role, or application role). Although the schema owner can own other schemas, the owner cannot use this schema as the default schema. If the schema owner is set as a role or Windows group, multiple users will own the schema.

5.  Click OK to create the schema.

The Transact-SQL command for creating schemas is CREATE SCHEMA. Sample 10-1 shows the syntax and usage for this command. The *schema_element* for the command allows you to use CREATE TABLE, CREATE VIEW, GRANT, REVOKE, and DENY statements to define tables, views, and permissions that should be created and contained within the schema you are defining.

**Note**   To specify another user as the owner of the schema being created, you must have IMPERSONATE permission on that user. If a database role is specified as the owner, you must be a member of the role or have ALTER permission on the role.

**Sample 10-1**   CREATE SCHEMA Syntax and Usage

```
Syntax
CREATE SCHEMA schema_name_clause [ < schema_element > [ , ...n ] ]
< schema_name_clause >::=
    { schema_name | AUTHORIZATION owner_name
    | schema_name AUTHORIZATION owner_name }
< schema_element >::=
    { table_definition | view_definition | grant_statement
    revoke_statement | deny_statement }


Usage
CREATE SCHEMA Employees AUTHORIZATION DataTeam
```

# Modifying Schemas

You might need to change the schema ownership or modify its permissions. One of the primary reasons for changing the schema owner is because the owner cannot use the schema as the default schema. You might also want to allow or deny specific permissions on a per-user or per-role basis. After a schema is created, however, you cannot change the schema name. You must drop the schema and create a new schema with the new name.

In SQL Server Management Studio, you can change the schema owner by completing the following steps:

1.  In SQL Server Management Studio, connect to the server instance that contains the database in which you want to work.

2. In Object Explorer, expand the Databases node, and then select a database and expand the view to show its resource nodes.

3. Expand the database's Security node, and then the Schemas node. Right-click the schema you want to work with. From the shortcut menu, choose Properties to display the Schema Properties dialog box.

4. To change the schema owner, click Search on the General page to display the Search Roles And Users dialog box, and then click Browse to open the Browse For Objects dialog box. Select the user or role to act as the schema owner, and then click OK twice.

You can manage granular permissions for a schema on the Permissions page in the Schema Properties dialog box. Any user or roles that are directly assigned permissions on the object are listed under Users Or Roles. To configure permissions for a user or role, complete the following steps:

1. Select the Permissions page from the Select A Page list in the Schema Properties dialog box.

2. Click Search to add specific permissions for users, roles, or both. This opens the Select Users Or Roles dialog box.

3. In the Select Users Or Roles dialog box, enter the names of the users or roles to add. Separate names with semicolons. You can enter partial names, and then click Check Names to expand the names. To search for names, click Browse. When you've selected the users or roles to add, click OK.

4. Select a user or role in the Users Or Roles list box. Use the Permissions For list box to Grant or Deny permissions as appropriate. If you grant a permission and also want the user to be able to grant the permission, select the With Grant option. Clear both check boxes to revoke a previously granted or denied permission.

5. When you are finished, click OK to assign the permissions.

## Moving Objects to a New Schema

As discussed previously, schemas are containers for objects, and there are times when you will want to move an object from one container to another. Objects can be moved from one schema to another only within the same database. When you do this, you change the namespace associated with the object, which changes the way the object is queried and accessed.

Moving the object to a new schema also affects permissions on the object. All permissions on the object are dropped when it is moved to a new schema. If the object owner is set to a specific user or role, that user or role will continue to be the owner of the object. If the object owner is set to SCHEMA OWNER, the ownership will remain as

SCHEMA OWNER, and after the move, the owner will become the owner of the new schema.

To move objects between schemas, you must have CONTROL permissions on the object and ALTER permissions on the schema to which you are moving the object. If the object has an EXECUTE AS OWNER specification on it and the owner is set to SCHEMA OWNER, you must also have IMPERSONATE permission on the owner of the target schema.

In SQL Server Management Studio, you can move an object to a new schema by completing the following steps:

1. In SQL Server Management Studio, connect to the server instance that contains the database in which you want to work.

2. In Object Explorer, expand the Databases node, and then select a database and expand the view to show its resource nodes.

3. Right-click the table, view, or other object you want to move. From the shortcut menu, choose View Dependencies. The Object Dependencies dialog box shows the database objects that must be present for this object to function properly and the objects that depend on the selected object. Use this dialog box to understand any dependencies that might be affected by moving the selected object. Click OK.

4. Right-click the table, view, or other object, and then select Design. One of several views displayed in the right pane is the Properties view for the selected object. If this view is not displayed, press F4.

5. Under Identity, click in the Schema drop-down list and select a new schema to contain the selected object.

**Caution**   All permissions on the object are dropped immediately and irreversibly if you have previously selected the option Don't Warn Me Again, Proceed Every Time. If you see the warning prompt, click Yes to continue and move the object to the designated schema, or click No to cancel the move.

The Transact-SQL command for moving objects between schemas is ALTER SCHEMA. Sample 10-2 shows the syntax and usage for this command. When you alter a schema, make sure you are using the correct database and are not using the *master* database.

**Sample 10-2**   ALTER SCHEMA Syntax and Usage

```
Syntax
ALTER SCHEMA target_schema TRANSFER source_schema.object_to_move


Usage
ALTER SCHEMA Employees TRANSFER Location.Department
```

## Dropping Schemas

If you no longer need a schema, you can drop it, and in this way, remove it from the database. To drop a schema, you must have CONTROL permission on the schema. Before dropping a schema, you must first move or drop all the objects that it contains. If you try to delete a schema that contains other objects, the drop operation will fail.

In SQL Server Management Studio, you can drop a schema by completing the following steps:

1. In SQL Server Management Studio, connect to the server instance that contains the database in which you want to work.

2. In Object Explorer, expand the Databases node, and then select a database and expand the view to show its resource nodes.

3. Expand the database's Security and Schemas nodes. Right-click the schema you want to drop. From the shortcut menu, choose Delete. This displays the Delete Object dialog box.

4. Click OK to confirm the deletion.

The Transact-SQL command for deleting schemas is DROP SCHEMA. Sample 10-3 shows the syntax and usage for this command. When you drop a schema, make sure you are using the correct database and are not using the *master* database.

**Sample 10-3**  DROP SCHEMA Syntax and Usage

```
Syntax
DROP SCHEMA schema_name


Usage
DROP SCHEMA Employees
```

# Getting Started with Tables

In Microsoft SQL Server 2008, the structures of tables and indexes are just as important as the database itself, especially when it comes to performance. Tables are collections of data about a specific entity, such as a customer or an order. To describe the attributes of these entities, you use named columns. For example, to describe the attributes of a customer, you could use these columns: cust_name, cust_address, and cust_phone.

Each instance of data in a table is represented as a single data entry or row. Typically, rows are unique and have unique identifiers called *primary keys* associated with them. However, a primary key is not mandatory in ANSI SQL, and it is not required in SQL Server. The job of the primary key is to set a unique identifier for each row in the table and to allow SQL Server to create a unique index on this key. Indexes are user-defined data structures that provide fast access to data when you search on an indexed column. Indexes are separate from tables, and you can configure them automatically with the Database Engine Tuning Advisor.

Most tables are related to other tables. For example, a *Customers* table might have a cust_account column that contains a customer's account number. The cust_account column might also appear in tables named *Orders* and *Receivables*. If the cust_account column is the primary key of the *Customers* table, a foreign key relationship can be established between *Customers* and *Orders* as well as between *Customers* and *Receivables*. The foreign key creates a link between the tables that you can use to preserve referential integrity in the database.

After you have established the link, you will not be able to delete a row in the *Customers* table if the cust_account identifier is referenced in the *Orders* or *Receivables* tables. This feature prevents you from invalidating references to information used in other tables. You would first need to delete or change the related references in the *Orders* or *Receivables* tables, or both, before deleting a primary key row in the *Customers* table. Foreign key relationships allow you to combine data from related tables in queries by matching the foreign key constraint of one table with the primary or unique key in another table. Combining tables in this manner is called a *table join*, and the keys allow SQL Server to optimize the query and quickly find related data.

# Table Essentials

Tables are defined as objects in SQL Server databases. Tables consist of columns and rows of data, and each column has a native or user-defined data type. Tables have two units of data storage: data pages and extents. *Data pages* are the fundamental units of data storage. *Extents* are the basic units in which space is allocated to tables and indexes. Data within tables can be organized using partitions.

## Understanding Data Pages

For all data types except large-value data types and variable-length columns when the data exceeds 8 KB, table data is stored in data pages that have a fixed size of 8 KB (8192 bytes). Each data page has a page header, data rows, and free space that can contain row offsets. The page header uses the first 96 bytes of each page, leaving 8096 bytes for data and row offsets. Row offsets indicate the logical order of rows on a page, which means that offset 0 refers to the first row in the index, offset 1 refers to the second row, and so on. If a table contains the large object data types varchar(max), nvarchar(max), or varbinary(max), the data might not be stored with the rest of the data for a row. Instead, SQL Server can store a 16-byte pointer to the actual data, which is stored in a collection of 8-KB pages that are not necessarily contiguous. A similar technique is used with variable-length columns when the row data exceeds 8 KB (except that 24-byte pointers are used).

SQL Server 2008 supports eight types of data pages:

- **Bulk Changed Map**   Contains information about extents modified by bulk operations since the last log file backup

- **Data**   Contains data rows with all data except for nvarchar(max), varchar(max), varbinary(max), and xml data (as well as text, ntext, and image data when *text in row* is set to ON)

- **Differential Changed Map**   Contains information about extents that have changed since the last database backup

- **Global Allocation Map, Shared Global Allocation Map**   Contains information about extents that have been allocated by SQL Server

- **Index Allocation Map**   Contains information about extents used by a table or index

- **Index**   Contains index entries

- **Page Free Space**   Contains information about free space available in data pages

- **Text/Image (large object data types)**   Contains text, ntext, image, nvarchar(max), varchar(max), varbinary(max), and xml data, as well as data for variable-length columns when the data row exceeds 8 KB (varchar, nvarchar, varbinary, sql_variant, and CLR user-defined)

**Note**   The ntext, text, and image data types are being deprecated in favor of nvarchar(max), varchar(max), and varbinary(max) data types.

Within data pages, SQL Server stores data in rows. Data rows do not normally span more than one page. The maximum size of a single data row is 8096 bytes (including any necessary overhead). Effectively, this means that the maximum size of a column is 8000 bytes, not including large object data types, and that a column can store up to 8000 ASCII characters or up to 4000 2-byte Unicode characters. Large object data type values can be up to 2 GB in size, which is too large to be stored in a single data row. With large object data types, data is stored in a collection of 8-KB pages, which might or might not be stored contiguously.

Although collections of pages are ideal for large object data that exceeds 8096 bytes, this storage mechanism is not ideal when the total data size is 8096 bytes or less. In this case, you will want to store the data in a single row, and to do this, you must set the *text in row* table option. The *text in row* option allows you to place small nvarchar(max), varchar(max), varbinary(max), text, ntext, and image values directly in a data row instead of in separate pages. This can reduce the amount of space used to store data and can also reduce the amount of disk input/output (I/O) needed to retrieve the values.

**Note**   A table that has fixed-length rows always stores the same amount of rows on each page. A table with variable-length rows, however, stores as many rows as possible on each page, based on the length of the data entered. As you might expect, there is a distinct performance advantage to keeping rows compact and allowing more rows to fit on a page. With more rows per page, you will have an improved cache-hit ratio and reduce I/O.

## Understanding Extents

An extent is a set of eight contiguous data pages, which means extents are allocated in 64-KB blocks and there are 16 extents per megabyte. SQL Server 2008 has two types of extents:

- **Mixed extents**   With mixed extents, different objects can own pages in the extent. This means that up to eight objects can own a page in the extent.

- **Uniform extents**   With uniform extents, a single object owns all the pages in the extent. This means that only the owning object can use all eight pages in the extent.

When you create a new table or index, SQL Server allocates pages from a mixed extent to the new table or index. The table or index continues to use pages in the mixed extent until it grows to the point at which it uses eight data pages. When this happens, SQL Server changes the table or index to uniform extents. As long as the table or index continues to use at least eight data pages, it will use uniform extents.

## Understanding Table Partitions

In SQL Server 2008, tables are contained in one or more partitions, and each partition contains data rows in either a heap or clustered index structure. Partitioning large tables allows you to manage subsets of the table data and can improve response times when working with the table data. To improve read/write performance, you can place partitions into multiple filegroups as well.

By default, tables have only one partition. When a table has multiple partitions, the data is partitioned horizontally so that groups of rows are mapped into individual partitions based on a specific column. For example, you might partition a *Customer_Order* table by purchase date. In this example, you would split the partition on date ranges, and each partition could hold yearly, quarterly, or monthly data.

For a *Customer* table, you might partition by customer ID. You would split the partition on name ranges, and each partition would store customer data that starts with a certain character—such as A, B, C, D, and so on—or a character sequence, such as Aa to Ez, Fa to Jz, Ka to Oz, Pa to Tz, and Ua to Zz.

SQL Server 2008 Enterprise Edition supports on-disk storage compression in both row and page format for tables stored as heaps, tables stored as clustered indexes, nonclustered indexes, and indexed views. You can configure compression of partitioned tables and indexes independently for each partition, regardless of whether partitions are for the same object. This allows different partitions of the same object to use different compression settings. Although enabling compression changes the physical storage format of data, compression does not require application changes. When you plan to use compression, as part of server sizing and capacity planning, you'll need to carefully consider the additional overhead required to compress and uncompress data.

With partition switching, you can use the Transact-SQL ALTER TABLE...SWITCH statement to transfer subsets of your data. This statement allows you to assign a table as a partition to an already existing partitioned table, switch a partition from one partitioned table to another, or reassign a partition to form a single table. When you transfer a partition, the Database Engine doesn't move the data; it only changes the metadata about the location of the data.

# Working with Tables

SQL Server provides many ways to work with tables. You can create new tables by using the New Table feature in SQL Server Management Studio or the CREATE TABLE command. You can modify existing tables by using the Modify Table feature in SQL Server Management Studio or the ALTER TABLE command. You can also perform other table management functions, including copy, rename, and delete.

## Creating Tables

Before you create a table, you should consider the table name carefully. Table names can be up to 128 characters long. Table names must begin with an alphabetic character, but they can also contain underscores (_), "at" symbols (@), pound signs (#), and numerals. The exceptions to this rule are temporary tables. Local temporary tables have names that begin with # and are accessible to you only during the current user session. Global temporary tables have names that begin with ## and are accessible to anyone as long as your user session remains connected. Temporary tables are created in the *tempdb* database and are automatically deleted when your user session ends.

Table names must be unique for each schema within a database. Different schemas, however, can contain like-named tables. This means you can create multiple *contacts* tables as long as they are defined in separate schemas. Thus, the *Customers*, *Employees*, and *Services* schemas all could have a *contacts* table.

Each table can have up to 1024 columns. Column names follow the same naming rules as tables and must be unique only on a per-table basis. That is, a specific table can have only one StreetAddress column, but any number of other tables can have this same column.

In SQL Server Management Studio, you create a new table by completing the following steps:

1. In SQL Server Management Studio, connect to the server instance that contains the database in which you want to work. You must have CREATE TABLE permission in the database and ALTER permission on the schema in which the table is being created.

2. In Object Explorer, expand the Databases node, and then select a database and expand the view to show its resource nodes.

3. To create a new table, right-click the Tables node, and then select New Table from the shortcut menu. Then access the Table Designer in SQL Server Management Studio, and you will see a window similar to Figure 10-2.

**Figure 10-2**   Create and modify tables in SQL Server Management Studio.

4. You can now design the table using the views provided:

   ❑ **Active File/Table view**   Provides quick access tabs for switching between open files and a summary. If you select the Table view in the Active File view, you will see an overview of the table's columns. Each column is listed by Column Name, Data Type, and Allow Nulls. For fixed or variable-length data types, you follow the data type designator with the field length. If you select the Summary view in the Active File view, you will see all the tables in the current database listed by name, associated schema, and creation date. You can double-click a listed table to see the objects it contains.

❑ **Column Properties view**    When you select a column in the Table view, you can use the Column Properties view to configure the settings for that column. Column properties that appear dimmed are fixed in value and cannot be changed. The values of these fixed properties typically depend on the column data type and properties inherited from the Database object itself.

❑ **Table Properties view**    Allows you to view and set general table properties, including the table name, description, and schema. You can open this view by pressing F4. Any dimmed properties cannot be changed at the table level and must be managed at the database level.

5. The Table Designer menu also provides options for designing the table. Because the options apply to the selected column in the Table view, you can apply them by selecting a column first and then choosing the appropriate option on the Table Designer menu. The same options are displayed when you right-click a column in the Table view.

When you have started the table creation process, you will want to do the following:

■ Use the Table Properties view to set the table name, description, and schema. Type the name and description in the boxes provided. Use the drop-down list to select the schema that will contain this table.

■ Use the Table Properties view to specify the filegroup (or filegroups) in which the table data will be stored. Regular data and large object data are configured separately.

❑ To specify the storage location for regular data, expand the Regular Data Space Specification node, and then use the Filegroup Or Partition Schema Name drop-down list to specify the filegroup.

❑ Use the Text/Image Filegroup drop-down list to specify the storage location for large object data.

■ Use the Table view to create and manage columns.

❑ Rows in the Table view correspond to columns in the table in which you are working. In Figure 10-2, columns listed include CustomerID, CustomerType, and AccountNumber.

❑ Columns in the Table view correspond to column properties in the table in which you are working. In Figure 10-2, column properties listed include Name, Data Type, and Allow Nulls.

■ Use Table Designer menu options to work with a selected column. You can mark the column as the primary key, establish foreign key relationships, check constraints, and more.

- Use the Column Properties view to specify the characteristics for the column you are creating. The characteristics include

  - ❑ **Name**   Shows or determines the name of the column.

  - ❑ **Allow Nulls**   Shows or determines whether or not null values are allowed in this column.

  - ❑ **Data Type**   Shows or determines the data type for the column.

  - ❑ **Default Value Or Binding**   Shows or determines the default value or binding for the column, which is used whenever a row with a null value for this column is inserted into the database and nulls are not allowed in this column.

  - ❑ **Length**   Shows or determines the maximum number of characters for values in the column. This property applies only when the column contains fixed-length data type values.

  - ❑ **Size**   Shows the storage size in bytes for values in the column. This property applies only when the column contains fixed-length data type values.

  - ❑ **Precision**   Shows or determines the maximum number of digits for values in the column. This property applies only when the column contains numeric or decimal data type values.

  - ❑ **Scale**   Shows or determines the maximum number of digits that can appear to the right of the decimal point for values in the column. This property applies only when the column contains numeric or decimal data type values.

  - ❑ **Is Identity**   Shows or determines if the column is used as an identifier column.

  - ❑ **Identity Seed**   Shows or sets the base value for generating unique identifiers. This property applies only to columns whose Is Identity option is set to Yes.

  - ❑ **Identity Increment**   Shows or sets the increment for generating unique identifiers. This property applies only to columns whose Is Identity option is set to Yes.

  - ❑ **Is Sparse**   Shows or determines whether the column is sparse. Sparse columns are optimized for null values and reduce space requirements for null values while increasing the overhead required to retrieve non-null values. However, with filtered indexes on sparse columns, the index size is reduced because only the populated values are indexed and this can increase index and search efficiency.

❑ **RowGuid**   Shows or determines if the column contains globally unique identifiers. This property applies only to columns whose Is Identity option is set to Yes or Yes (Not For Replication).

❑ **Formula**   Shows or sets the formula for a computed column.

❑ **Collation**   Shows or sets the default collating sequence that SQL Server applies to the column whenever the column values are used to sort rows of a query result.

■ When you are finished creating the table, click Save or press Ctrl+S.

You can create tables with Transact-SQL using the CREATE TABLE command. Sample 10-4 shows the syntax and usage for this command. Here you create the *Customers* table under the *Sales* schema. You must have CREATE TABLE permission in the database and ALTER permission on the schema in which the table is being created.

**Sample 10-4**   CREATE TABLE Syntax and Usage

```
Syntax
CREATE TABLE
[ database_name . [ schema_name ] . | schema_name . ] table_name
  ( { <col_def> | <comp_col_def> | <column_set_def> }
  [ <table_constraint> ] [ ,...n ] )
[ ON { part_scheme_name ( part_column_name ) | filegroup
    | "default" } ]
[ { TEXTIMAGE_ON { filegroup | "default" } ]
[ FILESTREAM_ON { part_scheme_name | filegroup | "default" } ]
[ WITH ( <table_option> [ ,...n ] ) ] [ ; ]

<col_def> ::=
column_name <data_type>
[ FILESTREAM ] [ COLLATE collation_name ] [ NULL | NOT NULL ]
[ [ CONSTRAINT constraint_name ] DEFAULT constant_expression ]
  | [ IDENTITY [ ( seed ,increment ) ] [ NOT FOR REPLICATION ] ]
[ ROWGUIDCOL ] [ <column_constraint> [ ...n ] ] [ SPARSE ]

<data type> ::=
[ type_schema_name . ] type_name
  [ ( precision [ , scale ] | max
  | [ { CONTENT | DOCUMENT } ] xml_schema_collection ) ]

<column_constraint> ::=
[ CONSTRAINT constraint_name ]
{ { PRIMARY KEY | UNIQUE } [ CLUSTERED | NONCLUSTERED ]
  [ WITH FILLFACTOR = fillfactor
    | WITH ( < index_option > [ , ...n ] ) ]
  [ ON { part_scheme_name ( part_column_name ) | filegroup
    | "default" } ]
```

```
| [ FOREIGN KEY ]
REFERENCES [ schema_name . ] referenced_table_name
[ ( ref_column )]
[ ON DELETE { NO ACTION | CASCADE | SET NULL | SET DEFAULT } ]
[ ON UPDATE { NO ACTION | CASCADE | SET NULL | SET DEFAULT } ]
[ NOT FOR REPLICATION ]
| CHECK [ NOT FOR REPLICATION ] ( logical_expression )
}


<comp_col_def> ::=
column_name AS computed_column_expression
[ PERSISTED [ NOT NULL ] ]
[ [ CONSTRAINT constraint_name ]
  { PRIMARY KEY | UNIQUE }
  [ CLUSTERED | NONCLUSTERED ] [ WITH FILLFACTOR = fillfactor
    | WITH ( <index_option> [ , ...n ] ) ]
  | [ FOREIGN KEY ]
  REFERENCES referenced_table_name [ ( ref_column ) ]
  [ ON DELETE { NO ACTION | CASCADE } ] [ ON UPDATE { NO ACTION } ]
  [ NOT FOR REPLICATION ]
  | CHECK [ NOT FOR REPLICATION ] ( logical_expression )
  [ ON { part_scheme_name ( part_column_name )
    | filegroup | "default" } ]
]


<column_set_def> ::=
column_set_name XML COLUMN_SET FOR ALL_SPARSE_COLUMNS


< table_constraint > ::=
[ CONSTRAINT constraint_name ]
{ { PRIMARY KEY | UNIQUE }
  [ CLUSTERED | NONCLUSTERED ] (column [ ASC | DESC ] [ ,...n ] )
  [ WITH FILLFACTOR = fillfactor |WITH ( <index_option> [ , ...n ] )]
  [ ON { part_scheme_name (part_column_name) | filegroup
    | "default"}]
  | FOREIGN KEY ( column [ ,...n ] )
  REFERENCES referenced_table_name [ ( ref_column [ ,...n ] ) ]
  [ ON DELETE { NO ACTION | CASCADE | SET NULL | SET DEFAULT } ]
  [ ON UPDATE { NO ACTION | CASCADE | SET NULL | SET DEFAULT } ]
  [ NOT FOR REPLICATION ]
  | CHECK [ NOT FOR REPLICATION ] ( logical_expression )
}


<table_option> ::=
{ DATA_COMPRESSION = { NONE | ROW | PAGE }
  [ ON PARTS ( { <part_number_expression> | <range> } [ , ...n ] ) ]
}
```

```
<index_option> ::=
{ PAD_INDEX = { ON | OFF } | FILLFACTOR = fillfactor
  | IGNORE_DUP_KEY = { ON | OFF } | STATISTICS_NORECOMPUTE
    = { ON | OFF}
  | ALLOW_ROW_LOCKS = { ON | OFF} | ALLOW_PAGE_LOCKS ={ ON | OFF}
  | DATA_COMPRESSION = { NONE | ROW | PAGE }
  [ ON PARTS ( { <part_number_expression> | <range> }
    [ , ...n ] ) ]
}
<range> ::=
<part_number_expression> TO <part_number_expression>


Usage
USE OrderSystemDB
CREATE TABLE Sales.Customers
(
    cust_lname varchar(40) NOT NULL,
    cust_fname varchar(20) NOT NULL,
    phone char(12) NOT NULL,
    uid uniqueidentifier NOT NULL
    DEFAULT newid()
)
```

## Modifying Existing Tables

When you are working with the Table Properties view, you can use the Lock Escalation option to configure lock escalation using the following settings:

- **Auto**  With Auto, the Database Engine selects the lock escalation granularity that is appropriate for the table schema. If the table is partitioned, lock escalation will be allowed to the heap or B-tree level and the lock will not then be escalated later to the table level, which can improve concurrency by reducing lock contention. If the table is not partitioned, the Database Engine will use lock escalation at the table level.

- **Table**  With Table, the Database Engine uses lock escalation at the table level regardless of whether the table is partitioned. Table is the default value.

- **Disable**  With Disable, the lock escalation is prevented in most cases and the Database Engine uses lock escalation only when required. For example, when you are scanning a table that has no clustered index under the serializable isolation level, the Database Engine must take a table lock to protect data integrity.

In SQL Server Management Studio, you modify an existing table by completing the following steps:

1. In SQL Server Management Studio, connect to the server instance that contains the database in which you want to work.

2. In Object Explorer, expand the Databases node, and then select a database and expand the view to show its resource nodes.

3. Expand the Tables node, and then right-click the table you want to modify. From the shortcut menu, choose Design. Then you can access the views for designing tables, which were shown previously in Figure 10-2.

4. Make any necessary changes to the table, and then click Save or press Ctrl+S. If the changes you make affect multiple tables, you will see a prompt showing which tables will be updated and saved in the database. Click Yes to continue and complete the operation.

The Transact-SQL command for modifying tables is ALTER TABLE. Sample 10-5 shows the syntax and usage for this command. Here you alter the *Customers* table under the *Sales* schema. You must have ALTER TABLE permission. Most of the subset elements are the same as defined for CREATE TABLE. Important exceptions are listed.

**Sample 10-5**   ALTER TABLE Syntax and Usage

```
Syntax
ALTER TABLE [ database_name . [ schema_name ] . | schema_name . ]
            table_name
{   ALTER COLUMN column_name
    {
        [ type_schema_name. ] type_name [ ( { precision [ , scale ]
        | max | xml_schema_collection } ) ]
        [ COLLATE collation_name ]
        [ NULL | NOT NULL ]
      | {ADD | DROP }
        { ROWGUIDCOL | PERSISTED | NOT FOR REPLICATION | SPARSE }
    }
      | [ WITH { CHECK | NOCHECK } ]
      | ADD
    { <column_definition>
      | <computed_column_definition>
      | <table_constraint>
      | <column_set_definition>
    } [ ,...n ]
    | DROP
    {   [ CONSTRAINT ] constraint_name
        [ WITH ( <drop_clustered_constraint_option> [ ,...n ] ) ]
        | COLUMN column_name
    } [ ,...n ]
    | [ WITH { CHECK | NOCHECK } ] { CHECK | NOCHECK } CONSTRAINT
        { ALL | constraint_name [ ,...n ] }
    | { ENABLE | DISABLE } TRIGGER
        { ALL | trigger_name [ ,...n ] }
    | { ENABLE | DISABLE } CHANGE_TRACKING
        [ WITH ( TRACK_COLUMNS_UPDATED = { ON | OFF } ) ]
```

```
    | SWITCH [ PARTITION source_partition_number_expression ]
       TO target_table
       [ PARTITION target_partition_number_expression ]
    | SET ( FILESTREAM_ON = { partition_scheme_name | filegroup |
       "default" | "NULL" } )
    | REBUILD
       [ [ WITH ( <rebuild_option> [ ,...n ] ) ]
         | [ PARTITION = partition_number
            [ WITH ( <single_partition_rebuild_option> [ ,...n ] ) ] ]
       ]
    | (<table_option>)
}
[ ; ]

<drop_clustered_constraint_option> ::=
{ MAXDOP = max_degree_of_parallelism
  | ONLINE = {ON | OFF }
  | MOVE TO { partition_scheme_name ( column_name ) | filegroup
  | "default" }
}

<range> ::=
<partition_number_expression> TO <partition_number_expression>

<rebuild_option> ::=
{ PAD_INDEX = { ON | OFF }
  | FILLFACTOR = fillfactor
  | IGNORE_DUP_KEY = { ON | OFF }
  | STATISTICS_NORECOMPUTE = { ON | OFF }
  | ALLOW_ROW_LOCKS = { ON | OFF }
  | ALLOW_PAGE_LOCKS = { ON | OFF }
  | SORT_IN_TEMPDB = { ON | OFF }
  | ONLINE = { ON | OFF }
  | MAXDOP = max_degree_of_parallelism
  | DATA_COMPRESSION = { NONE |ROW | PAGE}
    [ ON PARTITIONS ( { <partition_number_expression> | <range> }
      [ , ...n ] ) ]
}

<single_partition_rebuild_option> ::=
{ SORT_IN_TEMPDB = { ON | OFF }
  | MAXDOP = max_degree_of_parallelism
  | DATA_COMPRESSION = { NONE | ROW | PAGE} }
}

<table_option> ::=
  { SET ( LOCK_ESCALATION = { AUTO | TABLE | DISABLE } ) }
```

**Usage**
```
USE OrderSystemDB
ALTER TABLE Sales.Customers
ADD uid2 uniqueidentifier NOT NULL DEFAULT newid()
ALTER TABLE Sales.Customers
ALTER COLUMN cust_fname CHAR(10) NOT NULL
ALTER TABLE Sales.Customers
DROP Address2
```

## Viewing Table Row and Size Information

In SQL Server Management Studio, you can view table row and size information by completing the following steps:

1. In SQL Server Management Studio, connect to the server instance that contains the database in which you want to work.

2. In Object Explorer, expand the Databases node, and then select a database and expand the view to show its resource nodes.

3. Expand the Tables node, right-click the table you want to examine, and then select Properties from the shortcut menu. This displays the Table Properties dialog box shown in Figure 10-3.

**Figure 10-3**  The Table Properties dialog box.

4. On the General page, entries under the Misc section provide details about space used:

   ❑ Data Space shows the amount of space the table uses on disk.

   ❑ Index Space shows the size of the table's index space on disk.

   ❑ Row Count shows the number of rows in the table.

You can also view row, size, and space statistics for individual tables using the sp_spaceused stored procedure. The following code accesses the OrderSystemDB database and then checks the statistics for the *Customers* table under the *Sales* schema:

```
USE OrderSystemDB
EXEC sp_spaceused 'Sales.Customers'
```

## Displaying Table Properties and Permissions

In SQL Server Management Studio, you can display table properties and permissions by completing the following steps:

1. In SQL Server Management Studio, connect to the server instance that contains the database in which you want to work.

2. In Object Explorer, expand the Databases node, and then select a database and expand the view to show its resource nodes.

3. Expand the Tables node, right-click the table you want to examine, and then select Properties from the shortcut menu to display the Table Properties dialog box shown previously in Figure 10-3.

4. Use the General, Permissions, and Extended Properties pages of the dialog box to view the table's properties and permissions.

## Displaying Current Values in Tables

In SQL Server Management Studio, you view a table's current data by completing the following steps:

1. In SQL Server Management Studio, connect to the server instance that contains the database in which you want to work.

2. In Object Explorer, expand the Databases node, and then select a database and expand the view to show its resource nodes.

3. Expand the Tables node, right-click the table you want to examine, and then select Open Table from the shortcut menu to display all the row data contained in the table.

4. The lower portion of the Query Results pane provides buttons for moving between the rows and a status area. If you select a read-only cell, the status area displays "Cell Is Read Only." If you have modified a cell, the status area displays "Cell Is Modified."

You can also list a table's current data using the SELECT FROM statement. In the following example, you are selecting from the *Department* table under the *Human-Resources* schema in the Personnel database:

```
SELECT * FROM [Personnel].[HumanResources].[Department]
```

or

```
SELECT DepartmentID,Name,GroupName,ModifiedDate
  FROM [Personnel].[HumanResources].[Department]
```

## Copying Tables

The easiest way to create a copy of a table is to use a Transact-SQL command. Use SELECT INTO to extract all the rows from an existing table into the new table. The new table must not exist already. The following example will copy the *Customers* table under the *Sales* schema to a new table called *CurrCustomers* under the *BizDev* schema:

```
SELECT * INTO BizDev.CurrCustomers FROM Sales.Customers
```

You can also create the new table from a specific subset of columns in the original table. In this case, you specify the names of the columns to copy after the SELECT keyword. Any columns not specified are excluded from the new table. The following example copies specific columns to a new table:

```
SELECT CustName, Address, Telephone, Email INTO BizDev.CurrCustomers
FROM Sales.Customers
```

## Renaming and Deleting Tables

In SQL Server Management Studio, the easiest way to rename or delete a table is to complete the following steps:

1.  In SQL Server Management Studio, access a database, and then expand the Tables node to list the tables in the database.

2.  Right-click the table you want to rename or delete. From the shortcut menu, choose View Dependencies. The Object Dependencies dialog box shows the database objects that must be present for this object to function properly and the objects that depend upon the selected object. Use the information in this dialog box to understand any dependencies that might be affected by renaming or deleting the selected table. Click OK to close the Object Dependencies dialog box.

3.  To rename a table, right-click the table, and then choose Rename from the shortcut menu. You can now type a new name for the table.

4.  To delete a table, right-click the table, and then choose Delete from the shortcut menu to display the Delete Object dialog box. Click OK.

You can also rename tables using the sp_rename stored procedure. You must have ALTER TABLE permission and be a member of the sysadmin or dbcreator fixed server roles to rename a table with sp_rename. In the following example, you rename the *Customers* table under the *Sales* schema *CurrCustomers*:

```
EXEC sp_rename 'Sales.Customers', 'CurrCustomers'
```

As long as you have ALTER permission on the schema to which the table belongs or CONTROL permission on the table, you can remove a table from the database using the DROP TABLE command:

```
DROP TABLE Sales.CurrCustomers
```

If you want to delete the rows in a table but leave its structure intact, you can use DELETE. The following DELETE command deletes all the rows in a table but does not remove the table structure:

```
DELETE Sales.CurrCustomers
```

To use DELETE, you must be a member of the sysadmin fixed server role, the db_owner or db_datawriter fixed database roles, the table owner, or be granted DELETE permission.

## Adding and Removing Columns in a Table

You learned how to add or remove columns in a table in SQL Server Management Studio in "Working with Tables" on page 326. In Transact-SQL, you modify table columns using the ALTER TABLE command, which was shown previously in Sample 10-5.

### Adding Columns

The following example adds a unique identifier column to the *Customers* table under the *Sales* schema:

```
USE OrderSystemDB
ALTER TABLE Sales.Customers
ADD uid uniqueidentifier NOT NULL DEFAULT newid()
```

### Modifying Columns

To change the characteristics of an existing column, use the ALTER COLUMN command, such as in the following example:

```
USE OrderSystemDB
ALTER TABLE Sales.Customers
ALTER COLUMN cust_fname CHAR(10) NOT NULL
```

### Removing Columns

The following example removes the Address2 column from the *Customers* table:

```
USE OrderSystemDB
ALTER TABLE Sales.Customers
DROP COLUMN Address2
```

## Scripting Tables

You can re-create and store all the SQL commands used to create tables in a database in an .sql file for later use. To do this, complete the following steps:

1. In SQL Server Management Studio, access a database, and then expand the Tables node to list the tables in the database.

2. Select a table, right-click its name, and then select Script Table As from the shortcut menu.

3. Point to CREATE TO and select File to open the Select A File dialog box.

4. In the dialog box, set a folder and file path for the .sql script, and then click Save.

If you open the .sql file, you will find all the Transact-SQL statements required to re-create the table structure. The actual data in the table is not stored with this procedure, however.

# Managing Table Values

In this section, you will learn about the techniques and concepts you need to work with table values. Whether you want to create a new table or modify an existing one, the techniques and concepts you need to understand are similar.

## Using Native Data Types

Native data types are those built into SQL Server and supported directly. All data types have a length value, which is either fixed or variable. The length for a numeric or binary data type is the number of bytes used to store the number. The length for a character data type is the number of characters. Most numeric data types also have precision and scale. *Precision* is the total number of digits in a number. *Scale* is the number of digits to the right of the decimal point in a number. For example, the number 8714.235 has a precision of seven and a scale of three.

Table 10-1 summarizes native data types that work with numbers and money. The first column shows the general data type or data type synonym for SQL-92 compatibility. The second column shows the SQL Server data type. The third column shows the valid range. The fourth column shows the amount of storage space used.

Table 10-1 Native Data Types for Numbers and Money

| SQL-92 Name—Type | SQL Server Name | Range—Description | Storage Size |
|---|---|---|---|
| **Integers** | | | |
| Bit | bit | 0, 1, or NULL | 1 byte (for each 1-bit to 8-bit column) |
| Big integer | bigint | $-2^{63}$ through $2^{63} - 1$. | 8 bytes |
| Integer | int | $-2^{31}$ ($-2,147,483,648$) through $2^{31} - 1$ (2,147,483,647) | 4 bytes |
| small integer | smallint | $-2^{15}$ ($-32,768$) through $2^{15} - 1$ (32,767) | 2 bytes |
| tiny integer | tinyint | 0 through 255 | 1 byte |
| **Money** | | | |
| Money | money | $-922,337,203,685,477.5808$ through $+922,337,203,685,477.5807$ | 8 bytes |
| small money | smallmoney | $-214,748.3648$ through $+214,748.3647$ | 4 bytes |
| **Decimal** | | | |
| dec, decimal | decimal | $-10^{38} + 1$ through $10^{38} - 1$ | 5 to 17 bytes |
| Numeric | decimal | $-10^{38} + 1$ through $10^{38} - 1$ | 5 to 17 bytes |
| **Approximate Numeric** | | | |
| Double precision | float | $-1.79E + 308$ through $1.79E + 308$ | 4 to 8 bytes |
| Float | float | $-1.79E + 308$ through $1.79E + 308$. float[($n$)] for $n = 1 - 53$ | 4 to 8 bytes |
| Float | real | $-1.18E - 38$, 0 and $-1.18E - 38$ through $3.40E + 38$. float[($n$)] for $n = 1 - 24$ | 4 bytes |
| **Spatial Data** | | | |
| | geometry | A variable-length Common Language Runtime (CLR) data type for storing planar (flat-earth) data; represents points, lines, and polygons within a coordinate system | Varies |
| | geography | A variable-length CLR data type for storing ellipsoidal (round-earth) data; represents geographic objects on an area of the Earth's surface | Varies |

Table 10-1   Native Data Types for Numbers and Money

| SQL-92 Name—Type | SQL Server Name | Range—Description | Storage Size |
|---|---|---|---|
| **Other Numerics** | | | |
| Cursor | cursor | A reference to a cursor | Varies |
| | Hierarchyid, Sql-Hierarchyid | A variable-length CLR data type that logically encodes information about a single node in a hierarchy tree; represents the encoded path from the root of the tree to the node | Varies |
| Rowversion | rowversion, timestamp | A database-wide unique number that indicates the sequence in which modifications took place in the database (*Rowversion* is a synonym for *timestamp*.) | 8 bytes |
| SQL Variant | sql_variant | A special data type that allows a single column to store multiple data types (except text, ntext, sql_variant, image, timestamp, xml, varchar(max), varbinary(max), nvarchar(max), and .NET CLR user-defined types) | Varies |
| Table | table | A special data type that is used to store a result set temporarily for processing; can be used only to define local variables and as the return type for user-defined functions | Varies |
| Uniqueidentifier | unique-identifier | A globally unique identifier (GUID) | 16 bytes |
| Xml | xml | A special data type that allows you to store XML data; XML markup is defined using standard text characters | Varies |

Table 10-2 summarizes native data types for dates, characters, and binary data. Again, the first column shows the general data type or data type synonym for SQL-92 compatibility. The second column shows the SQL Server data type. The third column shows the valid range. The fourth column shows the amount of storage space used.

Table 10-2    Native Data Types for Dates, Characters, and Binary Values

| SQL-92 Name—Type | SQL Server Name | Range—Description | Storage Size |
|---|---|---|---|
| **Date** | | | |
| Datetime | datetime | January 1, 1753 through December 31, 9999; accuracy of three-hundredths of a second | Two 4-byte integers |
| small datetime | smalldatetime | January 1, 1900 through June 6, 2079; accuracy of one minute | Two 2-byte integers |
| Date | date | 0001-01-01 through 9999-12-31 | 3 bytes |
| Time | time | 00:00:00.0000000 through 23:59:59.9999999 | 3 to 5 bytes |
| | datetime2 | 0001-01-01 00:00:00.0000000 through 9999-12-31 23:59:59.9999999 | 6 to 8 bytes |
| | datetimeoffset | 0001-01-01 00:00:00.0000000 through 9999-12-31 23:59:59.9999999 (in UTC) | 8 to 10 bytes |
| **Character** | | | |
| Character | char | Fixed-length non-Unicode character data with a maximum length of 8000 characters | 1 byte per character |
| character varying | varchar | Variable-length non-Unicode data with a maximum length of 8000 characters | 1 byte per character |
| | varchar(max) | Variable-length data to $2^{31} - 1$ (2,147,483,647) characters | 1 byte per character + 2-byte pointer |
| Text | text | Variable-length non-Unicode data with a maximum length of $2^{31} - 1$ (2,147,483,647) characters | 1 byte per character |
| national character | nchar | Fixed-length Unicode data with a maximum length of 4000 characters | 2 bytes per character |
| national char varying | nvarchar | Variable-length Unicode data with a maximum length of 4000 characters | 2 bytes per character |
| | nvarchar(max) | Variable-length Unicode data with a maximum length of $2^{31} - 1$ (2,147,483,647) characters | 2 bytes per character plus 2-byte pointer |
| national text | ntext | Variable-length Unicode data with a maximum length of $2^{30} - 1$ (1,073,741,823) characters | 2 bytes per character |

**Table 10-2   Native Data Types for Dates, Characters, and Binary Values**

| SQL-92 Name—Type | SQL Server Name | Range—Description | Storage Size |
|---|---|---|---|
| **Binary** | | | |
| binary | binary | Fixed-length binary data with a maximum length of 8000 bytes | Size of data in bytes |
| binary varying | varbinary | Variable-length binary data with a maximum length of 8000 bytes | Size of data in bytes |
| | var-binary(max) | Variable-length binary data to $2^{31} - 1$ (2,147,483,647) bytes | Size of data in bytes + 2-byte pointer |
| Image | image | Variable-length binary data with a maximum length of $2^{31} - 1$ (2,147,483,647) bytes | Size of data in bytes |

When you create or modify a table in SQL Server Management Studio, you assign a native data type by clicking in the Data Type column and using the selection list to select a data type. In Transact-SQL, you set the data type when you create the table and populate its columns or when you alter a table and add or change columns. Sample 10-6 shows how you can use Transact-SQL commands to create a table and its columns.

**Sample 10-6**   Creating a Table and Its Columns

```
USE OrderSystemDB
CREATE TABLE Sales.Customers
    (CustomerID nchar(5) NOT NULL,
    CompanyName nvarchar(40) NOT NULL,
    ContactName nvarchar(30) NOT NULL,
    ContactTitle nvarchar(30) NOT NULL,
    Address nvarchar(60) NOT NULL,
    City nvarchar(15) NULL,
    Region nvarchar(15) NULL,
    PostalCode nvarchar(5) NULL,
    Country nvarchar(15) NULL,
    Phone nvarchar(24) NULL,
    Fax nvarchar(24) NULL)
```

# Using Fixed-Length, Variable-Length, and Max-Length Fields

You can create binary and character data types as fixed-length, variable-length, or max-length fields. When you use fixed-length data types, the column size you specify is reserved in the database and can be written to without manipulating the data in the column. This makes updates to the database quicker than with variable-length fields.

When you use variable-length data types, SQL Server will squeeze more rows into data pages, if possible. When there are more rows per data page, the process of reading data is usually more efficient, which can translate into improved performance for read operations. When you use max-length data types, SQL Server stores a 2-byte pointer to the actual data in the table's regular data space and stores the actual data in the large object data space. Generally speaking, you should

■ Use fixed-length data types when the size of the data is consistent.

■ Use variable-length data types when the size of the data varies.

■ Use max-length data types when the size of the data exceeds the fixed-length or variable-length limit.

To gain a better understanding of the performance implications, consider the following scenario. With fixed-length columns of 80, 120, 40, and 500 bytes each, rows would always be written using 750 bytes of storage (740 bytes for data plus 10 bytes of overhead for each row). In this example, 10 rows will fit on each data page (8096/750, without the remainder).

If you use variable-length columns, however, the number of bytes used per row and the of rows stored per page would vary. For example, assume that the average variable-length row uses 400 bytes. This includes 380 bytes of data and 20 bytes of overhead (12 bytes of overhead for rows that use variable-length data plus 2 bytes of overhead per variable-length column, thus 4 × 2 + 12 = 20). In this case, 20 rows will fit on each data page (8096/400, without the remainder), which would make data reads more efficient than the fixed-length example.

## Using User-Defined Data Types

User-defined data types are special data types that are based on a native data type. You will want to use user-defined data types when two or more tables store the same type of data in a column and these columns must have exactly the same data type, length, and nullability. You can create user-defined data types yourself, or you can let SQL Server do the job. For example, *sysname* is a user-defined data type that is used to reference database object names. The data type is defined as a variable Unicode character type of 128 characters, which is why object names are limited to 128 characters throughout SQL Server. You can apply this same concept to ensure that specific data is used exactly as you want it to be used.

### Creating User-Defined Data Types

You create user-defined data types at the database level rather than at the table level, which is why user-defined data types are static and immutable (unchangeable). This ensures that there is no performance penalty associated with user-defined data types. User-defined data types do have some limitations, however. You cannot declare a default value or check constraint as part of the user-defined data type. You also cannot create a user-defined data type based on a user-defined data type.

**Tip**   When you create user-defined data types in a user-defined database, they apply only to that database. If you want user-defined data types to apply to multiple databases, define the data type in the *model* database. Then the user-defined data type will exist in all new user-defined databases.

In SQL Server Management Studio, you create a user-defined data type by completing the following steps:

1. In SQL Server Management Studio, connect to the server instance containing the database in which you want to work.

2. In Object Explorer, expand the Databases node, and then select a database and expand the view to show its resource nodes.

3. Expand the Programmability node, right-click Types, point to New, and then select User-Defined Data Type. This opens the New User-Defined Data Type dialog box shown in Figure 10-4.

**Figure 10-4**   The New User-Defined Data Type dialog box.

4. The *dbo* schema is the default schema. To place the data type in a different schema, click the button to the right of the Schema box, and then click Browse. Select the schema you want to use, and then click OK twice.

5. Enter a name for the new data type.

6. In the Data Type list, select the data type on which you want to base the user-defined data type.

7. If the data type has a variable length, set the number of bytes or characters for the data type. For fixed-length variables, such as int, you will not be able to set a length.

8. To allow the data type to accept null values, select Allow Nulls.

9. Optionally, use the Default and Rule lists to select a default or rule to bind to the user-defined data type.

10. Click OK. If you open a new table or edit an existing table, you will see the new data type as one of the last entries in the Data Type selection list.

You can also create user-defined data types with the CREATE TYPE statement. Sample 10-7 shows the related syntax and usage.

**Sample 10-7**   CREATE TYPE Syntax and Usage for User-Defined Data Types

```
Syntax
CREATE TYPE [ schema_name. ] type_name
  { FROM base_type
  [ ( precision [ , scale ] ) ]
  [ NULL | NOT NULL ]
  | EXTERNAL NAME assembly_name [ .class_name ] } [ ; ]


Usage
USE master
CREATE TYPE USPhoneNumber
FROM char(12) NOT NULL
```

### Managing User-Defined Data Types

After you create user-defined data types, you often will need to manage their properties. To manage user-defined data types, complete the following steps:

1. In SQL Server Management Studio, connect to the server instance that contains the database in which you want to work.

2. In Object Explorer, expand the Databases node, and then select a database and expand the view to show its resource nodes.

3. Expand Programmability, Types, and User-Defined Data Types to list the current user-defined data types.

4. Right-click the user-defined data type you want to manage and then select from the following options:

   ❑ Properties, to view the data type's properties and set dependencies

   ❑ Delete, to delete the data type

❑   Rename, to rename the data type

5.   To see where the data type is used in the database, right-click the user-defined data type, and then select View Dependencies from the shortcut menu.

## Allowing and Disallowing Nulls

When you create columns in a table, you can specify whether or not nulls are allowed. A null means there is no entry in the column for that row; it is not the same as zero or an empty string. Columns defined with a primary key constraint or identity property cannot allow null values.

If you add a row but do not set a value for a column that allows null values, SQL Server inserts the value NULL–unless a default value is set for the column. When a default value is set for a column and you insert a null value, SQL Server replaces NULL with the default value. Additionally, if the column allows nulls, you can explicitly set a column to null using the NULL keyword. Do not use quotation marks when setting null explicitly.

In SQL Server Management Studio's Table view, you can

- Allow nulls in a column by selecting the Allow Nulls column property.

- Disallow nulls in a column by clearing the Allow Nulls column property.

For an example of how to allow and disallow nulls with Transact-SQL, refer to Sample 10-4 on page 330.

## Using Default Values

Null values are useful when you do not know a value or a value is missing. If the use of null values is not allowed according to the design specifications, however, a better alternative is to set a default value. The default value is used when no value is set for a column you are inserting into a table. For example, you might want a character-based column to have the value N/A rather than NULL, so you would set the default value as N/A.

Table 10-3 summarizes combinations of default values and nullability that are handled in different ways. The main thing to remember is that if you set a default value, the default is used whenever a value is not specified for the column entry. This is true even if you allow nulls.

**Table 10-3   Default Values and Nullability**

| Column Definition | No Entry, No DEFAULT Definition | No Entry, DEFAULT Definition | Enter a Null Value |
|---|---|---|---|
| Allows null values | Sets NULL | Sets default value | Sets NULL |
| Disallows null values | Error occurs | Sets default value | Error occurs |

## Using Sparse Columns

The Database Engine uses the SPARSE keyword in a column definition to optimize the storage of values in that column. When a value in a sparse column is NULL for any row in the table, the value requires no additional storage space. In this way, sparse columns are optimized for null values and reduce space requirements for null values. However, sparse columns increase the overhead required to retrieve non-null values. They also increase the storage space required for fixed-length data types.

Sparse columns are especially appropriate for filtered indexes because sparse columns have many null values. With filtered indexes on sparse columns, the index size is reduced because only the populated values are indexed and this can increase index and search efficiency. INSERT, UPDATE, and DELETE statements can reference sparse columns by name. You also can view and work with all the sparse columns of a table that are combined into a single XML column called a column set.

The text, ntext, timestamp, image, geography, geometry, and user-defined data types cannot be set as SPARSE. Although a computed column can contain a sparse column, a computed column cannot be marked as SPARSE. A sparse column cannot be used as a partition key of a clustered index or heap. However, a sparse column can be used as the partition key of a nonclustered index. Persisted and nonpersisted computed columns that are defined on sparse columns also can be part of a clustered key.

Sparse columns reduce the maximum size of a row from 8060 bytes to 8018 bytes. The following also applies to sparse columns:

- Cannot have the FILESTREAM, ROWGUIDCOL, or IDENTITY properties
- Cannot have default values or be bound to a rule
- Cannot be part of a clustered index or a unique primary key index
- Cannot be used as the partition key of a clustered index or heap
- Cannot be part of a user-defined table type

In SQL Server Management Studio's Column Properties view, you can do the following:

- Set a column as sparse by setting the option Is Sparse to Yes.
- Set a column as not sparse by setting the option Is Sparse to No.

## Using Identities and Globally Unique Identifiers

When you design tables, you will often need to think about unique identifiers that can be used as primary keys or can ensure that merged data does not conflict with existing data. Unique identifiers for primary keys can include customer account numbers or Social Security numbers. However, if a unique identifier is not available, you might want to use the identity property to generate sequential values that are unique for each row in a table. You can also use this unique identifier to automatically generate a customer account number, an order number, or whatever other unique value you need.

Although the identity property provides a local solution for a specific table, it does not guarantee that the value used as an identifier will be unique throughout the database. Other tables in the database might have identity columns with the same values. In most cases, this is not a problem because the identity values usually are used only within the context of a single table and do not relate to other tables. However, in some situations, you might want to use a value that is unique throughout one or more databases, and then globally unique identifiers provide the solution you need.

Globally unique identifiers are guaranteed to be unique across all networked computers in the world, which is extremely useful in merge replication. When you are merging data from multiple databases, globally unique identifiers ensure that records are not inadvertently associated with each other. For example, a company's New York, Chicago, and San Francisco offices might have customer account numbers that are unique within those local offices but are not unique at the national level. Globally unique identifiers would ensure that account XYZ from New York and account XYZ from Chicago are not merged as the same account.

Identities and globally unique identifiers are not mutually exclusive. Each table can have one identifier column and one globally unique identity property. These values are often used together. For example, all clustered indexes in SQL Server should be unique, but they do not have to be unique.

In SQL Server Management Studio's Table view, you set identity values for a table by completing the following steps:

1. Create or modify other columns in the table as appropriate, and then start a new column for the identity value.

2. Give the identity column a name, and then select a data type. Identifier columns must use one of the following data types: tinyint, smallint, int, bigint, decimal, or numeric. Globally unique identifier columns must have a data type of uniqueidentifier.

   > **Tip**   When you set the data type for an identifier column, be sure to consider how many rows are in the table as well as how many rows might be added in the future. A tinyint identifier provides only 256 unique values (0 to 255). A smallint identifier provides 32,768 unique values (0 to 32,767).

3. Clear the Allow Nulls check box for the identity column.

4. To assign a globally unique identifier, select the identity column in the Table view. In the Column Properties view, set RowGuid to Yes. A default value of newid is created automatically for you.

**Note**   The newid function is used to generate new unique identifier values by combining the identification number of a network card with a unique number from the CPU clock. If a server process generates the identifier, the server's network card identification number is used. If the identifier is returned by application programming interface (API) function calls, the client's network card is used. Network card manufacturers guarantee that no other network card in the next 100 years will have the same number.

5. To assign a unique identifier, select the identity column in the Table view, expand Identity Specification in the Column Properties view, and then set (Is Identity) to Yes.

6. Type a value in the Identity Increment field. This value is the increment that is added to the Identity Seed for each subsequent row. If you leave this field blank, the value 1 is assigned by default.

7. Type a value in the Identity Seed field. This value is assigned to the first row in the table. If you leave this field blank, the value 1 is assigned by default.

8. If you are replicating a database—as discussed in Chapter 13, "Implementing Snapshot, Merge, and Transactional Replication"—and do not want the column to be replicated, set Is Not For Replication to Yes. Otherwise, you'll typically want to set Is Not For Replication to No to allow the column to be replicated.

**Note**   The identity seed and increment values are used to determine the identifier for rows. If you enter a seed value of 100 and an increment of 10, the first row has a value of 100, the second has a value of 110, and so on.

When you create a table in Transact-SQL, globally unique identifiers are not generated automatically. You must reference the newid function as the default value for the identifier column, as shown in this example:

```
USE OrderSystemDB
CREATE TABLE Sales.Customers
    (cust_lname varchar(40) NOT NULL,
    cust_fname varchar(20) NOT NULL,
    phone char(12) NOT NULL,
    uid uniqueidentifier NOT NULL DEFAULT newid())
```

Then when you insert a new row into the table, you call newid to generate the globally unique identifier:

```
INSERT INTO Sales.Customers
Values ('Stanek', 'William', '123-555-1212', newid())
```

# Using User-Defined Table Types

A user-defined table type is a special data type that represents the definition of a table structure. You will want to use user-defined table types when you want to declare table-valued parameters to send multiple rows of data to a Transact-SQL statement, stored procedure, or function without having to create a temporary table or many parameters.

## Understanding User-Defined Table Types

Table-valued parameters are similar to parameter arrays in Open Database Connectivity (ODBC) and OLE DB, but they are more efficient. A table-valued parameter is scoped to the stored procedure, function, or dynamic Transact-SQL statement, exactly like other parameters, and has a scope like any other local variable that is created by using a DECLARE statement. You can declare table-valued variables within dynamic Transact-SQL statements and pass these variables as table-valued parameters to stored procedures and functions. Transact-SQL passes table-valued parameters to stored procedures or functions by reference to avoid making a copy of the input data.

In many cases, table-valued parameters offer better performance than temporary tables or other techniques you can use to pass a list of parameters. Table-valued parameters perform well when you are using any of the following:

- Complex server logic to insert fewer than 1000 rows from formatted data files on the server

- Complex remote client processes to insert any number of rows

- Direct insert with remote client processes to insert fewer than 1000 rows

However, you are better off using BULK INSERT operations when you are using any of the following:

- Direct inserts from formatted data files on the server to insert any number of rows

- Complex server logic to insert more than 1000 rows from formatted data files on the server

- Direct inserts of more than 1000 rows with remote client processes

You create user-defined table types at the database level rather than at the table level. To create and use table-valued parameters, follow these steps:

1. Create a table type using CREATE TYPE and then define the table structure using CREATE TABLE.

2. Create a procedure using CREATE PROCEDURE or a function using CREATE FUNCTION that has a parameter of the table type.

3. Declare a variable of the table type using DECLARE @local_variable, and then reference the table type.

4. Add rows to the table variable using an INSERT statement. After the table variable is created and filled, you can pass the variable to a procedure or function. When the procedure or function is out of scope, the table-valued parameter is no longer available. However, the type definition remains until it is dropped.

Table-valued parameters are strongly typed, do not acquire locks for the initial population of data from a client, and do not cause a statement to recompile. They also enable the client to specify sort order and unique keys, and they reduce back and forth communications between the client and server. You can obtain information that is associated with table-valued parameters using the sys.parameters, sys.types, and sys.table_types catalog views.

SQL Server does not maintain statistics on columns of table-valued parameters, and table-valued parameters must be passed as input READONLY parameters to Transact-SQL routines. You cannot perform data manipulation language (DML) operations such as UPDATE, DELETE, or INSERT on a table-valued parameter in the body of a routine. Additionally, although a table-valued parameter can be in the FROM clause of SELECT INTO or in the INSERT EXEC string or stored-procedure, you cannot use a table-valued parameter as the target of a SELECT INTO or INSERT EXEC statement.

### Creating User-Defined Table Types

In SQL Server Management Studio, you create a user-defined table type by completing the following steps:

1. In SQL Server Management Studio, connect to the server instance containing the database in which you want to work.

2. In Object Explorer, expand the Databases node, and then select a database and expand the view to show its resource nodes.

3. Expand the Programmability node, right-click Types, point to New, and then select User-Defined Table Type. This creates a Transact-SQL query with the basic structure of the required CREATE TYPE statement.

Sample 10-8 shows how you can use the CREATE TYPE statement to create user-defined table types.

**Sample 10-8**   Creating User-Defined Table Types

```
Syntax
CREATE TYPE [ schema_name. ] type_name
{
  AS TABLE ( { <col_def> | <comp_col_def> }
    [ <table_constraint> ] [ ,...n ] )
}
[ ; ]
```

```
<col_def> ::=
  column_name <data_type>
  [ COLLATE collation_name ] [ NULL | NOT NULL ]
  [ DEFAULT constant_expression ]
    | [ IDENTITY [ ( seed ,increment ) ] ]
  [ ROWGUIDCOL ] [ <column_constraint> [ ...n ] ]

<data type> ::=
  [ type_schema_name . ] type_name
  [ ( precision [ , scale ] | max |
    [ { CONTENT | DOCUMENT } ] xml_schema_collection ) ]

<column_constraint> ::=
{ { PRIMARY KEY | UNIQUE } [ CLUSTERED | NONCLUSTERED ]
  [ WITH ( <index_option> [ ,...n ] ) ]
  | CHECK ( logical_expression )
}

<comp_col_def> ::=
{ column_name AS computed_column_expression
  [ PERSISTED [ NOT NULL ] ]
  [ { PRIMARY KEY | UNIQUE } [ CLUSTERED | NONCLUSTERED ]
  [ WITH ( <index_option> [ ,...n ] ) ]
  | CHECK ( logical_expression ) ]
}

<table_constraint> ::=
{ { PRIMARY KEY | UNIQUE }
  [ CLUSTERED | NONCLUSTERED ] ( column [ ASC | DESC ] [ ,...n ] )
  [ WITH ( <index_option> [ ,...n ] ) ]
  | CHECK ( logical_expression )
}

<index_option> ::=
{ IGNORE_DUP_KEY = { ON | OFF } }
```

**Usage**
```
USE CustomerDB
CREATE TYPE StoreTableType AS TABLE
    ( StoreName VARCHAR(60)
    , StoreNumeric INT )
GO
```

### Managing User-Defined Table Types

After you create user-defined table types, you often will need to manage their properties. To manage user-defined table types, complete the following steps:

1. In SQL Server Management Studio, connect to the server instance that contains the database in which you want to work.

2. In Object Explorer, expand the Databases node, and then select a database and expand the view to show its resource nodes.

3. Expand Programmability, Types, and User-Defined Table Types to list the current user-defined table types.

4. As with any table, the user-defined table type can have associated columns, keys, constraints, and indexes. Right-click the user-defined table type you want to manage and then select from the following options:

   ❑ Properties, to view the data type's properties and set dependencies

   ❑ Delete, to delete the data type

   ❑ Rename, to rename the data type

5. To see where the data type is used in the database, right-click the user-defined table type, and then select View Dependencies from the shortcut menu.

# Using Views

Views can be thought of as virtual tables because the result sets returned by views have the same general form as a table, with columns and rows, and views can be referenced much like tables in queries. Several types of views can be created. Most views are used to join data from multiple tables so that it can be accessed in a single result set. For example, you could create a CustOrder view that gets the customer's first name, last name, address, account number, and telephone number from the *Customers* table and the last order details from the *Orders* table, which makes the information more manageable for your company's sales representatives.

Views can be created from other views as well, which allows you to extract subsets of data from views and to create supersets that combine data from multiple views. For example, you could create a subset view of the CustOrder view that shows only the customer's first name, last name, and telephone number. You could also create a superset view that combines elements of the CustOrder view, AllCustOrders view, and LastOrder view.

## Working with Views

To create a view, you use a SELECT statement to select the data in one or more tables and display it as a view. Like tables, views can be partitioned and indexed. A partitioned view joins horizontally partitioned data from a set of base tables from one or more servers. A partitioned view in which all base tables reside in the same database is referred to as a local partitioned view. A partitioned view in which one or more base tables reside on one or more different remote servers is referred to as a distributed partitioned view.

> **Tip**  Typically, you will use distributed partitioned views rather than local partitioned views because the preferred method for partitioning data locally is through partitioned tables (and local partitioned views are supported only for backward compatibility). Distributed partitioned views are used to create a federation of database servers. A *federation* is a group of servers that are managed separately, but which cooperate to share the query processing load of a large application or Web site.

Partitioned views also can be updatable or read-only. Updatable partitioned views are updatable copies of the underlying tables. Read-only partitioned views are read-only copies of the underlying tables. To perform updates on a partitioned view, the partitioning column must be part of the base table's primary key. If this is not possible (or to make read-only partitioned views updatable), you can use INSTEAD OF triggers. INSTEAD OF triggers execute whenever a user attempts to modify data using INSERT, UPDATE, or DELETE. Views comprising multiple base tables must use an INSTEAD OF trigger to support inserts, updates, and deletes that reference data in more than one table.

You index views to improve query performance. The first index created on a view must be a unique clustered index. After the unique clustered index is created, you can create additional nonclustered indexes on the view. A view for which you want to create a unique clustered index must not reference any other views. It can reference only base tables, and those base tables must be in the same database as the view and have the same owner as the view.

The query processor handles indexed and nonindexed views in different ways. The rows of an indexed view are stored in the database in the same format as a table. If the query optimizer uses an indexed view in a query plan, the indexed view is handled the same way as a base table. With nonindexed views, only the view definition is stored in the database, not the rows of the view. If the query optimizer uses a nonindexed view in an execution plan, only the logic from the view definition is used.

When an SQL statement references a nonindexed view, the parser and query optimizer analyze the source of both the SQL statement and the view and resolve them into a single execution plan. This means that there is not one plan for the SQL statement and a separate plan for the view—there is only one execution plan.

As with tables, views are contained in schemas, and you can assign permissions to views. Typically, you want the base tables and the related views to be in the same schema. It is also important to note that permissions assigned to views are separate from the table permissions.

## Creating Views

Views can have up to 1024 columns. If you understand tables, creating views is a straightforward process. However, there are a few rules to follow. Although the SELECT statement used to create a view can use more than one table and other views, you must have appropriate permissions to select from the referenced objects. The view definition cannot include COMPUTE or COMPUTE BY clauses, an ORDER BY clause (unless there is also a TOP clause), the INTO keyword, the OPTION clause, or a reference to a temporary table or a table variable.

You can create a view in SQL Server Management Studio by completing the following steps:

1. In SQL Server Management Studio, select a database, and then expand the Views node to list the current views in the database. Two types of views are available: system and user. System views provide a summarized report of database information, such as table constraints and table privileges. User views are defined by you or by other database users.

2. To create a new view, right-click the Views node. From the shortcut menu, choose New View to display the Add Table dialog box shown in Figure 10-5. The Add Table dialog box has tabs that allow you to work with tables, views, functions, and synonyms. If you select Add New Derived Tables from the Query Designer menu and display the dialog box again, you will see a Local Tables tab containing derived tables.

**Figure 10-5** The Add Table dialog box.

3. In the Add Table dialog box, select a table or other object that contains data you want to add to the view, and then click Add. This displays a view pane for the

selected object, which you can use to add columns, fields, and so on to the view you are creating.

4. When you are finished working with the Add Table dialog box, click Close. You can display this dialog box again at any time by selecting Add Table on the Query Designer menu.

5. Use the view panes provided to select the columns and fields to use in the view, as shown in Figure 10-6. Your actions create a SELECT statement that can be used to generate the view.

**Figure 10-6**   Select columns and fields to use for a view.

6. The View Properties pane is not displayed by default. In the right pane, click the tab with the name of the view, and then press F4 to display the View Properties pane.

7. Set the view name, description, and schema. Type the name and description in the fields provided. Use the drop-down list to select the schema that will contain this view.

8. You might want to create a dependency within a schema to ensure that any modifications to the underlying structures that the view comprises are not changed without first changing the view. You do this by binding the view to the schema. If you want to bind the view to the schema, set Bind To Schema to Yes.

> **Note**   When you bind a view to the schema, views or tables used in the view
> cannot be dropped unless that view is dropped or changed so that it no
> longer has schema binding. Furthermore, executing ALTER TABLE statements
> on tables that participate in views that have schema binding will fail when
> these statements affect the view definition.

9.  If you want to ensure that the view shows only distinct rows and filters out dupli-
    cate rows, set Distinct Values to Yes.

10. If you want the view to return a partial result set containing the top matches, set
    Top to Yes, and then define the number of top matches to return as either a fixed
    maximum or a percentage of total results.

    ❑  To define a fixed maximum, set Expression to the maximum number of
       results to return and set Percent to No. For example, set Expression to 50
       to return the top 50 results.

    ❑  To define a percentage of the total results to return, set Expression to the
       percentage of results to return and set Percent to Yes. For example, set
       Expression to 10 and Percent to Yes to return the top 10 percent of the
       result set.

11. If you want to create an updatable view, set Update Using View Rules to Yes.
    Updatable views cannot be created with distinct values or from top result sets. To
    make sure data remains visible through the view after a modification is commit-
    ted, set Check Option to Yes. Remember, however, that updates performed
    directly to a view's base tables are not verified against the view even when you
    select the Check Option.

12. When you are finished configuring the view, verify the SQL syntax by selecting
    Verify SQL Syntax from the Query Designer menu. Correct any errors or issues
    reported during the verification process before continuing.

13. To create the view, press Ctrl+R or select Execute SQL on the Query Designer
    menu.

14. After you run the view to update it for the latest changes, save the view. Press
    Ctrl+S or click Save on the toolbar.

You can also create views using the CREATE VIEW statement. You can create a simple
view by selecting all the values in a table:

```
CREATE VIEW Sales.CustomView As
SELECT *
FROM Sales.Customers
```

Then you can work directly with the view:

```
SELECT * FROM Sales.CustomView
```

Sample 10-9 shows the full syntax and usage for CREATE VIEW.

**Sample 10-9**   CREATE VIEW Syntax and Usage

```
Syntax
CREATE VIEW [ schema_name . ] view_name [ (column [ ,...n ] ) ]
[ WITH <view_attribute> [ ,...n ] ]
AS select_statement
[ WITH CHECK OPTION ] [ ; ]

<view_attribute> ::=
{    [ ENCRYPTION ]
     [ SCHEMABINDING ]
     [ VIEW_METADATA ]      }

Usage
CREATE VIEW Sales.CustomView As
SELECT cust_id AS Account, cust_lname AS [Last Name],
     cust_fname AS [First Name], state AS Region
FROM Sales.Customers
WHERE (state = 'WA') OR
      (state = 'HI') OR
      (state = 'CA')
```

## Modifying Views

You can modify a view in SQL Server Management Studio by completing the following steps:

1. In SQL Server Management Studio, select a database, and then expand the Views node to list the current views in the database.

2. To modify an existing view, right-click the view, and then select Design.

3. If you want to add tables, views, and so on, you can display the Add Table dialog box by selecting Add Table from the Query Designer menu.

4. If you want to set view properties, click the tab with the name of the view and then press F4 to display the View Properties pane.

To change an existing view without having to reset its permissions and other properties, you use ALTER VIEW. The following example changes the definition of the Sales Custom view used in previous examples:

```
ALTER VIEW Sales.CustomView As
    SELECT cust_id AS Account, cust_lname AS [Customer Last Name],
    cust_fname AS [Customer First Name], state AS Region
    FROM Sales.Customers
    WHERE (state = 'WA') OR
        (state = 'CA')
```

Sample 10-10 shows the full syntax for ALTER VIEW.

**Sample 10-10** ALTER VIEW Syntax

```
Syntax
ALTER VIEW [ schema_name . ] view_name [ ( column [ ,...n ] ) ]
[ WITH <view_attribute> [ ,...n ] ]
AS select_statement
[ WITH CHECK OPTION ] [ ; ]

<view_attribute> ::=
{   [ ENCRYPTION ]
    [ SCHEMABINDING ]
    [ VIEW_METADATA ]   }
```

## Using Updatable Views

SQL Server supports updatable views as well. With an updatable view, you can change the information in the view using INSERT, UPDATE, and DELETE statements. You can create updatable views if the table columns being modified are not affected by GROUP BY, HAVING, or DISTINCT clauses. Furthermore, an updatable view can be modified only when the columns from one base table are being modified and those columns directly reference the underlying data. This means the data cannot be derived from an aggregate function or computed from an expression that uses other columns.

With updatable views, you will usually want to set Check Option to Yes. If you do not set the option, changes to the view might result in rows that are no longer displayed in the view. For example, consider the view created as an example previously. The view included customer information from Washington (WA), Hawaii (HI), and California (CA). If you change a state value to GA, the row would disappear from the view because Georgia-based customers are not displayed in the view.

## Managing Views

You can examine view properties, set view permissions, and perform other management tasks, just as you do with tables. To get started managing views, complete the following steps:

1. In SQL Server Management Studio, select a database, and then expand the Views node to list the current views in the database.

2. Select a view, and then right-click it to open a shortcut menu that gives you the following choices to manage the view:

   ❑ **Select Top 1000 Rows** Displays up to 1000 rows in the result set for the view.

- ❑ **Edit Top 200 Rows**   Displays up to 200 rows in the result set for the view, and allows you to edit the related values.

- ❑ **Properties**   Examine view properties.

- ❑ **Rename**   Rename the view.

- ❑ **Delete**   Delete the view.

- ❑ **View Dependencies**   View objects that depend on the view or objects on which the view depends.

3. To set permissions for a view, right-click the view, and then select Properties. In the View Properties dialog box, select the Permissions page. You can now manage the permissions for the view.

# Creating and Managing Indexes

Indexes provide quick access to data without searching through an entire database. With SQL Server 2008, you can create indexes on tables, views, and columns. By creating indexes on tables, you can search through the data in a table quickly. By creating indexes on views, you can generate a result set of the view that is stored and indexed in the database. By creating indexes on computed columns, you can evaluate expressions and index the results (if certain criteria are met).

Indexes are separate from tables, and you can configure them automatically using the Database Engine Tuning Advisor. This section examines the techniques you will use to work with indexes.

## Understanding Indexes

Indexes, like tables, use pages. The structure of index pages is similar to the structure used for table data pages. Index pages are 8 KB (8192 bytes) in size and have a 96-byte header. But unlike data pages, they do not have row offsets. Each index has a corresponding row in the sys.indexes catalog view with an index ID value (index_id) of 1 for clustered indexes or 2 through 250 for nonclustered indexes. An index ID value of 255 indicates large object data such as image, ntext, text, varchar(max), nvarchar(max), varbinary(max), or xml data. (Large object data types cannot be index key columns; varchar(max), nvarchar(max), varbinary(max), and xml data types can be included columns, however.)

SQL Server maintains indexes using a BTree structure, which is a basic tree structure consisting of a root node, intermediate-level nodes, and leaf nodes. Because indexes use a tree structure, you can search them quickly and efficiently. Without the tree structure, SQL Server would need to read each table data page in the database in turn, searching for the correct record.

To put this in perspective, consider a simple table in which each data page contains a single row. In this case, if SQL Server searches for data in row 800 and there is no index, SQL Server might have to search 799 other rows before finding the right row. With a tree structure, SQL Server navigates the nodes down the index searching for the row that matches the corresponding index key. In the best-case scenario, in which the index keys have been arranged in a full tree, the number of nodes that need to be searched is proportional to the height of the tree. For example, 27,000 rows might be represented by 30 levels of nodes, and if so, SQL Server would have to navigate a maximum of 15 nodes to find the matching row.

**Note** You might have noticed that I simplified this example to demonstrate the power of indexing. Nevertheless, indexing can improve performance by orders of magnitude, and accessing a database without indexing can seem extremely slow. You must be careful, however; indexing the wrong information also can make the database perform slowly, which is why it is so important to select the most referenced/used column in the table to index.

In SQL Server 2008, indexing performance has been enhanced in many ways:

- Index operations can be performed online, and online indexing depends on the amount of memory allocated for indexing. Online indexing makes it possible for users to access table data and use other indexes on a table while an index is being created, modified, or dropped.

- Columns that are not part of the index key can be included in nonclustered indexes to improve query performance by making all the required data available without the need to access the table data rows. These included columns can exceed the index size limitations of 16 key columns and the maximum key size of 900 bytes.

- Both row-level and page-level index locks are allowed when accessing the index. If you allow row locks, page locks, or both, the Database Engine determines when the locks are used.

- The maximum degree of parallelism can be set using MAXDOP. This controls the number of parallel operations when creating, alerting, or dropping an index.

- Indexes can be partitioned on value ranges using existing partition schemes. When you partition a nonunique, clustered index, the Database Engine adds the partitioning column to the list of clustered index keys if it is not already specified. When you partition a nonunique, nonclustered index, the Database Engine adds the partitioning column as a nonkey (included) column of the index if it is not already specified.

SQL Server 2008 supports two main types of indexing:

- Clustered indexes
- Nonclustered indexes

You can create clustered and nonclustered indexes on almost any column. Exceptions include CLR user-defined types and very large object data types—you cannot create indexes on these data types. If you want to create indexes on computed columns, you must ensure the computed column expression always returns the same result for a specific set of inputs. Although you can create an index on any other type of column, you should always select the index column carefully. Selecting the correct column to index improves response time dramatically. Selecting the wrong column to index actually can degrade response time. For more information about which column to index, use the Database Engine Tuning Advisor.

SQL Server 2008 also supports several special types of indexing:

- **XML indexes**   An XML index can be either a nonclustered index (the default) or a clustered index. A clustered index is created for XML data from the clustering key of the user table and an XML node identifier. Each table can have up to 249 XML indexes. You will learn more about XML indexes in "Using XML Indexes" on page 364.

- **Filtered indexes**   A filtered index is an optimized nonclustered index on a sub-set of table data. Well-designed filtered indexes reduce index storage costs because you don't need to index full tables, improve query performance and execution plan quality because they are smaller than full-table indexes, and reduce maintenance overhead because they are maintained only when the data in the index is modified. You will learn more about filtered indexes in "Using Filtered Indexes" on page 364.

- **Spatial indexes**   A spatial index is defined on a table column that contains geometric or geographic data. A spatial index on geographic data maps the geographic data to a two-dimensional space. Each table can have up to 249 spatial indexes. You can define spatial indexes only on a table that has a primary key. Primary key metadata cannot be changed while a spatial index is defined on a table, and the maximum number of primary key columns on the table is 15. You can create more than one spatial index on the same spatial column, such as might be necessary to index different grid parameters in a single column.

## Using Clustered Indexes

A clustered index stores the actual table data pages at the leaf level, and the table data is physically ordered around the key. A table can have only one clustered index, and when this index is created, the following events also occur:

- Table data is rearranged.
- New index pages are created.
- All nonclustered indexes within the database are rebuilt.

As a result, there are many disk I/O operations and extensive use of system and memory resources. So if you plan to create a clustered index, make sure you have enough free space, equal to at least 1.5 times the amount of data in the table. The extra free space ensures that you have enough space to complete the operation efficiently.

Normally, you create a clustered index on a primary key. You can, however, create a clustered index on any named column, such as cust_lname or cust_id. When you create a clustered index, the values you are indexing should be unique. If the values are not unique, SQL Server creates secondary sort keys on rows that have duplicates of their primary sort keys.

## Using Nonclustered Indexes

In a nonclustered index, pages at the leaf level contain a bookmark that tells SQL Server where to find the data row corresponding to the key in the index. If the table has a clustered index, the bookmark indicates the clustered index key. If the table does not have a clustered index, the bookmark is an actual row locator.

When you create a nonclustered index, SQL Server creates the required index pages but does not rearrange table data, and other indexes for the table are not deleted. Each table can have up to 249 nonclustered indexes.

## Using XML Indexes

As mentioned earlier, an XML index is a special type of index that can be either clustered or nonclustered. Before you can create an XML index, there must be a clustered index based on the primary key of the user table, and this key is limited to 15 columns. Two types of XML indexes can be created: primary and secondary. Each xml column in a table can have one primary XML index and one or more secondary XML indexes. However, there must be a primary XML index before a secondary XML index can be created on a column, and you cannot create a primary XML index on a computed xml column.

Also note that an XML index can be created only on a single xml column. You cannot create an XML index on a non-xml column, nor can you create a relational index on an xml column. You cannot create an XML index on an xml column in a view, on a table-valued variable with xml columns, or on an xml type variable. Finally, the SET options must be the same as those required for indexed views and computed-column indexes. This means ARITHABORT must be set to ON when an XML index is created and when inserting, deleting, or updating values in the xml column.

## Using Filtered Indexes

As mentioned earlier, a filtered index is a special type of nonclustered index on a subset of table data. Filtered indexes are useful in several situations. When a table column has only a limited number of relevant values and a query selects only from the relevant values, you can create a filtered index for the relevant data rows. When a table column has multiple categories of data and a query selects only from a particular category or categories, you can create a filtered index for the relevant category or categories.

Filtered indexes are useful when your queries use simple comparison logic in a predicate and are not a replacement for views, which have broader scope and functionality. For example, you could create a filtered index for non-null data rows using a query that selects only from non-null values. Or you could create a filtered index for a subset of categories within the data using a query that selects only the desired categories.

> **Note**   You cannot create filtered indexes on views. You cannot drop, rename, or alter the definition of a table column that is defined in a filtered index expression. You can track dependencies for filtered index expressions using the sys.sql_expression_dependencies catalog view.

In some cases, a parameterized query does not contain enough information at compile time for the query optimizer to choose a filtered index. You might be able to rewrite the query to provide the missing information. For example, you could modify the query so that the query results are empty when a parameterized expression is not a subset of the filter predicate.

When creating filtered indexes, you should include only the columns that are necessary for the query optimizer to choose the filtered index for the query execution plan. Although the filtered index doesn't have to cover the query, it should. The primary key of the table does not need to be specifically included in the filtered index definition. The primary key is automatically included in all nonclustered indexes, including filtered indexes.

When the filtered index expression is equivalent to the query predicate and the query does not return the column in the filtered index expression with the query results, a column in the filtered index expression does not need to be a key or included column in the filtered index definition. When the query predicate uses the column in a comparison that is not equivalent to the filtered index expression, a column in the filtered index expression should be a key or included column in the filtered index definition.

When the comparison operator specified in the filtered index expression results in an implicit or explicit data conversion, an error will occur if the conversion occurs on the left side of a comparison operator. A workaround is to write the filtered index expression with the data conversion operator (CAST or CONVERT) on the right side of the comparison operator. However, this can change the meaning of the conversion.

## Determining Which Columns Should Be Indexed

Now that you know how indexes work, you can focus on which columns you should index. Ideally, you will select columns for indexing based on the types of queries executed on the database. SQL Server Profiler can help you determine the types of queries being run. You use SQL Server Profiler to create a trace that contains a good snapshot of activities performed by users on the database.

You can examine this trace manually to see what types of queries are executed, or you can use the trace file as a saved workload file in the Database Engine Tuning Advisor. Regardless of which method you use, keep in mind that the maximum length of all key columns that an index comprises is 900 bytes. This means that the total size in bytes of all columns must be 900 or less. (Columns that are not part of the index key can be included, and these included columns can exceed the index size limitations of 16 key columns and maximum key size of 900 bytes.) Table 10-4 offers some guidelines about the kinds of tables and columns that can be successfully indexed and those that do not result in useful indexes.

**Table 10-4   Guidelines for Selecting Tables and Columns to Index**

| Index | Do Not Index |
|---|---|
| Tables with lots of rows | Tables with few rows |
| Columns that are often used in queries | Columns that are rarely used in queries |
| Columns that have a wide range of values and have a high likelihood of rows being selected in a typical query | Columns that have a wide range of values but have a low likelihood of rows being selected in a typical query |
| Columns used in aggregate functions | Columns that have a large byte size |
| Columns used in GROUP BY queries | Tables with many modifications but few actual queries |
| Columns used in ORDER BY queries | |
| Columns used in table joins | |

Table 10-5 provides suggestions for the types of columns that should use clustered or nonclustered indexes.

**Table 10-5   Guidelines for Using Clustered and Nonclustered Indexes**

| Use Clustered Index for | Use Nonclustered Index for |
|---|---|
| Primary keys that are searched for extensively, such as account numbers | Primary keys that are sequential identifiers, such as identity columns |
| Queries that return large result sets | Queries that return small result sets |
| Columns used in many queries | Columns used in aggregate functions |
| Columns with strong selectivity | Foreign keys |
| Columns used in ORDER BY or GROUP BY queries | |
| Columns used in table joins | |

## Indexing Computed Columns and Views

With SQL Server 2008, you can index computed columns and views as well as tables. Indexes on computed columns and views involve storing results in the database for future reference. With computed columns, the column values are calculated and then used to build the keys stored in the index. With views, the result set is stored by creating a clustered index on the view. In both cases, the stored results are valid only if all connections referring to the results can generate an identical result set, which puts specific restrictions on how you can create indexes on computed columns and views.

You must establish connections referring to the results using specific SET options, and these options must have the same settings. The options you must set are as follows:

- ANSI_NULLS must be set to ON.
- ANSI_PADDING must be set to ON.
- ANSI_WARNINGS must be set to ON.
- ARITHABORT must be set to ON.
- CONCAT_NULL_YIELDS_NULL must be set to ON.
- QUOTED_IDENTIFIER must be set to ON.
- NUMERIC_ROUNDABORT must be set to OFF.

Furthermore, all operations referencing the view must use the exact same algorithm to build the view result set, including

- The CREATE INDEX statement that builds the initial result set or is used to calculate the initial keys
- Any subsequent INSERT, UPDATE, or DELETE statements that affect the data used to build the view result set or are used to calculate keys
- All queries for which the query optimizer must determine if the indexed view is useful

## Viewing Index Properties

Both tables and views can have indexes. In SQL Server Management Studio, you can view indexes associated with a table or view by completing the following steps:

1. In SQL Server Management Studio, select a database, and then expand the Tables or Views node as appropriate.

2. Select a table or view and expand its node to list the objects it contains.

3. Expand the Indexes node to list the indexes associated with the selected table or view (if any).

4.  Right-click an index, and then select Properties from the shortcut menu to open the Index Properties dialog box shown in Figure 10-7. This dialog box has several pages that you can select to view and manage index properties:

    ❏  **General**    Shows general properties, including the index name and type. You can change the index type and add or remove key columns.

    ❏  **Options**    Allows you to set options for rebuilding the index, recomputing statistics, using row or page locks, setting the fill factor, and determining maximum degree of parallelism.

    ❏  **Included Columns**    Allows you to view and manage the included columns (with nonclustered indexes).

    ❏  **Storage**    Lists the current storage configuration. Allows you to configure filegroups and partition schemes.

    ❏  **Spatial**    Lists spatial properties for columns that include geometric or geographic data.

    ❏  **Filter**    Lists the filter expression for a filtered index.

    ❏  **Fragmentation**    Lists the index fragmentation data, which you can use to determine if you need to reorganize or rebuild the index.

    ❏  **Extended Properties**    Lists extended properties. Allows you to add or remove extended properties.

Figure 10-7    Index Properties dialog box.

Using the sp_statistics stored procedure, you can examine the indexes for a specific table or view. To do this, you simply specify the name of the table or view whose indexes you want to examine, as shown in the following example:

```
USE OrderSystemDB
EXEC sp_statistics Sales.Customers
```

## Creating Indexes

Only the owner of a table or view can create indexes on that table or view. You can create indexes with a design tool in SQL Server Management Studio or with the Transact-SQL CREATE INDEX statement. To create indexes with the design tool, complete the following steps:

1.  In SQL Server Management Studio, connect to the server instance containing the database in which you want to work.

2.  In Object Explorer, expand the Databases node, and then select a database and expand it to show the database's resource nodes.

3.  Expand the Tables or Views node as appropriate. Right-click the table or view for which you are creating the index, and then select Design from the shortcut menu.

4.  On the Table Designer menu, select Indexes/Keys to display the Indexes/Keys dialog box shown in Figure 10-8.

**Figure 10-8**    The Indexes/Keys dialog box.

5.  Any current primary/unique keys and indexes are listed in the left pane of the dialog box, and you can manage the properties of any of the keys by selecting it and making the necessary changes. To add an index, click Add.

6. Click in the Columns text box and then click the button to the right of the Columns box. This displays the Index Columns dialog box shown in Figure 10-9.

7. Under Column Name, select the column or columns you want to include in the index. You can select only columns that have valid data types for indexing.

**Figure 10-9** The Index Columns dialog box.

8. Each column can have a separate sort order for the index. By default, the sort order is set to Ascending. You can set the sort order to Descending.

9. When you have finished selecting columns to index, click OK to close the Index Columns dialog box.

10. If you want to ensure that data entered into this index is unique, set the option Is Unique to Yes. This ensures the uniqueness of values stored in the index. You cannot set this option for XML indexes.

11. Type should be set to Index by default. Under Identity, use the text boxes provided to type the index name and description. You can use up to 128 characters for the index name. Ideally, the index name should be short and easy to associate with its purpose, such as [*Index for Cust ID*].

12. Set the option Create As Clustered to Yes to create a clustered index on the columns selected. Otherwise, a nonclustered index is created. Remember that you can have only one clustered index per table, so if the table already has a clustered index, this option is shaded and you cannot select it.

13. To specify the storage location for the index, expand the Data Space Specification node, and then use the Filegroup Or Partition Schema drop-down list to specify the filegroup.

14. To set the fill parameters, expand the Fill Specification node. Set the Fill Factor to 0 (the default value) to let SQL Server use an optimized fill, as described in "Setting the Index Fill" on page 168. Refer to this same section for information about setting the Fill Factor to a different value to set a specific index fill.

15. If you want to ignore duplicate keys, set the option Ignore Duplicate Keys to Yes. When this option is on, any attempt to insert rows that violate the unique index fails with a warning, and the rows are not inserted. Whether this option is set on or off, however, SQL Server does not allow you to create a unique index on columns that already have duplicate values. Columns that are used in a unique index should be set so that they do not allow nulls. Furthermore, you cannot use the Ignore Duplicate Keys option with XML indexes or indexes created on views.

16. Optionally, turn on automatic statistics updating by setting the option Re-Compute Statistics to Yes. If you set Re-Compute Statistics to No, out-of-date statistics are not automatically recomputed.

17. When you are finished configuring the index, click Close. Select File, Save or press Ctrl+S to save the table, which in turn saves the index you created.

18. With nonclustered indexes, you can create filtered indexes by adding the WHERE clause to the CREATE INDEX statement. In SQL Server Management Studio, right-click a nonclustered index, and then select Properties from the shortcut menu to open the Index Properties dialog box shown previously in Figure 10-7. You can then enter the filter on the Filter page.

Use the Transact-SQL CREATE INDEX command to create indexes with the syntax shown in Sample 10-11. With a nonclustered index, you can create a filtered index by adding a WHERE clause.

**Sample 10-11**   CREATE INDEX Syntax

```
Syntax Relational Index
CREATE [ UNIQUE ] [ CLUSTERED | NONCLUSTERED ] INDEX index_name
    ON <object> ( column [ ASC | DESC ] [ ,...n ] )
    [ INCLUDE ( column_name [ ,...n ] ) ]
    [ WHERE <filter_predicate> ]
    [ WITH ( <relational_index_option> [ ,...n ] ) ]
    [ ON { partition_scheme_name ( column_name )
         | filegroup_name
         | default
         }
    ]
    [ FILESTREAM_ON { filestream_filegroup_name
        | partition_scheme_name | "NULL" } ]
[ ; ]
```

```
<object> ::=
{ [ database_name. [ schema_name ] . | schema_name. ]
        table_or_view_name
}

<relational_index_option> ::=
{ PAD_INDEX = { ON | OFF }
  | FILLFACTOR = fillfactor
  | SORT_IN_TEMPDB = { ON | OFF }
  | IGNORE_DUP_KEY = { ON | OFF }
  | STATISTICS_NORECOMPUTE = { ON | OFF }
  | DROP_EXISTING = { ON | OFF }
  | ONLINE = { ON | OFF }
  | ALLOW_ROW_LOCKS = { ON | OFF }
  | ALLOW_PAGE_LOCKS = { ON | OFF }
  | MAXDOP = max_degree_of_parallelism
  | DATA_COMPRESSION = { NONE | ROW | PAGE}
    [ ON PARTITIONS ( { <partition_number_expression> | <range> }
    [ , ...n ] ) ]
}

<filter_predicate> ::=
    <conjunct> [ AND <conjunct> ]

<conjunct> ::=
    <disjunct> | <comparison>

<disjunct> ::=
        column_name IN (constant ,…)

<comparison> ::=
        column_name <comparison_op> constant

<comparison_op> ::=
    { IS | IS NOT | = | <> | != | > | >= | !> | < | <= | !< }

<range> ::=
<partition_number_expression> TO <partition_number_expression>
```

**Syntax XML Index**
```
CREATE [ PRIMARY ] XML INDEX index_name
    ON <object> ( xml_column_name )
    [ USING XML INDEX xml_index_name
        [ FOR { VALUE | PATH | PROPERTY } ] ]
    [ WITH ( <xml_index_option> [ ,...n ] ) ]
[ ; ]
```

```
<object> ::=
{ [ database_name. [ schema_name ] . | schema_name. ] table_name }

<xml_index_option> ::=
{ PAD_INDEX  = { ON | OFF }
  | FILLFACTOR = fillfactor
  | SORT_IN_TEMPDB = { ON | OFF }
  | IGNORE_DUP_KEY = OFF
  | STATISTICS_NORECOMPUTE = { ON | OFF }
  | DROP_EXISTING = { ON | OFF }
  | ONLINE = OFF
  | ALLOW_ROW_LOCKS = { ON | OFF }
  | ALLOW_PAGE_LOCKS = { ON | OFF }
  | MAXDOP = max_degree_of_parallelism
}
```

**Syntax Spatial Index**

```
CREATE SPATIAL INDEX index_name
  ON <object> ( spatial_column_name )
    {
        [ USING <geometry_grid_tessellation> ]
            WITH ( <bounding_box>
                    [ [,] <tesselation_parameters> [ ,...n ] ]
                    [ [,] <spatial_index_option> [ ,...n ] ] )
      | [ USING <geography_grid_tessellation> ]
            [ WITH ( [ <tesselation_parameters> [ ,...n ] ]
                    [ [,] <spatial_index_option> [ ,...n ] ] ) ]
    }
  [ ON { filegroup_name | "default" } ]
;

<object> ::=
    [ database_name. [ schema_name ] . | schema_name. ] table_name

<geometry_grid_tessellation> ::=
{ GEOMETRY_GRID }

<bounding_box> ::=
BOUNDING_BOX = ( {
        xmin, ymin, xmax, ymax
    | <named_bb_coordinate>, <named_bb_coordinate>,
      <named_bb_coordinate>, <named_bb_coordinate>
  } )

<named_bb_coordinate> ::= { XMIN = xmin | YMIN = ymin | XMAX = xmax
    | YMAX=ymax }
```

```
<tesselation_parameters> ::=
{ GRIDS = ( { <grid_density> [ ,...n ] | <density>, <density>,
<density>, <density>  } )
  | CELLS_PER_OBJECT = n
}

<grid_density> ::=
{  LEVEL_1 = <density>
  | LEVEL_2 = <density>
  | LEVEL_3 = <density>
  | LEVEL_4 = <density>
}

<density> ::= { LOW | MEDIUM | HIGH }

<geography_grid_tessellation> ::=
{ GEOGRAPHY_GRID }

<spatial_index_option> ::=
{ PAD_INDEX = { ON | OFF }
  | FILLFACTOR = fillfactor
  | SORT_IN_TEMPDB = { ON | OFF }
  | IGNORE_DUP_KEY = OFF
  | STATISTICS_NORECOMPUTE = { ON | OFF }
  | DROP_EXISTING = { ON | OFF }
  | ONLINE = OFF
  | ALLOW_ROW_LOCKS = { ON | OFF }
  | ALLOW_PAGE_LOCKS = { ON | OFF }
  | MAXDOP = max_degree_of_parallelism
}
```

## Managing Indexes

After you create an index, you might need to change its properties, rename it, or delete it. You handle these tasks in SQL Server Management Studio by completing the following steps:

1. In SQL Server Management Studio, select a database, and then expand the Tables or Views node as appropriate.

2. Select a table or view and expand its node to list the objects it contains.

3. Expand the Indexes node to list the indexes associated with the selected table or view.

4. Right-click an index. You can now choose from the following options:

   ❑ Select Properties to view the index properties, including details on space usage and fragmentation.

❑   Select Rename to rename an index.

❑   Select Rebuild to rebuild the index. In the Rebuild Indexes dialog box, use the Total Fragmentation and Status values to help you determine whether or not to proceed. Click OK to proceed with the rebuild. Click Cancel to exit without performing the rebuild. SQL Server 2008 performs online index rebuilds and reorganizations.

❑   Select Reorganize to reorganize the index. In the Reorganize Indexes dialog box, check the Total Fragmentation of the index to determine if the index needs to be reorganized. By default, both regular data and large object data are reorganized. Clear the Compact Large Object Column Data option if you want to compact only regular index data. Click OK to proceed with the reorganization. Click Cancel to exit without performing the reorganization.

❑   Select Delete to drop the index (as long as it is not a primary key or unique constraint).

You can also manage indexes with the Transact-SQL commands ALTER INDEX and DROP INDEX. Unfortunately, you must use these commands cautiously because there are several limitations to them. For example, you cannot drop an index that was created by defining a primary key or unique constraints. You must instead drop the constraint with ALTER TABLE. Sample 10-12 shows the syntax for ALTER INDEX, and Sample 10-13 shows the syntax for DROP INDEX.

**Note**   ALTER INDEX supports filtered indexes. You can modify the filtered index expression using the CREATE INDEX WITH DROP_EXISTING statement.

**Sample 10-12**   ALTER INDEX Syntax

```
Syntax
ALTER INDEX { index_name | ALL }
    ON <object>
    { REBUILD
      [ [PARTITION = ALL]
        [ [ WITH ( <rebuild_index_option> [ ,...n ] ) ]
          | [ PARTITION = partition_number
                [ WITH ( <single_partition_rebuild_index_option>
                        [ ,...n ] )
                ]
            ]
        ]
      | DISABLE
      | REORGANIZE
          [ PARTITION = partition_number ]
          [ WITH ( LOB_COMPACTION = { ON | OFF } ) ]
    | SET ( <set_index_option> [ ,...n ] )
    }
[ ; ]
```

```
<object> ::=
{ [ database_name. [ schema_name ] . | schema_name. ]
        table_or_view_name
}

<rebuild_index_option > ::=
{ PAD_INDEX = { ON | OFF }
  | FILLFACTOR = fillfactor
  | SORT_IN_TEMPDB = { ON | OFF }
  | IGNORE_DUP_KEY = { ON | OFF }
  | STATISTICS_NORECOMPUTE = { ON | OFF }
  | ONLINE = { ON | OFF }
  | ALLOW_ROW_LOCKS = { ON | OFF }
  | ALLOW_PAGE_LOCKS = { ON | OFF }
  | MAXDOP = max_degree_of_parallelism
  | DATA_COMPRESSION = { NONE | ROW | PAGE }
    [ ON PARTITIONS ( { <partition_number_expression> | <range> }
    [ , ...n ] ) ]
}
<range> ::=
{ <partition_number_expression> TO <partition_number_expression>
}

<single_partition_rebuild_index_option> ::=
{ SORT_IN_TEMPDB = { ON | OFF }
  | MAXDOP = max_degree_of_parallelism
  | DATA_COMPRESSION = { NONE | ROW | PAGE } }
}

<set_index_option>::=
{ ALLOW_ROW_LOCKS = { ON | OFF }
  | ALLOW_PAGE_LOCKS = { ON | OFF }
  | IGNORE_DUP_KEY = { ON | OFF }
  | STATISTICS_NORECOMPUTE = { ON | OFF }
}
```

**Sample 10-13**   DROP INDEX Syntax

**Syntax**
```
DROP INDEX
{ <drop_relational_or_xml_or_spatial_index> [ ,...n ]
| <drop_backward_compatible_index> [ ,...n ]
}
```

```
<drop_relational_or_xml_or_spatial_index> ::=
        index_name ON <object>
    [ WITH ( <drop_clustered_index_option> [ ,...n ] ) ]


<drop_backward_compatible_index> ::=
    [ owner_name. ] table_or_view_name.index_name


<object> ::=
{
    [ database_name. [ schema_name ] . | schema_name. ]
        table_or_view_name
}


<drop_clustered_index_option> ::=
{ MAXDOP = max_degree_of_parallelism
  | ONLINE = { ON | OFF }
  | MOVE TO { partition_scheme_name ( column_name )
      | filegroup_name
      | "default" }
  [ FILESTREAM_ON { partition_scheme_name
      | filestream_filegroup_name
      | "default" } ]
}
```

## Using the Database Engine Tuning Advisor

The Database Engine Tuning Advisor is one of the best tools a database administrator can use to facilitate the indexing and optimization process. But before you start this wizard, you should create a trace containing a representative snapshot of database activity. You will use this snapshot as the workload file in the Database Engine Tuning Advisor. For specific pointers on creating a trace file, see See "Creating and Managing Data Collector Sets" on page 506. To use the Database Engine Tuning Advisor, complete the following steps:

1. In SQL Server Management Studio, select Database Engine Tuning Advisor on the Tools menu. Use the Connect To Server dialog box to connect to the server you want to use.

2. The Database Engine Tuning Advisor opens to start a new session, as shown in Figure 10-10. In the Workload panel, type a name for the session, such as **Personnel DB Check**. Using the Database For Workload Analysis drop-down list provided, select a database to which the Database Engine Tuning Advisor will connect for analyzing the workload:

   ❑ If you saved the trace data to a file, select File in the Workload panel, and then click the Browse For A Workload File button (the binoculars icon).

Next, use the Select Workload File dialog box to select the trace file you previously created, and then click Open.

❑ If you saved the trace data to a table, select Table in the Workload panel, and then click the Browse For A Workload Table button (the binoculars icon). Next, use the Select Workload Table dialog box to specify which SQL Server instance to connect to and the source table to use.

**Figure 10-10** The Database Engine Tuning Advisor.

3. Select the database you want to analyze. You can analyze multiple databases as well as individual tables within specific databases if you want. In most cases, you will want to examine a single database and possibly a subset of tables to reduce the analysis time. Because you are using a trace file, the analysis does not have to be performed on the server where the database or databases you are tuning are located.

4. Select the tables to analyze. If you select a database for tuning, all tables are selected for tuning by default. Click in the appropriate field under Selected Tables to display a list of tables in the selected database. Select the check box for the associated table you want added, or select the Name check box to add all tables.

5. Select the Tuning Options tab, as shown in Figure 10-11. You can limit the tuning time by setting a specific stop time. By default, the stop time is approximately one hour from the time you created the session.

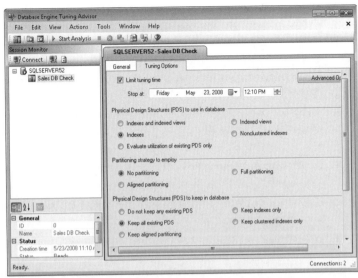

**Figure 10-11**   The Tuning Options tab of the Database Engine Tuning Advisor.

6. From the Physical Design Structures (PDS) To Use In Database options, select the type of structures that you want the tuning wizard to recommend:

❑ **Indexes And Indexed Views**   The Database Engine Tuning Advisor will recommend both clustered and nonclustered indexes, as well as indexed views, to improve performance.

❑ **Indexes**   The Database Engine Tuning Advisor will recommend clustered and nonclustered indexes to improve performance.

❑ **Indexed Views**   The Database Engine Tuning Advisor will recommend only indexed views to improve performance.

❑ **Nonclustered Indexes**   The Database Engine Tuning Advisor will recommend only nonclustered indexes to improve performance.

❑ **Evaluate Utilization Of Existing PDS Only**   The Database Engine Tuning Advisor will not recommend options for improving performance, and instead will analyze only the usage of existing structures. (This option cannot be used with the Keep All Existing PDS option under Physical Design Structure To Keep In Database.)

7. Use the Partitioning Strategy To Employ options to determine if the Database Engine Tuning Advisor should consider partitioning strategies:

❑ **No Partitioning**   The Database Engine Tuning Advisor will not consider any partitioning strategies.

❑ **Aligned Partitioning** Newly recommended structures will be partition aligned to make partitions easy to maintain. (This option cannot be used with the Keep Indexes Only option under Physical Design Structure To Keep In Database.)

❑ **Full Partitioning** Newly recommended structures will be partitioned to provide the best performance for the workload.

8. Use the Physical Design Structures (PDS) To Keep In Database options to determine which (if any) existing structures will be considered for removal from the database:

❑ **Do Not Keep Any Existing PDS** The Database Engine Tuning Advisor will consider all existing structures for possible removal from the database.

❑ **Keep All Existing PDS** The Database Engine Tuning Advisor will not consider any existing structures for possible removal from the database.

❑ **Keep Aligned Partitioning** The Database Engine Tuning Advisor will retain existing partition-aligned structures, and any recommended new structures will be aligned with the existing partitioning scheme. (Aligned Partitioning must also be selected as the Partitioning Strategy To Employ option.)

❑ **Keep Indexes Only** The Database Engine Tuning Advisor will keep existing clustered and nonclustered indexes. All other structures will be considered for possible removal from the database.

❑ **Keep Clustered Indexes Only** The Database Engine Tuning Advisor will keep existing clustered indexes. All other structures will be considered for possible removal from the database.

**Tip** If you have selected a strong, representative snapshot of database activity in the trace, you will probably want to select an option other than Keep All Existing PDS and let the Database Engine Tuning Advisor make the appropriate suggestions for you to ensure that existing structures do not conflict with the recommendations the wizard might make.

9. Click the Advanced Options button to set advanced options, as shown in Figure 10-12. The advanced tuning options are as follows:

❑ **Define Max. Space For Recommendations (MB)** Sets the maximum space that can be used by recommended structures. The default value depends on the database and structures selected.

❑ **Max. Columns Per Index** Sets the maximum number of columns that can be used in a single index. The default is 1023, which allows all the columns in a table to be considered.

❑ **Online Index Recommendations**   Sets the type of indexing recommendations. By default, the Database Engine Tuning Advisor uses recommendations that require the server to be taken offline. Alternatively, you can elect to generate online recommendations when possible or to generate only online recommendations. Online recommendations can be performed when the server is online.

**Figure 10-12**   Advanced Tuning Options for the Database Engine Tuning Advisor.

10. Click OK to close the Advanced Tuning Options dialog box. When you are ready to proceed, click the Start Analysis button or press F5. The Database Engine Tuning Advisor will begin analyzing your workload file. Progress is shown on the Progress tab. You can click Stop Analysis to stop the analysis at any time.

11. When it has finished the analysis, the wizard displays recommendations on the Recommendations tab. The recommendations are listed in two separate panels, Partition Recommendations and Index Recommendations. You can view a tuning summary and tuning reports on the Reports tab of the Database Engine Tuning Advisor. Be sure to note the percentage of estimated improvement by making the recommended changes. If the estimated improvement is 0%, this can be an indicator that the trace file might not accurately reflect the database workload.

12. You can now do the following:

❑ Select Save Recommendations on the Actions menu to save the recommended changes as an SQL script file. You can review or edit the script using a text editor and schedule a job to implement the changes later.

❑ Select Apply Recommendations on the Actions menu to apply the recommendations or schedule the recommendations to be applied later. In Apply Recommendations, select Apply Now or Schedule For Later as appropriate, and then click OK. If you schedule for later, you can set the run date and time as well.

13. If you choose to apply the changes, the status of each change is displayed in the Applying Recommendations dialog box. The status of each change should be listed as Success. If you see a failure status, read the related error message to determine why the change failed.

# Column Constraints and Rules

Column constraints and rules are important aspects of database administration. You use constraints to control the way column values are used, such as whether a value must be unique or whether it must have a specific format. Although you usually apply constraints directly to a specific column, you also can use rules to create constraints that you can apply to multiple tables in a database.

## Using Constraints

SQL Server enforces the uniqueness of column values using unique and primary key constraints. You will often use unique constraints to create secondary keys (for non-clustered indexes) that you can use in conjunction with the primary key. Foreign key constraints identify the relationships between tables and ensure that referential integrity is maintained. Other types of constraints that you might want to use are check and not null constraints. Check constraints restrict the format or range of acceptable values for columns. Not null constraints prevent null values in a column.

Constraints can apply to columns or to entire tables. A column constraint is specified as part of a column definition and applies only to that column. A table constraint is declared independently from a column definition and can apply to several columns in the table. You must use table constraints when you want to include more than one column in a constraint. For example, if a table has three columns in the primary key, you must use a table constraint to include all three columns in the primary key.

### Setting Unique Constraints

When you set a unique constraint on a column or columns, SQL Server automatically creates a unique index and then checks for duplicate values. If duplicate key values exist, the index creation operation is cancelled and an error message is displayed. SQL Server also checks the data each time you add data to the table. If the new data contains duplicate keys, the insert or update operation is rolled back and an error message is generated. You can specify that duplicate keys should be ignored by using the IGNORE_DUP_KEY option.

In SQL Server Management Studio, you make a unique index by setting the option Is Unique to Yes when creating the index, as described in "Creating Indexes" on page 369, or by selecting the Unique check box on the General page of the Index Properties dialog box. In Transact-SQL, you can set the unique constraint when you create the index, as shown in the following example:

```
USE OrderSystemDB
CREATE UNIQUE INDEX [Cust ID Index]
ON Sales.Customers(cust_id)
```

A nonclustered index is created unless a clustered index is explicitly specified, such as:

```
USE Customer
CREATE UNIQUE CLUSTERED INDEX [Cust ID Index]
ON Sales.Customers(cust_id)
```

## Designating Primary Key Constraints

SQL Server also allows you to designate any column or group of columns as a primary key, but primary keys are often defined for identity columns. A table can have only one primary key, and because unique values are required, no primary key column can accept null values. Also, when you use multiple columns, the values of all the columns are combined to determine uniqueness.

As with unique constraints, SQL Server creates a unique index for the primary key columns. With primary key constraints, however, the index is created as a clustered index—unless a clustered index already exists on the table or a nonclustered index is explicitly specified.

In SQL Server Management Studio, you set the primary key when designing a new table or modifying an existing table by completing the following steps:

1. Clear the Allow Nulls check box for any columns that will be used in the primary key.

2. Select the column or columns that you want to use as the primary key by pressing Ctrl and clicking the shaded box to the left of the column name.

3. Click Set Primary Key on the toolbar, or select Set Primary Key on the Table Designer menu.

You can also set the primary key when you create or alter tables using Transact-SQL. Examples are shown in Sample 10-14.

**Sample 10-14**   Creating a Table and Its Columns with a Primary Key Constraint

```
USE CUSTOMER
CREATE TABLE Sales.Customers
    (cust_id int NOT NULL,
    cust_lname varchar(40) NOT NULL,
    cust_fname varchar(20) NOT NULL,
    phone char(12) NOT NULL,
    CONSTRAINT PK_Cust PRIMARY KEY (cust_id))

USE CUSTOMER
ALTER TABLE Sales.Customers
    ADD CONSTRAINT PK_Cust PRIMARY KEY (cust_id)
```

## Using Foreign Key Constraints

Foreign key constraints identify the relationships between tables and ensure that referential integrity is maintained. A foreign key in one table points to a candidate key in another table. Foreign keys prevent changes that would leave rows with foreign key values when there are no candidate keys with that value in the related table. You cannot insert a row with a foreign key value if there is no candidate key with that value. The exception is when you insert a null foreign key value.

In the following example, the *Orders* table establishes a foreign key referencing the *Customer* table defined earlier:

```
CREATE TABLE Sales.Orders
    (order_nmbr int,
    order_item varchar(20),
    qty_ordered int,
    cust_id int
        FOREIGN KEY REFERENCES Sales.Customers(cust_id)
        ON DELETE NO ACTION
)
```

The ON DELETE clause defines that actions are taken if you try to delete a row to which existing foreign keys point. The ON DELETE clause has several options:

- **NO ACTION**   Specifies that the deletion fails with an error and the delete action on the row is rolled back.

- **CASCADE**   Specifies that all rows with foreign keys pointing to the deleted row are to be deleted as well. (CASCADE cannot be used if there is an INSTEAD OF trigger ON DELETE clause.)

- **SET NULL**   Specifies that all values that make up the foreign key are set to NULL if the corresponding row in the parent table is deleted. (Foreign key columns must be nullable.)

- **SET DEFAULT**   Specifies that all the values that make up the foreign key are set to their default values if the corresponding row in the parent table is deleted. (Foreign key columns must have default definitions. If a column is nullable and there is no explicit default, the column is set to NULL.)

You can also set an ON UPDATE clause in Transact-SQL, as shown in the following example:

```
CREATE TABLE Sales.Orders
    (order_nmbr int,
    order_item varchar(20),
    qty_ordered int,
    cust_id int
        FOREIGN KEY REFERENCES Sales.Customers(cust_id)
        ON UPDATE CASCADE
)
```

The ON UPDATE clause defines the actions that are taken if you try to update a row to which existing foreign keys point. The clause also supports the NO ACTION, CASCADE, SET NULL, and SET DEFAULT options.

## Using Check Constraints

Check constraints allow you to control the format or range of values, or both, that are associated with tables and columns. For example, you could use this type of constraint to specify that postal codes must be entered in the format 99999 or that phone numbers must be entered as 9999999999. Be careful when using check constraints that perform implicit or explicit data type conversion because these types of check constraints might cause partition switching or filtered indexes to fail.

In SQL Server Management Studio, you set check constraints when designing a new table or modifying an existing table by completing the following steps:

1. Select Check Constraints from the Table Designer menu. This displays the Check Constraints dialog box shown in Figure 10-13.

2. You can now do the following:

   ❑ Edit an existing constraint. First select it in the Selected Check Constraint selection list, and then modify the existing constraint expression and definition using the boxes provided.

   ❑ Delete a constraint. First select it in the Selected Check Constraint selection list, and then click Delete. In the Delete Object dialog box, confirm the deletion by clicking OK.

   ❑ Create a new constraint. Click Add, and then type a name and description of the constraint in the boxes provided. Click the button to the right of the Expression box, enter the check constraint expression, and then click OK.

3. Click Close when you are finished working with check constraints.

**Figure 10-13**   The Check Constraints dialog box.

Check constraint expressions specify the permitted characters using regular expressions:

- Use [0–9] to indicate that any numeral from 0 through 9 is permitted in the designated position. As an example, to format a column to accommodate a nine-digit postal code, you would use the following expression:

```
PostalCode LIKE '[0-9][0-9][0-9][0-9][0-9][0-9][0-9][0-9][0-9]'
```

- Use [a–z] or [A–Z] to indicate that any lowercase letter from *a* through *z* or any uppercase letter from *A* through *Z* is permitted in the designated position. As an example, to format a column to accommodate any five-letter word with the first letter capitalized, you would use the following expression:

```
PostalCode LIKE '[A-Z][a-z][a-z][a-z][a-z]'
```

- Use [a–zA–Z0–9] to indicate that any letter or numeral is permitted in the designated position. As an example, to format a column to accommodate any five-character value, you would use the following expression:

```
PostalCode LIKE '[a-zA-Z0-9][a-zA-Z0-9][a-zA-Z0-9][a-zA-Z0-9]
    [a-zA-Z0-9]'
```

You can also add and remove constraints in Transact-SQL by using the CREATE TABLE or ALTER TABLE command, such as in the following example:

```
USE CUSTOMER
ALTER TABLE Sales.Customers
ADD CONSTRAINT CheckZipFormat
CHECK ((([PostalCode] like '[0-9][0-9][0-9][0-9][0-9][0-9][0-9][0-9]
    [0-9]'))
```

### Using Not Null Constraints

Not null constraints specify that the column does not accept null values. Normally, you set not null constraints when you create the table. You can also set not null constraints when you alter a table. In SQL Server Management Studio, the Allow Nulls column in the Table view controls the use of this constraint. If the Allow Nulls column is cleared, the related table column does not accept nulls.

## Using Rules

A *rule* is a constraint that you can apply to multiple columns or tables. Rules perform the same function as check constraints and are maintained in SQL Server 2008 for backward compatibility with early versions of SQL Server. Microsoft recommends that you use check constraints rather than rules. Check constraints are more customizable and more concise than rules. For example, although you can apply only one rule to a column, you can apply multiple check constraints to a column.

Rules can be useful in certain situations, however. Constraints are defined within table definitions, whereas rules are independently defined objects, and therefore, are not limited to only one particular table. Rules are also bound to a table after the table is created, and they are not deleted if the table is deleted. Another advantage of rules is that they can be bound to any user-defined data type.

If you use care when you apply rules, you can still use rules in situations that make them a better choice than constraints. To view existing rules in SQL Server Management Studio, complete the following steps:

1.  In SQL Server Management Studio, connect to the server instance that contains the database in which you want to work.

2.  In the Object Explorer view, expand the Databases node, and then expand the database to show its resource nodes.

3.  Expand the Programmability and Rules nodes. You will see any existing rules listed.

The Transact-SQL commands for creating and managing rules are CREATE RULE and DROP RULE. You can use CREATE RULE as follows:

```
CREATE RULE CheckFormatZip
AS @value LIKE '[09][09][09][09][09][09][09][09][09]'
```

After you have created a rule, you must activate the rule to use it. You use a special stored procedure called sp_bindrule to bind the rule to a particular table column or user-defined data type. You can also use sp_unbindrule to remove a rule that is bound to a table column or user-defined data type. Use the following syntax when binding and unbinding rules:

```
sp_bindrule <'rule'>, <'object_name'>, [<'futureonly_flag'>]
sp_unbindrule 'object name'
```

# Creating Partitioned Tables and Indexes

You create partitioned tables and indexes using a multistep process that requires the following actions:

1.  Creating a partition function to specify how a table or index that uses the function can be partitioned

2.  Creating a partition scheme to specify the placement of the partitions within filegroups

3.  Creating tables or indexes using the partition scheme

I discuss each of these processes in the sections that follow.

## Creating Partition Functions

You use a partition function to specify how a table or index is partitioned. The function maps to a set of partitions. To create a partition function, you specify the number of partitions, the partitioning column, and the range of partition column values for each partition.

Each partition function identifies a single partitioning column. Any data type that is valid for use as an index column can be used as a partitioning column, except timestamp. This means you cannot specify the ntext, text, image, xml, varchar(max), nvarchar(max), varbinary(max), alias, or CLR user-defined types. Computed columns that participate in a partition function must be explicitly marked as PERSISTED.

You can create a partition function using the CREATE PARTITION FUNCTION statement. Sample 10-15 shows the syntax and usage.

**Sample 10-15** CREATE PARTITION FUNCTION Syntax and Usage

```
Syntax
CREATE PARTITION FUNCTION partition_function_name
    ( input_parameter_type )
AS RANGE [ LEFT | RIGHT ]
FOR VALUES ( [ boundary_value [ ,...n ] ] )
[ ; ]


Usage
CREATE PARTITION FUNCTION rangePF1 (int)
AS RANGE LEFT FOR VALUES (1, 2000, 4000, 6000);
```

## Creating Partition Schemes

You use a partition scheme to map the partitions produced by a partition function to a set of filegroups. A partition scheme can use only one partition function. However, a partition function can participate in more than one partition scheme.

When you create a partition scheme, you define the filegroups where the table partitions are mapped, based on the parameters of the partition function. Although you must specify enough filegroups to hold the number of partitions, you can do the following:

- Map all partitions to the same filegroup.

- Map multiple partitions to the same filegroup.

- Map each partition to a different filegroup.

Using NEXT USED, you also can specify additional, unassigned filegroups in case you want to add more partitions later. When you do this, SQL Server marks one of the filegroups with the NEXT USED property. This means that the filegroup will hold the next partition that is added.

You can create a partition scheme using the CREATE PARTITION SCHEME statement. Sample 10-16 shows the syntax and usage.

**Sample 10-16** CREATE PARTITION SCHEME Syntax and Usage

```
Syntax
CREATE PARTITION SCHEME partition_scheme_name
AS PARTITION partition_function_name
[ ALL ] TO ( { file_group_name | [ PRIMARY ] } [ ,...n ] )
[ ; ]
```

```
Usage
CREATE PARTITION SCHEME rangePS1
AS PARTITION rangePF1
TO (filegroup1, filegroup2, filegroup3, filegroup4, filegroup5);
```

## Creating Partitions

When you create a table or index, you can partition it by specifying the partition scheme that the table will use to map the partitions to filegroups and the partitioning column in the CREATE TABLE or CREATE INDEX statement. The partitioning column must match what you've specified in the partition function and in the partition scheme with regard to data type, length, and precision. If the column is computed, you must mark it as PERSISTED.

You can turn an existing nonpartitioned table into a partitioned table using one of two techniques:

- Create a partitioned clustered index on the table by using the CREATE INDEX statement. When you do this, SQL Server re-creates the table in a clustered index format. If the table already has a partitioned clustered index applied to it, you can drop the index and rebuild it on a partition scheme by using CREATE INDEX with the DROP EXISTING = ON clause.

- Use the ALTER TABLE...SWITCH statement to switch the data of the table to a range-partitioned table that has only one partition. However, this partitioned table must already exist before the conversion occurs, and its single partition must be empty.

After you modify the table to create a partitioned table, you can modify the related partition function to add partitions as necessary. You can turn an existing partition table into a nonpartitioned table by modifying the table's partition function so that the table has only one partition. If a table has a partitioned clustered index applied to it, you can obtain the same result by dropping the index and rebuilding it as a nonpartitioned index using the CREATE INDEX statement with the DROP EXISTING = ON clause.

With SQL Management Studio, you can create partitions after you create a table or index by completing the following steps:

1. In SQL Server Management Studio, select a table and expand its node to list the objects it contains. Expand the Indexes node to list the indexes associated with the selected table.

2. Right-click the table or index that you want to partition, point to Storage, and then select Create Partition. This starts the Create Partition Wizard. If you see the Welcome page, click Next.

3. On the Select A Partitioning Column page, select the one partitioning column that you want to use. Optionally, you can elect to collocate the table to a selected partitioned table, to storage-align indexes with the indexed partitioning column, or both. Click Next.

4. On the Select A Partition Function page, you can type the required definition for a new function or select an existing partition function. Click Next.

5. On the Select A Partition Scheme page, you can type the required definition for a new scheme or select an existing partition scheme. Click Next.

6. On the Map Partitions page, select the partition range as either Left Boundary or Right Boundary. Next, select each filegroup in turn and specify the boundary values. Be sure to enter an additional filegroup in addition to the boundary values.

7. Click Estimate Storage to determine the required space. Click Next.

8. You can now create a script for adding partitioning, run the script immediately, or schedule a job for partitioning. If you want to create a script, you can set scripting options. If you want to schedule these activities for later, you can click Change Schedule to set the run date and time. Click Next.

9. Review your selections and then click Finish. If you choose to run immediately, the status of each action is displayed on the Create Partition Wizard Progress page. The status of each action should be listed as Success. If you see a failure status, read the related error message to determine why the change failed. You can generate a report by clicking Report and then selecting a report option.

## Viewing and Managing Partitions

When you query data or perform updates, there is no difference in the way you reference a partitioned table versus a table that is not partitioned. That said, however, you can focus queries on individual partitions using the $PARTITION function together with the partition function name. This allows you to examine how many rows exist in each partition, access all rows in a subset of partitions, and determine in which partition a row with a particular partition key value currently resides or will reside when inserted.

You can query individual partitions of a partitioned table or index using $PARTITION. The syntax and usage is shown as Sample 10-17.

**Sample 10-17**    $PARTITION Syntax and Usage

```
Syntax
[ database_name. ] $PARTITION.partition_function_name(expression)


Usage
USE CustomerDB;
GO
CREATE PARTITION FUNCTION rangePF1 ( int )
```

```
AS RANGE FOR VALUES (100, 2000, 4000, 8000) ;
GO
SELECT $PARTITION.rangePF1 (100) ;
GO
```

Catalog views that contain partitioning information include

- sys.destination_data_spaces, which gets information about individual partition schemes

- sys.partition_functions, which gets information about individual partition functions

- sys.partition_parameters, which gets information about individual parameters of partition functions

- sys.partition_range_values, which gets information about the boundary values of a partition function

- sys.partition_schemes, which gets information about all the partition schemes in a database

- sys.partitions, which gets partitioning information about a table or index

With SQL Management Studio, you can manage existing partitions by completing the following steps:

1. In SQL Server Management Studio, select a table and expand its node to list the objects it contains. Expand the Indexes node to list the indexes associated with the selected table.

2. Right-click the table or index that you want to partition, point to Storage, and then select Manage Partition. This starts the Manage Partition Wizard. If you see the Welcome page, click Next.

3. On the Select A Partition Action page, you can elect to create a staging table for partition switching or manage a sliding-window partition. However, if you are using non-storage-aligned indexes, you cannot switch out or switch in data, which means you can only create a staging table. Click Next.

4. Set the staging table or sliding window options as necessary and then click Next.

5. You can now create a script for modifying partitioning, run the script immediately, or schedule a job for modifying partitioning. If you want to create a script, you can set scripting options. If you want to schedule these activities for later, you can click Change Schedule to set the run date and time. Click Next.

6. Review your selections and then click Finish. If you choose to run immediately, the status of each action is displayed on the Manage Partition Wizard Progress page. The status of each action should be listed as Success. If you see a failure status, read the related error message to determine why the change failed. You can generate a report by clicking Report and then selecting a report option.

# Compressing Tables, Indexes, and Partitions

SQL Server 2008 Enterprise Edition supports on-disk storage compression for tables stored as heaps, tables stored as clustered indexes, nonclustered indexes, and indexed views. Because you can configure compression of partitioned tables and indexes independently for each partition, different partitions of the same object can use different compression settings.

## Using Row and Page Compression

The storage engine handles all aspects of compression. SQL Server 2008 supports two types of compression:

- Row compression
- Page compression

Row compression affects the physical storage of data within rows. Most data types are affected in some unique way, but no application changes are required because of these changes. Row compression reduces the metadata overhead associated with records and uses variable-length storage for numeric types and fixed-character strings. For example, if a value can be reduced to 1 byte through compression, storage of the value will use only 1 byte.

When you use page compression with non–leaf-level pages of indexes, the storage engine performs only row compression. When you use page compression with leaf-level pages of tables and indexes, the storage engine uses three different operations to compress the data: row compression, followed by prefix compression, followed by dictionary compression. Typically, with prefix compression, the storage engine finds repeated prefix values for each column, moves the prefixes new row immediately following the page header and within the compression information structure, and then changes column values to references to the prefix. Typically, with dictionary compression, the storage engine finds repeated values anywhere on the page and stores them within the compression information structure.

When you create a new table with page compression, the metadata for the table indicates that page compression should be used but no actual compression occurs. As you add data to the first data page, data is row-compressed until you fill the first row. The next row you add initiates page compression using prefix compression and dictionary compression. If page compression has created enough room on the page for an additional row, the storage engine adds the row, and the related data is page-compressed, meaning the storage engine applies row, prefix, and dictionary compression. Keep in mind that if the space gained by page compression minus the space that is required for the compression information structure is not significant, the storage engine won't use page compression for a particular page. As you add rows, those rows either fit onto the page or require the storage engine to add a new page. Similar to the first page, the new page is compressed using row compression first and then as you fill rows, the prefix and dictionary are compressed.

When you convert an existing table that contains data-to-page compression, the storage engine rebuilds and reevaluates each page. Rebuilding all the pages causes the storage engine to rebuild the related table, index, or partition.

Compression is not available for system tables. When you compress or uncompress a user table, the storage engine doesn't automatically apply the compression settings to the table's nonclustered indexes. You must configure compression settings for each nonclustred index individually. However, when a clustered index is created on a heap, the clustered index inherits the compression state of the heap unless you specify otherwise.

When you are compressing indexes, leaf-level pages can be compressed with both row and page compression. However, non–leaf-level pages do not receive page compression. Additionally, when the existing data in an index is fragmented, you might be able to reduce the size of the index by rebuilding the index instead of using compression. The fill factor of an index will be applied during an index rebuild, which also could potentially increase the size of the index.

Although the storage engine handles all aspects of compression, the storage engine presents data to most other SQL Server components in an uncompressed state. This means that when a heap is configured for page-level compression, pages receive page-level compression only when data is inserted by using BULK INSERT or INSERT INTO ... WITH (TABLOCK) or a table is rebuilt by executing the ALTER TABLE ... REBUILD statement with the PAGE compression option. Changing the compression setting of a heap requires all nonclustered indexes on the table to be rebuilt so that they have pointers to the new row locations in the heap.

Although compression can allow more rows to be stored on a page, it does not change the maximum row size of a table or index. You cannot enable a table for compression when the maximum row size plus the compression overhead exceeds the maximum row size of 8060 bytes. The storage engine checks the row size when the object is initially compressed as well as whenever a row is inserted or modified, and it prevents updates that would not fit on the row when the row is uncompressed. Additionally, with large-value data types and variable-length columns, when the data exceeds 8 KB data compression is not available for the data that is stored separately.

The disk space requirements for enabling or disabling row or page compression are the same as for creating or rebuilding an index. For partitioned data, you can reduce the space that is required by enabling or disabling compression for one partition at a time. You can determine the compression state of partitions in a partitioned table by querying the data_compression column of the sys.partitions view.

## Setting or Changing Compression Settings

With SQL Management Studio, you manage compression after you create a table or index by completing the following steps:

1. In SQL Server Management Studio, select a table and expand its node to list the objects it contains. Expand the Indexes node to list the indexes associated with the selected table.

2. Right-click the table or index that you want to compress, point to Storage, and then select Manage Compression. This starts the Data Compression Wizard. If you see the Welcome page, click Next.

3. On the Select Compression Type page, you can configure compression in one of two ways:

   ❑ **Select a partition type for each partition**    Each partition is listed by its partition number, boundary, row count, and current space. Use the Compression Type list for each partition to set the desired compression level.

   ❑ **Use the same compression type for each partition**    Select the Use Same Compression Type For All Partitions check box, and then use the related drop-down list to set the desired compression level.

4. Click Calculate to determine the compressed space for the partition or partitions.

5. You can now create a script for adding compression, run the script immediately, or schedule a job for compressing the partition or partitions. If you want to create a script, you can set scripting options. If you schedule for later, you can click Change Schedule to set the run date and time. Click Next.

6. Review your selections and then click Finish. If you choose to run immediately, the status of each change is displayed on the Compression Wizard Progress page. The status of each action should be listed as Success. If you see a failure status, read the related error message to determine why the change failed. You can generate a report by clicking Report and then selecting a report option.

You can compress tables and indexes when you create them using the CREATE TABLE and CREATE INDEX statements. To do this, set the DATA_COMPRESSION clause to the desired value. By default, data compression is disabled and set to NONE. If you want tables or indexes to be compressed, you can specify ROW to enable row-level compression or PAGE to enable page-level compression.

You can change the compression state of a table, index, or partition using the ALTER TABLE or ALTER INDEX statement. If you modify a table without specifying a compression state, the existing compression state is preserved.

You can determine how changing the compression state will affect tables and indexes using the sp_estimate_data_compression_savings stored procedure. To monitor compression statistics for a SQL Server instance, use the Page compression attempts/sec and Pages compressed/sec counters of the SQL Server, Access Methods Object. To monitor compression statistics for individual partitions, use the sys.dm_db_index_operational_stats function.

## Chapter 11
# Importing, Exporting, and Transforming Data

Whether you need to move data from a legacy system to a new system permanently or you want to continually move data back and forth for data warehousing, Microsoft SQL Server 2008 Integration Services (SSIS) should be your first choice. With Integration Services, you have access to an Extraction, Transformation, and Loading (ETL) platform that can be fully customized for your specific application and is optimized for high-performance data movement and transformation. You can use Integration Services to copy and transform data to or from almost any data source, including flat file, OLE DB, and Open Database Connectivity (ODBC) data sources. In addition, BULK COPY (BCP) remains available in SQL Server 2008 as a basic means of importing and exporting data.

## Working with Integration Services

As an administrator, you will most often perform the following Integration Services tasks:

- Installing the Integration Services components using SQL Server 2008 Setup

- Using the SQL Server Import And Export Wizard to move data

- Upgrading, managing, or migrating existing Data Transformation Services (DTS) 2000 Packages to Integration Services as necessary

- Upgrading SQL Server 2005 Integration Services to SQL Server 2008 Integration Services

- Creating and managing Integration Services packages using Business Intelligence Development Studio

- Running Integration Services packages using Business Intelligence Development Studio, SQL Server Management Studio, or the Dtexec command-line utility

Before you try to perform any of these tasks, you should know how the Integration Services feature works and how it is used. After you are familiar with Integration Services, its tools, and its structures, you will be better prepared to manage its components.

## Getting Started with Integration Services

Integration Services are designed to move data accurately and efficiently, as well as to convert or transform data between heterogeneous data sources. You can use Integration Services when you want to perform any of the following tasks:

- Move data between heterogeneous systems, such as from Oracle to SQL Server or from SQL Server to Oracle

- Move data between instances of SQL Server, including primary and foreign keys

- Move data from Microsoft Access or Microsoft Office Excel to SQL Server or from SQL Server to Access or Excel

- Extract data; transform the data by performing column mappings, filling in missing values, and so on; and then import the data on the destination system

- Copy views from one database to another

Although SQL Server 2008 supports existing DTS packages and provides an upgrade/migration path for those packages, Integration Services are the functional replacement for DTS. The architecture of Integration Services is very different from that of DTS. With DTS, the workflow controls and the data movement were all managed through a single component: the DTS engine. The Integration Services process separates workflow controls and data movement using two separate components:

- **Integration Services runtime engine**    Stores package layout, executes packages, controls workflow between tasks, and provides other essential runtime services

- **Integration Services data flow engine**    Manages data movement and transformation, and supports multiple sources, multiple transformations, and multiple destinations

Integration Services has an extensible object model that includes a runtime application programming interface (API) and a data-flow API that supports the Microsoft .NET Framework. These APIs allow developers to extend and customize the Integration Services object model. Custom extensions can be developed for tasks, log providers, connection managers, data flow components, and more.

## Integration Services Tools

The primary tools for working with Integration Services are Business Intelligence Development Studio and SQL Server Management Studio. Business Intelligence Development Studio is used to build data-transformation solutions, and SQL Server Management Studio is used to manage Integration Services packages. Within Business Intelligence Development Studio, you can access Integration Services Designer, the graphical tool for creating Integration Services packages.

The SQL Server Import And Export Wizard is the new face of the old DTS Import/Export Wizard. The wizard has been updated to support Integration Services and has been extended to provide better support for data in flat files and for real-time preview of data. Integration Services packages created by using the Import And Export Wizard can be opened in Business Intelligence Development Studio and then extended using Integration Services Designer.

> **Tip**   The SQL Server Import And Export Wizard can run the import/export process between any of the available data sources; you do not have to set SQL Server as either the source or the destination. For example, you can use the SQL Server Import And Export Wizard to copy data from a text file to an Excel spreadsheet.

As with DTS, Integration Services packages are stored in either the *msdb* database or in the file system. The SQL Server Integration Services service is responsible for managing package storage. You can manage packages from the command line using the Dtutil command-line utility. You can use Dtutil to copy, move, sign, and delete packages. To run packages, you can use Business Intelligence Development Studio or SQL Server Management Studio to access the Execute Package Utility (Dtexecui). The command-line counterpart is the Dtexec command-line utility.

On a 64-bit computer, Integration Services installs both a 32-bit and a 64-bit version of the Dtexec utility and the Dtutil utility. Using either the Dtexec utility or the Dtutil utility, you can create debug dump files that provide information about the execution of a package. You can then use the information in these files to help you diagnose and resolve package execution issues. Integration Services creates the following debug dump files:

- A debug dump file in binary format with the .mtmp file extension
- A debug dump file in text format with the .tmp file extension

Integration Services includes the Package Configuration Wizard to assist with configuration management. By running the Integration Services package deployment utility from within Business Intelligence Development Studio, you can install packages to the *msdb* database in an instance of SQL Server 2008 or to the file system. The deployment utility automatically detects and includes all package dependencies, making it easier to deploy packages.

SQL Server 2008 includes tools for managing and migrating DTS packages from previous versions of SQL Server. When you connect to a server in SQL Server Management Studio's Object Explorer, you can expand the Legacy\Data Transformation Services node to list available DTS 2000 packages. You can edit or execute these packages and migrate the packages to the Integration Services format. In Integration Services Designer, select Migrate DTS 2000 Package on the Project menu to start the Package Migration Wizard. You can then use the wizard to migrate DTS 2000 packages stored in SQL Server or in structured storage files.

When you upgrade an instance of SQL Server 2005 to SQL Server 2008, SQL Server doesn't automatically upgrade existing SQL Server 2005 Integration Services packages to the package format that SSIS uses. You will have to select an upgrade method and manually upgrade SQL Server 2005 packages by doing one or more of the following:

- Use the Dtexec utility that comes with SQL Server 2008 to run the SQL Server 2005 package. When you use this method to run a SQL Server 2005 package, the upgrade is temporary, and you cannot save the changes that result from the upgrade.

- Add the SQL Server 2005 package to an existing project using the Add Existing Package option on the Project menu in Integration Services Designer. Integration Services will automatically upgrade the package. The upgrade is temporary unless you save the changes to make the upgrade permanent.

- Upgrade all open packages in the project using the SSIS Package Upgrade Wizard. To start this wizard, select Upgrade All Packages in Integration Services Designer. Integration Services will automatically upgrade open packages that need to be upgraded. This upgrade process is permanent.

When you upgrade a SQL Server 2005 package, Integration Services

- Migrates the scripts in any Script task and Script component to Microsoft Visual Studio Tools for Applications (VSTA). In SQL Server 2005, the scripts in Script tasks or Script components used Microsoft Visual Studio for Applications (VSA).

- Migrates the Lookup transformation to the SQL Server 2008 version. The Lookup transformation performs lookups by joining data in input columns with columns in a reference dataset. For SQL Server 2008, there are additional options that you might want to use.

- Does not migrate third-party components. You will need to manually recompile third-party components to enable them to work with SQL Server 2008 Integration Services.

With SQL Server 2008 Integration Services, some connection strings require different values because the names of certain providers have changed. Although the SSIS Package Upgrade Wizard upgrades connection strings automatically, the other techniques might not and you might need to do this manually.

## Integration Services and Data Providers

Data providers are a key part of Integration Services. Without these data providers, you would not be able to communicate with other systems. SQL Server includes data providers for the following files and applications:

- SQL Server

- Oracle

- Microsoft Access and Excel

- Microsoft Analysis Services

- Microsoft Data Mining Services

- SQLXML

- Text files

The flat file source driver is the all-purpose driver for import and export procedures. If you do not have a native provider for your legacy database and you cannot use the generic ODBC providers, you can usually export your data to a text file and then import it into SQL Server. You can go from SQL Server to a legacy system using the same technique.

## Integration Services Packages

The SQL Server Import And Export Wizard is the fastest, easiest way to move data between systems. You use the SQL Server Import And Export Wizard to create basic Integration Services packages, which you can later view or modify using Integration Services Designer. Packages are simply sets of tasks for importing, transforming, and exporting data that you can reuse or schedule to run as often as needed. You can do the following with packages:

- Store them in the *msdb* database on a local or remote server.

- Save them to the file system in DTSX, XML, XMLA, or TXT files, which is useful when you want to copy, move, and e-mail packages to another location.

  **Note**   Integration Services does not support storage in Microsoft Visual Basic files. DTS 2000 packages that are stored in Visual Basic files cannot be migrated to SQL Server 2008 Integration Services.

You execute packages directly from SQL Server Management Studio or Business Intelligence Development Studio. You can also execute packages from the command prompt using the Dtexec command-line utility. Within Integration Services packages, you will find the following features:

- **Connections**   Store information about the source or destination of data. In a connection, you specify the data provider to use (such as the Microsoft OLE DB

Data Provider for SQL Server), the server to which you want to connect, the login to use for the connection, and the database to work with for the import/export operation. In Integration Services Designer, you select connections using the Data menu.

■ **Tasks**   Set the operations that need to be performed within the package. Tasks can consist of ActiveX scripts, SQL scripts, SQL queries, commands to transfer SQL Server objects, data-driven queries, bulk insert commands, and external processes to execute. You can even have Integration Services send e-mail when a package completes.

■ **Workflow containers**   Set when and how a particular task should be executed, such as on completion, on failure, or on success. For example, you can schedule a task that sends e-mail on failure or on success.

■ **Control flow procedures**   A control flow consists of one or more tasks and containers that execute sequentially or in parallel when the package runs. Precedence constraints connect the package's tasks and containers and define the conditions for running the next task or container in the package control flow. Tasks and containers can also be grouped in a loop and run repeatedly as a unit within the package control flow.

■ **Data flow procedures**   Set the step-by-step transformation process for the data. Before you can add a data flow to a package, the package control flow must include a Data Flow task that is responsible for running the data flow. A data flow consists of the source and destination adapters that extract and load data, the transformations that modify and extend data, and the paths that link adapters and transformations.

You can store an Integration Services package on any computer running SQL Server, and you do not need to create or store it on the source or destination server associated with the package. If you are editing, modifying, scheduling, or just viewing an Integration Services package, you need to use the user account of the package owner or an account that operates under the sysadmin role on the server on which the package is actually stored.

# Creating Packages with the SQL Server Import And Export Wizard

Creating an Integration Services package can be one of the most complex tasks you perform as a database administrator. Fortunately, the SQL Server Import And Export Wizard is designed to help you build Integration Services packages with minimal difficulty, but it is still an involved process. To help reduce complexity, we can divide the creation process into stages and then examine each stage individually. The stages you use to create Integration Services packages are as follows:

■ Stage 1: Source and Destination Configuration

- Stage 2: Copy or Query

- Stage 3: Formatting and Transformation

- Stage 4: Save and Execute

To begin using Integration Services, start the SQL Server Import And Export Wizard and then click Next to advance to the source selection page. You start the SQL Server Import And Export Wizard in SQL Server Management Studio by completing the following steps:

1. In SQL Server Management Studio, connect to the server instance containing the database with which you want to work.

2. In the Object Explorer view, expand the Databases node. Select a database, and then right-click its name, point to Tasks, and select either Import Data or Export Data.

You can also run the SQL Server Import And Export Wizard by clicking Start, typing **dtswizard** in the Search box, and pressing Enter.

> **Real World**   On 64-bit computers, you'll find a 32-bit and a 64-bit version of the Import And Export Wizard. You'll find that the 64-bit version can in many cases perform import and export operations faster than its 32-bit counterpart. The 64-bit version will run by default when you start the wizard at the command line or from the Start menu.
>
> With the 32-bit wizard, you can work with .NET Framework Data Providers for ODBC, Oracle, and SQL Server. You can work with OLE DB Providers for Analysis Services, Data Mining Services, Oracle, and SQL Server. You also can work with Microsoft Access, Microsoft Excel, flat file, and SQL Server Native Client sources.
>
> With the 64-bit wizard, you only can work with the available 64-bit sources and destinations. In most installations, this does not include Microsoft Access, Microsoft Excel, and some OLE DB providers (unless you've updated the SQL Server installation with the related clients).

## Stage 1: Source and Destination Configuration

The first task associated with creating an Integration Services package is to choose the source and destination for the import/export operation. If you started the SQL Server Import And Export Wizard and clicked Next, you will see the Choose A Data Source page. At this point, complete the following steps:

1. Use the Data Source drop-down list box to select the source for the import/export operation. SQL Server has .NET Framework, OLE DB, and other data providers. These data providers allow you to work with SQL Server, Oracle, Access and Excel, Analysis Services, Data Mining Services, SQLXML, and flat files. Select the data source that matches the type of file, application, or database you want to use as the source. For example, if you are copying from an Excel spreadsheet, choose Excel as the source for the import/export operation.

2. Fill in any additional information required to establish a connection to the source. (The source you select determines what additional information you need to supply.) Click Next.

3. Use the Destination drop-down list box to select the destination for the import/ export operation.

4. Fill in any additional information required to establish a connection to the destination. As with the source, the destination you select determines what additional information you need to supply.

5. Click Next to proceed to the next stage of the operation: Copy or Query.

If choosing a source and destination were as easy as these simple steps appear, this task would require very little effort. But sometimes it is not clear what additional information you need to provide because there are several different kinds of sources and destinations that you can select. These sources include

■ .NET Framework Data Provider connections

■ File-based data connections

■ Server-based connections to databases other than SQL Server

■ Server-based connections to SQL Server

■ Flat files

We will examine each of these connection categories more closely.

### .NET Framework Data Provider Connections

SQL Server 2008 includes .NET Framework Data Providers for ODBC, Oracle, and SQL Server. The .NET Framework Data Provider for ODBC is the only ODBC driver supported. You configure the .NET Framework Data Providers through a dialog box similar to the one shown in Figure 11-1. You must provide the following information, depending on the .NET Framework Data Provider you are using:

■ If you are using .NET Framework Data Provider for ODBC, you must specify the connection string, the data source name (DSN), and the name of the ODBC driver to use when connecting to the data source.

■ If you are using .NET Framework Data Provider for Oracle, you must specify the user ID and password to use in establishing the connection, and the name of the database to which you want to connect in the Data Source text box. As necessary, you can configure other initialization, pooling, and security parameters as well. To work with Oracle databases, you'll need to install the Oracle client software version 8.1.7 or higher.

■ If you are using .NET Framework Data Provider for SQL Server, you must specify the network library (options are provided in a drop-down list when you click in the text box), the user ID and password to use in establishing the connection, and the name of the database to which you want to connect in the Data Source text box. As necessary, you can configure other initialization, pooling, and security parameters as well.

**Figure 11-1**   SQL Server Import And Export Wizard page for .NET Framework Data Provider connections.

### File-Based Data Connections

You use file-based data connections with applications and databases that are file based. For example, you use this type of connection with Access and Excel. You use a dialog box similar to the one shown in Figure 11-2 to configure file-based connections. For Access, you must provide the following information:

- **File Name**   The full file name or Universal Naming Convention (UNC) path to the source or destination file, such as //omega/data/access/data.mdb

- **User Name**   A valid user name for accessing the source or destination file

- **Password**   A valid password for accessing the source or destination file

For Excel, you must provide the following information:

- **Excel File Path**   The full file name or UNC path to the source or destination file, such as //omega/data/excel/cust.xls

- **Excel Version**   The version of Excel from which you are copying data

**Note**   If the first row of the Excel spreadsheet does not have column names, be sure to clear the First Row Has Column Names check box.

**Figure 11-2**    SQL Server Import And Export Wizard page for an Access file-based data connection.

## Server-Based Connections to Databases Other Than SQL Server

You use server-based data connections to connect to databases other than SQL Server. Use this type of connection with Microsoft OLE DB Provider for Oracle, Microsoft OLE DB Provider for Analysis Services 10.0, Microsoft OLE DB Provider for Data Mining Services, Microsoft OLE DB Provider for OLAP Services 8.0, and SQLXMLOLEDB. You configure server-based connections by setting Data Link properties that connect to a data source. Data Link properties have four components:

- An OLE DB provider, which you select from the Source or Destination selection list in the SQL Server Import And Export Wizard.

- Connection options, which you set using the Connection tab in the Data Link Properties dialog box. Connection options typically include a data source name or server name accompanied by the user name and password information needed to log on to the database.

- Advanced options, which you set using the Advanced tab in the Data Link Properties dialog box. Advanced options let you configure network settings, timeouts, and access permissions (as long as these options are configurable).

- Initialization properties, which you view using the All tab in the Data Link Properties dialog box. The initialization properties display all the options you have configured for the provider and provide a central location for editing values. Simply double-click a value to edit the associated settings.

If you are using Oracle, the Oracle client and networking components must be installed on the system running SQL Server. If these components are not installed, you will not be able to use the OLE DB provider. Assuming that the Oracle client is installed on your system, you can set the Data Link properties for Oracle by completing the following steps:

1. In the SQL Server Import And Export Wizard, select Microsoft OLE DB Provider for Oracle in the Source or Destination selection list, and then click Properties to display the Connection tab of the Data Link Properties dialog box, as shown in Figure 11-3.

**Figure 11-3**   The Connection tab of the Data Link Properties dialog box for Oracle.

2. Type the name of the Oracle server to which you want to connect in the Enter A Server Name text box.

3. Then type the user name and password needed to log on to the database in the appropriate text boxes.

4. To test the connection to the server, click Test Connection. If the connection fails, you might have improperly configured the Oracle client.

5. You can use the Advanced and All tabs to view additional options. Change these options as necessary.

6. When you have finished setting the Data Link properties for Oracle, click OK.

## Server-Based Connections to SQL Server

In addition to using the .NET Framework Data Provider for SQL Server, you can connect to SQL Server using the SQL Native Client or Microsoft OLE DB Provider for SQL Server. The options you have available using either of these alternate connections are shown in Figure 11-4, and you can configure the connection by completing the following steps:

1.  Use the Server Name drop-down list box to select the computer running SQL Server for the connection. If the server you want to use is not listed, type in the server name.

2.  Next, select an authentication method. Type a user name and password, if necessary.

3.  Use the Database drop-down list box to select a database. You must provide valid credentials, and those credentials must have sufficient privileges.

**Figure 11-4**  SQL Server Import And Export Wizard page for SQL Native Client or Microsoft OLE DB Provider for SQL Server.

## Importing and Exporting Flat Files

You can use flat files as a data source or destination. When you do, you must provide additional information about the input or output formatting. The steps in the process are similar when using flat files as either the source or the destination. To use text files as a data source, use the following process as an example and complete these steps:

1. In the SQL Server Import And Export Wizard, choose the Flat File Source option. Then enter the full file name or UNC path to the file with which you want to work.

   **Tip**   If the file is in use, you will get an error message. Click OK, and then select the file again. (This forces the SQL Server Import And Export Wizard to try to read the file again. Otherwise, you will not be able to edit the Format specifications for the file.)

2. After you enter the text file information, the wizard page is updated as shown in Figure 11-5.

**Figure 11-5**   SQL Server Import And Export Wizard page for a flat file data source.

3. The values in the Locale and Code Page boxes are set based on the file you have selected. If the values are incorrect, select the appropriate values.

4. Select the file type using the Format drop-down list box. The file must be formatted in an acceptable flat file format, such as ANSI (ASCII text), IBM EBCDIC, MAC, OEM (original equipment manufacturer), UTF-7, or UTF-8.

   **Note**   When you are importing data, OEM normally refers to the native SQL Server format. If the file contains Unicode characters, select the Unicode check box.

5. Specify how the file is delimited. If the file has fixed-width columns, select the Fixed Width option from the Format selection list. If the columns are delimited

with commas, tabs, semicolons, or other unique characters, select the Delimited option from the Format selection list.

6. Use the Text Qualifier box to specify the qualifier for text as Double Quote ("), Single Quote ('), or <None>.

7. Specify the header row delimiter using the Header Row Delimiter drop-down list box. The available options are

   ❑ {CR} {LF} for carriage return and line feed

   ❑ {CR} for carriage return only

   ❑ {LF} for line feed only

   ❑ Semicolon

   ❑ Colon

   ❑ Comma

   ❑ Tab

   ❑ Vertical bar for the | character

8. To skip rows at the beginning of a file, use the Header Rows To Skip box to set the number of rows to skip.

   **Note** If you indicated that the first row contains column names, the first row is read and then the specified number of rows is skipped.

9. If the first row contains column headers, select the check box for the option Column Names In The First Data Row.

   **Tip** Column headers make it easier to import data. If the file does not contain column names, you might want to click Cancel, add the column names to the first line, and then restart the import/export procedure.

10. This completes the General page options. For an export, the other pages are not available or applicable, so skip to step 17.

11. Select Columns from the Data Source list in the left pane of the wizard to proceed. The wizard will attempt to determine the row and column delimiters, and then it will display a preview of the data.

12. If you selected fixed-width columns, you must indicate to the SQL Server Import And Export Wizard where columns start and end. Vertical lines indicate the start and end of columns. Add column markers by clicking in the Source Data Columns area to create a column marker. Remove column markers by double-clicking them. Move column markers by clicking them and dragging them to a new position.

13. If necessary, specify the end-of-row delimiter using the Row Delimiter drop-down list box.

14. If necessary, specify the column delimiter within rows.

15. Select the Advanced page from the Data Source list in the left pane of the wizard to configure the output properties for each column, including the output column name, output column width, and output data type. If there are different delimiters between columns, you can specify the delimiter on a per-column basis.

16. Select the Preview page from the Data Source list to see the data format for the options you have chosen. If you notice data elements out of place, you should reconfigure the options before continuing. You might also need to modify the source file. In this case, click Cancel, modify the file, and then restart the SQL Server Import And Export Wizard.

17. Click Next when you are ready to select the destination for the import/export operation. After selecting the destination, you are ready to move on to the second stage of creating an Integration Services package.

## Stage 2: Copy or Query

With most import or export procedures, the second stage of the process involves specifying tables and views to copy or build a query to specify the objects to transfer. You first select the operation using the dialog box shown in Figure 11-6, and then depending on the choice you have made, you proceed as described in the following sections.

**Figure 11-6**   The Specify Table Copy Or Query page of the SQL Server Import And Export Wizard.

### Specifying Tables and Views to Copy

If you want to copy tables and views to the destination, you must select which tables and views you want to copy. When a text file is the data source, making the selection is easy—only one table is available, and you cannot select any views. If you are using any other data sources, however, you must select the tables and views you want to copy. You use the Select Source Tables And Views page of the wizard, shown in Figure 11-7, to make your selections.

**Figure 11-7**    The Select Source Tables And Views page of the SQL Server Import And Export Wizard.

To select tables and views, complete the following steps:

1. On the Specify Table Copy Or Query page (shown in Figure 11-6), select Copy Data From One Or More Tables Or Views and then click Next.

2. On the Select Source Tables And Views Page (shown in Figure 11-7), select a table or view by clicking its entry, and then preview the data the table contains by clicking Preview.

3. When you find a table or view you want to copy, select the check box next to it in the Source column.

4. By default, the destination name of the table is set to be the same as the source table name. If you want to change the table name, edit the corresponding value in the Destination column.

5. If you want to manipulate the row values in a table, select the table and then click the Edit Mappings button. Mapping row values is covered in "Stage 3: Formatting and Transformation" on page 413.

## Building a Query

Another way to select data for exporting is to build a query and execute it against the source file, spreadsheet, or database. Regardless of the type of data source you select, you build the query in the same way by completing the following steps:

1. On the Specify Table Copy Or Query page (shown in Figure 11-6), select Write A Query To Specify The Data To Transfer, and then click Next.

2. On the Provide A Source Query page, you can do the following:

   ❑ Type a query directly in the text box provided, and then parse it to check for accuracy using the Parse button.

   ❑ Click Browse to open a previously saved query.

   > **Tip**   You can also create a query in your favorite query designer, and then paste the results into the SQL Statement text box. See the discussion that follows for details on using Query Designer, which is provided in SQL Server Management Studio.

3. Click Next. On the Select Source Tables And Views page, the tables and views selected by the previously defined query are listed and selected.

4. By default, the destination name of the table is set to be the same as the source table name. If you want to change the table name, edit the corresponding value in the Destination column.

5. If you want to manipulate the row values in a table, select the table and then click the Edit Mappings button. Mapping row values is covered in "Stage 3: Formatting and Transformation" on page 413.

Query Designer in SQL Server Management Studio provides the easiest way to design a query to export data. You can start and work with Query Designer by completing the following steps:

1. In SQL Server Management Studio, connect to the server instance containing the database in which you want to work.

2. In the Object Explorer view, expand the Databases node. Select a database, right-click it, and then select New Query to display a Query window with its own toolbar. A similar list of options (with more selections) is provided on the Query menu.

3. Access Query Designer by selecting Design Query In Editor on the Query menu or by pressing Ctrl+Shift+Q.

4. When you first start Query Designer, the Add Table dialog box shown in Figure 11-8 is displayed. The Add Table dialog box has tabs that allow you to select the tables, views, functions, and synonyms you want to work with.

**Figure 11-8** The Add Table dialog box.

5. In the Add Table dialog box, select a table or other object that contains data you want to add to the query, and then click Add. This displays a view pane for the selected object, which you can use to add columns, fields, and so on to the query you are building. When you are finished working with the Add Table dialog box, click Close. You can display this dialog box again at any time by selecting Add Table on the Query Designer menu.

6. Use the view panes provided to select the columns and fields to use in the view, as shown in Figure 11-9. Your actions create a SELECT statement that can be used to generate the query.

7. When you have finished designing the query, click OK to close the Query Designer window. The query you have generated is then added to the Query window.

8. The result of the Query Designer procedure is a complete SQL statement that you can use to select data for exporting. Click Parse to ensure that the query runs properly. If necessary, rebuild the query or remove statements that are causing errors.

9. Copy the query to the SQL Server Import And Export Wizard.

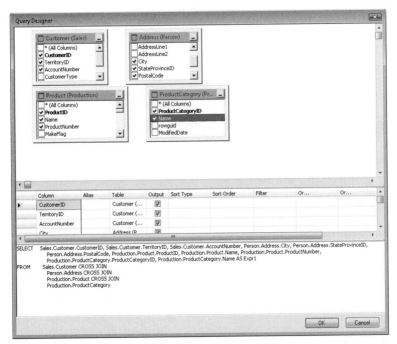

**Figure 11-9**   Query Designer.

## Stage 3: Formatting and Transformation

*Transformation* is the process of manipulating the source data and formatting it for the chosen destination. The way you transform and format data depends on the destination you chose. With most types of files, databases, and spreadsheets, you are guided through a column-mapping and transformation process. But if you have chosen a text file as the destination, you must also specify the format of the output file. Because the formatting options are essentially the same as those used for importing, you can find more information about these options in "Importing and Exporting Flat Files" on page 406.

Unless you specify otherwise, the SQL Server Import And Export Wizard sets the default mapping for all selected tables. This default mapping does the following:

- Specifies that every column in the source table is copied

- Maps the original column name, data type, nullability, size, precision, and scale to the destination table

- Appends the source data to the destination table, or creates the destination table if it does not exist

You can override the default mapping by completing the following steps:

1. The Select Source Tables And Views page lists the results of your query or all of the available tables in the source database, spreadsheet, or file that you have selected. If you have selected a particular table, you can edit its mapping by clicking the Edit Mappings button. This opens the Column Mappings dialog box shown in Figure 11-10.

**Figure 11-10**    The Column Mappings dialog box.

2. In the Column Mappings dialog box, set the general transfer options:

   ❑ **Create Destination Table**    Creates the destination table before copying source data. If the destination table exists, you must select the check box for the Drop And Re-create Destination Table option or an error will occur.

   ❑ **Delete Rows In Destination Table**    Deletes all rows in the destination table before copying the source data. Indexes and constraints on the destination table remain.

   ❑ **Append Rows To The Destination Table**    Inserts the source data into the destination table instead of overwriting existing data. This option does not affect existing data, indexes, or constraints in the destination table.

   > **Note**    Rows might not necessarily be inserted at the end of the destination table. To determine where rows will be inserted, use a clustered index on the destination table.

❏ **Drop And Re-create Destination Table**    Drops and re-creates the destination table before attempting to copy data into it, which permanently deletes all existing data and indexes.

> **Tip**    If the table exists at the destination, you must drop and re-create it to map new column values to the destination table. Otherwise, you can only map source columns to different destination columns.

❏ **Enable Identity Insert**    Allows you to insert explicit values into the identity column of a table. This option is available only on SQL Server and only if an identity column is detected.

❏ **Edit SQL**    Displays the Create Table SQL Statement dialog box, which allows you to customize the default CREATE TABLE statement.

3.   After you set the general transfer options, use the fields in the Mappings list box to determine how values are mapped from the source to the destination. The fields are all set to default values based on the source column. If you want to override these values for a new table, or if you are dropping and re-creating an existing table, you can modify these values. The Mappings fields are used as follows:

❏ **Source**    Sets the source column to map to a destination column.

❏ **Destination**    Click in this column, and then select an existing column name or type a new column name for the destination table. Use the <Ignore> option if a destination column should not be created.

> **Note**    If a destination column already exists and you choose <Ignore>, the source data will not be copied into this column.

❏ **Type**    Select a data type for the destination column. If you select a different data type than the data type of the source column, the data is converted to the new data type during the transfer.

> **Note**    Make sure you select a valid conversion option. The SQL Server Import And Export Wizard will not let you truncate data, and if you try to do so, an error will occur.

❏ **Nullable**    Select this check box if the destination allows NULL values.

❏ **Size**    Sets the length of the destination column. This value is applicable only for the char, varchar, nchar, nvarchar, binary, and varbinary data types.

> **Note**   Setting the size smaller than the length of the source data can result in data truncation. If this happens, the SQL Server Import And Export Wizard will generate an error and will not complete the data transfer.

- ❑ **Precision**   Sets the maximum number of decimal digits, including decimal places. This option is for decimal and numeric data types only.

- ❑ **Scale**   Sets the maximum number of digits to the right of the decimal point. This value must be less than or equal to the Precision value, and it applies to decimal and numeric data types only.

4. Click OK, and then repeat this process for other tables you want to transform.

5. When you are ready to continue, click Next.

## Stage 4: Save and Execute

You have nearly completed the process of creating an Integration Services package. At this stage, you specify when to use the package you have created and decide if the package should be saved for future use. After you click Next in the Select Source Tables And Views dialog box, the Save And Run Package page, shown in Figure 11-11, will appear. To use this page, complete the following steps:

1. By default, the Run Immediately option is selected so that you can run the package. If you do not want to run the package immediately, simply clear the check box for this option.

2. Use the options for saving the package to save it for future use. If you want to save the package to use later, select the Save SSIS Package check box and then specify where the package should be saved. The available locations are as follows:

- ❑ **SQL Server**   Saves as a local package in the *msdb* database so that the package is accessible for use on the designated server.

- ❑ **File System**   Saves as a DTSX file. You can add more packages to the file as long as they have a different package name. You can then copy, move, or e-mail the file to a different location.

**Figure 11-11**   The Save And Run Package page of the SQL Server Import And Export Wizard.

3. When you have finished configuring the run and save options, use the Package Protection Level options to set the encryption options for the package. The options are as follows:

- ❑ **Do Not Save Sensitive Data**   Creates the package, but does not save sensitive data in the package.

- ❑ **Encrypt Sensitive Data With User Key**   Creates the package with sensitive data encrypted. The package can be opened or executed only by the user who created the package (the current login account).

- ❑ **Encrypt Sensitive Data With Password**   Creates the package with sensitive data encrypted. The package can be opened or executed with the password you specify. This means that anyone with the password can open or execute the package.

- ❑ **Encrypt All Data With User Key**   Creates the package with all data encrypted. The package can be opened only by the user who created the package (the current login account).

- ❑ **Encrypt All Data With Password**   Saves the package with all data encrypted. The package can be opened or executed with the password you specify. This means that anyone with the password can open or execute the package.

❑ **Rely On Server Storage And Roles For Access Control**   Creates a package that uses SQL Server permissions and roles to control access (available only if you save the package to SQL Server).

4. If you have opted to save the package, the next page lets you set the save location. (See Figure 11-12.) The options might differ slightly from those shown, depending on the save location you previously selected.

**Figure 11-12**   The Save SSIS Package page of the SQL Server Import And Export Wizard.

5. Type a name for the package and a description of it in the Name and Description boxes. The name should be unique for the target location.

6. If you are saving the package to SQL Server, use the Server Name drop-down list to select the name of the computer running SQL Server to which you want to save the package. The package is saved in the *msdb* database on the designated server.

7. Select the type of authentication to use by selecting the option for either Windows Authentication or SQL Server Authentication. Provide an authorized user name and password if you select the Use SQL Server Authentication option.

8. If you selected to save the package to a file, set the file location using the File Name box.

9. Click Next. Review the actions that will be performed, and then click Finish.

If you have elected to run the package immediately, SQL Server runs the package. As each step is completed (or fails), the status is updated as shown in Figure 11-13. If an error occurs, you can click its message entry to view a detailed report of the error. Errors might halt execution of the package, and if they do, you will have to redesign the package using Integration Services Designer or re-create the package using the SQL Server Import And Export Wizard.

**Figure 11-13**   Check the execution status.

SQL Server stores Integration Services packages as local packages in a designated server's *msdb* database and as file-based packages. You manage packages by using SQL Server Management Studio, Business Intelligence Development Studio, or the Execute Package Utility (Dtexecui). Two command-line utilities are provided as well: Dtutil for copying, moving, signing, and deleting packages; and Dtexec for executing packages.

# Understanding BCP

BULK COPY (BCP) offers a command-line alternative to the SQL Server Import And Export Wizard. The Transact-SQL counterpart to BCP import is BULK INSERT. You will find that BULK INSERT has a similar syntax when used for importing data. To learn more about BCP, we will examine its features:

- Basics
- Syntax
- Permissions
- Modes

- Importing data
- Exporting data

## BCP Basics

BCP might continue to be a favorite of database administrators because of its great performance and minimal overhead. You will find that import and export processes tend to be very fast and that BCP requires very little memory to operate. BCP does not have a graphical user interface (GUI) and is best used in two situations:

- To import data from a text file to a single SQL Server table or view
- To export data to a text file from a single SQL Server table or view

When transferring data to or from SQL Server, BCP uses ODBC.

> **Tip**   Dates are written in ODBC format. You will find that the *datetime* format is yyyymmdd hh:mm:ss rather than mmm dd yyy hh:mm (A.M./P.M.), and the *money* format has no commas with four digits after the decimal (instead of commas and two digits after the decimal).

> **Note**   When you import data using BCP, columns with computed values and time stamps are ignored. SQL Server can automatically assign values. To do this, use a format file to specify that the computed values or time-stamp columns in the table should be skipped; SQL Server then automatically assigns values for the column. During export, computed values and time stamps are handled like other values.

## BCP Syntax

Before we examine how to use BCP, let's look at the command syntax, shown in Sample 11-1 and extended in Tables 11-1 and 11-2. As you can see, the syntax is extensive. BCP switches are case sensitive and order sensitive. You must use these switches exactly as indicated, or you will have problems executing the BCP command.

**Sample 11-1**   BCP Syntax and Usage

```
Syntax
bcp {[[dbname.][owner].]{tablename | viewname } | "query"}
    {in | out | queryout | format} datafile
    [switch1 [parameter1]] [switch2 [parameter2]]
    [switchN [parameterN]]


Usage
bcp pubs..customer out customers.txt -c -U sa -P"guerilla"
bcp pubs..customer in customers.txt -f customers.fmt
    -U sa -P"guerilla"
```

Table 11-1 provides a summary of key BCP parameters.

**Table 11-1   Key Parameters Used with BCP**

| Parameter | Description |
|---|---|
| Dbname | The name of the database. This parameter is optional, and if it is not supplied, the user's default database is used. |
| Owner | The schema (owner) of the table or view being used. Use the .. syntax for a default schema, such as *pubs..authors* instead of *pubs.dbo.authors*. |
| Tablename | The name of the table to access. Use the # or ## syntax to copy a temporary table. |
| Viewname | The name of the destination view when copying data into SQL Server; the source view when copying data from SQL Server. |
| Query | T-SQL statement that generates a result set. You must use double quotation marks around the query and specify the queryout parameter; these are mandatory with this option. |
| In | Specifies an import process. |
| Out | Specifies an export process. |
| Format | Sets the creation of a format file. You must set the name of the format file with the –f switch and also specify the format for this file with –n, –c, –w, –6, or –N. When creating an XML file, you must also specify –x. |
| Queryout | Must be used when exporting output from an SQL query or stored procedure. |
| Datafile | The name of the file for importing, or the name of the file to create when exporting. This can include the full file path. |

BCP also supports a wide variety of switches. These switches and their associated parameters are summarized in Table 11-2.

**Table 11-2   Switches Used with BCP**

| Switch | Description |
|---|---|
| –a *packetsize* | Sets the number of bytes in a network packet. The default is 4096 bytes. The valid range is 512 bytes through 65,535 bytes. |
| –b *batchsize* | The number of rows to transfer in the batch. Each batch is copied to the server as one transaction. By default, all rows are copied in a single batch. Do not use with the –h ROWS_PER_BATCH option. |
| –c | Character data mode (ASCII text) for transfers to and from non–SQL Server products. |
| –C *codepage* | Code page being used by the import file. This is relevant only when the data contains char, varchar, or text columns with character values greater than 127 or less than 32. Use the code page value ACP with ANSI ISO 1252 data, use RAW when no conversion should occur, use OEM to use the client's default code page, or type a specific code page value, such as 850. |

Table 11-2  Switches Used with BCP

| Switch | Description |
| --- | --- |
| −e errfile | Stores error messages in the specified error file. |
| −E | Uses identity values. Otherwise, identity values are ignored and automatically assigned new values. |
| −F firstrow | Sets the number of the first row to use. |
| −f formatfile | Sets the name and path to a BCP format file. The default file name is BCP.FMT. If you use −n, −c, −w, −6, or −N and do not specify −f, you will be prompted for format information, and your responses will be saved in a format file (named BCP.FMT by default). |
| −h loadhints | Used to set load hints: FIRE_TRIGGERS, ROWS_PER_BATCH, KILOBYTES_PER_BATCH, TABLOCK, CHECK_CONSTRAINTS, and ORDER. |
| −i inputfile | Sets the name of a response file that contains responses to the command prompt questions for each field when performing a bulk copy using interactive mode. |
| −k | Preserves null values. |
| −L lastrow | Sets the last row to use. |
| −m maxerrors | Sets the maximum number of errors that can occur before terminating BCP. The default is 10. |
| −N | Sets native export for noncharacter data and Unicode character export for character data. |
| −n | Sets native data mode, which is SQL Server specific. |
| −o outfile | File to redirect output of BCP during unattended operation. |
| −P password | Password to use to log in. Do not store passwords in files because this is a poor security practice. |
| −q | Uses quoted identifiers. |
| −R | Enables regional format copy for currency, date, and time data. |
| −r rowterminator | Sets the row terminator. The default is the new line character (\n). |
| −S servername | Sets the name of the computer running SQL Server. You can also follow the server name by the instance name: −S servername\instancename. |
| −t fieldterminator | Sets the field terminator. The default is the tab character (\t). |
| −T | Uses a trusted connection, which is a good security practice. |
| −U username | Sets the user name for login. |
| −V | Sets the data type version for native and character formats to a previous SQL Server version. For SQL Server 7.0, use 70; for SQL Server 2000, use 80; for SQL Server 2005, use 90. |

Table 11-2   Switches Used with BCP

| Switch | Description |
|--------|-------------|
| –v | Displays the BCP version number. |
| –w | Sets wide character (Unicode) mode. |
| –x | Used with the format and –f options to create an XML format file instead of a standard text-based format file. |

# BCP Permissions and Modes

Although any user can run BCP, only users with appropriate permissions can access SQL Server and the specified database objects. When you run BCP, you can set login information using the –U and –P switches or you can use a trusted connection that is more secure. For unattended operations, it is essential to use these switches to ensure that permissions are granted appropriately. To import data into a table, the user needs INSERT permission on the target table. To export data from a table, the user needs SELECT permission for the source table.

BCP can use three different modes:

- **Character mode**   Used when you want to import or export data as ASCII text. The switch to set this mode is –c.

- **Native mode**   Used when you want to import or export data in native format. The switch to set this mode is –n or –N.

- **Wide mode**   Used when you want to import or export data as Unicode text. The switch to set this mode is –w.

The character and wide modes are the best choices when you are copying to a non–SQL Server product. Use native mode when you are copying data between SQL Server tables. These modes all have their strengths and weaknesses. With character or wide mode files, you can view the contents and make sure that you have the right data set; however, for imports, you must also tell SQL Server how this data is formatted. You can do this through interactive prompts or by using a format file containing the responses to these prompts. With native mode, you cannot view the contents of native data files, but you do not have to specify data formatting information when importing files either.

# Importing Data with BCP

You can import data with BCP in two ways. You can start an interactive session, or you can set the necessary responses in a format file. The following example shows how to start an interactive session using a trusted connection:

```
bcp pubs..customer in customers.txt -T
```

To specify a format file, use the −f flag, such as in the following example:

```
bcp pubs..customer in customers.txt -w -f customers.fmt -T
```

In an interactive session, BCP prompts you for information needed to complete the import or export process. BCP starts an interactive session when either of the following situations occurs:

- You import without specifying the −c, −n, −w, or −N parameters.
- You export without specifying the −c, −n, −w, or −N parameters.

The interactive session allows you to customize the BCP process, much as you do with a format file. In fact, before you try to create a format file, you should run BCP in interactive mode, and then choose to have BCP create the necessary format file for you. This operation will show you the best way to configure the format file.

For each column in a table you are importing, you will see prompts similar to the following during an interactive session:

```
Enter the file storage type of field [nchar]:
Enter prefix length of field [0]:
Enter length of field [5]:
Enter field terminator [none]:
```

> **Note**   Pressing Enter accepts the default values. To skip a column in an import file, type **0** for the prefix length, **0** for the field length, and **none** for the terminator type. You cannot skip a column when exporting data.

These prompts ask you to type various kinds of information, and in every case the default value for the current column is shown in brackets. At the end of the interactive session, you will be asked if you want to save your responses in a format file. If you answer yes (by typing **Y**), you can type the name of the format file when prompted, as shown here:

```
Do you want to save this format information in a file? [Y/N]
Host filename [bcp.fmt]: customers.fmt
```

You can then use the format file for other BCP sessions by setting the −f switch as explained previously. Because the format file has a rigid syntax that you must follow, I recommend creating a sample file to get started. As Sample 11-2 shows, each line in the file contains information fields that determine how data should be imported.

**Sample 11-2**   BCP Non-XML Format File

```
10.0
50
1 SQLINT    0 8    ""  1  CUSTOMERID  ""
2 SQLNCHAR 2 25    ""  2  CUSTNAME    SQL_Latin1_General_CP1_CI_AS
3 SQLNCHAR 2 20    ""  3  CUSTORG     SQL_Latin1_General_CP1_CI_AS
..
50 SQLNCHAR 2 9    ""  3  POSTALCODE  SQL_Latin1_General_CP1_CI_AS
```

The lines give you the following information:

- The first line sets the version of BCP used. Here the version is 10.0, indicating SQL Server 2008.

- The second line sets the number of columns in the table you are importing. In the example, the table contains 50 columns.

- Subsequent lines set the formats for each column in the table, from the first column to the last column.

The lines defining table columns are broken down into fields, and each field sets a different input parameter. Normally, these fields are separated by spaces. The number of spaces does not really matter—provided there is at least one space. BCP treats one or more spaces as a field separator. File format fields operate in the following manner:

- Field 1 sets the column number you are describing from the data file.

- Field 2 sets the file storage type, which is simply the data type of the column.

- Field 3 sets the prefix length for compacted data. A value of zero specifies that no prefix is used.

- Field 4 sets the field length, which is the number of bytes required to store the data type. Use the default value provided whenever possible.

- Field 5 sets the field terminator. By default, BCP separates all fields but the last one with tabs (\t) and separates the last field with a carriage return and newline field (\r\n).

- Field 6 sets the table column number in the database. For example, a value of 1 means that the column corresponds to the first column in the database.

- Field 7 sets the table column name.

- Field 8 sets the column collation.

## Exporting Data with BCP

When you export data, BCP creates a data file using the name you specify. If you are exporting data from non-native files (ASCII and Unicode text), the columns in this file are separated with tabs by default, and the last column has a carriage return and newline. You specify a tab as a terminator with \t and a carriage return and newline with \r\n. In a format file, a tab can be an actual tab character or a series of five or more spaces.

As when importing data, you can handle data export interactively. For example, if you start an export session without specifying format information, you are prompted for this information. In the following example, you export a table to a file called customers.txt and use semicolons as the delimiter:

```
bcp pubs..customer out customers.txt -c -t -T;
```

# BCP Scripts

A BCP script is simply a batch file or a Windows Script Host file that contains BCP commands. Sample 11-3 shows examples of how to run BCP using various scripting options. If you do not know how to use batch files or Windows Script Host, two great resources are *Windows Command-Line Administrator's Pocket Consultant,* 2nd Edition (Microsoft Press, 2008) and *Windows 2000 Scripting Guide* (Microsoft Press, 2003).

**Sample 11-3**    Using BCP in a Script

```
sched-export.bat
@echo off
@if not "%OS%"=="Windows_NT" goto :EXIT
bcp pubs..customer out customers.txt -c -t, -T
:EXIT


sched-export.vbs
'Nightly Bulk Copy export for the customers table
'Writes output to cust.txt and errors to err.txt
Set ws = WScript.CreateObject("WScript.Shell")
ret = ws.Run("bcp pubs..customers out cust.txt -c -t, -T
    -eerr.txt",0,"TRUE")


sched-export.js
\\Nightly Bulk Copy export for the customers table
\\Writes output to cust.txt and errors to err.txt
var ws = WScript.CreateObject("WScript.Shell");
ret = ws.Run("bcp pubs..customers out cust.txt -c -t, -T
    -eerr.txt",0,"TRUE")
```

After you create a script file for the bulk copy command, you can schedule it as a task to run on your system. To schedule these scripts to run every night at midnight, for example, use the following commands:

```
AT 00:00 /every:M,T,W,Th,F,S,Su "sched-export.bat"
AT 00:00 /every:M,T,W,Th,F,S,Su "cscript //B sched-export.js"
AT 00:00 /every:M,T,W,Th,F,S,Su "cscript //B sched-export.vbs"
```

**Note**    For more information on scheduling tasks, refer to *Microsoft Windows Command-Line Administrator's Pocket Consultant,* 2nd Edition (Microsoft Press, 2008) or *Microsoft Windows Vista Administrator's Pocket Consultant,* (Microsoft Press, 2007).

# Using the BULK INSERT Command

A Transact-SQL command for importing data into a database is BULK INSERT. You can use BULK INSERT in much the same way that you use BCP. In fact, most of the parameters for BULK INSERT are the same as those used with BCP—they just have a different syntax. This syntax is shown in Sample 11-4.

**Sample 11-4**   BULK INSERT Syntax and Usage

```
Syntax
BULK INSERT [database_name.[schema_name ][table_name|view_name]
    FROM 'data_file'
    [ WITH (
    [ [ , ] BATCHSIZE = batch_size ]
    [ [ , ] CHECK_CONSTRAINTS ]
    [ [ , ] CODEPAGE = { 'ACP' | 'OEM' | 'RAW' | 'code_page' } ]
    [ [ , ] DATAFILETYPE  =
        { 'char' | 'native'| 'widechar' | 'widenative' } ]
    [ [ , ] FIELDTERMINATOR = 'field_terminator' ]
    [ [ , ] FIRSTROW = first_row ]
    [ [ , ] FIRE_TRIGGERS ]
    [ [ , ] FORMATFILE = 'format_file_path' ]
    [ [ , ] KEEPIDENTITY ]
    [ [ , ] KEEPNULLS ]
    [ [ , ] KILOBYTES_PER_BATCH = kilobytes_per_batch ]
    [ [ , ] LASTROW = last_row ]
    [ [ , ] MAXERRORS = max_errors ]
    [ [ , ] ORDER ( { column [ ASC | DESC ] } [ ,...n ] ) ]
    [ [ , ] ROWS_PER_BATCH = rows_per_batch ]
    [ [ , ] ROWTERMINATOR = 'row_terminator' ]
    [ [ , ] TABLOCK ]
    [ [ , ] ERRORFILE = 'file_name' ]
    )]

Usage
BULK INSERT pubs..customers FROM 'c:\data\customer.txt'
BULK INSERT pubs..customers FROM 'c:\cust.txt' with
    (DATAFILETYPE = 'char ',
    FORMATFILE='c:\cust.fmt')
```

To use BULK INSERT, you must have INSERT and ADMINISTER BULK OPERATION permissions. You might also need ALTER TABLE permission if any of the following conditions are true:

- Constraints are disabled (the default setting). To keep constraints enabled, use the CHECK_CONSTRAINTS option.

- Triggers are disabled (the default setting). To fire triggers, use the FIRE_ TRIGGER option.

- KEEPIDENTITY is used to import identity values from the specified data file.

Additionally, before using BULK INSERT, you might want to set the database recovery model to Bulk-Logged. This mode minimally logs bulk operations and increases performance when bulk inserting. To set this option, select a database, open its Properties dialog box, choose the Options page, and then select Bulk-Logged under Recovery Model. You might also want to use sp_tableoption to set the table lock on the bulk load value. When this option is set to FALSE (the default setting), the bulk load process obtains row locks when inserting into user-defined tables. If you set this option to TRUE, the bulk load process obtains a bulk update lock instead. Members of the sysadmin fixed server role, members of the db_owner and db_ddladmin fixed database roles, and the table owner can modify the table lock on a bulk load value.

Sample 11-5 shows how to set the table lock on a bulk load value using sp_tableoption.

**Sample 11-5** sp_tableoption Syntax and Usage

```
Syntax
sp_tableoption [ @TableNamePattern = ] 'table'
         , [ @OptionName = ] 'option_name'
         , [ @OptionValue = ] 'value'


Usage
EXEC sp_tableoption Sales.Customers 'table lock on bulk load', 'true'
```

# Chapter 12

# Linked Servers and Distributed Transactions

Networking environments are becoming more and more complex. Organizations that managed with a single server now need additional servers, or they need to integrate their existing server with other heterogeneous data sources. Microsoft SQL Server 2008 provides several features for integrating SQL Server databases with other SQL Server databases and with other data sources, including distributed data, linked servers, and replication. This chapter focuses on linked servers and distributed data. Distributed data includes support for distributed queries, distributed transactions, and remote stored procedure execution. These distributed data features are handled through linked servers, which can be computers running SQL Server or computers running other database server software, such as Oracle Database Enterprise Edition. You will learn about replication in the next chapter, "Implementing Snapshot, Merge, and Transactional Replication."

## Working with Linked Servers and Distributed Data

Before you use distributed data, you must configure the linked servers you want to use. Linked servers depend on OLE DB providers to communicate with one another. Through OLE DB, you can link instances of SQL Server to other instances of SQL Server as well as to other data sources.

You use linked servers to handle distributed queries, distributed transactions, remote stored procedure calls, and replication. Basically, queries and transactions are *distributed* when they make use of two or more database server instances. For example, if a client is connected to one server instance and starts a query that accesses a different server instance, the query is distributed. On the other hand, if the same client queries two different databases on the same server instance, the query is considered a local query and is handled internally.

You can define linked servers that point back to the server on which they are defined. This type of linked server is called a *loopback linked server* because Transact-SQL statements loop through the SQL Native Client Interface provider and back to the local server. You'll find that loopback linked servers are most useful when you are testing an application that uses distributed queries on a single server network.

**Note**  You cannot use loopback linked servers in distributed transactions. You'll get an error if you try to execute a distributed query against a loopback linked server from within a distributed transaction. In SQL Server 2008, an INSERT...EXE-CUTE statement can execute against a loopback linked server when the connection does not have Multiple Active Result Sets (MARS) enabled.

## Using Distributed Queries

When you execute a distributed query, SQL Server interprets the command and then breaks it down for the destination OLE DB provider using rowset requests. A *rowset* is a type of database object that enables OLE DB data providers to support data with a tabular format. As their name implies, rowset objects represent a set of rows and columns of data. After creating the rowset objects, the OLE DB provider calls the data source, opens the necessary files, and returns the requested information as rowsets. SQL Server then formats the rowsets as result sets and adds any applicable output parameters.

**Note**  With SQL-92, the user connections must have the ANSI_NULLS and ANSI_WARNINGS options before they can execute distributed queries. Be sure to configure these options, if necessary. For more information, see "Configuring User and Remote Connections" on page 161.

You can create simple distributed queries quickly by making your own rowsets. To do this, you use the Openrowset function. When you use this function, you do not need to use linked servers, and you can use the Openrowset function in place of a table in a query if you pass parameters that identify the OLE DB data source and provider.

You use the Openrowset function in the same way that you use virtual tables; simply replace the virtual table reference with an Openrowset reference. Sample 12-1 shows the syntax and usage of Openrowset.

The BULK rowset provider is similar to the BULK INSERT statement. The data_file parameter is used to specify the data file from which data will be copied into the target table. A format file is required to define the column types in the result set, except when you use SINGLE_BLOB, SINGLE_CLOB, or SINGLE_NCLOB. SINGLE_BLOB returns the contents of the data file as a single-row, single-column rowset of type varbinary(max). SINGLE_CLOB reads the data file as ASCII text and returns the contents of the data file as a single-row, single-column rowset of type varchar(max). SINGLE_NCLOB reads the data file as Unicode text and returns the contents as a single-row, single-column rowset of type nvarchar(max). Both SINGLE_CLOB and SINGLE_NCLOB use the collation of the current database.

**Sample 12-1**   OPENROWSET Syntax and Usage

**Syntax for SELECT with Table Alias**
```
SELECT selection FROM OPENROWSET(rowset_options) AS table_alias
```

**Syntax for OPENROWSET**
```
OPENROWSET
( { 'provider_name' , { 'datasource' ; 'user_id' ; 'password'
  | 'provider_string' }
    , { [ catalog. ] [ schema. ] object
  | 'query' }
  | BULK 'data_file' ,
      { FORMATFILE = 'format_file_path' [ <bulk_options> ]
      | SINGLE_BLOB | SINGLE_CLOB | SINGLE_NCLOB }
} )

<bulk_options> ::=
  [ , CODEPAGE = { 'ACP' | 'OEM' | 'RAW' | 'code_page' }]
  [ , ERRORFILE = 'file_name' ]
  [ , FIRSTROW = first_row ]
  [ , LASTROW = last_row ]
  [ , MAXERRORS = maximum_errors ]
  [ , ROWS_PER_BATCH = rows_per_batch ]
  [ , ORDER ( { column [ ASC | DESC ] } [ ,...n ] ) [ UNIQUE ]
```

**Usage**
```
USE pubs
GO
SELECT a.*
FROM OPENROWSET('SQLOLEDB','Pluto';'netUser';'totem12',
'SELECT * FROM pubs.dbo.authors ORDER BY au_lname, au_fname')
AS a
GO
SELECT o.*
FROM OPENROWSET('Microsoft.Jet.OLEDB.4.0','C:\
customers.mdb';'Admin';'', 'Orders')
AS o
```

When the OPENROWSET BULK option is used with an INSERT statement, you can use standard table hints, such as TABLOCK, as well as the special BULK INSERT table hints: IGNORE_CONSTRAINTS, IGNORE_TRIGGERS, KEEPDEFAULTS, and KEEP-IDENTITY. When you use the BULK rowset provider with OPENROWSET, you must either specify column aliases in the FROM clause or specify column names in the format file. The syntax for the SELECT statement with the table alias then becomes:

```
SELECT selection FROM OPENROWSET(BULK rowset_options) AS
    table_alias[(column1_alias, column2_alias,...)]
```

Simple distributed queries using the Openrowset function are useful for infrequent references. For frequent references to OLE DB data sources, use linked servers instead. After you create a linked server as discussed in "Adding Linked Servers" on page 435, you can access the linked server using several different techniques. You can use the EXECUTE statement to execute both commands and stored procedures on a linked server. EXECUTE statements that pass through a command with the AT linked_server_name extension can include data definition language (DDL) and data manipulation language (DML) statements, as well as commands that return more than one result. Sample 12-2 shows the syntax for using EXECUTE in this way.

**Sample 12-2**   EXECUTE at linked_server

```
Syntax
EXEC [UTE] ( { @string_variable | [ N ] 'command_string' } [ + ...n ]
    [ {, { value | @variable [ OUTPUT ] } } [...n] ] )
    [ AS { LOGIN | USER } = ' name ']
    [ AT linked_server_name ] [;]


Usage
EXEC ( 'SELECT * FROM william.sales') AT ORADBSVR38;
```

You also can use remote stored procedures that execute against the linked server or distributed queries that access tables in the linked server through SELECT, INSERT, UPDATE, and DELETE statements that reference the linked server using a four-part name. The syntax for a four-part name is

*LinkedServerName.DatabaseName.TableName.ColumnName*

In this example, *LinkedServerName* is the name of a previously defined linked server, *DatabaseName* is the name of a database, *TableName* is the name of a database table, and *ColumnName* is the name of a table column, such as

```
SELECT * FROM ORADBSVR38.Customers.Employees.EmployeeID
```

Distributed queries can use four-part names only if the OLE DB provider you are using meets certain minimum requirements. The provider must support the IDBSchema-Rowset interface as well as restrictions on name parts. SQL Server uses a period (.) for catalog and schema separators and the double-quotation character for a string literal delimiter, and the provider must support these literals. If the provider provides Unicode string literal prefixes and Unicode string literal suffixes, SQL Server uses these. If the provider does not meet these minimum requirements, you can reference the provider only by using pass-through queries in the OPENDATASOURCE or OPEN-ROWSET function.

## Using Distributed Transactions

Distributed transactions are transactions that use distributed queries or remote procedure calls (RPCs). As you might expect, distributed transactions are more involved than distributed queries, primarily because you need a mechanism that ensures that transactions are committed uniformly or rolled back on all the linked servers. For example, if you start a transaction that updates databases on three different server instances, you want to make certain that the transaction is committed when it has completed successfully, or that the transaction is rolled back if an error occurs. In this way, you ensure the integrity of the databases involved in the distributed transaction.

In SQL Server, three components are required for distributed transactions to be handled properly:

- **Resource managers**   You must configure resource managers, which are the linked servers used in the distributed transactions. For details about how to configure resource managers, see "Managing Linked Servers" on page 435.

- **Distributed Transaction Coordinator service**   The Microsoft Distributed Transaction Coordinator (MS DTC) service must be running on all servers that are handling distributed transactions. If it is not, distributed transactions will not work properly.

- **Transaction manager**   The transaction manager coordinates and manages distributed transactions. The transaction manager on SQL Server is the Distributed Transaction Coordinator.

**Note**   Applications other than SQL Server can use the Distributed Transaction Coordinator. If you try to analyze Distributed Transaction Coordinator performance, you should note which applications besides SQL Server are using the Distributed Transaction Coordinator.

Each server instance involved in a distributed transaction is known as a *resource manager*. Resource managers coordinate transactions through a transaction manager, such as the Distributed Transaction Coordinator. You can use other transaction managers if they support the X/Open XA specification for distributed transaction processing.

You handle distributed transactions in much the same manner as local transactions. Applications start distributed transactions in several ways:

- Explicitly, by using BEGIN DISTRIBUTED TRANSACTION

- Explicitly, by using the methods or functions available with ODBC, OLE DB, ADO, or the .NET Framework to join a distributed transaction started by the application

- Implicitly, by executing a distributed query within a local transaction

- Implicitly, by calling a remote stored procedure within a local transaction (provided the REMOTE_PROC_TRANSACTIONS option is set to ON)

At the end of the transaction, the application requests that the transaction be either committed or rolled back. To ensure that the transaction is handled properly on all servers, even if problems occur during the transaction, the transaction manager uses a commit process with two phases:

- **Phase 1: The prepare phase** The transaction manager sends a "prepare to commit" request to all the resource managers involved in the transaction. Each resource manager performs any necessary preparatory tasks and then reports its success or failure to the transaction manager. If all the resource managers are ready to commit, the transaction manager broadcasts a commit message and the transaction enters phase 2, the commit phase.

- **Phase 2: The commit phase** The resource managers attempt to commit the transaction. Each resource manager then sends back a success or failure message. If all the resource managers report success, the transaction manager marks the transaction as completed and reports this to the application. If a resource manager fails in either phase, the transaction is rolled back and the failure is reported.

SQL Server applications manage distributed transactions either through Transact-SQL or through the SQL Server database application programming interface (API). SQL Server itself supports distributed transactions using the ITransactionLocal (local transactions) and ITransactionJoin (distributed transactions) OLE DB interfaces, as well as the rowset objects discussed previously. If an OLE DB provider does not support ITransactionJoin, only read-only procedures are allowed for that provider. Similarly, the types of queries you can execute on a linked server depend on the OLE DB provider you are using.

With distributed queries and transactions, you can use most data manipulation language (DML) commands, such as SELECT, INSERT, UPDATE, and DELETE. You cannot, however, use data definition language (DDL) commands, such as CREATE, DROP, or ALTER. If you need to use DDL commands on linked servers, you might want to create stored procedures and then execute these stored procedures remotely, as necessary.

## Running the Distributed Transaction Coordinator Service

The Distributed Transaction Coordinator service must run on each server that handles distributed transactions, and you usually will want the service to start automatically when the system starts. This ensures that the distributed transactions are executed as expected. By using SQL Server Configuration Manager, you can control the Distributed Transaction Coordinator service just as you do other SQL Server–related services. For details, see "Configuring SQL Server Services" on page 56.

You can view the Distributed Transaction Coordinator service in SQL Server Management Studio by completing the following steps:

1. In SQL Server Management Studio, connect to the server instance you want to use.

2. In the Object Explorer view, expand the Management node. You will see the status of the Distributed Transaction Coordinator service. A green circle with a triangle indicates that the service is running. A red circle with a square indicates that the service is stopped.

# Managing Linked Servers

To work properly, distributed queries and transactions depend on linked servers. You configure the linked servers you are using by registering their connection and data source information in SQL Server. Then you will be able to reference the linked server by using a single logical name. If you no longer need to link to a server, you can remove the linked server connection.

## Adding Linked Servers

If you want a server to be able to use distributed queries, distributed transactions, or remote command execution, you must configure linked server connections to other servers. For example, if clients that access a server named Zeta make distributed queries to Pluto and Omega, you must configure Pluto and Omega as linked servers on Zeta. If clients that connect to Pluto make distributed queries to Zeta and Omega, you must configure Zeta and Omega as linked servers on Pluto. To add a linked server, complete the following steps:

1. In SQL Server Management Studio, connect to the server instance you want to configure.

2. In the Object Explorer view, expand the Server Objects node.

3. Right-click the Linked Servers entry, and then choose New Linked Server from the shortcut menu to open the dialog box shown in Figure 12-1.

4. In the Linked Server text box, type the name of the linked server to create.

5. If you are linking to a computer running SQL Server, select the SQL Server option.

**Figure 12-1** The New Linked Server dialog box.

6. If you are linking to a different data source, select the Other Data Source option and then configure the data source using the text boxes provided. If there is no text box available in the dialog box for a specific option, you cannot configure that option for the selected provider. Provide information in the text boxes as follows:

❑ **Provider** Select the name of the OLE DB provider to use when communicating with the specified linked server from the drop-down list box.

❑ **Product Name** Set the server product name for the OLE DB data source.

❑ **Data Source** Provide the OLE DB data source, which is used to initialize the OLE DB provider.

❑ **Provider String** Type a provider-specific connection string that identifies a unique data source.

❑ **Location** Set the location of the database for the OLE DB provider.

❑ **Catalog** Indicate the catalog to use when connecting to the OLE DB provider.

**Real World**    The most commonly used option combinations are provider name and data source. For example, if you were configuring a linked server for a Microsoft Access database or a Microsoft Office Excel spreadsheet, you would select Microsoft Jet 4.0 OLE DB Provider and then set the data source name. With Oracle, you would select Microsoft OLE DB Provider For Oracle and then set the data source name.

7. Select the Server Options page from the Select A Page list in the left pane of the dialog box to configure server-specific settings as follows:

   ❏ **Collation Compatible**    Set this option to enable SQL Server to send comparisons on character columns to the provider. Otherwise, SQL Server evaluates comparisons on character columns locally. Set this option only when the linked server has the same collation as the local server.

   > **Note**    The Collation Compatible option controls the sort order settings. If you do not select this option, SQL Server uses the local sort order. This affects the order of result sets, and you should note it when you develop SQL Server applications or configure clients that support distributed transactions.

   ❏ **Data Access**    Set this option to enable the linked server for distributed query access.

   ❏ **RPC**    Set this option to enable remote procedure calls from the linked server.

   ❏ **RPC Out**    Set this option to enable remote procedure calls to the linked server.

   ❏ **Use Remote Collation**    Set this option to have SQL Server use the collation from the linked server's character columns. If you do not set this option, SQL Server interprets data from the linked server using the default collation of the local server instance. Note that only SQL Server databases take advantage of this option.

   ❏ **Collation Name**    Set this option to assign a specific collation for queries and transactions. You must set the Collation Compatible option to False before you can set this option.

   ❏ **Connection Timeout**    Use this text box to set the time-out value for connections made to the remote server.

   ❏ **Query Timeout**    Use this text box to set the time-out value for queries made to the remote server.

❑ **Enable Promotion Of Distributed Transactions** Use this text box to enable calling a remote stored procedure and then automatically starting a distributed transaction and enlisting the transaction with MS DTC. After a distributed transaction has been started, remote stored procedure calls can be made to other instances of SQL Server that have been defined as linked servers. The linked servers are all enlisted in the distributed transaction, and MS DTC ensures that the transaction is completed against each linked server.

8. Click OK to create the linked server. Next, you must configure security settings for the linked server, as discussed in "Configuring Security for Linked Servers" on page 440.

The corresponding Transact-SQL command for adding linked servers is sp_addlinkedserver. Use this stored procedure as shown in Sample 12-3.

**Sample 12-3** sp_addlinkedserver Syntax and Usage

```
Syntax
sp_addlinkedserver [@server =] 'server'
    [, [@srvproduct =] 'product_name']
    [, [@provider =] 'provider_name']
    [, [@datasrc =] 'data_source']
    [, [@location =] 'location']
    [, [@provstr =] 'provider_string']
    [, [@catalog =] 'catalog']


Usage
EXEC sp_addlinkedserver
        @server='ORADBSVR38',
        @srvproduct='Oracle',
        @provider='OraOLEDB.Oracle',
        @datasrc='ORACLE10';
GO
```

Table 12-1 provides a summary of parameter values you can use when configuring various OLE DB providers. The table also shows the sp_addlinkedserver parameter values to use for each OLE DB provider. Because some providers have different configurations, there might be more than one row for a particular data source type.

**Note** When you want to access a mirrored SQL Server database, the connection string must contain the database name to enable failover attempts by the data access provider. You can specify the database name in the @provstr or @catalog parameter. Optionally, the connection string also can provide a failover partner name.

Table 12-1   Parameter Values for Configuring OLE DB Providers

| Remote OLE DB Data Source | OLE DB Provider | product_ name | provider_ name | data_source | Other |
|---|---|---|---|---|---|
| SQL Server | Microsoft SQL Native Client OLE DB Provider | SQL Server (default) | — | — | — |
| SQL Server | Microsoft SQL Native Client OLE DB Provider | — | SQLNCLI | Network name of SQL Server (for default instance) | Database name optional for catalog field |
| SQL Server | Microsoft SQL Native Client OLE DB Provider | — | SQLNCLI | *Servername\ instancename* (for specific instance) | Database name optional for catalog field |
| Oracle | Microsoft OLE DB Provider for Oracle | Any | MSDAORA | SQL*Net alias for Oracle database | — |
| Oracle 8.0 and later | Oracle Provider for OLE DB | Any | OraOLEDB. Oracle | Alias for the Oracle database | — |
| Access/Jet | Microsoft OLE DB Provider for Jet | Any | Microsoft. Jet.OLEDB. 4.0 | Full path name of Jet database file | — |
| ODBC data source | Microsoft OLE DB Provider for ODBC | Any | MSDASQL | System DSN of ODBC data source | — |
| ODBC data source | Microsoft OLE DB Provider for ODBC | Any | MSDASQL | — | ODBC connection string for *provider_ string* |
| File system | Microsoft OLE DB Provider for Indexing Service | Any | MSIDXS | Indexing Service catalog name | — |
| Microsoft Office Excel Spreadsheet | Microsoft OLE DB Provider for Jet | Any | Microsoft. Jet.OLEDB. 4.0 | Full path name of Excel file | Excel 5.0 for *provider_ string* |
| IBM DB2 Database | Microsoft OLE DB Provider for DB2 | Any | DB2OLEDB | — | Catalog name of DB2 database in catalog field |

## Configuring Security for Linked Servers

You use linked server security to control access and to determine how local logins are used. By default, new linked servers are set to have no security context when a user login is not defined. This blocks access to all logins not explicitly mapped to the linked server.

To change the security settings for a linked server, complete the following steps:

1. Start SQL Server Management Studio, and then access the local server that contains the linked server definitions you want to change.

2. In the Object Explorer view, expand the Server Objects node, and then expand the Linked Servers node. You should now see an entry for each linked server that you created on the currently selected server.

3. Right-click the icon for the linked server you want to configure, and then choose Properties from the shortcut menu to open the Linked Server Properties dialog box.

4. In the Linked Server Properties dialog box, click the Security page, as shown in Figure 12-2.

**Figure 12-2**  The Security page of the Linked Server Properties dialog box.

5. Map local logins to remote logins by clicking Add.

6. Configure the following options on a per-login basis:

   ❑ **Local Login**   Sets the ID of a local login that can connect to the linked server.

   ❑ **Impersonate**   Select this check box to use the local login ID to connect to the linked server. The local login ID must match a login ID on the linked server exactly.

   > **Note**   If you select the Impersonate check box, you cannot map the local login to a remote login.

   ❑ **Remote User**   Sets the remote user to which the local login ID maps on the linked server.

   ❑ **Remote Password**   Sets the password for the remote user. If it is not provided, the user might be prompted for a password.

7. Use the options and text boxes in the lower portion of the Security page to set a default security context for all users who do not have a specific login setting for the linked server. These options are used as follows:

   ❑ **Not Be Made**   Users without logins are not allowed access to the linked server.

   ❑ **Be Made Without Using A Security Context**   Blocks access to all logins not explicitly mapped to the linked server.

   ❑ **Be Made Using The Login's Current Security Context**   Logins not explicitly mapped to the linked server use their current login and password to connect to the linked server. Access is denied if the login and password do not exist on the linked server.

   ❑ **Be Made Using This Security Context**   Logins not explicitly mapped to the linked server will use the login and password provided in the Remote Login and With Password text boxes.

8. When you have finished configuring logins, click OK.

The related Transact-SQL command for configuring logins is sp_addlinkedsrvlogin. Use this stored procedure as shown in Sample 12-4.

Sample 12-4 sp_addlinkedsrvlogin Syntax and Usage

```
Syntax
sp_addlinkedsrvlogin [@rmtsrvname =] 'rmtsrvname'
[,[@useself =] 'TRUE' | 'FALSE' | 'NULL']
[,[@locallogin =] 'locallogin']
[,[@rmtuser =] 'rmtuser']
[,[@rmtpassword =] 'rmtpassword']


Usage
EXEC sp_addlinkedsrvlogin
    @rmtsrvname='ORADBSVR38',
    @useself='false',
    @locallogin=null,
    @rmtuser='william',
    @rmtpassword='tango98';
GO
```

# Setting Server Options for Remote and Linked Servers

You set server options for remote and linked servers using sp_serveroption. Use this stored procedure as shown in Sample 12-5. Key options are summarized in Table 12-2.

Sample 12-5 sp_serveroption Syntax and Usage

```
Syntax
sp_serveroption [@server =] 'server'
    ,[@optname =] 'option_name'
    ,[@optvalue =] 'option_value' ;


Usage
EXEC sp_serveroption 'ORADBSVR38', 'rpc out', true;
```

Table 12-2   Key Options for sp_serveroption

| Option Name | Option Usage/Description |
|---|---|
| collation compatible | If TRUE, compatible collation is assumed with regard to character set and collation sequence (or sort order) and SQL Server sends comparisons on character columns to the provider. Otherwise, SQL Server always evaluates comparisons on character columns locally. |
| collation name | Sets the name of the collation used by the remote data source if Use Remote Collation is TRUE and the data source is not a SQL Server data source. The name must be a specific, single collation supported by SQL Server. |
| connect timeout | Sets the time-out value for connecting to the linked server. Set this option to 0 (zero) to use the sp_configure default. |
| data access | Set to TRUE to enable a linked server for distributed query access. Set this option to FALSE to disable the linked server for distributed query access. |
| lazy schema validation | If this option is TRUE, SQL Server skips schema checking of remote tables at the beginning of a query. |
| query timeout | Sets the time-out value for queries against a linked server. Set this option to 0 (zero) to use the sp_configure default. |
| remote proc transaction promotion | If this option is set to TRUE, calling a remote stored procedure starts a distributed transaction and enlists the transaction with MS DTC. Otherwise, a local transaction will not be promoted to a distributed transaction while calling a remote procedure call on a linked server. |
| rpc | Set to TRUE to enable RPC from the linked server. |
| rpc out | Set to TRUE to enable RPC to the linked server. |
| use remote collation | If this option is set to TRUE, the collation of remote columns is used for SQL Server data sources, and the collation specified in Collation Name is used for non–SQL Server data sources. Otherwise, distributed queries will always use the default collation of the local server, while the collation name and the collation of remote columns are ignored. |

## Deleting Linked Servers

If you do not need a linked server anymore, you can delete it by completing the following steps:

1. Start SQL Server Management Studio, and then access the local server that contains the linked server definitions you want to delete.

2. In the Object Explorer view, expand the Server Objects node, and then expand the Linked Servers node. You should now see an entry for each linked server that you created on the currently selected server.

3. Right-click the icon for the linked server you want to remove, and then choose Delete to open the Delete Object dialog box.

4. In the Delete Object dialog box, click OK.

The Transact-SQL command to drop linked servers is sp_dropserver. The Transact-SQL command to drop linked server logins is sp_droplinkedsrvlogin. Use these stored procedures as shown in Samples 12-6 and 12-7.

**Sample 12-6** sp_dropserver Syntax and Usage

```
Syntax
sp_dropserver [@server =] 'server'
[, [@droplogins =]{'droplogins' | NULL}]

Usage
EXEC sp_dropserver 'ORADBSVR38', 'droplogins'
```

**Sample 12-7** sp_droplinkedsrvlogin Syntax and Usage

```
Syntax
sp_droplinkedsrvlogin [@rmtsrvname =] 'rmtsrvname',
[@locallogin =]'locallogin'

Usage
EXEC sp_droplinkedsrvlogin 'ORADBSVR38', 'william'
```

# Implementing Snapshot, Merge, and Transactional Replication

Data replication allows you to distribute data from a source database to one or more destination databases. The source and destination databases can be on computers running different instances of Microsoft SQL Server or on other database systems as long as an OLE DB provider is available for each destination database. You have precise control over when replication occurs, what data is replicated, and how other aspects of replication are handled. For example, you can configure replication to happen continuously or periodically. Before we examine how to implement replication, let's look at why you would want to use replication and review the main concepts it involves.

## An Overview of Replication

You use replication to copy data on one server and distribute it to other servers. You can also use replication to copy data, transform it, and then distribute the customized data to multiple servers. You generally use replication when you need to manage data on multiple servers on a recurring basis. If you need to create a copy of a database just once, you do not need replication—instead you should copy the database as discussed in "Tips and Techniques" on page 223 or in "Restoring a Database to a Different Location" on page 558." If you need to copy and transform data from one server to another server, you do not need replication either; instead, you should use the import and export procedure discussed in Chapter 11, "Importing, Exporting, and Transforming Data." Some reasons to use replication include

- To synchronize changes to remote databases with a central database. For example, if the sales team uses remote laptops, you might need to create a copy of data for its sales region on the laptops. Later, a salesperson in the field might add information or make changes when she is disconnected from the network. By using replication, these modifications can be synchronized with the central database.

■ To create multiple instances of a database so that you can distribute the workload. For example, if you have a central database that is updated regularly, you might want to push changes out to departmental databases as they occur. Employees can then access data through these departmental databases instead of trying to connect to the central database.

■ To move specific data sets from a central server and distribute them to several other servers. For example, you would use replication if you had a central database and needed to distribute sales data to all the databases in your company's department stores.

■ To customize data and distribute it to multiple subscribers. For example, if your company sold subscriptions to your consumer credit database, you could replicate the data for subscribers, customizing the data for each subscriber.

Replication is designed to meet the needs of a wide variety of environments. Replication architecture is divided into several different processes, procedures, and components, each of which is used to customize replication for a particular situation. The replication architecture includes the following items:

■ **Replication components**   The server and data components used in replication

■ **Replication agents**   Applications that assist in the replication process

■ **Replication variants**   The types of replication you can configure

## Replication Components

Before working with replication, you need to know the main components of the process and how you use them. Servers in the replication model can have one or more of the following roles:

■ **Publisher**   Publishers are servers that make data available for replication to other servers. Publishers also track changes to data and maintain other information about source databases. Each data grouping has only one publisher.

■ **Distributor**   Distributors are servers that distribute replicated data. Distributors store the *distribution* database, metadata, historical data, and (for transactional replication) transactions.

■ **Subscriber**   Subscribers are the destination servers for replication. These servers store the replicated data and receive updates. Subscribers can also make changes to data. You can publish data to multiple subscribers.

The data being published for replication is referred to as *articles* and *publications*. Articles are the basic units for replication and can consist of a table, a subset of a table, or other database objects. Publications are collections of articles that subscribers can receive. You should associate articles with a publication and then publish the publication. Articles can contain

- An entire table
- Only certain columns from a table, obtained by using a vertical filter
- Only certain rows from a table, obtained by using a horizontal filter
- A table subset containing certain rows and columns
- A view, indexed view, or user-defined function
- A stored procedure

You can also specify whether schema objects are replicated. Schema objects include constraints, indexes, triggers, collation, and extended properties. When you alter tables, views, procedures, functions, or triggers using data definition language (DDL) statements such as ALTER TABLE or ALTER VIEW on a published object, the changes are propagated by default to all SQL Server subscribers. You cannot publish any of the following for replication:

- The *model*, *tempdb*, and *msdb* databases
- System tables in the *master* database

In the publication and subscription model, setting up replication involves the following steps:

1. Selecting a replication type and model
2. Performing any necessary preliminary tasks
3. Configuring a distributor, and enabling publishers and *publication* databases
4. Creating a publication
5. Creating subscriptions to the publication, and designating subscribers

## Replication Agents and Jobs

SQL Server uses various helper applications to assist in the replication process. These applications are called *replication agents*:

- **Snapshot Agent (snapshot.exe)**   Creates snapshots of data. It includes schema and data, which are stored for distribution. The Snapshot Agent is also responsible for updating status information in the *distribution* database. The Snapshot Agent runs on the distributor. Each published database has its own Snapshot Agent that runs on the distributor and connects to the publisher. Snapshot Agents are used with all types of replication.

- **Distribution Agent (distrib.exe)**   Applies data from snapshot replication or transactions from transaction replication to subscribers. The Distribution Agent can run on the distributor or on subscribers. It runs on the distributor for push subscriptions and on the subscriber for pull subscriptions. This agent is not used with merge replication. (Push and pull subscriptions are discussed in "Subscribing to a Publication" on page 478.)

- **Merge Agent (replmerg.exe)**   Synchronizes changes that occur after the initial snapshot is created. If any conflicts occur when the changes are being synchronized, the conflicts are resolved using the rules set with the conflict resolver. Depending on the configuration, Merge Agents run on the publisher or on subscribers. Merge Agents are used only with merge replication.

- **Log Reader Agent (logread.exe)**   Moves transactions marked for replication from the transaction log on the publisher to the distributor. Each database that is published using transactional replication has its own Log Reader Agent that runs on the distributor and connects to the publisher. Log Reader Agents are used only with transactional replication.

- **Queue Reader Agent (qrdrsvc.exe)**   Stores database changes in a queue where the updates can be asynchronously propagated to the publisher. This allows subscribers to modify published data and synchronize those changes without having an active network connection to the publisher. Queue Reader Agents are used only with transactional replication with the queued updating option.

SQL Server 2008 does not have a separate cleanup agent. Instead, the following replication maintenance jobs are used to perform cleanup tasks:

- **Agent History Clean Up: *DistributionDBName***   Removes replication agent history from the *distribution* database. By default, this runs every 10 minutes.

- **Distribution Clean Up: *DistributionDBName***   Deactivates subscriptions that have not been synchronized within the maximum distribution-retention period, and removes replicated transactions from the *distribution* database. By default, this runs every 10 minutes.

- **Expired Subscription Clean Up**   Removes expired subscriptions from *publication* databases. By default, this runs every day at 1:00 A.M.

- **Reinitialize Subscriptions Having Data Validation Failures**   Flags all subscriptions that have data validation failures. The next time the Merge Agent or Distribution Agent runs, a new snapshot is applied at the subscriber. By default, this job is not enabled.

- **Replication Agents Checkup**   Detects replication agents that are not actively logging history, and writes an error to the Microsoft Windows event logs if a job step fails. By default, this runs every 10 minutes.

- **Replication Monitoring Refresher For *DistributionDBName***   Refreshes cached queries used by the Replication Monitor. By default, this starts automatically when SQL Server Agent starts and runs continuously.

## Replication Variants

SQL Server supports several types of replication:

- **Snapshot replication**   Takes a snapshot of current data, and replaces the entire copy of the data on one or more subscribers. With subsequent snapshots, the entire copy of the data is again distributed to subscribers. Although exact copies are a benefit of snapshot replication, this technique increases the amount of overhead and traffic on the network. Another disadvantage of snapshot replication is that it runs only periodically, which usually means that subscribers do not have the most current information.

  In SQL Server 2008, snapshot preparation has been enhanced to allow processing of multiple articles while scripting schema or bulk copying data. This technique, referred to as *parallel processing*, is used automatically when possible. SQL Server 2008 also features resumable snapshot delivery, which allows an interrupted snapshot delivery to be resumed automatically. When the delivery is resumed, only files that have not been transferred or were partially transferred are transferred—any snapshot files that have been completely transferred are not retransferred.

- **Transactional replication**   Uses transactions to distribute changes, primarily in server-to-server environments. When replication starts, a snapshot of the data is sent to subscribers. After the snapshot is sent, selected transactions in the publisher's transaction log are marked for replication and then distributed to each subscriber separately. Snapshots are then taken periodically to ensure that the databases are synchronized. Distributed transactions are used to ensure that incremental changes are applied consistently.

  A benefit of transactional replication is that you replicate individual transactions rather than an entire data set. Transactional replication can also occur continuously or periodically, which makes the procedure more versatile than snapshot replication by itself. To allow for easier implementation of transactional replication of large databases, SQL Server 2008 allows you to initialize a transactional subscription from backup. Thus, rather than using a snapshot to initialize a subscription, you can restore any backup taken after the creation of the publication on a subscriber. SQL Server 2008 also creates concurrent snapshots whenever possible to reduce the amount of time that locks are held during snapshot generation. This limits the impact on users that are working with the database while the snapshot is being generated.

- **Merge replication**   Allows subscribers to make changes to replicated data independently, and primarily in a server-to-client environment. Later, you can merge these changes into all the related source and destination databases. The snapshots needed to initialize merge replication can be pregenerated for each subscriber, or you can specify that subscribers can initiate snapshot generation during the initial synchronization. Merge replication does not use distributed transactions and cannot guarantee transactional consistency. Instead, merge replication uses a conflict resolver to determine which changes are applied. By default, merge replication processes changes on a row-by-row basis. You can also group sets of related rows as a logical record. This ensures that related sets of records are always processed in their entirety at the same time on a subscriber.

SQL Server 2008 provides article-level statistics during merge replication. This feature provides better tracking of the merge phase and also allows you to define the order of article processing during merge synchronization. This technique, referred to as *declarative ordering*, is useful if you use triggers or rely on triggers firing in a specific order.

In snapshot and transactional replication, subscribers normally do not change data. However, with transactional replication, you have several options for allowing subscribers to change data:

- **Immediate updating**   Allows subscribers to make changes and then immediately update the publisher. The publisher then replicates these changes to other subscribers.

- **Queued updating**   Allows subscribers to make changes and then store the changes in a queue until they can be applied to the publisher. The publisher then replicates the changes to other subscribers. Immediate and queued updating is supported only in snapshot and transactional publications.

Queued updating provides fault tolerance that might be needed when databases are geographically separated. Immediate updating requires an active connection to the publisher, but queued updating does not. By using queued updating, subscribers can asynchronously apply changes, which means that they can store changes when a link is inactive, and then when the link is active, they can submit the changes to the publisher.

You can also use immediate updating with queued updating as a failover method when you expect publishers and subscribers to be connected but do not want to lose the ability to make updates if a link fails. Here, you configure both updating options, using immediate updating as the primary update mechanism and then switching to queued updating when needed. You can invoke failover at any time. However, you cannot fail back afterward until the subscriber and publisher are connected and the Queue Reader Agent has applied all pending updates in the queue.

Both immediate updating and queued updating use transactions and the standard two-phase commit process to apply updates to the publisher. Transactions ensure that the update can be committed if it is successfully applied or rolled back if there is a problem. The transactions are applied from a specific subscriber to the publisher. After changes are made to the publisher, the publisher replicates the changes to other subscribers.

Transactions are completed automatically through the update process and are managed by the Distributed Transaction Coordinator (DTC). Custom applications that modify subscriber data can be written as though they were updating a single database. In a standard (default) configuration, updates to the subscriber are applied only when they can be replicated through a transaction. If the update cannot be replicated through a transaction, the subscriber will not be able to modify the subscription data.

SQL Server detects subscriber changes that would conflict with changes on the publisher. If it detects a conflict, it rejects the transaction and does not allow the data changes. Usually, a rejection means that the subscriber needs to synchronize with the publisher before attempting to update the data locally.

When you include stored procedures as articles in a snapshot publication, SQL Server replicates the entire stored procedure from the publisher to the subscribers. Changes caused by the execution of the stored procedures are replicated with new snapshots. If you use transactional replication, however, you can replicate execution of the stored procedure instead of replicating the changes that the execution causes. By sending an execute command rather than data changes, you reduce the amount of data that needs to flow across the network and improve the performance of SQL applications that use replication.

If you replicate the execution of stored procedures, you have two configuration settings. You can use *standard* procedure execution, or you can use *serialized* procedure execution. With standard procedure execution, procedure execution is replicated to all subscribers, even if those procedures are executed in different transactions. Because multiple transactions might be executing at a particular time, subscribers' data cannot be guaranteed to be consistent with the publisher's data. With serialized stored procedures, procedures are executed in sequence if they are referenced within serialized transactions. If the procedures are executed outside of serialized transactions, changes to the data are replicated instead. This behavior guarantees that the subscribers' data is consistent with the publisher's data.

# Planning for Replication

As you have learned, the architecture for the replication process is extensive. This ensures that the architecture is versatile enough to meet the needs of almost any replication situation. Unfortunately, this versatility also makes replication tricky to configure. To make the replication go smoothly, you should do a bit of planning, which involves selecting a specific replication model and performing any necessary preliminary tasks before you start configuring replication.

## Replication Models

The main decision to make when you select a replication model involves the physical layout of the publisher, distributor, and subscriber databases. Replication models you might want to use include

- **Peer-to-peer model**   Allows replication between identical participants in the topology. The advantage of this model is that it permits roles to move between replicated nodes dynamically for maintenance or failure management. The disadvantage is the additional administration overhead involved with moving roles.

- **Central publisher model**   Maintains the publisher and distributor databases on the same server, with one or more subscribers configured on other servers. The advantages of this model are manageability and ease of maintenance. The disadvantages include the extra workload and resource usage on the publication server.

  > **Tip**   The central publisher model is the most commonly used replication model. Unfortunately, you will often find that the extra load on the publication server slows down server performance. To reduce the server load, you should put the distributor on its own server. Be aware, however, that doing this will not entirely eliminate the workload on the publication server. The publisher and distributor still need to communicate, and they still need to pass data back and forth.

- **Central publisher with remote distributor model**   Maintains the publisher and distributor databases on different servers, with one or more subscribers configured on other servers. The advantage of this model is that the workload is more evenly distributed. The disadvantage is that you have to maintain an additional server.

- **Central subscriber model**   A single subscriber database that collects data from several publishers. For example, if you have ServerA, ServerB, and ServerC, ServerA and ServerB act as central publishers and ServerC acts as the central subscriber. In this configuration, when updates are distributed from ServerA and ServerB, they are collected on ServerC. A central subscriber can then republish the combined data to other servers. To use this model, all tables used in replication must have a unique primary key; otherwise, the replication model will not work properly.

- **Publishing subscriber model**   Relays the distribution of data to other subscribers; you can use this with any of the other models. For example, if you have two geographically separated sites, a publisher can replicate data to servers at site A and then have a publishing subscriber at site B that distributes the data to servers at site B.

## Preliminary Replication Tasks

After selecting the replication type and model you want to use, you prepare for the replication by performing preliminary tasks. The following sections describe the main tasks involved, according to replication type.

## Preparing for Snapshot Replication

If you use snapshot replication, the data being replicated is copied in full to data files on the distributor. Normally, these snapshot files are the same size as the data you are replicating, and they are stored in the SQL Server Repldata folder by default. You should make sure that the drive on which the replication data is stored has adequate free space. For example, if you are using snapshot replication to distribute publication A with 500 MB of data, publication B with 420 MB, and publication C with 900 MB, you should have at least 2 GB of free space. Some of the free space is needed for processing overhead; the rest is required for the actual data.

You can also store snapshot data in an alternate location where subscribers can retrieve it at a later time. If you use an alternate location, you have the option of compressing the snapshot file, which reduces the disk space requirements only for the files you are compressing. It does not change the overall space requirements, and it does not always reduce the initial and final space requirements. With compression, the Snapshot Agent generates the necessary data files and then uses the Microsoft CAB utility to compress the files. When the subscriber receives compressed snapshot files, the files are written to a temporary location, which is either the default client working directory or an alternate location specified in the subscription properties. The subscriber uses the CAB utility to decompress the files before reading them.

> **Real World**    When you create snapshot files in the default location and in an alternate location on different drives, the files are created separately. This means that the total disk space required typically is what you would expect, based on the size of the files. However, when you create snapshot files in the default location and in an alternate location on the same drive, both files are initially created in the default location and then the alternate location file is copied to its final destination. This means that the total disk space required in the default location is twice what you might expect. Compression does not help, because the Snapshot Agent generates the necessary data files and then compresses them.

Replication timing is another important consideration in snapshot replication. When the Snapshot Agent creates a snapshot of a published table, the agent locks the entire table while it bulk copies the data from the publisher to the distributor. As a result, users cannot update any data in the table until the lock is released. To reduce the impact on operations, you should carefully schedule when replication occurs. Some actions that might help include

- Identifying times when operations are at their lowest levels or users do not need write access to the tables you are replicating

- Identifying times when snapshots must be made and scheduling users to do work during that time that does not require write access to the tables you are replicating

SQL Server 2008 processes multiple articles while scripting schema or bulk copying data. This parallel processing can increase the speed and efficiency of the snapshot generation process. SQL Server 2008 also features resumable snapshot delivery, which allows an interrupted snapshot delivery to be automatically resumed. When the delivery is resumed, only files that have not been transferred yet or have been transferred partially are transferred—any snapshot files that have been completely transferred already are not retransferred.

### Preparing for Transactional Replication

Because transactional replication builds on the snapshot replication model, you will want to prepare for both snapshot and transactional replication. When you use transactional replication, an initial snapshot is sent to the distributor, and this snapshot is then updated on a periodic basis, such as once a month. Between snapshots, transactions are used to update subscribers. These transactions are logged in the distributor's database and are cleared out only after a new snapshot is created.

Transaction logs for published databases are extremely important to successful replication. As long as replication is enabled, pending transactions cannot be cleared out of a published database until they have been passed to the distributor. Because of this, you might need to increase the size of a published database's transaction log. Furthermore, if the publisher cannot contact the distributor, or if the Log Reader Agent is not running, transactions will continue to build up in the publisher's transaction logs.

With transactional replication, all published tables must have a declared primary key. You can add a primary key to an existing table using the ALTER TABLE statement. (See Chapter 10, "Manipulating Schemas, Tables, Indexes, and Views.") Additionally, if a publication uses very large data types, you must make sure that you keep the following limitations in mind:

- When updating varchar(max), nvarchar(max), and varbinary(max) data types, you should use the WRITE clause of the UPDATE statement to perform a partial or full update. If you are performing a partial update of a varchar(max) column, you might update the first 100 characters of a column. If you are performing a full update, you might modify all the data in a column. @Offset and @Length values for the WRITE clause are specified in bytes for varbinary(max) and varchar(max) data types and in characters for the nvarchar(max) data type.

  **Tip** For best performance, you should insert or update data in multiples of 8040 bytes, which ensures the data is written using whole data pages. Any WRITE updates that insert or append new data are minimally logged when the database recovery model is set to Simple or Bulk Logged. Minimal logging is not used when you update existing values.

- When modifying text, ntext, or image data types, UPDATE initializes the column, assigns a valid text pointer to it, and allocates at least one data page unless the column is being updated with NULL. If you need to replace or modify large blocks of text, ntext, or image data, Microsoft recommends that you use WRITE-TEXT or UPDATETEXT instead of the UPDATE statement. However, support for WRITETEXT and UPDATETEXT is deprecated and might be removed in future versions of SQL Server.

■ The SQL Server configuration option MAX TEXT REPL SIZE controls the maximum byte size of the text and image data that can be replicated. Operations that exceed this limit will fail. Set the maximum text replication size with the sp_configure system stored procedure.

The snapshot process can be modified for transactional replication in several important ways. To allow for easier implementation of transactional replication of large databases, SQL Server 2008 allows you to initialize a transactional subscription from backup. Thus, rather than using a snapshot to initialize a subscription, you can restore on a subscriber any backup taken after the creation of the publication. SQL Server 2008 also creates concurrent snapshots whenever possible to reduce the amount of time that locks are held during snapshot generation. This limits the impact on users that are working with the database while the snapshot is being generated.

### Preparing for Merge Replication

For merge replication, all published tables must have primary keys. If a table contains foreign keys or is used in validation, you must include the reference table in the publication. Otherwise, update operations that add new rows will fail because SQL Server cannot find the required primary key. Additionally, merge replication affects time-stamp column usage. Time stamps are generated automatically and are guaranteed to be unique only in a specific database. Because of this, SQL Server replicates time-stamp columns but does not replicate the literal time-stamp values contained in the columns. These values are regenerated when the initial snapshot rows are applied at the subscriber.

Like transactional replication, merge replication has a few limitations when it comes to text and image columns. For example, you must explicitly update text and image columns with an UPDATE statement. When using merge replication, subscribers can make changes to replicated data independently, and these changes can be merged into all of the related source and destination databases. The Merge Agent watches for changes that conflict with other changes. If it detects a conflict, a conflict resolver is used to determine which change is applied and which change is rolled back. The Merge Agent can track changes at a column level or at a row level. In column-level tracking, a conflict exists when changes are made to the same column in a table in more than one copy. In row-level tracking, a conflict exists when changes are made to the same row in a table in more than one copy.

Normally, subscribers to merge publications synchronize updates only with the publisher. Subscribers can also synchronize with other servers, and they do this by designating alternate synchronization partners. It is useful to have an alternate synchronization partner when you want to ensure that updates can be made even if the primary publisher is offline or otherwise unavailable.

> **Note**   By default, merge replication processes changes on a row-by-row basis. You can group sets of related rows as a logical record. This ensures that related sets of records are always processed in their entirety at the same time on a subscriber. You can also use declarative ordering to define the order of article processing during merge synchronization.

# Distributor Administration

As the name indicates, you use distributors to distribute replicated data. When you work with distributors, the core set of administration tasks you will perform includes setting up new distributors, enabling publishers, enabling *publication* databases, updating existing distributors, and deleting distributors.

## Setting Up a New Distributor

Setting up a new distributor is the first major step in configuring replication. Before you get started, you should prepare as follows:

- Select a replication type—either snapshot, transactional, or merge.

- Select a replication model, such as the central publisher model.

- Perform any necessary preliminary tasks. To meet certain limitations, you might need to update clients and applications that modify published databases directly.

When you are ready to proceed, configure the distributor by completing the following steps:

1. Start SQL Server Management Studio. In the Object Explorer view, connect to the server you want to use, and then work your way down to the Replication folder.

   > **Tip**   If you cannot successfully connect to a remote server, the server might not be configured to accept remote connections. As discussed in Chapter 3, "Managing the Surface Security, Access, and Network Configuration," you will need to use the SQL Server 2008 Surface Area Configuration tool to allow remote connections.

2. Right-click the Replication folder, and then select Configure Distribution. This starts the Configure Distribution Wizard.

3. Click Next to move past the Welcome screen. On the Distributor page of the wizard, you can select a distributor, as shown in Figure 13-1.

**Figure 13-1**   The Configure Distribution Wizard.

4. Because you want to set up a new distributor, accept the default to allow the current server to act as its own distributor and then click Next.

5. If SQL Server Agent isn't already started and configured to start automatically, you'll see the SQL Server Agent Start page. Select Yes, Configure The SQL Server Agent Service To Start Automatically and then click Next.

6. On the Snapshot Folder page, set the location of the folder used to store snapshots and then click Next. The default path is to the %*ProgramFiles*%\Microsoft SQL Server\MSSQL10.MSSQLSERVER\MSSQL\ReplData folder on the server designated as the distributor. To guarantee that Distribution and Merge agents running on subscribers can access snapshots of their push and pull subscriptions, you must place the snapshot folder on a network share and specify the network path by typing it in the text box provided, such as \\**CorpSvr09\ReplData**.

   **Tip**   Because the wizard cannot validate the path you enter, you should ensure the path is correct before continuing.

7. On the Distribution Database page, provide information for the *distribution* database as shown in Figure 13-2. Enter a name for the *distribution* database, and then set folder locations for the corresponding data and log files. Click Next when you are ready to continue.

**Tip**    You cannot use mapped network drives as folder locations for the data and log files.

**Note**    Be sure to use a descriptive name for the database, such as EmployeeDistribution or EmpDistr.

**Figure 13-2**    The Distribution Database page of the Configure Distribution Wizard.

8. As shown in Figure 13-3, you need to enable publishers for this *distribution* database. Only registered servers in the current domain are shown. If you want to add a server so that it can use this distributor when it becomes a publisher, click Add, and then do the following:

- ❑ Choose Add SQL Server Publisher to configure a connection to an instance of SQL Server using the Connect To Server dialog box. Registered servers are listed in the Server Name drop-down list, and you can browse for others. The default authentication is Windows Authentication, which uses your current login and password. Click Connect.

- ❑ Choose Add Oracle Publisher to configure a connection to an Oracle server using the Connect To Server dialog box. Registered servers are listed in the Server Name drop-down list, and you can browse for others. The default authentication is Oracle Standard Authentication, which requires a user login and password. Click Connect.

**Figure 13-3**   The Publishers page of the Configure Distribution Wizard.

9. To the right of registered publisher entries, you will see the Properties button
   (...). Click this button to open the Properties dialog box to set publisher options
   for the related server. As Figure 13-4 shows, the following options are available:

   ❑ **Agent Connection Mode**   Distributors use SQL Server Agent to handle
   replication tasks. SQL Server Agent must be configured to start automatically. By default, synchronization agents log in to the publishers using the
   SQL Server Agent account (determined by selecting the Impersonate The
   Agent Process Account option). If you want synchronization agents to use
   a specific login when connecting to publishers, select SQL Server Authentication from the drop-down list, and then enter the login and password
   to use.

   ❑ **Default Snapshot Folder**   Sets the location of the folder used to store
   snapshots. The Snapshot folder is stored on the *distribution* database and
   can be in a different location for each publisher that uses the *distribution*
   database.

10. Click Next. If you specified a remote server as a possible publisher, you next
    must specify and confirm the password that remote publishers will use to con-
    nect to the distributor. This password must be provided when a remote pub-
    lisher connects to the distributor to perform replication administrative
    operations. The password must meet the Windows policy requirements for
    length and complexity. Click Next.

**Figure 13-4**   The Publisher Properties dialog box.

11. By default, the wizard will configure the distributor immediately when you click Finish. If you would rather have the wizard generate a script that you can run at a later time or can schedule to be run, clear the Configure Distribution check box and select the Generate A Script File check box.

12. Click Next, and then click Finish. The wizard will configure the distributor or generate the script according to the option you specified. The success or failure of each step is shown in the related dialog box. If a step fails, click the link provided to display the error details. Click Close.

When you establish a server as a distributor, many areas of the server are updated. You might note that there is a new *distribution* database; additional jobs, alerts, and proxies for replication can now be listed, and other updates might be evident. The Replication Monitor tool also becomes available. To learn how to work with this SQL Server feature, see Chapter 14, "Profiling and Monitoring Microsoft SQL Server 2008."

Configure publications and subscriptions as explained in "Enabling and Updating Publishers" on page 463, "Enabling Publication Databases" on page 464, and "Creating Subscriptions" on page 479.

## Updating Distributors

When you configure a new distributor, you can set up a new *distribution* database, as discussed in "Setting Up a New Distributor" on page 456. If you have already configured a distributor, you can update the distributor and create additional *distribution* databases by completing the following steps:

1. Start SQL Server Management Studio. In the Object Explorer view, connect to the server you want to use, and then work your way down to the Replication folder.

2. Right-click the Replication folder, and then select Distributor Properties. This opens the dialog box shown in Figure 13-5.

**Figure 13-5**   The Distributor Properties dialog box.

3. You can use the options in the dialog box to change publisher and distributor data properties for the currently selected distributor. Use the Select A Page options in the left pane as follows:

   ❑ **General**   Configure *distribution* databases, agent profiles, and properties for retention and queuing.

   ❑ **Publishers**   Enable and disable publishers for the distributor, set publisher properties, and configure passwords for administrative links.

4. On the General page, you will see a list of current *distribution* databases and their settings for transaction and history retention. By default, new *distribution* databases store transactions only as long as they are needed—determined by the retention setting of at least zero (0) hours—but not for more than 72 hours, and they retain replication performance history data for at least 48 hours.

5. To view the current location of database and log files for a selected *distribution* database or change the retention settings, click the Properties button (...) in the

third column to right of the database name. This displays the Distribution Database Properties dialog box shown in Figure 13-6. Use the text boxes and options provided to manage the retention settings as necessary. Click OK when you are finished to apply the changes.

**Figure 13-6** The Distribution Database Properties dialog box.

6. On the Publishers page, you will see a list of current publishers for this distributor and the *distribution* databases they use. A check mark next to a publisher's name indicates that the publisher is enabled.

7. Click OK to close the dialog box and apply any changes.

## Creating Distribution Databases

Distribution databases are used to store the information being distributed to subscribers. Each publisher that uses a distributor is assigned a *distribution* database to which it can connect. Publishers can share *distribution* databases, and you also can create additional databases as necessary. If you have already configured a distributor, you can create additional *distribution* databases by completing the following steps:

1. Start SQL Server Management Studio. In the Object Explorer view, connect to the server you want to use, and then work your way down to the Replication folder.

2. Right-click the Replication folder, and then select Distributor Properties. This opens the dialog box shown previously in Figure 13-5.

3. On the General page, click New. You can now configure the *distribution* database.

4. Enter a name for the *distribution* database, and then set folder locations for the corresponding data and log files. You cannot use mapped network drives.

5. Use the options in the Transaction Retention and History Retention columns to determine how long transactions and performance history are retained for the *distribution* database.

6. Click OK twice to close the open dialog boxes and create the *distribution* database.

You can assign the new *distribution* database to any new publishers you configure.

## Enabling and Updating Publishers

Distributors can work only with servers and databases that are enabled for their use. You can enable publishers when you create a new distributor or by completing the following steps:

1. Start SQL Server Management Studio. In the Object Explorer view, connect to the server you want to use, and then work your way down to the Replication folder.

2. Right-click the Replication folder, and then select Distributor Properties.

3. In the Distributor Properties dialog box, select the Publishers page. Use the check boxes provided to enable or disable publishers. Only registered publishers are shown. If you want to add a server so that it can use this distributor when it becomes a publisher, click Add and then do the following:

    ❑ Choose Add SQL Server Publisher to configure a connection to an instance of SQL Server using the Connect To Server dialog box. Registered servers are listed in the Server Name drop-down list, and you can browse for others. The default authentication is Windows Authentication, which uses your current login and password. Click Connect. If there is more than one *distribution* database available, the Distribution Database box will have a drop-down list allowing you to choose the database to use.

    ❑ Choose Add Oracle Publisher to configure a connection to an Oracle server using the Connect To Server dialog box. Registered servers are listed in the Server Name drop-down list, and you can browse for others. The default authentication is Oracle Standard Authentication, which requires a user login and password. Click Connect. If there is more than one *distribution* database available, the Distribution Database box will have a drop-down list allowing you to choose the database to use.

4. To the right of the registered publisher entries, you will see the Properties button (...). Click this button to set publisher options for the related server. The following options are available:

   ❑ **Agent Connection Mode** Distributors use SQL Server Agent to handle replication tasks. SQL Server Agent must be configured to start automatically. By default, synchronization agents log in to the publishers using the SQL Server Agent account (determined by selecting the Impersonate The Agent Process Account option). If you want synchronization agents to use a specific login when connecting to publishers, select SQL Server Authentication in this box, and then enter the login and password to use. (This is the Administrative Link Password, which also can be set by selecting the publisher on the Publishers page, and then using the boxes and options provided in the lower-right area of the dialog box.)

   ❑ **Default Snapshot Folder** Sets the location of the folder used to store snapshots. The Snapshot folder is stored on the *distribution* database and can be in a different location for each publisher that uses the *distribution* database.

## Enabling Publication Databases

After you configure distributors and publishers, you can enable publication databases by completing the following steps:

1. Start SQL Server Management Studio. In the Object Explorer view, connect to the server you want to use, and then work your way down to the Replication folder.

2. Right-click the Replication folder, and then select Publisher Properties. This opens the Publisher Properties dialog box.

3. To enable *publication* databases, select the Publication Databases page. Then select entries under the Transactional column to enable a database for snapshot or transactional replication, or select entries under the Merge column to enable a database for merge replication.

4. To enable a *publication* database for any type of replication, select both the corresponding Transactional and Merge check boxes.

## Deleting Distribution Databases

Before you can delete a *distribution* database, you must remove all publications and disable all the publishers using the *distribution* database. After you have done this, you can delete *distribution* databases by completing the following steps:

1. Start SQL Server Management Studio. In the Object Explorer view, connect to the server you want to use, and then work your way down to the Replication folder.

2. Right-click the Replication folder, and then select Distributor Properties. This opens the Distributor Properties dialog box.

3. On the General page, select the *distribution* database you want to delete and then click Delete.

4. Click OK to close the dialog box and perform the delete operation.

## Disabling Publishing and Distribution

By using the Disable Publishing And Distribution Wizard in SQL Server Management Studio, you can disable publishing and distribution. When you disable publishing

- All publications on the selected server are dropped.
- All subscriptions to the affected publications are dropped.
- The server is disabled as a distributor.

You can disable publishing and distribution by completing the following steps:

1. Start SQL Server Management Studio. In the Object Explorer view, connect to the server you want to use, and then work your way down to the Replication folder.

2. Right-click the Replication folder, and then select Disable Publishing And Distribution. This starts the Disable Publishing And Distribution Wizard.

3. Click Next to skip the Welcome screen, and then choose Yes, Disable Publishing On This Server.

4. Click Next. Review the publishers that will be disabled.

5. Click Next and then click Finish.

# Creating and Managing Publications

After you have configured a distributor and enabled publishers, *publication* databases, and subscribers, you can create publications. You will manage the publications you create as you would any other SQL Server resource.

## Creating Publications

The easiest way to create publications is by using SQL Server Management Studio. To do this, complete the following steps:

1. Start SQL Server Management Studio. In the Object Explorer view, connect to the server you want to use, and then work your way down to the Replication folder.

2. Right-click the Local Publications folder, and then select New Publication. This starts the New Publication Wizard. Click Next to skip the Welcome screen.

> **Note**  If you want to create an Oracle publication, select New Oracle Publication. This starts the New Oracle Publication Wizard, which is similar to the New Publication Wizard.

3. Choose the database on the selected server that contains the data or objects you want to publish. You can select user databases only. Click Next.

4. Choose the type of replication you want to use for the publication:

   ❏ **Snapshot Publication**  Creates a publication setup for snapshot replication

   ❏ **Transactional Publication**  Creates a publication setup for transactional replication

   ❏ **Transactional Publication With Updatable Subscriptions**  Creates a publication setup for transactional replication with subscriptions that can be updated

   ❏ **Merge Publication**  Creates a publication setup for merge replication

5. If you are creating a snapshot or transactional publication, continue using the steps listed in "Snapshot and Transactional Publications" below.

6. If you are creating a merge publication, continue using the steps listed in "Merge Publications" on page 470.

### Snapshot and Transactional Publications

Snapshot and transactional publications are the most commonly used types of publications. With snapshot publications, the publisher periodically replaces subscriber data with an updated snapshot. With transactional publications, the publisher updates data and changes are sent to subscribers through transactions.

After you have started a new publication as discussed in "Creating Publications" on the preceding page, you can create a snapshot or transactional publication by completing the following steps:

1. Click Next to continue. On the Articles page, shown in Figure 13-7, select the objects for replication. The Objects To Publish pane shows the types of objects that are available for replication. Click the plus sign (+) next to the object to see a list of available objects of the specified type.

2. To select all the columns in a table or view, select the table or view name entry. Which objects are available depends on the types of objects in the database and can include tables, stored procedures, user-defined functions, and views. Tables without primary keys cannot be published for transactional replication, and you will see a key surrounded by a red circle with a line through it in the Specify Articles dialog box. Additionally, tables referenced by views are required.

**Figure 13-7**   The Articles page of the New Publication Wizard.

3. To select individual columns in a table or view, expand the table or view entry and then select the appropriate entries for the columns to include. If you are using transactional replication and selecting individual columns, keep in mind that primary key columns are required and must be published. Primary key columns are indicated by a key with a green asterisk. By clearing a column check box, you exclude the related column from replication (which was previously referred to as vertically filtering a table).

4. Default properties are set for each selected object (article), including the destination object name and object owner, action to use if the object exists, and whether user triggers and extended properties should be copied. You can manage these default properties by setting global defaults, by setting defaults for an individual article, or both:

   ❑ To set defaults for an individual article, select it under Objects To Publish, click Article Properties, and then select Set Properties Of Highlighted...Article. Refer to "Setting Publication Properties" on page 474 for details.

   ❑ To set defaults for all articles of a particular type, select the object type under Objects To Publish, click Article Properties, and then select Set Properties Of All...Articles. Refer to "Setting Publication Properties" for details.

5. After you select objects to use in the publication, click Next. If there are any issues that require changes to the publication, you will see a prompt similar to the one shown in Figure 13-8. Read the description carefully to determine how to

resolve the issue, and make changes as necessary. Some important issues that might be described in a prompt include the following:

❏ Tables referenced by views are required and so are objects referenced by stored procedures. If you do not select referenced tables or objects, you must create them manually at the subscriber.

❏ SQL Server adds uniqueidentifier columns to any tables you have selected for replication. Adding a uniqueidentifier column will cause INSERT statements without column lists to fail and will increase the time needed to generate the first snapshot.

❏ IDENTITY columns require the NOT FOR REPLICATION option. If a published IDENTITY column does not use this option, INSERT commands might not replicate properly.

**Figure 13-8** Article Issues page of the New Publication Wizard.

6. Click Next. By default, all rows are published. If you want to filter your data, you can use the Filter Table Rows page to exclude unwanted rows from published tables. As you define filters, they are added to the Filtered Tables list. Selecting a filter shows the related WHERE clause in the Filter box. When a filter is selected, you can click Edit to modify the settings or click Delete to delete the filter. To define a new filter, click Add to display the Add Filter dialog box shown in Figure 13-9. Select a table to filter and then create a filter statement that identifies which rows subscribers will receive. Enter a WHERE clause for the corresponding SELECT *published_columns* FROM *TableName* statement. Click OK to close the Add Filter dialog box and return to the Filter Table Rows page.

**Figure 13-9**   The Add Filter dialog box.

7. Click Next. The Snapshot Agent initializes subscriptions by creating a snapshot of publication schema and data that can be pushed to subscribers or pulled by subscribers. You can create a snapshot immediately by selecting Create A Snapshot Immediately. If you want the Snapshot Agent to create snapshots periodically, select Schedule The Snapshot Agent To Run. By default, snapshots are made every day at one-hour intervals. To change this schedule, click Change and then set a new schedule.

8. Click Next. Set a login for each agent used in replication, which can include the Snapshot, Log Reader, and Queue Reader agents. To configure the login for the Snapshot Agent, click the related Security Settings button and then do the following:

   ❑ Specify the Windows account under which the agent runs at the distributor. This account is referred to as the process account. The account must be a member of the db_owner fixed database role in the *distribution* database and must have write permissions on the snapshot share. Be sure to type domain account names in the form *domain\account*, such as **cpandl\ sqlserver**. Then type and confirm the account password.

   ❑ Specify whether the agent should make connections to the publisher by impersonating the account specified in the Process Account text box or by using a SQL Server account. If you choose to use a SQL Server account, enter a SQL Server login and password. Typically, you will want to impersonate the Windows account rather than use a SQL Server account.

9. The Log Reader Agent is used with updatable and nonupdatable transactional publications. By default, the Log Reader Agent uses the same login as the Snapshot Agent. To specify separate security settings for the Log Reader Agent, clear the Use The Security Settings From The Snapshot Agent check box, and then click the related Security Settings button. You can then specify the process account and how connections to the publisher are made.

10. The Queue Reader Agent is used with updatable transactional publications. By default, the Queue Reader Agent has a separate security context from the other agents. To configure security, click the related Security Settings button and then specify the process account.

11. Click Next. Choose the wizard action upon completion. By default, the wizard creates the publication. You can also generate a script file with the steps to create the publication. If you want to only generate a script, clear Create The Publication. Click Next.

12. On the Complete The Wizard page, type a name for the publication and then click Finish. You will see a dialog box that shows the progress of the creation process. If errors occur, you must resolve any problems before you can continue; otherwise, you must restart the publication-definition process.

## Merge Publications

After you have started a new publication as discussed in "Creating Publications" on page 465, you can create a merge publication by completing the following steps:

1. Click Next to continue. Select the types of subscribers that will subscribe to the publication. You can choose any or all of the following:

   ❏ **SQL Server 2008**  With this type of subscriber, snapshots are formatted using Native SQL Server format.

   ❏ **SQL Server 2005**  With this type of subscriber, newer data types are not supported, including Filestream, Date, and Geography data types.

   ❏ **SQL Server 2005 Mobile, SQL Server Compact 3.1 And Higher**  With this type of subscriber, snapshots are formatted using Character format.

   ❏ **SQL Server 2000**  With this type of subscriber, logical records, replication of DDL changes, and some filter optimizations are not supported.

2. Click Next to continue. On the Articles page, shown previously in Figure 13-7, select the objects for replication. The Objects To Publish pane shows the types of objects that are available for replication. Click the plus sign (+) next to the object to see a list of available objects of the specified type.

3. To select all the columns in a table or view, select the table or view name entry. The objects available depend on the types of objects in the database; they can be tables, stored procedures, user-defined functions, and views. Tables referenced by views are required.

4. To select individual columns in a table or view, expand the table or view entry and then select the appropriate entries for the columns to include. If you are selecting individual columns, keep in mind that both primary key and Rowguid columns are required and must be published. Primary key columns are indicated by a key and a green asterisk. Rowguid columns are indicated by a green asterisk. By clearing a column check box, you exclude the related column from replication (which was previously referred to as vertically filtering a table).

5. Default properties are set for each selected object (article), including the destination object name and object owner, action to use if the object exists, and whether user triggers and extended properties should be copied. You can manage these default properties by setting global defaults, by setting defaults for an individual article, or both:

   ❑ To set defaults for an individual article, select it under Objects To Publish, click Article Properties, and then select Set Properties Of Highlighted... Article. Refer to "Setting Publication Properties" on page 474 for details.

   ❑ To set defaults for all articles of a particular type, select the object type under Objects To Publish, click Article Properties, and then select Set Properties Of All...Articles. Refer to "Setting Publication Properties" for details.

6. After you select objects to use in the publication, click Next. If there are any issues that require changes to the publication, you will see a prompt, similar to the one shown previously in Figure 13-8, describing the issue or issues. Read the description carefully to determine how to resolve the problems indicated, and then make changes as necessary. Common issues include

   ❑ Tables referenced by views are required and so are objects referenced by stored procedures. If you do not select referenced tables or objects, you must create them manually at the subscriber.

   ❑ SQL Server adds uniqueidentifier columns to any tables you have selected for replication. Adding the uniqueidentifier column will cause INSERT statements without column lists to fail and will increase the time needed to generate the first snapshot.

   ❑ IDENTITY columns require the NOT FOR REPLICATION option. If a published IDENTITY column does not use this option, INSERT commands might not replicate properly.

7. Click Next. Use the Filter Table Rows page to exclude unwanted rows from published tables. As you define filters, they are added to the Filtered Tables list. Selecting a filter shows the related WHERE clause in the Filter text box. You can define filters manually and then extend those filters to other tables, or you can attempt to automate the process.

8. If you want to define a new filter, complete the following steps:

   ❑ Click Add, and then select Add Filter to display the Add Filter dialog box. By default, all rows are published. To change this behavior, select a table to filter and then create a filter statement that identifies which rows subscribers will receive. Enter a WHERE clause for the corresponding SELECT *published_columns* FROM *TableName* statement.

   ❑ Specify how many subscribers will receive data from this table: one or many. Merge publications use static or parameterized filters. Static filters are evaluated when the publication is created, and all subscribers to the publication receive the same data. Parameterized filters are evaluated during replication synchronization, and different subscribers can receive different partitions of data based on the subscriber login or computer name.

   ❑ Click OK to close the Add Filter dialog box.

9. After you define a filter, you can extend the filtering to a related table by defining a join. To do this, create a filter on a table as discussed in the previous step. On the Filter Table Rows page, select the filter, click Add, and select Add Join To Extend The Selected Filter. This displays the Add Join dialog box shown in Figure 13-10. You must now do the following:

   ❑ Select the joined table from the list of published tables available in the Joined Table drop-down list, and then define the INNER JOIN clause using the builder or manually.

   ❑ Specify the join options. If there is a one-to-one or one-to-many relationship between rows in the joined table, select Unique Key. If rows in the joined table do not relate to exactly one row in the filtered table, clear the Unique Key check box. Additionally, if related changes should be handled as a logical record and you are working with a unique key, select Logical Record.

   ❑ Click OK to close the Add Join dialog box.

10. An alternative to defining filters manually is to generate filters automatically. On the Filter Table Rows page, click Add, and then select Automatically Generate Filters. In the Generate Filters dialog box, you must then define a new filter as explained previously. SQL Server will then use defined relationships to add joins that extend the filter to other tables.

11. Click Next. The Snapshot Agent initializes subscriptions by creating a snapshot of publication schema and data that can be pushed to subscribers or pulled by subscribers. You can create a snapshot immediately by selecting Create A Snapshot Immediately. If you want the Snapshot Agent to create a snapshot periodically, select Schedule The Snapshot Agent To Run. By default, snapshots are made once every 14 days. To change this schedule, click Change, and then set a new schedule.

**Figure 13-10**   The Add Join dialog box.

12. Click Next. Configure the login for the Snapshot Agent. Click the related Security Settings button.

13. Specify the Windows account under which the agent runs at the distributor. This account is referred to as the *process account*. The account must be a member of the db_owner fixed database role in the *distribution* database and must have write permissions on the snapshot share. Be sure to type domain account names in the form *domain\account*, such as **cpandl\sqlserver**. Then type and confirm the account password.

14. Specify whether the agent should make connections to the publisher by impersonating the account specified in the Process Account text box or by using a SQL Server account. If you choose to use a SQL Server account, enter a SQL Server login and password. Typically, you will want to impersonate the Windows account rather than use a SQL Server account. Click OK.

15. Click Next. Choose the wizard action upon completion. By default, the wizard creates the publication. You can also generate a script file with the steps to create the publication. If you want to generate only a script, clear Create The Publication. Click Next.

16. On the Complete The Wizard page, type a name for the publication and then click Finish. You will see a dialog box that shows the progress of the creation process. If errors occur, you must resolve any problems before you can continue or you must restart the publication-definition process.

## Viewing and Updating Publications

You can view or change the properties of publications at any time. To do so, complete the following steps:

1. Start SQL Server Management Studio. In the Object Explorer view, connect to the server you want to use, and then work your way down to the Replication folder.

2. Click the Local Publications folder to see a list of publications for the replicated database. The icon associated with a publication tells you its type:

   ❑ **Snapshot**  Purple book icon with a blue circle

   ❑ **Transactional**  Blue book icon with a green arrow pointing right

   ❑ **Merge**  Yellow book icon with a green arrow pointing right and a blue arrow pointing left

3. Right-click the publication you want to change, and then select Properties to display the Publication Properties dialog box.

4. Use the Publication Properties dialog box to configure all of the publication options discussed in "Creating Publications" on page 465.

## Setting Publication Properties

Publication properties control the behavior of replication. You can modify the properties at any time. To edit the properties of an existing publication, follow these steps:

1. Start SQL Server Management Studio. In the Object Explorer view, connect to the server you want to use, and then work your way down to the Replication folder.

2. Click the Local Publications folder to see a list of publications for the replicated database.

3. Right-click the publication you want to edit, and then select Properties.

4. Choose the properties you want from the list of properties in the Publication Properties dialog box. The available publication properties depend on the replication type. You might see one or more of the following pages:

   ❑ **General**  Allows you to configure basic options, and is available for all replication types. You can view the article name, source database, and type. You can set the description and the subscription expiration. By default, subscriptions do not expire, but you can set an expiration interval in hours.

   ❑ **Articles**  Allows you to view and configure published articles.

   ❑ **Filter Rows**  Allows you to view and work with row filters.

   ❑ **Snapshot**  Sets options for snapshots, which are used with all replication types. You can set options that control the snapshot format, either Native

SQL Server or Character. Native SQL Server can be used only when all sub-scribers are running SQL Server. Character format is required when a pub-lisher or subscriber is not running SQL Server. You can also specify where to put snapshot files and additional scripts to run before or after applying a snapshot.

❑ **FTP Snapshot And Internet**   Allows subscribers to download snapshot files using File Transfer Protocol (FTP) or Web synchronization. If you select the FTP option, snapshot files are placed in the FTP root folder by default and anonymous login is used. With FTP, you also can specify an alternate path from the root folder and provide a login and password. If you select the Web Synchronization option, you allow subscribers to synchronize subscriptions by connecting to the IIS server you specify. The IIS server must use Secure Sockets Layer and you must enter the fully qualified Web address in the text box provided, such as **https://wserver2.cpandl.com/synchronize**.

> **Real World**   After you enable a publication for Web synchronization, you must configure the IIS server by installing the SQL Server client components and SQL Server Management Studio. Next, start SQL Server Management Studio on the IIS server. Right-click the publication, select Configure Web Synchronization, and then follow the prompts to create a virtual directory for synchronization on the Web server.
>
> On the Web Server page, create a new folder. On the Virtual Directory Information page, set the virtual directory alias, such as **synchronize**, and the local path, such as **c:\Inetpub\wwwroot\websync**. When prompted, copy the SQL Server Internet Server API DLL to this folder. On the Authenticated Access page, select Basic Authentication, clear Integrated Windows Authentication, and then clear Digest Authentication. Configure the Default Domain and Realm by entering the domain of the computer that is running IIS. On the Directory Access page, add the accounts that subscribers will use to make connections to the IIS server. On the Snapshot Share Access page, specify the share to use for snap-shots. On 64-bit computers, you must copy Microsoft SQL Server\100\ COM\replisapi.dll to the virtual directory and then execute the follow-ing command: **regsvr32 replisapi.dll**.

❑ **Subscription Options**   Provides options for allowing or disallowing anon-ymous subscriptions, attachable *subscription* databases, pull subscriptions, non–SQL Server subscribers, and replication of schema changes. By default, anonymous subscriptions, pull subscriptions, and replication of schema changes are allowed.

❑ **Publication Access List**   Controls who can access the publication. By default, only sa, local administrators, the database owner, the process accounts, and distributor_admin have access to the publication data.

❏ **Agent Security**   Allows you to view or change the process account for agents used by the publication.

## Setting Agent Security and Process Accounts

All publications use one or more replication agents, including the Snapshot, Log Reader, and Queue Reader agents. The Snapshot Agent is used with all publication types. The Log Reader Agent is used with updatable and nonupdatable transactional publications. By default, the Log Reader Agent uses the same login as the Snapshot Agent. The Queue Reader Agent is used with updatable transactional publications. By default, the Queue Reader Agent has a security context that is separate from the other agents.

If agent security is not configured properly, replication will fail. You can configure security for these agents by completing the following steps:

1. Start SQL Server Management Studio. In the Object Explorer view, connect to the server you want to use, and then work your way down to the Replication folder.

2. Click the Local Publications folder to see a list of publications for the replicated database.

3. Right-click the publication you want to configure, and then select Properties to display the Publication Properties dialog box.

4. Select the Agent Security page.

5. To configure the login for the Snapshot Agent or Log Reader Agent, click the related Security Settings button, and then do the following:

   ❏ Specify the Windows account under which the agent runs. This account is referred to as the process account. Be sure to type domain account names in the form *domain\account*, such as **cpandl\sqlserver**. Then type and confirm the account password.

   ❏ Specify whether the agent should make connections to the publisher by impersonating the account specified in the Process Account text box or by using a SQL Server account. If you choose to use a SQL Server account, enter a SQL Server login and password. Typically, you will want to impersonate the Windows account rather than use a SQL Server account.

6. To configure security for the Queue Reader Agent, which is used for transaction replication with updating, click the related Security Settings button and then specify the process account.

## Controlling Subscription Access to a Publication

All publications have access control lists (ACLs). For publications, access control lists determine which logins can be used by a pull subscription and immediately update subscribers to access the publication. By default, only sa, local administrators, the database owner, the process accounts, and distributor_admin have access to the publication data. To add or remove users, complete the following steps:

1. Start SQL Server Management Studio. In the Object Explorer view, connect to the server you want to use, and then work your way down to the Replication folder.

2. Click the Local Publications folder to see a list of publications for the replicated database.

3. Right-click the publication you want to change, and then select Properties to display the Publication Properties dialog box.

4. Select the Publication Access List page. Use the buttons provided to add or remove logins.

## Creating a Script for a Publication

Scripts can help you manage publications. You can generate scripts to create the objects specified in a publication and enable the publication, or you can use them to drop the objects specified in a publication and disable the publication.

To create a script for a publication, complete the following steps:

1. Start SQL Server Management Studio. In the Object Explorer view, connect to the server you want to use, and then work your way down to the Replication folder.

2. Click the Local Publications folder to see a list of publications for the replicated database.

3. Right-click the publication you want to edit, and then select Generate Scripts.

4. In the Generate SQL Script dialog box, specify the type of script to generate. Typically, you'll want to create or enable the replicated objects rather than drop or disable them.

5. The script will call replication stored procedures to perform the necessary tasks, and it creates any necessary jobs when executing. To script the jobs and create a record of the jobs, select the Replication Jobs check box.

6. Click Generate Script and then select Save To File. Use the Script File Location dialog box to select the location where you want to save the script to an .sql file, and then click Save. By default, the file is saved as Unicode text. The file can be executed in the Query view to re-create or drop the publication.

7. Click Close.

**Note**   In the Query view, you can access scripts by clicking the Open File button on the toolbar and then entering the location of the script file.

## Deleting a Publication

When you are finished using a publication, you can delete it to release resources that it is using. But before you do this, you might want to create a script that allows you to re-create the publication automatically if you need it again. After creating the script, you can delete the publication by completing the following steps:

1. Start SQL Server Management Studio. In the Object Explorer view, connect to the server you want to use, and then work your way down to the Replication folder.

2. Click the Local Publications folder to see a list of publications for the replicated database.

3. Right-click the publication you want to remove, and then select Delete.

4. When prompted to confirm the action, click Yes.

# Subscribing to a Publication

The final step in the replication process is having servers subscribe to the publication. You can do this using *push* or *pull* subscriptions.

## Subscription Essentials

With push subscriptions, the publisher is responsible for replicating all changes to subscribers without subscribers asking for the changes. You will usually use push subscriptions when you need to send changes to subscribers immediately or when you want to schedule updates periodically. Because the publisher initiates the replication, push subscriptions also offer more security than pull subscriptions. Making the publisher responsible for replicating changes, however, increases overhead on the publisher and might not be the ideal subscription model for a server with a heavy workload.

With pull subscriptions, subscribers request periodic updates of all changes from the publisher. You will usually use pull subscriptions when you have a large number of subscribers or when you need to reduce overhead on the publisher. You also might want to use pull subscriptions for independent mobile users. A single publication can support a mixture of push and pull subscriptions.

You can also use a special type of pull subscription called an *anonymous* subscription. With an anonymous subscription, the publisher and distributor do not maintain subscription information. Instead, the subscriber is responsible for maintaining and synchronizing the subscription, which increases the load on the subscriber but reduces the load on the publisher and distributor. Accordingly, anonymous subscriptions are most useful when you have a large number of subscribers or when you allow subscriptions using the Internet.

> **Note**   You create anonymous subscriptions to publications in the same way you
> create pull subscriptions. You enable anonymous subscriptions using the Subscrip-
> tion Options page of the Publication Properties dialog box. Set the Allow Anony-
> mous Subscriptions option to True to allow anonymous subscriptions. Set Allow
> Anonymous Subscriptions to False to prevent anonymous subscriptions.

The Distribution Agent and Merge Agent are responsible for synchronizing subscriptions and resetting their retention period. If these agents are not running, subscriptions become incompatible with their publications and are marked as deactivated. A
deactivated subscription is a subscription that has exceeded the publication-retention
period. Deactivated subscriptions no longer receive updates during synchronization,
and you must mark these subscriptions for reinitialization to enable them again. If you
do not reenable deactivated subscriptions before they expire, the Expired Subscription
Clean Up job will delete them.

## Creating Subscriptions

The main difference between push and pull subscriptions involves how they are initiated. The subscriber initiates pull subscriptions. The distributor initiates push subscriptions. You configure subscriptions by completing the following steps:

1. Start SQL Server Management Studio. In the Object Explorer view, connect to
   the database server instance that will act as a subscriber or distributor, and then
   work your way down to the Replication folder.

2. Right-click the Local Subscriptions folder and select New Subscriptions. This
   starts the New Subscription Wizard.

3. Click Next. You use the Publication page, shown in Figure 13-11, to specify where
   you want to look for a publication. Select Find SQL Server Publisher, Find Oracle
   Publisher, or a registered server as appropriate.

4. After you select a server, you can browse available publications on that server.
   Select the publication to which you want to subscribe, and then click Next.

5. The next page you see depends on the type of publication. With merge publications, on the Merge Agent Location page, select Run All Agents At The Distributor
   to create push subscriptions or select Run Each Agent At Its Subscriber to create
   pull subscriptions. With other publication types, on the Distribution Agent Location page, choose where to run the Distribution Agent or agents used with this
   publication. If you want the agents to run on the distributor, and therefore create
   a push subscription, select Run All Agents At The Distributor. If you want the
   agents to run on each subscriber, and therefore create a pull subscription, select
   Run Each Agent At Its Subscriber.

**Figure 13-11**    The Publication page of the New Subscription Wizard.

6. Click Next. On the Subscribers page shown in Figure 13-12, choose one or more subscribers for the publication.

**Figure 13-12**    The Subscribers page of the New Subscription Wizard.

7. If you are using updatable transactional replication and a server you want to act as a subscriber is not listed, click Add SQL Server Subscriber and then configure a connection to a SQL Server using the Connect To Server dialog box.

8. If you are using merge, snapshot, or nonupdatable transactional replication and a server you want to act as a subscriber is not listed, click Add Subscriber, and then do the following:

   ❏ Choose Add SQL Server Subscriber to configure a connection to a computer that is running SQL Server by using the Connect To Server dialog box. Registered servers are listed in the Server Name drop-down list, and you can browse for others. The default authentication is Windows Authentication, which uses your current login and password. Click Connect. Specify the destination database in which to create the subscription or select New Database to create a new database for the subscription.

   ❏ Choose Add Non-SQL Subscriber to configure a connection to an Oracle or IBM DB2 server using the Add Non-SQL Server Subscriber dialog box. Enter the data source name that can be used to locate the database on the network. SQL Server generates a connection string for the database using the data source name, combined with the login, password, and any connection options you specify on the Distribution Agent Security page in this wizard. The data source name and connection string are not validated until the Distribution Agent attempts to initialize the subscription. Click OK. The *subscription* database is set as the default destination, which is the database you specified in the data source name.

9. The next page you see depends on the type of publication. With other publications, you configure security for the Distribution Agent. With merge publications, you configure security for the Merge Agent. With merge publications, you set the process account and connection options for each Merge Agent running on subscribers (for pull subscriptions) or for the distributor (for push subscriptions) by clicking the related Properties button (...). With non-merge publications, you set the process account and connection options for each subscriber (for pull subscriptions) or for the distributor (for push subscriptions) by clicking the related Properties button (...). After you click the Properties button (...), do the following:

   ❏ Specify the Windows account under which the Merge Agent/Distribution Agent runs for the selected server (which is either a subscriber or a distributor). This account is referred to as the process account. Be sure to type domain account names in the form *domain\account*, such as **cpandl\ sqlserver**. Then type and confirm the account password. The account must be a member of the Publication Access List. (To check or modify the access list, access the Local Publications folder. In the Object Explorer view, right-click the publication and then select Properties. This displays the Publication Properties dialog box. Select the Publication Access List page.)

❑   Specify whether the agent should make connections to the publisher/distributor by impersonating the account specified in the Process Account text box or by using a SQL Server account. If you choose to use a SQL Server account, enter a SQL Server login and password. Typically, you will want to impersonate the Windows account rather than use a SQL Server account. The account must be a member of the Publication Access List.

❑   Specify whether the agent should make connections to the subscriber by impersonating the account specified in the Process Account text box or by using a SQL Server account. If you choose to use a SQL Server account, enter a SQL Server login and password. Typically, you will want to impersonate the Windows account rather than use a SQL Server account. The account must be a database owner of the *subscription* database.

10.   Click OK to close the Properties dialog box. Click Next. On the Synchronization Schedule page, set the synchronization schedule for Distribution Agents or Merge Agents using one of the following options:

❑   **Run Continuously**   Select this option to continuously check for updates on the publisher.

❑   **Run On Demand Only**   Select this option if you want to update the *subscription* database manually.

❑   **Define Schedule**   Select this option to set a periodic schedule, such as once an hour.

11.   If you selected a publication that uses updatable transactions, the next wizard page will be titled Updatable Subscriptions. Specify if you want the *subscription* databases to be initialized.

❑   Clear the Replicate check box for a subscriber if you do not want to create an updatable subscription at this time.

❑   Set the Commit At Publisher option to Simultaneously Commit Changes to enforce immediate updating. Changes are committed on both the subscriber and the publisher at the same time, which requires a dedicated connection.

❑   Set the Commit At Publisher option to Queue Changes And Commit When Possible to allow queuing of changes. Queued changes are committed on the subscriber immediately and on the publisher during the next online synchronization.

12.   If you choose to create an updatable subscription, the next page allows you to configure the technique that will be used by the subscriber to access the publisher. You can use an existing linked server or remote server to establish the connection if you have already configured these options as described in Chapter 12,

"Linked Servers and Distributed Transactions." Or you can use a SQL Server login and password, provided the login is listed on the Publication Access List.

> **Tip**  To check or modify the access list, access the Local Publications folder. In the Object Explorer view, right-click the publication and then select Properties. This displays the Publication Properties dialog box. Select the Publication Access List page.

13. Use the Initialize Subscriptions page to determine whether or not the *subscription* databases should be initialized:

   ❑ Clear the Initialize check box if you have already initialized the subscription or will initialize a transactional subscription from backup.

   ❑ Set the Initialize When option to Immediately to initialize the *subscription* database with a snapshot of the publication data and schema as soon as possible after the Snapshot Agent generates the snapshot.

   ❑ Set the Initialize When option to At First Synchronization to initialize the *subscription* database with a snapshot of the publication data and schema the first time the subscription is synchronized.

   > **Note**  With merge publications, initialization is handled by the Snapshot Agent and Merge Agent. The Snapshot Agent creates the initial view of the schema and data, and then the Merge Agent applies the snapshot either immediately or at first synchronization.
   >
   > With non-merge publications, initialization is handled by the Snapshot Agent and Distribution Agent. The Snapshot Agent creates the initial view of the schema and data, and then the Distribution Agent applies the snapshot either immediately or at first synchronization.

14. If you are using merge replication, use the Subscription Type page to specify whether the subscription type is server or client. With a server subscription, subscribers can republish data to other subscribers, act as alternate sync partners, and resolve conflicts according to the relative priority you set. With a client subscription, subscribers cannot replicate data to other subscribers or act as alternate sync partners. Additionally, with a client subscription, the first subscriber to submit a change to a publisher wins any conflicts that might arise from that change. Note that you cannot change the subscription type later.

15. Click Next. On the Wizard Actions page, choose the wizard action upon completion. By default, the wizard creates the subscription or subscriptions. You can also generate a script file with the steps to create the subscription or subscriptions. If you want to generate only a script, clear Create The Subscription(s). Click Next.

16. Click Next. Check the setup and click Finish when you are ready to create the subscription or subscriptions. The Creating Subscription(s) dialog box shows you the status of the creation process. Click the message link provided for any errors to read the error text.

## Viewing Subscription Properties

To view the configuration properties of a subscription, complete the following steps:

1. Start SQL Server Management Studio. In the Object Explorer view, connect to the database server instance that will act as a subscriber or distributor, and then work your way down to the Replication folder.

2. Click the Local Publications folder to see a list of publications for the server instance. Click Refresh or press F5 if you don't see a list of publications.

3. Double-click a publication to show its current subscriptions.

4. To view the properties of a subscription, right-click the subscription name and choose Properties to display the Subscription Properties dialog box.

## Updating, Maintaining, and Deleting Subscriptions

To update, maintain, or delete a subscription, complete the following steps:

1. Start SQL Server Management Studio. In the Object Explorer view, connect to the database server instance that will act as a subscriber or distributor, and then work your way down to the Replication folder.

2. Click the Local Subscriptions folder to see a list of subscriptions for the server instance.

3. Right-click a subscription, and then choose one of the following options:

   ❑ **View Synchronization Status**   Displays a status of the synchronization process for the selected subscription.

   ❑ **Set Update Method**   For updatable subscriptions only, this option allows you to switch between immediate updating and queued updating.

   ❑ **Delete**   Deletes the subscription. Confirm the action by clicking Yes when prompted.

4. You validate and reinitialize subscriptions through the associated publication. For more details, refer to the following two sections.

## Validating Subscriptions

You can validate subscriptions to verify that the subscribers have the same number of rows of replication data as the publisher. When you mark a subscription for validation, the validation occurs the next time the Distribution Agent runs, and the results are available in the Replication Monitor.

To validate one or more subscriptions, follow these steps:

1. Start SQL Server Management Studio. In the Object Explorer view, connect to the database server instance that will act as a subscriber or distributor, and then work your way down to the Replication folder.

2. Click the Local Publications folder to see a list of publications for this server instance.

3. If you want to validate subscriptions for a transactional publication, right-click the transactional publication you want to use and then choose Validate Subscriptions. This displays the Validate Subscriptions dialog box. You can validate all SQL Server subscriptions or the specified subscriptions on computers running instances of SQL Server. Non–SQL Server subscriptions cannot be validated. Optionally, click Validation Options to configure how the Distribution Agent computes row counts, whether or not the Distribution Agent compares checksums, and whether or not the Distribution Agent is stopped after the validation is completed.

4. If you want to validate all subscriptions for the selected merge publication, select Validate All SQL Server Subscriptions. This displays the Validate All Subscriptions dialog box. By default, the distributor validates only the row counts on the subscriber. If all subscribers are running SQL Server, you can also verify the data in rows by comparing checksum values.

5. Click OK. The validation occurs the next time the Distribution Agent runs, and the results are available in the Replication Monitor. More information about how to work with the Replication Monitor is provided in Chapter 14.

## Reinitializing Subscriptions

You can reinitialize snapshots in a publication's *subscription* database by using the current snapshot or a new snapshot. To reinitialize all subscriptions, complete the following steps:

1. Start SQL Server Management Studio. In the Object Explorer view, connect to the database server instance that will act as a subscriber or distributor, and then work your way down to the Replication folder.

2. Click the Local Publications folder to see a list of publications for this server instance.

3. Right-click the publication you want to work with, and then choose Reinitialize All Subscriptions. This displays the Reinitialize Subscription(s) dialog box.

4. To use the current snapshot to reinitialize the subscriptions, select Use The Current Snapshot.

5. To generate a new snapshot to reinitialize the subscriptions, select Use A New Snapshot. If you want to generate the snapshot immediately, select Generate The New Snapshot Now.

6. Click Mark For Reinitialization.

To reinitialize a specific subscription, complete the following steps:

1. Start SQL Server Management Studio. In the Object Explorer view, connect to the database server instance that will act as a subscriber or distributor, and then work your way down to the Replication folder.

2. Click the Local Publications folder to see a list of publications for this server instance.

3. Double-click the publication you want to use to show its current subscriptions.

4. Right-click the subscription you want to reinitialize, and then choose Reinitialize. This displays the Reinitialize Subscription(s) dialog box.

5. Select Use The Current Snapshot or Use A New Snapshot as appropriate. If you want to generate a new snapshot immediately, select Generate The New Snapshot Now.

6. Click Mark For Reinitialization.

Part IV

# Microsoft SQL Server 2008 Optimization and Maintenance

This part of the book covers administration tools that you'll use to enhance and maintain Microsoft SQL Server 2008. Chapter 14 provides the essentials for working with server logs, monitoring SQL Server performance, and solving performance problems. Chapter 15 starts by explaining how to create a backup and recovery plan and then discusses common tasks for creating and restoring backups. Chapter 16 explores database automation. You'll learn how to configure alerts, schedule jobs, and manage database operators. You'll also learn how to create maintenance plans and resolve database consistency problems. Chapter 17 discusses log shipping and database mirroring. Log shipping and database mirroring are disaster recovery solutions designed to help improve availability and quickly recover SQL Server 2008. In Chapter 18, you will learn about essential tasks for working with Policy-Based Management. Policy-Based Management defines management policies that not only configure SQL Server settings but also control whether and how settings can be changed. Before you deploy SQL Server 2008, you should familiarize yourself with the available options and determine whether your servers will be put into specific management groups.

# Chapter 14
# Profiling and Monitoring Microsoft SQL Server 2008

| In this chapter: | |
|---|---|

Monitoring server performance, tracking user activity, and troubleshooting errors are essential parts of database administration, and Microsoft SQL Server has several tools that you can use to perform these tasks. Reliability And Performance Monitor, the standard Microsoft Windows Server 2008 tool for monitoring servers, has updated counters for SQL Server. These counters allow you to track many different server resources and activities. SQL Server Profiler, an analysis and profiling tool, allows you to trace server events. Other tools and resources are available, such as stored procedures and the SQL Server logs.

## Monitoring Server Performance and Activity

Monitoring SQL Server is not something you should do haphazardly. You need to have a plan—a set of goals that you hope to achieve. Let's look at some reasons you might want to monitor SQL Server and the tools you can use to do this.

### Reasons to Monitor SQL Server

One of the main reasons you monitor SQL Server performance is to troubleshoot problems. For example, if users are having problems connecting to the server, you will want to monitor the server to find out more about what is causing these problems. Your goal is to track down the problem using the available monitoring resources and then solve the problem effectively.

Another common reason to monitor SQL Server is to improve server performance. To achieve optimal performance, you need to minimize the time it takes for users to see the results of queries and maximize the total number of queries that the server can handle simultaneously. You do this by using the following techniques:

- Resolve hardware issues that might be causing problems. For example, if disk read/write activity is slower than expected, work on improving disk input/ output (I/O).

- Monitor memory and CPU usage, and take appropriate steps to reduce the load on the server. For example, other processes running on the server might be using memory and CPU resources needed by SQL Server.

- Cut down the network traffic load on the server. With replication, for example, you can configure remote stored procedure execution rather than transmit large data changes individually.

Unfortunately, you often have to make tradeoffs in resource usage. For example, as the number of users accessing SQL Server grows, you might not be able to reduce the network traffic load, but you might be able to improve server performance by optimizing queries or indexing.

## Getting Ready to Monitor

Before you start monitoring SQL Server, it is a good idea to establish baseline performance metrics for your server. To do this, you measure server performance at various times and under different load conditions. You can then compare the baseline performance with subsequent performance to determine how SQL Server is performing. Performance metrics that are well above the baseline measurements might indicate areas in which the server needs to be optimized or reconfigured.

After you establish the baseline metrics, prepare a monitoring plan. A comprehensive monitoring plan involves the following steps:

1. Determine which server events should be monitored to help you accomplish your goal.

2. Set filters to preferentially select the amount of information that is collected.

3. Configure monitors and alerts to watch the events.

4. Log the event data so that it can be analyzed.

5. Analyze the event data, and replay the data to find a solution.

These procedures will be examined later in this chapter in "Monitoring SQL Server Performance" on page 502. Although you should develop a monitoring plan in most cases, sometimes you might not want to go through all these steps to monitor SQL Server. For example, if you want to check only current user activity levels, you might not want to use Reliability And Performance Monitor and you might decide to run the stored procedure sp_who instead. Or you can examine this information in the Activity Monitor window in SQL Server Management Studio.

**Note** The stored procedure sp_who reports on current users and processes. When you execute sp_who, you can pass a login name as an argument. If you do not specify a login name, NULL is passed in this argument, so all logins are returned. If you use the keyword *active* as the login name, you will see only active processes; any processes waiting for the next command from a user will be excluded. Instead of a specific login name, such as *sa*, you can use the numeric value for a system process ID as well.

## Monitoring Tools and Resources

The primary monitoring tools you will use are Reliability And Performance Monitor and SQL Server Profiler. Other resources for monitoring SQL Server include

- **Activity Monitor** This monitor provides information on current users, processes, and locks, as discussed in "Managing Server Activity" on page 134. To display Activity Monitor, use the Object Explorer view to access an instance of the Database Engine. Right-click the Database Engine instance and then select Activity Monitor.

- **Replication Monitor** This monitor provides details on the status of SQL Server replication and allows you to configure replication alerts. To display Replication Monitor, use the Object Explorer view to access an instance of the Database Engine. Right-click the Replication node and then select Launch Replication Monitor.

- **SQL Server logs** The information in these event logs allows you to view informational, auditing, warning, and error messages that can help you troubleshoot SQL Server problems. To access the server logs, use the Object Explorer view to access an instance of the Database Engine. Expand the server node and the Management node. Under the Management node, expand the SQL Server Logs node and then double-click the log you want to examine.

- **Job Activity Monitor** This monitor provides details on the status of SQL Server Agent jobs. To display Job Activity Monitor, use the Object Explorer view to access an instance of the Database Engine. Expand the server node and the SQL Server Agent node, and then double-click Job Activity Monitor.

- **SQL Server Agent logs** The information in these event logs allows you to view informational, auditing, warning, and error messages that can help you troubleshoot SQL Server Agent problems. To access agent logs, use the Object Explorer view to access an instance of the Database Engine. Expand the server node and the SQL Server Agent node. Under the SQL Server Agent node, expand the Error Logs node and then double-click the log you want to examine.

**Note**   SQL Server documentation refers to the SQL Server and SQL Server Agent logs as *error logs*. In their current implementation, however, the logs are more accurately called *event logs*, which is the terminology used in this chapter. Similar to event logs in Microsoft Windows, these logs in SQL Server contain informational and security messages as well as error messages.

- **Event logs**   The information in the event logs allows you to troubleshoot systemwide problems, including SQL Server and SQL Server Agent problems. To access event logs, click Start, click Administrative Tools, and then select Event Viewer.

- **DBCC statements**   This set of commands allows you to check SQL Server statistics, to trace activity, and to check database integrity.

- **sp_helpdb**   This stored procedure displays information about databases.

- **sp_helpindex**   This stored procedure reports information about indexes on a table or view.

- **sp_helpserver**   This stored procedure provides information in SQL Server instances configured for remote access or replication.

- **sp_monitor**   This stored procedure shows key SQL Server usage statistics, such as CPU idle time and CPU usage.

- **sp_spaceused**   This stored procedure shows an estimate of disk space used by a table, indexed view, or Service Broker queue in the current database.

- **sp_who**   This stored procedure shows a snapshot of current SQL Server users and processes.

- **sys.dm_tran_locks**   This dynamic management view shows information about object locks.

**Note**   The sys.dm_tran_locks view replaces the sp_lock stored procedure.

In addition to having the use of log files and Transact-SQL statements, you will find a set of built-in functions that return system information. Table 14-1 provides a summary of key functions and their usages. The values returned by these functions are cumulative from the time SQL Server was last started.

Table 14-1   Built-in Functions for Monitoring SQL Server Performance and Activity

| Function | Description | Example |
|---|---|---|
| @@connections | Returns the number of connections or attempted connections | select @@connections as 'Total Login Attempts' |
| @@cpu_busy | Returns CPU processing time in milliseconds for SQL Server activity | select @@cpu_busy as 'CPU Busy', getdate() as 'Since' |
| @@idle | Returns SQL Server idle time in milliseconds | select @@idle as 'Idle Time', getdate() as 'Since' |
| @@io_busy | Returns I/O processing time in milliseconds | select @@io_busy as 'IO Time', getdate() as 'Since' for SQL Server |
| @@pack_received | Returns the number of input packets read from the network by SQL Server | select @@pack_received as 'Packets Received' |
| @@pack_sent | Returns the number of output packets written to the network by SQL Server | select @@pack_sent as 'Packets Sent' |
| @@packet_errors | Returns the number of network packet errors for SQL Server connections | select @@packet_errors as 'Packet Errors' |
| @@timeticks | Returns the number of microseconds per CPU clock tick | select @@timeticks as 'Clock Ticks' |
| @@total_errors | Returns the number of disk read/write errors encountered by SQL Server | select @@total_errors as 'Total Errors', getdate() as 'Since' |
| @@total_read | Returns the number of disk reads by SQL Server | select @@total_read as 'Reads', getdate() as 'Since' |
| @@total_write | Returns the number of disk writes by SQL Server | select @@total_write as 'Writes', getdate() as 'Since' |
| fn_virtualfilestats | Returns input/output statistics for data and log files | select * from fn_virtualfilestats(null,null) |

# Working with Replication Monitor

When you have configured replication as discussed in Chapter 13, "Implementing Snapshot, Merge, and Transactional Replication," you will use Replication Monitor to track the status of replication throughout the enterprise. By default, only the currently selected publisher is displayed in the Replication Monitor window, but you can add any publishers that you want to monitor and organize them into publisher groups as necessary.

## Starting and Using Replication Monitor

To start Replication Monitor, right-click the Replication folder in the Object Explorer view, and then select Launch Replication Monitor. Replication Monitor uses icons to indicate the general status of replication. If any publication has an error status, the error status is indicated by a red circle around an X at all levels within Replication Monitor.

When you select a publisher in the left pane, the right pane shows the replication details for that publisher. By default, this information is refreshed every five seconds, and it can be refreshed immediately by pressing F5. As Figure 14-1 shows, the publisher view has three tabs:

- **Publications**   Shows individual entries for each configured publication. An icon indicates the type and status of the publication:

  - A purple book icon with a blue circle in it for snapshot replication

  - A blue book icon with a right-facing green arrow in it for transactional replication

  - A yellow book icon with a left-facing green arrow and a right-facing blue arrow in it for merge replication

  - A red circle around an X for error status

  At a glance, you can also see the number of subscriptions to the publication, the number of subscriptions being synchronized, the current average performance for subscribers, and the current worst performance for subscribers.

- **Subscription Watch List**   Shows the status of individual subscriptions by type. Use the first drop-down list to specify the type of subscriptions to display and the second drop-down list to specify whether to display all subscriptions of the specified type or some subset, such as the 25 worst-performing subscriptions. Note the status, such as running, error, and so on; the performance level, such as excellent, good, poor, and so on; and the latency.

- **Agents**   Shows the SQL Server Agent jobs common to all publications on the selected publisher. To determine if there are potential replication problems, note the status, last start time, and duration. There might be a problem with jobs that have a status of Never Started and with jobs that have been running for a long time.

**Figure 14-1**  Replication Monitor.

## Adding Publishers and Publisher Groups

When you first start Replication Monitor, only the currently selected publisher is displayed in Replication Monitor. You can add publishers that you want to monitor and organize them into publisher groups as necessary.

To start monitoring additional publishers and create publisher groups, follow these steps:

1. Start Replication Monitor. In the left pane, right-click the Replication Monitor node and select Add Publisher from the shortcut menu. This displays the Add Publisher dialog box, shown in Figure 14-2.

2. Click Add, and then do the following:

   ❑ Choose Add SQL Server Publisher to configure a connection to a server running SQL Server by using the Connect To Server dialog box. Registered servers are listed in the Server Name drop-down list, and you can browse for others. The default authentication is Windows Authentication, which uses your current login and password. Click Connect.

   ❑ Choose Specify A Distributor And Add Its Publishers to configure a connection to a distributor using the Connect To Server dialog box. Registered servers are listed in the Server Name drop-down list, and you can browse for others. The default authentication is Windows Authentication, which uses your current login and password. When you click Connect, Replication Monitor connects to the distributor, obtains a list of publishers for the distributor, and then connects to these publishers as well.

❑   Choose Add Oracle Publisher to configure a connection to an Oracle server using the Connect To Server dialog box. Registered servers are listed in the Server Name drop-down list, and you can browse for others. The default authentication is Oracle Standard Authentication, which requires a user login and password. Click Connect.

**Note**   Before you can add an Oracle publisher, you must first configure a connection to the Oracle publisher's distributor by choosing Specify A Distributor And Add Its Publishers.

3.   Publisher groups make it easier to manage monitoring in complex enterprise environments. Select the publisher group to which to add the publisher or publishers. If you want to create a new group, click New Group, specify the group name, and then click OK. Then select the new group under Show This Publisher(s) In The Following Group.

4.   Click OK.

**Figure 14-2**   The Add Publisher dialog box.

# Working with the Event Logs

Event logs provide historical information that can help you track down problems with SQL Server. SQL Server writes events to the SQL Server event logs, the SQL Server Agent event logs, and the Windows application log. You can use all three logs to track messages related to SQL Server. However, there are some things you should know about these logs:

■   Only the application log provides additional information on all applications running on the server, and only the application log provides features for filtering events based on type. For example, you can filter events so that only error and warning messages are displayed.

- If you start the MSSQLServer or MSSQL$*instancename* service from the command prompt, events are logged to the SQL Server event log and to standard output. No events are recorded in the Windows application log.

- Windows has additional logs that can be helpful when tracking issues. If you are tracking security issues, start with the SQL Server event logs and also examine the Windows security log. If you are having trouble finding the source of a problem that is preventing proper operation of SQL Server, start with the SQL Server logs and also examine the Windows application and system logs.

SQL Server error messages can be cryptic and difficult to read if you do not understand the formatting. Error messages logged by SQL Server can have the following information:

- **An error number that uniquely identifies the error message**   System error numbers have one to five digits. System errors are numbered from 1 to 50,000. User-defined errors start at 50,001.

- **A severity level that indicates how critical the message is**   Severity levels range from 1 to 25. Messages with a severity level of 0 to 10 are informational messages. Severity levels from 11 to 16 are generated by users and users can correct them. Severity levels from 17 to 25 indicate software or hardware errors that you should examine.

- **An error state number that indicates the source of the error**   Error state numbers have one to three digits and a maximum value of 127. Normally, error state numbers indicate the line number in the SQL Server code that generated the message.

- **A message that provides a brief description of the error**   Read the message to get more information about the error, which will help you in troubleshooting problems.

You might see ODBC (Open Database Connectivity) and OLEDB (object linking and embedding database) return errors from SQL Server that contain similar information as well. The sys.messages catalog view in the *master* database contains a list of error messages and descriptions that can be returned by SQL Server. To see all error messages that can be returned by SQL Server, you can execute the following T-SQL statement:

```
USE master
GO
SELECT * FROM sys.messages
GO
```

## Examining the Application Log

The application log contains entries for all database server instances running on the computer, as well as entries for other business applications. You access the application log by completing the following steps:

1. Click Start, click All Programs, click Administrative Tools, and then choose Event Viewer. This starts Event Viewer.

2. Event Viewer displays logs for the local computer by default. If you want to view logs on a remote computer, right-click the Event Viewer node in the console tree (left pane), and then select Connect To Another Computer to display the Select Computer dialog box. In the dialog box, enter the name of the computer you want to access, and then click OK.

3. In the console tree (left pane), expand the Windows Logs node and then click Application. You should see an application log similar to the one shown in Figure 14-3. Use the information in the Source column to determine which service or database server instance logged a particular event.

**Figure 14-3**   A Windows application log.

**Note**   Windows Server 2003 and Windows Server 2008 have different versions of Event Viewer. On Windows Server 2003, Event Viewer doesn't have additional nodes and you can access the application log directly from the console tree.

The entries in the main window of Event Viewer provide a quick overview of when, where, and how an event occurred. To obtain detailed information on an event, review the details provided on the General tab in the lower portion of the main window. The event level or keyword precedes the date and time of the event. Event levels include

- **Information**  An informational event that is generally related to a successful action.

- **Audit Success**  An event related to the successful execution of an action.

- **Audit Failure**  An event related to the failed execution of an action.

- **Warning**  A noncritical error that provides a warning. Details for warnings are often useful in preventing future system problems.

- **Error**  An error, such as the failure of a service to start.

In addition to the date, time, and event type indicator, the summary and detailed event entries provide the following information:

- **Source**  The application, service, or component that logged the event

- **Event ID**  An identifier for the specific event

- **Task Category**  The category of the event, which is sometimes used to further describe the related action

- **User**  The user account that was logged on when the event occurred, if applicable

- **Computer**  The computer name on which the event occurred

- **Description**  A text description of the event, provided in detailed entries

- **Data**  Any data or error code output by the event, provided in detailed entries

Warnings and errors are the two main types of events that you want to examine closely. Whenever one of these types of events occurs and you are unsure of the cause, review the detailed event description. If you want to see only warnings and errors, you can filter the log. To filter a selected log on Windows Server 2003, complete the following steps:

1. From the View menu, choose the Filter option.

2. Clear the following check boxes: Information, Success Audit, and Failure Audit.

3. Select the Warning and Error check boxes if they are not already selected.

4. Click OK. You should now see a list of warning and error messages only. Remember that these messages are for all applications running on the server and not just for SQL Server.

To filter a selected log on Windows Server 2008, complete the following steps:

1. In the actions pane or on the Action menu, click Filter Current Log.

2. Use the Logged list to select the included time frame for logged events. You can choose to include events from the Last Hour, Last 12 Hours, Last 24 Hours, Last 7 Days, or Last 30 Days.

3. Use the Event Level check boxes to specify the level of events to include. Select Verbose to get additional detail.

4. Use the Event Source list to select event sources to include. If you select specific event sources, all other event sources are excluded.

5. Optionally, use the User and Computer(s) boxes to specify users and computers that should be included. If you do not specify the users and computers to be included, events generated by all users and computers are included.

6. Click OK. You should now see a filtered list of events. Review these events carefully, and take steps to correct any problems that exist. To clear the filter and see all events for the log, click Clear Filter in the actions pane or on the Action menu.

## Examining the SQL Server Event Logs

The SQL Server logs record information, warnings, errors, and auditing messages pertaining to SQL Server activity. New logs are created when you start the SQL Server service or when you run the sp_cycle_errorlog stored procedure. When a new log is created, the current log is cycled to the archive. SQL Server maintains up to five archived logs (by default).

You can view the SQL Server event logs in SQL Server Management Studio or through a text editor. In SQL Server Management Studio, you access the event logs by completing the following steps:

1. Start SQL Server Management Studio. In the Object Explorer view, connect to the database server of your choice, and then work your way down to the Management folder.

2. Expand the Management folder, and then double-click the SQL Server Logs entry. The current log is shown with the label *Current*. Archived logs are shown with descriptive labels such as *Archive #1*.

3. Double-click the log you want to view to open it in Log File Viewer.

4. With Log File Viewer open, you can add other logs to the log file summary by selecting their check boxes, as shown in Figure 14-4.

**Figure 14-4**   Log File Viewer.

To access the event logs in a text editor, complete the following steps:

1. Start a text editor, such as WordPad, and then use its Open dialog box to access the SQL Server Log folder, normally located in MSSQL10.MSSQLSERVER\ MSSQL\LOG or MSSQL10.*InstanceName*\MSSQL\LOG.

2. Open the log you want to examine. The current log file is named ERRORLOG with no file extension. The most recent log backup has the extension .1, the second most recent has the extension .2, and so on.

To change the number of logs that SQL Server maintains, right-click the SQL Server Logs entry in the Object Explorer view and select Configure. In the Configure SQL Server Error Logs dialog box, select Limit The Number Of Error Log Files and then set the maximum number of error log files to retain using the Maximum Number Of Error Log Files combo box. The default number of log files maintained is six: one current log and five archive logs. You can change the number of logs maintained to any value from 6 through 99.

## Examining the SQL Server Agent Event Logs

The SQL Server Agent logs record information, warnings, and errors pertaining to SQL Server Agent activity. New logs are created only when you start the SQL Server Agent service. When a new log is created, the current log is cycled to the archive. SQL Server maintains up to five archived agent logs (by default).

In SQL Server Management Studio, you access the current SQL Server Agent log by completing the following steps:

1. Start SQL Server Management Studio. In the Object Explorer view, connect to the database server of your choice, and then work your way down to the SQL Server Agent node.

2. Expand the SQL Server Agent node, and then double-click the Error Logs entry. The current log is shown with the label *Current*. Archived logs are labeled *Archive # 1* and so on.

3. Double-click the log you want to view to open it in Log File Viewer.

4. With Log File Viewer open, you can add other logs to the log file summary by selecting their check boxes.

To access archived SQL Server Agent event logs in a text editor, complete the following steps:

1. Start the text editor, and then use its Open dialog box to access the SQL Server Log folder, which is normally located in MSSQL10.MSSQLSERVER\MSSQL\ LOG or MSSQL10.*InstanceName*\MSSQL\LOG.

2. Open the log you want to examine. The current log file is named SQLAGENT.OUT. The most recent log backup has the extension .1, the second most recent has the extension .2, and so on.

You can manage the SQL Server Agent logs in several ways. You can force the SQL Server Agent to recycle the current log by right-clicking the SQL Server Agent\Error Logs node in the Object Explorer view, selecting Recycle, and then clicking OK. When you do this, SQL Server closes out the current agent log, moves it to an archive log, and starts a new agent log. You can control the level of logging and set the log file location as well. To do this, complete the following steps:

1. Right-click the SQL Server Agent\Error Logs node in the Object Explorer view, and then select Configure.

2. Use the Error Log File box to set the folder path and file name of the agent log. The default path is MSSQL10.MSSQLSERVER\MSSQL\LOG\SQLAGENT.OUT or MSSQL10.*InstanceName*\MSSQL\LOG\SQLAGENT.OUT. New archive files will also be created in the folder specified as part of the path.

3. Use the Agent Log Level check boxes to control the level of logging for the SQL Server Agent. By default, only error and warning messages are logged. If you want to view informational messages in the logs, select the Information check box as well.

4. Click OK.

# Monitoring SQL Server Performance

Reliability And Performance Monitor is the tool of choice for monitoring SQL Server performance. Reliability And Performance Monitor graphically displays statistics for the set of performance parameters you select. These performance parameters are referred to as *counters*.

When you install SQL Server on a system, Reliability And Performance Monitor is updated with a set of counters for tracking SQL Server performance parameters. These counters also can be updated when you install services and add-ons for SQL Server. For example, when you configure replication on a server, Replication Monitor is added and made available through SQL Server Management Studio, and Reliability And Performance Monitor is again updated with a set of objects and counters for tracking replication performance.

Reliability And Performance Monitor creates a graph depicting the various counters you are tracking. You can configure the update interval for this graph, but it's set to three seconds by default. As you will see when you work with Reliability And Performance Monitor, the tracking information is most valuable when you record the information in a log file and when you configure alerts to send messages when certain events occur or when certain thresholds are reached, such as when a database log file gets close to running out of free space.

The following sections examine the procedures you will use with Reliability And Performance Monitor.

> **Note** On Windows Server 2003, you can use Performance Monitor to configure counters to monitor using similar techniques. However, only Reliability And Performance Monitor includes data collector sets for collecting performance data. Data collector sets replace performance monitor logs and alerts.

## Choosing Counters to Monitor

Performance Monitor displays information only for counters you are tracking. More than one hundred SQL Server counters are available—and if you have configured other SQL Server features, such as replication, you can use even more counters. These counters are organized into object groupings. For example, all lock-related counters are associated with the SQLServer:Locks object.

To select which counters you want to monitor, complete the following steps:

1. You can access a standalone console by clicking Start, pointing to Administrative Tools, and then clicking Reliability And Performance Monitor. In Server Manager, you can access this tool as a snap-in under the Diagnostics node. Double-click the Diagnostics node to expand it. Finally, double-click and then select the Reliability And Performance node.

2. In the Reliability And Performance console, expand Monitoring Tools and then select Performance Monitor, as shown in Figure 14-5. Any default counters are shown in the lower portion of the Performance Monitor window. To delete a default counter, click its entry in the Performance Monitor window, and then press the Delete key.

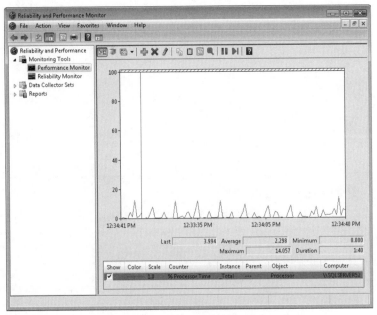

**Figure 14-5**   The Performance Monitor window.

3. The Performance Monitor tool has several views and view types. Ensure that you are viewing current activity by clicking View Current Activity on the toolbar or pressing Ctrl+T. You can switch between the view types (Line, Histogram Bar, and Report) by clicking Change Graph Type or pressing Ctrl+G.

4. To add counters, click the Add button on the toolbar or press Ctrl+I. This displays the Add Counters dialog box shown in Figure 14-6.

> **Tip**   The easiest way to learn what you can track is by exploring the objects and counters available in the Add Counters dialog box. Select an object in the Performance Object list, select the Show Description check box, and then scroll through the list of counters for the object.

**Figure 14-6**   The Add Counters dialog box.

5.  In the Select Counters From Computer box, enter the Universal Naming Convention (UNC) name of the computer running SQL Server that you want to work with, such as \\SQLServer52, or choose *<Local computer>* to work with the local computer.

> **Note**   You need to be at least a member of the Performance Monitor Users group in the domain or the local computer to perform remote monitoring. When you use performance logging, you need to be at least a member of the Performance Log Users group in the domain or the local computer to work with performance logs on remote computers.

6.  In the Available Counters panel, performance objects are listed alphabetically. If you select an object entry by clicking it, all related counters are selected. If you expand an object entry, you can see all the related counters and can then select individual counters by clicking them. For example, you could expand the entry for the SQLServer:Locks object and then select the Average Wait Time (ms), Lock Requests/sec, and Lock Timeouts (timeout > 0)/sec counters.

7.  When you select an object or any of its counters, you see the related instances. Choose All Instances to select all counter instances for monitoring. Or select one or more counter instances to monitor. For example, you could select instances of Application or Database locks.

8.  When you've selected an object or a group of counters for an object as well as the object instances, click Add to add the counters to the graph. Repeat steps 5 through 8 to add other performance parameters.

9. Click Close when you're finished.

**Tip**   Don't try to chart too many counters or counter instances at once. You'll make the display too difficult to read, and you'll use system resources—namely, CPU time and memory—that might affect server responsiveness.

## Performance Logging

Windows Server 2008 introduces data collector sets and reports. Data collector sets allow you to specify sets of performance objects and counters that you want to track. After you've created a data collector set, you can easily start or stop monitoring the performance objects and counters included in the set. In a way, this makes data collector sets similar to the performance logs used in earlier releases of Windows. However, data collector sets are much more sophisticated. You can use a single data set to generate multiple performance counter and trace logs. You can also perform the following tasks:

- Assign access controls to manage who can access collected data.

- Create multiple run schedules and stop conditions for monitoring.

- Use data managers to control the size of collected data and reporting.

- Generate reports based on collected data.

In the Reliability And Performance console, you can review currently configured data collector sets and reports under the Data Collector Sets and Reports nodes, respectively. As shown in Figure 14-7, you'll find data sets and reports that are user defined and system defined. User-defined data sets are created by users for general monitoring and performance tuning. System-defined data sets are created by the operating system to aid in automated diagnostics.

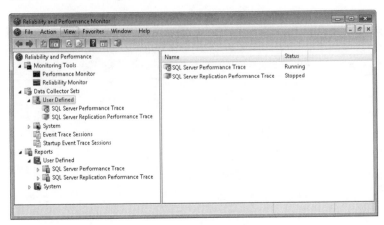

**Figure 14-7**   Access data collector sets and reports.

**Note** With SQL Server 2008, you can create several special-purpose data collector sets automatically and then generate periodic reports to get a better understanding of disk usage, query statistics, and server activity. See "Configuring a Management Data Warehouse" on page 511 for details.

## Creating and Managing Data Collector Sets

To view the currently configured data collector sets, access Reliability And Performance Monitor by selecting the Reliability And Performance Monitor option on the Administrative Tools menu and then expanding the Data Collector Sets node. You can work with data collectors in a variety of ways:

- You can view currently defined user or system data collector sets by selecting either User Defined or System as appropriate. When you select a data collector set in the left pane, you'll see a list of the related data collectors in the main pane listed by name and type. The Trace type is for data collectors that record performance data whenever related events occur. The Performance Counter type is for data collectors that record data on selected counters when a predetermined interval has elapsed. The Configuration type is for data collectors that record changes to particular registry paths.

- You can view running event traces by selecting Event Trace Sessions. You can then stop a data collector running a trace by right-clicking it and selecting Stop.

- You can view the enabled or disabled status of event traces configured to run automatically when you start the computer by selecting Startup Event Trace Sessions. You can start a trace by right-clicking a startup data collector and selecting Start As Event Trace Session. You can delete a startup data collector by right-clicking it and then selecting Delete.

- You can save a data collector as a template that can be used as the basis of other data collectors by right-clicking the data collector and selecting Save Template. In the Save As dialog box, select a directory, type a name for the template, and then click Save. The data collector template is saved as an XML file that can be copied to other systems.

- You can delete a user-defined data collector by right-clicking it and then selecting Delete. If a data collector is running, you'll need to stop collecting data first and then delete the collector. Deleting a collector deletes the related reports as well.

## Collecting Performance Counter Data

Data collectors can be used to record performance data on the selected counters at a specific sample interval. For example, you could sample performance data for the CPU every 15 minutes.

To collect performance counter data, follow these steps:

1. In Reliability And Performance Monitor, under the Data Collector Sets node, right-click the User-Defined node in the left pane, point to New, and then choose Data Collector Set.

2. In the Create New Data Collector Set Wizard, type a name for the data collector, such as SQL Server Performance Monitor or Replication Performance Monitor.

3. Select the Create Manually option and then click Next.

4. On the What Type Of Data Do You Want To Include page, the Create Data Logs option is selected by default. Select the Performance Counter check box and then click Next.

5. On the Which Performance Counters Would You Like To Log page, click Add. This displays the Add Counters dialog box, which you can use as previously discussed to select the performance counters to track. When you are finished selecting counters, click OK.

6. On the Which Performance Counters Would You Like To Log page, type in a sample interval and select a time unit in seconds, minutes, hours, days, or weeks. The sample interval specifies when new data is collected. For example, if you sample every 15 minutes, the data log is updated every 15 minutes. Click Next when you are ready to continue.

7. On the Where Would You Like The Data To Be Saved page, type the root path to use for logging collected data. Alternatively, click Browse and then use the Browse For Folder dialog box to select the logging directory. Click Next when you are ready to continue.

   **Best Practices**   The default location for logging is *%SystemRoot%*\Perf-Logs\Admin. Log files can grow in size very quickly. If you plan to log data for an extended period, be sure to place the log file on a drive with lots of free space. Remember, the more frequently you update the log file, the higher the drive space and CPU resource usage on the system.

8. On the Create New Data Collector Set page, the Run As box lists <Default> as the user to indicate that the log will run under the privileges and permissions of the default system account. To run the log with the privileges and permissions of another user, click Change. Type the user name and password for the desired account, and then click OK. User names can be entered in *DOMAIN\Username* format, such as CPANDL\WilliamS for the WilliamS account in the CPANDL domain.

9. Select the Open Properties For This Data Collector Set option and then click Finish. This saves the data collector set, closes the wizard, and then opens the related Properties dialog box.

10. By default, logging is configured to start manually. To configure a logging schedule, click the Schedule tab and then click Add. You can now set the active range, start time, and run days for data collection.

11. By default, logging stops only if you set an expiration date as part of the logging schedule. Using the options on the Stop Condition tab, you can configure the log file to stop manually after a specified period of time, such as seven days, or when the log file is full (if you've set a maximum size limit).

12. Click OK when you've finished setting the logging schedule and stop conditions. You can manage the data collector as explained in "Creating and Managing Data Collector Sets" on page 506.

**Note**   You can configure Windows to run a scheduled task when data collection stops. You configure tasks to run on the Task tab in the Properties dialog box.

### Collecting Performance Trace Data

You can use data collectors to record performance trace data whenever events related to their source providers occur. A source provider is an application or operating system service that has traceable events.

To collect performance trace data, follow these steps:

1. In Reliability And Performance Monitor, under the Data Collector Sets node, right-click the User-Defined node in the left pane, point to New, and then choose Data Collector Set.

2. In the Create New Data Collector Set Wizard, type a name for the data collector, such as Database Locks Trace or Database Mirroring Trace.

3. Select the Create Manually option and then click Next.

4. On the What Type Of Data Do You Want To Include page, the Create Data Logs option is selected by default. Select the Event Trace Data check box and then click Next.

5. On the Which Event Trace Providers Would You Like To Enable page, click Add. Select an event trace provider to track, such as Active Directory Domain Services: Core. By selecting individual properties in the Properties list and clicking Edit, you can track particular property values rather than all values for the provider. Repeat this process to select other event trace providers to track. Click Next when you are ready to continue.

6. Complete steps 7 through 12 from the previous procedure, "Collecting Performance Counter Data."

### Collecting Configuration Data

You can use data collectors to record changes in registry configuration. To collect configuration data, follow these steps:

1. In Reliability And Performance Monitor, under the Data Collector Sets node, right-click the User-Defined node in the left pane, point to New, and then choose Data Collector Set.

2. In the Create New Data Collector Set Wizard, type a name for the data collector, such as SQL Server Registry or Registry Adapter Info.

3. Select the Create Manually option and then click Next.

4. On the What Type Of Data Do You Want To Include page, the Create Data Logs option is selected by default. Select the System Configuration Information check box and then click Next.

5. On the Which Registry Keys Would You Like To Record page, click Add. Type the registry path to track. Repeat this process to add other registry paths to track. Click Next when you are ready to continue.

6. Complete steps 7 through 12 from the earlier procedure, "Collecting Performance Counter Data."

## Viewing Data Collector Reports

When you're troubleshooting problems, you'll often want to log performance data over an extended period of time and then review the data to analyze the results. For each data collector that has been or is currently active, you'll find related data collector reports. As with data collector sets themselves, data collector reports are organized into two general categories: user-defined and system.

You can view data collector reports in Reliability And Performance Monitor. Expand the Reports node and then expand the individual report node for the data collector you want to analyze. Under the data collector's report node, you'll find individual reports for each logging session. A logging session begins when logging starts and ends when logging is stopped.

The most recent log is the one with the highest log number. If a data collector is actively logging, you won't be able to view the most recent log. You can stop collecting data by right-clicking a data collector set and selecting Stop. Collected data is shown by default in a graph view from the start of data collection to the end of data collection.

You can modify the report details using the following techniques:

1. In the monitor pane, press Ctrl+Q or click the Properties button on the toolbar. This displays the Performance Monitor Properties dialog box.

2. Click the Source tab.

3. Specify data sources to analyze. Under Data Source, click Log Files and then click Add to open the Select Log File dialog box. You can now select additional log files to analyze.

4. Specify the time window that you want to analyze. Click Time Range, and then drag the Total Range bar to specify the appropriate starting and ending times. Drag the left edge to the right to move up the start time. Drag the right edge to the left to move down the end time.

5. Click the Data tab. You can now select counters to view. Select a counter and then click Remove to remove it from the graph view. Click Add to display the Add Counters dialog box, which you can use to select the counters that you want to analyze.

> **Note**   Only counters that you selected for logging are available. If you don't see a counter that you want to work with, you'll need to modify the data collector properties, restart the logging process, and then check the logs at a later date.

6. Click OK. In the monitor pane, click the Change Graph Type button to select the type of graphing.

## Configuring Performance Counter Alerts

You can configure alerts to notify you when certain events occur or when certain performance thresholds are reached. You can send these alerts as network messages and as events that are logged in the application event log. You can also configure alerts to start application and performance logs.

To configure an alert, follow these steps:

1. In Reliability And Performance Monitor, under the Data Collector Sets node, right-click the User-Defined node in the left pane, point to New, and then choose Data Collector Set.

2. In the Create New Data Collector Set Wizard, type a name for the data collector, such as DB Application Locks Alert or SQL Server Replication Alert.

3. Select the Create Manually option and then click Next.

4. On the What Type Of Data Do You Want To Include page, the Create Data Logs option is selected by default. You don't want to use this option or its related check boxes. Instead, select the Performance Counter Alert option and then click Next.

5. On the Which Performance Counters Would You Like To Monitor page, click Add to display the Add Counters dialog box. This dialog box is identical to the Add Counters dialog box discussed previously. Use the Add Counters dialog box to add counters that trigger the alert. Click OK when you're finished.

6.  In the Performance Counters panel, select the first counter and then use the Alert When text box to set the occasion when an alert for this counter is triggered. Alerts can be triggered when the counter is above or below a specific value. Select Above or Below, and then set the trigger value. The unit of measurement is whatever makes sense for the currently selected counter or counters. For example, to alert if processor time is over 95 percent, you would select Over and then type **95**. Repeat this process to configure other counters you've selected.

7.  Click Next. Complete steps 8 through 12 from the earlier procedure, "Collecting Performance Counter Data."

# Configuring a Management Data Warehouse

SQL Server 2008 has a built-in feature called the management data warehouse. This feature uses several special-purpose data collector sets to automatically collect disk usage, query statistics, and server activity information. To use this feature, you must configure a data collection host and then set up data collection for SQL Server instances you want to track.

## Understanding Management Data Warehouses

When you configure a management data warehouse, you can enable data collection whenever you want to monitor SQL Server performance and then generate reports to review the collected information. When you are finished evaluating SQL Server performance, you should free server resources used for collection by disabling data collection.

To enable data collection, you must create a management data warehouse. The warehouse is a database that stores the collected data as well as related report data. As the selected SQL Server instance will then act as a data collection host, you must also ensure that SQL Server Agent is properly configured. SQL Server Agent jobs are used to collected data at periodic intervals on any SQL Server instance for which you've subsequently configured data collection.

Any database you use as a management data warehouse has three special-purpose roles:

- **mdw_reader**   Members of this role are able to access the management data warehouse and read reports.

- **mdw_writer**   Members of this role are able to write and upload data to the management data warehouse. All data collectors must have this role.

- **mdw_admin**   Members of this role have full access and can perform read, write, update, and delete operations in the management data warehouse.

These special-purpose roles are stored in the *msdb* database on the data collection host and no user is a member of these roles by default. While users who are members of the sysadmin role have full access to data collector views, administrators must be explicitly added to the appropriate role or roles to perform other operations.

## Creating the Management Data Warehouse

A management data warehouse stores your data collector information. You can create a management data warehouse by completing the following steps:

1. Start SQL Server Management Studio. In the Object Explorer view, connect to the server you want to use, and then expand the Management folder. If data collection hasn't been configured, you'll see a red down arrow on the Data Collection icon. Right-click Data Collection and then select Configure Management Data Warehouse.

2. Select Create Or Upgrade A Management Data Warehouse and then click Next.

3. SQL Server stores the collected data in a database. If you want to use an existing database to store the data, select the database using the selection list provided. Otherwise, click New and create a database for storing the collected data. Click Next.

4. On the Map Logins And Users page, you can map logins and users to management data warehouse roles. Later, by configuring logins for the *msdb* database, you can modify membership in these roles as discussed in "Managing Server Logins" on page 285. Click Next and then click Finish.

## Setting Up Data Collection

You can set up data collection by completing the following steps:

1. In SQL Server Management Studio's Object Explorer view, expand the Management folder, right-click Data Collection, and then select Configure Management Data Warehouse.

2. Select Set Up Data Collection and then click Next.

3. Click the Options (...) button to the right of the Server Name box. Connect to the data collection host. Next, select the collection database using the selection list provided.

4. Optionally set a cache directory that is used to store collected data before it is uploaded to the specified database. If you don't specify a directory, the TEMP directory is used.

5. Click Next and then click Finish.

## Managing Collection and Generating Reports

When you set up collection, data collection is enabled automatically. You can turn data collection on or off by right-clicking the Data Collection node and selecting Enable Data Collection or Disable Data Collection as appropriate. In SQL Server Management

Studio's Object Explorer view, you can generate data collection reports by expanding the Management folder, right-clicking Data Collection, pointing to Reports, pointing to Management Data Warehouse, and then selecting the type of report to generate. You can generate the following reports: Server Activity History, Disk Usage History, or Query Statistics History.

# Solving Performance Problems with Profiler

Whether you are trying to track user activity, troubleshoot connection problems, or optimize SQL Server, SQL Server Profiler is one of the best utilities available. Profiler enables you to trace events that occur in SQL Server. Events you can track in Profiler are similar to counters you can monitor in Performance Monitor. They are organized into groups called *event classes*, and you can track one or more events for any of the available event classes. The strengths of Profiler are its advanced features and extensive customization capabilities.

You can record and replay Profiler traces when you want to analyze the data—and this is one area in which Profiler excels. You can use Profiler to do the following:

- Use the information to find slow-running queries and then determine what is causing the queries to run slowly.

- Go through statements a step at a time to find the cause of a problem.

- Track a series of statements that cause a particular problem, and then replay the trace on a test server to determine the cause.

- Use trace information to determine the cause of deadlocks.

- Monitor user and application activity to discover actions that are using CPU time or queries that are taking a long time to process.

Let's look at how you can work with Profiler. Then we will examine how to create and manage traces.

## Using Profiler

You can start Profiler in two ways:

- Click Start, click All Programs, click Microsoft SQL Server 2008, click Performance Tools, and then choose SQL Server Profiler.

- In SQL Server Management Studio, select SQL Server Profiler from the Tools menu.

Figure 14-8 shows Profiler in the process of running a trace. The columns shown for the trace, such as EventClass, are completely configurable when you are setting up the trace, allowing you to select or clear columns as necessary. Two columns you will want to pay particular attention to are Duration and CPU. The Duration column shows how long a particular event has been running in milliseconds. The CPU column shows the amount of CPU processing time the event requires in milliseconds.

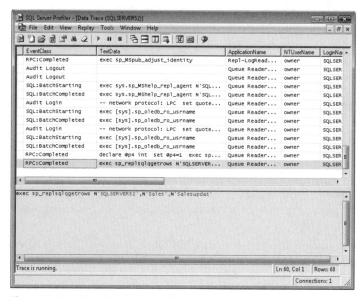

**Figure 14-8** Using SQL Server Profiler to trace SQL Server events.

Stored procedures provide an alternative to Profiler. Using these stored procedures gives you some options that you do not have with SQL Server Profiler. You can

- Store traces in the Windows application log.
- Autostart a trace when SQL Server starts.
- Forward event data to another computer running SQL Server (Windows only).

To create traces with stored procedures, complete the following steps:

1. Create a trace definition using sp_trace_create.
2. Set events to capture using sp_trace_setevent.
3. Set event filters using sp_trace_setfilter.

## Creating New Traces

You use traces to record events generated by local and remote SQL servers. You run traces in the Profiler window and store them for later analysis.

To start a new trace, complete the following steps:

1. Start SQL Server Profiler, and then click the New Trace button. Or select File, New Trace.
2. Use the Connect To Server dialog box to connect to the server you want to trace.
3. You will see the Trace Properties dialog box, shown in Figure 14-9.

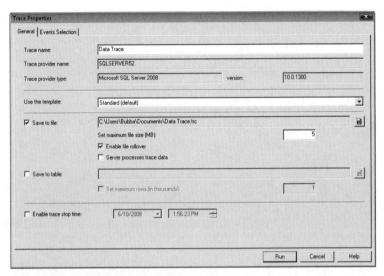

**Figure 14-9**    The Trace Properties dialog box.

4. In the Trace Name text box, type a name for the trace, such as Data Trace or Deadlock Trace For CustomerDB.

5. You can store traces as they are being created by selecting the Save To File or the Save To Table check box, or both. Or you can store a running trace later by selecting File, selecting Save As, and then choosing either the Trace File option or the Trace Table option.

> **Best Practices**    There are advantages and disadvantages to using trace files and trace tables. You can use trace files to store traces quickly and efficiently using minimal system resources. Trace tables make it easy to store a trace directly in a table on another server, but you use much more of the system resources and usually have slower response times. Note also that storing a trace saves only the trace data. It does not save the trace definition. To reuse the trace definition, you will have to export the trace definition.

6. SQL Profiler templates are used to save trace definitions that contain the events, data columns, and filters used in a trace. The Use The Template drop-down list enables you to choose a template to use as the basis of the trace. Select the TSQL_ Replay template if you want to replay the trace.

> **Note**    SQL Profiler templates end with the .tdf file extension.

7. Click the Events Selection tab, as shown in Figure 14-10. The currently selected template determines the events that are selected for tracking by default. The best way to learn the types of events you can trace is to select each event or event class and read its description at the bottom of the Events Selection tab. Move the pointer to a specific column to see details about that data column.

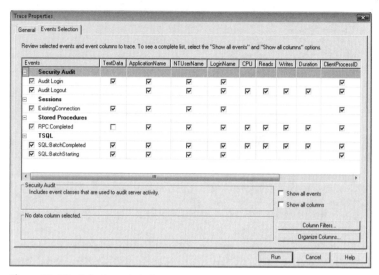

**Figure 14-10** Select events to trace.

8. Only a subset of the traceable events and event classes is displayed by default. To see all event classes available, select Show All Events. The event classes that can be traced include Broker, CLR, Cursors, Database, Deprecation, Errors And Warnings, Full Text, Locks, OLEDB, Objects, Performance, Progress Report, Query Notifications, Scans, Security Audit, Server, Sessions, Stored Procedures, TSQL, Transactions, and User Configurable.

9. Only a subset of the traceable data columns is displayed by default. To see all data columns, select Show All Columns.

10. Select event subclasses to add to the trace. If you select a subclass, all data columns for that class are tracked.

11. As necessary, select individual data columns for event subclasses to track specific data columns for an event subclass (versus all data columns for a subclass). At a minimum, you should track

   ❑ Cursors, CursorExecute

   ❑ Cursors, CursorOpen

   ❑ Cursors, CursorPrepare

   ❑ Sessions, ExistingConnection

   ❑ Stored Procedures, RPC:OutputParameter

   ❑ Stored Procedures, RPC:Starting

   ❑ TSQL, Exec Prepared SQL

❑ TSQL, Prepare SQL

❑ TSQL, SQL:BatchStarting

> **Tip** If you are tracking distributed queries, be sure to add the HostName column that corresponds to the ServerName in the display window. For transactions, be sure to add the TransactionID column. Also, if you plan to replay the trace for troubleshooting, refer to "Replaying a Trace" on page 518 for specific event classes and data columns that you need to select.

12. To focus the trace on specific types of data, you might want to set criteria that exclude certain types of events. If so, select an event category you want to filter, click the Column Filters button to open the Edit Filter dialog box, and then set filter criteria. For each event category, you can use different filtering criteria. To use the criteria, you click on the related plus sign and then enter the appropriate value in the text box provided. When you are finished, click OK to close the Edit Filter dialog box. You use the filter criteria as follows:

❑ **Equals, Not Equal To, Greater Than Or Equal, or Less Than Or Equal** Use these criteria to set the values that trigger the event. Events with values outside the specified range are excluded. For example, with the CPU event category you can specify that only events using greater than or equal to 1000 milliseconds of CPU time are captured. If events use less CPU time than specified, they are excluded.

❑ **Like or Not Like** Enter strings to include or exclude for this event category. Use the wildcard character (%) to match a series of characters. Use the semicolon (;) to separate multiple strings. For example, you can use the Application Name category to exclude all application names that start with *MS* and *SQL Server* by typing **MS%;SQL Server%**.

13. When you are finished configuring the trace, click Run to start the trace.

## Working with Traces

Profiler displays information for multiple traces in separate windows that can be cascaded or tiled. Use the buttons on the Profiler toolbar to control work with traces. Create a new trace by clicking the New Trace button, and then use the options in the New Trace dialog box to configure the trace. Create a trace template by clicking New Template, setting trace properties, and then clicking Save. Once you have an active trace, you can do the following:

■ Start the trace by clicking the Start Selected Trace button.

■ Pause the trace by clicking the Pause Selected Trace button. You can then use the Start Selected Trace button to resume the trace at the point at which it was stopped.

- Stop the trace by clicking the Stop Selected Trace button. If you start the trace again with the Start Selected Trace button, the Profiler displays data again from the beginning of the trace process; new data is appended to the files or tables to which you are capturing data.

- Edit trace properties by clicking the Properties button.

## Saving a Trace

When you create traces in Profiler, you create trace data and trace definitions. The Profiler window displays trace data, and you can also store it in a file or a table, or both. The trace data records a history of events that you are tracking, and you can use this history to replay the events for later analysis. The Trace Properties dialog box displays the trace definition. You can use the trace definition to create a new trace based on the existing trace.

To save trace data, complete the following steps:

1. Access the Profiler window that displays the trace you want to save.

2. Select File, point to Save As, and then select Trace File or Trace Table.

3. Use the Save As dialog box to select a folder location. Type a file name, and then click Save. Trace files end with the .trc extension.

To save a trace definition, complete the following steps:

1. Access the Profiler window that displays the trace with the definition you want to save.

2. Select File, point to Save As, and then select Trace Template.

3. Use the Select Template Name dialog box to select a folder location. Type a file name, and then click OK. Trace templates end with the .tdf extension.

## Replaying a Trace

One of the main reasons you will want to create traces is to save them and replay them later. When replaying traces, Profiler can simulate user connections and authentication, which allows you to reproduce the activity recorded in the trace. You can replay traces in different ways to help you troubleshoot different kinds of problems:

- Execute traces step by step to closely monitor each step in the trace.

- Execute traces using the original timeline to simulate user loads.

- Execute traces with a high replay rate to stress-test servers.

As you monitor the trace execution, you can look for problem areas. Then, when you identify the cause of problems you are trying to solve, you can correct them and rerun the original trace definition. If you are still having problems, you will need to reanalyze the trace data or look at other areas that might be causing problems. Keep in mind that you might need to specify different events to capture in the subsequent trace.

## Requirements for Replaying Traces

Traces that you want to replay must contain a minimum set of events and data columns. If the trace does not contain the necessary elements, you will not be able to replay the trace. The required elements are in addition to any other elements that you want to monitor or display with traces.

> **Tip**   If you select the TSQL_Replay template, the required event classes and data classes are enabled for tracing by default. If you select another template, you might need to manually select the required event classes and data columns.

You should capture the following event classes to allow a trace to be replayed and analyzed correctly: Audit Login, Audit Logout, ExistingConnection, RPC Output Parameter, RPC:Completed, RPC:Starting, SQL:BatchCompleted, and SQL:BatchStarting. When you are replaying server-side cursors, you must add CursorClose, CursorExecute, CursorOpen, CursorPrepare, and CursorUnprepare. When you are replaying server-side prepared SQL statements, you must add Exec Prepared SQL and Prepare SQL.

You should capture the following data columns to allow a trace to be replayed and analyzed correctly: ApplicationName, Binary Data, ClientProcessID, DatabaseID, DatabaseName, EndTime, Error, EventClass, EventSequence, HostName, IsSystem, LoginName, NTDomainName, NTUserName, ServerName, SPID, StartTime, and TextData.

## Replaying Traces on a Different Server

You can replay a trace on a server other than the server originally traced. When you replay a trace on another server, this server is called the *target system*. To replay traces on the target, you should ensure that all logins contained in the trace meet the following criteria:

- Are created on the target system, and are in the same database as the source system

- Have the same permissions they had originally

- Have the same passwords they had originally

- Are set to use a default database that matches the database on the source system

If these settings are not the same, you will see errors, but the replay operation will continue. Also, database IDs on the target system must be the same as those on the source system. The easiest way to set up databases on the target is to complete the following steps:

1. Back up the *master* database on the source and any user databases used in the trace.

2. Restore the databases on the target as explained in "Restoring a Database to a Different Location" on page 558.

### Replaying and Analyzing a Trace

Replaying a trace allows you to analyze problems. To begin, start Profiler, and then select the Open Trace File or Open Trace Table option, as appropriate for the type of trace you want to replay. After you select the trace to replay, the trace is then loaded into the Profiler window. Events and commands recorded in the trace are summarized in the Profiler window, as shown in Figure 14-11. You can select an entry to see an expanded list of commands executed.

As Figure 14-11 also shows, the toolbar in the replay window differs from the standard toolbar. The buttons provide just about everything that you need to debug traces, including

- **Start Replay**   Starts executing the trace

- **Pause Replay**   Pauses execution of the trace

- **Stop Replay**   Stops execution of the trace

- **Execute One Step**   Allows you to move through the trace one step at a time

- **Run To Cursor**   Allows you to move through the trace using cursor sets

- **Toggle Breakpoint**   Allows you to set breakpoints for the trace execution

**Figure 14-11**   The Profiler window.

When you start the replay, you will need to connect to the server, and then the initial dialog box is displayed to configure replay options. (See Figure 14-12.) You configure the options in the Replay Configuration dialog box to control where and how the play-back takes place. Start by setting the destination server for the replay operation. By default, the replay server is set to the current (local) server. Click Change to use a different replay server, and then set the replay options.

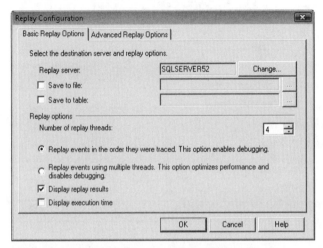

**Figure 14-12**   The Replay Configuration dialog box.

The replay options determine how closely the replay mirrors the original event execution. You can choose from the following options in the dialog box:

- **Replay Events In The Order They Were Traced**   Events are started in the order in which they originally started. This enables debugging, but it does not guarantee timing of event execution. Events might be executed sooner than their original start time or after their original start time, depending on current activity levels, the current speed of connections, and other factors.

- **Replay Events Using Multiple Threads**   Events are replayed as quickly as they can be processed. No timing is maintained between events. When one event completes, the next event is started. This optimizes performance and disables debugging.

The Display Replay Results check box controls whether or not the replay results are displayed in the Profiler window. To display results, select this option. Otherwise, clear this option.

You can also select an output file to save the result of the replay for later viewing. The output file allows you to review the replay just as you would any other trace file.

# Backing Up and Recovering Microsoft SQL Server 2008

Information is the fuel that drives the enterprise, and the most critical information is often stored in databases. Databases are where you will find an organization's customer account information, partner directories, product knowledge base, and other important data. To protect an organization's data and to ensure the availability of its databases, you need a solid database backup and recovery plan.

Backing up databases can protect against accidental loss of data, database corruption, hardware failures, and even natural disasters. It is your job as a database administrator to perform backups and store the backups you create in a safe and secure location.

## Creating a Backup and Recovery Plan

Creating and implementing a backup and recovery plan is one of your most important duties as a database administrator. Think of database backup as an insurance plan for the future—and for your job. Important data is deleted accidentally all the time. Mission-critical data can become corrupt. Natural disasters can leave your office in ruins. With a solid backup and recovery plan in place, you can recover from any of these situations. Without one, you are left with nothing after a disaster of any kind.

## Initial Backup and Recovery Planning

Creating and implementing a backup and recovery plan takes time. You will need to figure out which databases need to be backed up, how often the databases should be backed up, and more. To help you create a plan, consider the following questions:

- **What type of databases are you backing up?**   System and user databases often have different backup and recovery needs. For example, the *master* database is essential for all Microsoft SQL Server operations. If the *master* database fails or becomes corrupt, it takes the whole server down with it. But you do not need to back up *master* every hour, as you might need to do with a critical user database that handles real-time customer transactions. You need to back up *master* only after you create a database, change configuration values, configure SQL logons, or perform similar activities that make changes to databases on a server.

- **How important is the data in the database?**   How you judge the data's importance can help determine *when* and *how* you should back it up. Although you might back up a development database weekly, you would probably back up a production database at least daily. The data's importance also drives your decision about the *type* of backup. To protect the data in that development database, you would probably want to make a full backup once a week. For an in-house customer order database that is updated throughout each weekday, you would probably want to perform full backups twice a week and supplement this with daily differential backups and hourly backups for the transaction logs. You might even want to set named log marks that allow recovery up to a specific point in the work.

- **How often are changes made to the database?**   The frequency of change can drive your decision about how often the database should be backed up. Because a read-only database does not ordinarily change, it does not need to be backed up regularly. On the other hand, a database that is updated nightly should be backed up after the nightly changes are posted. A database that is updated around the clock should be backed up continually.

- **How quickly do you need to recover the data?**   It is important to consider the amount of time it will take to recover lost data when you create a backup plan. For mission-critical databases, you might need to get the database back online swiftly; to do this, you might need to alter your backup plan. Instead of backing up to tape, for example, you might want to back up to disk drives or use multiple backup devices. Both options are much faster than restoring from a single tape device.

- **Do you have the equipment to perform backups?**   You need backup hardware to perform backups. If you do not have the hardware, you cannot perform backups. To perform timely backups, you might need several backup devices and several sets of backup media. Backup hardware includes a tape drive, optical drives, removable disk drives, and plain old disk drives.

- **Can you compress backups?**  SQL Server 2008 Enterprise Edition and later supports compression backups, and any SQL Server 2008 or later edition can restore compressed backups. Because a compressed backup is smaller than an uncompressed backup of the same data, SQL Server requires less device input/output (I/O) and the backup itself requires less storage space. Typically, this increases backup and restore speed significantly. However, compression and decompression can significantly increase processor overhead and this could adversely affect server performance.

- **What is the best time to schedule backups?**  You will want to schedule backups when database usage is as low as possible. Using this approach will speed the backup process. However, in the real world, you cannot always schedule backups for off-peak hours. So you will need to carefully plan when important databases are backed up.

- **Do you need to store backups off site?**  Storing copies of backup tapes at an off-site location is essential to the recovery of your systems in the case of a natural disaster. In your off-site storage location, you should also include copies of the software required to restore operations on a new system.

**Note**  Availability options, such as log shipping, are not a substitute for backups. Even if you use log shipping, mirroring, or clustering, you will still need to create backups.

Backing up a database differs from backing up a server or a workstation, primarily because you often need to combine all (or nearly all) of the available techniques to ensure that you can recover a database completely. The basic types of backups you can perform include

- **Full database backups**  Used to perform a full backup of the database, including all objects, system tables, and data. When the backup starts, SQL Server copies everything in the database and also includes portions of the transaction log that are needed while the backup is in progress. Because of this, you can use a full backup to recover the complete state of the data in the database at the time the backup operation finishes.

- **Differential backups**  Designed to back up data that has changed since the last full backup. Because you store only the changes, this type of backup is faster and you can perform it more often. As with full backups, differential backups include portions of the transaction logs that are needed to restore the database to the time when the backup operation finishes.

> **Tip**   You can use differential backups only in conjunction with full backups, and you cannot perform differential backups on the *master* database. Do not confuse differential backups with incremental backups. Differential backups record all changes since the last full backup (which means the amount of data that is backed up grows over time). Incremental backups record changes since the most recent full or incremental backup (which means the size of the data backed up incrementally is usually much smaller than a full backup).

- **Transaction log backups**   Transaction logs are serial records of all database modifications and are used during recovery operations to commit completed transactions and to roll back uncompleted transactions. When you back up a transaction log, the backup stores the changes that have occurred since the last transaction log backup and then truncates the log, which clears out transactions that have been committed or aborted. Unlike full and differential backups, transaction log backups record the state of the transaction log at the time the backup operation starts (not when it ends).

- **File and filegroup backups**   Allow you to back up database files and filegroups rather than the entire database. This type of backup is useful if you are dealing with large databases and you want to back up individual files rather than the entire database to save time. Many factors affect file and filegroup backups. When you use file and filegroup backups, you must back up the transaction log as well. Because of this dependency, you cannot use this backup technique if Truncate Log On Checkpoint is enabled. Furthermore, if objects in the database span multiple files or filegroups, you must back up all the related files and filegroups at the same time.

**Real World**   When you create full-text indexes, you can specify the filegroup in which an index should be created. If you don't specify a filegroup, the index will be part of the primary filegroup for the database. However, you might want to store full-text indexes in secondary filegroups because this can give you additional recovery options. You can view the filegroup ID of the filegroup that contains a full-text index by selecting the data_space_id column of the sys.fulltext_indexes view.

If the filegroup that contains the full-text index is brought online after the filegroup that contains the table data, users might experience problems with full-text queries. Specifically, full-text queries will fail because the index is not available. When change tracking is enabled, user data manipulation language (DML) will fail until the index filegroup is available. Any status functions that ordinarily access the full-text index fail. As soon as you bring both the full-text index filegroup and the table data filegroup online, full-text index queries will succeed and all other full-text operations will be restored.

**Tip** With databases that have one or more read-only filegroups, you might want to include contingencies for partial backups and partial differential backups in your planning. With a partial backup, you back up all the data in the primary filegroup and every read/write filegroup automatically. Partial backups do not, however, automatically include read-only filegroups. SQL Server includes read-only filegroups only when you explicitly specify them. With a partial differential backup, you back up only the data extents that were modified since the most recent partial backup of the same set of filegroups.

SQL Server 2008 uses recovery models to help you plan backups. The types of databases you are backing up and the types of backups you perform drive the choices for recovery models. Three recovery models are available:

- **Simple** The simple recovery model is designed for databases that need to be recovered to the point of the last backup. The backup strategy with this model should consist of full and differential backups. You cannot perform transaction log backups when the simple recovery model is enabled. SQL Server 2008 turns on the Truncate Log On Checkpoint option, which clears out inactive entries in the transaction log on checkpoint. Because this model clears out transaction logs, it is ideal for most system databases.

- **Full** The full recovery model is designed for databases that need to be recovered to the point of failure or to a specific point in time. Using this model, all operations are logged, including bulk operations and bulk loading of data. The backup strategy with this model should include full, differential, and transaction log backups or full and transaction log backups only.

- **Bulk-logged** The bulk-logged recovery model reduces the log space usage yet retains most of the flexibility of the full recovery model. With this model, bulk operations and bulk loads are minimally logged and cannot be controlled on a per-operation basis. You will need to manually redo bulk operations and bulk loads if the database fails before you perform a full or differential backup. The backup strategy with this model should include full, differential, and transaction log backups or full and transaction log backups only.

Each database can have a different recovery model. By default, *master*, *msdb*, and *tempdb* use the simple recovery model, and the *model* database uses the full recovery model. The *model* database is the template database for all new databases, so if you change the default setting, all new databases for the database server instance use the new default model. You set the recovery model by completing the following steps:

1. Start SQL Server Management Studio. In the Object Explorer view, connect to the appropriate server.

2. If you plan to switch from bulk-logged recovery to simple recovery, perform a transaction log backup prior to making the change, and then change your backup strategy so that you no longer perform transaction log backups.

3. Expand the Databases folder. If you are configuring recovery for a system database, expand the System Databases folder as well.

4. Right-click the database you want to change and choose Properties. This displays the Database Properties dialog box.

5. Use the Recovery Model drop-down list on the Options page to change the recovery model, and then click OK.

6. If you switched from simple recovery to full or bulk-logged recovery, add transaction log backups to your backup strategy for the database.

SQL Server 2008 includes several features that allow you to create standby servers. Following are the three general types of standby servers:

- **Hot standby server**   An automatically updated server that automatically comes online if a primary server/database fails

- **Warm standby server**   An automatically updated server that must be brought online manually if a primary server/database fails

- **Cold standby server**   A manually updated server that must be brought online manually if a primary server/database fails

Database mirroring, log shipping, and database copies allow you to create standby servers. You use database mirroring to establish a hot standby server, called a *mirror server*, on which the database is continuously brought up to date and to which failover can occur automatically if the primary database fails. You use log shipping to establish a warm standby server, called a *secondary server*, on which the database is automatically updated from log backups, but which must be brought online manually if the primary database fails. You create a copy of a database to establish a cold standby server, on which the database is manually updated and which must be brought online manually if the primary database fails.

## Planning for Mirroring and Mirrored Database Backups

Mirroring allows you to create hot standby servers. You can mirror any database except for *master*, *msdb*, *temp*, and *model*. You can configure and enable mirroring using the Mirroring page in the Database Properties dialog box. As discussed in "Ensuring Availability and Scalability" on page 33, mirroring requires up to three servers: a principal server, a mirror server, and a witness server.

Backups are not used with mirrored databases in the same way as they are with other databases. When mirroring is configured, backups of a principal database are used to initialize the mirror database on the mirror server. As part of the mirror creation process, you can back up and restore individual files and filegroups. However, you must restore all files and filegroups before you begin mirroring. If you want to work only with a subset of a database and its objects, use replication instead, as discussed in Chapter 13, "Implementing Snapshot, Merge, and Transactional Replication."

When mirroring databases, remember the following information:

- While database mirroring is active, you cannot back up or restore the mirror database.

- Although you can back up the principal database, you cannot use BACKUP LOG WITH NORECOVERY.

- You cannot restore the principal database (that is what mirroring is for). The mirror will correct itself after failover.

## Planning for Backups of Replicated Databases

Databases that are replicated present a special problem for backup and restoration planning, primarily because the traditional database architecture is extended to include three server roles (which all have related databases):

- **Publisher**   A server that makes data available for replication, tracks changes to data, and maintains other information about source databases. Each publisher has a *publication* database.

- **Distributor**   A server that distributes replicated data and stores the *distribution* database. Each distributor has a *distribution* database.

- **Subscriber**   A destination server for replication. The subscriber databases store the replicated data, receive updates, and in some cases can also make changes to data. Each subscriber has a *subscription* database.

As you do with other system databases, you should regularly back up the *publication*, *distribution*, and *subscription* databases. At the publisher, distributor, and all subscriber servers, you should back up both the *master* and *msdb* system databases at the same time as you back up the replication databases. When you restore the *publication* database, you should also restore the *master* and *msdb* databases at the publisher server. When you restore the *distribution* database, you should also restore the *master* and *msdb* databases at the distributor server. When you restore the *subscription* database, you should also restore the *master* and *msdb* databases at the subscriber server.

The *subscription* database backups should be no older than the shortest retention period of all publications to which the subscriber subscribes. If the shortest retention period is 10 days, the backup you plan to restore should be no older than 10 days. To ensure successful recovery of a *subscription* database, subscribers should synchronize with the publisher before the *subscription* database is backed up. They should also synchronize after the *subscription* database is restored. Synchronizing prior to backup helps ensure that if a subscriber is restored from backup, the subscription is still within the publication retention period.

You can restore replicated databases to the same server and database from which the backup was created or to another server or database. If you restore a backup of a replicated database to another server or database, replication settings are not preserved, and you will need to re-create all publications and subscriptions after backups are restored, except in the case of log shipping. If you use log shipping, you can restore a replicated database to a standby server and the replication settings are preserved.

With merge replication, any replication-related changes should be captured in the log backups. If you do not perform log backups, the *publication* database should be backed up whenever a setting relevant to replication is changed. After restoring the *publication* database from a backup, you should either synchronize the *publication* database with a *subscription* database or reinitialize all subscriptions to the publications in the *publication* database. You can synchronize the *publication* database or reinitialize subscriptions as discussed in "Subscribing to a Publication" on page 478. Be sure to check the identity ranges in tables that contain IDENTITY columns after restoring a database.

> **Note**   In merge replication, the *distribution* database has a limited role. It does not store any data used in change tracking, and it does not provide temporary storage of merge replication changes to be forwarded to *subscription* databases (as it does in transactional replication).

With transactional replication, you set the Sync With Backup option on the *distribution* and *publication* databases for the following reasons:

- Turn this option on for the *distribution* databases to ensure that transactions in the log of the *publication* database will not be truncated until they have been backed up at the *distribution* database. This allows the *distribution* database to be restored to the last backup, and any missing transactions then can be delivered from the *publication* database to the *distribution* database while replication continues unaffected. Although this has no effect on replication latency, it can delay the truncation of the log on the *publication* database until the corresponding transactions in the *distribution* database have been backed up.

- Turn this option on for the *publication* database if your application can tolerate additional latency to ensure that transactions are not delivered to the *distribution* database until they are backed up at the *publication* database. This allows you to restore the last *publication* database backup at the publisher without any possibility of the *distribution* database having transactions that the restored *publication* database does not have. Latency and throughput are affected because transactions cannot be delivered to the *distribution* database until they have been backed up at the publisher.

## Planning for Backups of Very Large Databases

If you must develop a plan to back up and restore very large databases, you might want to take advantage of parallel backup and restore. The parallel backup and restore process allows SQL Server to use multiple threads to read and write data. This means SQL

Server can read data from, and write data to, multiple data sources. The backup and restore process uses parallel I/O in different ways:

- Backup uses one thread per disk device to read data from the database when a database has files on several disk devices.

- Restore uses one thread per disk device as it initializes a database that it is creating for the restore process if the database is defined with files on several disks.

- Both backup and restore use one thread per backup device when a backup set is stored on multiple backup devices.

As you can see from this information, to take advantage of parallel I/O, you must implement your backup strategy so that databases do the following:

- Use multiple disk drives for storing data
- Use multiple backup devices for backing up and restoring data

After you determine the backup operations to use on each database and how often you want to back up each database, you can select backup devices and media that meet these requirements. The next section covers backup devices and media.

## Planning for Backup Compression

Backup compression is disabled by default. You can set a global default with compression on or off on a per-instance basis by completing the following steps:

1. Start SQL Server Management Studio. In the Object Explorer view, connect to the appropriate server.

2. Right-click the server entry and then select Properties. This displays the Server Properties dialog box.

3. On the Database Settings page, select the Compress Backup check box to turn on backup compression. Clear the Compress Backup check box to turn off backup compression. Click OK.

Using Transact-SQL, you can set the global default for compression using the server configuration option Backup Compression Default for the sp_configure stored procedure. As shown in the following example, use a value of 1 to turn compression on:

```
EXEC sp_configure 'backup compression default', '1'
GO
RECONFIGURE WITH OVERRIDE
GO
```

You can override the global default when creating or scheduling database backups. However, the global setting is extremely important because the server-level setting for compression determines whether the data SQL Server sends is compressed when you use log shipping and database mirroring. Specifically, you must enable backup compression at the server level to enable log backup compression for log shipping and database mirroring.

You can calculate the compression ratio of a database backup by dividing the original backup size by the compressed backup size. You can obtain both values from the backupset column in the *msdb* database as shown in the following example:

```
SELECT backup_size/compressed_backup_size FROM msdb..backupset
```

The compression ratio of a compressed backup depends on the type of data you have compressed. For example, although you can compress encrypted data, encrypted data has a significantly lower compression ratio than unencrypted data. Additionally, if the database itself is already compressed, compressing the backup won't necessarily reduce the backup size.

In a standard configuration, backup compression—whether used for database backups, log shipping, or log mirroring—can significantly increase processor utilization and this can have an impact on SQL Server performance. To reduce the performance impact for long-running database backups, you can compress backups by using a user session for which CPU utilization has been limited by using the Resource Governor.

## Selecting Backup Devices and Media

Many different solutions are available for backing up data. Some are fast and expensive. Others are slow but very reliable. The backup solution that is right for your organization depends on many factors, including the following:

- **Capacity**   This refers to the amount of data that you need to back up on a routine basis. Can the backup hardware support the required load given your time and resource constraints?

- **Reliability**   The reliability of the backup hardware and media determines how useful the backups you create will be when you need them to restore lost data. Can you afford to sacrifice reliability to meet budget or time needs?

- **Extensibility**   The extensibility of the backup solution refers to its ability to expand beyond its original capacity. Will this solution meet your needs as your organization grows?

- **Speed**   Consider the speed with which data can be backed up and recovered when selecting an appropriate solution. Can you afford to sacrifice speed to reduce costs?

- **Cost**   The cost of backup solution choices will affect your decision. Does the solution fit within your budget?

Capacity, reliability, extensibility, speed, and cost are the main issues that will influence your choice of a backup plan. If you determine the relative value of these issues to your organization, you will be able to select an appropriate backup solution for your situation. Some of the most commonly used backup solutions include the following hardware and media:

- **Tape drives** Tape drives are the most common backup devices. Tape drives use magnetic tape cartridges to store data. Magnetic tapes are relatively inexpensive, but they are not highly reliable. Tapes can break or stretch. They can also lose information over time. The average capacity of tape cartridges ranges from 4 GB to 10 GB. Compared with other backup solutions, tape drives are fairly slow. Their biggest advantage is their low cost.

- **Digital Audio Tape (DAT) drives** DAT drives are quickly replacing standard tape drives as the preferred type of backup devices. Many DAT formats are available. The most commonly used format is Digital Linear Tape (DLT) or Super DLT. With DLT IV, tapes have a capacity of either 35 GB or 40 GB uncompressed (70 GB or 80 GB compressed). If yours is a large organization, you might want to look at Linear Tape Open (LTO) or Advanced Intelligent Tape (AIT) tape technologies. Typically, LTO tapes have a capacity of 100 GB uncompressed (200 GB compressed), and AIT-3 tapes also have a capacity of 100 GB uncompressed (260 GB compressed).

  **Tip** To perform faster backup and recovery operations, you can use multiple backup devices with SQL Server. For example, if it normally takes four hours to perform a full backup or restoration of the database, you can cut the backup and restoration time in half by using two backup devices; with four backup devices, you could fully back up or restore the database in an hour.

- **Autoloader tape systems** Autoloader tape systems use a magazine of tapes to create extended backup volumes capable of meeting an enterprise's high-capacity needs. With an autoloader system, tapes within the magazine are automatically changed as needed during the backup or recovery process. Most autoloader tape systems use DAT tapes formatted for DLT, LTO, or AIT. Typical DLT drives can record up to 45 GB per hour, and you can improve that speed by purchasing a tape library system with multiple drives. In this way, you can record on multiple tapes simultaneously. In contrast, most LTO and AIT drives record over 100 GB per hour, and by using multiple drives in a system, you can record hundreds of GB per hour.

- **Optical jukeboxes** Optical jukeboxes are similar to autoloader tape systems. Jukeboxes use magnetic optical discs rather than DAT tapes to offer high-capacity solutions. These systems load and unload discs stored internally for backup and recovery operations. The main disadvantage of optical jukeboxes is their high cost.

- **Removable disk drives** Removable disks, such as external USB drives or eSATA drives, are increasingly being used as backup devices. Removable disks offer good speed and ease of use for a single drive or single system backup. However, the disk drives and the removable disks tend to be more expensive than standard tape or DAT drive solutions.

- **Disk drives**   Disk drives provide the fastest way to back up and restore files. Using disk drives, you can often accomplish in minutes what takes a tape drive hours. So when business needs mandate a speedy recovery, nothing beats a disk drive. The cost of disk drives, however, might be higher compared to tape library systems.

Selecting a backup device is an important step in implementing a backup and recovery plan, but it is not the only step. You also need to purchase the tapes or the disks, or both, that will allow you to implement your backup and recovery plan. The number of tapes, disks, or drives you need depends on the following factors:

- How much data you will be backing up

- How often you will be backing up the data

- How long you need to keep additional data sets

Typically, you implement backups by using a rotation schedule with two or more sets of tapes, disks, or files on a drive. Having more than one set of media allows you to increase media longevity by reducing media usage, and at the same time it reduces the number of actual tapes, disks, or files you need to ensure that you have data available when necessary.

> **Best Practices**   For important databases, I recommend using four media sets. Use two sets in regular rotation. Use the third set for the first rotation cycle at the beginning of each month, and use the fourth set for the first rotation cycle of each quarter. This technique allows you to recover the database in a wide variety of situations.

# Using Backup Strategies

Table 15-1 lists backup strategies you might want to use. As you can see, these backup strategies are based on the type of database as well as the type of data. When planning a backup strategy, remember the following:

- The *master* database stores important information about the structure of other databases, including the database size. Any time database information or structure changes, *master* might be updated without your knowing about it. For example, the size of most databases changes automatically, and when this happens *master* is updated. Because of this, often the best backup strategy for *master* is to schedule backups every other day and to rotate through several backup sets so that you can go back to several different versions of *master* if necessary.

- You can use transaction logs to recover databases up to the point of failure and up to a point of work. To recover a database to a point of work, you must insert named log marks into the transaction log using BEGIN TRANSACTION WITH

MARK. You can then recover to a mark in the log using RESTORE LOG WITH STOPATMARK or RESTORE LOG WITH STOPBEFOREMARK.

**Table 15-1**  Backup Strategies for System and User Databases

| Database Type | Details | Strategy |
| --- | --- | --- |
| User | Recovery up to the minute | Run full backups twice a week if possible. Use nightly differential backups, and back up the recovery transaction log every 10 minutes during business hours. Do not use Truncate Log On Checkpoint, as this will make it impossible to recover some transactions. To improve backup/restore speed, use multiple backup devices whenever possible. |
| | Recovery up to a point of work | Run full backups twice a week if possible. Use nightly differential backups, and back up the recovery transaction log every 10 minutes during business hours. Do not use Truncate Log On Checkpoint. Use named transactions to insert named marks into the transaction logs. To improve backup/restore speed, use multiple backup devices whenever possible. |
| | Recovery up to the hour | Run full backups twice a week if possible. Use nightly differential backups, and back up the recovery transaction log every 30 minutes during business hours. Do not use Truncate Log On Checkpoint. To improve backup/restore speed, use multiple backup devices whenever possible. |
| | Recovery of daily changes | Run full backups at least once a week. Use nightly differential backups, and back up the changes transaction log every four hours during business hours. Do not use Truncate Log On Checkpoint. |
| | Read-only | Schedule a full backup of the database every 30 days, and supplement this with an additional full backup whenever the database is modified. |
| System | *distribution* | Available when you configure replication and the server is acting as a distributor. Schedule full backups after snapshots. With transactional replication, schedule regular log backups. |
| | *master* | Run full backups immediately after creating or removing databases, changing the size of a database, adding or removing logins, or modifying server configuration settings. Do not forget to maintain several backup sets for *master*. |
| | *msdb* | If you schedule jobs through the SQL Server Agent, back up this database regularly because this is where the job schedule and history are maintained and backup history is stored. |
| | *model* | Treat like a read-only database. |

**Table 15-1   Backup Strategies for System and User Databases**

| Database Type | Details | Strategy |
|---|---|---|
| System (continued) | *publication* | Available when you configure replication and the server is acting as a distributor. If you do not perform log backups, the *publication* database should be backed up whenever a setting relevant to replication is changed. |
| | *subscription* | Available when you configure replication and the server is acting as a subscriber. *Subscription* database backups should be no older than the shortest retention period of all publications to which the subscriber subscribes. |
| | *tempdb* | Normally does not need to be backed up. This database is re-created each time you start SQL Server. |

# Creating a Backup Device

Early versions of SQL Server required you to configure backup devices before you could back up databases. With SQL Server 2008, you do not need to explicitly define backup devices. Nevertheless, backup devices do provide an easy way to ensure that you create backups that have the same file name and location time after time. By using consistent names and locations, you can more easily manage the backup and recovery process.

To create a backup device using SQL Server Management Studio, complete the following steps:

1.  Start SQL Server Management Studio. In the Object Explorer view, connect to the appropriate server.

2.  Expand the server's Server Objects folder.

3.  Right-click Backup Devices, and then choose New Backup Device to open the dialog box shown in Figure 15-1.

4.  In the Device Name box, type the name of the logical backup device. Use a short but descriptive name, such as Customer Device or Master Device.

5.  If you have installed a tape drive and want to back up to the tape drive, select the Tape option, and then use the related drop-down list box to select the target drive.

6.  If you are backing up to a file, select the File option, and then type the full path to the backup file you want to associate with this device, such as E:\MSSQL\ BACKUP\PERSONNEL.BAK.

7.  Click OK. SQL Server will attempt to verify the backup file location. If there is a problem, you will see a prompt notifying you of any issues.

**Figure 15-1**    The Backup Device dialog box.

With Transact-SQL, you create backup devices using sp_addumpdevice. Sample 15-1 shows the syntax and usage for this command, which uses many different arguments, including device_type, logical_name, physical_name, controller_type, and device_status. The device_type is the type of device you are using—disk or tape. The logical_name is the name of the backup device. The physical_name is the full path to the backup file. The controller_type is 2 for a disk, or 5 for a tape. The device_status is either noskip, to read ANSI tape headers, or skip, to skip ANSI tape headers.

**Sample 15-1**    sp_addumpdevice Syntax and Usage

```
Syntax
sp_addumpdevice [@devtype =]'device_type',
    [@logicalname =] 'logical_name',
    [@physicalname =] 'physical_name'
    [, {
        [@cntrltype =] controller_type |
        [@devstatus =] 'device_status' }
    ]


Usage
EXEC sp_addumpdevice 'disk', 'Customer', 'c:\mssql\backup\cust.bak'
EXEC sp_addumpdevice 'disk', 'Customer on Backup Server',
    '\\omega\backups\cust.bak'
EXEC sp_addumpdevice 'tape', 'Customer on Tape', '\\.\tape0'
```

# Performing Backups

Backups are an essential part of database administration. They are so important that SQL Server provides multiple backup procedures and several ways to create backups—all designed to help you manage database backup and recovery easily and effectively. In this section, you will learn about standard backup procedures and the Transact-SQL backup process. The final component in a successful backup strategy involves database maintenance plans, which you will learn about in Chapter 16, "Database Automation and Maintenance."

## Creating Backups in SQL Server Management Studio

In SQL Server Management Studio, you can start the backup process by right-clicking the database you want to back up, pointing to Tasks, and then selecting Back Up. I will focus on how you use the Back Up Database dialog box to perform backups in these situations:

- When you want to create a new backup set
- When you want to add to an existing backup set

### Creating a New Backup Set

Whenever you back up a database for the first time or start a new rotation on an existing backup set, follow these steps to create the backup:

1. Start SQL Server Management Studio. In the Object Explorer view, connect to the appropriate server.

2. Expand the Databases folder. Right-click the database you want to back up, point to Tasks, and then select Back Up. This opens the Back Up Database dialog box shown in Figure 15-2.

3. The database you want to back up should be selected in the Database drop-down list in the dialog box. The current recovery model for this database is also shown, but it is shaded because the recovery model cannot be changed. You cannot create transaction log backups when the recovery model is set to Simple.

4. Because this is a new backup set, select the type of backup you want to perform. Typically, for a first backup, you will want to perform a full backup. Then you can add to the backup set later using other types of backups.

5. You can back up the entire database or a subset of its files and filegroups. By default, Backup Component is set to Database to create a database backup. If you want to create a file and filegroup backup, select the Files And Filegroups option. The Select Files And Filegroups dialog box opens, and you can choose the files and filegroups you want to back up. Click OK after making your selections.

**Note** The only available backup option for the *master* database is Full. That is because you can run only full backups on *master*.

**Figure 15-2** The Back Up Database dialog box.

6. In the Name text box in the Backup Set area, type a name for the backup set you are creating. This is an ordinary, nontechnical name that will help you tell at a glance what the backup contains. For example, name the first backup set for the Customer database Customer Backup Set 1. Then you can add the full, differential, and transaction log backups for this rotation to the set.

7. In the Description box, type a description of the backup, such as **Set 1 contains the weekly full, daily differential, and hourly transaction log backups. This is the full backup for the week.**

8. Use the Backup Set Will Expire options to set an expiration interval or date. This allows the backup to overwrite the media after a specified period or date.

9. If a backup set exists and is listed in the Destination area, select it and click Remove.

10. Click Add to display the Select Backup Destination dialog box shown in Figure 15-3. To use a new file as the backup destination, select the File Name option and type the full path to the backup file, such as E:\DATA\BACKUPS\CUST.BAK or \\OMEGA\BACKUPS\CUST.BAK. To use a backup device, select the Backup

Device option, and then choose the backup destination using the drop-down list box. Click OK when you are ready to continue.

**Figure 15-3**   The Select Backup Destination dialog box.

11. To set additional options for the backup, select the Options page. You use the available options as follows:

   ❑ **Back Up To The Existing Media Set**   Select this option if you are using an existing media set. You can specify whether to append to the existing backup set or overwrite all existing backup sets.

   ❑ **Check Media Set Name And Backup Set Expiration**   Use this option to ensure that you are writing to the correct tape set and that the tape expiration date has not been reached. If you select this option, enter the media set name that should be verified.

   ❑ **Back Up To A New Media Set, And Erase All Existing Backup Sets**   Select this option if you want to create a new media set and erase all existing media sets. Then enter the media set name and an optional description.

   ❑ **Verify Backup When Finished**   Choose this option to verify the entire backup and check for errors. Generally, it is a very good idea to verify your backups.

   ❑ **Perform Checksum Before Writing To Media**   Use this option to check the data you are backing up prior to writing. This is the same as using the CHECKSUM or NOCHECKSUM options with the BACKUP statement. If you perform a checksum, you can also specify to continue on checksum error.

   ❑ **Continue On Error**   Select this option to continue backup after encountering one or more errors. If you do not select this option, SQL Server cancels the backup upon encountering an error.

❑ **Truncate The Transaction Log** Select this option to clean out entries that are no longer needed after the backup. These entries are for transactions that have been committed or rolled back. (This option is set by default for transaction log backups.)

❑ **Back Up The Tail Of The Log** Use this option to back up the active transaction log (those transactions that have not been completed and are at the tail of the log). When you use the full or bulk-logged recovery model, you must back up the active transaction log before you can restore the database using SQL Server Management Studio.

> **Tip** You will usually want to perform one last log backup before you try to restore a corrupt database. When you do, you will want to clear this option and perform the log backup without truncation. This option is the same as running BACKUP LOG NO_TRUNCATE.

❑ **Unload The Tape After Backup** Select this option to eject the tape after the backup. Optionally, you also can elect to rewind the tape before unloading. Both options are only valid with tape devices.

❑ **Set Backup Compression** Use these settings to set the desired compression option. You can use the server-level default setting or explicitly turn compression on or off.

12. Click OK to start the backup. If you opted to verify the data, the verification process starts immediately after the backup ends.

## Adding to an Existing Backup Set

When you want to add to an existing backup set, complete the following steps:

1. Start SQL Server Management Studio. In the Object Explorer view, connect to the appropriate server.

2. Expand the Databases folder. Right-click the database you want to back up, point to Tasks, and then select Back Up to open the Back Up Database dialog box (shown previously in Figure 15-2).

3. The database you want to back up should be selected in the Database drop-down list.

4. Select the type of backup you want to perform: Full, Differential, or Transaction Log. Typically, when you are adding to an existing set, you do so using a differential or transaction log backup. You cannot create transaction log backups when the recovery model is set to Simple.

5. You can back up the entire database or a subset of its files and filegroups. By default, Backup Component is set to Database to create a database backup. If you

want to create a file and filegroup backup, select the Files And Filegroups option. The Select Files And Filegroups dialog box is then displayed, allowing you to choose the files and filegroups to back up. Click OK after making your selections.

6. In the Backup Set panel's Name box, type a name for the backup you are creating. In the Description box, type a description of the backup, such as **Daily differential backup**.

7. Use the Backup Set Will Expire options to set an expiration interval or date. This allows the backup to overwrite the media after a specified period or date.

8. A backup set should be listed in the Destination area. If so, click Contents to see the current contents of this backup set. If a backup set is not listed, click Add to display the Select Backup Destination dialog box, and then enter the location of the existing backup. Click OK when you are ready to continue.

9. Select the Options page. Because you are adding more data to the existing backup set, the options Backup To The Existing Media Set and Append To The Existing Backup Set should be selected.

> **Real World**    Because compressed and uncompressed backups cannot co-exist in a media set, be sure to set the same compression option. Whether you back up data to a tape or disk drive, you should use the tape rotation technique. Create multiple sets, and then write to these sets on a rotating basis. With a disk drive, for example, you could create these backup files on different network drives and use them as follows:
>
> > **\\omega\data1drive\backups\cust_set1.bak**   Used in weeks 1, 3, 5, and so on for full and differential backups of the customer database
> >
> > **\\omega\data2drive\backups\cust_set2.bak**   Used in weeks 2, 4, 6, and so on for full and differential backups of the customer database
> >
> > **\\omega\data3drive\backups\cust_set3.bak**   Used in the first week of the month for full backups of the customer database
> >
> > **\\omega\data4drive\backups\cust_set4.bak**   Used in the first week of the quarter for full backups of the customer database
>
> Do not forget that each time you start a new rotation on a tape set, you should overwrite the existing media. For example, you would append all backups in week 1. Then, when starting the next rotation in week 3, you would overwrite the existing media for the first backup, and then append the remaining backups for the week.

10. For transaction log backups, you usually will want to select the Truncate The Transaction Log check box. This ensures that inactive entries are cleared out of the transaction log after a backup.

11. Click OK to start the backup. If you opted to verify the data, the verify process starts immediately after the backup ends.

## Using Striped Backups with Multiple Devices

Through a process called *parallel striped backups*, SQL Server can perform backups to multiple backup devices simultaneously. As you can imagine, writing multiple backup files at the same time can dramatically speed backup operations. The key to this speed, however, is having physically separate devices, such as three different tape devices or three different drives that you are using for the backup. You cannot write parallel backups to a single tape device, and you cannot write parallel backups to the same drive.

Multiple devices used in a backup operation are referred to as a *media set*. SQL Server allows you to use from 2 to 32 devices to form the media set. These devices must be of the same type. For example, you cannot create a striped backup with one backup tape device and one backup drive device.

The two main operations involved in parallel striped backups are

- Creating a new media set
- Adding to an existing media set

### Creating a New Media Set

To create a new media set using multiple devices, complete the following steps:

1. Select the server you want to use, and then create each of the backup devices you need in the media set, as described in "Creating a Backup Device" on page 535.

2. Right-click the database you want to back up, point to Tasks, and then select Back Up to display the Back Up Database dialog box.

3. Follow the steps outlined in "Creating a New Backup Set" on page 537. Repeat step 10 for each backup device you want to use in the media set.

### Adding to an Existing Media Set

To add to an existing media set, complete the following steps:

1. Right-click the database you want to back up, point to Tasks, and then select Back Up to display the Back Up Database dialog box.

2. Follow the steps outlined in "Adding to an Existing Backup Set" on page 540. The only difference is that in step 8 you should see a list of all the backup devices used in the media set. If you do not, you will need to add them one by one using the Add button and the related Select Backup Destination dialog box.

## Using Transact-SQL Backup

An alternative to using the backup procedures in SQL Server Management Studio is to use the T-SQL BACKUP statement. You use BACKUP DATABASE to back up databases and BACKUP LOG to back up transaction logs.

**Best Practices**   If you back up databases using Transact-SQL, you lose one of the biggest benefits of SQL Server—the automated recovery process. With automated recovery, you do not have to worry about which backup to apply in which situation, which command flags to use, and so on. Furthermore, because you can schedule automated and unattended backups, you do not really need to run backups manually through SQL as often as in the past. I recommend using the SQL Server Management Studio backup and restore process whenever possible.

BACKUP DATABASE has dual syntax. Sample 15-2 shows the syntax and usage for full and differential backups. A full backup is the default operation.

**Sample 15-2**   BACKUP DATABASE Syntax and Usage for Full and Differential Backups

```
Syntax
BACKUP DATABASE { database_name | @database_name_var }
TO < backup_device > [ ,...n ]
[ [ MIRROR TO < backup_device > [ ,...n ] ] [ ...next-mirror ] ]
[ WITH
    [ BLOCKSIZE = { blocksize | @blocksize_variable } ]
    [ [ , ] { CHECKSUM | NO_CHECKSUM } ]
    [ [ , ] { COMPRESSION | NO_COMPRESSION } ]
    [ [ , ] { STOP_ON_ERROR | CONTINUE_AFTER_ERROR } ]
    [ [ , ] DESCRIPTION = { 'text' | @text_variable } ]
    [ [ , ] DIFFERENTIAL ]
    [ [ , ] NAME = { backup_set_name | @backup_set_name_var } ]
    [ [ , ] PASSWORD = { password | @password_variable } ]
    [ [ , ] EXPIREDATE = { date | @date_var }
      | RETAINDAYS = { days | @days_var } ]
    [ [ , ] { FORMAT | NOFORMAT } ]
    [ [ , ] { INIT | NOINIT } ]
    [ [ , ] { NOSKIP | SKIP } ]
    [ [ , ] MEDIADESCRIPTION = { 'text' | @text_variable } ]
    [ [ , ] MEDIANAME = { media_name | @media_name_variable } ]
    [ [ , ] MEDIAPASSWORD = { mediapassword |
        @mediapassword_variable } ]
    [ [ , ] { NOREWIND | REWIND } ]
    [ [ , ] { NOUNLOAD | UNLOAD } ]
    [ [ , ] BUFFERCOUNT = { buffercount | @buffercount_variable }
        | MAXTRANSFERSIZE = { maxtransfersize |
        @maxtransfersize_variable }]
    [ [ , ] RESTART ]
    [ [ , ] STATS [ = percentage ] ]
    [ [ , ] COPY_ONLY ]
```

```
]
<backup_device> ::=
{
  { logical_backup_device_name | @logical_backup_device_name_var }
  |
    { DISK | TAPE } = { 'physical_backup_device_name' |
    @physical_backup_device_name_var }
}
```

**Usage**
```
USE master
EXEC sp_addumpdevice 'disk', 'Customer Backup Set 1',
    'f:\data\backup\Cust2.dat'
BACKUP DATABASE 'Customer' TO 'Customer Backup Set 1'
```

Sample 15-3 shows the BACKUP DATABASE syntax for file and filegroup backups.

**Sample 15-3**   BACKUP DATABASE Syntax and Usage for File or Filegroup Backups

```
Syntax
BACKUP DATABASE { database_name | @database_name_var }
     <file_or_filegroup> [ ,...f ]
TO <backup_device> [ ,...n ]
[ [ MIRROR TO <backup_device> [ ,...n ] ] [ ...next-mirror ] ]
[ WITH
     [ BLOCKSIZE = { blocksize | @blocksize_variable } ]
     [ [ , ] { CHECKSUM | NO_CHECKSUM } ]
     [ [ , ] { COMPRESSION | NO_COMPRESSION } ]
     [ [ , ] { STOP_ON_ERROR | CONTINUE_AFTER_ERROR } ]
     [ [ , ] DESCRIPTION = { 'text' | @text_variable } ]
     [ [ , ] DIFFERENTIAL ]
     [ [ , ] NAME = { backup_set_name | @backup_set_name_var } ]
     [ [ , ] PASSWORD = { password | @password_variable } ]
     [ [ , ] EXPIREDATE = { date | @date_var }
         | RETAINDAYS = { days | @days_var } ]
     [ [ , ] { FORMAT | NOFORMAT } ]
     [ [ , ] { INIT | NOINIT } ]
     [ [ , ] { NOSKIP | SKIP } ]
     [ [ , ] MEDIADESCRIPTION = { 'text' | @text_variable } ]
     [ [ , ] MEDIANAME = { media_name | @media_name_variable } ]
     [ [ , ] MEDIAPASSWORD = { mediapassword |
         @mediapassword_variable } ]
     [ [ , ] { NOREWIND | REWIND } ]
     [ [ , ] { NOUNLOAD | UNLOAD } ]
     [ [ , ] BUFFERCOUNT = { buffercount | @buffercount_variable }
         | MAXTRANSFERSIZE = { maxtransfersize |
         @maxtransfersize_variable }]
     [ [ , ] RESTART ]
```

```
        [ [ , ] STATS [ = percentage ] ]
        [ [ , ] COPY_ONLY ]
]
<file_or_filegroup> :: =
        { FILE = { logical_file_name | @logical_file_name_var }
        |
        FILEGROUP = { logical_filegroup_name |
          @logical_filegroup_name_var }
        | READ_WRITE_FILEGROUPS }
<backup_device> ::=
{
  { logical_backup_device_name | @logical_backup_device_name_var }
        |
        { DISK | TAPE } = { 'physical_backup_device_name' |
          @physical_backup_device_name_var }
}
```

**Usage**
```
USE master
EXEC sp_addumpdevice 'disk', 'Customer Backup Set 1',
    'f:\data\backup\Cust2.dat'
BACKUP DATABASE Customer
    FILE = 'Customer_data',
    FILEGROUP = 'Primary',
    FILE = 'Customer_data2',
    FILEGROUP = 'Secondary'
    TO 'Customer Backup Set 1'
```

Sample 15-4 shows the syntax for BACKUP LOG. By default, this command truncates the log after the backup.

**Sample 15-4**  BACKUP LOG Syntax and Usage

**Syntax for Backing Up the Log**
```
BACKUP LOG { database_name | @database_name_var }
{
    TO <backup_device> [ ,...n ]
[ [ MIRROR TO <backup_device> [ ,...n ] ] [ ...next-mirror ] ]
    [ WITH
    [ BLOCKSIZE = { blocksize | @blocksize_variable } ]
    [ [ , ] { CHECKSUM | NO_CHECKSUM } ]
    [ [ , ] { COMPRESSION | NO_COMPRESSION } ]
    [ [ , ] { STOP_ON_ERROR | CONTINUE_AFTER_ERROR } ]
    [ [ , ] DESCRIPTION = { 'text' | @text_variable } ]
    [ [ , ] EXPIREDATE = { date | @date_var }
        | RETAINDAYS = { days | @days_var } ]
    [ [ , ] PASSWORD = { password | @password_variable } ]
```

```
        [ [ , ] { FORMAT | NOFORMAT } ]
        [ [ , ] { INIT | NOINIT } ]
        [ [ , ] { NOSKIP | SKIP } ]
        [ [ , ] MEDIADESCRIPTION = { 'text' | @text_variable } ]
        [ [ , ] MEDIANAME = { media_name | @media_name_variable } ]
        [ [ , ] MEDIAPASSWORD = { mediapassword |
            @mediapassword_variable } ]
        [ [ , ] NAME = { backup_set_name | @backup_set_name_var } ]
        [ [ , ] NO_TRUNCATE ]
        [ [ , ] { NORECOVERY | STANDBY = undo_file_name } ]
        [ [ , ] { NOREWIND | REWIND } ]
        [ [ , ] { NOUNLOAD | UNLOAD } ]
        [ [ , ] BUFFERCOUNT = { buffercount | @buffercount_variable }
            | MAXTRANSFERSIZE = { maxtransfersize |
            @maxtransfersize_variable }]
        [ [ , ] RESTART ]
        [ [ , ] STATS [ = percentage ] ]
        [ [ , ] COPY_ONLY ]
        ]
}
<backup_device> ::=
{
    { logical_backup_device_name | @logical_backup_device_name_var }
        |
        { DISK | TAPE } = { 'physical_backup_device_name' |
            @physical_backup_device_name_var }
}
```

**Syntax for Truncating the Log**
```
BACKUP LOG { database_name | @database_name_var }
{
    WITH
        { NO_LOG | TRUNCATE_ONLY } ]
}
```

**Usage**
```
USE master
EXEC sp_addumpdevice 'disk', 'Customer_log1',
    'f:\data\backup\Cust_log.dat'
BACKUP LOG Customer
    TO Customer_log1
```

# Performing Transaction Log Backups

Transaction logs are essential to the timely recovery of SQL Server databases. Unlike database backups, which can be full or differential, transaction log backups are usually incremental. This means that each transaction log backup has a record of transactions only within a certain time frame. Transaction logs are always applied in sequence—with the completion time of the last full or differential backup marking the beginning of a transaction log sequence.

Consequently, to restore the database you must apply each transaction log in sequence up to the point of failure. For example, if you run a full backup at 1:00 P.M. and the database fails at 1:46 P.M., you restore the last full backup and then apply each transaction log created after the last full backup, such as the backups at 1:15 P.M., 1:30 P.M., and 1:45 P.M. As you can see, without the incremental transaction log backups, you would lose all the transactions that took place after the 1:00 P.M. full backup.

You can perform transaction log backups like any other backup. Still, there are a few details that you should know before beginning this kind of backup, and the following sections cover these details.

### Options and Commands That Invalidate Log Sequences

Although the normal backup process for transaction logs is fairly straightforward, SQL Server has some tricky features involving the option flags that you can set for the backup or the database, or both. The following database options prevent you from using a transaction log sequence to recover a database:

- **Truncate Log On Checkpoint**   Clears out inactive entries in the transaction log on checkpoint, which means you cannot use the log for recovery.

- **Using Non-Logged Operations**   Commands that bypass the log invalidate a log backup sequence.

- **ALTER DATABASE**   Adding or deleting files with ALTER DATABASE invalidates a backup sequence.

> **Tip**   As mentioned previously, the completion time of the last full or differential backup marks the beginning of a transaction log sequence. If you use any of the previous commands and invalidate a log sequence, perform a full or differential backup to start a new sequence.

### Log Truncation Options

When you back up transaction logs, you have several options that determine how the backups are made. With SQL Server Backup in SQL Server Management Studio, you can use the Truncate The Transaction Log option. Setting this option clears committed transactions out of the log after a log backup. The BACKUP LOG command normally clears out committed or aborted transactions after a log backup as well. However, you can override this behavior with these options:

- **TRUNCATE_ONLY**   Removes inactive entries from the log without creating a backup. This option invalidates the log sequence.

- **NO_LOG**   Same as TRUNCATE_ONLY, but this option does not log the BACKUP LOG command in the transaction log. This option is designed for a situation in which the transaction log or its home drive is full and you must truncate the log without writing to the log device.

- **NO_TRUNCATE**   Writes all the transaction log entries from the last backup to the point of failure. Use this option when the database is corrupt and you are about to restore it.

**Tip**   After you use TRUNCATE_ONLY or NO_LOG, always perform a full or differential backup. This revalidates the log sequence. Additionally, because you can grow logs automatically, you should rarely encounter a situation in which you need to truncate the log without logging. The log can run out of space only if you set a maximum size or the drive or drives that the log uses run out of space.

# Restoring a Database

Occasional database corruption, hardware failure, and natural disasters do happen, and as a database administrator, you need to be able to restore the database if any of these events occur. Even if you are a pro at backup and restore procedures, keep in mind that restoring a database is different from restoring an operating system or recovering other types of applications. The mix of full, differential, and transaction log backups ensures that you can get up-to-the-minute recovery of a database, but it complicates the recovery process.

In the following section, you will find tips and advice on troubleshooting database corruption. After that, you will find step-by-step procedures for restoring a database in various situations, including

- Restoring a database using backups created in SQL Server Management Studio

- Restoring a file or filegroup

- Restoring a database to a different location

- Restoring a database using Transact-SQL

**Note**   You cannot restore SQL Server 2008 backups using any earlier version of SQL Server. In SQL Server 2008, you cannot restore system database backups that were created by using SQL Server 2000 or SQL Server 2005 to SQL Server 2008. In SQL Server 2008, you can, however, restore user database backups that were created by using SQL Server 2000, SQL Server 2005, or SQL Server 2008. After you restore a SQL Server 2005 or SQL Server 2000 database to SQL Server 2008, the database becomes available immediately and is then automatically upgraded to SQL Server 2008.

## Database Corruption and Problem Resolution

All the knowledge you have accumulated as a database administrator is most important in one defining moment. That is the moment when you attempt to restore a database. The techniques you use to restore a database depend on the backup options you have used and the state of the database. As you know, the backup techniques available are full, differential, transaction log, and file/filegroups. What you might not know is how to restore a database by combining these techniques.

Table 15-2 lists some suggested recovery strategies for corrupted databases. These strategies show how to recover a database with various combinations of the available backup operations. If you use SQL Server Management Studio for backup and restore operations, these procedures are done for you automatically in most cases. The actual step-by-step process is covered later in this chapter.

**Table 15-2   Recovery Strategies for Databases**

| Backup Type | Restore Process |
| --- | --- |
| Full backups only | Restore the database using the last full backup. |
| Full and differential backups | Restore the last full backup with NORECOVERY. Then restore the last differential backup with RECOVERY. |
| Full and transaction log backups | Back up the current transaction log with NO_TRUNCATE. Restore the last full backup with NORECOVERY. Apply log backups from that time forward in sequence, using NORECOVERY. Apply the last differential backup with the RECOVERY option. |
| Full, differential, and transaction log backups | Back up the current transaction log with NO_TRUNCATE. Restore the last full backup with NORECOVERY and transaction log backups and then the last differential backup with NORECOVERY. Apply log backups from that time forward in sequence using NORECOVERY. Apply the last backup using the RECOVERY option. |

Now you know how to restore a database in theory. But before you begin, you should make sure the database is really corrupt and cannot be recovered by other means. To troubleshoot database problems and potential corruption, complete the following steps:

1. Start with the SQL Server logs. See what types of error messages are in the logs, paying particular attention to errors that occur during database startup. Also take a look at user-related errors. If you find errors, you can look up the error numbers in SQL Server Books Online or the Microsoft Online Support Web site (*http://search.support.microsoft.com*). You access the server logs through the Management folder in SQL Server Management Studio as discussed in Chapter 14, "Profiling and Monitoring Microsoft SQL Server 2008."

2. Check the state of the database. Every time you start SQL Server, it goes through a recovery process on each database. If the recovery process has problems, the mode or state of the database might be abnormal. To check the mode or state, use these properties of the databaseproperty function:

- ❑ **IsShutDown** If this property is set to 1, the database is shut down because of problems during startup.

- ❑ **IsEmergencyMode** If this property is set to 1, the database is in emergency mode, which allows a suspect database to be used.

- ❑ **IsSingleUser, IsDboOnly, IsReadOnly, or IsOffline** If these properties are set to 1, the database is in a limited or no access mode and needs to be made operational so that it can be accessed.

- ❑ **IsSuspect** If this property is set to 1, the database is suspect, which means it is possibly corrupted.

- ❑ **IsInLoad** If this property is set to 1, the database is going through the loading process.

- ❑ **IsInRecovery** If this property is set to 1, the database is going through the recovery process.

- ❑ **IsNotRecovered** If this property is set to 1, the database failed to recover and is in an unstable state.

3. If possible, try to use the DBCC command to further troubleshoot or repair the database. DBCC is covered in Chapter 16.

4. If these procedures indicate that you have a corrupt database that cannot be repaired, restore the database from backup.

You can use the databaseproperty function as shown in Sample 15-5.

**Sample 15-5** The databaseproperty Function Syntax and Usage

```
Syntax
databaseproperty('database','property')


Usage
select databaseproperty('Customer','IsEmergencyMode')
```

## Restoring a Database from a Normal Backup

SQL Server Management Studio tracks all the backups you create for each database; when you need to restore a database, SQL Server Management Studio automatically configures the restore. You can restore a database using these default settings or fine-tune the restore operation as necessary.

To restore a database, complete the following steps:

1. If you are using transaction logs and the database is still running, you should back up the current transaction log with NO_TRUNCATE. When you are using the SQL Server Backup dialog box, this means you should select Back Up The Tail Of The Log on the Options page of the Back Up Database dialog box when performing the transaction log backup.

2. In SQL Server Management Studio, connect to the appropriate server in the Object Explorer view.

3. Expand the Databases folder. Right-click the database you want to restore. On the shortcut menu, point to Tasks, select Restore, and then select Database. This opens the Restore Database dialog box shown in Figure 15-4.

**Figure 15-4**   The Restore Database dialog box.

4. The database currently selected is displayed in the To Database list box in the Destination For Restore area at the top of the dialog box. If you are restoring the database to its original location, leave the database in the To Database box as it is. If you want to restore the database to an alternate location, select a different database to use as the destination or type the name of a new database for the restore operation.

> **Note**   This option is provided to allow you to restore a database to a different location, as described in "Restoring a Database to a Different Location" on page 558. All databases on the server are included in the drop-down list as possible values except *master* and *tempdb*.

5.  By default, the database is restored to the most recent possible point in time. If multiple backups are available, you might be able to select a point in time for the restore. For example, if you know that GOTEAM accidentally deleted the Accounts table at 12:16 P.M., you could restore the database to a point just prior to this transaction, such as 12:15 P.M. To use the point in time option, click the Properties (...) button to the right of the To A Point In Time text box. This opens the Point In Time Restore dialog box. Choose the option A Specific Date And Time, select a date and time using the text boxes provided, and then click OK.

6.  The database currently selected is displayed in the From Database list box under Source For Restore. If you are restoring a different database, choose this database instead. Only databases that have backup history in the *msdb* are listed.

> **Note**   Restoring a database from a tape device or other backup device differs from a normal backup. This is primarily because you have to work with backup media (tapes) that might contain multiple backups, as well as multiple backup media sets (tape sets). If you are restoring from a device, select From Device, and then click the related Properties (...) button. You can then use the Specify Backup dialog box to specify the backup media and its location for the restore operation. You can add multiple locations and view the contents of added backup sets as well.

7.  Use the Select The Backup Sets To Restore option to select the backup set to restore. By default, the last full set (including the last full backup, differential backups since the last full backup, and transaction log backups since the last full backup) should be selected. The selected backups can also represent the most current backup set (according to a recovery plan) that meets the point-in-time recovery requirements.

> **Real World**   Normally, you will want to start with the last complete backup set. However, if you know that the last backup set is bad or contains transactions that you do not want to apply, such as a massive table deletion, go back to a previous backup set by selecting a different full backup and its related differential and transaction log backups as the starting point.

8.  The lower portion of the Restore Database dialog box provides a backup history for the selected database. You can use the information in the history as follows:

❑ **Restore**   Allows you to select which backup sets to restore. Default selections are based on the first backup to restore, and they go forward in time through differential and transaction log backups. You should rarely need to change the default selections.

❑ **Name**   Indicates the name of the backup set.

❑ **Component**   Shows the backed-up component as Database, File, or a blank entry. A blank entry indicates a transaction log backup.

❑ **Type**   Indicates the type of backup performed as Full, Differential, or Transaction Log.

❑ **Server**   Shows the Database Engine instance that performed the backup.

❑ **Database**   Displays the name of the database backed up.

❑ **Position**   Shows the position of the backup set in the volume.

❑ **First LSN**   For log backups, this is the log sequence number (LSN) of the first transaction in the backup set, which helps with ordering transaction logs for the restore operation.

❑ **Last LSN**   For log backups, this is the log sequence number of the last transaction in the backup set, which helps with ordering transaction logs for the restore operation.

❑ **Checkpoint LSN**   For log backups, this is the log sequence number of the most recent checkpoint at the time the backup was created, which helps with ordering transaction logs for the restore operation.

❑ **Full LSN**   The log sequence number of the most recent full database backup.

❑ **Start Date**   Displays a date and time stamp that indicates when the backup operation started.

❑ **Finish Date**   Displays a date and time stamp that indicates when the backup operation finished.

❑ **Size**   Shows the size of the backup.

❑ **User Name**   Displays the name of the user who performed the backup operation.

❑ **Expiration**   Indicates the date and time the backup set expires.

9. Select the Options page to configure options for the restore operation. The Options page is shown in Figure 15-5. You use the available options as follows:

   ❑ **Overwrite The Existing Database**   Allows the restore operation to overwrite any existing databases and their related files. (This is the same as using RESTORE with the REPLACE option.)

- ❏ **Preserve The Replication Settings** Ensures that any replication settings are preserved when restoring a published database to a server other than the server where the database was originally created. You must select the Leave The Database Ready For Use By Rolling Back Uncommitted Transactions option. (This is the same as using RESTORE with the PRESERVE_ REPLICATION option.)

- ❏ **Prompt Before Restoring Each Backup** Automatically prompts after completing a successful restore and before starting the next restore. The prompt includes a Cancel button, which is useful to cancel the restore operation after a particular backup is restored. This is a good option to use when you need to swap tapes for different media sets.

- ❏ **Restrict Access To The Restored Database** Sets the database in restricted-user mode so that only dbo, dbcreator, and sysadmin can access it. (This is the same as using RESTORE with the RESTRICTED_USER option.)

- ❏ **Restore The Database Files As** Allows you to change the restore location for database files.

**Figure 15-5** The Options page of the Restore Database dialog box.

10. Set the recovery state using one of the following options:

   ❑ **Leave The Database Ready To Use**   Completes the entire restore process, and applies all the selected backups, which can include a full backup, a differential backup, and multiple transaction log backups. All completed transactions are applied, and any uncompleted transactions are rolled back. When the restore process is completed, the database is returned to ready status and you can use it for normal operations. (This is the same as using RESTORE WITH RECOVERY.)

   ❑ **Leave The Database Non-Operational**   This is essentially a manual restore that allows you to go step-by-step through the backups. SQL Server completes the entire restore process and applies all the selected backups, which can include a full backup, a differential backup, and multiple transaction log backups. When the restore is completed, the database is not returned to ready status, and you cannot use it for normal operations. All transactions have not been processed, and the database is waiting for you to apply additional transaction logs. Apply these transaction logs using this mode, and then for the last transaction log, set the mode to Leave Database Operational. All completed transactions are then applied, and any uncompleted transactions are rolled back. (This is the same as using RESTORE WITH NORECOVERY.)

   ❑ **Leave The Database In Read-Only Mode**   This is similar to the Leave The Database Non-Operational option, with some exceptions. When the restore process ends, the database is in Read-Only mode, and it is ready for additional transaction logs to be applied. With the database in Read-Only mode, you can check the data and test the database. If necessary, apply additional transaction logs. Then for the last transaction log, set the mode to Leave Database Operational. All completed transactions are then applied, and any uncompleted transactions are rolled back. (This is the same as using RESTORE WITH STANDBY.)

   **Real World**   When you use the option Leave The Database In Read-Only Mode, SQL Server also creates an Undo file, which you can use to undo the restore operation. To commit the restore operations and the final transactions without restoring another transaction log, you could use the following code:

   ```
   RESTORE DATABASE Customer
   WITH RECOVERY
   ```

   This commits final transactions (if possible), deletes the Undo file, and puts the database back in operational mode. Although you might want to use WITH RECOVERY at this stage, you probably do not want to use WITH NORECOVERY because you will undo all the changes from the restore and might end up with an empty database.

11. When you are ready to start the restore operation, click OK. Stop the restore at any time by clicking Stop Action Now. If an error occurs, you will see a prompt with an error message.

## Restoring Files and Filegroups

You can restore files and filegroups from database backups or file backups either individually, in combination with each other, or all together. If any changes were made to the files or filegroups, you must also restore all transaction log backups that were created after the files or filegroups were backed up.

Although you can usually recover individual files or filegroups, there are exceptions. If tables and indexes are created that span multiple filegroups, all the related filegroups must be restored together. Do not worry, because SQL Server generates an error prior to starting the restore if a needed filegroup is missing. Further, if the entire database is corrupted, you must restore all files and filegroups in the database. In both cases, you must also apply transaction log backups created after the file or filegroup backups you are restoring.

To restore files or filegroups, complete the following steps:

1. If you are using transaction logs and the database is still running, you should back up the current transaction log with NO_TRUNCATE. When you are using the SQL Server Backup dialog box, this means you should select Back Up The Tail Of The Log on the Options page of the Back Up Database dialog box when performing the transaction log backup.

2. In SQL Server Management Studio, connect to the appropriate server in the Object Explorer view.

3. Expand the Databases folder. Right-click the database you want to restore. On the shortcut menu, point to Tasks, select Restore, and then select Files And Filegroups. This opens the Restore Files And Filegroups dialog box, shown in Figure 15-6.

4. The database currently selected is listed in the To Database box under Destination To Restore. If you are restoring a file or filegroup to its original database, this is what you want to use. If you want to restore the file or filegroup to a different database, select the different database to use as the destination or type the name of a new database for the restore operation.

> **Note** This option is provided to allow you to restore a database to a different location, as described in "Restoring a Database to a Different Location" on page 558. All databases on the server are listed as possible values except *master* and *tempdb*.

**Figure 15-6**   The Restore Files And Filegroups dialog box.

5. The database currently selected is listed in the From Database box under Source For Restore. If you are restoring files and filegroups for a different database, choose this database instead. Only databases that have backup history in the *msdb* are listed.

6. The lower portion of the Restore Files And Filegroups dialog box provides a backup history for the files and filegroups in the selected database. You can use the information in the history as follows:

   ❑ **Restore**   The selected check boxes indicate backup files to restore.

   > **Note**   No default selections are made in the Restore text box; you must choose the files manually.

   ❑ **Name**   The name of the backup set.

   ❑ **File Type**   The type of data in the backup. Data that is contained in tables is Rows Data. Binary large object (BLOB) data that is stored in the file system is Filestream Data. Transaction log data is Log.

   ❑ **Type**   The type of backup performed as Full, Differential, or Transaction Log.

❏ **Server**   The Database Engine instance that performed the backup.

❏ **File Logical Name**   The logical name of the file.

❏ **Database**   The name of the file that was backed up.

❏ **Start Date**   A date and time stamp indicating when the backup operation started.

❏ **Finish Date**   A date and time stamp indicating when the backup operation finished.

❏ **Size**   The size of the backup.

❏ **User Name**   The name of the user who performed the backup operation.

7. Select the backup files you want to restore.

8. Select the Options page to configure options for the restore operation. The available options are the same as those discussed in "Restoring a Database from a Normal Backup" on page 550.

9. When you are ready to start the restore operation, click OK. You can stop the restore at any time by clicking Stop.

## Restoring a Database to a Different Location

When you restore a database to a different location, you are essentially copying the database from backups. If you use this procedure to copy a database to a new location on the same computer, you create a copy of the database that can have separate files and a different database name. Restoring a database to a different location is similar to the process of restoring files and filegroups discussed previously. The main differences are as follows:

1. On the General page under Destination To Restore, type a new name for the database in the To Database box. For example, if you are restoring the Customer database to a new location, name the copy *Customer 2* or *CustomerCopy*.

2. When you access the Options page, you must override the default destination paths and enter new destination paths for all of the files you are restoring. Simply click in the Restore As box, and then enter a new file path. Or you can click the related Properties (...) button to select a new Restore As location.

If you use this procedure to copy a database to a different computer, you can create a working copy of the database on another server. You do not need to create a new database or perform any preliminary work, with one exception—if you want to use backup devices on the destination server, you should set them up beforehand. Also, before you begin the restore, you should ensure that the destination computer is using the same code page, sort order, Unicode collation, and Unicode locale as the source server. If these configuration settings are not identical, you will not be able to run the database on the destination server.

## Recovering Missing Data

If you suspect part of the database is missing or corrupted, you can perform a partial restore to a new location so that you can recover the missing or corrupted data. To do this, use the PARTIAL option with the RESTORE DATABASE statement as discussed in "Using Transact-SQL Restore Commands" on page 561. You can restore partial databases only at the filegroup level. The primary file and filegroup are always restored along with the files that you specify and their corresponding filegroups. Files and filegroups that are not restored are marked as offline, and you cannot access them.

To carry out the restore and recovery process, complete the following steps:

1. Perform a partial database restore. Give the database a new name and location in the RESTORE DATABASE statement, and use MOVE/TO to move the original database source files to new locations, such as

```
RESTORE DATABASE new_custdb_partial
    FILEGROUP = 'Customers2'
    FROM DISK='g:\cust.dmp'
    WITH FILE=1,NORECOVERY,PARTIAL,
    MOVE 'cust' TO 'g:\cu2.pri',
    MOVE 'cust_log' TO 'g:\cu2.log',
    MOVE 'cust_data_2' TO 'g:\cu2.dat2'
GO
```

2. Extract any needed data from the partial restore, and insert it into the database from which it was deleted.

## Creating Standby Servers

The notion of restoring a backup to a different computer can be extended to create a standby backup server that you can bring online if the primary server fails. When you create a standby server, you have two options:

- You can create a *cold* standby that you synchronize manually.

- Or you can create a *warm* standby that SQL Server synchronizes automatically.

### Creating a Cold Standby

To create a standby that you synchronize manually, complete the following steps:

1. Install SQL Server on a new server system using an identical configuration. This means that the destination server should use the same code page, sort order, Unicode collation, and Unicode locale as the source server.

2. Copy all of the databases on the primary server to this new system by specifying a different restore location in the Restore Database dialog box.

3. Maintain the copies of the databases by periodically applying the transaction log backups from the primary server to the standby server.

4. You might want to leave the standby server in Standby mode so that the database is read only. This allows users to access the database but not make changes.

If one or more databases on the primary server fail for any reason, you can make the corresponding databases on the standby server available to users. However, before you do this, you should synchronize the primary server and the standby servers by completing the following steps:

1. On the standby server, apply any transaction log backups created on the primary server that have not been applied yet. You must apply these backups in the proper time sequence.

2. Create a backup of the active transaction log on the primary server, and apply this backup to the database on the standby server. This ensures up-to-the-minute synchronization. Be sure to recover the database or specify that the database should be put in operational mode after this backup is applied.

> **Tip**   If you need to make the standby server appear to be the primary server, you might need to take the primary server off the network and rename it. Then rename the standby so that it appears to be the primary.

3. After you restore the primary server to working condition, any changes to the standby server's databases need to be restored to the primary server. Otherwise, those changes are lost when you start using the primary server again.

> **Note**   Standby servers are not the same as a SQL Server failover cluster, which is created using the SQL Server Failover Cluster Wizard and Microsoft Cluster Service. Standby servers store a second copy of a database on their hard disk drives. Virtual servers use a single copy of a database that is accessed from a shared storage device.

### Creating a Warm Standby

SQL Server 2008 Enterprise Edition includes a feature called *log shipping*. You can use log shipping to create a standby server that is automatically synchronized with the primary server. To do this, follow these steps:

1. Install SQL Server on a new server system using an identical configuration. This means that the destination server should use the same code page, sort order, Unicode collation, and Unicode locale as the source server.

2. Copy all of the databases on the primary server to this new system by specifying a different restore location in the Restore Database dialog box.

3. On the primary server, configure log shipping as described in Chapter 17, "Managing Log Shipping and Database Mirroring."

The primary server is referred to as the *source server*. The servers receiving the logs are referred to as *destination servers*. After configuring log shipping, you should check the status of log shipping on the source server and destination servers periodically.

If one or more databases on the primary server fail for any reason, you can make the corresponding databases on the standby server available to users. To do that, follow these steps:

1. Make sure that the most recent logs have been applied by checking the status of log shipping on the destination server.

2. Take the primary server off the network and rename it.

3. Rename the standby server so that it appears to be the primary server.

4. Check connections to the new primary server.

After you restore the primary server to working condition, any changes to the standby server's databases need to be restored to the primary server. Otherwise, those changes are lost when you start using the primary server again.

## Using Transact-SQL Restore Commands

You can also restore databases using Transact-SQL. The commands you will use are RESTORE DATABASE and RESTORE LOG. You can use RESTORE DATABASE to restore an entire database, specific files and filegroups, or part of a corrupted database. Sample 15-6 shows the syntax and usage for a complete restore. The option WITH RECOVERY is the default mode.

**Sample 15-6**   RESTORE DATABASE Syntax and Usage for a Complete Restore

```
Syntax
RESTORE DATABASE { database_name | @database_name_var }
[ FROM <backup_device> [ ,...n ] ]
[ WITH
    [ BUFFERCOUNT = { buffercount | @buffercount_variable } ]
    [ [ , ] { CHECKSUM | NO_CHECKSUM } ]
    [ [ , ] { STOP_ON_ERROR | CONTINUE_AFTER_ERROR } ]
    [ [ , ] MAXTRANSFERSIZE = { maxtransfersize |
        @maxtransfersize_variable }]
    [ [ , ] { CONTINUE_AFTER_ERROR | STOP_ON_ERROR } ]
    [ [ , ] ENABLE_BROKER ]
    [ [ , ] ERROR_BROKER_CONVERSATIONS ]
    [ [ , ] NEW_BROKER ]
    [ [ , ] FILE = { file_number | @file_number } ]
    [ [ , ] PASSWORD = { password | @password_variable } ]
    [ [ , ] KEEP_CDC ]
    [ [ , ] KEEP_REPLICATION ]
    [ [ , ] MEDIANAME = { media_name | @media_name_variable } ]
```

```
    [ [ , ] MEDIAPASSWORD = { mediapassword |
        @mediapassword_variable } ]
    [ [ , ] BLOCKSIZE = { blocksize | @blocksize_variable } ]
    [ [ , ] MOVE 'logical_file_name' TO 'operating_system_file_name' ]
        [ ,...n ]
    [ [ , ] { RECOVERY | NORECOVERY | STANDBY =
        {standby_file_name | @standby_file_name_var } }
    ]
    [ [ , ] REPLACE ]
    [ [ , ] RESTART ]
    [ [ , ] RESTRICTED_USER ]
    [ [ , ] { REWIND | NOREWIND } ]
    [ [ , ] STATS [ =percentage ] ]
    [ [ , ] STOPAT = { date_time | @date_time_var } |
      [ , ] STOPATMARK = { 'lsn:lsn_number' } [ AFTER 'datetime' ] |
      [ , ] STOPBEFOREMARK = { 'lsn:lsn_number' } [ AFTER 'datetime' ]
    ]
    [ [ , ] { UNLOAD | NOUNLOAD } ]
]
[;]
<backup_device> ::=
{ { 'logical_backup_device_name' | @logical_backup_device_name_var }
    | { DISK | TAPE } = { 'physical_backup_device_name' |
        @physical_backup_device_name_var } }


Usage
RESTORE DATABASE Customer
    FROM TAPE = '\\.\tape0'


Usage
RESTORE DATABASE Customer
    FROM Customer_1
    WITH NORECOVERY,
        MOVE 'CustomerData1' TO 'F:\mssql7\data\NewCust.mdf',
        MOVE 'CustomerLog1' TO 'F:\mssql7\data\NewCust.ldf'
RESTORE LOG Customer
    FROM CustomerLog1
    WITH RECOVERY
```

Using RESTORE DATABASE, you also can restore files and filegroups. Sample 15-7 shows the related syntax and usage.

**Sample 15-7**   RESTORE DATABASE Syntax and Usage for File and Filegroup Restore

```
Syntax
RESTORE DATABASE { database_name | @database_name_var }
    <file_or_filegroup_or_pages> [ ,...f ]
[ FROM <backup_device> [ ,...n ] ]
[ WITH [ RECOVERY | NORECOVERY ]
    [ BUFFERCOUNT = { buffercount | @buffercount_variable } ]
    [ [ , ] { CHECKSUM | NO_CHECKSUM } ]
    [ [ , ] { STOP_ON_ERROR | CONTINUE_AFTER_ERROR } ]
    [ [ , ] MAXTRANSFERSIZE = { maxtransfersize |
      @maxtransfersize_variable }]
    [ [ , ] { CONTINUE_AFTER_ERROR | STOP_ON_ERROR } ]
    [ [ , ] FILE = { file_number | @file_number } ]
    [ [ , ] PASSWORD = { password | @password_variable } ]
    [ [ , ] MEDIANAME = { media_name | @media_name_variable } ]
    [ [ , ] MEDIAPASSWORD = { mediapassword |
      @mediapassword_variable }]
    [ [ , ] BLOCKSIZE = { blocksize | @blocksize_variable } ]
    [ [ , ] MOVE 'logical_file_name' TO 'operating_system_file_name' ]
      [ ,...n ]
    [ [ , ] RECOVERY | NORECOVERY ]
    [ [ , ] REPLACE ]
    [ [ , ] RESTART ]
    [ [ , ] RESTRICTED_USER ]
    [ [ , ] { REWIND | NOREWIND } ]
    [ [ , ] STATS [ =percentage ] ]
    [ [ , ] { UNLOAD | NOUNLOAD } ]
]
[;]
<backup_device> ::=
{  { logical_backup_device_name|
      @logical_backup_device_name_var }
    | { DISK | TAPE } = { 'physical_backup_device_name' |
      @physical_backup_device_name_var } }
<file_or_filegroup_or_pages> ::=
{  FILE = { logical_file_name | @logical_file_name_var }
    | FILEGROUP = { logical_filegroup_name |
      @logical_filegroup_name_var } }
    | PAGE = 'file:page [ ,...p ]'  }


Usage
RESTORE DATABASE Customer
    FILE = 'Customerdata_1',
    FILE = 'Customerdata_2',
    FILEGROUP = 'Primary'
    FROM Customer_1
    WITH NORECOVERY
RESTORE LOG Customer
    FROM CustomerLog1
```

Sample 15-8 shows the syntax for performing a partial restore. This command creates a new database that is based on a partial copy of the backup data. When you use this procedure, the database_name represents the new name for the database, and the MOVE/ TO command is used to move the original database source files to new locations.

**Sample 15-8**   RESTORE DATABASE Syntax and Usage for Partial Restore

```
Syntax
RESTORE DATABASE { database_name | @database_name_var }
        <files_or_filegroups>
[ FROM <backup_device> [ ,...n ] ]
[ WITH PARTIAL
    [ BUFFERCOUNT = { buffercount | @buffercount_variable } ]
    [ [ , ] { CHECKSUM | NO_CHECKSUM } ]
    [ [ , ]  { STOP_ON_ERROR | CONTINUE_AFTER_ERROR } ]
    [ [ , ] MAXTRANSFERSIZE = { maxtransfersize |
        @maxtransfersize_variable }]
    [ [ , ] { CONTINUE_AFTER_ERROR | STOP_ON_ERROR } ]
    [ [ , ] FILE = { file_number | @file_number } ]
    [ [ , ] PASSWORD = { password | @password_variable } ]
    [ [ , ] MEDIANAME = { media_name | @media_name_variable } ]
    [ [ , ] MEDIAPASSWORD = { mediapassword |
        @mediapassword_variable } ]
    [ [ , ]  BLOCKSIZE = { blocksize | @blocksize_variable } ]
    [ [ , ] MOVE 'logical_file_name' TO 'operating_system_file_name' ]
        [ ,...n ]
    [ [ , ] NORECOVERY ]
    [ [ , ] REPLACE ]
    [ [ , ] RESTART ]
    [ [ , ] RESTRICTED_USER ]
    [ [ , ] { REWIND | NOREWIND } ]
    [ [ , ] STATS [ =percentage ] ]
      [ [ , ] STOPAT = { date_time | @date_time_var } |
        [ , ] STOPATMARK = { 'lsn:lsn_number' } [ AFTER datetime ] |
        [ , ] STOPBEFOREMARK = { 'lsn:lsn_number' } [ AFTER datetime ]
      ]
    [ [ , ] { UNLOAD | NOUNLOAD } ]
]
[;]
<backup_device> ::=
{ { logical_backup_device_name | @logical_backup_device_name_var }
  | { DISK | TAPE } = { 'physical_backup_device_name' |
        @physical_backup_device_name_var } }

<files_or_filegroups> ::=
   { FILE = { logical_file_name | @logical_file_name_var }
   | FILEGROUP = { logical_filegroup_name |
        @logical_filegroup_name_var }}
   [ ,...f ]
```

```
Usage
RESTORE DATABASE cust_part
    FILEGROUP = 'Customers2'
    FROM DISK = 'g:\cust.dmp'
    WITH FILE = 1,NORECOVERY,PARTIAL,
    MOVE 'cust' TO 'g:\cu2.pri',
    MOVE 'cust_log' TO 'g:\cu2.log',
    MOVE 'cust_data_2' TO 'g:\cu2.dat2'
GO
RESTORE LOG cust_part
    FROM DISK = 'g:\cust.dmp'
    WITH FILE = 2,RECOVERY
GO
```

Sample 15-9 shows how you can use RESTORE LOG.

**Sample 15-9**   RESTORE LOG Syntax and Usage

```
Syntax
RESTORE LOG { database_name | @database_name_var }
    <file_or_filegroup_or_pages> [ ,...f ]
[ FROM <backup_device> [ ,...n ] ]
[ WITH
  [ BUFFERCOUNT = { buffercount | @buffercount_variable } ]
  [ [ , ] { CHECKSUM | NO_CHECKSUM } ]
  [ [ , ] { STOP_ON_ERROR | CONTINUE_AFTER_ERROR } ]
  [ [ , ] MAXTRANSFERSIZE = { maxtransfersize |
      @maxtransfersize_variable }]
  [ [ , ] { CONTINUE_AFTER_ERROR | STOP_ON_ERROR } ]
  [ [ , ] FILE = { file_number | @file_number } ]
  [ [ , ] PASSWORD = { password | @password_variable } ]
  [ [ , ] KEEP_REPLICATION ]
  [ [ , ] MEDIANAME = { media_name | @media_name_variable } ]
  [ [ , ] MEDIAPASSWORD = { mediapassword |
      @mediapassword_variable } ]
  [ [ , ] BLOCKSIZE = { blocksize | @blocksize_variable } ]
  [ [ , ] MOVE 'logical_file_name' TO 'operating_system_file_name' ]
      [ ,...n ]
  [ [ , ] { RECOVERY | NORECOVERY | STANDBY =
        {standby_file_name | @standby_file_name_var } } }
  ]
  [ [ , ] REPLACE ]
  [ [ , ] RESTART ]
  [ [ , ] RESTRICTED_USER ]
  [ [ , ] { REWIND | NOREWIND } ]
  [ [ , ] STATS [ =percentage ] ]
    [ [ , ] STOPAT = { date_time | @date_time_var } |
```

```
        [ , ] STOPATMARK = { 'mark_name' | 'lsn:lsn_number' }
               [ AFTER datetime ] |
        [ , ] STOPBEFOREMARK = { 'mark_name' | 'lsn:lsn_number' }
               [ AFTER datetime ]
        ]
    [ [ , ] { UNLOAD | NOUNLOAD } ]
]
[;]
<backup_device> ::=
{ { logical_backup_device_name |
            @logical_backup_device_name_var }
    | { DISK | TAPE } = { 'physical_backup_device_name' |
            @physical_backup_device_name_var } }
<file_or_filegroup_or_pages> ::=
{  FILE = { logical_file_name | @logical_file_name_var }
    | FILEGROUP = { logical_filegroup_name |
            @logical_filegroup_name_var } }
    | PAGE = 'file:page [ ,...p ]'  }


Usage
RESTORE DATABASE Customer
    FROM Customer_1, Customer_2
    WITH NORECOVERY
RESTORE LOG Customer
    FROM CustomerLog1
    WITH NORECOVERY
RESTORE LOG Customer
    FROM CustomerLog2
    WITH RECOVERY, STOPAT = 'Dec 11, 2006 3:30 PM'
```

## Restoring the *master* Database

The *master* database is the most important database in the SQL Server database management system. This database stores information about all the databases on the server, server configuration, server logons, and other important information. If *master* gets corrupted, operations on the server might grind to a halt, and you will have to recover *master* using one of two techniques.

If you can start SQL Server, you can restore *master* from backup using a process similar to what you would use to restore any other database. To do this, complete the following steps:

1. You can back up *master* only by using a full backup. As a result, no differential or transaction log backups will be available. This means you might not be able to restore *master* exactly as it was before the failure, and that normally you should use the Recovery state of Leave Database Operational.

2. When you finish restoring the *master* database, you might need to manually apply any changes made since the last full backup.

3. After you check the server and verify that everything is okay, make a full backup of *master*.

If you cannot start SQL Server and you know *master* is the cause of the problem, you can restore *master* by completing the following steps:

1. Rebuild the *master* database by running Setup. Use Setup to rebuild, verify, and repair the SQL Server instance and its system databases.

2. After you rebuild *master* and get SQL Server back online, you can restore the last backup of *master* to return the server to its most current state.

3. Because Rebuild Master rebuilds the *msdb* and *model* databases, you might need to restore these databases from backup as well.

4. Re-create any backup devices if necessary.

5. Re-enter logins and other security settings if necessary.

6. Restore replication databases if necessary.

7. Restore or attach user databases if necessary.

8. Restore other server configuration settings if necessary.

As you can see from this step-by-step procedure, restoring *master* can take a lot of time and work, which is why it is so important to back up *master* regularly. When you finish recovering the server, be sure to make a full backup of the *master* database.

# Chapter 16
# Database Automation and Maintenance

Automation and maintenance go hand in hand. You can automate many routine database administration tasks, most of which have to do with maintenance issues, such as backing up databases or running consistency checks. Automation allows you to increase productivity, complete tasks while away from your computer, and more. You can configure the server to monitor processes and user activities, to check for errors, and to alert you when related events occur. If you configure alerts properly, Microsoft SQL Server 2008 can monitor itself and you can focus on other areas of administration. You can also schedule jobs to automate routine administration tasks. You can configure these jobs to run once or on a recurring basis, such as once a week or the third Tuesday of every month.

## Overview of Database Automation and Maintenance

SQL Server 2008 has four main database automation and maintenance components:

- **Database Mail**   Enables e-mail alerts and notifications.

- **SQL Server Agent**   Enables self-monitoring by using alerts, operator notifications, and scheduled jobs.

- **Database Maintenance Plans**   Enables automated maintenance.

- **Log Shipping**   Enables automatic synchronization with standby servers as discussed in Chapter 17, "Managing Log Shipping and Database Mirroring."

Typically, when you want to use these automation and maintenance features, you will select the following configurations:

1. Configure Database Mail for *msdb* and other databases. The *msdb* database is used by SQL Server Agent for scheduling alerts and jobs and to track operators. When you enable Database Mail, Database Mail objects are created in the *msdb* database. These objects allow *msdb* to act as a mail host server for sending alerts, notifications, and other types of messages.

2. Configure the SQL Server Agent service for your environment. Typically, you want to ensure that the service is automatically started with the operating system, that it uses the correct startup account, and that it has the correct mail profile so that it can be used with Database Mail.

3. Configure SQL Server Agent alerts, jobs, and operators to enable automatic alerts and scheduled jobs. *Alerts* are automatically generated messages that bring an error or issue to the attention of an administrator or other user. *Jobs* are scheduled tasks that run automatically when triggered or at a specific interval. *Operators* are individuals to whom you want to send alerts and notifications.

4. Configure Database Maintenance Plans to automate routine database optimization and maintenance. Even though you can automate many routine tasks, you should regularly review report histories to track maintenance plan execution. Additionally, you might find that occasionally you need to perform some optimization and maintenance tasks manually, and you can do this with database maintenance plans as well.

5. Optionally, configure log shipping to enable other computers running SQL Server to act as standby servers that can be brought online manually in case of primary server failure. Typically, log shipping is used as an alternative to database mirroring, which was discussed in Chapter 15, "Backing Up and Recovering Microsoft SQL Server 2008." However, both features can be configured, enabled, and in use simultaneously on any given SQL Server instance.

# Using Database Mail

Database Mail is an essential part of database automation. You must configure Database Mail so that alerts and other types of messages can be sent to administrators or other users. Database Mail provides SQL Server with the ability to generate and send e-mail messages as a mail client using the Simple Mail Transfer Protocol (SMTP). The Database Mail configuration process performs the following tasks:

- Installs database messaging objects in the *msdb* database
- Configures database mail accounts and profiles
- Configures database mail security

Database Mail is a full-featured replacement for SQL Mail. Database Mail acts as a mail client and sends its messages to designated SMTP servers. Any SMTP server, including Microsoft Exchange servers, can receive and deliver messages generated by Database Mail.

## Performing the Initial Database Mail Configuration

Like most mail clients, Database Mail uses mail profiles and mail accounts to send e-mail messages. The profile defines the mail environment Database Mail will use and can be associated with one or more SMTP mail accounts. Because the mail accounts are used in priority order, you can configure multiple accounts on different mail servers as a safeguard against mail-server failure or network problems that could prevent message delivery, and you can then configure the Database Mail profile to use these separate accounts. If mail cannot be delivered to the first account listed in the profile, the second one is tried, and so on.

The mail profile can be public or private. A public profile is available to any user or application for any configured database mail host on the current server instance. A private profile is available only to explicitly defined users and applications. If you are configuring Database Mail for SQL Server Agent or a specific application, you will usually want to use a private profile. If you are configuring Database Mail for general use, you will usually want to use a public profile.

Before you configure Database Mail, you should create the SMTP accounts Database Mail will use or have your organization's mail administrator do this. If you are configuring Database Mail for SQL Server Agent, it is a good idea to have the e-mail address and account name reflect this. For example, set the user name as SQL Agent and the e-mail address as sqlagent@yourcompany.com. To configure Database Mail, you need the account user name, e-mail address, and SMTP server name. If the SMTP server requires authentication, and most do, you will also need the logon user name and password for the account.

**Real World**   Some database maintenance tasks might require exclusive access to SQL Server. For example, if a database on the current server instance is in single-user mode and there is an active connection to the database, you might not be able to perform a maintenance task. You need to put the database back in multiuser mode before continuing. If you cannot get access to the database to put it back in multiuser mode, you can force the database mode change by following these steps:

1. Log on to the server and start a command prompt. Use the NET STOP command to stop the SQL Server instance you want to change. For example, if you want to stop the default SQL Server instance, you type **net stop mssqlserver**.

2. Use the CD command to change to the Binn directory for the SQL Server instance. For example, type **cd "C:\Program Files\Microsoft SQL Server\ MSSQL10.MSSQLSERVER\MSSQL\Binn"**.

3. Put the database in single-user mode by typing **sqlservr –m**.

4. Start a second command prompt, and open a dedicated administrator connection to SQL Server by typing **sqlcmd –A**. Be sure to provide a user name and password if necessary, using the –U and –P parameters.

5. Perform the necessary maintenance tasks by using sqlcmd.

6. Set the database in single-user mode back to normal mode using sp_dboption. For example, if the database is named *cust*, you type

   ```
   use master
   exec sp_dboption 'cust', 'single user', 'FALSE';
   go
   ```

7. At the first command prompt (where SQL Server is running), press Ctrl+C to stop SQL Server. When prompted to confirm, type **Y**.

8. Start the SQL Server instance you are working with by using NET START. For example, if you want to start the default SQL Server instance, you type **net start mssqlserver**.

You can use SQL Server Management Studio to configure Database Mail for the first time by completing the following steps:

1. Start SQL Server Management Studio. In the Object Explorer view, connect to the server instance of your choice, and then expand the server's Management folder.

2. Right-click Database Mail, and then select Configure Database Mail. This starts the Database Mail Configuration Wizard. Click Next.

3. To configure Database Mail for the first time, accept the default value of Setup Database Mail and then click Next.

4. When prompted to enable the Database Mail feature, click Yes.

5. On the New Profile page, type the name and description of the mail profile that Database Mail will use, such as Mail Profile For SQL Server Agent. The profile is used to define the mail environment Database Mail will use.

6.  To specify an SMTP account the profile will use to send e-mail messages, click Add. This displays the New Database Mail Account dialog box shown in Figure 16-1.

**Figure 16-1**   The New Database Mail Account dialog box.

7.  In the Account Name and Description text boxes, enter the name and description of the account you are configuring for use with Database Mail. This information is used only with Database Mail and is shown in SQL Server dialog boxes.

8.  In the E-Mail Address box, type the e-mail address of the Database Mail account, such as sqlagent@cpandl.com.

9.  In the Display Name box, type the name that will appear in the From field of outgoing messages.

10. In the Reply E-Mail box, type the e-mail address to which replies to Database Mail messages can be sent. For example, if you want administrators to send follow-up information to a lead administrator, you would put the administrator's e-mail address in the Reply E-Mail text box.

11. In the Server Name box, type the host name of the mail server, such as smtp. You can also type the fully qualified domain name of the mail server, such as smtp.cpandl.com. Using the full domain name ensures a successful connection when the mail server is in a different domain.

12. By default, most SMTP servers use TCP port 25 for communications. If your SMTP server uses a different TCP port for communications, enter the TCP port number in the field provided. Additionally, select This Server Requires A Secure Connection if you've installed a Secure Sockets Layer (SSL) certificate for SQL Server and want to encrypt SMTP communications using SSL.

13. Database Mail will need to log on to the mail server to submit mail for delivery. Select the appropriate SMTP Authentication option, based on your mail server configuration:

   ❑ **Windows Authentication Using Database Engine Service Credentials**   SQL Mail logs in to the designated mail server using the credentials of the SQL Server service (MSSQLService) for the current Database Engine instance.

   ❑ **Basic Authentication**   SQL Mail logs in to the designated mail server using the user name and password you have provided. Enter a user name for the account. Type and confirm the password for the account in the text boxes provided.

   ❑ **Anonymous Authentication**   SQL Mail logs in to the designated mail server as an anonymous user. The mail server must be configured to allow anonymous login (which is not a good security practice).

14. Click OK to close the New Database Mail Account dialog box.

15. Repeat steps 6 through 13 to specify other mail accounts to associate with the Database Mail profile. The account listed first is the account that Database Mail will try to use first. As necessary, use the Move Up and Move Down buttons to set the usage priority for multiple accounts. Click Next.

16. If you are creating a public profile, select the Public check box on the Public Profiles tab. To make the profile the default for all mail host databases and users, set Default Profile to Yes. (See Figure 16-2.)

**Figure 16-2**   The Public Profiles tab.

17. If you are creating a private profile, select the Private Profiles tab. Use the User Name drop-down list to select a user to which you will grant profile access. The default user is the SQL Server Agent service account. After you select a user in the drop-down list, select the Access check box to grant access to the profile, and then repeat this action as necessary to grant access to other users. To make the profile the default for the selected mail host database and user, set Default Profile to Yes. Click Next.

18. System parameters are used by all database mail hosts configured for a SQL Server instance. Configure the default system parameters using the following options, and then click Next:

   ❑ **Account Retry Attempts**   Sets the number of times to retry sending the message. The default is 1. If you have configured multiple accounts, this might be sufficient, because it provides for one retry. However, when you are configuring mail for SQL Server Agent, you usually want to set this to try three to five times to send a message.

   ❑ **Account Retry Delay**   Sets the delay (in seconds) between retry attempts. The default is 60 seconds, which is far too long if Database Mail is trying to deliver critical alerts. A retry delay of 30 to 60 seconds might be preferred when you are configuring mail for SQL Server Agent.

   ❑ **Maximum File Size**   Sets the maximum size (in bytes) for any generated message, including headers, message text, and included attachments. The default is 1,000,000 bytes (976 KB). When you are configuring mail for SQL Server Agent, this is usually sufficient. If applications generate messages that include graphics or multimedia, however, this might not be sufficient.

   ❑ **Prohibited Attachment File Extensions**   Sets the types of files that cannot be sent as attachments according to their file extension. To prevent abuse of Database Mail, a more inclusive list would include all file extensions designated as high risk by Attachment Manager in Group Policy, including .ade, .adp, .app, .asp, .bas, .bat, .cer, .chm, .cmd, .com, .cpl, .crt, .csh, .exe, .fxp, .hlp, .hta, .inf, .ins, .isp, .its, .js, .jse, .ksh, .lnk, .mad, .maf, .mag, .mam, .maq, .mar, .mas, .mat, .mau, .mav, .maw, .mda, .mdb, .mde, .mdt, .mdw, .mdz, .msc, .msi, .msp, .mst, .ops, .pcd, .pif, .prf, .prg, .pst, .reg, .scf, .scr, .sct, .shb, .shs, .tmp, .url, .vb, .vbe, .vbs, .vsmacros, .vss, .vst, .vsw, .ws, .wsc, .wsf, and .wsh.

   ❑ **Database Mail Executable Minimum Lifetime**   Sets the minimum time for Database Mail to run while generating a message. The lifetime should be set to optimize usage of the Database Mail executable file. You do not want the server to create the related objects in memory and then remove them from memory over and over again. You do want the related objects to be cleared out when they are not needed. The default 600 seconds (10 minutes) is typically sufficient.

❑ **Logging Level**   Determines the level of logging with regard to Database Mail. The default value, Extended, configures Database Mail to perform extended logging of related events. To reduce logging, you can set the level to Normal so that only important events, such as warnings and errors, are logged.

**Note**   The logging level also can be set to Verbose. However, this setting should be used only for troubleshooting Database Mail. When you are finished troubleshooting, reset the logging level to Extended or Normal.

19. Review the setup actions that will be performed, and then click Finish. The Configuring page shows the success or failure of each action. Click the link provided for any error message to see details about the error that occurred, and then take any necessary corrective action. Click Close.

**Tip**   If you are enabling Database Mail for use with the SQL Server Agent service, you must ensure the service is running and configured for automatic startup. See "Configuring the SQL Server Agent Service" on page 578 for details. You can check the status of SQL Server Agent in the Object Explorer view in SQL Server Management Studio. If the service is not running, right-click the SQL Server Agent node and then select Start.

## Managing Database Mail Profiles and Accounts

Database Mail can be configured to use one or more mail profiles, and each of those mail profiles can have one or more mail accounts associated with it. Database Mail profiles can be either of the following:

■ **Public**   Available to any user or application on the current server instance

■ **Private**   Available only to explicitly defined users and applications

Database Mail accounts are used in priority order and are a safeguard against mail server failure or network problems that could prevent message delivery. If mail cannot be delivered to the first account listed in the profile, the second one is tried, and so on.

To manage profiles and their accounts or add a profile, follow these steps:

1. Start SQL Server Management Studio. In the Object Explorer view, connect to the server instance of your choice, and then expand the server's Management folder.

2. Right-click Database Mail, and then select Configure Database Mail to display the Database Mail Configuration Wizard. Click Next.

3. Select Manage Database Mail Accounts And Profiles, and then click Next.

4. If you have configured multiple database mail hosts on this server instance and want to define separate profiles for these database mail hosts, select Create A New Profile, click Next, and then follow steps 5 through 13 in "Performing the Initial Database Mail Configuration" on page 570 to define the new profile and the accounts associated with this profile.

5. If you want to modify an existing profile or add an account to an existing profile, select View, Change, Or Delete An Existing Profile, and then click Next. Use the Profile Name drop-down list to select the profile to manage. You can then add, remove, or prioritize accounts for this profile, as discussed in steps 6 through 13 in "Performing the Initial Database Mail Configuration" to define the new profile and the accounts associated with this profile.

6. Click Next, and then click Finish. The Configuring page shows the success or failure of each action. Click the link provided for any error message to see details about the error that occurred, and then take any necessary corrective action. Click Close.

To set a mail profile as public or private, follow these steps:

1. Start SQL Server Management Studio. In the Object Explorer view, connect to the server instance of your choice, and then expand the server's Management folder.

2. Right-click Database Mail, and then select Configure Database Mail to display the Database Mail Configuration Wizard. Click Next.

3. Select Manage Profile Security, and then click Next.

4. The Public Profiles tab shows public profiles. Clear the Public check box if you want to make a profile private. To make a public profile the default for all mail host databases and users, set Default Profile to Yes.

5. The Private Profiles tab shows private profiles that are accessible only to a specific database and user. Use the drop-down lists to select the database and user for which you want to configure a private profile. After selecting a user in the drop-down list, select the Access check box to grant access to the profile and repeat this action as necessary to grant access to other users. To make a private profile the default for the selected mail host database and user, set Default Profile to Yes.

6. Click Next, and then click Finish. The Configuring page shows the success or failure of each action. Click the link provided for any error message to see details about the error that occurred, and then take any necessary corrective action. Click Close.

## Viewing or Changing Database Mail System Parameters

Database Mail system parameters are set globally for each SQL Server instance. If you want to manage the global system parameters for Database Mail, follow these steps:

1. Start SQL Server Management Studio. In the Object Explorer view, connect to the server instance of your choice, and then expand the server's Management folder.

2. Right-click Database Mail, and then select Configure Database Mail to display the Database Mail Configuration Wizard. Click Next.

3. Select View Or Change System Parameters. Click Next.

4. Make changes as appropriate to the system parameters. See "Performing the Initial Database Mail Configuration" on page 570 for details about configuring individual parameters.

5. Click Next, and then click Finish. The Configuring page shows the success or failure of each action. Click the link provided for any error message to see details about the error that occurred, and then take any necessary corrective action. Click Close.

# Using SQL Server Agent

SQL Server Agent is the driving force behind database automation. It is responsible for processing alerts and running scheduled jobs. When alerts are triggered and when scheduled jobs fail, succeed, or complete, you can notify SQL Server operators. Operator notifications are also processed through SQL Server Agent.

## Accessing Alerts, Operators, and Jobs

You can use SQL Server Management Studio to access resources related to SQL Server Agent by completing the following steps:

1. Start SQL Server Management Studio. In the Object Explorer view, connect to the server instance of your choice, and then expand the server's SQL Server Agent folder. (SQL Server Agent must be running to expand the related node.)

2. You should see entries for Alerts, Operators, and Jobs. Select one of these entries in the left pane to display its properties. If the Object Explorer Details window is not displayed automatically, press F7 or choose Object Explorer Details on the View menu.

3. Any jobs or alerts that are dimmed are configured but not enabled. Double-click an alert, operator, or job entry to access its associated Properties dialog box.

**Note**  If you have configured replication on the server, you will see many alerts and jobs that you configure to make it easier to monitor replication. To start these alerts or jobs, you need to enable them and set the appropriate property settings.

## Configuring the SQL Server Agent Service

The SQL Server Agent service executes scheduled jobs, triggers alerts, and performs other automated tasks. Each SQL Server Database Engine instance has its own SQL Server Agent service. You can control the related service (SQLServerAgent or SQLAgent$*instancename*) just as you do the SQL Server service. For SQL Server Agent to work properly, you should configure the SQL Server Agent service to run automatically. The startup account used by the SQL Server Agent service determines access permissions for SQL Server Agent. If the startup account does not have appropriate permissions, SQL Server Agent will not run properly. In most cases, you will want to use a Microsoft Windows domain account that is a member of the sysadmin role. This ensures that SQL Server Agent can generate alerts, run jobs, and restart services, as necessary.

To configure the SQL Server Agent service, complete the following steps:

1.  In SQL Server Configuration Manager, select the SQL Server Services node in the left pane to see the related SQL Server services in the right pane.

2.  Right-click the SQL Server Agent service for the Database Engine instance you are configuring and select Properties.

3.  SQL Server Agent can run using a built-in system account or a designated Windows account:

    ❑   Choose Built-In Account to use one of the built-in system accounts as the startup account. The drop-down menu gives you three options: Local System, Local Service, and Network Service. Local System grants access to the local system and certain systemwide privileges, such as Act As Part Of The Operating System. Local Service grants access to the local system as a regular service account. Network Service grants access to the local system and allows SQL Server Agent to access the network, such as when it is necessary to connect to remote systems.

    ❑   Choose This Account to control permissions and privileges using a Windows account. Type the user name and password of a Windows domain account. You can also click Browse to search for an account using the Select User Or Group dialog box.

4.  If you changed the service account, you must stop and then start the service. Do this by clicking Restart. If the service is stopped already, click Start instead.

5.  On the Service tab, Start Mode should be set to Automatic. If it is not, click in the Start Mode drop-down list and select Automatic.

6.  Click OK.

# Setting the SQL Server Agent Mail Profile

The SQL Server Agent service sends alerts and notifications through e-mail messages. Two options are allowed. You can use Database Mail or SQL Mail (which has been deprecated). When you initially set Database Mail to send alerts and notifications, you configure one or more databases as mail hosts and define client settings so that users and applications, such as SQL Server Agent, can send SMTP e-mail messages through your organization's SMTP mail server. To use Database Mail for SQL Server Agent alerts and notifications, you must do the following:

1. Configure *msdb* as a database mail host.

2. Designate a profile for this database.

3. Grant profile access to the SQL Server Agent service account.

SQL Mail configures SQL Server Agent as a mail client to send mail by using the Messaging Application Programming Interface (MAPI) through your organization's MAPI-compliant mail server. To use SQL Mail with SQL Server Agent, you must configure SQL Mail, create a MAPI profile on the system (such as a Microsoft Office Outlook mail profile), and then modify the SQL Server Agent properties so that the SQL Mail profile is enabled for the MAPI profile.

You designate the SQL Mail profile by completing the following steps:

1. Right-click the SQL Server Agent entry in the SQL Server Management Studio Management folder, and then select Properties.

2. On the Alert System page, select Enable Mail Profile.

3. Select SQL Mail as the Mail System, and then select the appropriate mail profile. If you want to test the configuration, click Test.

4. Click OK.

   **Tip**   If you are using Database Mail with SQL Server Agent, Enable Mail Profile should not be selected. The mail profile is configured through Database Mail.

# Using SQL Server Agent to Restart Services Automatically

You can configure SQL Server Agent to restart the SQL Server and SQL Server Agent services automatically if they stop unexpectedly. Configuring automatic restart of these services is a good idea, because it might keep you from getting paged if the server stops for some reason at 3:00 A.M. on a Tuesday morning.

To configure automatic service restart, complete the following steps:

1. Right-click the SQL Server Agent entry in the SQL Server Management Studio Management folder, and then select Properties.

2. On the General page, select Auto Restart SQL Server If It Stops Unexpectedly and select Auto Restart SQL Server Agent If It Stops Unexpectedly.

3. Click OK.

# Managing Alerts

Using alerts, you can send e-mail, pager, or Net Send alerts when errors occur or when performance conditions are reached. For example, you can configure an alert to send a message when a Log File Is Full error occurs, or when the number of deadlocks per second is more than five. You can also execute a job on an alert event.

## Using Default Alerts

Default alerts are configured when you configure features such as replication. The names of alerts configured when you set up replication begin with *Replication:* and include the following:

- **Replication: Agent Success**   An alert that tells you that the replication agent was successful

- **Replication: Agent Failure**   An alert that tells you that the replication agent failed

- **Replication: Agent Retry**   An alert that tells you that the replication agent failed and is retrying

- **Replication: Expired Subscription Dropped**   An alert that tells you that an expired subscription was dropped, which means the subscriber will not be updated anymore

- **Replication: Subscriber Has Failed Data Validation**   An alert that tells you that data in the subscriber's subscription could not be validated

- **Replication: Subscriber Has Passed Data Validation**   An alert that tells you that data in the subscriber's subscription was validated

- **Replication: Subscription Reinitialized After Validation Failure**   An alert that tells you that data in the subscriber's subscription was reinitialized with a new snapshot

These replication alerts are disabled and do not have operators assigned either. So if you want to use these alerts, you will need to enable them and assign operators. Other default alerts for replication are used to issue warnings and are enabled in a standard configuration.

## Creating Error Message Alerts

Error message alerts are triggered when SQL Server generates an error message. You can create an error message alert by completing the following steps:

1. In SQL Server Management Studio, access the SQL Server Agent entry on the server running SQL Server Agent.

2. Expand the SQL Server Agent entry in the left pane by double-clicking it.

3. Right-click Alerts, and then select New Alert from the shortcut menu. This displays the New Alert dialog box, shown in Figure 16-3.

**Figure 16-3**   The New Alert dialog box.

4. Type a short but descriptive name for the alert in the Name text box. In Figure 16-3, the alert is named Database Consistency Error.

5. In the Type selection list, choose SQL Server Event Alert. You can now set alerts according to the number or severity level of error messages.

6. Use the Database Name selection list to choose the database in which the error must occur in order to trigger the alert. To specify all databases on the server, select the <All Databases> option.

7. To set alerts by error number, choose Error Number, and then type an error number in the related text box. To see all error messages that can be returned by SQL Server, you query the *master* database by using SELECT * FROM SYS.MESSAGES, as discussed in Chapter 14, "Profiling and Monitoring Microsoft SQL Server 2008."

8. To set alerts by severity level, choose Severity, and then use the related selection list to choose a severity level that triggers the alert. You will usually want to configure alerts for severity levels 19 through 25 (which are the levels for fatal errors).

9. To restrict alerts to messages containing specific text strings, select the Raise Alert When Message Contains check box and then type the filter text in the Message Text box.

10. Configure the alert response as explained in the next section, "Handling Alert Responses." Click OK to create the alert.

## Handling Alert Responses

In response to an alert, you can execute SQL Server jobs or notify operators of the alert, or both. To configure the alert response, complete the following steps:

1. In SQL Server Management Studio, access the SQL Server Agent entry on the server running SQL Server Agent.

2. Expand the SQL Server Agent and Alerts folders.

3. Double-click the alert you want to configure. Then select the Response page, as shown in Figure 16-4.

**Figure 16-4**    The Response page of the New Alert dialog box.

4. To execute a job in response to the alert, select Execute Job.

5. If you want to execute an existing job, use the Jobs list to select it. You can enter the full or partial job name to display matches. To be sure you have the right job, you can click View Job to view the job properties.

6. If you want to create a new job, click New Job, and then configure the job as discussed in "Scheduling Jobs" on page 586.

7. To notify designated operators of an alert rather than just logging the alert, select Notify Operators.

8. Operators configured to handle alerts and schedule jobs are shown in the Operator List area. The available notification methods depend on how the operator account is configured. You can select the E-Mail, Pager, or Net Send notification, or all three. Click New Operator to configure a new operator or View Operator to view the properties of an operator currently selected in the Operator List area.

9. Select the Options page.

10. Use the Include Alert Error Text In check boxes to specify whether error text should be sent with the notification message. By default, error text is sent only with E-Mail and Net Send notifications.

11. Set an additional message to send to operators by using the Additional Notification Message To Send text box.

12. Set the delay between responses for subsequent alert notifications by using the Delay Between Responses boxes labeled Minutes and Seconds.

> **Tip**   To limit the number of alert responses triggered, you will probably want to set a delay response value of five minutes or more.

13. Click OK to complete the configuration.

## Deleting, Enabling, and Disabling Alerts

Deleting an alert removes its entry from the alerts list. Because old alerts might be useful to you (or another database administrator) in the future, you might want to disable them instead of deleting them. When an alert is disabled, no alerts are triggered if the related event occurs.

To delete, enable, or disable an alert, complete the following steps:

1. In SQL Server Management Studio, access the SQL Server Agent entry on the server running SQL Server Agent.

2. Expand the SQL Server Agent and Alerts folders.

3. Any alerts that are dimmed are configured but not enabled. To enable or disable an alert, right-click it, and then select Enable or Disable as appropriate. Click Close.

4. To delete an alert, click it, and then press Delete. In the Delete Object dialog box, click OK to confirm the deletion.

# Managing Operators

Operators are special accounts that can be notified when alerts are triggered and when scheduled jobs fail, succeed, or complete. Before operators become available, you need to register them. After you register operators, you can enable or disable them for notifications.

## Registering Operators

You register operators by completing the following steps:

1. In SQL Server Management Studio, access the SQL Server Agent entry on the server running SQL Server Agent.

2. Expand the SQL Server Agent folder.

3. Right-click the Operators entry in the left pane, and then choose New Operator to display the New Operator dialog box shown in Figure 16-5.

**Figure 16-5**   New Operator dialog box.

4. Type a name for the operator in the Name text box.

5. Specify the e-mail, net send, or pager account (or all three) to notify.

**Tip**   If you specify a pager account for the operator, you can set a duty schedule for the pager using the Pager On Duty Schedule area's text boxes and check boxes. This option is helpful if you have operators who should be notified only during working hours. To set default configuration settings for pagers, access the Alert System page of the SQL Server Agent Properties dialog box.

6. Select the Notifications page to specify existing alerts that the operator should receive (if any). Existing alerts are listed in the Alert Name column. If you find an alert that the operator should receive, select the corresponding check boxes in the E-Mail, Pager, and Net Send columns as appropriate.

7. Click OK to register the operator.

## Deleting and Disabling Notification for Operators

When database administrators leave the organization or go on vacation, you might want to delete or disable their associated operator accounts. To do this, complete the following steps:

1. In SQL Server Management Studio, access the SQL Server Agent entry on the server running SQL Server Agent.

2. Expand the SQL Server Agent and Operators folders.

3. To disable an operator, double-click the operator entry in the right pane to display the Operator Properties dialog box. Clear Enabled on the General page. Click OK.

4. To delete an operator, click its entry in the right pane, and then press Delete. The Delete Object dialog box is displayed.

5. If the operator has been selected to receive alert or job notifications, you will see a Reassign To option in the Delete Object dialog box. To reassign notification duty, select a different operator using the Reassign To drop-down list. You can view or change the properties of this operator by clicking Properties.

6. Click OK to delete the operator.

## Configuring a Fail-Safe Operator

When things go wrong with notification, operators do not get notified and problems might not be corrected in a timely manner. To prevent this, you might want to designate a fail-safe operator. The fail-safe operator is notified in the following situations:

- SQL Server Agent cannot access system tables in the *msdb* database, which is where operator definitions and notification lists are stored.

- All pager notifications to designated operators have failed, or the designated operators are off duty (as defined in the pager schedule).

**Note**   Using the fail-safe operator on pager notification failure might seem strange, but it is a good way to ensure that alerts are handled efficiently. E-mail and net send messages almost always reach their destination—but the people involved are not always watching their mail or sitting at their computer to receive net send messages, so the fail-safe operator is a way to guarantee notification.

To configure a fail-safe operator, complete the following steps:

1. Right-click the SQL Server Agent entry in SQL Server Management Studio, and then select Properties.

2. In the SQL Server Agent Properties dialog box, select the Alert System page.

3. Select Enable Fail-Safe Operator to define a fail-safe operator.

4. Use the Operator drop-down list to choose an operator to designate as the fail-safe operator. You can reassign the fail-safe duty by selecting a different operator, or you can disable the feature by clearing Enable Fail-Safe Operator.

5. Use the Notify Using check boxes to determine how the fail-safe operator is notified.

6. Click OK.

# Scheduling Jobs

Job scheduling is a key part of database automation. You can configure SQL Server jobs to handle almost any database task.

## Creating Jobs

You create jobs as a series of steps that contain actions in the sequence in which you want to execute them. When you schedule jobs in conjunction with other SQL Server facilities, such as database backups or data transformation, the necessary commands are configured for you. Normally, these commands are set as step 1, and all you need to do is set a run schedule for the job. You can add extra steps to these jobs and thus perform other tasks. For example, after importing data, you might want to back up the related database. To do this, in the SQL Server Import And Export Wizard, you schedule the import and then edit the associated job in SQL Server Management Studio to add an additional step for backing up the database. By coordinating the two processes, you ensure that the import operation is completed before starting the backup.

Another reason for editing a job created by another SQL Server facility is to add notifications based on success, failure, and completion of the job. In this way, you can notify operators of certain conditions, and you do not have to search through logs to determine if the job executed properly.

When you schedule jobs to execute for alerts, you configure the entire job process from start to finish by performing the following tasks:

- Create a job definition.
- Set steps to execute.
- Configure a job schedule.
- Handle completion, success, and failure notification messages.

## Assigning or Changing Job Definitions

Whether you are creating a new job or editing an existing job, the steps for working with job definitions are the same:

1. In SQL Server Management Studio, access the SQL Server Agent entry on the server running SQL Server Agent.

2. Expand the SQL Server Agent and Jobs folders.

3. Existing jobs are shown in the right pane. Double-click a job to access its related Properties dialog box, which is essentially the same as the New Job dialog box shown in Figure 16-6.

**Figure 16-6**   The General page of the New Job dialog box.

4. To create a new job, right-click the Jobs entry and, from the shortcut menu, choose New Job to display the New Job dialog box shown in Figure 16-6.

5. In the Name text box, type a descriptive name for the job. The name can be up to 128 characters long. If you change the name of an existing job, the job is displayed with the new name. Any references to the old job name in logs or history files remain the same and are not modified.

6. Job categories allow you to organize jobs so that they can be easily searched and differentiated. The default category is Uncategorized (Local). Use the Category selection list to choose a different category for the job.

> **Note**   Job categories are created and managed through a separate process. To create a new job category or update an existing category, use the techniques described in "Managing Job Categories" on page 597.

7. By default, the current user owns the job. Administrators can reassign jobs to other users. To do this, use the Owner selection list. You can use only predefined logons. If the logon you want to use is not available, you will need to create a logon for the account.

8. Type a description of the job in the Description text box. You can use up to 512 characters.

9. If job scheduling across multiple servers is configured, select the Targets page, and then designate the target server. The target server is the server on which the job runs. To run on the currently selected server, select Target Local Server. To run on multiple servers, select Target Multiple Servers and then choose the target servers.

10. Set Steps, Schedules, and Notifications as explained in the following sections.

## Setting Steps to Execute

Jobs can have one or more steps. SQL Server Agent always attempts to execute the start step, but additional steps can be executed conditionally, such as only when the start step succeeds or fails. You work with steps using the Steps page in the New Job dialog box, as shown in Figure 16-7. The page displays any existing steps for the job. You can use the boxes and buttons in this dialog box as follows:

- **New**   Creates a new step.
- **Insert**   Inserts a step before the currently selected step.
- **Edit**   Allows edits to the selected step.
- **Delete**   Deletes the selected step.
- **Move Step Up/Down**   Changes the order of the selected step.
- **Start Step**   Sets which step is executed first. The green flag icon highlights the start step in the step list.

**Figure 16-7**   The Steps page of the New Job dialog box.

When you create or edit a step, you see a dialog box similar to the one in Figure 16-8.

**Figure 16-8**   The New Job Step dialog box.

To configure this dialog box, complete the following steps:

1. Type a short but descriptive name for the step in the Step Name text box.

2. Use the Type drop-down list to choose a step type from the following choices:

   ❑ **Transact-SQL Script (T-SQL)**    Execute Transact-SQL commands. Type Transact-SQL commands in the Command area, or load the statements from a Transact-SQL script. To load commands from a script, click Open, and then select the Transact-SQL script you want to use. The entire contents of the script are then stored with this step.

   ❑ **ActiveX Script**    Run ActiveX scripts. You can write ActiveX scripts in VBScript, JScript, or another active scripting language configured for use on the system. Enter script statements directly into the Command area, or load the statements from a script file. Again, the entire contents of the script are then stored with this step, and later changes to the script file are not updated automatically.

   ❑ **Operating System (CmdExec)**    Execute operating system commands. Enter the operating system commands on a separate line, making sure that you specify the full path to commands and in command parameters. Commands can run batch scripts, Windows scripts, command-line utilities, or applications.

   ❑ **Replication [Agent Name]**    Pass Transact-SQL commands to designated replication agents. You can script the Distributor, Snapshot, Merge, Queue Reader, and Transaction–Log Reader agents with Transact-SQL commands. To see examples, refer to the existing jobs that are configured to handle replication, distribution, and subscription processes on the server (if available).

   ❑ **SQL Server Analysis Services Command/Query**    Pass commands or queries to SQL Server Analysis Services. Type commands and queries in the Command area, or load the commands and queries from an Analysis Server file. To load from a file, click Open, and then select the Analysis Server Command (.xmla) or Analysis Server Query (.mdx) file to use. The entire contents of the file will be stored with this step.

   ❑ **SQL Server Integration Services Package**    Execute SQL Server Integration Services packages stored on a specific server.

   **Tip**    Subsequent changes to scripts are not updated automatically. You will need to edit the step properties and reload the script file. Additionally, you should not edit existing replication jobs. Instead, modify the replication process as described in Chapter 13, "Implementing Snapshot, Merge, and Transactional Replication."

3. When executing Transact-SQL commands or scripts, use the Database drop-down list to set the database on which the commands are executed.

4. Select the Advanced page as shown in Figure 16-9.

5. Use the On Success Action drop-down list to set the action to take when the step succeeds. You can choose from the following options:

   ❑ Go To The Next Step continues sequential execution of the job.

   ❑ Go To Step .... continues execution of the job on a specified step.

   ❑ Quit The Job Reporting Success halts execution of the job and reports success.

   ❑ Quit The Job Reporting Failure halts execution of the job and reports failure.

**Figure 16-9**   The Advanced page of the New Job Step dialog box.

6. By default, Retry Attempts is set to zero and SQL Server Agent does not try to execute steps again. You can change this behavior by setting the number of retry attempts and a retry interval. You do this by using the Retry Attempts and Retry Interval (Minutes) boxes, respectively. The retry interval is the delay in minutes between retries.

7. If the job fails on all retry attempts (if any), the action set in the On Failure Action drop-down list is executed. The available options are the same as those for success.

8. If desired, configure a file for logging output from Transact-SQL and CmdExec commands. Type the file name and path in the Output File text box, or click the related Options button (...) to search for an existing file.

> **Tip** You might want to create a central log file for the output of all jobs or only all jobs in a particular category. If you do this, be sure to select the Append Output To Existing File option rather than allowing the file to be over-written. This ensures that the output file does not get overwritten. An alternative is to include the step output in the job history.

9. Click the Options button (...) next to the Run As User box to set the login to use when executing commands. By default, commands are run using the current login ID.

10. Click OK to complete the step configuration.

## Configuring Job Schedules

You track schedules on the Schedules page of the New Job dialog box, as shown in Figure 16-10. Jobs can have one or more schedules associated with them, and just as you can enable or disable jobs and their individual steps, you can enable or disable individual schedules. This makes the job scheduling process very flexible. For example, you could set one schedule to execute the job on weekdays at 2 A.M., another to execute the job every Sunday at 8 A.M., and another for execution at 10 P.M. only when needed.

**Figure 16-10**  The Schedules page of the New Job dialog box.

Whether you are creating a new job or editing an existing job, you work with schedules on the Schedules page as follows:

- **Create a new schedule**   Click New to configure a new schedule.

- **Pick a schedule**   Click Pick to select an existing schedule, and then click Edit to view or modify its properties.

- **Edit a schedule**   Select a previously selected schedule, and then click Edit to view or modify its properties.

- **Delete a schedule**   Select a previously selected schedule, and then click Remove to remove the schedule.

You create or edit schedules by completing the following steps:

1. Click New to open the New Job Schedule dialog box, or click Edit to open the Edit Job Schedule dialog box. These dialog boxes are essentially the same except for the title. Figure 16-11 shows the New Job Schedule dialog box.

**Figure 16-11**   The New Job Schedule dialog box.

2. Type a name for the schedule, and then select one of the following schedule types:

   ❑ **Start Automatically When SQL Server Agent Starts**   Runs the job automatically whenever SQL Server Agent starts.

- ❑ **Start Whenever The CPUs Become Idle**   Runs the job whenever the CPU is idle. CPU idle time is specified on the Advanced page of the SQL Server Agent Properties dialog box.

- ❑ **One Time**   Runs the job once at the date and time specified in the Date and Time boxes.

- ❑ **Recurring**   Runs the job according to the recurring schedule displayed.

3. Recurring jobs are the ones that need the most explanation. You can schedule recurring jobs to run on a daily, weekly, or monthly basis. To run the job on a daily basis, choose Daily from the Occurs drop-down list. Then use the Recurs Every box to set the run interval. Daily recurring jobs can run every day, every other day, or every Nth day.

4. To run the job on a weekly basis, choose Weekly from the Occurs drop-down list. Then configure the job using these boxes:

   - ❑ **Recurs Every *N*th Week(s)**   Allows you to run the task every week, every other week, or every Nth week

   - ❑ **Check boxes for days of the week**   Set the day or days of the week when the task runs, such as on Monday or on Monday, Wednesday, and Friday

5. To run the job on a monthly basis, choose Monthly from the Occurs drop-down list. Then configure the job using these boxes:

   - ❑ **Day *N* Of Every *N*th Month**   Sets the day of the month, and specifies in which months the job runs. For example, if you select Day 15 of every second month, the job runs on the 15th day of alternating months.

   - ❑ **The *N*th Day Of Every *N*th Month**   Sets the job to run on the Nth occurrence of a day in a given month, such as the second Monday of every month or the third Sunday of every other month.

6. Set the Daily Frequency for the daily, weekly, or monthly job. You can configure jobs to run one or more times on their scheduled run date. To run the job once on a given date, select Occurs Once At and then set a time. To run the job several times on a given date, select Occurs Every and then set a time interval in hours or minutes. Afterward, set a start and end time, such as from 7:30 A.M. to 5:30 P.M.

7. By default, schedules begin on the current date and do not have a designated end date. To change this behavior, select the End Date option, and then use the Start Date and End Date boxes to set a new duration for the schedule.

8. Click OK again to complete the schedule process.

## Handling Job Alerts

Alerts can be generated when jobs are run. You can define and manage job-specific alerts using the Alerts page of the New Job dialog box. To configure alerts, complete the following steps:

1. Access the Alerts page of the job you want to configure.

2. Any current alerts are listed by name and type. You can take the following actions for an alert:

   ❑  Edit an alert by selecting it and clicking Edit.

   ❑  Add an alert by clicking Add to display the New Alert dialog box, and then using the dialog box features to define the alert as discussed previously.

   ❑  Remove an alert by selecting it and clicking Remove.

## Handling Notification Messages

Notification messages are generated when a job succeeds, fails, or completes. You can handle these messages in several ways. You can notify operators, log the related event, automatically delete the job, or do all three. To configure notification, complete the following steps:

1. Access the Notifications page of the job you want to configure. This page is shown in Figure 16-12.

**Figure 16-12**   The Notifications page of the New Job dialog box.

2. You can notify operators by an e-mail, a pager, or a net send message. Select the check box for the technique you want to use. Choose an operator to handle the notification. Then choose a notification type. Repeat this process to configure other notification methods.

3. To log a particular type of notification message in the event log, select Write To The Windows Application Event Log and then select the notification type to log. Usually, you will want to log failure, so select When The Job Fails.

4. To delete a job upon notification, select Automatically Delete Job and then choose the notification type that triggers the deletion.

5. Click OK.

## Managing Existing Jobs

In SQL Server Management Studio, you manage jobs with SQL Server Agent. To do that, complete the following steps:

1. In SQL Server Management Studio, access the SQL Server Agent entry on the server running SQL Server Agent.

2. Expand the SQL Server Agent and Jobs folders.

3. You can now double-click a job entry to access its related Properties dialog box or right-click a job entry to display a shortcut menu. The following commands are available on the shortcut menu:

   ❑ **Delete**   Deletes the job definition. Before deleting a complex job, you might want to create a script that can be used to re-create the job.

   ❑ **Disable**   Disables the job so that it will not run.

   ❑ **Enable**   Enables the job so that it will run.

   ❑ **Rename**   Allows you to rename the job. Type the new name and then press Enter or Tab.

   ❑ **Script Job As**   Choose Create To, and then select File to generate a Transact-SQL script file that you can use to re-create the job.

   ❑ **Start Job At Step**   Starts the selected job if it is not already running.

   ❑ **Stop Job**   Stops the selected job if it is running.

   ❑ **View History**   Displays the Log File Viewer dialog box. This dialog box enables you to view summary or detail information on the job execution.

## Managing Job Categories

You use job categories to organize jobs into topical folders. When you install SQL Server, default job categories are created automatically. You can add new job categories and change the existing categories at any time.

### Working with Job Categories

To create a new job category or update an existing category, complete the following steps:

1. In SQL Server Management Studio, access the SQL Server Agent entry on the server running SQL Server Agent.

2. Expand the SQL Server Agent folder. Right-click Jobs, and then choose Manage Job Categories. This displays the Manage Job Categories dialog box.

3. You can delete a category by selecting it and clicking Delete.

4. You can view the jobs associated with a category by selecting it and clicking View Jobs.

5. To add categories or to change the properties of a category, follow the steps outlined in the following "Creating Job Categories" and "Updating Job Categories" sections, respectively.

### Creating Job Categories

You can create a new job category by completing the following steps:

1. Access the Manage Job Categories dialog box as explained previously. Click Add to display a Properties dialog box.

2. Type a name for the category in the Name text box, and then select Show All Jobs.

3. All jobs defined on the current server should now be listed. Add a job to the new category by selecting the corresponding check box in the Select column. Remove a job from the new category by clearing the corresponding check box in the Select column.

4. Click OK when you are finished.

### Updating Job Categories

You can update an existing job category by completing the following steps:

1. Access the Manage Job Categories dialog box as explained previously. Click View Jobs to display a New Job Category Properties dialog box.

2. Select Show All Jobs. All jobs defined on the current server should now be listed.

3. Add a job to a new category by selecting the corresponding check box in the Select column. Remove a job from the category by clearing the corresponding check box in the Select column.

4. Click OK when you are finished.

# Automating Routine Server-to-Server Administration Tasks

Anytime you deploy multiple computers that run SQL Server or multiple instances of SQL Server within an organization, you will need a way to handle routine server-to-server administration tasks. For example, if you have a database on one server, you might need to copy users from one server to another. SQL Server 2008 allows you to automate routine server-to-server administration tasks using scripts. You can write the scripts to the Query Editor or save them to a file for later use.

The server-to-server administration tasks you can automate include

- Copying users, tables, views, and other objects from one database to another
- Copying alerts, jobs, and scheduled jobs from one server to another

The sections that follow explain how you can automate these administration tasks.

## Copying Users, Tables, Views, and Other Objects from One Database to Another

Using the Script Wizard, you can generate T-SQL scripts that allow you to re-create the objects contained in a specified database. Scripts can be written to the Query Editor window so that you can run them immediately, or they can be saved to files so that you can run them later. By running the script against a database other than the one from which it was generated, you can create copies of objects in other databases.

You can create copies of objects by completing the following steps:

1. Start SQL Server Management Studio and then access the server of your choice.

2. In the Object Explorer view, right-click the Management folder, and then select Generate Scripts. This starts the Generate SQL Server Scripts Wizard. Click Next.

3. Select the database you want to script, and then click Next.

4. Set the script options summarized in Table 16-1 to determine how the copy operation works, and then click Next.

5. Select the objects you want to script, and then click Next. Objects you can script include database triggers, database roles, schemas, stored procedures, tables, user-defined functions, users, and views.

6. You will have one Choose page for each type of object you selected. Use this page to choose the individual objects to script. For example, if you are scripting tables

and views, you will be able to choose the tables to script and then the views to script.

7. Choose an output option. You can create the script as a file, copy it to the Windows Clipboard, or send it to the New Query Editor window. Click Next when you are ready to continue.

8. When you click Finish, the script is created and copied to your chosen destination. Click Close. You can then run the script as needed against a specified database. For example, if you are copying users from Customer to Projects, you insert USE PROJECTS at the beginning of the script before running it on the server containing the Projects database.

**Table 16-1   Script Options for the Script Wizard**

| Script Option | Default | When True... |
| --- | --- | --- |
| ANSI Padding | True | Generates statements about ANSI padding. |
| Append To File | False | Appends the script to an existing file rather than overwriting the file. |
| Continue Scripting On Error | False | Continues writing the script if an error occurs. |
| Convert UDDTs To Base Types | False | Converts user-defined data types (UDDTs) to base types. |
| Generate Script For Dependent Objects | False | Scripts dependent objects. |
| Include Descriptive Headers | True | Includes descriptive header comments for each object scripted. (Does not affect how objects are created later; it only sets comments.) |
| Include If NOT EXISTS | False | Scripts the objects so that they are re-created only if they do not already exist. |
| Include System Constraint Names | False | Includes system-generated constraint names to enforce declarative referential integrity. |
| Schema Qualify Object Names | True | Prefixes object names with the object schema. |
| Script Bindings | False | Includes options to set binding. |
| Script Change Tracking | False | Includes the change-tracking information. |
| Script Check Constraints | True | Script checks constraints for each table or view scripted. |

**Table 16-1** Script Options for the Script Wizard

| Script Option | Default | When True... |
| --- | --- | --- |
| Script Collation | False | Writes the collation settings of the object to the script. |
| Script Create | True | Script creates designated objects (as opposed to dropping designated objects). |
| Script Data | False | Scripts the data for each table scripted. |
| Script Data Compression Options | False | Includes the data-compression information. |
| Script Defaults | True | Scripts the default values for the object. |
| Script Drop | False | Script drops designated objects (as opposed to creating designated objects). |
| Script Extended Properties | True | Scripts the extended properties of objects. |
| Script For Server Version | SQL Server 2008 | Creates the script to be compatible with the specified SQL Server version. |
| Script Foreign Keys | True | Scripts foreign keys for each table or view scripted. |
| Script Full-Text Indexes | False | Scripts full-text indexes for each table or view scripted. |
| Script Indexes | False | Scripts indexes for each table or view scripted. |
| Script Logins | False | Scripts all logins available on the server. Passwords are not scripted. |
| Script Object-Level Permissions | False | Scripts permissions for the object as per the original database. |
| Script Primary Keys | True | Scripts primary keys for each table or view scripted. |
| Script Statistics | Do not script statistics | Controls whether statistics for table or indexed view objects are scripted. |
| Script Triggers | True | Scripts triggers for each table or view scripted. |
| Script Unique Keys | True | Scripts unique keys for each table or view scripted. |
| Script Use Database | True | Sets a USE statement with the name of the original database at the top of the script. |

### Copying Alerts, Operators, and Scheduled Jobs from One Server to Another

You use alerts, operators, and scheduled jobs to automate routine administration tasks. If you have already created alerts, operators, and jobs on one server, you can reuse them on another server. To do this, you create a script for the alert, operator, or job you want to copy, and then run the script against a target server. You then need to edit the job properties to ensure that they make sense for the target server. For example, if you created a set of jobs to periodically check the Support database and then added custom steps to handle various database states, you could copy these jobs to another server and then edit the job properties to apply the tasks to the Customer database on the target server.

You can copy alerts, operators, or jobs from one server to another server by completing the following steps:

1. In SQL Server Management Studio, access the SQL Server Agent entry on the server running SQL Server Agent.

2. Expand the SQL Server Agent folder, and then expand the Alerts, Jobs, or Operators folder as appropriate for the type of object you are copying.

3. Right-click the alert, operator, or job; point to Script...As, Create To; and then select File. In the Select A File dialog box, specify the save location and name for the T-SQL script file. Click Save.

4. Connect to the server on which you want to create the new alert, operator, or job in the Object Explorer view. Right-click the server in the Object Explorer view, and then select New Query.

5. Click the Open File button or press Ctrl+O. Select the script file you previously created.

6. The script is set to use the *msdb* database because alert, job, and operator objects are stored in that database.

7. Click Execute or press F5 to run the script and create the object in the *msdb* database.

## Multiserver Administration

Multiserver administration allows you to use one server to manage alerts and job scheduling for other servers from a central location. You centrally manage alerts through event forwarding. You centrally manage job scheduling by designating master servers and target servers.

## Event Forwarding

If you have multiple instances of SQL Server running on multiple systems throughout the network, event forwarding is a time and resource saver. With event forwarding, you can forward application log events to a central server and then process those events on this server. Thus, rather than having to configure alerts on 12 different server instances, you configure event forwarding on 11 servers and have one server handle all the incoming events. You can then use the application log's Computer field to determine the system on which the event occurred and take the appropriate corrective actions by using scripts or remote procedure calls.

To configure event forwarding, complete the following steps:

1. In SQL Server Management Studio, access the SQL Server Agent entry on the server running SQL Server Agent.

2. Right-click the SQL Server Agent entry and select Properties.

3. Access the Advanced page of the SQL Server Agent Properties dialog box, as shown in Figure 16-13.

**Figure 16-13**   The Advanced page of the SQL Server Agent Properties dialog box.

4. Select Forward Events To A Different Server.

5.  Use the Server selection list to choose a registered server that will handle the events. If the server you want to use is not listed, you will need to register it. Then access the SQL Server Agent Properties dialog box again.

6.  Set the type of events to forward by selecting Unhandled Events or All Events. An unhandled event is one that you have not configured alerts for on the current server.

7.  From the If Event Has Severity At Or Above drop-down list, select the severity threshold for events that are forwarded.

> **Tip**   To reduce network traffic caused by event forwarding, set the severity threshold to a fairly high value. Fatal errors have a severity level of 19 through 25.

8.  Click OK.

## Multiserver Job Scheduling

When you want to centrally manage job scheduling, you will need to create a master server and one or more target servers. The SQL Server Agent running on the master server can do the following:

-   Centrally manage jobs for the target servers. Then you create jobs on the master server that run on the targets. For details, see "Assigning or Changing Job Definitions" on page 587.

-   Download jobs to a target. For details, see "Managing Existing Jobs" on page 596.

### Multiserver Scheduling Requirements

For the master/target relationship to work correctly, you must do the following:

-   Make sure that the master server and all target servers are running SQL Server 2008.

-   Use domain accounts, not local accounts, when configuring the master and target.

-   Make sure that SQL Server Agent is running on the master server and all target servers.

### Configuring Master Servers

To create a master server, complete the following steps:

1.  In SQL Server Management Studio, access the SQL Server Agent entry on the server running SQL Server Agent.

2.  Right-click the SQL Server Agent entry, point to Multi Server Administration, and then select Make This A Master. This starts the Master Server Wizard.

3. Read the welcome page, and then click Next.

4. As shown in Figure 16-14, create a special operator to handle multiserver job notifications. This operator, called the Master Server Operator, is created on the master and on all target servers that use this master. Set an e-mail, a pager, and a net send address as appropriate. You can change this information later by editing the Master Server Operator properties on the master server. Click Next.

**Figure 16-14**   The Master Server Operator page of the Master Server Wizard.

5. Select the target servers to associate with this master server. If a server is not registered, you can add a connection for it by clicking Add Connection. The process of associating target servers with a master is called *enlisting*. Later, you can remove the association by right-clicking SQL Server Agent in SQL Server Management Studio, selecting Multi Server Administration, and then selecting Manage Target Servers.

6. When you click Next, the wizard will check to make sure that the versions of SQL Server running on the master and target servers are compatible. If target servers are running different versions of SQL Server, note any compatibility issues listed. Click Close.

7. Specify the account that the target server will use to connect to the master server and download jobs. If Windows authentication is allowed on the master server, the new login will be created automatically.

8. Click Next, and then click Finish. The wizard performs the necessary tasks and reports its progress. You will be notified of any errors.

9. Click Close when the configuration is finished.

### Configuring Target Servers

You can configure one or more target servers for each master server. You create target servers by completing the following steps:

1. In SQL Server Management Studio, access the SQL Server Agent entry on the server running SQL Server Agent.

2. Right-click the SQL Server Agent entry, point to Multi Server Administration, and then select Make This A Target. This starts the Make TSX Wizard.

3. Read the welcome page, and then click Next.

4. Click Pick Server to select a master server for this target server. Use the Connect To Server dialog box to connect to the master server. The master server is the source server from which SQL Server Agent jobs will be downloaded.

5. When you click Next, the wizard will check to make sure that the versions of SQL Server running on the master and target servers are compatible. If target servers are running different versions of SQL Server, note any compatibility issues listed. Click Close.

6. Specify the account that the target server will use to connect to the master server and download jobs. If Windows authentication is allowed on the master server, the new login will be created automatically.

7. Click Next, and then click Finish. The wizard performs the necessary tasks and reports its progress. You will be notified of any errors.

8. Click Close when the configuration is finished.

# Database Maintenance

Database maintenance involves different tasks. Most of these tasks have been discussed in previous chapters; this section does not go into detail about tasks already covered. Instead, there is a checklist that you can use as a starting point for your maintenance efforts. The rest of the section explains how to set up maintenance plans and run database consistency checks.

## Database Maintenance Checklist

The following checklists provide recommended daily, weekly, and monthly maintenance tasks.

*Daily*

✔ Monitor application, server, and agent logs.

✔ Configure alerts for important errors that are not configured for alert notification.

✔ Check for performance and error alert messages.

✔ Monitor job status, particularly jobs that back up databases and perform replication.

✔ Review the output from jobs in the job history or output file, or both.

✔ Back up databases and logs (as necessary, and if not configured as automatic jobs).

*Weekly*

✔ Monitor available disk space on drives.

✔ Monitor the status of linked, remote, master, and target servers.

✔ Check the maintenance plan reports and history to determine the status of maintenance plan operations.

✔ Generate an updated record of configuration information by executing sp_configure.

*Monthly*

✔ Monitor server performance, tweaking performance parameters to improve response time.

✔ Manage logins and server roles.

✔ Audit server, database, and object permissions to ensure that only authorized users have access.

✔ Review alert, job, and operator configurations.

*As Needed*

✔ Back up the SQL Server registry data.

✔ Run database integrity checks, and update database statistics. (SQL Server 2008 handles this automatically in most cases.)

## Using Maintenance Plans

Maintenance plans provide an automated way to perform essential maintenance tasks. You can run a maintenance plan against a single database or multiple databases running on a designated target server. You can also generate report histories for maintenance plan execution.

You create maintenance plans with the Maintenance Plan Wizard or with the Maintenance Plan Package Designer. Both techniques are similar:

■ With the wizard, the wizard pages guide you through the steps of selecting maintenance tasks to perform, configuring execution history logging, and setting an execution schedule. When you complete the wizard steps, the wizard generates the package that will perform the designated maintenance tasks.

■ With the package designer, you specify servers, add tasks to perform from a predefined list of maintenance tasks, and configure execution history logging as necessary. After you configure connections to the server on which you want to perform maintenance, you build the maintenance plan by dragging tasks from the Maintenance Plan Tasks toolbox to the design window. The order in which you add tasks sets the order of execution. If a task requires additional input, such as database or server names, double-clicking the task opens a Properties dialog box that lets you specify the needed information.

The set of maintenance tasks you can perform is similar whether you are working with the wizard or the designer:

■ **Back Up Database**   Allows you to specify the source databases, destination files or tapes, and overwrite options for a full, differential, or transaction log backup. In the wizard interface, there are separate task listings for each backup type.

■ **Check Database Integrity**   Performs internal consistency checks of the data and index pages with the designated databases.

■ **Execute SQL Server Agent Job**   Allows you to select SQL Server Agent jobs to run as part of the maintenance plan.

■ **Execute T-SQL Statement**   Allows you to run any T-SQL script as part of the maintenance plan. (Available only in the Maintenance Plan Package Designer.)

■ **Clean Up History**   Deletes historical data about Backup and Restore, SQL Server Agent, and Maintenance Plan operations.

■ **Maintenance Cleanup**   Deletes files created when executing maintenance plans.

■ **Notify Operator**   Sends an e-mail message to a designated SQL Server Agent operator. (Available only in the Maintenance Plan Package Designer.)

■ **Rebuild Index**   Rebuilds indexes to improve the performance of index scans and seeks. This task also optimizes the distribution of data and free space on the index pages, allowing for faster future growth.

■ **Reorganize Index**   Defragments and compacts clustered and nonclustered indexes on tables and views to improve index-scanning performance.

■ **Shrink Database**   Reduces the disk space used by the designated databases by removing empty data and log pages.

■ **Update Statistics**    Updates the query optimizer statistics regarding the distribution of data values in the tables. This improves the query optimizer's ability to determine data access strategies, which can ultimately improve query performance.

When you first start working with maintenance plans, you will probably want to run the Maintenance Plan Wizard and let the wizard design the necessary package for you. After you have created a package, you modify it in the Maintenance Plan Package Designer view.

> **Tip**    For most installations, I recommend configuring separate maintenance plans for system and user databases. This gives you greater flexibility when determining how and when maintenance operations are performed. For large installations, you might want to have separate maintenance plans for each database so that you can work with different databases on different days or at different times of the day.

### Creating Maintenance Plans

You can create a maintenance plan by completing the following steps:

1. In SQL Server Management Studio, access the Management folder on the server where you want to create the maintenance plan. This can be a different server from the one on which the maintenance plan will run.

2. Right-click Maintenance Plans, and then select Maintenance Plan Wizard. This starts the Maintenance Plan Wizard.

3. Read the welcome page, and then click Next. Type a name and description for the maintenance plan, such as **Engineering DB Server Maintenance** and **Backup Plan**.

4. By default, maintenance plans run on demand, which means you must start them manually. You also can schedule maintenance plans to run automatically. If you want each maintenance task to have a separate run schedule, select Separate Schedule For Each Task and then when you configure each task later, create the necessary schedule by clicking the Change button, setting a run schedule, and then clicking OK. If you want to use a single run schedule for the entire plan, select Single Schedule For The Entire Plan Or No Schedule, click Change, set a run schedule, and then click OK. Click Next when you are ready to continue.

5. As shown in Figure 16-15, select the maintenance tasks you want to perform, and then click Next. The order in which tasks are listed on the Select Maintenance Task Order page determines the order in which the tasks are executed. Select a task and then click the Move Up or Move Down button as appropriate to change the task's order. When the tasks are in the desired run order, click Next.

**Figure 16-15**    The Select Maintenance Tasks page of the Maintenance Plan Wizard.

6. Next, for each task that can be applied to one or more databases, you will need to choose the database or databases on which the tasks will be performed. Typically, you can perform a task on all databases, all system databases, all user databases, or a combination of one or more individual databases. You might also need to configure individual task parameters. When you are finished configuring tasks, click Next. Following are guidelines for each task:

❑ **Back Up Database**    Select the databases for which you want to create a full, differential, or transaction log backup. You can back up to disk or tape, and either append or overwrite existing backup files. Typically, you will want to create a backup file for every selected database. With disk-based backups, you can set a specific backup directory and create subdirectories for each database being backed up. You can also set the file extension for the backups. The default extension is .bak. To verify the integrity of backups upon completion, select Verify Backup Integrity.

❑ **Check Database Integrity**    Select the databases on which you want to perform internal consistency checks. By default, both data and index pages are checked. If you want to check only data pages, clear Include Indexes.

❑ **Execute SQL Server Agent Job**    Select SQL Server Agent jobs to run as part of the maintenance plan. Any available jobs on the server are listed, and you can select the related check box to execute the job whenever the maintenance plan runs.

❑ **Cleanup History**   Historical data about backup and restore, SQL Server Agent, and maintenance plan operations is stored in the *msdb* database. When the history cleanup task runs, any historical data older than four weeks is deleted on the target server by default. You can modify the type of historical data cleaned up and set the Older Than criteria to different values. For example, you might find that you need to maintain historical data for a full quarter. If so, you set Remove Historical Data Older Than to 3 Months.

❑ **Rebuild Index**   Select the databases on which you want to rebuild indexes. If you select specific databases, you can specify whether all table and view indexes are rebuilt or only a specific table or view index is rebuilt. For example, if you want to rebuild the NWCustomer view in the Orders database, you click in the Databases drop-down list, select These Databases, choose the Orders database, and then click OK.

Next, under Object, select View, and then click in the Selection drop-down list, select These Objects, choose dbo.NWCustomers, and click OK. The affected indexes are dropped and re-created with a new fill factor. You can chose Reorganize Pages With The Default Amount Of Free Space to re-create indexes with the original fill factor that was specified when the indexes were created. Or you can choose Change Free Space Per Page Percentage To if you want to specify a new fill factor. The higher the percentage, the more free space is reserved on the index pages and the larger the index grows. The default is 10 percent. Valid values are from 0 through 100.

> **Note**   Fill factors are discussed in "Setting the Index Fill" on page 168. Reorganizing pages changes table indexes and thus invalidates existing statistics. You cannot reorganize data and update statistics in the same plan, and you might want to create separate maintenance plans for handling each of these important tasks.

❑ **Reorganize Index**   Select the databases you want to defragment and compact. If you select specific databases, you can specify whether all tables and views are reorganized or only a specific table or view is reorganized. For example, if you want to reorganize the *Customer* table in the Orders database, you click in the Databases drop-down list, select These Databases, choose the Orders database, and then click OK. Next, under Object, select Table, and then click in the Selection drop-down list, select These Objects, choose dbo.Customers, and click OK.

❑ **Shrink Database**   Select the databases on which you want to reduce the disk space by removing empty data and log pages. Use Shrink Database

When It Grows Beyond to specify the database size that triggers this task. Free space in a database is removed only when the size of the database file exceeds this value. The default value is 50 MB, which means that if there is more than 50 MB of free space, SQL Server will shrink the database to the size specified. Use Amount Of Free Space To Remain After Shrink to set the amount of unused space that should remain after the database is reduced in size. The value is based on the percentage of the actual data in the database. The default value is 10 percent. Valid values are from 0 through 100. Free space can be returned to the operating system or retained for future use by the database.

❑ **Update Statistics**    Select the databases on which you want to update query optimizer statistics. If you select specific databases, you can specify whether statistics for all tables and views are updated or only a specific table or view is updated. By default, both column and index statistics are updated. You also can specify to update only column or index statistics.

7. Use the Select Report Options page, shown in Figure 16-16, to determine how maintenance plan reports are handled. By default, whenever a maintenance plan runs, a report is generated. The report can be written to a file in any designated folder location, can be sent by e-mail to a SQL Server Agent operator, or both. Click Next.

**Figure 16-16**    The Select Report Options page of the Maintenance Plan Wizard.

8. Review the maintenance plan. Click Finish to complete the process and generate the SQL Server Agent job to handle the designated maintenance tasks. These jobs are labeled according to the name of the maintenance plan. Click Close.

## Checking Maintenance Reports and History

Creating a maintenance plan is only the beginning. After you create the plan, you will need to check the maintenance reports and history periodically. Maintenance reports are stored as text files in a designated directory, are sent as e-mail messages to designated SQL Server Agent operators, or both. You can view file-based reports in a standard text editor or word processor. To access the maintenance history through SQL Server Management Studio, complete the following steps:

1. In SQL Server Management Studio, access the Management folder on the server of your choice.

2. Right-click Maintenance Plans, and then select View History. This displays the Log File Viewer as shown in Figure 16-17.

**Figure 16-17** The Log File Viewer.

3. Under Select Logs in the left pane, Maintenance Plans should be selected by default. There should also be a log entry for each maintenance plan configured on the server.

4. Choose the maintenance plan or plans for which you want to review a job history.

5. Use the summary in the right pane to review the job history. Click Close when you are finished.

### Viewing, Editing, Running, and Deleting Maintenance Plans

You can view, edit, run, or delete maintenance plans by completing the following steps:

1. In SQL Server Management Studio, access the Management folder on the server of your choice.

2. Select Maintenance Plans in the left pane. You will see the existing maintenance plans in the right pane.

3. You can now do the following:

   ❑ View or edit a maintenance plan by double-clicking the maintenance plan entry in the right pane. This opens the plan in the Maintenance Plan Package Designer.

   ❑ Delete a maintenance plan by selecting its entry and pressing Delete. In the Delete Object dialog box, click OK to confirm the deletion.

   ❑ Execute the maintenance plan by right-clicking it and selecting Execute.

## Checking and Maintaining Database Integrity

You rarely have to perform database integrity checks with SQL Server 2008, and when you do, you can use maintenance plans to handle most of the work. On those rare occasions when you want to perform consistency checks manually, you will use the DBCC command. DBCC stands for *database consistency check*. There are many different DBCC commands, and the ones you will use most often to maintain a database are covered in the following sections.

### Using DBCC CHECKDB

The DBCC CHECKDB command checks the consistency of the entire database and is the primary method used to check for database corruption. The command ensures that

- Index and data pages are linked correctly.
- Indexes are up to date and sorted properly.
- Pointers are consistent.
- The data on each page is up to date.
- Page offsets are up to date.
- Indexed views, varbinary(max) data in the file system, and Service Broker data are validated.

**Note**   When you run DBCC CHECKDB you do not have to run DBCC
CHECKALLOC on the database, DBCC CHECKTABLE on every table and view in
the database, or DBCC CHECKCATALOG on database catalogs. DBCC CHECKDB
performs similar validation tasks for you.

Sample 16-1 shows the syntax and usage for the DBCC CHECKDB command. When
you run the command without a repair option, errors are reported but not corrected.
To correct errors, you need to put the database in single-user mode, and then set a
repair option. After you repair the database, create a backup.

**Sample 16-1**   DBCC CHECKDB Syntax and Usage

```
Syntax
DBCC CHECKDB
(    'database_name' | database_id | 0
     [ , NOINDEX
     | { REPAIR_ALLOW_DATA_LOSS
     | REPAIR_FAST
     | REPAIR_REBUILD
     } ] )
     [ WITH          {
                     [ ALL_ERRORMSGS ]
                     [ , ESTIMATEONLY ]
                     [ , EXTENDED_LOGICAL_CHECKS ]
                     [ , NO_INFOMSGS ]
                     [ , TABLOCK ]
                     [ , { PHYSICAL_ONLY | DATA_PURITY } ]
     ]

Usage
DBCC CHECKDB ('customer', NOINDEX)
DBCC CHECKDB ('customer', REPAIR_REBUILD)
```

The REPAIR_FAST option performs minor repairs that do not consume a lot of time
and will not result in data loss. The REPAIR_REBUILD option performs comprehensive error checking and correction that requires more time to complete but does not
result in data loss (but the database must be in single-user mode). The REPAIR_
ALLOW_DATA_LOSS option performs all the actions of REPAIR_REBUILD and adds
new tasks that might result in data loss. These tasks include allocating and deallocat-
ing rows to correct structural problems and page errors as well as deleting corrupt text
objects.

**Tip**   When trying to fix database problems, start with REPAIR_FAST or REPAIR_
REBUILD. If these options do not resolve the problem, use REPAIR_ALLOW_DATA_
LOSS. Remember that running the REPAIR_ALLOW_DATA_LOSS option might result
in unacceptable loss of important data. To ensure that you can recover the database
in its original state, place the DBCC command in a transaction so that you can
inspect the results and roll back the transaction, if necessary.

## Using DBCC CHECKTABLE

To correct problems with individual tables, you can use the DBCC CHECKTABLE command. As shown in Sample 16-2, the syntax and usage for this command are almost the same as for DBCC CHECKDB. The database you want to work with must be selected for use.

**Sample 16-2**   DBCC CHECKTABLE Syntax and Usage

```
Syntax
DBCC CHECKTABLE
(    'table_name' | 'view_name'
     [ , NOINDEX
     | index_id
     | { REPAIR_ALLOW_DATA_LOSS
     | REPAIR_FAST
     | REPAIR_REBUILD }
     ] )
     [ WITH
        { ALL_ERRORMSGS ]
           [ , ESTIMATEONLY ]
           [ , EXTENDED_LOGICAL_CHECKS ]
           [ , NO_INFOMSGS ]
           [ , TABLOCK ]
           [ , { PHYSICAL_ONLY | DATA_PURITY } ]
        }
     ]

Usage
DBCC CHECKTABLE ('receipts')
DBCC CHECKTABLE ('receipts', REPAIR_REBUILD)
```

## Using DBCC CHECKALLOC

To check the consistency of database pages, you can use DBCC CHECKALLOC. Again, the syntax for this command is nearly identical to the previous DBCC commands. One item worth noting is that although Sample 16-3 shows a NOINDEX option, it is maintained only for backward compatibility with previous SQL Server versions. The command always checks the consistency of page indexes.

**Sample 16-3**   DBCC CHECKALLOC Syntax and Usage

```
Syntax
DBCC CHECKALLOC
(     [ 'database_name' | database_id | 0 ]
          [ , NOINDEX
     |
     { REPAIR_ALLOW_DATA_LOSS
     | REPAIR_FAST
```

```
      | REPAIR_REBUILD
      } ] )
      [ WITH { [ ALL_ERRORMSGS ]
               [ , NO_INFOMSGS ]
               [ , TABLOCK ]
               [ , ESTIMATEONLY ] }
      ]
```

**Usage**
```
DBCC CHECKALLOC ('customer')
DBCC CHECKALLOC ('customer', REPAIR_REBUILD)
```

## Using DBCC CHECKCATALOG

Another useful DBCC command is CHECKCATALOG. You use this command to check the consistency of a database's systems tables. Sample 16-4 shows the syntax and usage of this command.

**Sample 16-4**   DBCC CHECKCATALOG Syntax and Usage

**Syntax**
```
DBCC CHECKCATALOG
[ ( 'database_name' | database_id | 0 ) ]
    [ WITH NO_INFOMSGS ]
```

**Usage**
```
DBCC CHECKCATALOG ('customer')
```

## Using DBCC CHECKIDENT

You use the CHECKIDENT command to check a table's identity value and set a new identity value. Sample 16-5 shows the syntax and usage of this command.

**Sample 16-5**   DBCC CHECKIDENT Syntax and Usage

**Syntax**
```
DBCC CHECKIDENT
( table_name
    [ , { NORESEED
    | { RESEED [ , new_reseed_value ] } }
    ] )
    [ WITH NO_INFOMSGS]
```

**Usage**
```
DBCC CHECKIDENT ('customer', NORESEED)
DBCC CHECKIDENT ('customer', RESEED, 50)
```

## Using DBCC CHECKFILEGROUP

To check the allocation and structural integrity of all table and index views in a file-group, you can use the DBCC CHECKFILEGROUP command. Sample 16-6 shows the syntax and usage of this command.

**Sample 16-6**   DBCC CHECKFILEGROUP Syntax and Usage

```
Syntax
DBCC CHECKFILEGROUP
[
    [ ( { filegroup | filegroup_id | 0 }
        [ , NOINDEX ]
    ) ]
    [ WITH
        {
            [ ALL_ERRORMSGS | NO_INFOMSGS ]
            [ , TABLOCK ]
            [ , ESTIMATEONLY ]
        }
    ]
]

Usage
USE CUSTOMER
GO
DBCC CHECKFILEGROUP (1, NOINDEX)
GO
```

## Using DBCC UPDATEUSAGE

To report and correct pages and row count inaccuracies in catalog views, you can use DBCC UPDATEUSAGE. Sample 16-7 shows the syntax and usage of this command.

**Sample 16-7**   DBCC UPDATEUSAGE Syntax and Usage

```
Syntax
DBCC UPDATEUSAGE
    (   { database_name | database_id | 0 }
    [ , { table_name | table_id | view_name | view_id }
    [ , { index_name | index_id } ] ]
        ) [ WITH [ NO_INFOMSGS ] [ , ] [ COUNT_ROWS ]
    ]

Usage
DBCC UPDATEUSAGE ('CustomerDB')
DBCC UPDATEUSAGE ('CustomerDB', 'Inventory.Item')
```

# Chapter 17

# Managing Log Shipping and Database Mirroring

You'll want to strongly consider using log shipping and database mirroring in just about any environment where you deploy Microsoft SQL Server 2008. Log shipping and database mirroring are disaster-recovery solutions designed to help improve availability and quickly recover SQL Server 2008. They do this by establishing a standby database that can be used if your production database becomes unavailable because of an outage or disaster. Because log shipping and database mirroring create a copy of a database, they can help protect you against many types of data loss as well. For example, with a delayed log shipping configuration, you can protect the production database against physical corruption of data and accidental deletion of data. Whether you use log shipping, database mirroring, or a combination of the two is a design choice that will depend on your availability and recovery needs.

## Log Shipping

You use log shipping to establish one or more secondary databases that can be brought online manually if a primary database fails. Following is an overview of log shipping and then a discussion of how it is implemented.

### Log Shipping: How It Works

Log shipping consists of a source database and a target database. Any changes that are made to the source database are backed up, copied to the target database, and then applied. Because of the way log shipping works, you can use log shipping only with either the full or bulk-logged recovery model.

Log shipping requires at least two separate SQL Server instances:

- A primary server instance on which you have configured a database to act as the primary database for log shipping

- A secondary server instance on which you have configured a database to act as the secondary database for log shipping

**Real World**   As part of your planning, you should consider carefully the hardware configuration of your secondary servers. Although a secondary server often will sit idle most of the time, you ideally will want to use hardware that can handle the normal workload of the primary server. This will ensure the secondary server can act as the primary server during an extended outage.

While you are determining whether log shipping and database mirroring are right for your organization, you also might want to consider whether you should establish geographically separate primary and secondary servers as a safeguard against natural disasters. In the past, because of bandwidth limitations and other constraints, it wasn't always feasible to use log shipping or database mirroring with geographically dispersed servers. With SQL Server 2008 Enterprise Edition, however, you can configure compression with log shipping and database mirroring to dramatically reduce the amount of data transferred over networks.

All administration of the log shipping configuration is performed on the primary server. You can extend log shipping in several ways:

- By configuring multiple secondary databases on multiple secondary servers, you can establish multiple standbys that can be brought online in case the primary database fails. You can think of each secondary database as a cold standby.

- By configuring an optional monitoring server, you can track the history and status of log shipping. The monitoring server can also be configured to raise alerts if log shipping operations fail to occur as scheduled.

- By configuring secondary servers for query processing, you can reallocate query processing from a primary server to one or more secondary servers.

Log shipping uses a backup folder for logs. Because all log shipping servers must have access to this folder, this folder should be on a network or distributed share and the secondary server proxy accounts (which are by default the SQL Server Agent accounts used on the secondary servers) must have Read and Write permissions on this folder.

SQL Server Agent is the essential ingredient that enables log shipping. A SQL Server Agent job is scheduled to copy the primary server's transaction logs to the backup folder. This job is referred to as the backup job. Other SQL Server Agent jobs also are used to copy the transaction logs from the backup share to the secondary server and to restore the transaction logs on the secondary server. These jobs are referred to as copy and restore jobs. By default, the backup, copy, and restore jobs run every 15 minutes.

When you enable and configure log shipping, the related SQL Server Agent jobs are created automatically. There will always be only one of each job on a server, even if you have configured log shipping on multiple databases. You should never edit the job properties directly. Instead, edit the backup settings on the primary database for log shipping.

**Real World** When a database is updated frequently, a short interval between backup, copy, and restore operations helps ensure that the secondary databases are synchronized with the primary database. In some situations, however, you might want to set a longer interval to reduce the workload and resource usage associated with the backup, copy, and restore operations. For example, if the primary database is overworked and has few resources available, you might want to set a longer interval for each of the jobs. If the primary database is updated infrequently, you might want to set a longer interval for each of the jobs. If you want to protect against possible data loss on the primary database that can occur because of physical corruption of data and accidental deletion of data, you might want to set a longer interval for each of the jobs as well. Then if you catch the problem and SQL Server hasn't replicated the errors to the secondary database, you should be able to recover the lost data from the secondary.

When you configure log shipping, tables are created in the *msdb* database on the servers acting as primary, secondary, and monitoring servers. Stored procedures also are created to perform the necessary operations, cleanup, and monitoring. Related alerts are configured automatically to help you monitor log shipping.

## Preparing for Log Shipping

Log shipping requires a very specific configuration to work properly. To prepare your servers for log shipping, follow these general steps:

1. Log shipping is set on a per-database basis. Access the Database Properties dialog box for the primary database. On the Options page, ensure that the Recovery Model is set to Full or Bulk-Logged. Log shipping databases cannot use the Simple recovery model.

2. You should configure the service-related accounts for SQL Server 2008 so that they can access the network. See "Setting the Startup Service Account" on page 62.

   **Note** Preferably, the SQL Server service and the SQL Server Agent service for the Database Engine instance will use a domain account with appropriate permissions. The SQL Server Agent service for the related Database Engine instance running on the primary server will back up the transaction logs to the backup folder you specify in the log shipping configuration. The SQL Server Agent service for the related Database Engine instance running on the secondary server will copy files from the backup location to a designated copy folder.

3. You'll need to ensure that remote connections to SQL Server 2008 are enabled on the primary and secondary servers. See "Managing the Connections Configuration" on page 69.

4. Create a shared resource to use as the backup folder for log shipping. Set permissions so that secondary server proxy accounts (which are by default the SQL

Server Agent accounts used on the secondary servers) have Read and Write permissions on this folder.

> **Tip**   A good resource for creating shared folders and setting shared folder permissions is *Microsoft Windows Server 2008 Administrator's Pocket Consultant* (Microsoft Press, 2008). See the "Configuring Standard File Sharing" and "Managing Share Permissions" sections in Chapter 15 of this reference.

5. Enable log shipping on the primary database as discussed in "Enabling Log Shipping on the Primary Database" on the next page.

6. Specify the log shipping secondary databases as discussed in "Adding Log Shipping Secondary Databases" on page 626.

7. Optionally, add a monitoring server to track job history and alerts. The monitoring server runs an alert job that generates alerts when backup operations have not completed successfully within the predefined intervals.

## Upgrading SQL Server 2000 Log Shipping to SQL Server 2008 Log Shipping

Unlike SQL Server 2000 log shipping, which is configured using maintenance plans, SQL Server 2008 log shipping is configured as part of the standard database properties. Because of this, you cannot directly update SQL Server 2000 log shipping to SQL Server 2008 log shipping. You can, however, migrate your SQL Server 2000 log shipping configuration to SQL Server 2008 log shipping.

To upgrade the log shipping configuration easily, complete the following steps:

1. Upgrade all secondary server instances to SQL Server 2008. When you upgrade the secondary server instances, any log shipping databases will remain SQL Server 2000 databases because they will be in an offline state.

2. Upgrade the primary server to SQL Server 2008. The primary database will be unavailable while the upgrade is in progress, and you will not be able to failover to a secondary server.

3. Enable the primary database for log shipping. To ensure that backup logs are applied properly, use the same backup share that you used with your SQL Server 2000 log shipping configuration.

4. Specify the secondary servers. In the Secondary Database Settings dialog box, you must select the option No, The Secondary Database Is Initialized during the configuration. The secondary database is upgraded automatically to a SQL Server 2008 database when you start shipping logs.

SQL Server 2008 does not use any of the log shipping tables used by SQL Server 2000. After the migration, you can remove the following SQL Server 2000 log shipping tables:

- *log_shipping_databases*
- *log_shipping_monitor*
- *log_shipping_plan_databases*
- *log_shipping_plan_history*
- *log_shipping_plans*
- *log_shipping_primaries*
- *log_shipping_secondaries*

You can also delete any log shipping SQL Server Agent jobs created by SQL Server 2000.

## Enabling Log Shipping on the Primary Database

You can enable log shipping by completing the following steps:

1. In SQL Server Management Studio, access the primary server in the Object Explorer view.

2. Right-click the database you want to be the primary database and select Properties.

3. On the Transaction Log Shipping page, select Enable This As A Primary Database In A Log Shipping Configuration, as shown in Figure 17-1.

4. Click Backup Settings to display the Transaction Log Backup Settings dialog box shown in Figure 17-2.

5. Type the UNC path for the network share where the transaction logs are created on the primary server, such as \\ENGSQL\Data\Logs.

6. If the network share location is an actual folder on the local server, you can set the local path for the primary server to use. Otherwise, leave the related box blank.

7. Use the Delete Files Older Than boxes to configure how long old transaction logs copied to the backup folder will be retained. The default value is 72 hours (3 days). Before you change this value, consider the amount of available space in the backup location and the size of the logs. You don't want the backup location to run out of available free space. However, you also want to ensure that you keep old transaction logs for a sufficient period of time.

8. By default, the backup job runs every 15 minutes, and you can modify this as necessary by clicking Schedule and setting a new backup schedule. SQL Server monitors backup jobs. If no backup occurs within a specified time, you can configure log shipping to generate an alert. Set the Alert If No Backup Occurs Within option to the time to wait before generating an alert for failed backup operations.

**Figure 17-1**  The Transaction Log Shipping page in the Database Properties dialog box.

**Figure 17-2**  The Transaction Log Backup Settings dialog box.

**Note** The default value for alerts is one hour. If you are using delayed log shipping, you'll want to adjust this value appropriately. For example, if you are delaying log shipping for one hour, you might want SQL Server to alert within two hours of backup failure.

9. With SQL Server 2008 Enterprise Edition, you can configure backup compression by using one of the following options in the Set Backup Compression drop-down list:

- ❑ **Use The Default Server Setting** Uses the default server setting for compression to determine whether backup compression will be used.

- ❑ **Compress Backup** Enables backup compression. Typically, you'll want to enable backup compression when you want to reduce the size of the backups and thereby reduce the amount of data transmitted over the network.

- ❑ **Do Not Compress Backup** Disables backup compression. Typically, you'll want to disable backup compression when you are concerned about resource usage on the primary and secondary servers. By disabling compression, you reduce any overhead associated with compressing or uncompressing backups.

10. Optionally, to better track statistics, status, and error messages related to log shipping, you should configure a log shipping monitor. Although the monitor server can be any computer running SQL Server 2008, you might want to use a separate, centralized monitor server. By centralizing monitoring, you can more easily keep track of log shipping status and shift the associated workload to another server. The steps for configuring a log shipping monitor are as follows:

   a. On the Transaction Log Shipping page, select the Use A Monitor Server Instance check box and then click Settings. This displays the Log Shipping Monitor Settings dialog box shown in Figure 17-3.

   b. Click Connect. Use the Connect To Server dialog box to connect to the secondary server. The account you use must be a member of the sysadmin fixed server role on the secondary server.

   c. During the backup, copy, and restore processes, SQL Server must be able to connect to the monitor server to update the status of these log shipping operations. SQL Server can do this either by impersonating the SQL Server Agent proxy account or by using a specific SQL Server login. Choose the related Monitor Connections option as appropriate.

   d. Use the Delete History After boxes to configure how long log shipping history information is retained on the monitor server before it is deleted. The default value is 96 hours. Typically, you will want to retain copies for at least this long or longer. To enable more in-depth troubleshooting, you might need want to retain at least seven days of history information.

e.  Optionally, set the name of the related SQL Server Agent job. Click OK to complete the log shipping monitor configuration.

**Figure 17-3**   Optionally, configure a monitor server.

11. When you click OK to complete the log shipping configuration, SQL Server creates all the jobs needed for log shipping and performs related actions. As shown in Figure 17-4, SQL Server lists the success or error status of each action. If an error occurs, click the related error message to get details, make any necessary changes to resolve the problem, and then begin the configuration process again from step 1.

**Figure 17-4**   Check the action status, and resolve any errors.

12. Click Close. Click OK to close the Database Properties dialog box.

## Adding Log Shipping Secondary Databases

After you enable log shipping, you can add a log shipping secondary database by completing the following steps:

1. In SQL Server Management Studio, access the primary server in Object Explorer.

2. Right-click the database you want to be the primary database and select Properties.

3. On the Transaction Log Shipping page, click Add under Secondary Databases. This displays the Secondary Database Settings dialog box shown in Figure 17-5.

**Figure 17-5**    Initialize the secondary database.

4. Click Connect. Use the Connect To Server dialog box to connect to the secondary server.

5. To initialize the secondary database, you must restore a full backup of the primary database on the secondary server by using WITH NORECOVERY. This initializes the secondary database. If you have already done this, select the option No, The Secondary Database Is Initialized. Otherwise, select one of the following options to initialize the secondary database:

   ❑ **Yes, Generate A Full Backup**    Creates a full backup of the primary database, and restores it by using WITH NORECOVERY on the secondary server. Click Restore Options to set the folder paths for data and log files.

❑ **Yes, Restore An Existing Backup**   Uses the full backup of the primary database specified in the Backup File box. Click Restore Options to set the folder paths for data and log files.

**Tip**   SQL Server can back up the primary database and copy it to the secondary server, or you can manually copy a backup of the primary database to the secondary server and then restore it. If you have a very large database, you will probably want to manually copy the backup and then restore it. Otherwise, a copy/restore operation over the network might take too long. Keep in mind the restore operation will fail if a database with the same name as the primary database exists on the secondary server.

6. On the Copy Files tab, shown in Figure 17-6, specify the local folder to use as the destination folder for transaction log copy operations. A SQL Server Agent job running on the secondary server handles this copy task, and the SQL Server Agent service account must have access to the specified folder.

**Figure 17-6**   Configure the copy options.

7. Use the Delete Copied Files After boxes to configure how long transaction log copies are retained. Typically, you will want to retain copies for at least 72 hours. Before you change this value, consider the amount of available space in the copy location and the size of the logs. You don't want the copy location to run out of available free space. However, you also want to ensure that you keep old transaction logs for a sufficient period of time.

8. By default, the copy job runs every 15 minutes. Click Schedule to change the run schedule.

9. On the Restore Transaction Log tab, shown in Figure 17-7, specify the database state when restoring backups as either No Recovery Mode or Standby Mode. With No Recovery Mode, the transaction logs are applied by using WITH NORECOVERY, and the database is left in a nonoperational state. With Standby Mode, the database is in an operational standby state.

**Figure 17-7** Configure the restore options.

10. By default, the restore job runs every 15 minutes. Click Schedule to change the run schedule.

11. By default, the delay value for restoring backups is set to zero (0) minutes. This means backups are restored whenever the restore job runs. If you want to delay restoring backups, you can set a specific delay in minutes, hours, or days. The delay should never be longer than the Delete Copied Files After setting on the Copy Files tab (and be sure to account for the restore job run interval).

12. If no restore occurs within a specified time, you can configure log shipping to generate an alert. Set the Alert If No Restore Occurs Within option to the time to wait before generating an alert for failed restore operations.

13. Click OK to start the secondary configuration. The progress of the configuration is displayed. If an error occurs, click the related link to read the error message, take corrective action as necessary, and then begin the configuration process again from step 1.

14. Click Close when the configuration is complete. Click OK to close the Database Properties dialog box.

## Changing the Transaction Log Backup Interval

By default, transaction log backups are created every 15 minutes. To change the frequency of backup creation, follow these steps:

1. In SQL Server Management Studio, access the primary server in the Object Explorer view.

2. Right-click the database you want to be the primary database and select Properties.

3. On the Transaction Log Shipping page, select Backup Settings. This displays the Transaction Log Backup Settings dialog box.

4. Note the Job Name under Backup Job. Click Edit Job to display the Job Properties dialog box.

5. Set the schedule type and run frequency for the backup job. Typically, you'll want to use a recurring, daily job and a daily run frequency in hours or minutes. To work with schedules, access the Scheduled page in the Job Properties dialog box, and then click Edit under Schedule List.

6. Click OK three times to close all open dialog boxes and apply the settings.

## Changing the Copy and Restore Intervals

By default, transaction logs copied from backup and restore operations are performed every 15 minutes. To change the frequency of the copy and restore operations, follow these steps:

1. In SQL Server Management Studio, access the primary server in the Object Explorer view.

2. Right-click the database you want to be the primary database and select Properties.

3. On the Transaction Log Shipping page, secondary servers and databases are listed by server instance and database name. Select the secondary database you want to modify, and then click the related Properties (...) button. This displays the Secondary Database Settings dialog box.

4. On the Copy Files tab, click Schedule to display the Job Schedule Properties dialog box. Set the run frequency for the copy job, and then click OK.

5. On the Restore Transaction Log tab, click Schedule to display the Job Schedule Properties dialog box. Set the run frequency for the restore job. Typically, you'll want to use a recurring, daily job and a daily run frequency in hours or minutes. Click OK.

## Monitoring Log Shipping

The easiest way to monitor log shipping is through the SQL Server Agent job history. Anytime you suspect a server is having problems with log shipping, these jobs are the first place you should look to help you identify the root cause of the problem. In Object Explorer, expand SQL Server Agent, and then expand the Jobs folder to see a list of jobs. Look for jobs related to log shipping. If you right-click a job, you can select View History to get more detailed information that will include error messages useful for troubleshooting.

Another way to check the status of log shipping is to run a status report. In the status report, you'll see information about recent log shipping activities. Any alerts are shown as well, so you'll know immediately about recent failed jobs. You can run a status report by following these steps:

1. In Object Explorer, right-click the SQL Server instance acting as a primary server, secondary server, or monitor server.

2. Point to Reports, point to Standard Reports, and then click Transaction Log Shipping Status.

Log shipping can fail for a number of reasons, but the most common reasons are related to disk space and permissions. The disks used for backup and copy operations must have enough free space to retain files through the retention period. The SQL Server Agent service for the related Database Engine instance running on the primary server will back up the transaction logs to the backup folder, and it must have read and write permissions on the folder. The SQL Server Agent service for the related Database Engine instance running on the secondary server will copy files from the backup location to a designated copy folder, and it must have read permissions on the backup folder and both read and write permissions on the copy folder.

Network connectivity and server problems also can cause log shipping to fail. For these types of problems, you often will have to dig into the Microsoft Windows event logs and the SQL Server logs. As discussed in Chapter 14, "Profiling and Monitoring Microsoft SQL Server 2008," look through the logs for errors and warnings. Use the related error messages to help you diagnose and resolve the problem.

## Failing Over to a Secondary Database

In most cases, when you manually failover from a primary database to a secondary database, the two databases will not be fully synchronized. This lack of synchronization can occur for either or both of the following reasons:

- Some transaction log backups created on the primary server might not yet have been copied or applied to the secondary server.

- Changes to the databases on the primary server might have occurred since the last transaction log backup.

Because of this possible lack of full synchronization, before using a secondary database, you should synchronize the primary database with the secondary database and then bring the second server online. To do this, follow these steps:

1. Back up the *syslogins* table in the *master* database to a text file. You will use this file to synchronize *sysusers* to *syslogins* on the secondary server when failover occurs. If you do not do this, you will have orphaned connections and users will not be able to properly connect to the secondary database after failover. The best way to handle this issue is to create a SQL Server Agent job that runs daily after the backup and uses Bulk Copy to back up the *syslogins* table in the *master* database to a text file on the secondary server or any available network share, such as

   ```
   bcp master..syslogins out \\sqlserver52\data\syslogins.dat -N -S . -T
   ```

   **Note**   The –T option specifies that you want to use trusted Windows authentication. In this situation, this means the job will run under the SQL Server Agent service account's credentials.

2. Copy any remaining transaction log backup files from the backup share location to the copy destination folder on the secondary server. You can do this manually or by starting the copy job on each secondary server. To start the copy job on a secondary server, expand the SQL Server Agent and Jobs nodes, right-click the copy job, and then select Start Job.

3. Apply any unapplied transaction log backups. You can do this manually or by running the restore job on the secondary server. To start the restore job on a secondary server, expand the SQL Server Agent and Jobs nodes, right-click the restore job, and then select Start Job.

4. If possible, back up the active transaction log on the primary server by using NO_TRUNCATE. When you are using the SQL Server Backup dialog box, you should select the Back Up The Tail Of The Log option on the Options page of the Back Up Database dialog box when performing the transaction log backup. Alternatively, use the following commands:

   ```
   USE master
   GO
   BACKUP LOG database_name TO device_name
   WITH NO_TRUNCATE,INIT
   ```

   Such as:

   ```
   USE master
   GO
   BACKUP LOG personnel TO DISK='\\sqlserver52\backup\logtail.trn'
   WITH NO_TRUNCATE,INIT
   ```

5. If you are able to back up the active transaction log, apply the log backup to the secondary server. This ensures that the secondary server has the most up-to-date version of the data. Regardless, uncommitted transactions from the primary server are lost. You can apply the log on the secondary server by using the following commands:

```
USE master
GO
RESTORE LOG database_name FROM device_name
WITH RECOVERY
```

Such as:

```
USE master
GO
RESTORE LOG personnel FROM DISK='\\sqlserver52\backup\logtail.trn'
WITH RECOVERY
```

6. Resolve the logins between the primary and the secondary servers. You can do this by using the following commands:

```
EXEC sp_resolve_logins @dest_db= 'database_name'
  @dest_path= 'path'
  @filename= 'filename'
```

Such as:

```
EXEC sp_resolve_logins @dest_db= 'personnel'
  @dest_path= '\\sqlserver52\data\'
  @filename= 'syslogins.dat'
```

7. Users can now log in to the database by using the logins and passwords that they normally use with the primary database server. To complete the configuration, you will need to modify any applications that connect to the primary database and point them to the secondary database. You can do this by specifying the new database server by name or IP address, or by modifying the connection string or other settings in the ODBC data source name (DSN).

After you have failed over to the secondary server, you can configure the secondary database to act as the primary database. Then, you will be able to swap primary and secondary databases as needed. The steps required for the initial role change are different from those required on subsequent role changes.

The first time you want to failover to the secondary database and make it your new primary database, you must follow these steps:

1. Manually failover from the primary database to a secondary database, as discussed previously.

2. Disable the log shipping backup job on the original primary server and the copy and restore jobs on the original secondary server.

3. Configure log shipping on the secondary database, which is now acting as the primary database. You must use the same backup share as the original primary server, add the original primary server as a secondary server in the log shipping configuration, and choose No, The Secondary Database Is Initialized.

After you have completed the steps for an initial role change, you can perform subsequent role changes by completing these steps:

1. Perform the manual failover steps, and bring the secondary database online. When you are backing up the active transaction log on the primary server, you must use WITH NORECOVERY.

2. Disable the log shipping backup job on the original primary server and the copy and restore jobs on the original secondary server.

3. Enable the log shipping backup job on the secondary server, which is now acting as the primary server, and enable the copy and restore jobs on the primary server, which is now acting as the secondary server.

## Disabling and Removing Log Shipping

When you remove log shipping from a primary database, SQL Server disables log shipping and removes all jobs and history from the primary, secondary, and monitor server instances. You can remove log shipping by following these steps:

1. In SQL Server Management Studio, access the primary server in the Object Explorer view.

2. Right-click the database you want to be the primary database and select Properties.

3. On the Transaction Log Shipping page, clear the Enable This As A Primary Database In A Log Shipping Configuration option and then click OK.

4. When prompted to confirm, click Yes. SQL Server removes all jobs and history from the primary, secondary, and monitor server instances.

# Database Mirroring

Mirroring allows you to create hot standby servers. SQL Server 2008 allows you to mirror any database except for *master*, *msdb*, *temp*, and *model*. You can configure and enable mirroring by using the Mirroring page in the Database Properties dialog box. As discussed in "Ensuring Availability and Scalability" on page 33, mirroring requires up to three servers: a principal server, a mirror server, and a witness server.

## Database Mirroring Essentials

The principal server is the source server with the principal database in the mirror pair. The mirror server is the target server with the target database in the mirror pair. The witness server is an optional monitoring server that is preferably physically separate from the principal and mirror.

SQL Server 2008 has three operating modes for database mirroring:

- Synchronous mirroring that requires a witness and provides a high-availability solution with transaction safety set to FULL

- Synchronous mirroring that doesn't require a witness and provides a high-protection solution with transaction safety set to FULL

- Asynchronous mirroring that doesn't require a witness and provides a high-performance solution with transaction safety set to OFF

Synchronous mirroring with a witness is the only operating mode that allows automatic failover. Synchronous mirroring requires that the mirror receives data, confirms committing the data, and sends an acknowledgment back to the principal prior to the principal committing the data and proceeding to the next operation. On a fast network, this arrangement works well in most cases. However, on a slow network, having to wait for acknowledgment can cause serious performance issues.

On the other hand, asynchronous mirroring does not require acknowledgment. The principal sends data to the mirror as resources are available but does not wait for acknowledgment before proceeding to the next operation. Although transactional consistency is always maintained between the principal and mirror, the mirror typically is not current with the principal. For example, when the principal is experiencing heavy transactional volume, the mirror could lag behind the principal by several minutes or more.

As you do with log shipping, you must ensure logins are synchronized between the principal and mirror databases. You can synchronize logins by backing up the *syslogins* table in the *master* database to a text file. You will use this file to synchronize *sysusers* to *syslogins* on the secondary server when failover occurs. Without this, you will have orphaned connections and users will not be able to properly connect to the secondary database after failover. The best way to handle this is to create a SQL Server Agent job that runs daily after the backup and uses Bulk Copy to back up the *syslogins* table in the *master* database to a text file on the secondary server or any available network share, such as

```
bcp master..syslogins out \\sqlserver52\data\syslogins.dat -N -S . -T
```

**Note**    The –T option specifies that you want to use trusted Windows authentication. In this situation, this means the job will run under the SQL Server Agent service account's credentials.

When you need to resolve the logins between the principal database and mirror database, you can do this by using the following commands:

```
EXEC sp_resolve_logins @dest_db= 'database_name'
  @dest_path= 'path'
  @filename= 'filename'
```

Such as:

```
EXEC sp_resolve_logins @dest_db= 'personnel'
  @dest_path= '\\sqlserver52\data\'
  @filename= 'syslogins.dat'
```

Users will then be able to log in to the mirror database by using the logins and passwords that they normally use with the principal database.

## Configuring Database Mirroring

After you have installed SQL Server 2008 on the servers that will be used in mirroring, you must prepare for mirroring by doing the following:

1. Start SQL Server Management Studio. In the Object Explorer view, connect to the server you want to act as the principal.

2. Right-click the database you want to work with and choose Properties. This displays the database's Properties dialog box. On the Options page, set the Recovery Model to Full. Click OK.

3. In the Registered Server view, right-click the principal server and choose SQL Server Configuration Manager. This starts SQL Server Configuration Manager with the server selected for configuration.

4. Select the SQL Server Services node in the left pane. In the right pane, note the Log On As account for the SQL Server service on the instance that will act as the principal.

5. Perform a full backup of the principal database.

6. In the Object Explorer view, connect to the server you want to act as the mirror.

7. Restore a full backup of the principal database on the mirror server instance by using NORECOVERY.

8. Right-click the database you want to work with on the mirror and choose Properties to display the database's Properties dialog box. On the Options page, set the Recovery Model to Full. Click OK.

9. In the Registered Server view, right-click the mirror server and choose SQL Server Configuration Manager. This starts SQL Server Configuration Manager with the server selected for configuration.

10. Select the SQL Server Services node in the left pane. In the right pane, note the Log On As account for the SQL Server service on the instance that will act as the mirror.

11. In the Object Explorer view, connect to the server you want to act as the witness (if any).

12. In the Registered Server view, right-click the witness server and choose SQL Server Configuration Manager. This starts SQL Server Configuration Manager with the server selected for configuration.

13. Select the SQL Server Services node in the left pane. In the right pane, note the Log On As account for the SQL Server service on the instance that will act as the witness (if any).

After you prepare for mirroring, you then must configure the mirror endpoints and mirror security. To do this, complete the following steps:

1. Start SQL Server Management Studio. In the Object Explorer view, connect to the server you want to act as the principal.

2. Expand the Databases folder. Right-click the database you want to work with and choose Properties to display the database's Properties dialog box.

3. On the Mirroring page, click Configure Security. When the wizard starts, click Next on the opening page. If you are using a witness server to allow synchronous mode with automatic failover, accept the default answer of Yes on the Include Witness Server page of the wizard, and then click Next. Otherwise, click No to specify that you will not be using a witness server.

4. Typically, you will want to configure security on all the servers that are part of the mirror set, so accept the default (which has the appropriate server types selected) on the Choose Servers To Configure page of the wizard and click Next.

5. On the Principal Server Instance page, the current server is selected by default as the principal as shown in Figure 17-8. Set a listener port and endpoint name for this server as part of the mirror set. If the principal, mirror, and witness are instances on the same server, the related endpoints must use different listener ports. Otherwise, the endpoints can use the same listener ports. The default is TCP port 5022. By default, data sent through the endpoint is encrypted to ensure your data is secure. If you don't want to use encryption, clear the Encrypt Data Sent Through This Endpoint check box. Click Next.

   **Tip**   To enable automatic decryption of the database master key of a mirror database, you must provide the password used to encrypt the master key to the mirror server instance. Use sp_control_dbmasterkey_password to create a credential for the database master key before you start database mirroring. You must repeat this process for every database you want to mirror.

6.  On the Mirror Server Instance page, use the Mirror Server Instance drop-down list to select the server that will act as the mirror. The principal and mirror cannot be the same server instance. As necessary, click Connect and then use the Connect To Server dialog box to connect to the server you want to use.

**Figure 17-8**   Configure the principal server instance.

7.  Set a listener port and endpoint name. The default endpoint name is Mirroring. If the principal, mirror, or witness are instances on the same server, the related endpoints must use different listener ports. Otherwise, the endpoints can use the same listener ports. The default is TCP port 5023. Click Next.

8.  If you aren't using a witness server, skip to step 10. Otherwise, on the Witness Server Instance page, use the Witness Server Instance drop-down list to select the server that will act as the witness. The principal and witness cannot be the same server instance; the mirror and witness cannot be the same server instance.

9.  Set a listener port and endpoint name for the witness server. The default endpoint name is Mirroring. If the principal, mirror, or witness are instances on the same server, the related endpoints must use different listener ports. Otherwise, the endpoints can use the same listener ports. The default is TCP port 5023. Click Next.

10. On the Service Accounts page, shown in Figure 17-9, you can configure service accounts. If the server instances use different domain accounts for their SQL Server service accounts and those accounts are in the same domain or trusted

domains, enter the account names in the boxes provided. For domain accounts, be sure to enter the account name in *DOMAIN\username* format. If the service accounts are different, the wizard will grant CONNECT permissions on the endpoints for each account.

**Figure 17-9**    Configure service accounts in the same or trusted domains.

11. Click Next, and then click Finish. The wizard then configures security for mirroring. As shown in Figure 17-10, the wizard lists the success or error status of each action. If an error occurs, click the related error message to get details, make any necessary changes to resolve the problem, and then begin the configuration process again from step 1.

12. Click Close. Click Do Not Start Mirroring.

13. The Database Properties dialog box should still be open to the Mirroring page. Set the mirror operating mode you want to use. If you have configured a witness server, you can use High Safety With Automatic Failover mode to ensure high availability.

14. Prior to starting database mirroring, you must ensure the mirror server has a copy of the principal's database in a recovery state. If you've restored the principal database on the mirror and put it in a recovery state, click Start Mirroring and then click Yes when prompted. Otherwise, perform any necessary actions, and then click Start Mirroring on the Mirroring page in the Database Properties dialog box.

**Figure 17-10**   Check the action status and resolve any errors.

If you need to restore the principal database on the mirror and put it in a recovery state, you can do this by using the following commands:

```
RESTORE DATABASE database_name FROM device_name
WITH MOVE 'data_file' TO 'mirror_data_file'
MOVE 'log_file' TO 'mirror_log_file'
NORECOVERY
```

Such as:

```
RESTORE DATABASE personnel FROM DISK='\\sqlserver52\backup\db.bak'
WITH MOVE 'data_file' TO 'c:\sql\data\data_file.mdf'
MOVE 'log_file' TO 'c:\sql\data\data_file.ldf'
NORECOVERY
```

Here, the NORECOVERY clause keeps the database closed so that the transaction log can be applied. To initialize the database, you must then apply a transaction log to the mirror database. As shown in this example, you again leave the database in NORECOVERY mode so that when mirroring is started, the log records from the principal can be applied properly:

```
RESTORE LOG personnel FROM DISK='\\sqlserver52\backup\logtail.trn'
WITH NORECOVERY
```

You can then start mirroring by clicking Start Mirroring on the Mirroring page in the Database Properties dialog box.

## Managing and Monitoring Mirroring

You can view the current status of mirroring by completing the following steps:

1. Start SQL Server Management Studio. In the Object Explorer view, connect to the server you want to act as the principal.

2. Expand the Databases folder. Right-click the database you want to work with and choose Properties to display the database's Properties dialog box.

3. Select the Mirroring page. The current mirroring status is displayed at the bottom of the page.

After you have configured and started mirroring, you can manage mirroring on the Mirroring page by using the following options:

- Click Pause to temporarily stop mirroring. When prompted to confirm, click Yes. Click Resume to resume mirroring.

- Click Stop Mirroring to stop mirroring. When prompted to confirm, click Yes. Click Start Mirroring to start mirroring again.

- If you are using a witness, failover occurs automatically. You can also force failover by clicking the Failover button.

Mirroring details can be obtained using the following catalog views:

- **sys.database_mirroring**   This catalog view displays the database mirroring metadata for each mirrored database in a server instance.

- **sys.database_mirroring_endpoints**   This catalog view displays information about the database mirroring endpoint of the server instance.

- **sys.database_mirroring_witnesses**   This catalog view displays the database mirroring metadata for each of the sessions in which a server instance is the witness.

In Performance Monitor, you can use the SQLServer:Database Mirroring object to monitor mirroring performance:

- Use the Log Bytes Sent/sec counter to monitor the amount of log data sent per second.

- Use the Transaction Delay counter to determine whether mirroring is affecting performance on the principal server.

- Use the Redo Queue and Log Send Queue counters to determine whether the mirror database is keeping up with the principal database.

Although related catalog views and performance counters are helpful, they are no substitute for the Database Mirroring Monitor utility, which provides an overview and status of all mirroring activities. You can access and use Database Mirroring Monitor by completing the following steps:

1. Start SQL Server Management Studio. In the Object Explorer view, connect to the server you want to act as the principal.

2. Expand the Databases folder. Right-click the principal database, point to Tasks, and then select Launch Database Mirroring Monitor.

3. By default, no mirrored databases are registered for monitoring, so you'll need to register the databases you want to monitor. Click the Register Mirrored Database link.

4. In the Register Mirrored Database dialog box, use the Server Instance list to select a mirrored database to monitor and then click Connect. Use the Connect To Server dialog box to connect to the related server instance. You can register principals, mirrors, and witnesses as necessary. Click OK.

5. You will then see a mirroring entry for each mirrored pair or grouping. By selecting the related entry in the left pane, you will see details in the right pane. On the Status tab, you'll find summary details regarding the current state of database mirroring. On the Warning tab, you will find any related warnings regarding database mirroring.

Like log shipping, database mirroring can fail for a number of reasons. To help you diagnose and resolve problems with database mirroring, use the status, error, and warning messages provided in Database Mirroring Monitor. Network connectivity and server problems also can cause database mirroring to fail. For these types of problems, you often will have to dig into the Windows event logs and the SQL Server logs. As discussed in Chapter 14, look through the logs for errors and warnings. Use the related error messages to help you diagnose and resolve the problem.

**Tip**   With SQL Server 2008 Enterprise Edition, database mirroring partners automatically try to resolve certain types of errors that prevent reading a data page. If the partner is unable to read a page and is in a synchronized state, the partner requests a fresh copy from the other partner. If this request succeeds, the unreadable page is replaced by the copy, which will resolve the error in most cases. Specific error types that can be automatically repaired include error number 823 for cyclic redundancy checks, error number 824 for logical data errors (such as torn write or bad page checksum), and error number 829 for pages marked as restore pending.

The transaction safety property determines whether a database runs synchronously or asynchronously. A database owner can change the transaction safety level at any time from FULL, the highest availability mode that supports automatic failover when a witness is present, to OFF, the highest performance mode that doesn't support automatic failover. During a database mirroring session, the mirrored database is always in a specific mirroring state, which indicates the communication status and data flow. The partners use the mirroring state to monitor the mirrored database. The principal and mirror database are always in the same state except when there is a pending failover. If a witness is set for the session, each of the partners monitors the witness by using its connection state.

The relationship between the principal, mirror, and optional mirror is referred to as the *quorum*. If a witness exists, the witness has one of several states. When the witness is connected to a partner, the witness is in the CONNECTED state relative to that partner and has quorum with that partner. In this case, the database can be made available, even if one of the partners is unavailable. On the other hand, when the witness exists but is not connected to a partner, the witness is in the UNKOWN or DISCONNECTED state relative to that partner. In this case, the witness lacks quorum with that partner, and if the partners are not connected to each other, the database becomes unavailable.

The possible mirroring states for databases are as follows:

- **DISCONNECTED**   Indicates the partner has lost communication with the other partner.

- **PENDING_FAILOVER**   Indicates failover has begun but the server has not transitioned into the mirror role. When a failover is initiated, the principal database goes into the PENDING_FAILOVER state, terminates any user connections, and takes over the mirror role.

- **SUSPENDED**   Indicates the mirror copy of the database is not available. The principal database is running without sending any logs to the mirror server, a condition known as *running exposed*. This is the state after a failover. A mirroring session can also go into a SUSPENDED state as a result of redo errors or if the administrator pauses the session. SUSPENDED is a persistent state that survives partner shutdowns and startups.

- **SYNCHRONIZED**   Indicates the principal and mirror are fully synchronized. The database remains in this state as long as the principal server continues to send changes to the mirror server and the mirror server continues to apply changes to the mirror database without lagging behind. When transaction safety is set to FULL, automatic failover and manual failover are both supported in the SYNCHRONIZED state and there is no data loss after a failover. However, when transaction safety is OFF, some data loss is always possible, even in the SYNCHRONIZED state.

- **SYNCHRONIZING**   Indicates that the contents of the mirror database are lagging behind the contents of the principal database. The principal server is sending log records to the mirror server, which is in the process of applying the changes to the mirror database to roll it forward.

You can view the safety level and state of the witness for a database by using the sys.database_mirroring catalog view. The relevant columns are mirroring_safety_level, mirroring_safety_level_desc, mirroring_witness_name, and mirroring_witness_state_ desc. Here is an example:

```
SELECT mirroring_safety_level, mirroring_safety_level_desc,
mirroring_witness_name, mirroring_witness_state_desc FROM
sys.database_mirroring
```

## Recovering by Using Failover

Each operating mode has different quorum states and recovery scenarios depending on which node in the relationship is lost. The quorum states and recovery scenarios are as follows:

- **Full quorum**    A full quorum relationship exists when the principal, mirror, and witness can all communicate with each other. If the principal is lost and the witness is up and running, SQL Server will automatically failover to the mirror.

- **Quorum**    A quorum relationship exists when the witness is available and either partner can communicate with it. If the mirror is lost, the principal retains control. If the principal is lost and the mirror is available, you have to manually failover. If the witness is lost and the principal and mirror are up and running, a partner-to-partner quorum is established.

- **Partner-to-partner quorum**    A partner-to-partner quorum exists when only the principal and mirror can communicate with each other. Because only the witness is missing, no failover occurs. If the principal is lost and the mirror is available, you have to manually failover.

With synchronous mirroring in a high-performance solution with transaction safety set to FULL, you can failover to the mirror in the event the principal fails by using the following steps:

1. On the mirror, run the command ALTER DATABASE *database_name* SET PARTNER FORCE_SERVICE_ALLOW_DATA_LOSS, where *database_name* is the name of the database to failover, such as

   ```
   ALTER DATABASE personnel SET PARTNER FORCE_SERVICE_ALLOW_DATA_LOSS
   ```

   If the principal is still available and you run this command, you will get an error telling you the mirror is not in the correct state to become the principal database.

2. The mirror becomes the new principal and database mirroring stops. When the original principal becomes available, it is marked as mirroring in a suspended state. You can ensure that the users and logins are synchronized by running the sp_resolve_logins stored procedure or restoring the master database from a previous backup of the original principal. Be sure to repoint any applications to the new principal server as necessary.

With asynchronous mirroring in a high-protection solution with transaction safety set to OFF, you can failover to the mirror in the event the principal fails by using the following steps:

1. On the mirror, run the command ALTER DATABASE *database_name* SET PARTNER OFF, where *database_name* is the name of the database to failover, such as

   ```
   ALTER DATABASE personnel SET PARTNER OFF
   ```

2. To recover the database, run the command RESTORE DATABASE *database_name* WITH RECOVERY, such as

   ```
   RESTORE DATABASE personnel WITH RECOVERY
   ```

3. The mirror becomes the new principal, and database mirroring stops. When the original principal becomes available, it is marked as mirroring in a suspended state. You can ensure that the users and logins are synchronized by running the sp_resolve_logins stored procedure or restoring the master database from a previous backup of the original principal. Be sure to repoint any applications to the new principal server as necessary.

## Removing Database Mirroring

The database owner can manually stop a database mirroring session at any time, at either partner. When you remove mirroring, all information about the mirroring session is dropped, each partner server instance is left with a separate copy of the database, and the relationship between the partners and between each partner and the witness breaks permanently. If the partners are connected and communicating with each other when the session is stopped, their relationship is immediately broken on both computers. If the partners are disconnected and not communicating, the relationship is broken immediately on the partner from which mirroring is stopped. When the other partner tries to reconnect, it discovers that the database mirroring session has ended and the mirroring relationship is then broken.

You can remove database mirroring by completing the following steps:

1. Start SQL Server Management Studio. In the Object Explorer view, connect to the principal server.

2. Expand the Databases folder. Right-click the principal database, point to Tasks, and then select Mirror. This opens the Mirroring page of the Database Properties dialog box.

3. To remove mirroring, click Remove Mirroring. When prompted to confirm, click Yes. The session is stopped and mirroring is removed from the database.

Because the mirror database was created by using the RESTORE WITH NORECOVERY option, the mirror database is left in the RESTORING state. At this point, you can drop the former mirror database or restore it using WITH RECOVERY. When you recover the database, its data will not necessarily be identical to that in the former principal database.

To continue mirroring after stopping a session, you must establish a new database mirroring session and at least one log backup must be taken on the principal database and applied to the mirror database. Any additional log backups taken since mirroring was removed also must be applied to the mirror database. Therefore, if you created log backups after stopping mirroring, apply them to the mirror database before restarting mirroring.

# Using Mirroring and Log Shipping

Mirroring and log shipping are two different options that you can use to improve availability. The principal database used in database mirroring can act as the primary database in log shipping as well. You might want to do this is in a situation in which you have a critical database and you want to have multiple standby servers available. For example, you might use either of the following options:

- Mirroring, to establish a single standby that will come online if the principal fails. With a fully synchronous mirroring configuration, automatic failover occurs if the principal database is lost, as long as the mirror server and witness can communicate with each other. Automatic failover causes the mirror server to assume the principal role and bring its database online as the principal database. When the former principal comes back online, it comes online as the mirror.

- Log shipping, to establish one standby or more, which can be manually brought online in case the primary and mirror both fail. Transaction logs are shipped from a primary database to a central backup folder. Secondary servers access the backup folder and restore the transaction logs in their secondary databases to keep the servers synchronized. If the primary database fails, any secondary database can be brought online manually as the new primary database.

If you want to use both mirroring and log shipping, you will usually configure mirroring first and then log shipping by following these general steps:

1. Restore backups of the principal database onto the server that will act as the mirror by using the NORECOVERY option.

2. Set up database mirroring by configuring the principal and mirror servers and, as necessary, the witness server (required for synchronous mirroring and automatic failover).

3. Restore backups of the principal database to servers that will act as log shipping secondary (destination) databases.

4. Create a shared resource to use as the backup folder for log shipping.

5. Configure the principal database as the log shipping primary database for one or more secondary (destination) databases.

6. Configure the mirror server as a log shipping primary server with the same log shipping configuration as the primary server. This allows log shipping to continue after database mirroring fails over.

7. If mirroring fails over, the former mirror server comes online as the primary server. If the backup folder is not available to both the primary and mirror servers, log shipping backup jobs will fail when the mirror server takes over as the primary server. To prevent this, create the backup folder on a shared network resource.

# Chapter 18

# Implementing Policy-Based Management

Policy-Based Management is an extensible and scalable configuration framework that you can use to manage servers, databases, and other objects in your data environments. As an administrator, you'll need to be very familiar with how Policy-Based Management technology works, and that's exactly what this chapter is about. If you haven't worked with Policy-Based Management technology before, one thing you'll notice immediately is that the technology is fairly advanced and has many features. To help you manage this complex technology, I'll start with an overview of Policy-Based Management and then explore its components.

## Introducing Policy-Based Management

Just about every administrative task you'll perform will be affected by the policy-based framework in some way. The policy-based framework provides the ability to define policies that apply to servers, databases, and other objects in your data environment. You use these policies to help you control and manage the configuration of data services throughout the enterprise. Through intelligent monitoring and proactive responses, you can prevent changes that deviate from desired configurations. You also can scale management across multiple servers, which makes it easy to enforce consistent configuration policies.

Within the policy-based framework, you use the following objects to configure policy management:

- **Facet** Defines a management area within the policy-based framework. Each management area has a set of related properties that you can configure. For example, the Backup Device facet has the following properties: BackupDeviceType, Name, PhysicalLocation, and SkipTapeLabel.

- **Condition**   Defines the permitted states for one or more properties of a single facet. For example, you can create a condition called Limit Backup Devices to specify that the BackupDeviceType for the Backup Device facet can be a hard disk or tape, and that SkipTapeLabel should always be set to True.

- **Policy**   Contains a single condition that you want to enforce. For example, you can create a policy named Standard Backup Device Policy that assigns the Limit Backup Devices condition.

- **Category**   Contains one or more policies that you want to enforce together. For example, you can create a category named Standard DB Policies that contains all the standard policies that you want to enforce within your Microsoft SQL Server databases.

- **Target**   Defines the servers, databases, or other database objects for which policies are applied. For example, a target set could include all of the databases on an instance of SQL Server.

You create and manage policies in SQL Server Management Studio. The policy creation process includes the following steps:

1. Select a facet that contains the properties you want to configure.

2. Define a condition that specifies the permitted states of the facet.

3. Define a policy that contains the condition and sets one of the evaluation modes listed in Table 18-1.

4. Determine whether an instance of SQL Server is in compliance with the policy, and take appropriate action.

**Table 18-1   Evaluation Modes for Policy-Based Management**

| Policy Evaluation Mode | Description | Execution Type |
|---|---|---|
| On Demand | Evaluates the policy only when you directly execute the policy. | Manual |
| On Change: Prevent | When nested triggers are enabled, uses data definition language (DDL) triggers to prevent policy violations by detecting changes that violate policy and rolling them back. | Automatic |
| On Change: Log Only | Evaluates a policy when a relevant change is made and logs policy violations in the event logs. | Automatic |
| On Schedule | Uses SQL Server Agent jobs to periodically evaluate policies. Logs policy violations in the event logs and generates a report. | Automatic |

**Note**   All facets support the On Demand and On Schedule modes. Facets support the On Change: Log Only mode only if the change of the facet state can be captured by related system events. Facets support the On Change: Prevent mode only if there is transactional support for the DDL statements that change the facet state. Only automatic policies can be enabled or disabled.

Policy categories apply to databases and servers. At the database level, database owners can subscribe a database to a set of policy categories and those policies govern the database. All databases implicitly subscribe to the default policy category. At the server level, you can apply policy categories to all databases.

You can mark categories as Active or Inactive at the server or database level. By default, all databases implicitly subscribe to the default category. Although you can classify policies into different policy categories, a policy can belong only to one policy category.

All objects defined on a SQL Server instance form a target hierarchy. Within a policy, you define a target when you apply filters to the target hierarchy. For example, a target set with a large scope could include all of the databases on an instance of SQL Server, while a target set with a small scope could include only the tables and indexes owned by the Sales schema in the Customers database.

The effective policies of a target are those policies that govern the target. For a policy to be effective with regard to a target, the policy must be enabled and the target must be subject to the policy. Within your data services environment, you enforce Policy-Based Management using configuration servers. A designated configuration server is responsible for monitoring and enforcing policies as appropriate. By default, each instance of SQL Server acts as its own configuration server. This means each SQL Server instance normally handles its own policy monitoring and enforcement.

**Real World**   To be notified when messages from automatically executed policies are written to the event logs, you can create alerts to detect these messages and perform necessary actions. The alerts should detect the messages according to their message number. Look for message numbers 34050, 34051, 34052, and 34053. You can configure alerts as discussed in "Managing Alerts" on page 580.

When policies are executed automatically, they execute as a member of the sysadmin role. This allows the policy to write to the event logs and raise an alert. When policies are evaluated on demand, they execute in the security context of the current user. To write to the event log, the user must have ALTER TRACE permissions or be a member of the sysadmin fixed server role. Otherwise, Microsoft Windows will not write to the event log and will not fire an alert.

# Working with Policy-Based Management

You must be a member of the PolicyAdministratorRole role in the *msdb* database to configure Policy-Based Management settings. This role has complete control of all policies and can create policies and conditions, edit policies and conditions, and enable or disable policies.

When working with policies, keep the following in mind:

- A system administrator or database owner can subscribe a database to a policy or policy group.

- Ad hoc policy execution occurs in the security context of the user.

- Members of the PolicyAdministratorRole role can create policies that they do not have permission to execute on an ad hoc basis.

- Members of the PolicyAdministratorRole role can enable or disable policies.

- Policies that are in the On Schedule mode use SQL Server Agent jobs that are owned by the sa login.

Although you certainly can manage policies for each instance of SQL Server, you'll likely want to reuse policies you've defined and then apply them to other instances of SQL Server. With Policy-Based Management, you can apply policies to multiple instances of SQL Server in several ways. As discussed in "Importing and Exporting Policies" on page 656, you can export the policies you've defined on a particular instance of SQL Server and then import the policies on another instance of SQL Server. During the import process, you can specify whether policies are enabled or disabled and whether the exported state of the policies are preserved.

Being able to export and import policies is useful. However, you don't necessarily need to move policies around to enforce the policies on multiple computers running SQL Server. Instead, you might want to manage policies centrally, and you can do this using a central management server. A central management server is a special type of configuration server that is responsible for monitoring and enforcing policy on any instance of SQL Server registered as a subordinate server. As discussed in "Configuring Central Management Servers" on page 658, you designate central management servers and their subordinates using SQL Server Management Studio. Because the central management architecture already is an execution environment for Transact-SQL statements related to policies, you also can execute Transact-SQL statements on multiple instances of SQL Server at the same time from a central management server.

Because SQL Server stores policy-related data in the *msdb* database, you should back up *msdb* after you change conditions, policies, or categories. Policy history for policies evaluated in the current instance of the Database Engine is maintained in *msdb* system tables. Policy history for policies applied to other instances of the Database Engine or applied to Reporting Services or Analysis Services is not retained.

As summarized in Table 18-2, SQL Server 2008 includes several sets of predefined policies, including those for the Database Engine, Analysis Services, and Reporting Services. By default, the policies are stored as XML files in the following locations and you must import them into SQL Server:

- Microsoft SQL Server\100\Tools\Policies\DatabaseEngine\1033

- Microsoft SQL Server\100\Tools\Policies\AnalysisServices\1033

- Microsoft SQL Server\100\Tools\Policies\ReportingServices\1033

**Note**  On 64-bit computers, policies are under Program Files (x86) rather than Program Files when you install SQL Server in the default file system location. Note also that surface area configuration is discussed in "Managing SQL Server Component Feature Access" on page 53.

Table 18-2   Predefined Policies for SQL Server 2008

| Predefined Policy Name | Description |
| --- | --- |
| Asymmetric Key Encryption Algorithm | Checks whether asymmetric keys were created by using 1024-bit or stronger encryption. As a best practice, you should use RSA 1024-bit or stronger encryption to create asymmetric keys for data encryption. |
| Backup And Data File Location | Checks whether database files are on devices separate from the backup files. As a best practice, you should put the database and backups on separate backup devices. This approach helps safeguard the data in case of device failure and also optimizes the input/output (I/O) performance for both the production use of the database and the writing of backups. |
| CmdExec Rights Secured | Checks an instance of SQL Server 2000 to determine whether only members of the sysadmin server role can run CmdExec and ActiveX Script job steps, which is a recommended best practice. |
| Data And Log File Location | Checks whether data and log files are placed on separate logical drives. As a best practice, placing the files on separate drives allows the I/O activity to occur at the same time for both the data and log files. |
| Database Auto Close | Checks whether the AUTO_CLOSE option is set to OFF. When AUTO_CLOSE is set to ON, this option can cause performance degradation on frequently accessed databases because of the increased overhead of opening and closing the database after each connection. AUTO_CLOSE also flushes the procedure cache after each connection. Therefore, as a best practice, you should set the AUTO_CLOSE option to OFF on a database that is accessed frequently. |
| Database Auto Shrink | Checks whether the AUTO_SHRINK database option is set to OFF. Because frequently shrinking and expanding a database can lead to fragmentation on the storage device, you should set the AUTO_SHRINK database option to OFF in most instances. |

Table 18-2 Predefined Policies for SQL Server 2008

| Predefined Policy Name | Description |
|---|---|
| Database Collation | Checks whether user-defined databases are defined by using a database collation that is the same as the collation for the *master* and *model* databases, which is a recommended best practice. Otherwise, collation conflicts can occur that might prevent code from executing. You can resolve collation conflicts by exporting the data from the user database and importing it into new tables that have the same collation as the *master* and *model* databases, and then rebuilding the system databases to use a collation that matches the user database collation. Or you can modify any stored procedures that join user tables to tables in *tempdb* to create the tables in *tempdb* by using the collation of the user database. |
| Database Page Status | Checks for user databases that have the database status set to Suspect. The Database Engine marks a database as Suspect when it reads a database page that contains an 824 error. Error 824 indicates that a logical consistency error was detected during a read operation, and it frequently indicates data corruption caused by a faulty I/O subsystem component. Resolve this situation by running DBCC CHECKDB. |
| Database Page Verification | Checks whether the PAGE_VERIFY database option is set to CHECKSUM. This recommended best practice helps provide a high level of data-file integrity by forcing the Database Engine to calculate a checksum over the contents of the whole page and store the value in the page header when a page is written to disk. When the page is read from disk, the checksum is recomputed and compared to the checksum value that is stored in the page header. |
| File Growth For SQL Server 2000 | Checks an instance of SQL Server 2000 for data files that are 1 gigabyte or larger and are set to autogrow by a percentage instead of a fixed size. As a recommended best practice, large databases should autogrow by a fixed size. Otherwise, growing a data file by a percentage can cause performance problems with SQL Server because of progressively larger growth increments. |
| Guest Permissions | Checks whether the guest user has permission to access a user database. As a best practice, you should revoke the guest user permission to access a database if it is not required. Although the guest user cannot be dropped, the guest user can be disabled by revoking its CONNECT permission. Execute REVOKE CONNECT FROM GUEST within any database other than *master* or *tempdb*. |

**Table 18-2   Predefined Policies for SQL Server 2008**

| Predefined Policy Name | Description |
| --- | --- |
| Last Successful Backup Date | Checks to ensure that a database has recent backups. Scheduling regular backups protects a database against data loss. If there are no recent backups, you should schedule backups using a database maintenance plan. |
| Public Not Granted Server Permissions | Checks whether the public server role has server permissions. Every login that is created on the server is a member of the public server role and will have server permissions. As a best practice, however, do not grant server permissions directly to the public server role. |
| Read-Only Database Recovery Model | Checks for read-only user databases that have recovery set to Full. As a best practice, these databases should use the Simple recovery model because they aren't frequently updated. |
| SQL Server 32-Bit Affinity Mask Overlap | Checks whether the 32-bit instance of SQL Server has one or more processors that are assigned to be used with both the Affinity Mask and Affinity I/O Mask options. Enabling a CPU with both the affinity mask and the affinity I/O mask can slow performance by forcing the processor to be overused. |
| SQL Server 64-Bit Affinity Mask Overlap | Checks whether the 64-bit instance of SQL Server has one or more processors that are assigned to be used with both the Affinity Mask and Affinity I/O Mask options. Enabling a CPU with both the affinity mask and the affinity I/O mask can slow performance by forcing the processor to be overused. |
| SQL Server Affinity Mask | Checks whether the Affinity Mask option is set to 0. This is the default value, which dynamically controls CPU affinity. Using the default value is a recommended best practice. |
| SQL Server Blocked Process Threshold | Checks the Blocked Process Threshold option, and ensures it is set to 0 (disabled) or to a value higher than or equal to 5 (seconds). Setting the Blocked Process Threshold option to a value from 1 through 4 can cause the deadlock monitor to run constantly, and this state is desirable only when you are troubleshooting. |
| SQL Server Default Trace | Determine whether the Default Trace option is disabled. When this option is enabled, default tracing provides information about configuration and DDL changes to the SQL Server Database Engine. |
| SQL Server Dynamic Locks | Checks whether the Locks option is set to 0. This is the default value, which dynamically controls locks. Using the default value is a recommended best practice. Otherwise, if the maximum number of locks is reached, batch jobs will stop and SQL Server will generate "out of locks" errors. |

Table 18-2 Predefined Policies for SQL Server 2008

| Predefined Policy Name | Description |
| --- | --- |
| SQL Server Lightweight Pooling | Checks whether the Lightweight Pooling option is set to 0. This is the default value, which prevents SQL Server from using lightweight pooling. Using the default value is a recommended best practice. |
| SQL Server Login Mode | Checks the login security configuration to ensure Windows authentication is being used. Using Windows authentication is a recommended best practice because this mode uses the Kerberos security protocol, provides support for account lockout, and supports password expiration. For Windows Server 2003 and Windows Server 2008, Windows authentication also provides password policy enforcement in terms of complexity validation for strong passwords. |
| SQL Server Max Degree Of Parallelism | Checks whether the Max Degree Of Parallelism (MAXDOP) option is set to a value greater than 8. Because setting this option to a value larger than 8 often causes unwanted resource consumption and performance degradation, you'll usually want to reduce the value to 8 or less. |
| SQL Server Max Worker Threads For SQL Server 2005 And Above | Checks the Max Worker Threads Server option for potentially incorrect settings. Setting the Max Worker Threads option to a small value might prevent enough threads from servicing incoming client requests in a timely manner. Setting the option to a large value can waste address space, because each active thread consumes 512 KB on 32-bit servers and up to 4 MB on 64-bit servers. For instances of SQL Server 2005 and SQL Server 2008, you should set this option to 0, which allows SQL Server to automatically determine the correct number of active worker threads based on user requests. |
| SQL Server Network Packet Size | Determines whether the network packet size of any logged-in user is more than 8060 bytes. As a best practice, the network packet size should not exceed 8060 bytes. Otherwise, SQL Server performs different memory allocation operations, and this can cause an increase in the virtual address space that is not reserved for the buffer pool. |
| SQL Server Password Expiration | Checks whether password expiration is enabled for each SQL Server login. As a best practice, you should enable password expiration for all SQL Server logins using ALTER LOGIN. Additionally, if SQL Server authentication is not required in your environment, you should enable only Windows authentication. |

**Table 18-2   Predefined Policies for SQL Server 2008**

| Predefined Policy Name | Description |
|---|---|
| SQL Server Password Policy | Checks whether the Enforce Password policy is enabled for each SQL Server login. As a best practice, you should enable the Enforce Password policy for all the SQL Server logins by using ALTER LOGIN. |
| SQL Server System Tables Updatable | Checks whether system tables for SQL Server 2000 can be updated. As a best practice, you shouldn't allow updates to system tables. |
| Symmetric Key Encryption For User Databases | Checks whether encryption keys that have a length of less than 128 bytes do not use the RC2 or RC4 encryption algorithm. As a best practice, you should use AES 128 bit or larger to create symmetric keys for data encryption. If AES is not supported by your operating system, you should use 3DES encryption. |
| Symmetric Key For *master* Database | Checks for user-created symmetric keys in the *master* database. |
| Symmetric Key For System Databases | Checks for user-created symmetric keys in the *msdb*, *model*, and *tempdb* databases. As a best practice, you should not create symmetric keys in the system databases. |
| Trustworthy Database | Checks whether the dbo role for a database is assigned to the sysadmin fixed server role and the database has its trustworthy bit set to ON. As a best practice, you should turn off the trustworthy bit or revoke sysadmin permissions from the dbo database role. Otherwise, a privileged database user can elevate privileges to the sysadmin role and then create and run unsafe assemblies that could compromise the system. |
| Windows Event Log Cluster Disk Resource Corruption Error | Checks the system event log for EventId 1066. This error can occur when a device is malfunctioning and also as a result of SCSI host adapter configuration issues. |
| Windows Event Log Device Driver Control Error | Checks the system event log for EventId 11. This error can be caused by a corrupt device driver, a hardware problem, faulty cabling, or connectivity issues. |
| Windows Event Log Device Not Ready Error | Checks the system event log for EventId 15. This error can be caused by SCSI host adapter configuration issues or related problems. |
| Windows Event Log Disk Defragmentation | Checks the system event log for EventId 55. This error occurs when the Disk Defragmenter tool cannot move a particular data element and as a result Chkdsk.exe is scheduled to run. |
| Windows Event Log Failed I_O Request Error | Checks the system event log for EventId 50. This error is caused by a failed I/O request. |

Table 18-2 Predefined Policies for SQL Server 2008

| Predefined Policy Name | Description |
| --- | --- |
| Windows Event Log I_O Delay Warning | Checks the event log for error message 833. This message indicates that SQL Server has issued a read or write request from disk, and that the request has taken longer than 15 seconds to return. You can troubleshoot this error by examining the system event log for hardware-related error messages. Look also for hardware-specific logs. |
| Windows Event Log I_O Error During Hard Page Fault Error | Checks the system event log for EventId 51. This error is caused by an error during a hard page fault. |
| Windows Event Log Read Retry Error | Checks the event log for SQL Server error message 825. This message indicates that SQL Server was unable to read data from the disk on the first try. You'll need to check the disks, disk controllers, array cards, and disk drivers. |
| Windows Event Log Storage System I_O Timeout Error | Checks the system event log for EventId 9. This message indicates that an I/O time-out has occurred in the storage system. |
| Windows Event Log System Failure Error | Checks for the system event log for EventId 6008. This event indicates an unexpected system shutdown. |

# Managing Policies Throughout the Enterprise

As discussed previously, you create and manage policies in SQL Server Management Studio. Implementing Policy-Based Management is a multistep process that involves selecting a facet that contains the properties you want to configure, defining a condition that specifies the permitted states of the facet, and defining a policy that contains the condition and sets an evaluation mode. The evaluation mode you set determines whether SQL Server uses automated policy monitoring, reporting, and compliance enforcement.

## Importing and Exporting Policies

SQL Server 2008 includes predefined policies for the Database Engine, Analysis Services, and Reporting Services. You can import these predefined policies with their preconfigured conditions if you want to use them with a particular instance of the Database Engine, Analysis Services, or Reporting Services. If you create your own policies, you can export the policies with their conditions to XML files and then import from the XML files on another instance of SQL Server.

You can export a policy by completing the following steps:

1. In SQL Server Management Studio, access the Management folder on the instance of the Database Engine you want to work with.

2. In Object Explorer, under the Management node, expand Policy Management, Policies; right-click a policy; and then click Export Policy. This displays the Export Policy dialog box shown in Figure 18-1.

3. Use the options in the Export Policy dialog box to select a save location, and then type the desired name of the XML file.

4. Click Save. By default, SQL Server preserves the current state of the policy and this state will be set when the policy is imported. Note that any condition associated with the policy is exported as well.

**Figure 18-1**   The Export Policy dialog box.

You can import a policy by completing the following steps:

1. In SQL Server Management Studio, access the Management folder on the instance of the Database Engine you want to work with.

2. In Object Explorer, under the Management node, expand Policy Management, right-click Policies, and then click Import Policy.

3. In the Import dialog box, shown in Figure 18-2, click the Options (...) button and then use the Select Policy dialog box to locate the XML file that contains the policy. Select a policy by clicking it and then click Open. You can select multiple files using Shift+click or Ctrl+click.

**Figure 18-2**    The Import dialog box.

4. Click Open and then click OK. Note that any condition associated with the policy is imported as well.

5. If identically named policies (and conditions) already exist, the import process will fail with an error stating the policies already exist. To force SQL Server to overwrite existing policies, you must select the Replace Duplicates With Items Imported check box.

6. By default, SQL Server preserves the policy state on import. If a policy was enabled when it was exported, it will be enabled. If a policy was disabled when it was exported, it will be disabled. You can modify this behavior by explicitly setting the state. To enable the policies you are importing, select Enable All Policies On Import. To disable the policies you are importing, select Disable All Policies On Import.

## Configuring Central Management Servers

By default, each instance of SQL Server is responsible for monitoring and enforcing its own policies. Although this configuration is useful in standalone deployments, you'll often want a more robust solution in the enterprise, and this is where central management servers are useful. Central management servers take over the responsibility of monitoring and enforcing policy from any instance of SQL Server registered as a subordinate server. From a central management server, you also can execute Transact-SQL statements on multiple instances of SQL Server simultaneously.

You can specify a SQL Server instance that you want to act as a central management server by registering the server in the Registered Servers view. Afterward, you can specify the subordinate servers that you will manage via the central management server.

After you register the central management servers you want to use, you must register the subordinate servers. Although you must register subordinate servers individually, you can manage subordinate servers collectively using subordinate server groups.

**Note**   You must register all central management servers and subordinate servers using Windows authentication. Only members of the ServerGroupAdministrator-Role role can manage the central management server. Membership in the Server-GroupReaderRole role is required to connect to a central management server.

### Registering Central Management Servers

A central management server cannot be a subordinate server or a member of a subordinate group that it maintains. You can register a central management server by following these steps:

1. In SQL Server Management Studio, you use the Registered Servers view to work with central management servers. To use this view, or to display it if it is hidden, press Ctrl+Alt+G.

2. Under the Central Management Servers node, you'll see a list of previously registered central management servers. To register a new server, right-click the Central Management Servers node and then select Register Central Management Server. This displays the New Server Registration dialog box shown in Figure 18-3.

**Figure 18-3**   The New Server Registration dialog box.

3. In the Server Name box, type the fully qualified domain name or host name of the central management server, such as dbsvr23.cpandl.com or DBSvr23.

4. Choose Windows Authentication as the authentication type.

5. The registered server name is filled in for you based on the previously entered server name. Change the default name only if you want SQL Server Management Studio to use an alternate display name for the server.

6. To test the settings, click Test. If you successfully connect to the server, you will see a prompt confirming this. If the test fails, verify the information you provided, make changes as necessary, and then test the settings again.

7. Click Save.

### Registering Subordinate Servers

After you register a central management server, you can register subordinate servers and create subordinate server groups. You can register a subordinate server by following these steps:

1. In the Registered Servers view, expand the Central Management Servers node. You'll see a list of previously registered central management servers.

2. Right-click the central management server that will have management responsibility for the subordinate server, and then select New Server Registration.

3. In the Server Name box, type the fully qualified domain name or host name of the central management server, such as DatabaseServer12.cpandl.com or DatabaseServer12.

4. Choose Windows Authentication as the authentication type.

5. The registered server name is filled in for you based on the previously entered server name. Change the default name only if you want SQL Server Management Studio to use an alternate display name for the server.

6. To test the settings, click Test. If you successfully connect to the server, you will see a prompt confirming this. If the test fails, verify the information you provided, make changes as necessary, and then test the settings again.

7. Click Save.

### Registering Subordinate Server Groups

You can create a subordinate server group by completing the following steps:

1. In the Registered Servers view, expand the Central Management Servers node. You'll see a list of previously registered central management servers.

2. Right-click the central management server that will have management responsibility for the subordinate server, and then select New Server Group.

3. In the New Server Group Properties dialog box, type a name and description for the new group in the boxes provided. Click OK.

## Moving Subordinate Servers and Server Groups

Sometimes, you'll need to move a subordinate server or server group to a new location in the central management server hierarchy. You can do this by completing the following steps:

1. In the Registered Servers view, expand the Central Management Servers node and the related server and group nodes as necessary.

2. Right-click the subordinate server or server group that you want to move, point to Tasks, and then select Move To.

3. In the Move Server Registration dialog box, you can move the server or server group to a different level by selecting the node into which you want to place the server or group.

4. Click OK.

The Move To process will not let you move a subordinate server or server group to a different central management server. To move a subordinate server or server group to a different central management server, you'll need to export the related registration settings and then import them in the desired location. The export and import process works like this:

1. In the Registered Servers view, right-click the node with the settings to export, point to Tasks, and then select Export.

2. Click the Options (...) button to the right of the Export File box.

3. Use the Save As dialog box to select and save the location, type a name for the exported registered servers file, and then click Save.

4. Click OK to close the Export Registered Servers dialog box.

5. Right-click the node where you want to import the settings, point to Tasks, and then select Import.

6. Click the Options (...) button to the right of the Import File box.

7. Use the Open dialog box to navigate to the save location and select the exported registered servers file, and then click Open.

8. Click OK to close the Import Registered Servers dialog box. Note that if you no longer need the original server and server group settings, you should remove them to avoid possible conflicts.

## Deleting Subordinate Servers and Server Groups

If you no longer want to use a subordinate server or server group, you can remove the server or server group. Right-click the server or server group and then select Delete. When prompted to confirm, click Yes. Note that when you delete a server group, SQL Server Management Studio removes the group and all the subordinate server registrations it contains.

## Executing Statements Against Multiple Servers

You can query multiple servers at the same time via central management servers. You can also execute Transact-SQL statements against local server groups in the Registered Servers view. Keep the following in mind:

■ To query all subordinate servers of a central management server, right-click the central management server in the Registered Servers view and select New Query. In Query Editor, type and execute your Transact-SQL statements.

■ To query every server in a server group, right-click the server group in the Registered Servers view and select New Query. In Query Editor, type and execute your Transact-SQL statements.

By default, the results pane will combine the query results from all the servers. Because the connections to subordinate servers execute using Windows authentication in the context of the currently logged-on user, the effective permissions might vary. If a connection cannot be established to one or more servers, those servers are ignored and results against the other servers are displayed.

The combined results will have the server name but will not have any login names. If you want, you can modify multiserver results using the Options dialog box. Click Options on the Tools menu. Expand Query Results, expand SQL Server, and then click Multiserver Results. On the Multiserver Results page, do one or more of the following and then click OK:

■ Configure the Add Login Names To The Results option. Use True to add login names to the results. Use False to remove login names from the results.

■ Configure the Add Server Names To The Results option. Use True to add server names to the results. Use False to remove server names from the results.

■ Configure the Merge Results option. Use True to merge results in a single results pane. Use False to display results in a separate pane for each server.

## Configuring and Managing Policy Facets

Facets define management areas within the policy-based framework. Each management area has a set of related properties that you can configure using a particular facet. You can view or modify the current state of any facet properties via the related object.

To view an object's current state and modify this state, follow these steps:

1. In Object Explorer, right-click a server instance, database, or database object, and then click Facets.

2. In the View Facets dialog box, shown in Figure 18-4, use the Facet drop-down list to select a facet related to the object. You will then see a list of properties that shows the names and values of the facets.

3. Click in the box next to the property to select a desired property value. If a property is dimmed, you cannot modify the property value.

4. Click OK.

**Figure 18-4**   Modify property values as necessary.

Exporting an object's current state as policy allows you to use the current configuration of a server instance, database, or other database object to define policies that you want to implement throughout the enterprise. After you export an object's current state as policy, you can save the policy to the Policy Management\Policies node on the local server or to a policy file that you can import on another server.

Exporting an object's current state as policy creates a condition and a policy. To view an object's current state and export this state as policy, follow these steps:

1. In Object Explorer, right-click a server instance, database, or database object, and then click Facets.

2. In the View Facets dialog box, use the Facet drop-down list to select a facet related to the object. You will then see a list of properties that shows the names and values of the facets.

3. Click Export Current State As Policy to display the Export As Policy dialog box, shown in Figure 18-5.

**Figure 18-5**    Export the property settings as a policy.

4.  Type a name for the policy, and then type a name for the condition.

5.  To save the policy to the Policy Management\Policies node on the local server, select To Local Server and then click OK to close the Export As Policy dialog box. The related policy and related condition are created under the appropriate nodes within Policy Management.

6.  To save the policy to a file that you can import on another server, click To File. Click the Options (...) button. Use the Export Policy dialog box to select a save location and name for the policy file and then click Save. Click OK to close the Export As Policy dialog box. Later, you can import the policy using the technique discussed in "Importing and Exporting Policies" on page 656.

## Creating and Managing Policy Conditions

Facets represent management areas within SQL Server. Most facets have multiple properties that you can manage using conditions. Conditions define the permitted states for properties. Although you can use a single condition in multiple policies, you define conditions for each facet individually.

When you are defining conditions, you join property evaluation expressions using And or Or clauses to form a logical statement. For example, with the database facet, you might want to establish the condition shown in Figure 18-6. In this example, the evaluation expression specifies the following:

■  AutoClose must be True

■  And AutoShrink must be False

■  And PageVerify must be set to either TornPageDetection or Checksum

■  And Trustworthy must be True

■  And AutoUpdateStatisticsEnabled must be True

**Figure 18-6**   Define the condition by joining property expressions.

Although the allowed values depend on the property you are configuring, values generally can be numeric, strings, or a fixed list. With properties that are either ON (TRUE) or OFF (FALSE), you can set the operator to equals (=) or not equals (!=). When you set a property to equals, the property must equal the specified value. When you set a property to not equals, the property cannot equal the specified value but can be set to other permitted values.

With multivalued properties, other operators you can use are as follows:

> Greater than; the property must be greater than the value specified.

>= Greater than or equal to; the property must be greater than or equal to the value specified.

< Less than; the property must be less than the value specified.

<= Less than or equal to; the property must be less than or equal to the value specified.

**Like**   Pattern match as with the LIKE clause in Transact-SQL; the property must match a specified pattern. Enclose the LIKE value in single quotation marks, such as '%computer%' or '[D-Z]arwin'.

**Not Like**   Pattern match as with the NOT LIKE clause in Transact-SQL; the property must not match a specified pattern. Enclose the NOT LIKE value in single quotation marks.

**In**     Query or list match as with the IN clause for Transact-SQL; the property must match a value in the specified query or list. Enclose the IN clause in parentheses, enclose individual values in single quotation marks, and separate values with commas, such as ('Hawaii', 'Idaho', 'Nebraska').

**Not In**   Query or list match as with the NOT IN clause for Transact-SQL; the property must not match a value in the specified query or list.

You can create a condition by completing the following steps:

1. In SQL Server Management Studio, access the Management folder on the instance of the Database Engine you want to work with.

2. In Object Explorer, under the Management node, expand Policy Management, expand Facets, right-click the facet that contains the properties that you want, and then click New Condition.

3. On the General page of the Create New Condition dialog box, type the name of the new condition, such as Standard Database Settings, in the Name box.

4. Confirm the correct facet in the Facet box, or select a different facet.

5. In the Expression area, construct condition expressions by selecting a facet property in the Field box, together with its associated operator and value. When you add multiple expressions, the expressions can be joined by using And or Or.

6. To create complex expressions, press the Shift or Ctrl key, and then click two or more clauses to select a range. Right-click the selected area, and then click Group Clauses. Grouping clauses is like putting parentheses around an expression in a mathematical expression, forcing the clauses to operate as a single unit that is separate from the rest of the condition.

7. Optionally, on the Description page, type a description of the new condition.

8. Click OK to create the condition.

After creating a condition, you can view or modify its settings by completing these steps:

1. In SQL Server Management Studio, access the Management folder on the instance of the Database Engine you want to work with.

2. In Object Explorer, under the Management node, expand Policy Management, expand Conditions, right-click the condition that you want to view or modify, and select Properties.

3. View the condition settings on the General page. Make changes as necessary. Click OK.

Although you cannot delete a condition referenced in a policy, you can delete unreferenced conditions as necessary. You delete a condition by right-clicking it and then selecting Delete. When prompted to confirm, click OK.

## Creating and Managing Policies

You use policies to check and optionally enforce conditions. When you create a policy, you can use a condition that you created earlier, or you can create a new condition when you are creating the policy. Although you can use a single condition in many policies, a policy can contain only a single condition.

When you create a policy, the policy normally is associated with the current instance of the Database Engine. If the current instance is a central management server, the policy can be applied to all subordinate servers. You also can directly create a policy by choosing the New on the File menu, and then saving the policy to a file. This enables you to create policies when you are not connected to the instance of the Database Engine that you want to work with.

You can create a policy and associate it with a particular instance of the Database Engine by completing the following steps:

1. In SQL Server Management Studio, access the Management folder on the instance of the Database Engine you want to work with.

2. In Object Explorer, under the Management node, expand Policy Management, right-click Policies, and then click New Policy. This displays the Create New Policy dialog box shown in Figure 18-7.

**Figure 18-7**   Create the policy and specify the condition that applies.

3. In the Name box, type the name of the new policy, such as Standard Database Settings Policy.

4. Use the Check Condition drop-down list to select one of the existing conditions, or select New Condition. To edit a condition, select the condition and then click the Options (...) button.

5. In the Against Targets box, select one or more target types for this policy. Some conditions and facets can be applied only to certain types of targets. The available target sets appear in the associated box. If no targets appear in this box, the check condition is scoped at the server level. To select a filtering condition for some types of the targets, click the Every entry and then select an existing filter condition or define a condition by selecting New Condition and then specifying the settings for the condition.

6. Use the Evaluation Mode drop-down list to select how this policy will behave. Different conditions can have different valid evaluation modes. Available modes can include On Demand, On Change: Prevent, On Change: Log Only, and On Schedule. If you specify a mode other than On Demand, you can enable the policy by selecting the Enabled check box. If you specify On Schedule as the mode, click Pick to select an existing run schedule or click New to create a new schedule.

7. To limit the policy to a subset of the target types, select a limiting condition from the Server Restriction drop-down list or select New Condition to create a new condition.

8. By default, policies are assigned to the Default category. On the Description page, in the Category box, you can select a different default policy category. (See Figure 18-8.) Otherwise, to create a new category, click New, type a category name, and then click OK.

9. On the Description page, type an optional description of the policy. Click OK to create the policy.

**Real World**   To help administrators understand your policies, you can publish help documents on a Web site and then refer administrators to the help documentation using a help hyperlink. You can define a help hyperlink using the Additional Help Hyperlink option on a policy's Description page. Enter the help text for the link in the Text To Display box, and then in the Address box type the hyperlink address. You can provide a link to a Web page that starts with http:// or https://, or you can provide a mail link that starts with mailto://. After you type a hyperlink, click the Test Link button to check the validity of the hyperlink. When you are evaluating a server instance, database, or other object for policy compliance, the help text and link are displayed as part of the detailed results.

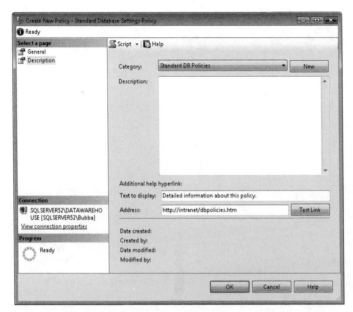

**Figure 18-8**   Assign the policy to a category.

After creating a policy, you can view or modify its settings by completing these steps:

1. In SQL Server Management Studio, access the Management folder on the instance of the Database Engine you want to work with.

2. In Object Explorer, under the Management node, expand Policy Management, expand Policies, right-click the policy that you want to view or modify, and select Properties.

3. View the policy settings on the General and Description pages. Make changes as necessary. Click OK.

You can manage policies you've created by using the following techniques:

■ Delete a policy by right-clicking it and then selecting Delete. When prompted to confirm, click OK.

■ Disable a policy by right-clicking it and then selecting Disable.

■ Enable a policy by right-clicking it and then selecting Enable.

## Managing Policy Categories and Mandating Policies

SQL Server 2008 uses policy categories to help you organize your policies. In a large organization, grouping policies into categories will make policy management easier. You can assign a policy to a category in several ways. By default, any policy you create will belong to the Default category. When you create a policy, you can assign the policy to an available or new category as well. To move a policy to a different policy category, complete the following steps:

1. Right-click the policy that you want to view or modify and select Properties.

2. On the Description page, in the Category box, you can select a different default policy category. Otherwise, to create a new category, click New, type a category name, and then click OK.

3. Click OK to apply the changes.

In addition to helping you organize policies, policy categories also help with policy application. Policies within categories are either mandated or not mandated. If a policy is mandated, it means that all databases on the instance of SQL Server must enforce the policy. If a policy is not mandated, it means that you must manually apply the policy as appropriate.

By default, any policy assigned to the Default category is a mandated policy. You can control whether a policy category and its related policies are mandated or not mandated by completing the following steps:

1. In SQL Server Management Studio, access the Management folder on the instance of the Database Engine you want to work with.

2. In Object Explorer, under the Management node, right-click the Policy Management node and then select Manage Categories.

3. The available categories are listed by name. To create a new policy category, simply click in an empty text box in the Name column and type the category name.

4. In the Manage Policy Categories dialog box, shown in Figure 18-9, select or clear the Mandate Database check box for each category as appropriate. Click OK.

**Figure 18-9**   Specify whether policies within categories are mandated.

You can determine the policies that are applied to a server instance, database, or other object by completing the following steps:

1. In Object Explorer, right-click a server instance, database, or database object; point to Policies; and then click Categories.

2. In the Categories dialog box, expand the category entries to determine which policies are being applied. As shown in Figure 18-10, the following information is available:

   ❑ **Name**   Shows the name of the policy category.

   ❑ **Subscribed**   Indicates whether the selected object has subscribed to the policy category. If the related check box is dimmed, the policy category is mandated and applies to all databases on the server.

   ❑ **Policy**   Shows the policies in the policy category, provided that you've expanded the related category node.

   ❑ **Enabled**   Indicates whether the policy is enabled or disabled.

   ❑ **Evaluation Mode**   Shows the evaluation mode of the policy.

   ❑ **History**   Click the View History link to open the Log File viewer and display the creation and change history for the policy.

**Figure 18-10**   Determine which policies are being applied.

## Evaluating Policies

Using automatically evaluated modes, you can check policy compliance when changes are made or on a regularly scheduled basis. You also can evaluate a policy manually to determine whether a server instance, database, or other object complies with the policy. If you later apply or enforce the policy, you can configure the selected database instance or database object to comply with the policy.

Because the connections to subordinate servers execute using Windows authentication in the context of the currently logged-on user, the effective permissions might vary. If a connection cannot be established to one or more servers, those servers are ignored and evaluation against the other servers continues independently.

You can determine whether a particular object complies with a policy by completing the following steps:

1. In Object Explorer, right-click a server instance, database, or database object; point to Policies; and then click Evaluate.

2. The Evaluate Policies dialog box shows only the policies that are appropriate for the object. (See Figure 18-11.) In the Evaluate Policies dialog box, select one or more policies, and then click Evaluate to run the policy in evaluation mode. Note that the evaluation mode is defined as part of the policy and cannot be changed in the Evaluate Policies dialog box.

**Figure 18-11**   Evaluate an object against policies to determine compliance.

3. If there are compliance issues, you'll see a red warning icon. You can click the View link that appears in the Details column under Target Details to view the detailed compliance results. As shown in Figure 18-12, the Result column shows whether each property in the joined evaluation expression is in compliance or out of compliance. Expected and actual values are also shown. Note that help text is provided if you've previously defined it. Click Close when you are finished reviewing the detailed results.

**Figure 18-12**   Review compliance issues.

4. Clicking Evaluate generates a compliance report for the target set but does not reconfigure SQL Server or enforce compliance. For targets that do not comply with the selected policies and have properties that can be reconfigured by Policy-Based Management, you can enforce policy compliance by selecting the policy or policies to apply on the Evaluation Results page and then clicking Apply.

5. The first time you try to apply a policy, you'll see a Policy Evaluation Warning dialog box prompting you to confirm the action. Click Yes to proceed. If you don't want to see the warning in the future, select the Do Not Show This Message Again check box before clicking Yes.

6. After you apply a policy, you can review the detailed results by clicking the View link that appears in the Details column under Target Details. If the properties can be reconfigured using Policy-Based Management, the properties will be changed. Click Close when you are finished reviewing the detailed results.

7. Optionally, you can export the results to a policy results file for later review. Click the Export button. Use the Export Results dialog box to select a save location for the results file, type a file name, and then click Save.

You can determine whether the targets of a policy are in compliance by completing the following steps:

1. In Object Explorer, expand Management, expand Policy Management, expand Policies, right-click a policy, and then click Evaluate.

2. Follow steps 2 through 7 in the previous procedure.

You can determine whether the targets of a policy are in compliance with a schedule by completing the following steps:

1. In Object Explorer, expand Management, expand Policy Management, expand Policies, right-click a policy, and then click Properties.

2. On the General page, specify On Schedule as the mode.

3. Click Pick to select an existing run schedule, or click New to create a new schedule.

To view the history of compliance checks in the future, right-click the policy and then select View History. In Log File Viewer, expand the available run dates to show additional details. Review the related details in the detailed view by clicking the link provided in the Details column.

Each property in the joined evaluation expression is listed according to whether it is in or out of compliance. If there are compliance issues, you'll see a red warning icon to show properties not in compliance and a green OK icon to show properties in compliance. Expected and actual values are also shown. Note that help text is provided if you've previously defined it. Click Close when you are finished reviewing the detailed results.

## Troubleshooting Policy-Based Management Policies

In the *msdb* database, you'll find the following views for displaying policy information:

- syspolicy_conditions
- syspolicy_policies
- syspolicy_policy_execution_history
- syspolicy_policy_execution_history_details
- syspolicy_policy_group_subscriptions
- syspolicy_policy_groups
- syspolicy_system_health_state
- syspolicy_target_filters

These views are owned by the dbo schema. SQL Server records compliance issues in the Windows event logs. For scheduled policies, compliance issues are recorded in the SQL Server Agent log as well. To view the history information recorded in the SQL Server Agent logs, right-click the policy and then select View History. Review the related details in the detailed view by clicking the link provided in the Details column. Note that if policies are not enabled or do not affect a target, the failure is not considered an error and is not logged. See "Evaluating Policies" on page 671 for more information.

Remember that compliance checks for scheduled policies occur only during scheduled run times and that on-demand policies run only when you manually execute them. If you are having problems with On Change: Log or On Change: Prevent policies, ensure that the policies are enabled and that the desired target is not excluded by a filter. As discussed in "Managing Policy Categories and Mandating Policies" on page 669, you can determine the policies that are applied to a server instance, database, or other object by right-clicking a server instance, database, or database object; pointing to Policies; and then clicking Categories.

You can determine whether a policy ran by right-clicking the policy and then selecting View History. The policy execution history in the msdb.dbo.syspolicy_policy_execution_history view also provides information about whether a policy ran. And you can determine whether the policy executed for the specific target by checking the policy execution history for the specific target in the msdb.dbo.syspolicy_policy_execution_history_details view. You can determine the execution time for policies by querying the start_date and end_date columns in the msdb.dbo.syspolicy_policy_execution_history view.

For policies that use the On Change: Prevent mode, Service Broker handles the rollback of changes. You should ensure Service Broker is running and configured properly. If it is, you can check the Service Broker Queue to ensure it is monitoring for the correct events by using the following query:

```
SELECT * FROM sys.server_event_notifications
WHERE name = N'syspolicy_event_notification';
GO
```

Keep in mind that if the nested triggers server configuration option is disabled, On Change: Prevent mode will not work correctly. Policy-Based Management relies on DDL triggers to detect and roll back DDL operations that do not comply with policies that use this evaluation mode. Removing the Policy-Based Management DDL triggers or disabling nested triggers will cause this evaluation mode to fail.

Because On Schedule policies rely on SQL Server Agent jobs, you should always check to ensure SQL Server Agent is running and configured properly. You should also check to ensure the related SQL Server Agent jobs are enabled and configured properly. Working with SQL Server Agent jobs is discussed in Chapter 16, "Database Automation and Maintenance."

# Index

## A

access. *See also* logins
  accounts with. *See* accounts
  assigning roles to logins, 297–299
  component feature access, 52–56
  database user accounts, 271
  group access. *See* groups
  permissions for. *See* permissions
  revoking user rights to database roles, 302
  server login. *See* server logins
  Transact-SQL management of, 303–304
accounts
  Administrator user account, 271
  dbo (database owner) accounts, 273
  guest user, 272–273
  Local Server, 11, 44
  NETWORK SERVICE account, 272
  sa login, 272–285
  service, types of, overview, 10–11
  startup service account settings, 62–63
  SYSTEM account, 272
Active Directory, 9, 57, 86, 172
Activity Monitor
  command execution, tracking, 142–143
  displaying, 490
  lock data, 138–140
  process information, 135–136
  wait data, 137
administration tools
  command line. *See* command-line tools
  graphical menu options, 12
  graphical, table of, 15
Administrator user account, 271
Administrators group, 271
affinity, processor, 156–158
Agent. *See* SQL Server Agent
alerts
  copying to another server, 601
  default replication alerts, 580
  error message alert creation, 580–582
  event forwarding as substitute in
    multiserver systems, 602–603
  jobs, generating from, 595
  managing, 583
  performance, configuration of, 510–511

  policy execution, 649
  purpose of, 580
  response configuration, 582–583
ALTER DATABASE statements
  ANSI compliance, 201–203
  automatic options configuration, 199–201
  capabilities of, 194–195
  chaining settings, 209
  database options, tables of, 97–99,
    106–110
  database state, setting, 207–208
  modifying database configurations with,
    194–199
  moving database files, 227–228
  syntax, 195–199
Analysis Services
  backups, 29
  caching, 28
  cell writeback, 28–29
  data mining enhancements, 27–29
  Deployment Wizard, 15
  groups created by Setup for, 60
  installing, 41
  manageable features, 55–56
  memory requirements, 4
  options, selecting during installation, 47
  purpose of, 2, 9
  SSD (scalable shared database) feature, 29
  startup state management of, 58
  UDM, 28
  XML as data definition language, 28
anonymous subscriptions, 478–479
ANSI compliance, 201–203
application logs, 497–499, 602–603
application schemas, 317
articles, replication, 446–447
attaching databases, 220–223
auditing levels, 148
authentication
  Database Mail, configuring, 573
  mixed security mode, 270–271
  mode selection, 148, 269
  options, choosing during installation,
    45–46

# About the Author

**William R. Stanek** (*http://www.williamstanek.com/*) has over 20 years of hands-on experience with advanced programming and development. He is a leading technology expert, an award-winning author, and a pretty-darn-good instructional trainer. Over the years, his practical advice has helped millions of programmers, developers, and network engineers all over the world. He has written over 75 books. Current or forthcoming books include *Microsoft Exchange Server 2007 Administrator's Pocket Consultant Second Edition* (Microsoft Press, 2007), *Microsoft Windows Server 2008 Administrator's Pocket Consultant* (Microsoft Press, 2008), *Internet Information Services (IIS) 7.0 Administrator's Pocket Consultant* (Microsoft Press, 2007), and *Windows Server 2008 Inside Out* (Microsoft Press, 2008).

William has been involved in the commercial Internet community since 1991. His core business and technology experience comes from over 11 years of military service. He has substantial experience in developing server technology, encryption, and Internet solutions. He has written many technical white papers and training courses on a wide variety of topics. He frequently serves as a subject matter expert and consultant.

William has an M.S. with distinction in information systems and a B.S. in computer science, magna cum laude. He is proud to have served in the Persian Gulf War as a combat crew member on an electronic warfare aircraft. He flew on numerous combat missions into Iraq and was awarded nine medals for his wartime service, including one of the United States of America's highest flying honors, the Air Force Distinguished Flying Cross. Currently, he resides in the Pacific Northwest with his wife and children.

# What do you think of this book?

# We want to hear from you!

Do you have a few minutes to participate in a brief online survey?

Microsoft is interested in hearing your feedback so we can continually improve our books and learning resources for you.

To participate in our survey, please visit:

**www.microsoft.com/learning/booksurvey/**

...and enter this book's ISBN-10 number or ISBN-13 number (located above barcode on back cover*). As a thank-you to survey participants in the United States and Canada, each month we'll randomly select five respondents to win one of five $100 gift certificates from a leading online merchant. At the conclusion of the survey, you can enter the drawing by providing your e-mail address, which will be used for prize notification only.

Thanks in advance for your input. Your opinion counts!

**Microsoft®**
*Press*

\*Where to find the ISBN on back cover

ISBN-13: 000-0-0000-0000-0
ISBN-10: 0-0000-0000-0

Example only. Each book has unique ISBN.

No purchase necessary. Void where prohibited. Open only to residents of the 50 United States (includes District of Columbia) and Canada (void in Quebec). For official rules and entry dates see:

**www.microsoft.com/learning/booksurvey/**